Lecture Notes in Computer Science 1722

Edited by G. Goos, J. Hartmanis and J. van Leeuwen

Springer

Berlin
Heidelberg
New York
Barcelona
Hong Kong
London
Milan
Paris
Singapore
Tokyo

Aart Middeldorp Taisuke Sato (Eds.)

Functional and Logic Programming

4th Fuji International Symposium, FLOPS'99
Tsukuba, Japan, November 11-13, 1999
Proceedings

 Springer

Series Editors

Gerhard Goos, Karlsruhe University, Germany
Juris Hartmanis, Cornell University, NY, USA
Jan van Leeuwen, Utrecht University, The Netherlands

Volume Editors

Aart Middeldorp
University of Tsukuba
Institute of Information Sciences and Electronics
Tsukuba 305-8573, Japan
E-mail: ami@is.tsukuba.ac.jp

Taisuke Sato
Tokyo Institute of Technology
Graduate School of Information Science and Engineering
Ookayama 2-12-2, Meguro-ku, Tokyo 152-8552, Japan
E-mail: sato@cs.titech.ac.jp

Cataloging-in-Publication data applied for

Die Deutsche Bibliothek - CIP-Einheitsaufnahme

Functional and logic programming : 4th Fuji international
symposium ; proceedings / FLOPS '99, Tsukuba, Japan, November
11 - 13, 1999. Aart Middeldorp ; Taisuke Sato (ed.). - Berlin ;
Heidelberg ; New York ; Barcelona ; Hong Kong ; London ; Milan ;
Paris ; Singapore ; Tokyo : Springer, 1999
    (Lecture notes in computer science ; Vol. 1722)
    ISBN 3-540-66677-X

CR Subject Classification (1998): D.1.1, D.1.6, D.3, F.3, I.2.3

ISSN 0302-9743
ISBN 3-540-66677-X Springer-Verlag Berlin Heidelberg New York

© Springer-Verlag Berlin Heidelberg 1999
Printed in Germany

Typesetting: Camera-ready by author
SPIN: 10705424   06/3142 – 5 4 3 2 1 0   Printed on acid-free paper

Preface

This volume contains the papers presented at the *4th Fuji International Symposium on Functional and Logic Programming* (FLOPS'99) held in Tsukuba, Japan, November 11–13, 1999, and hosted by the Electrotechnical Laboratory (ETL). FLOPS is a forum for presenting and discussing all issues concerning functional programming, logic programming, and their integration. The symposium takes place about every 1.5 years in Japan. Previous FLOPS meetings were held in Fuji Susuno (1995), Shonan Village (1996), and Kyoto (1998).

There were 51 submissions from Austria ($\frac{1}{3}$), Belgium (2), Brazil (3), China (1), Denmark (2), France ($3\frac{3}{4}$), Germany (8), Ireland (1), Israel ($\frac{1}{3}$), Italy ($1\frac{7}{12}$), Japan ($9\frac{1}{3}$), Korea (1), Morocco (1), The Netherlands (1), New Zealand (1), Portugal ($\frac{1}{2}$), Singapore ($\frac{1}{3}$), Slovakia (1), Spain ($4\frac{3}{4}$), Sweden (1), UK ($4\frac{5}{6}$), and USA ($2\frac{1}{4}$), of which the program committee selected 21 for presentation. In addition, this volume contains full papers by the two invited speakers, Atsushi Ohori and Mario Rodríguez-Artalejo.

FLOPS'99 was organized in cooperation with the Special Interest Group on Principles of Programming of the Japan Society of Software Science and Technology. The following sponsors provided financial support: Grant-in-Aid for Scientific Research on Priority Area "Discovery Science" of the Ministry of Education, Science, Sports and Culture of Japan, Electrotechnical Laboratory (ETL), Tokyo Institute of Technology, University of Tsukuba. Springer-Verlag kindly agreed to publish the proceedings in their LNCS series.

August 1999   Aart Middeldorp
                                                      Taisuke Sato
                                           FLOPS'99 Program Chairs

Conference Organization

Program Chairs

Aart Middeldorp
Taisuke Sato

Program Committee

Zena Ariola	*Eugene*
Robert Glück	*Copenhagen*
Manuel Hermenegildo	*Madrid*
Herbert Kuchen	*Münster*
Michael Maher	*Brisbane*
Aart Middeldorp	*Tsukuba*
Gopalan Nadathur	*Chicago*
Masahiko Sato	*Kyoto*
Taisuke Sato	*Tokyo*
Peter Thiemann	*Freiburg*
Kazunori Ueda	*Tokyo*

Local Arrangements Chair

Yoshiki Kinoshita

List of Referees

G. Amato
N. Andersen
S. Antoy
H. Arimura
K. Asai
F. Baader
A. Banerjee
D. Billington
F. Bueno
D. Cabeza
M. Carro
I. Cervesato
M.M.T. Chakravarty
N.H. Christensen
K. Claessen
G. Delzanno
R. Echahed
M. García-de la Banda
J. Garcia-Martin
A.J. Glenstrup
J.C. Gonzalez-Moreno
B. Gramlich
M. Falaschi
M. Hagiya
M. Hamana
J. Hannan
M. Hanus
W. Harvey
S. Helsen
A. Herranz-Nieva
K. Hirata
C. Hosono
F. Huch

G. Hutton
Y. Isobe
B. Jayaraman
S. Kahrs
T. Kato
Y. Kameyama
Y. Kinoshita
J.W. Klop
T. Kurata
F. Lopez-Fraguas
P. Lopez-Garcia
W. Lux
M. Jones
L. Maranget
M. Marchiori
M. Marin
J. Marinno
D. Miller
T. Mogensen
J.J. Moreno-Navarro
S. Mukhopadhyay
P.M. Neergaard
L. Naish
T. Nipkow
S. Nishizaki
M. Odersky
E. Ohlebusch
S. Okui
J. Palsberg
L. Pareto
S. Peyton Jones
F. Piessens
D. Plump

C. Prehofer
G. Puebla
F. van Raamsdonk
I.V. Ramakrishnan
S. Romanenko
M. Saeki
K. Sagonas
C. Sakama
J.P. Secher
H. Seki
P. Sestoft
Y. Shen
O. Shivers
E. Shibayama
S. Skalberg
Z. Somogyi
H. Søndergaard
M.H. Sorensen
M. Sperber
R. Strandh
P. Stuckey
T. Suzuki
I. Takeuti
J. Tanaka
N. Tamura
A. Tolmach
Y. Toyama
H. Tsuiki
N. Yoshida
P. Wadler
A. Wright
N. Zhou

Table of Contents

Semantics and Types in Functional Logic Programming 1
J. C. González-Moreno, M. T. Hortalá-González and
M. Rodríguez-Artalejo

Polytypic Programming With Ease (Extended Abstract) 21
Ralf Hinze

Type Inference for Overloading without Restrictions,
Declarations or Annotations 37
Carlos Camarão and Lucília Figueiredo

Partial Evaluation and Non-interference for Object Calculi 53
Gilles Barthe and Bernard P. Serpette

Lazy Lexing is Fast 68
Manuel M. T. Chakravarty

A Functional-Logic Perspective of Parsing 85
Rafael Caballero and Francisco J. López-Fraguas

Implementing Encapsulated Search for a Lazy Functional Logic
Language 100
Wolfgang Lux

Comparison of Deforestation Techniques for Functional Programs
and for Tree Transducers 114
Armin Kühnemann

Automatic Verification Based on Abstract Interpretation 131
Mizuhito Ogawa

A Transformation System for Lazy Functional Logic Programs 147
María Alpuente, Moreno Falaschi, Ginés Moreno and Germán Vidal

Termination Analysis of Tabled Logic Programs Using Mode
and Type Information 163
Sofie Verbaeten and Danny De Schreye

On Quasi-Reductive and Quasi-Simplifying Deterministic
Conditional Rewrite Systems 179
Enno Ohlebusch

An Interval Lattice-Based Constraint Solving Framework for Lattices 194
Antonio J. Fernández and Patricia M. Hill

Higher Order Matching for Program Transformation 209
Oege de Moor and Ganesh Sittampalam

Automated Generalisation of Function Definitions 225
Adam Bakewell and Colin Runciman

An Extensional Characterization of Lambda-Lifting and
Lambda-Dropping 241
Olivier Danvy

Using Types as Approximations for Type Checking Prolog Programs 251
Christoph Beierle and Gregor Meyer

Typed Static Analysis: Application to Groundness Analysis
of PROLOG and λPROLOG 267
Olivier Ridoux, Patrice Boizumault and Frédéric Malésieux

A Space Efficient Engine for Subsumption-Based Tabled Evaluation
of Logic Programs 284
*Ernie Johnson, C. R. Ramakrishnan, I. V. Ramakrishnan and
Prasad Rao*

The Logical Abstract Machine: A Curry-Howard Isomorphism
for Machine Code 300
Atsushi Ohori

On Reducing the Search Space of Higher-Order Lazy Narrowing 319
Mircea Marin, Tetsuo Ida and Taro Suzuki

Typed Higher-Order Narrowing without Higher-Order Strategies 335
Sergio Antoy and Andrew Tolmach

A Semantics for Program Analysis in Narrowing-Based Functional Logic
Languages 353
Michael Hanus and Salvador Lucas

Author Index 369

Semantics and Types in Functional Logic Programming*

J. C. González-Moreno, M. T. Hortalá-González, and M. Rodríguez-Artalejo

Dpto. Sistemas Informáticos y Programación, UCM, Madrid
{jcmoreno,teresa,mario}@sip.ucm.es

Abstract. The rewriting logic CRWL has been proposed as a semantic framework for higher-order functional logic programming, using applicative rewriting systems as programs and lazy narrowing as the goal solving procedure. We present an extension of CRWL with a polymorphic type system, and we investigate the consequences of type discipline both at the semantic level and at the operational level. Semantically, models must be extended to incorporate a type universe. Operationally, lazy narrowing must maintain suitable type information in goals, in order to guarantee well-typed computed answers.

1 Introduction

Research on functional logic programming (FLP, for short) has been pursued for longer than ten years, aiming at the integration of the best features of functional programming (FP) and logic programming (LP). In this paper, we will investigate the integration of two fundamental characteristics: *logical semantics*, mainly developed in the LP field, and *type discipline*, best understood in FP languages. Regarding the FP side, we will restrict our attention to *non-strict* languages such as Haskell [17], whose adventages from the viewpoint of declarative programming are widely recognized. Thanks to lazy evaluation, functions in a non-strict language can sometimes return a result even if the values of some arguments are not known, or known only partially, and the semantic values intended for some expressions can be infinite objects. In the rest of the paper, "FP" must be understood as "non-strict FP".

Logical semantics characterizes the meaning of a pure logic program $\mathcal{P}$ (a set of definite Horn clauses) as its least Herbrand model, given by the set of all the atoms that are logical consequences of $\mathcal{P}$ in Horn logic [1]. Disregarding those proposals without a clear semantic basis, most early approaches to the integration of FP and LP, as e.g. [13,6] were based on the idea of adding equations to LP languages. This approach is appealing because equational logic is simple, well-known and widely applicable. Equational logic captures LP by representing Horn clauses as a particular kind of conditional equations, and it seems to capture also FP by viewing functional programs as sets of oriented equations, also known

---

* This research has been partially supported by the Spanish National Project TIC98-0445-C03-02 'TREND" and the Esprit BRA Working Group EP-22457 "CCLII".

A. Middeldorp, T. Sato (Eds.): FLOPS'99, LNCS 1722, pp. 1–20, 1999.
© Springer-Verlag Berlin Heidelberg 1999

as *term rewriting systems* (shortly, TRSs) [3]. Certainly, term rewriting serves as an operational model for FP, but in spite of this equational logic does not provide a logic semantics for FP programs. In general, the set of all equations that are logical consequences of a functional program in equational logic *do not* characterize the meaning of the program. As a simple example, let $\mathcal{P}$ be the FP program consisting of the following two equations:

repeat1(X) ≈ [X|repeat1(X)]   repeat2(X) ≈ [X,X|repeat2(X)]

Here [X|Xs] is intended to represent a list with head X and tail Xs, and the notation [X,X|repeat2(X)] is meant as an abbreviation for [X|[X|repeat2(X)]]. In a non-strict FP language, it is understood that the two expressions repeat1(0) and repeat2(0) have the same meaning, namely an infinite list formed by repeated occurrences of 0. If equational logic would characterize the meaning of $\mathcal{P}$, both expressions should be interchangeable for the purposes of equational deduction, which is not the case. In particular, the equation repeat1(0) = repeat2(0) cannot be deduced from $\mathcal{P}$ in equational logic.

Borrowing ideas from denotational semantics, [8] proposed a rewriting logic CRWL to characterize the logical meaning of higher-order FP and FLP programs. The main results in [8] are existence of least Herbrand models for all programs, in analogy to the LP case, as well as soundness and completeness of a lazy narrowing calculus CLNC for goal solving. No type discipline was considered.

Most functional languages use Milner's type system [14], which helps to avoid errors and to write more readable programs. This system has two crucial properties. Firstly, "well-typed programs don't go wrong", i.e., it is guaranteed that no type errors will occur during program execution, without any need of dynamic type checking. Secondly, types are polymorphic, because they include type variables with a universal reading, standing for any type. For instance, a function to compute the length of a list admits the polymorphic type $[\alpha] \rightarrow int$, meaning that it will work for a list of values of any type α. Polymorphism promotes genericity of programs.

Type discipline in LP is not as well understood as in FP. Often one finds a distinction between the so-called *descriptive* and *prescriptive* views of types. The descriptive approach is applied to originally untyped programs, and views types *a posteriori* as approximations (usually regular supersets) of the success sets of predicates. On the contrary, the prescriptive approach views types *a priori* as imposing a restriction to the semantics of a program, so that predicates only accept arguments of the prescribed types. Usually, the prescriptive view leads to explicit type annotations in programs. See [18] for more details on type systems for LP.

In our opinion, polymorphic type systems in Milner's style are also a good choice for LP and FLP languages. In the past, polymorphic type systems have been proposed for Prolog programs [15,10], for equational logic programs [11] and for higher-order logic programs in the language λ-Prolog [16]. Exactly as in Milner's original system, [15] guarantees that well-typed programs don't go wrong without any type checking at run time. On the contrary, the type systems in [10,11,16] can accept a wider class of well-typed programs, but type annotations at run time are needed.

Polymorphic type systems are implemented in some FLP languages, such as Curry [12] and $\mathcal{TOY}$ [4]. Currently, $\mathcal{TOY}$ performs no dynamic type checking. As a consequence, absence of type errors at run time is guaranteed for purely functional computations, but not for more complicated computations involving HO variables. This paper is intended as a contribution to a better understanding of polymorphic type discipline in FLP languages. Starting from the results in [8], we will extend the rewriting logic CRWL and the narrowing calculus CLNC with a polymorphic type system, and we will investigate the consequences of type discipline both at the semantic level and at the operational level. At the semantic level, we will modify the models from [8] to incorporate a type universe. At the operational level, we will modify CLNC to maintain type information in goals. The modified narrowing calculus will be sound and complete in a reasonable sense w.r.t. the computation of well-typed solutions. Moreover, dynamic type checking will take place only at those computation steps where some HO logic variable becomes bound.

The rest of the paper is organized as follows. In Section 2 we introduce Higher-Order (shortly, HO) FLP programs as a special kind of applicative TRSs, as well as a polymorphic type system. In Sections 3 and 4 we present the results concerning logical semantics and goal solving, respectively, and in Section 5 we summarize our conclusions. Due to lack of space, we have given only short proof hints. Detailed proofs will appear in an extended version of the paper.

2 Programming with Applicative Rewrite Systems

2.1 Types and Expressions

Since we are interested in HO FLP languages with a type discipline, we need a suitable syntax to represent types and expressions of any type. To introduce types, we assume a countable set $TVar$ of *type variables* α, β, ... and a countable ranked alphabet $TC = \bigcup_{n \in \mathbb{N}} TC^n$ of *type constructors* C. Types $\tau \in Type$ are built as $\tau ::= \alpha \ (\alpha \in TVar) \mid C\ \tau_1 \ldots \tau_n \ (C \in TC^n) \mid \tau \to \tau'$.

Types without any occurrence of $\to$ are called *datatypes*. By convention, $C\ \overline{\tau}_n$ abbreviates $C\ \tau_1 \ldots \tau_n$, "$\to$" associates to the right, and $\overline{\tau}_n \to \tau$ abbreviates $\tau_1 \to \cdots \to \tau_n \to \tau$. The set of type variables occurring in τ is written $tvar(\tau)$. A type τ is called *monomorphic* iff $tvar(\tau) = \emptyset$, and *polymorphic* otherwise. The type variables occurring in polymorphic types have an implicit universal reading. A *polymorphic signature* over TC is a triple $\Sigma = \langle TC, DC, FS \rangle$, where $DC = \bigcup_{n \in \mathbb{N}} DC^n$ resp. $FS = \bigcup_{n \in \mathbb{N}} FS^n$ are ranked sets of *data constructors* resp. *defined function symbols*. Moreover, each $c \in DC^n$ comes with a type declaration $c :: \overline{\tau}_n \to C\ \overline{\alpha}_k$, where n, k$\geq$0, $\alpha_1, \ldots, \alpha_k$ are pairwise different, τ_i are datatypes, and $tvar(\tau_i) \subseteq \{\alpha_1, \ldots, \alpha_k\}$ for all $1 \leq i \leq n$ (so-called *transparency property*).

Also, every $f \in FS^n$ comes with a type declaration $f :: \overline{\tau}_n \to \tau$, where τ_i, τ are arbitrary types.

In the sequel, we will use the notation $h :: \tau \in_{var} \Sigma$ to indicate that Σ includes the type declaration $h :: \tau$ up to a renaming of type variables. For any signature Σ, we write $\Sigma_\perp$ for the result of extending Σ with a new data constructor $\perp :: \alpha$, intended to represent an undefined value that belongs to every type. As notational conventions, we use $c, d \in DC$, $f, g \in FS$ and $h \in DC \cup FS$, and we define the *arity* of $h \in DC^n \cup FS^n$ as $ar(h) = n$. In the sequel, we always suppose a given signature Σ, that will not appear explicitly in our notation. Assuming a countable set $DVar$ of data *variables* $X, Y, \ldots$ (disjoint with $TVar$), *partial expressions* $e \in Exp_\perp$ are defined as follows:

$$e ::= X \ (X \in DVar) \mid \perp \mid h \ (h \in CS \cup FS) \mid (e \ e_1)$$

These expressions are usually called *applicative*, because $(e \ e_1)$ stands for the *application* operation (represented as juxtaposition) which applies the function denoted by e to the argument denoted by e_1. FO expressions can be translated to applicative expressions by means of so-called *curried notation*. For instance, $f(X, g(Y))$ becomes $(f \ X \ (g \ Y))$. The set of data variables occurring in e is written $var(e)$. An expression e is called *closed* iff $var(e) = \emptyset$, and *open* otherwise. Following a usual convention, we assume that application associates to the left, and we use the notation $e \ \overline{e}_n$ to abbreviate $e \ e_1 \ldots e_n$. Expressions $e \in Exp$ without occurrences of $\perp$ are called *total*. Two important subclasses of expressions are *partial data terms* $t \in Term_\perp$, defined as

$$t ::= X \ (X \in DVar) \mid \perp \mid (c \ \overline{t}_n) \ (c \in CS^n)$$

and *partial patterns* $t \in Pat_\perp$, defined as:

$$t ::= \ X \ (X \in DVar) \ \mid \ \perp \ \mid \ (c \ \overline{t}_m) \ (c \in DC^n, \ m \leq n) \ \mid \ (f \ \overline{t}_m) \ (f \in FS^n, \ m < n)$$

Total data terms $t \in Term$ and *total patterns* $t \in Pat$ are defined analogously, but omitting $\perp$. Note that $Term_\perp \subset Pat_\perp \subset Exp_\perp$. As usual in FP, data terms are used to represent data values. Patterns generalize data terms and can be used as an intensional representation of functions. Most functional languages allow also λ-*abstractions* of the form $\lambda X.e$ to represent functions. Some approaches to HO FLP also permit λ-abstractions, see [19]. We will avoid them because they give rise to undecidable unification problems [7], and applicative expressions are expressive enough for most programming purposes.

The next example illustrates some of the notions introduced so far.

Example 1. Let us consider a signature with
$TC^0 = \{\texttt{bool}, \texttt{nat}\}$, $DC^0 = \{\texttt{true}, \texttt{false}, \texttt{z}, \texttt{nil}\}$, $DC^1 = \{\texttt{s}\}$, $DC^2 = \{\texttt{cons}\}$, $FS^1 = \{\texttt{not}, \texttt{foo}\}$, $FS^2 = \{\texttt{and}, \texttt{or}, \texttt{plus}, \texttt{map}, \texttt{snd}, \texttt{twice}\}$, and with the following type declarations:

```
true, false :: bool    z :: nat  s :: nat → nat
nil :: list α  cons :: α → list α → list α
not :: bool → bool  and, or :: bool → bool → bool
plus :: nat → nat → nat  foo :: α → nat
map :: (α → β) → list α → list β
snd :: α → β → α  twice :: (α → α) → α → α
```

Then, we can build *data terms* such as (s X), (cons (s X) (cons Y nil)); *patterns* such as (plus z), (snd X), (twice twice), (twice (plus X)); and *expressions*, like (map (s X) (cons (s X) nil)), (twice (plus X) Y).

In the sequel, we will use Prolog notation for the list constructors, writing [ ] for nil and [X|Xs] for cons X Xs. The following classification of expressions is useful: $X\ \bar{e}_m$, with $X \in DVar$ and $m > 0$, is called a *flexible expression*, while $h\ \bar{e}_m$ with $h \in DC \cup FS$ is called a *rigid expression*. Moreover, a rigid expression is called *active* iff $h \in FS$ and $m \geq ar(h)$, and *passive* otherwise. Note that any pattern is either a variable or a passive rigid expression. As we will see in Section 3, outermost reduction makes sense only for active rigid expressions.

Following the spirit of denotational semantics [20], we view $Pat_\perp$ as the set of finite elements of a semantic domain, and we define the *approximation ordering* $\sqsubseteq$ as the least partial ordering over $Pat_\perp$ satisfying the following properties: $\perp \sqsubseteq t$, for all $t \in Pat_\perp$; $X \sqsubseteq X$, for all $X \in DVar$; and $h\ \bar{t}_m \sqsubseteq h\ \bar{s}_m$ whenever these two expressions are patterns and $t_i \sqsubseteq s_i$ for all $1 \leq i \leq m$. $Pat_\perp$, and more generally any partially ordered set (shortly, poset), can be converted into a semantic domain by means of a technique called *ideal completion*; see [9] for details.

In the sequel we will need substitutions. We define *type substitutions* $\sigma_t \in TSub$ as mappings $\sigma_t : TVar \rightarrow Type$ extended to $\sigma_t : Type \rightarrow Type$ in the natural way. Similarly, we consider *partial data substitutions* $\sigma_d \in DSub_\perp$ given by mappings $\sigma_d : DVar \rightarrow Pat_\perp$, *total data substitutions* $\sigma_d \in DSub$ given by mappings $\sigma_d : DVar \rightarrow Pat$, and *substitutions* given as pairs $\sigma = (\sigma_t, \sigma_d)$. By convention, we write $\tau\sigma_t$ instead of $\sigma_t(\tau)$, and $\theta_t\sigma_t$ for the composition of θ_t and σ_t, such that $\tau(\theta_t\sigma_t) = (\tau\theta_t)\sigma_t$ for any τ. We define the *domain* $dom(\sigma_t)$ as the set of all type variables α s.t. $\sigma_t(\alpha) \neq \alpha$, and the *range* $ran(\sigma_t)$ as $\bigcup_{\alpha \in dom(\sigma_t)} tvar(\sigma_t(\alpha))$. Similar notions can be defined for data substitutions. The *identity substitution* $id = (id_t, id_d)$ is such that $id_t(\alpha) = \alpha$ for all $\alpha \in TVar$ and $id_d(X) = X$ for all $X \in DVar$. The approximation ordering over $Pat_\perp$ induces another approximation ordering over $DSub_\perp$, defined by $\sigma_d \sqsubseteq \sigma'_d$ iff $\sigma_d(X) \sqsubseteq X\sigma'_d(X)$, for all $X \in DVar$. Another useful ordering over $DSub_\perp$ is *subsumption*, defined by $\theta_d \leq \theta'_d$ iff $\theta'_d = \theta_d\sigma_d$ for some $\sigma_d \in DSub_\perp$. For any set of variables $\mathcal{X}$, we use the notations $\theta_d \leq \theta'_d[\mathcal{X}]$ (resp. $\theta_d \leq \theta'_d[\backslash\mathcal{X}]$) to indicate that $X\theta'_d = X\theta_d\sigma_d$ holds for some $\sigma_d \in DSub_\perp$ and all $X \in \mathcal{X}$ (resp. all $X \notin \mathcal{X}$).

2.2   Well-Typed Expressions

Following Milner's type system [14], we will now introduce the notion of well-typed expression. We define an *type environment* as any set T of type assumptions $X :: \tau$ for data variables, such that T does not include two different assumptions for the same variable. The *domain* $dom(T)$ and the *range* $ran(T)$ of a type environment are the set of all data variables resp. type variables that occur in T. Given $\sigma_t \in TSub$, we define $T\sigma_t = \{X :: \tau\sigma_t \mid X :: \tau \in T\}$. We write $T' \leq T$ iff there is some $\sigma_t \in TSub$ s.t. $T' = T\sigma_t$. *Type judgements* $T \vdash e :: \tau$ are derived by means of the following inference rules:

VR $T \vdash X :: \tau$, if $X :: \tau \in T$.
ID $T \vdash h :: \tau\sigma_t$, if $h :: \tau \in_{var} \Sigma_\perp$, $\sigma_t \in TSub$.
AP $T \vdash (e\ e_1) :: \tau$, if $T \vdash e :: (\tau_1 \rightarrow \tau)$ and $T \vdash e_1 :: \tau_1$, for some τ_1.

An expression $e \in Exp_\perp$ is called *well-typed* in the type environment T iff there exists some type τ s.t. $T \vdash e :: \tau$. Expressions that admit more than one type in T are called *polymorphic*. A well-typed expression always admits a so-called *principal type* that is more general than any other. Adapting ideas from [14], we define a *type reconstruction* algorithm TR to compute principal types. Assume a expression e and a type environment T s.t. $var(e) \subseteq dom(T)$. Then $TR(T, e)$ returns a pair of the form (e^τ, E) where e^τ is a *type annotation* of e and E is a system of equations between types, expressing most general conditions for τ to be a valid type of e. The algorithm TR works by structural recursion on e:

VR $TR(T, X) = (X^\tau, \emptyset)$, if $X :: \tau \in T$.
ID $TR(T, h) = (h^\tau, \emptyset)$, if $h :: \tau \in_{var} \Sigma_\perp$ is a fresh variant of h's type declaration.
AP $TR(T, (e\ e_1)) = ((e^{\tau_1 \rightarrow \gamma}\ e_1^{\tau_1})^\gamma, E \cup E1 \cup \{\tau \approx \tau_1 \rightarrow \gamma\})$,
if $TR(T, e) = (e^\tau, E)$, $TR(T, e_1) = (e_1^{\tau_1}, E1)$, $tvar(E) \cap tvar(E1) \subseteq ran(T)$, $\gamma \notin tvar(E) \cup tvar(E1)$ fresh type variable.

Type annotated expressions, as those returned by TR, carry an obvious certification of their well-typed character. In particular, the annotations of their variables define an environment. Their syntactic specification is:

$$e ::= X^\tau\ (X \in DVar, \tau \in Type) \mid h^{\tau\sigma_t}\ (h\ ::\ \tau \in_{var} \Sigma_\perp, \sigma_t \in TSub) \mid (e^{\tau_1 \rightarrow \tau} e_1^{\tau_1})^\tau$$

Given a system E of equations between types, its set of *solutions* $TSol(E)$ consists of all $\sigma_t \in TSub$ s.t. $\tau\sigma_t = \tau'\sigma_t$ for all $\tau \approx \tau' \in E$. If E is *solvable* (i.e., $TSol(E) \neq \emptyset$), a most general solution $mgu(E) = \sigma_t \in TSol(E)$ can by computed by means of Robinson's unification algorithm (see e.g. [1]). The next result is easily proved by structural induction on e.

Proposition 1. *Assume* $TR(T, e) = (e^\tau, E)$. *Then, for any* $\sigma_t \in TSol(E)$ *one has* $T\sigma_t \vdash e :: \tau\sigma_t$. *Reciprocally, if* $T' \leq T$ *and* $T' \vdash e^{\tau'}$, *there is some* $\sigma_t \in TSol(E)$ *such that* $T' = T\sigma_t$ *and* $e^{\tau'}$ *is* $e^\tau\sigma_t$. □

Assuming $TR(T, e) = (e^\tau, E)$ with solvable E, and $\sigma_t = mgu(E)$, we will write $PT(T, e) = \tau\sigma_t$ for the *principal type* of e w.r.t. T, and $PA(e) = e^\tau\sigma_t$ for the *principal type annotation* of e w.r.t. T. All the expressions from Example 1 are well-typed in suitable environments, and some of them are polymorphic. For instance, the pattern twice twice is well-typed in the empty environment. Moreover, $PA(\emptyset, \text{twice twice})$ can be computed as

$$(\text{twice}^{((\alpha \rightarrow \alpha) \rightarrow \alpha \rightarrow \alpha) \rightarrow (\alpha \rightarrow \alpha) \rightarrow \alpha \rightarrow \alpha}\ \text{twice}^{(\alpha \rightarrow \alpha) \rightarrow \alpha \rightarrow \alpha})^{(\alpha \rightarrow \alpha) \rightarrow \alpha \rightarrow \alpha}$$

To compute a principal type for an expression e with $var(e) = \{X_1, \ldots, X_n\}$ one can invoke $TR(T, e)$ with $T = \{X_1 :: \alpha_1, \ldots, X_n :: \alpha_1\}$, where α_i are n pairwise different type variables.

Due to the transparency property required for the type declarations of data constructors, all data terms t are *transparent* in the sense that the type of the variables occurring in t can be deduced from the type of t. It is useful to isolate those patterns that have a similar property. We say that a pattern t is *transparent* iff for each subpattern of t of the form $f\ \bar{t}_m$, the type declared for f in Σ can be written as $\bar{\tau}_m \to \tau$ with $tvar(\bar{\tau}_m) \subseteq tvar(\tau)$. Note that the pattern snd X is not transparent. In fact, its principal type $\beta \to \beta$ gives no information on the type of X.

2.3 Programs

Following [8], we define CRWL programs as a special kind of applicative TRSs, but now requiring well-typedness. More precisely, assuming $f \in FS^n$ whose declared type (up to renaming of type variables) is of the form $f :: \bar{\tau}_n \to \tau$, a *well-typed* defining rule for f must have the following form:

$$\underbrace{f\ t_1\ \dots\ t_n}_{\text{left hand side } (l)} \to \underbrace{r}_{\text{right hand side}} \Leftarrow \underbrace{C}_{\text{Condition}} \ \Box \ \underbrace{T}_{\text{Type Environment}}$$

where l must be linear, t_i must be transparent patterns, r must be an expression s.t. $var(r) \subseteq var(l)$, the condition C must consist of finitely many (possibly zero) so-called *joinability statements* $a \bowtie b$ where a, b are expressions, and T must be a type environment whose domain is the set of all data variables occurring in the rewrite rule, and such that: $T \vdash t_i :: \tau_i$ for $1 \leq i \leq n$, $T \vdash r :: \tau$ and $T \vdash C ::$ bool. The symbol $\perp$ never occurs in a defining rule. A *well-typed* CRWL program can be any set of *well-typed* defining rules for different symbols $f \in FS$. Neither termination nor confluence is required. In particular, the lack of confluence means that CRWL programs can define non-deterministic functions, whose usefulness for FLP languages has been defended in [9].

The meaning of joinability statements will be explained in the next section. An additional explanation is needed to understand the previous definitions. In $T \vdash C ::$ bool, we view C as an "expression" built from symbols in the current signature Σ, plus the two additional operations $(\bowtie) :: \alpha \to \alpha \to$ bool and $(,)$ $::$ bool $\to$ bool $\to$ bool, used in infix notation to build conditions. We also agree to view the rewrite symbol as an operation $(\to) :: \alpha \to \alpha \to$ bool, used in infix notation to build "expressions" $l \to r$. This convention will be useful for typing purposes in Section 4.

Note that defining rules in a well-typed program are *type general* and *transparent*, in the sense left-hand sides use transparent patterns and have exactly the principal type declared for the corresponding function. Transparency of function definitions made no sense in [8], but it is important in a typed setting.

We consider also *untyped* programs, which are sets of untyped defining rules where the type environment T is missing. Given an untyped program $\mathcal{P}$, the type reconstruction algorithm TR can be used to decide whether it is possible to well-type the program by adding suitable type environments T to its rewrite rules. In practice, the user of FP languages such as Haskell [17] or FLP languages such as $\mathcal{TOY}$ [4] must provide type declarations only for data constructors.

Next we show a well-typed program, using the signature from Example 1, that will be useful for other examples in the rest of the paper.

Example 2. Well-typed program.

```
not :: bool → bool                    snd :: α → β → β
not  false → true ⇐ ∅ □ ∅             snd X Y → Y ⇐ ∅ □ {X :: α, Y :: β}
not  true → false ⇐ ∅ □ ∅

plus :: nat → nat → nat
plus  z  Y → Y ⇐ ∅ □ {Y :: nat}
plus (s X) Y → s (plus X Y) ⇐ ∅ □ {X, Y :: nat}

foo :: α → nat
foo X  →  z ⇐ F Y ⋈ X □ {X :: α, Y :: β, F :: β → α}

map :: (α → β) → [α] → [β]
map F [ ] → [ ] ⇐ ∅ □ {F :: α → β}
map F [X | Xs] → [F X | map F Xs] ⇐ ∅ □ {F :: α → β, X :: α, Xs :: [α]}

twice :: (α → α) → α → α
twice F X  → F (F X) ⇐ ∅ □ {F :: α → α, X :: α}
```

In this particular example, all patterns in the left-hand sides are data terms of FO type. See [8] for another example where HO patterns are used to represent logical circuits.

3   A Rewriting Logic for Program Semantics

In [8], a rewriting logic was proposed to deduce from an untyped CRWL program $\mathcal{P}$ certain statements that characterize the meaning of $\mathcal{P}$. More precisely, two kinds of statements must be considered: *approximation statements* $e \to t$, meaning that $t \in Pat_\perp$ approximates the value of $e \in Exp_\perp$; and *joinability statements* $a \bowtie b$, meaning that $a \to t$, $b \to t$ holds for some *total* $t \in Pat$. The collection of all t s.t. $e \to t$ can be deduced from $\mathcal{P}$ leads to a logical characterization of e's meaning. On the other hand, joinability statements are needed for conditions in rewrite rules, as well as for goals (see Section 4). They do not behave as equations in equational logic, for two reasons: t is required to be a total pattern rather than an arbitrary expression, and it is not required to be unique. Requiring unicity of t would lead to a deterministic version of joinability, which has been used under the name *strict equality* in several FLP languages.

Roughly, a deduction of $e \to t$ in CRWL corresponds to a finite sequence of rewrite steps going from e to t in the TRS $\mathcal{P} \cup \{X \to \perp\}$. Unfortunately, this simple idea does not work directly, because it leads to an unconvenient treatment of non-determinism. Therefore, a Goal-Oriented Rewriting Calculus (GORC for short) with special inference rules was given in [8] to formalize CRWL deducibility. We recall this calculus below. The inference rule (**OR**) uses the set of (possibly partial) instances of rewrite rules from $\mathcal{P}$, that is defined as follows, ignoring the type environments:

$$[\mathcal{P}]_\perp = \{(l \to r \Leftarrow C)\sigma_d \mid (l \to r \Leftarrow C \sqcap T) \in \mathcal{P}, \sigma_d \in DSub_\perp\}$$

$BT:$ $e \to \bot$ $RR:$ $X \to X$, if $X \in DVar$

$OR:$ $\dfrac{e_1 \to t_1 \ldots e_n \to t_n \quad C \quad r\ a_1 \ldots a_m \to t}{f\ e_1 \ldots e_n\ a_1 \ldots a_m \to t}$,

if $t \not\equiv \bot$ is a pattern, $m \geq 0$, and $f\ t_1 \ldots t_n \to r \Leftarrow C \in [\mathcal{P}]_\bot$

$DC:$ $\dfrac{e_1 \to t_1 \ldots e_n \to t_n}{h\ e_1 \ldots e_n \to h\ t_1 \ldots t_n}$ $JN:$ $\dfrac{a \to t \quad b \to t}{a \bowtie b}$

if $h\ t_1 \ldots t_n$ is a rigid pattern   if t is a total pattern

We use the notation $\mathcal{P} \vdash_{GORC} \varphi$ to assert that the statement φ can be deduced from the program $\mathcal{P}$ by means of a GORC proof. More detailed explanations about a FO version of GORC can be found in [9]. Note that $\mathcal{P} \vdash_{GORC} e \to t$ corresponds to a purely functional computation reducing e to t. Although the GORC calculus does not care about types, dynamic type checking is not needed for purely functional computations in the case of a well-typed program. This is shown by the next type preservation theorem. A similar result for a FO FLP language has been given in [2].

Theorem 1. Type preservation by reduction.
Consider a well-typed program $\mathcal{P}$, $e \in Exp_\bot$, $\tau \in Type$ and a type environment T such that $T \vdash e :: \tau$. Then, for every $t \in Pat_\bot$ such that $\mathcal{P} \vdash_{GORC} e \to t$, one has $T \vdash t :: \tau$.

Proof idea: Induction on the structure of the GORC proof that proves $\mathcal{P} \vdash_{GORC} e \to t$. A case distinction is needed according to the GORC inference rule applied at the last step. The **(OR)** case is the most interesting one; it uses type generality and transparency of the defining rules in $\mathcal{P}$.   □

To show that the previous theorem may fail if defining rules are not transparent, consider a function unpack :: $(\beta \to \beta) \to \alpha$, defined by the non-transparent rewrite rule unpack (snd X) $\to$ X $\Leftarrow \emptyset$ □ $\{X :: \alpha\}$. Then, taking the empty environment for T, we see that

$T \vdash$ unpack (snd z) $:: \alpha$ $\mathcal{P} \vdash_{GORC}$ unpack (snd z) $\to$ z

but not $T \vdash$ z $:: \alpha$, thus violating type preservation.

In Section 4 we will see that dynamic type checking is needed for solving goals that involve HO logic variables. There, the following notion will be useful. A *type-annotated* GORC proof is obtained from a given GORC proof Π by attaching a type annotation to all the expressions occurring in Π in a consistent way. More precisely, each approximation statement $e \to t$ occurring in Π must be annotated to become $e^\tau \to t^\tau$ for some type τ; and each step in Π where a joinability statement $a \bowtie b$ is infered from premises $a \to t$ and $b \to t$ by means of **(JN)**, must be annotated to become an inference of $a^\tau \bowtie b^\tau$ from $a^\tau \to t^\tau$ and $b^\tau \to t^\tau$, for some type τ. As seen in Subsection 2.2, only well-typed expressions can be type-annotated. Therefore, type-annotated GORC proofs always represent a well-typed computation. Some GORC proofs, however, cannot be type-annotated. Considering the well-typed program $\mathcal{P}$ from Example 2, we can show:

Example 3. A GORC proof that *cannot* be type-annotated.

1. foo true ⋈ z   by (JN), 2, 5 and z total pattern.
2. foo true → z   by (OR), 6, 5, 3.
3. plus z true ⋈ true   by (JN), 4, 6 and true total pattern.
4. plus z true → true   by (OR), 5, 6.
5. z → z   by (DC).
6. true → true   by (DC).

Note that foo true → z is type preserving as a functional reduction. The problem with the GORC proof above is that the GORC rule **(OR)** has guessed an ill-typed binding for the HO variable F.

Models for CRWL programs have been presented in [8] for an untyped HO language, and in [2] for a typed FO language with algebraic datatypes. It is possible to combine both approaches, using *intensional models* $\mathcal{A}$ with a poset $D^{\mathcal{A}}$ as data universe and a set $T^{\mathcal{A}}$ as type universe. The elements in $D^{\mathcal{A}}$ can be interpreted as intensional representations of functions by means of an application operation, although they are not true functions. Thanks to intensional semantics, one can work in a HO language while avoiding undecidability problems, especially undecidability of HO unification [7]. Variants of this idea have occured previously in some LP and equational LP languages, as e.g. in [5,10,11].

In particular, for any program $\mathcal{P}$ and any type environment T with $dom(T) = DVar$, we can define a *least Herbrand model* $\mathcal{M}_{\mathcal{P}}(T)$ whose data universe is $Pat_{\perp}$ and whose type universe is $Type$, and we can prove that $\mathcal{M}_{\mathcal{P}}(T)$ satisfies exactly those approximation and joinability statements φ that are true in all the models of $\mathcal{P}$ under all possible totally defined valuations. Moreover, if $\mathcal{P}$ is well-typed, then $\mathcal{M}_{\mathcal{P}}(T)$ is also well-typed in a natural sense. As a consequence of this result, GORC deducibility is sound and complete w.r.t. semantic validity. Moreover, $\mathcal{M}_{\mathcal{P}}(T)$ can be viewed as the logical semantics of $\mathcal{P}$, in analogy to the least Herbrand model of a LP program over a Herbrand universe with variables [1]. Least Herbrand models of FO CRWL programs can be also characterized as least fixpoints and free objects in a category of models [9,2]. These results can be extended to the present typed HO setting.

4   A Lazy Narrowing Calculus for Goal Solving

In this section we will extend the lazy narrowing calculus CLNC from [8] to prevent type errors at run time. All the examples used in the sequel implicitly refer to the well-typed program from Example 2.

We recall that initial goals G for CLNC are finite systems of joinability statements $a ⋈ b$. A correct solution for such a G is any total data substitution θ_d s.t. $\mathcal{P} \vdash_{GORC} a\theta_d ⋈ b\theta_d$ for all $a ⋈ b \in G$. Soundness and completeness of CLNC, proved for untyped programs in [8], is also valid for well-typed programs. In the typed setting, however, one would like to avoid the computation of ill-typed answers, whenever the program and the goal are well-typed. Unfortunately, there are problematic situations where run time type errors can occur in CLNC. A first kind of problem appears when a HO logic variable F occurs as head in some flexible expression $F \, \bar{e}_m$. In CLNC there are special transformations to guess a suitable pattern t as binding for F in such cases, and sometimes $t \, \bar{e}_m$ may become ill-typed. For instance, the goal F X ⋈ Y, not Y ⋈ X is well-typed, but the binding F↦plus z can lead to an ill-typed goal. As a second example, consider map F [true,X] ⋈ [Y,false]. This is also a well-typed goal, but CLNC can compute an ill-typed solution with bindings F↦plus z, X↦false, Y↦true.

A second kind of problematic situation is related to statements $h \, \bar{a}_m ⋈ h \, \bar{b}_m$, joining two *rigid and passive* expressions. In CLNC a *decomposition* transformation reduces such condition to a system of simpler conditions $a_i ⋈ b_i$. Assume that the declared type for h can be written as $\bar{\tau}_m \rightarrow \tau$. Then we will say that the forementioned decomposition step is *transparent* if $tvar(\bar{\tau}_m) \subseteq tvar(\tau)$, and *opaque* otherwise. In the case of an opaque decomposition step, some of the new conditions $a_i ⋈ b_i$ may become ill-typed. Consider for instance the two well-typed goals snd true ⋈ snd z and snd (map not [ ]) ⋈ snd (map s [ ]). Both of them become ill-typed after a decomposition step. In the first case the goal is unsolvable, while in the second case the computation ultimately succeeds, in spite of the type error. Opaque decomposition steps are also possible for approximation statements $h \, \bar{a}_m \rightarrow h \, \bar{t}_m$.

As shown in [10,11] for the case of FO typed SLD resolution and FO typed narrowing, respectively, a goal solving procedure that works with fully type-annotated goals can detect type errors at run time, since they cause failure at the level of type unification. Full type annotations have the disadvantage that goal solving becomes more complex and less efficient also for those computations that do not need any dynamic type checking. Some optimization techniques were proposed in [10,11] to alleviate this difficulty.

Here we will adopt a less costly solution to extend CLNC with dynamic type checking. Goals G will be similar to those from [8], but extended with a type environment T, and the notion of solution will be also extended so that solutions can provide bindings both for the data variables and for the type variables occurring in G. Moreover, those CLNC transformations that compute a binding t for some HO variable F will use type unification to ensure that t is type-compatible with the type expected for F in the goal type environment. The CLNC transformations not related to HO variable bindings will perform no dynamic type checking. In case of a computation that involves no HO logic variables, the only overhead w.r.t. untyped CLNC will consist in maintaining the goal type environment. This is not too costly, because it can be done on the basis of declared principal types, known at compilation time.

In the rest of this section we develop these ideas and we state the soundness, completeness and type preservation properties of the resulting lazy narrowing calculus. Unfortunately, we have found no way to prevent dynamic type errors due to opaque decomposition. Therefore, our soundness theorem guarantees well-typed computations only under the assumption that no opaque decomposition steps have occurred. Dually, our completeness theorem only ensures the well-typed computation of those solutions whose correctness is witnessed by some type-annotated GORC proof.

4.1 Admissible Goals and Solutions

The lazy narrowing calculus CLNC from [8] works with goals that include both joinability statements $a \bowtie b$ to be solved and approximation statements $e \to t$ to represent delayed unifications, introduced by lazy narrowing steps. Moreover, goals in G include a *solved part* to represent the answer data substitution computed so far, and they satisfy a number of *goal invariants*. Here we must extend this class of goals, adding a *type environment* and a second solved part to represent an answer type substitution. Those variables of a goal that have been introduced locally by previous CLNC steps will be viewed as *existential*. For technical convenience, in the rest of the paper we assume a countable set $EVar$ of existential data variables, and we use the notation $(l \to r \Leftarrow C \Box T) \in_{var} \mathcal{P}$ to indicate that $(l \to r \Leftarrow C \Box T)$ is a renaming of some defining rule from $\mathcal{P}$, using fresh type variables in T and fresh existential variables in place of data variables. We also write $a \asymp b$ for anyone of the conditions $a \bowtie b$ or $b \bowtie a$. The formal definition of goal follows. More motivation and explanations can be found in [9].

Definition 1. Admissible goals *have the form* $G = P \Box C \Box S_d \Box S_t \Box T$, *where:*

1. *The* **delayed part** $P = e_1 \to t_1, \ldots, e_k \to t_k$ *is a multiset of approximation statements, with* $e_i \in Exp$, $t_i \in Pat$. *The set of* **produced data variables** *of G is defined as* $pvar(P) = var(t_1) \cup \ldots \cup var(t_k)$, *and the* **production relation** *is defined over* $var(G)$ *by the condition* $X \gg_P Y$ *iff there is some* $1 \leq i \leq k$ *such that* $X \in var(e_i)$ *and* $Y \in var(t_i)$.

2. *The* **unsolved part** $C = a_1 \bowtie b_1, \ldots, a_l \bowtie b_l$ *is a multiset of joinability statements. The set of* **demanded data variables** *of G is defined as* $ddvar(C) = \{X \in DVar \mid X \, \bar{e}_m \bowtie b \in C, \text{for some } \bar{e}_m, b\}$.

3. *The* **data solved part** $S_d = \{X_1 \approx s_1, \ldots, X_n \approx s_n\}$ *is a set of equations in solved form, such that each* $s_i \in Pat$ *and each* X_i *occurs exactly once in G. We write* σ_d *for* $mgu(S_d)$.

4. *The* **type solved part** $S_t = \{\alpha_1 \approx \tau_1, \ldots, \alpha_m \approx \tau_m\}$ *is a set of type equations in solved form, such that each* $\tau_i \in Type$ *and each* α_i *occurs exactly once in G. We write* σ_t *for* $mgu(S_t)$.

5. $T = \{X_1 :: \tau_1, \ldots, X_k :: \tau_k\}$ *is called the* **type environment** *of G.*

6. *G must fulfil the following conditions, called* **goal invariants:**
   LN *The tuple* $(t_1, \ldots, t_k)$ *is linear.*
   EX *All produced variables are existential:* $pvar(P) \subseteq EVar$.
   NC *The transitive closure of the production relation* $\gg_P$ *is irreflexive.*
   SL *No produced variable enters the solved part:* $var(S_d) \cap pvar(P) = \emptyset$.   □

Note that any admissible goal verifies $(P \Box C)\sigma_d = (P \Box C)$ and $T\sigma_t = T$, because of the requirements in items 3. and 4. above. By convention, *initial goals* are of the form $G_0 = \emptyset \Box C \Box \emptyset \Box \emptyset \Box T_0$, and include no existential variables.

In what follows we use the type reconstruction algorithm TR explained in Subsection 2.2. We say that a goal $G = P \,\square\, C \,\square\, S_d \,\square\, S_t \,\square\, T$ is well-typed iff there is some $T' \leq T$ s.t. $T' \vdash (P, C)$ :: bool. In addition, G is called *type-closed* iff T itself can be taken as T'. Note that conditions of defining rules in well-typed programs, as defined in Subsection 2.3, are always well-typed and type-closed. More formally:

Definition 2. *Consider an admissible goal* $G \equiv P \,\square\, C \,\square\, S_d \,\square\, S_t \,\square\, T$.

1. *We say that* G *is* **well-typed** *iff* $TR(T, (P, C)) = ((-)^{bool}, E)$ *such that* $TSol(E) \neq \emptyset$ *with* $mgu(E) = \sigma'_t$. *In case that* $T = T\sigma'_t$, *we also say that* G *is* **type-closed**.
2. *If* G *is well-typed, but not type-closed, the* **type-closure** *of* G *is the new goal* $\hat{G} = P \,\square\, C \,\square\, S_d \,\square\, \hat{S}_t \,\square\, \hat{T}$ *where* $TR(T, (P, C)) = ((-)^{bool}, E)$ *and* $\hat{\sigma}_t = mgu(E \cup S_t)$ *and* $\hat{T} = T\hat{\sigma}_t$. *Note that* $\hat{G}$ *is again an admissible goal.* $\square$

Well-typed solutions for admissible goals, and GORC proofs witnessing their correctness, can be defined as follows:

Definition 3. *Let* $G = P \,\square\, C \,\square\, S_d \,\square\, S_t \,\square\, T$ *be an admissible goal for a program* $\mathcal{P}$.

1. *An* **answer** *for* G *is any pair* (R, θ) *formed by a type environment* R *and a substitution* $\theta = (\theta_t, \theta_d)$, *satisfying the following conditions:*

   (a) $dom(\theta_t) \cap dom(\sigma_t) = \emptyset$ *and* $dom(\theta_d) \cap dom(\sigma_d) = \emptyset$.

   (b) *If* $X \in dom(\theta_d) \setminus pvar(P)$ *then* $\theta_d(X)$ *is a total pattern.*

   (c) *If* $Z \in dom(R)$ *then* $Z \in ran(\theta_d) \setminus dom(T)$.

2. *An answer* (R, θ) *for* G *is a* **well-typed solution** *iff* $\theta_t \in Sol(S_t)$ *and* $\theta_d \in Sol(S_d)$, $\mathcal{P} \vdash_{GORC} (P \,\square\, C)\theta_d$ *and* $(T\theta_t \cup R) \vdash T\theta$. *We write* $Sol(G)$ *for the set of all well-typed solutions of* G.

3. *A* **witness** *of* $(R, \theta) \in Sol(G)$ *is a multiset containing a GORC proof for each condition* $(e \rightarrow t)\theta_d \in P\theta_d$ *and a GORC proof for each condition* $((a \bowtie b)\theta_d) \in (C\theta_d)$.

4. *Assume that* G *and* $\mathcal{P}$ *are well-typed. A* **type-annotated witness** *of* $(R, \theta) \in Sol(G)$, *if it exists, is obtained by performing a type annotation of the GORC proofs included in an ordinary witness. More precisely, if* $PA(T\theta_t \cup R, (P, C)\theta_d) = \dots e_i^{\tau_i} \rightarrow t_i^{\tau_i} \dots, \dots a_j^{\tau_j} \bowtie b_j^{\tau_j} \dots$, *then the type-annotated witness must contain a type-annottated GORC proof for each* $e_i^{\tau_i} \rightarrow t_i^{\tau_i}$ *and a type-annotated GORC proof for each* $a_j^{\tau_j} \bowtie b_j^{\tau_j}$. *We write* $ASol(G)$ *for the set of all the solutions of* G *which have a type-annotated witness.* $\square$

As part of the definition of well-typed solution, we have demanded $(T\theta_t \cup R) \vdash T\theta$. This is intended to mean that $(T\theta_t \cup R) \vdash X\theta_d :: \tau\theta_t$ must hold for each $X :: \tau \in T$. The rôle of the type environment R is to provide type assumptions for the new data variables introduced in $ran(\theta_d)$. As we will see, R is always empty in the case of computed solutions.

4.2   Lazy Narrowing Calculus

Now we are ready to extend the lazy narrowing calculus CLNC from [8] with dynamic type checking. We keep the CLNC denomination. As in [8], the notation $G \Vdash G'$ means that G is transformed into G' in one step. The aim when using CLNC is to transform an *initial goal* $G_0 = \emptyset \,\square\, C \,\square\, \emptyset \,\square\, \emptyset \,\square\, T_0$ into a *solved goal* $G_n = \emptyset \,\square\, \emptyset \,\square\, S_d \,\square\, S_t \,\square\, T_n$, and the return $(\emptyset, (\sigma_t, \sigma_d))$ as computed answer. Trivially, $(\emptyset, (\sigma_t, \sigma_d))$ is a solution of G_n in the sense of Definition 3. A sequence of transformation steps $G_0 \Vdash \ldots \Vdash G_n$ going from an initial goal to a solved goal, is called CLNC *derivation* and noted as $G_0 \Vdash^* G_n$.

Due to the convention that P and C are understood as multisets, CLNC assumes no particular *selection strategy* for choosing the goal statement to be processed in the next step. For writing failure rules we use **FAIL**, representing an irreducible inconsistent goal. We also use some hopefully self-explaining abbreviations for tuples. In particular, $\bar{a}_m \bowtie \bar{b}_m$ stands for m new joinability statements $a_i \bowtie b_i$, and similarly for approximation statements. Some CLNC rules use the notation "[...]" meaning an optional part of a goal, present only under certain conditions. Finally, some other rules (related to *occurs-check*) refer to the set $svar(e)$ of those data variables that occur in e at some position outside the scope of evaluable function calls. Formally, $svar(X) = \{X\}$ for any data variable X; for a rigid and passive expression $e = h\,\bar{e}_m$, $svar(e) = \bigcup_{i=1}^m svar(e_i)$; and $svar(e) = \emptyset$ in any other case.

The CLNC Calculus

Rules for the Unsolved Part

Identity: (ID)

$P \,\square\, X \bowtie X,\, C \,\square\, S_d \,\square\, S_t \,\square\, T \Vdash P \,\square\, C \,\square\, S_d \,\square\, S_t \,\square\, T$
- $X \notin pvar(P)$.

Decomposition: (DC1)

$P \,\square\, h\,\bar{a}_m \bowtie h\,\bar{b}_m,\, C \,\square\, S_d \,\square\, S_t \,\square\, T \Vdash P \,\square\, \bar{a}_m \bowtie \bar{b}_m,\, C \,\square\, S_d \,\square\, S_t \,\square\, T$
- $h\,\bar{a}_m,\, h\,\bar{b}_m$ rigid and passive.

Binding & Decomposition: (BD) ★ $(k \geq 0)$

$P \,\square\, X\,\bar{a}_k \preceq s\,\bar{b}_k,\, C \,\square\, S_d \,\square\, S_t \,\square\, T \Vdash (P \,\square\, \bar{a}_k \preceq \bar{b}_k, C \,\square\, S_d)\sigma_d, X \approx s\square S'_t \,\square\, T\sigma'_t$
- $s \in Pat;\, X \notin var(s);\, X \notin pvar(P);\, var(s) \cap pvar(P) = \emptyset$.   * $\sigma_d = \{X\,/\,s\}$.
- $k = 0$ and $S'_t = S_t$; or $k > 0$, $s\,\bar{b}_k$ rigid and passive, and $\sigma'_t = mgu(S_t, \tau \approx \tau')$ where $X :: \tau \in T, \tau' = PT(T, s)$.

Imitation & Decomposition: (IM) ★ $(k \geq 0)$

$P \,\square\, X\,\bar{a}_k \preceq h\,\bar{e}_m\,\bar{b}_k,\, C \,\square\, S_d \,\square\, S_t \,\square\, T$
$\quad \Vdash (P \,\square\, \bar{V}_m\bar{a}_k \preceq \bar{e}_m\,\bar{b}_k,\, C \,\square\, S_d)\sigma_d,\, X \approx h\,\bar{V}_m)\,\square\, S'_t \,\square\, (\bar{V}_m :: \bar{\tau}_m, T)\sigma'_t$
- $h\,\bar{e}_m\bar{b}_k$ rigid and passive; $X \notin pvar(P)$; $X \notin svar(h\,\bar{e}_m)$; $\bar{V}_m$ fresh existential vars; **(BD)** not applicable.   * $\sigma_d = \{X\,/\,h\,\bar{V}_m\}$.
- $k = 0$ and $S'_t = S_t$; or $k > 0$ and $\sigma'_t = mgu(S_t, \tau \approx \tau')$ where $X :: \tau' \in T$, $h :: \bar{\tau}_m \to \tau \in_{var} \Sigma$.

Outer Narrowing: (NR1) $(k \geq 0)$

$$\overline{P \; \square \; f \; \overline{e}_n \overline{a}_k \asymp b, \; C \; \square \; S_d \; \square \; S_t \; \square \; T \; \Vdash \; \overline{e}_n \to \overline{t}_n, P \; \square \; C', \; r\overline{a}_k \asymp b, C \; \square \; S_d \square S_t \square T', T}$$

- $(f \; \overline{t}_n \to r \Leftarrow C' \; \square \; T') \in_{var} \mathcal{P}$

Guess & Outer Narrowing: (GN) ★ ★ $(k \geq 0)$

$$\overline{\begin{array}{l} P \; \square \; X \; \overline{e}_q \overline{a}_k \asymp b, C \; \square \; S_d \; \square \; S_t \; \square \; T \\ \quad \Vdash \; (\overline{e}_q \to \overline{s}_q, P \; \square \; C', r\overline{a}_k \asymp b, C \; \square \; S_d)\sigma_d, \; X \; \approx \; f \; \overline{t}_p \; \square \; S'_t \; \square \; (T', \; T)\sigma'_t \end{array}}$$

- $q > 0$; $X \notin \text{pvar}(P)$; $(f \; \overline{t}_p \overline{s}_q \to r \Leftarrow C' \; \square \; T') \in_{var} \mathcal{P}$. *$\sigma_d = \{X \; / \; f \; \overline{t}_p\}$.
- $\circ \; \sigma'_t = \text{mgu}(S_t, \tau' \approx \overline{\tau}_q \to \tau)$ where $(f :: \overline{\tau}_p \to \overline{\tau}_q \to \tau) \in_{var} \Sigma$, $X :: \tau' \in T$.

Guess & Decomposition: (GD) ★ ★

$$\overline{\begin{array}{l} P \; \square \; X \; \overline{a}_p \bowtie Y \; \overline{b}_q, C \; \square \; S_d \; \square \; S_t \; \square \; T \\ \quad \Vdash \; (P \; \square \; \overline{V}_{m-p}, \overline{a}_p \bowtie \overline{W}_{m-q} \overline{b}_q, C \; \square \; S_d)\sigma_d, \; X \approx h \; \overline{V}_{m-p}, Y \approx h \; \overline{W}_{m-q} \; \square \; S'_t \\ \quad \quad \square \; (\overline{V}_{m-p} :: \overline{\tau'}_{m-p}, \overline{W}_{m-q} :: \overline{\tau''}_{m-q}, T)\sigma'_t \end{array}}$$

- $(p + q) > 0$; $X, Y \notin \text{pvar}(P)$; $\overline{V}_{m-p}, \overline{W}_{m-q}$ fresh existential vars; $(h \; \overline{V}_{m-p} \overline{a}_p)$, $(h \; \overline{W}_{m-q} \overline{b}_q)$ rigid and passive.   *$\sigma_d = \{X \; / \; h \; \overline{V}_{m-p}, \; Y \; / \; h \; \overline{W}_{m-q}\}$
- $\circ \; \sigma'_t = \text{mgu}(S_t, \tau' \approx \overline{\tau'}_p \to \tau, \tau'' \approx \overline{\tau''}_q \to \tau)$ where $X :: \tau', Y :: \tau'' \in T$, $(h :: \overline{\tau'}_{m-p} \to \overline{\tau'}_p \to \tau) = (h :: \overline{\tau''}_{m-q} \to \overline{\tau''}_q \to \tau) \in_{var} \Sigma$.

Conflict: (CF1)

$$\overline{P \; \square \; h \; \overline{a}_p \bowtie h' \; \overline{b}_q, C \; \square \; S_d \; \square \; S_t \; \square \; T \; \Vdash \; \textbf{FAIL}}$$

- $h \neq h'$ or $p \neq q$; $h \; \overline{a}_p$, $h' \; \overline{b}_q$ rigid and passive.

Cycle: (CY)

$$\overline{P \; \square \; X \bowtie a, C \; \square \; S_d \; \square \; S_t \; \square \; T \; \Vdash \; \textbf{FAIL}}$$

- $X \neq a$ and $X \in \text{svar}(a)$.

The CLNC Calculus

Rules for the Delayed Part

Decomposition: (DC2)

$$\overline{h \; \overline{e}_m \to h \; \overline{t}_m, P \; \square \; C \; \square \; S_d \; \square \; S_t \; \square \; T \; \Vdash \; \overline{e}_m \to \overline{t}_m, P \; \square \; C \; \square \; S_d \; \square \; S_t \; \square \; T}$$

- $h \; \overline{e}_m$ rigid and passive.

Output Binding & Decomposition: (OB) ★ $(k \geq 0)$

$$\overline{\begin{array}{l} X \; \overline{e}_k \to h \; \overline{t}_m \overline{s}_k, P \; \square \; C \; \square \; S_d \; \square \; S_t \; \square \; T \\ \quad \Vdash \; (\overline{e}_k \to \overline{s}_k, P \; \square \; C \; \square \; S_d)\sigma_d, [\; X \approx h \; \overline{t}_m \;] \; \square \; S'_t \; \square \; T\sigma'_t \end{array}}$$

- $[\; X \notin \text{pvar}(P) \;]$.   *$\sigma_d = \{X \; / \; h \; \overline{t}_m\}$
- $\circ \; k = 0$ and $S'_t = S_t$; or $k > 0$ and $\sigma'_t = \text{mgu}(S_t, \tau \approx \tau')$ where $X :: \tau' \in T$, $(h :: \overline{\tau}_m \to \tau) \in_{var} \Sigma$.

Input Binding: (IB)

$$\overline{t \to X, P \; \square \; C \; \square \; S_d \; \square \; S_t \; \square \; T \; \Vdash \; (P \; \square \; C)\sigma_d \square \; S_d \; \square \; S_t \; \square \; T}$$

- $t \in \text{Pat}$.   *$\sigma_d = \{X \; / \; t\}$.

Input Imitation: (IIM)

$$\overline{h \; \overline{e}_m \to X, P \; \square \; C \; \square \; S_d \; \square \; S_t \square T \; \Vdash \; (\overline{e}_m \to \overline{V}_m, P \; \square \; C)\sigma_d \square \; S_d \square \; S_t \square \; (\overline{V}_m :: \overline{\tau}_m), T}$$

- $h \; \overline{e}_m \notin \text{Pat}$ rigid and passive; $X \in \text{ddvar}(C)$; $\overline{V}_m$ fresh existential vars.
- *$\sigma_d = \{X \; / \; h \; \overline{V}_m\}$ $\circ \; (h :: \overline{\tau}_m \to \tau) \in_{var} \Sigma$

Elimination: (EL)

$e \rightarrow X, P \ \Box \ C \ \Box \ S_d \ \Box \ S_t \ \Box \ T \ \Vdash \ P \ \Box \ C \ \Box \ S_d \ \Box \ S_t \ \Box \ T$

- $X \notin \mathrm{var}(P \ \Box \ C)$.

Outer Narrowing: (NR2) $\quad (k \geq 0)$

$f\bar{e}_n\bar{a}_k \rightarrow t, P \Box C \Box S_d \Box S_t \Box T \ \Vdash \ \bar{e}_n \rightarrow \bar{t}_n, r\bar{a}_k \rightarrow t, P \Box C', C \Box S_d \Box S_t \Box T', T$

- $(t \notin \mathrm{DVar} \text{ or } t \in \mathrm{ddvar}(C)); (f \bar{t}_n \rightarrow r \Leftarrow C' \ \Box \ T') \in_{var} \mathcal{P}$.

Output Guess & Outer Narrowing: (OGN) ★ ★ $\quad (k \geq 0)$

$X \ \bar{e}_q\bar{a}_k \rightarrow t, P \ \Box \ C \ \Box \ S_d \ \Box \ S_t \ \Box \ T$

$\Vdash \ (\bar{e}_q \rightarrow \bar{s}_q, r\bar{a}_k \rightarrow t, P \ \Box \ C', C \ \Box \ S_d)\sigma_d, X \approx f \ \bar{t}_p \ \Box \ S'_t \ \Box \ (T', T)\sigma'_t$

- $q > 0; X \notin \mathrm{pvar}(P); (f \ \bar{t}_p\bar{s}_q \rightarrow r \Leftarrow C' \ \Box \ T') \in_{var} \mathcal{P}; t \notin \mathrm{DVar} \text{ or } t \in \mathrm{ddvar}(C)$.
- * $\sigma_d = \{X \ / \ f \ \bar{t}_p\}$.
- ○ $k = 0$ and $S'_t = S_t$; or $k > 0$ and $\sigma'_t = \mathrm{mgu}(S_t, \tau' \approx \overline{\tau}_q \rightarrow \tau)$ where $X :: \tau' \in T$, $(f :: \overline{\tau}_p \rightarrow \overline{\tau}_q \rightarrow \tau) \in_{var} \Sigma$.

Output Guess & Decomposition: (OGD) ★ ★

$X \ \bar{e}_q \rightarrow Y, P \ \Box \ C \ \Box \ S_d \ \Box \ S_t \ \Box \ T$

$\Vdash \ (\bar{e}_q \rightarrow \overline{W}_q, P \ \Box \ C \ \Box \ S_d)\sigma_d, [\ X \approx h \ \overline{V}_p \ ] \ \Box \ S'_t \ \Box \ (\overline{V}_p :: \overline{\tau}_p, \overline{W}_q :: \overline{\tau}_q, T)\sigma'_t$

- $q > 0; Y \in \mathrm{ddvar}(C); [\ X \notin \mathrm{pvar}(P) \ ]; \overline{V}_p, \overline{W}_q$ fresh existential vars; $(h \ \overline{V}_p \ \overline{W}_q)$ rigid and passive. $\quad$ * $\sigma_d = \{X \ / \ (h \ \overline{V}_p), Y \ / \ (h \ \overline{V}_p \ \overline{W}_q)\}$.
- ○ $\sigma'_t = \mathrm{mgu}(S_t, \tau' \approx \overline{\tau}_q \rightarrow \tau, \tau'' \approx \tau)$ where $(h :: \overline{\tau}_p \rightarrow \overline{\tau}_q \rightarrow \tau) \in_{var} \Sigma$, $X :: \tau', Y :: \tau'' \in T$.

Conflict: (CF2)

$h \ \bar{a}_p \rightarrow h' \ \bar{t}_q, P \ \Box \ C \ \Box \ S_d \ \Box \ S_t \ \Box \ T \ \Vdash \ \mathbf{FAIL}$

- $h \neq h'$ or $p \neq q; h \ \bar{a}_p$ rigid and passive.

In spite of their complex appearence, CLNC transformation rules are natural in the sense that they are designed to guess the shape of GORC derivations step by step. For instance, the transformations **(NR1)** and **(GN)** guess the shape of **(OR)** steps in GORC proofs. As a lazy narrowing calculus, CLNC emulates suspensions and sharing by means of the approximation statements in the delayed part of goals. This and other interesting features regarding occurs check and safe cases for eager variable elimination, have been discussed briefly in [8] and more widely in [9] for the FO untyped case. Here we will focus on the treatment of dynamic type checking. Each CLNC transformation has attached certain side conditions, labelled with the symbols •, * and ○, that must be checked before applying the transformation to the current goal G. In particular, those CLNC transformations whose name is marked with ★ or ★★, have a side condition of type ○ that performs dynamic type checking. In all such cases, the type stored in the goal type environment for some HO variable is compared to the type of a candidate binding by means of unification. In case of success, the type solved part of the goal is properly actualized. Moreover, the ★★ transformations must be applied to the type closure $\hat{G}$ of the current goal G, rather than to G itself, in the case that G is well-typed. Otherwise, it may happen that a type error is not detected. This caution is important because several CLNC transformations do not preserve type-closedness of goals, and the type environment in a type-closed goal bears more precise information in general.

Let us show the behaviour of CLNC by means ot two examples. The first one illustrates the opaque decomposition problem: a initially well-typed goal is eventually solved, but some intermediate goals become ill-typed due to opaque decomposition steps. The part of the current goal that is transformed at each step has been underlined.

Example 4. Opaque decomposition:

$$G = \hat{G} = \emptyset \,\square\, \underline{\text{snd (map s } [\,])} \,\bowtie\, \text{snd (map not } [\,]) \,\square\, \emptyset \,\square\, \emptyset \,\square\, \emptyset \,\Vdash_{DC1}$$

$$G' = \emptyset \,\square\, \underline{\text{map s } [\,]} \,\bowtie\, \text{map not } [\,] \,\square\, \emptyset \,\square\, \emptyset \,\square\, \emptyset \,\Vdash_{NR1}$$

$$\underline{\text{s} \,\to\, \text{F1}, [\,]} \,\to\, [\,] \,\square\, [\,] \,\bowtie\, \text{map not } [\,] \,\square\, \emptyset \,\square\, \emptyset \,\square\, \emptyset \,\{\text{F1} :: \alpha_1 \to \beta_1\} \,\Vdash_{IB,DC2}$$

$$\emptyset \,\square\, [\,] \,\bowtie\, \underline{\text{map not } [\,]} \,\square\, \emptyset \,\square\, \emptyset \,\square\, \emptyset \,\{\text{F1} :: \alpha_1 \to \beta_1\} \,\Vdash_{NR1}$$

$$\underline{\text{not} \,\to\, \text{F2}, [\,]} \,\to\, [\,] \,\square\, [\,] \,\bowtie\, [\,] \,\square\, \emptyset \,\square\, \emptyset \,\square$$
$$\{\text{F1} :: \alpha_1 \to \beta_1, \text{F2} :: \alpha_2 \to \beta_2\} \,\Vdash_{IB,DC2}$$

$$\emptyset \,\square\, \underline{[\,]} \,\bowtie\, \underline{[\,]} \,\square\, \emptyset \,\square\, \emptyset \,\square\, \{\text{F1} :: \alpha_1 \to \beta_1, \text{F2} :: \alpha_2 \to \beta_2\} \,\Vdash_{DC1}$$

$$\emptyset \,\square\, \emptyset \,\square\, \emptyset \,\square\, \emptyset \,\square\, \{\text{F1} :: \alpha_1 \to \beta_1, \text{F2} :: \alpha_2 \to \beta_2\} \,=\, G_f = \hat{G}_f$$

Note that the intermediate goal G' is ill-typed, but the final goal G_f is well-typed again. The computed answer, restricted to the variables in the initial goal, is $(\emptyset, id)$. This is a well-typed solution, but no type-annotated witness exists due to the opaque decomposition step.

The second example illustrates the need of computing the type-closure of a well-typed goal before applying a ★★ transformation. The following CLNC derivation is wrong because this prescription has been not obeyed in the step from G_2 to G_3 by the transformation (**GN**). As a consequence, the ill-typed binding F $\mapsto$ plus z for the HO variable F escapes dynamic type checking. Note that the side condition ∘ in (**GN**) would forbid this binding if (**GN**) were applied to $\hat{G}_2$ instead of G_2.

Example 5. Wrong application of (**GN**).

The initial goal is $G_0 = \emptyset \,\square\, \underline{\text{foo true}} \,\bowtie\, z \,\square\, \emptyset \,\square\, \emptyset \,\square\, \emptyset \,\Vdash_{NR1}$

$$\hat{G}_1 \,\ne\, G_1 \,=\, \underline{\text{true} \,\to\, \text{X}} \,\square\, \text{F Y} \,\bowtie\, \text{X}, z \,\bowtie\, z \,\square\, \emptyset \,\square\, \emptyset \,\square$$
$$\{\text{X} :: \alpha, \text{Y} :: \beta, \text{F} :: \beta \to \alpha\} \,\Vdash_{IB}$$

$$\hat{G}_2 \,\ne\, G_2 \,=\, \emptyset \,\square\, \underline{\text{F Y}} \,\bowtie\, \text{true}, z \,\bowtie\, z \,\square\, \emptyset \,\square\, \emptyset \,\square$$
$$\{\text{X} :: \alpha, \text{Y} :: \beta, \text{F} :: \beta \to \alpha\} \,\Vdash_{GN}$$

$$G_3 \,=\, \underline{\text{Y} \,\to\, \text{N}} \,\square\, \text{N} \,\bowtie\, \text{true}, z \,\bowtie\, z \,\square\, \text{F} \approx \text{plus z} \,\square\, \alpha \approx \text{nat}, \beta \approx \text{nat} \,\square$$
$$\{\text{X}, \text{Y}, \text{N} :: \text{nat}, \text{F} :: \text{nat} \to \text{nat}\} \,\Vdash_{IB}$$

$$G_4 \,=\, \emptyset \,\square\, \underline{\text{Y}} \,\bowtie\, \underline{\text{true}}, z \,\bowtie\, z \,\square\, \text{F} \approx \text{plus z} \,\square\, \alpha \approx \text{nat}, \beta \approx \text{nat} \,\square$$
$$\{\text{X}, \text{Y}, \text{N} :: \text{nat}, \text{F} :: \text{nat} \to \text{nat}\} \,\Vdash_{BD,DC1}$$

$$G_f \,=\, \emptyset \,\square\, \emptyset \,\square\, \text{F} \approx \text{plus z}, \text{Y} \approx \text{true} \,\square\, \alpha \approx \text{nat}, \beta \approx \text{nat} \,\square$$
$$\{\text{X}, \text{Y}, \text{N} :: \text{nat}, \text{F} :: \text{nat} \to \text{nat}\}$$

The computed answer, restricted to the variables of the initial goal, is again $(\emptyset, id)$. This is in fact a well-typed solution, but the ill-typed intermediate steps in the previous CLNC derivation correspond to the GORC proof from Example 3, that cannot be type-annotated. By guessing the binding $F \mapsto$ not instead of $F \mapsto$ plus z, itis possible to build a different CLNC derivation that computes the same solution while maintaining well-typed intermediate goals.

4.3   Soundness and Completeness

To finish our presentation of CLNC with dynamic type checking, we show soundness and completeness results relative to the computation of well-typed solutions, assuming well-typed programs and well-typed, type-closed initial goals. We use the notation $Sol(G') \subseteq_{ex} Sol(G)$, meaning that every well-typed solution of G' is identical to some well-typed solution of G, except for the bindings of existential variables. Similarly, $(R, \theta) \in_{ex} Sol(G')$ means that some well-typed solution of G' is identical to (R, θ) except for the bindings of existential variables.

Each CLNC transformation step is correct in the sense of the following lemma.

Lemma 1. Correctness lemma.
If G is an admissible goal G for a well-typed program $\mathcal{P}$ and $G \Vdash_{TR} G'$, then:
(a) G' is admissible and $Sol(G') \subseteq_{ex} Sol(G)$.
(b) Moreover, G' is well-typed, unless (TR) is an opaque decomposition step.

Proof idea: Items (a) and (b) can be checked separately for each CLNC transformation.   □

The next theorem guarantees the correctness of CLNC computed answers.

Theorem 2. Soundness Theorem.
Assume a well-typed and type-closed initial goal G_0 for a well-typed program $\mathcal{P}$, and a computed answer (T, σ). Then:
(a) $(T, \sigma) \in Sol(G_0)$.
(b) Moreover, if (T, σ) has been computed by a CLNC derivation without opaque decomposition steps, then $(T, \sigma) \in ASol(G_0)$.

Proof idea: the theorem follows from Lemma 1, using induction on the length of CLNC computations. A similar technique can be found in [8,9] for the case of untyped programs. Since CLNC transformations work by guessing the shape of GORC steps, every CLNC derivation leads naturally to a GORC witness, that can be type-annotated as long as no opaque decomposition steps occur.   □

Completeness of CLNC is proved with the help of a well-founded ordering for witnesses of solutions. Let $\prec$ be the well-founded multiset ordering for multisets of natural numbers [3]. Then:

Definition 4. *Multiset ordering for witnesses.*
Let $\mathcal{M}$, $\mathcal{M}'$ be finite multisets of (possibly type-annotated) GORC proofs. Let $\mathcal{SM}$, $\mathcal{SM}'$ be the corresponding multisets of natural numbers, obtained by replacing each GORC proof by its size, understood as the number of GORC inference steps. Then we define $\mathcal{M} \lhd \mathcal{M}'$ iff $\mathcal{SM} \prec \mathcal{SM}'$.   □

The next lemma guarantees that CLNC transformations can be chosen to make progress according to a given solution witness, avoiding opaque decomposition steps if the witness is type-annotated.

Lemma 2. Completeness lemma.
Assume a well-typed goal G for a well-typed program $\mathcal{P}$, not in solved form, as well as $(R, \theta) \in Sol(G)$ with witness $\mathcal{M}$. Then, we can choose some CLNC transformation rule (TR) applicable to G such that:
(a) $G \Vdash_{TR} G'$ and $(R, \theta) \in_{ex} Sol(G')$ with witness $\mathcal{M}' \lhd \mathcal{M}$.
(b) Moreover, if $(R, \theta) \in ASol(G)$ and $\mathcal{M}$ is a type-annotated witness, then we can guarantee that G' is also well-typed and the witness $\mathcal{M}'$ can be type-annotated.

Proof idea: Choose (TR) as a CLNC transformation suitable to guess the shape of the last inference step in one of the GORC proofs included in the given witness.   □

Finally, we can prove that CLNC computed answers subsume all possible well-typed solutions:

Theorem 3. Completeness Theorem.
Assume a well-typed and type-closed initial goal G_0 for a well-typed program $\mathcal{P}$, as well as $(R, \theta) \in Sol(G)$. Then:
(a) There exists a derivation $G_0 \Vdash^* G_n$ where $G_n = \emptyset \,\square\, \emptyset \,\square\, S_d \,\square\, S_t \,\square\, T$ is in solved form, $\sigma_d \leq \theta_d[dvar(G_0)]$ and $\sigma_t \leq \theta_t[tvar(G_0)]$.
(b) Moreover, if $(R, \theta) \in ASol(G_0)$ has a type-annotated witness, we can guarantee that all the intermediate goals along the CLNC derivation remain well-typed.

Proof idea: Starting with G_0 and $(R, \theta) \in Sol(G_0)$, Lemma 2 can be reiteratedly applied until a goal G_n in solved form is reached. This will eventually happen, because $\lhd$ is a well-founded ordering. The requested CLNC derivation is obtained in this way. Moreover, if the initially given witness is type-annotated, item (b) from Lemma 2 ensures that all the intermediate goals will be indeed well-typed.   □

5 Conclusions

We have presented a polymorphic type system that extends a previous approach to HO FLP, based on the rewriting logic CRWL [8]. Keeping a logical semantics even for the case of untyped programs, we have defined a natural class of well-typed programs, and we have extended both the models and the lazy narrowing calculus CLNC from [8] to take types into account. We have identified two possible sources of run-time type errors in CLNC computations, namely *opaque decompositions* and *ill-typed bindings for HO logic variables*. We have proposed dynamic type checking mechanisms to prevent the second problem, causing only a small overhead in computations that involve no use of HO logic variables. CLNC with dynamic type checking remains sound and complete for the computation of well-typed solutions, as long as no opaque decomposition steps occur.

Working out and testing an implementation of dynamic type checking in the $\mathcal{TOY}$ system [4] is obviously an interesting topic for future research.

References

1. K.R. Apt, *Logic Programming*, In J. van Leeuwen (ed.), *Handbook of Theoretical Computer Science*, vol. B, Chapter 10, Elsevier and The MIT Press, pp. 493–574, 1990.
2. P. Arenas-Sánchez and M. Rodríguez-Artalejo, *A Semantic Framework for Functional Logic Programming with Algebraic Polymorphic Types*, Proc. Int. Joint Conference on Theory and Practice of Software Development (TAPSOFT'97), Lille, Springer LNCS 1214, pp. 453–464, 1997.
3. F. Baader and T. Nipkow, *Term Rewriting and All That*, Cambridge University Press, 1998.
4. R. Caballero-Roldán, F.J. López-Fraguas and J. Sánchez-Hernández, *User's Manual for* $\mathcal{TOY}$, Technical Report SIP 57/97, Dpto. de Sistemas Informáticos y Programación, Univ. Complutense de Madrid. System available at http://mozart.sip.ucm.es/incoming/toy.html.
5. W. Chen, M. Kifer and D.S. Warren, *HiLog: A Foundation for Higher-Order Logic Programming*, Journal of Logic Programming 15, pp. 187–230, 1993.
6. J.A. Goguen and J. Meseguer, *Models and Equality for Logical Programming*, Proc. TAPSOFT'87, Springer LNCS 250, pp. 1–22, 1987.
7. W. Goldfarb, *The Undecidability of the Second-Order Unification Problem*, Theoretical Computer Science 13, pp. 225–230, 1981.
8. J.C. González-Moreno, M.T. Hortalá-González and M. Rodríguez-Artalejo, *A Higher Order Rewriting Logic for Functional Logic Programming*, Proc. Int. Conf. on Logic Programming, Leuven, the MIT Press, pp. 153–167, 1997.
9. J.C. González-Moreno, M.T. Hortalá-González, F.J. López-Fraguas and M. Rodríguez-Artalejo, *An Approach to Declarative Programming Based on a Rewriting Logic*, Journal of Logic Programming 40(1), pp. 47–87, 1999.
10. M. Hanus, *Polymorphic Higher-Order Programming in Prolog*, Proc. Int. Conf. on Logic Programming (ICLP'89), The MIT Press, pp. 382–397, 1989.
11. M. Hanus, *A Functional and Logic Language with Polymorphic Types*, Proc. Int. Symp. on Design and implementation of Symbolic Computation Systems, Springer LNCS 429, pp. 215–224, 1990.
12. M. Hanus (ed.), *Curry: an Integrated Functional Logic Language*, available at http://www-i2.informatik.rwth-aachen.de/ hanus/curry, 1998.
13. J. Jaffar, J.L. Lassez and M.J. Maher, *A Theory of Complete Logic Programs with Equality*, Journal of Logic Programming (1), pp. 211–223, 1984.
14. R. Milner, *A Theory of Type Polymorphism in Programming*, Journal of Computer and Systems Sciences, 17, pp. 348–375, 1978.
15. A. Mycroft and R.A. O'Keefe, *A Polymorphic Type System for Prolog*. Artificial Intelligence 23, pp. 295–307, 1984.
16. G. Nadathur and P. Pfenning, *The Type System of a Higher-Order Logic Programming Language*, In F. Pfenning (ed.), *Types in Logic Programming*, The MIT Press, pp. 245–283. 1992.
17. J. Peterson, and K. Hammond (eds.), *Report on the Programming Language Haskell, A Non-strict, Purely Functional Language*, Version 1.4, April 7, 1997.
18. F. Pfenning (ed.), *Types in Logic Programming*, The MIT Press. 1992.
19. C. Prehofer, *Solving Higher Order Equations: From Logic to Programming*, Birkhäuser, 1998.
20. D.S. Scott, *Domains for Denotational Semantics*, Proc. ICALP'82, Springer LNCS 140, pp. 577–613, 1982.

Polytypic Programming With Ease

(Extended Abstract)

Ralf Hinze

Institut für Informatik III, Universität Bonn
Römerstraße 164, 53117 Bonn, Germany
ralf@informatik.uni-bonn.de
http://www.informatik.uni-bonn.de/~ralf/

Abstract. This paper proposes a new framework for a polytypic extension of functional programming languages. A functional polytypic program is one that is parameterised by datatype. Since polytypic functions
are defined by induction on types rather than by induction on values,
they typically operate on a higher level of abstraction than their monotypic counterparts. However, polytypic programming is not necessarily
more complicated than conventional programming. In fact, a polytypic
function is uniquely defined by its action on constant functors, projection
functors, sums, and products. This information is sufficient to specialize
a polytypic function to arbitrary datatypes, including mutually recursive datatypes and nested datatypes. The key idea is to use infinite trees
as index sets for polytypic functions and to interpret datatypes as algebraic trees. This approach is simpler, more general, and more efficient
than previous ones that are based on the initial algebra semantics of
datatypes.

1 Introduction

This paper proposes a new framework for a polytypic extension of functional programming languages such as Haskell or Standard ML. A polytypic function is one
that is defined by induction on the structure of types. The archetypical example
of a polytypic function is $size :: f\ a \to Int$, which counts the number of values
of type a in a given value of type $f\ a$. The function $size$ can sensibly be defined
for each parameterised datatype and it is often—but not always—a tiresomely
routine matter to do so. A polytypic programming language enables the user to
program $size$ once and for all times. The specialization of $size$ to concrete instances of f is then handled automatically by the system. Polytypic programs are
ubiquitous: typical examples include equality and comparison functions, mapping functions, pretty printers (such as Haskell's *show* function), parsers (such
as Haskell's *read* function), data compression [9], and digital searching [6]. The
ability to define such programs generically for all datatypes greatly simplifies
the construction and maintenance of software systems.

Since polytypic functions are defined by induction on types rather than by
induction on values, they tend to be more abstract than their monotypic counterparts. However, once a certain familiarity has been gained, it turns out that

A. Middeldorp, T. Sato (Eds.): FLOPS'99, LNCS 1722, pp. 21–36, 1999.

polytypic programming is actually simpler than conventional programming. To support this claim let us define two simple functions, *size* and *sum*, for some illustrative datatypes. As a first example, consider the datatype of rose trees.[1]

$$\textbf{data } Rose \; a = Branch \; a \; (List \; (Rose \; a))$$
$$\textbf{data } List \; a \; = Nil \mid Cons \; a \; (List \; a)$$

The size of a rose tree can be determined as follows [2].

$$sizer \qquad\qquad\qquad :: Rose \; a \to Int$$
$$sizer \; (Branch \; a \; ts) = 1 + sum \; (map \; sizer \; ts)$$

This definition is already quite sophisticated: it makes use of a general combining form and an auxiliary function. The use of $map :: (a \to b) \to (List \; a \to List \; b)$, however, also incurs a slight run-time penalty: *map* produces an intermediate list, which is immediately consumed by *sum*. This inefficiency can be eliminated by fusing $sum \circ map \; sizer$ into a single function (called *sizef* below).

$$sizer \qquad\qquad\qquad :: Rose \; a \to Int$$
$$sizer \; (Branch \; a \; ts) = 1 + sizef \; ts$$
$$sizef \qquad\qquad\qquad :: List \; (Rose \; a) \to Int$$
$$sizef \; Nil \qquad\qquad = 0$$
$$sizef \; (Cons \; t \; ts) \quad = sizer \; t + sizef \; ts$$

Interestingly, this very definition naturally arises if we change the definition of rose trees to

$$\textbf{data } Rose' \; a \; = Branch \; a \; (Forest \; a)$$
$$\textbf{data } Forest \; a = Nil \mid Cons \; (Rose' \; a) \; (Forest \; a) \;.$$

The definition of *sum* proceeds completely analogously—it suffices, in fact, to replace '1' by '*a*' in the definitions above.

A slightly more complex datatype is the type of perfect binary search trees.

$$\textbf{data } Perfect \; a \; k = Zero \; a \mid Succ \; (Perfect \; (Node \; a \; k) \; k)$$
$$\textbf{data } Node \; a \; k \quad = Node \; a \; k \; a$$

The definition of *Perfect* is somewhat unusual in that the recursive component, *Perfect (Node a k) k*, is not identical to the left-hand side of the equation: *Perfect* is an example of a so-called *nested datatype*, a term coined by Bird and Meertens [4]. Since *Perfect* only encompasses perfect binary search trees, the size of a tree of type *Perfect a a* can be computed in logarithmic time.

$$sizep \qquad\qquad :: Perfect \; a \; k \to Int$$
$$sizep \; (Zero \; a) = 1$$
$$sizep \; (Succ \; t) = 2 * sizep \; t + 1$$

---

[1] Examples are given in the functional programming language Haskell 98 [21].

The function *sizep* counts the number of values of type *a* in a tree of type *Perfect a a*. However, *sizep* cannot be assigned the type *Perfect a a* → *Int* since the recursive call has type *Perfect (Node a k) k* → *Int*.

Summing up a perfect tree of integers is a bit more challenging.

$$
\begin{array}{ll}
sump & :: Perfect\ Int\ Int \rightarrow Int \\
sump\ (Zero\ a) & = a \\
sump\ (Succ\ t) & = sump\ (perfect\ sumn\ id\ t) \\
\\
sumn & :: Node\ Int\ Int \rightarrow Int \\
sumn\ (Node\ l\ k\ r) & = l + k + r
\end{array}
$$

Here, *perfect* :: $(a \rightarrow a') \rightarrow (k \rightarrow k') \rightarrow (Perfect\ a\ k \rightarrow Perfect\ a'\ k')$ denotes the mapping function of the binary functor *Perfect*. Improving the efficiency of *sump* by fusing *sump* ∘ *perfect sumn id* is left as an exercise to the reader.

Now, let us define *size* and *sum* once and for all times. To this end we must first take a closer look at the structure of types. Reconsider the datatype definitions given above. Haskell's **data** construct combines several features in a single coherent form: sums, products, and recursion. The structure of the types becomes more apparent if the definitions are rewritten as *functor equations*:

$$
\begin{array}{ll}
Rose & = Id \times List \cdot Rose \\
List & = K1 + Id \times List \\
Perfect & = Fst + Perfect \cdot (Node, Snd) \\
Node & = Fst \times Snd \times Fst \ ,
\end{array}
$$

where KT is the constant functor, *Id* is the identity functor, *Fst* and *Snd* are projection functors, and $F \cdot (F_1, \ldots, F_n)$ denotes the composition of an *n*-ary functor *F* with *n* functors, all of the same arity. Sum and product are defined pointwise: $(F_1 + F_2)\ a = F_1\ a + F_2\ a$ and $(F_1 \times F_2)\ a = F_1\ a \times F_2\ a$. In essence, functor equations are written in a compositional or 'point-free' style while **data** definitions are written in an applicative or 'pointwise' style. We treat 1, '+', and '×' as if they were given by the following datatype declarations.

$$
\begin{array}{ll}
\textbf{data } 1 & = () \\
\textbf{data } a_1 + a_2 & = Inl\ a_1\ |\ Inr\ a_2 \\
\textbf{data } a_1 \times a_2 & = (a_1, a_2)
\end{array}
$$

To define *size* it suffices to specify its action on constant functors, on the identity functor, on sums, and on products. Polytypic functions are written using angle brackets to distinguish them from ordinary functions.

$$
\begin{array}{ll}
size\langle f \rangle & :: \forall a.f\ a \rightarrow Int \\
size\langle Id \rangle\ x & = 1 \\
size\langle Kt \rangle\ x & = 0 \\
size\langle f_1 + f_2 \rangle\ (Inl\ x_1) & = size\langle f_1 \rangle\ x_1 \\
size\langle f_1 + f_2 \rangle\ (Inr\ x_2) & = size\langle f_2 \rangle\ x_2 \\
size\langle f_1 \times f_2 \rangle\ (x_1, x_2) & = size\langle f_1 \rangle\ x_1 + size\langle f_2 \rangle\ x_2
\end{array}
$$

Each equation is more or less inevitable: a value of type $Id\ a = a$ contains one element of type a; a value of type $Kt\ a = t$ contains no elements. To determine the size of an element of type $f_1\ a + f_2\ a$ we must either calculate the size of a structure of type $f_1\ a$ or that of a structure of type $f_2\ a$. The size of a structure of type $f_1\ a \times f_2\ a$ is given by the sum of the size of the two components. From this definition the following specializations can be automatically derived.

$$
\begin{array}{ll}
sizeRose & = sizeRose_1\ (const\ 1) \\
sizeRose_1\ \varphi\ (Branch\ a\ ts) & = \varphi\ a + sizeList_1\ (sizeRose_1\ \varphi)\ ts \\
sizeList_1\ \varphi\ Nil & = 0 \\
sizeList_1\ \varphi\ (Cons\ a\ as) & = \varphi\ a + sizeList_1\ \varphi\ as \\[4pt]
sizePerfect & = sizePerfect_2\ (const\ 1, const\ 1) \\
sizePerfect_2\ (\varphi_1, \varphi_2)\ (Zero\ a) & = \varphi_1\ a \\
sizePerfect_2\ (\varphi_1, \varphi_2)\ (Succ\ t) & = sizePerfect_2\ (sizeNode_2\ (\varphi_1, \varphi_2), \varphi_2)\ t \\
sizeNode_2\ (\varphi_1, \varphi_2)\ (Node\ l\ k\ r) & = \varphi_1\ l + \varphi_2\ k + \varphi_1\ r
\end{array}
$$

We postpone a detailed explanation of the specialization process until Section 3. For the moment it suffices to note that the different instances rigidly follow the structure of the respective datatypes. How do these functions relate to the hand-crafted definitions? Now, $sizeRose$ corresponds to the second, more efficient definition of $sizer$: we have $sizer = sizeRose_1\ (const\ 1)$ and $sizef = sizeList_1\ sizer$. On the negative side, $sizePerfect$ is a linear-time implementation as opposed to the logarithmic $sizep$. In general, a 'structure-strict', polytypic function has at least a linear running time. So we cannot reasonably expect to achieve the efficiency of a handcrafted implementation that exploits data-structural invariants.

The polytypic definition of sum is equally simple.

$$
\begin{array}{ll}
sum\langle f \rangle & :: f\ Int \to Int \\
sum\langle Id \rangle\ x & = x \\
sum\langle Kt \rangle\ x & = 0 \\
sum\langle f_1 + f_2 \rangle\ (Inl\ x_1) & = sum\langle f_1 \rangle\ x_1 \\
sum\langle f_1 + f_2 \rangle\ (Inr\ x_2) & = sum\langle f_2 \rangle\ x_2 \\
sum\langle f_1 \times f_2 \rangle\ (x_1, x_2) & = sum\langle f_1 \rangle\ x_1 + sum\langle f_2 \rangle\ x_2
\end{array}
$$

Specializing $sum\langle f \rangle$ to the various datatypes yields definitions similar to those obtained for $size\langle f \rangle$. In this case the generated functions are as efficient as the best handcoded implementations.

The moral of the story so far: giving ad-hoc definitions of polytypic functions like $size$ and sum is sometimes simple and sometimes involving. While the polytypic definition is slightly more abstract, it is also to a high degree inevitable. It is this feature that makes polytypic programming light and sweet.

The rest of this paper is organized as follows. Section 2 introduces the basic ingredients of polytypic programming: functor equations and algebraic trees. Section 3 explains how to specialize a polytypic function to concrete instances of datatypes. Section 4 presents several examples of polytypic functions, among others polytypic reduction and polytypic equality. Finally, Section 5 reviews related work and points out directions for future work.

2   Datatypes as Algebraic Trees

In the introduction we have seen that functor equations capture the essence of datatype definitions. In general, a system of functor equations has the form $f_1 = e_1; \ldots; f_p = e_p$ where the f_i are functor variables and the e_i are functor expressions. Given a ranked set of primitive functors, $\Sigma = \Sigma^0 \cup \Sigma^2$ with $\Sigma^0 = \{1, Int\}$ and $\Sigma^2 = \{+, \times\}$, the set of *functor expressions of arity* n is inductively defined as follows.

$$F^n ::= \Pi_i^n \mid \Sigma^n \mid F^k \cdot (F_1^n, \ldots, F_k^n)$$

Here Π_i^n denotes the n-ary projection functor selecting the i-th component. For unary and binary projection functors we use the following more familiar names: $Id = \Pi_1^1$, $Fst = \Pi_1^2$, and $Snd = \Pi_2^2$. The expression $F \cdot (F_1, \ldots, F_k)$ denotes the composition of a k-ary functor F with functors F_i, all of arity n. We omit the parentheses when $k = 1$ and we write $K T$ instead of $T \cdot ()$ when $k = 0$. Finally, we write $F_1 \oplus F_2$ instead of $\oplus \cdot (F_1, F_2)$ for $\oplus \in \Sigma^2$.

Each functor equation defines a unique infinite tree, whose inner nodes are labelled with primitive functors of arity $\geqslant 1$ and whose leaves are decorated with nullary functors and projection functors. Figure 1 displays the trees defined by the equations for *Rose* and *Perfect* given in the previous section. Note that

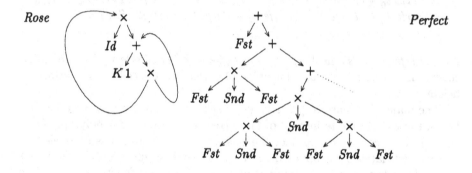

Fig. 1. Types interpreted as infinite trees

Rose is interpreted by a *rational tree* while *Perfect* denotes an *algebraic tree*. A rational tree is a possibly infinite tree that has only a finite number of subtrees. Algebraic trees are obtained as solutions of so-called algebraic equations, which are akin to functor equations. We will view infinite trees naively as a kind of 'infinite normal form' of functor expressions. Expressions in normal form are formed according to the following grammar.

$$T^n ::= \Pi_i^n \mid \Sigma^k \cdot (T_1^n, \ldots, T_k^n)$$

Thus, $P \cdot (F_1, \ldots, F_k)$ with $P \in \Sigma^k$ corresponds to a tree, whose root is labelled with P and which has subtrees $F_1, \ldots, F_k$, and Π_i^n corresponds to a leaf. For a more formal treatment the interested reader is referred to the full version of this paper [8]. Courcelle's article [5] provides a more detailed survey on the theory of infinite trees. Briefly, the set of infinite trees constitutes an initial continuous algebra. Systems of functor equations have least solutions in this complete partial order.

Roughly speaking, the infinite tree defined by a functor equation is obtained by unrolling the equation ad infinitum applying the following functorial laws.

$$F \cdot (\Pi_1, \ldots, \Pi_n) \quad = F \tag{1}$$

$$\Pi_i \cdot (F_1, \ldots, F_n) \quad = F_i \tag{2}$$

$$(F \cdot (G_1, \ldots, G_n)) \cdot \mathbf{H} = F \cdot (G_1 \cdot \mathbf{H}, \ldots, G_n \cdot \mathbf{H}) \tag{3}$$

In the latter equation $\mathbf{H}$ is a tuple of functor expressions. Functor composition can be seen as a substitution operation on trees. Eq. (2) defines the substitution of a leaf by a tree; Eq. (3) formalizes the propagation of a substitution to the subtrees of a node. As an example, consider the unfolding of *Perfect*:

$$
\begin{aligned}
&Perfect \\
={}& Perfect_0 + Perfect \cdot (Perfect_1, Snd) \\
={}& Perfect_0 + (Fst + Perfect \cdot (Node, Snd)) \cdot (Perfect_1, Snd) \\
={}& Perfect_0 + (Perfect_1 + Perfect \cdot (Perfect_2, Snd)) \\
={}& Perfect_0 + (Perfect_1 + (Fst + Perfect \cdot (Node, Snd)) \cdot (Perfect_2, Snd)) \\
={}& Perfect_0 + (Perfect_1 + (Perfect_2 + Perfect \cdot (Perfect_3, Snd))) \\
={}& \ldots \; ,
\end{aligned}
$$

where $Perfect_0 = Fst$ and $Perfect_{n+1} = Perfect_n \times Snd \times Perfect_n$. The unfolding shows that *Perfect* is the disjoint union of perfectly balanced trees of arbitrary height.

The major difference to previous approaches to polytypic programming [10] lies in the use of infinite instead of finite trees as index sets for polytypic functions. In essence, this means that the class of all datatypes is itself modeled by a *non-strict* datatype as opposed to an inductive datatype. This change is not as problematic as one might think at first sight. Polytypic functions can still be recursively defined. Of course, to make things work the functions involved must be continuous. This condition is, however, trivially satisfied since the functions are programs in Haskell or Standard ML.

Now, let us consider some examples of functors. A functor is called *polynomial* if it is represented by a finite tree.

$$
\begin{aligned}
\Delta \quad &= Id \times Id \\
Node23 &= Fst \times Snd \times Fst + Fst \times Snd \times Fst \times Snd \times Fst
\end{aligned}
$$

The functor Δ is called the diagonal or square functor; $Node23$ is used below in the definition of 2-3 trees.

A *regular* functor is one that is given by a rational tree.

$$Bintree = Fst + Bintree \times Snd \times Bintree$$

The functor *Bintree* models external, binary search trees. Further examples of regular functors are *Rose*, *List*, *Rose'*, and *Forest*.

The functor *Perfect* is an example of a *non-regular* or *nested* functor, which is given by an algebraic tree.

$$Sequ \quad = K1 + Sequ \cdot \Delta + Id \times Sequ \cdot \Delta$$
$$Tree23 = Fst + Tree23 \cdot (Node23, Snd)$$

Okasaki [19] uses the functor *Sequ* as the basis for a sequence implementation with an efficient indexing operation. The functor *Tree23* models 2-3 trees. The novelty of this definition is that the data-structural invariants of 2-3 trees—each interior node has two or three children and each path from the root to a leaf has the same length—are made manifest.

The same functor can usually be defined in a variety of ways. Take, for instance, the two definitions of rose trees given in Section 1.

$$Rose = Id \times List \cdot Rose \qquad Rose' \ = Id \times Forest$$
$$List \ = K1 + Id \times List \qquad Forest = K1 + Rose' \times Forest$$

Both *Rose* and *Rose'* denote the same rational tree depicted in Figure 1.

3 Polytypic Functions

We have already seen two examples of polytypic functions. In general, a polytypic function that is parameterised by m-ary functors is given by the following data (think of the following as a prototype for polytypic definitions).

$$
\begin{aligned}
poly\langle f \rangle & \quad :: \tau(f) \\
poly\langle \Pi_i \rangle & \ = poly_{\Pi_i} \\
poly\langle P \cdot (f_1, \ldots, f_k) \rangle & = poly_P \ (poly\langle f_1 \rangle, \ldots, poly\langle f_k \rangle)
\end{aligned}
$$

The type of $poly\langle f \rangle$ is specified by the type scheme $\tau(f)$. Since f is an m-ary functor, $poly_{\Pi_i}$ must be specified for $1 \leqslant i \leqslant m$. Furthermore, an equation specifying $poly_P$ must be given for each primitive functor $P \in \Sigma$. This information is sufficient to define a unique function $poly\langle f \rangle$ for each functor f [5]. Briefly, an inductively defined function like $poly\langle f \rangle$ can be uniquely extended to a continuous function on infinite trees.

The question we pursue in this section is how to derive specializations of $poly\langle f \rangle$ for given instances of f. The process of specialization is necessary since $poly\langle f \rangle$ cannot directly be implemented in languages such as Haskell or Standard ML. The reason is simply that the type of *poly* depends on the first argument, which is itself a type (or possibly, the encoding of a type). Even if we circumvented this problem by using encodings into a universal datatype [22] or by using dynamic types and a **typecase** [1], the result would be rather inefficient because *poly* would interpret its type argument at each stage of the recursion.

By specializing $poly\langle f\rangle$ for a given f we remove this interpretative layer. Thus, we can view the following as a very special instance of partial evaluation.

Since types correspond to algebraic trees, which may have an infinite number of different subtrees, the specialization cannot be based on the structure of types. However, using functor equations algebraic trees can be finitely represented so the idea suggests itself to carry out the specialization on the representation of trees. The main challenge lies in the treatment of functor composition. Assume, for instance, that an unary functor is defined in terms of a binary functor: $F = B \cdot (e_1, e_2)$. Now, if we want to specialize $size\langle F\rangle$, how can we generate code for the right-hand side? The central idea is to define an auxiliary function $size_2\langle B\rangle$ that satisfies $size_2\langle B\rangle \ (size\langle e_1\rangle, size\langle e_2\rangle) = size\langle B \cdot (e_1, e_2)\rangle$ for all e_1 and e_2. That is, $size_2\langle B\rangle$ takes $size\langle e_1\rangle$ and $size\langle e_2\rangle$ as arguments and implements $size\langle B \cdot (e_1, e_2)\rangle$. We have seen that functor composition corresponds to a substitution operation on trees. Using the function $size_2\langle B\rangle$ we imitate substitution on the function level. In general, we define, for each arity n, a polytypic function $poly_n\langle g\rangle :: (\tau(g_1), \ldots, \tau(g_n)) \to \tau(g \cdot (g_1, \ldots, g_n))$ satisfying

$$poly_n\langle g\rangle \ (poly\langle g_1\rangle, \ldots, poly\langle g_n\rangle) = poly\langle g \cdot (g_1, \ldots, g_n)\rangle \ . \tag{4}$$

Note the close correspondence between types and functions: g is an n-ary functor sending $g_1, \ldots, g_n$ to $g \cdot (g_1, \ldots, g_n)$; likewise $poly_n\langle g\rangle$ is an n-ary function sending $poly\langle g_1\rangle, \ldots, poly\langle g_n\rangle$ to $poly\langle g \cdot (g_1, \ldots, g_n)\rangle$.

For primitive functors $P \in \Sigma^n$ the function $poly_n\langle P\rangle$ is defined by $poly_n\langle P\rangle = poly_P$. The derivation of $poly_n\langle g\rangle$ for projection functors and for functor composition is a nice example in program calculation and proceeds almost mechanically. We assume that $\varphi = (poly\langle g_1\rangle, \ldots, poly\langle g_n\rangle)$ and reason:

$$poly_n\langle \Pi_i\rangle \ \varphi = poly\langle \Pi_i \cdot (g_1, \ldots, g_n)\rangle \tag{4}$$
$$= poly\langle g_i\rangle \ . \tag{2}$$

Generalizing $(poly\langle g_1\rangle, \ldots, poly\langle g_n\rangle)$ to the tuple $(\varphi_1, \ldots, \varphi_n)$ we have calculated $poly_n\langle \Pi_i\rangle \ (\varphi_1, \ldots, \varphi_n) = \varphi_i$. For functor composition we obtain

$$poly_n\langle h \cdot (h_1, \ldots, h_k)\rangle \ \varphi$$
$$= poly\langle (h \cdot (h_1, \ldots, h_k)) \cdot (g_1, \ldots, g_n)\rangle \tag{4}$$
$$= poly\langle h \cdot (h_1 \cdot (g_1, \ldots, g_n), \ldots, h_k \cdot (g_1, \ldots, g_n))\rangle \tag{3}$$
$$= poly_k\langle h\rangle \ (poly\langle h_1 \cdot (g_1, \ldots, g_n)\rangle, \ldots, poly\langle h_k \cdot (g_1, \ldots, g_n)\rangle) \tag{4}$$
$$= poly_k\langle h\rangle \ (poly_n\langle h_1\rangle \ \varphi, \ldots, poly_n\langle h_k\rangle \ \varphi) \ . \tag{4}$$

Thus, for each arity $n \geqslant 0$ the polytypic function $poly_n\langle g\rangle$ is given by

$$poly_n\langle g\rangle \qquad\qquad :: (\tau(g_1), \ldots, \tau(g_n)) \to \tau(g \cdot (g_1, \ldots, g_n))$$
$$poly_n\langle \Pi_i\rangle \qquad\qquad = \pi_i$$
$$poly_n\langle P\rangle \qquad\qquad = poly_P$$
$$poly_n\langle h \cdot (h_1, \ldots, h_k)\rangle = poly_k\langle h\rangle \star (poly_n\langle h_1\rangle, \ldots, poly_n\langle h_k\rangle) \ .$$

where $\pi_i\,(\varphi_1,\ldots,\varphi_n) = \varphi_i$ is the i-th projection function and '$\star$' denotes n-ary composition defined by $(\varphi \star (\varphi_1,\ldots,\varphi_n))\,a = \varphi\,(\varphi_1\,a,\ldots,\varphi_n\,a)$. Note that the g_i are m-ary functors while the h_i have arity n. Furthermore, note that the definition of $poly_n\langle g\rangle$ is *inductive on the structure of functor expressions*. On a more abstract level we can view $poly_n$ as an interpretation of functor expressions: Π_i is interpreted by π_i, P by $poly_P$, and '$\cdot$' by '$\star$'.

It remains to define $poly\langle f\rangle$ in terms of $poly_m\langle f\rangle$:

$$poly\langle f\rangle = poly\langle f \cdot (\Pi_1,\ldots,\Pi_m)\rangle \tag{1}$$
$$= poly_m\langle f\rangle\,(poly\langle\Pi_1\rangle,\ldots,poly\langle\Pi_m\rangle) \tag{4}$$
$$= poly_m\langle f\rangle\,(poly_{\Pi_1},\ldots,poly_{\Pi_m})\ . \qquad \text{definition } poly$$

By now we have the necessary prerequisites at hand to define the specialization of a polytypic function $poly\langle f\rangle$ for a given instance of f. The specialization works by transforming a system of functor equations that defines f into a system of function definitions that defines $poly_m\langle f\rangle$. In particular, recursion on the level of types is implemented by recursion on the function level.

$$
\begin{array}{ccc}
f_1 = e_1 & & poly_{k_1}\langle f_1\rangle = poly_{k_1}\langle e_1\rangle \\
\vdots & \implies & \vdots \\
f_p = e_p & & poly_{k_p}\langle f_p\rangle = poly_{k_p}\langle e_p\rangle
\end{array}
$$

Here k_i is the arity of f_i. The expression $poly_{k_i}\langle e_i\rangle$ is given by the inductive definition above, additionally setting $poly_{k_i}\langle f_i\rangle = poly\_f_i\_k_i$, where $poly\_f_i\_k_i$ is a new function symbol. Additionally, the defining equation for $poly\_f$, ie $poly\_f = poly\_f\_m\,(poly_{\Pi_1},\ldots,poly_{\Pi_m})$, must be added.

As an example, consider the datatype *Perfect* of Section 1.

$$Perfect = Fst + Perfect \cdot (Node, Snd)$$

Note that $size_+ = (\nabla)$, where (∇) is given by $(\varphi_1\ \nabla\ \varphi_2)\,(Inl\ x_1) = \varphi_1\ x_1$ and $(\varphi_1\ \nabla\ \varphi_2)\,(Inr\ x_2) = \varphi_2\ x_2$. Using this abbreviation the specialization of $size_2\langle Perfect\rangle$ proceeds as follows.

$$
\begin{aligned}
&size_2\langle Fst + Perfect \cdot (Node, Snd)\rangle\,(\varphi_1,\varphi_2) \\
&= size_2\langle+\rangle\,(size_2\langle Fst\rangle\,(\varphi_1,\varphi_2), size_2\langle Perfect \cdot (Node, Snd)\rangle\,(\varphi_1,\varphi_2)) \\
&= size_2\langle Fst\rangle\,(\varphi_1,\varphi_2)\ \nabla\ size_2\langle Perfect \cdot (Node, Snd)\rangle\,(\varphi_1,\varphi_2) \\
&= \varphi_1\ \nabla\ size_2\langle Perfect\rangle\,(size_2\langle Node\rangle\,(\varphi_1,\varphi_2),\varphi_2)
\end{aligned}
$$

Using the original constructor names we obtain

$$
\begin{aligned}
sizePerfect_2 \quad &::\ (\forall a.f_1\ a \to Int, \forall a.f_2\ a \to Int) \\
&\to (\forall a.Perfect\ (f_1\ a)\ (f_2\ a) \to Int) \\
sizePerfect_2\,(\varphi_1,\varphi_2)\,(Zero\ a) &= \varphi_1\ a \\
sizePerfect_2\,(\varphi_1,\varphi_2)\,(Succ\ t) &= sizePerfect_2\,(sizeNode_2\,(\varphi_1,\varphi_2),\varphi_2)\ t\ .
\end{aligned}
$$

Since $size\langle f\rangle$ has the polymorphic type $\tau(f) = \forall a.f\ a \to Int$, the auxiliary functions $size_n\langle g\rangle$ take polymorphic functions to polymorphic functions. In other words, $sizePerfect_2$ must be assigned a rank-2 type signature [15]. Unfortunately, the above definition passes neither the Hugs 98 [14] nor the GHC [20] type-checker though both accept rank-2 type signatures. The reason is that Haskell provides only a limited form of *type constructor polymorphism*. Consider the subexpression $sizeNode_2$ (φ_1, φ_2) in the last equation. It has type $\forall a. Node$ $(g_1\ a)$ $(g_2\ a) \rightarrow Int$, which is not unifiable with the expected type $\forall a. f_1\ a \rightarrow Int$. Since Haskell deliberately omits type abstractions from the language of types [13], we cannot instantiate f_1 to $\lambda u \rightarrow Node$ $(g_1\ u)$ $(g_2\ u)$. Fortunately, there is a way out of this dilemma. We simply replace each application of the functor variables f_1 and f_2 by a new type variable, ie $f_1\ a$ is replaced by x_1 and $f_2\ a$ by x_2.

$$sizePerfect_2 :: (x_1 \rightarrow Int, x_2 \rightarrow Int) \rightarrow (Perfect\ x_1\ x_2 \rightarrow Int)$$

This trick works for arbitrary type signatures and as a benevolent side effect the rank-2 type signature has turned into a standard rank-1 signature.

4   Examples

4.1   Polytypic *map*

Categorically speaking, a functor is the combination of a type constructor and a mapping function, which describes the action of the functor on functions. The mapping function can be generically defined for all datatypes.[2]

$$
\begin{aligned}
&fmap\langle f\rangle && :: \forall a. \forall b. (a \rightarrow b) \rightarrow (f\ a \rightarrow f\ b) \\
&fmap\langle f\rangle\ \varphi && = map\langle f\rangle \\
&\quad \textbf{where}\ map\langle f\rangle && :: f\ a \rightarrow f\ b \\
&\qquad map\langle Id\rangle\ x && = \varphi\ x \\
&\qquad map\langle K\,t\rangle\ x && = x \\
&\qquad map\langle f_1 + f_2\rangle\ (Inl\ x_1) && = Inl\ (map\langle f_1\rangle\ x_1) \\
&\qquad map\langle f_1 + f_2\rangle\ (Inr\ x_2) && = Inr\ (map\langle f_2\rangle\ x_2) \\
&\qquad map\langle f_1 \times f_2\rangle\ (x_1, x_2) && = (map\langle f_1\rangle\ x_1, map\langle f_2\rangle\ x_2)
\end{aligned}
$$

It is revealing to consider the typings of the subsidiary functions $map_n\langle g\rangle$.

$$
\begin{aligned}
map_n\langle g\rangle\ :: &\ (g_1\ a \rightarrow g_1\ b, \ldots, g_n\ a \rightarrow g_n\ b) \\
&\rightarrow (g\ (g_1\ a)\ \ldots\ (g_n\ a) \rightarrow g\ (g_1\ b)\ \ldots\ (g_n\ b))
\end{aligned}
$$

Replacing $g_i\ a$ by x_i and $g_i\ b$ by y_i we obtain the typings of n-ary mapping functions. And, in fact, $map_n\langle g\rangle$ corresponds to the mapping function of the n-ary functor g. Thus, to define $fmap\langle f\rangle$ generically for all types mapping functions of functors of arbitrary arity are required. The good news is that the programmer need not take care of their definition. Instead, they are generated automatically.

---

[2] We assume that type variables appearing in type signatures are scoped, ie the type variables a and b in the signature of $map\langle f\rangle$ are *not* universally quantified but refer to the occurrences in $fmap\langle f\rangle$'s signature.

4.2   Polytypic Reduction

The functions *size* and *sum* are instances of a more general concept, due to Meertens [16], termed *reduction* or *crush*. A reduction is a function of type $f\ a \to a$ that collapses a structure of values of type a into a single value of type a. To define a reduction two ingredients are required: a value $e :: a$ and a binary operation $op :: a \to a \to a$. Usually but not necessarily e is the neutral element of op.

$$
\begin{aligned}
&reduce\langle f\rangle && :: \forall a.a \to (a \to a \to a) \to f\ a \to a \\
&reduce\langle f\rangle\ e\ op && = red\langle f\rangle \\
&\quad \textbf{where}\ red\langle f\rangle && :: f\ a \to a \\
&\qquad red\langle Id\rangle\ x && = x \\
&\qquad red\langle K\,t\rangle\ x && = e \\
&\qquad red\langle f_1 + f_2\rangle\ (Inl\ x_1) && = red\langle f_1\rangle\ x_1 \\
&\qquad red\langle f_1 + f_2\rangle\ (Inr\ x_2) && = red\langle f_2\rangle\ x_2 \\
&\qquad red\langle f_1 \times f_2\rangle\ (x_1, x_2) && = red\langle f_1\rangle\ x_1\ `op`\ red\langle f_2\rangle\ x_2
\end{aligned}
$$

A number of useful functions can be defined in terms of $reduce\langle f\rangle$ and $fmap\langle f\rangle$, see Figure 2. Meertens [16], Jansson and Jeuring [12] give further applications.

$$
\begin{aligned}
&sum\langle f\rangle && :: \forall n.(Num\ n) \Rightarrow f\ n \to n \\
&sum\langle f\rangle && = reduce\langle f\rangle\ 0\ (+) \\[4pt]
&and\langle f\rangle && :: f\ Bool \to Bool \\
&and\langle f\rangle && = reduce\langle f\rangle\ True\ (\wedge) \\[4pt]
&minimum\langle f\rangle && :: \forall a.(Bounded\ a, Ord\ a) \Rightarrow f\ a \to a \\
&minimum\langle f\rangle && = reduce\langle f\rangle\ maxBound\ min \\[4pt]
&size\langle f\rangle && :: \forall a.\forall n.(Num\ n) \Rightarrow f\ a \to n \\
&size\langle f\rangle && = sum\langle f\rangle \circ fmap\langle f\rangle\ (const\ 1) \\[4pt]
&all\langle f\rangle && :: \forall a.(a \to Bool) \to (f\ a \to Bool) \\
&all\langle f\rangle\ p && = and\langle f\rangle \circ fmap\langle f\rangle\ p \\[4pt]
&flatten\langle f\rangle && :: \forall a.f\ a \to List\ a \\
&flatten\langle f\rangle && = reduce\langle f\rangle\ [\,]\ (+\!\!+) \circ fmap\langle f\rangle\ wrap\ \textbf{where}\ wrap\ a = [a] \\[4pt]
&\textbf{data}\ Tree\ a = Empty \mid Leaf\ a \mid Fork\ (Tree\ a)\ (Tree\ a) \\
&shape\langle f\rangle && :: \forall a.f\ a \to Tree\ a \\
&shape\langle f\rangle && = reduce\langle f\rangle\ Empty\ Fork \circ fmap\langle f\rangle\ Leaf
\end{aligned}
$$

Fig. 2. Examples of reductions

4.3   Polytypic Equality and Comparison

The equality function is a nice example of a function that is indexed by a nullary functor. In Haskell it can be automatically derived for datatypes of first-order kind and the following can be seen as a formalization of that process. We assume that a suitable equality function for *Int* is predefined.

$$
\begin{aligned}
&eq\langle f \rangle && :: f \to f \to Bool \\
&eq\langle 1 \rangle \; x \; y && = True \\
&eq\langle Int \rangle \; x \; y && = eqInt \; x \; y \\
&eq\langle f_1 + f_2 \rangle \; (Inl \; x_1) \; (Inl \; y_1) && = eq\langle f_1 \rangle \; x_1 \; y_1 \\
&eq\langle f_1 + f_2 \rangle \; (Inl \; x_1) \; (Inr \; y_2) && = False \\
&eq\langle f_1 + f_2 \rangle \; (Inr \; x_2) \; (Inl \; y_1) && = False \\
&eq\langle f_1 + f_2 \rangle \; (Inr \; x_2) \; (Inr \; y_2) && = eq\langle f_2 \rangle \; x_2 \; y_2 \\
&eq\langle f_1 \times f_2 \rangle \; (x_1, x_2) \; (y_1, y_2) && = eq\langle f_1 \rangle \; x_1 \; y_1 \land eq\langle f_2 \rangle \; x_2 \; y_2
\end{aligned}
$$

Varying the definition of $eq\langle f \rangle$ slightly we can also realize Haskell's *compare* function, which determines the precise ordering of two elements.

$$
\begin{aligned}
&\textbf{data } Ordering && = LT \mid EQ \mid GT \\
&cmp\langle f \rangle && :: f \to f \to Ordering \\
&cmp\langle 1 \rangle \; x \; y && = EQ \\
&cmp\langle Int \rangle \; x \; y && = cmpInt \; x \; y \\
&cmp\langle f_1 + f_2 \rangle \; (Inl \; x_1) \; (Inl \; y_1) && = cmp\langle f_1 \rangle \; x_1 \; y_1 \\
&cmp\langle f_1 + f_2 \rangle \; (Inl \; x_1) \; (Inr \; y_2) && = LT \\
&cmp\langle f_1 + f_2 \rangle \; (Inr \; x_2) \; (Inl \; y_1) && = GT \\
&cmp\langle f_1 + f_2 \rangle \; (Inr \; x_2) \; (Inr \; y_2) && = cmp\langle f_2 \rangle \; x_2 \; y_2 \\
&cmp\langle f_1 \times f_2 \rangle \; (x_1, x_2) \; (y_1, y_2) && = \textbf{case } cmp\langle f_1 \rangle \; x_1 \; y_1 \textbf{ of} \\
& && \quad \{ EQ \to cmp\langle f_2 \rangle \; x_2 \; y_2; ord \to ord \}
\end{aligned}
$$

5   Related and Future Work

This paper can be regarded as a successor to my previous work on polytypic programming [7], where a similar approach using *rational trees* is presented. The major difference between the two frameworks lies in the treatment of functor composition. In the 'rational tree approach' functor composition is regarded as a function symbol, which implies that a polytypic definition must specify the action on $g \cdot (g_1, \ldots, g_n)$ for each $n \geqslant 1$. Clearly, this cannot be done exhaustively. Furthermore, since the cases for functor composition are redundant, there is no guarantee that the polytypic function behaves the same on equal functors such as *Rose* and *Rose'*. Both problems disappear if we handle functor composition on the meta level generalizing rational trees to algebraic trees.

The classic approach to polytypic programming as realized in the polytypic programming language extension PolyP [10] is based on the initial algebra semantics of datatypes. Here, functors are modeled by the following grammar.

$$
\begin{aligned}
F &= \mu B \\
B &= K \, T \mid Fst \mid Snd \mid B + B \mid B \times B \mid F \cdot B
\end{aligned}
$$

Recursive datatypes are modeled by fixpoints of associated base functors: the functor μB, which is known as a *type functor*, denotes the unary functor F

given as the least solution of the equation $F\ a = B(a, F\ a)$. Polytypic functions are defined according to the above structure of types. In PolyP the polytypic function $size\langle f\rangle$ is defined as follows—modulo change of notation.

$$
\begin{aligned}
size\langle f\rangle && &:: \forall a.f\ a \to Int \\
size\langle \mu b\rangle && &= cata\langle \mu b\rangle\ (bsize\langle b\rangle) \\[4pt]
bsize\langle b\rangle && &:: \forall a.b\ a\ Int \to Int \\
bsize\langle K t\rangle\ x && &= 0 \\
bsize\langle Fst\rangle\ x && &= 1 \\
bsize\langle Snd\rangle\ n && &= n \\
bsize\langle b_1 + b_2\rangle\ (Inl\ x_1) && &= bsize\langle b_1\rangle\ x_1 \\
bsize\langle b_1 + b_2\rangle\ (Inr\ x_2) && &= bsize\langle b_2\rangle\ x_2 \\
bsize\langle b_1 \times b_2\rangle\ (x_1, x_2) && &= bsize\langle b_1\rangle\ x_1 + bsize\langle b_2\rangle\ x_2 \\
bsize\langle f \cdot b\rangle\ x && &= sum\langle f\rangle\ (fmap\langle f\rangle\ (bsize\langle b\rangle)\ x)
\end{aligned}
$$

The program is quite elaborate as compared to the one given in Section 1: it involves two general combining forms, $cata\langle f\rangle$ and $fmap\langle f\rangle$, and an auxiliary polytypic function, $sum\langle f\rangle$. The disadvantages of the initial algebra approach are fairly obvious. The above definition is redundant: we know that $size\langle f\rangle$ is uniquely defined by its action on constant functors, Id, sums, and products. The definition is incomplete: $size\langle f\rangle$ is only applicable to regular functors (recall that, for instance, $Perfect$ is not a regular functor). Furthermore, the regular functor may not depend on functors of arity $\geqslant 2$ since functor composition is only defined for unary functors. Finally, the definition exhibits a slight inefficiency: the combining form $fmap\langle f\rangle$ produces an intermediate data structure, which is immediately consumed by $sum\langle f\rangle$. In other words, $size\langle Rose\rangle$ corresponds to the first, less efficient definition of $sizer$.

An obvious advantage of PolyP is that it allows to define general recursion schemes like cata- and anamorphisms [17]. As an example, the recursion scheme $cata\langle f\rangle$, which is used in $size\langle f\rangle$, is given by

$$
\begin{aligned}
cata\langle f\rangle && &:: \forall a.\forall b.(f'\ a\ b \to b) \to (f\ a \to b) \\
cata\langle \mu b\rangle\ \varphi && &= \varphi \circ bmap\langle b\rangle\ id\ (cata\langle \mu b\rangle\ \varphi) \circ out\ .
\end{aligned}
$$

The operation $(\text{-})'$ (called $FunctorOf$ in PolyP) maps a type functor to its base functor, ie $F' = B$ for $F = \mu B$. The function $out :: f\ a \to f'\ a\ (f\ a)$ decomposes an element of type $f\ a$ by unfolding one level of recursion. While the explicit treatment of type recursion is unnecessary for many applications—all polytypic functions of PolyLib [12] can be implemented in our framework, except, of course, cata- and anamorphisms—it is indispensable for others. The polytypic unification algorithm described by Jansson and Jeuring [11], for instance, requires a function that determines the immediate subterms of a term. A similar function appears in the article of Bird, de Moor, and Hoogendijk [3], who present a generalization of the maximum segment sum problem. In both cases the recursive structure of a datatype must be known. Now, since our framework deals with type recursion on the meta level, one could feel tempted to conclude that we cannot deal with such applications. It appears, however, that the availability of operations on types is an orthogonal design issue. Hence, nothing prevents us from incorporating the operator $(-)'$ depicted above. Let us furthermore generalize $(-)'$ so that it maps an n-ary, regular functor to its associated $(n+1)$-ary base functor. Given two polytypic functions $in :: f' \, a_1 \ldots a_n \, (f \, a_1 \ldots a_n) \to f \, a_1 \ldots a_n$ and $out :: f \, a_1 \ldots a_n \to f' \, a_1 \ldots a_n \, (f \, a_1 \ldots a_n)$ we can define cata- and anamorphisms for functors of arbitrary arity. Here are the definitions for unary functors.

$$\begin{aligned}
cata\langle f \rangle &:: \forall a. \forall b.(f' \, a \, b \to b) \to (f \, a \to b) \\
cata\langle f \rangle \, \varphi &= \varphi \circ bmap\langle f' \rangle \, id \, (cata\langle f \rangle \, \varphi) \circ out \\
ana\langle f \rangle &:: \forall a. \forall b.(b \to f' \, a \, b) \to (b \to f \, a) \\
ana\langle f \rangle \, \psi &= in \circ bmap\langle f' \rangle \, id \, (ana\langle f \rangle \, \psi) \circ \psi
\end{aligned}$$

It is worth noting that the definition of the subsidiary function $bmap\langle b \rangle$ proceeds as before. In particular, there is no need to consider functor composition or type functors. Furthermore, the base functor may be a nested functor. The function that collects the immediate subterms of a term can be defined as follows.

$$\begin{aligned}
subterms\langle t \rangle &:: t \to List \, t \\
subterms\langle t \rangle &= flatten\langle t' \rangle \circ out
\end{aligned}$$

Directions for future work suggest themselves. In the full version of this paper [8] we show that polytypic functions satisfy fusion laws analogous to the fusion law for folds. The functorial properties of $fmap\langle f \rangle$ and the fusion law for reductions [16] are, for instance, consequences of the polytypic fusion laws. It remains to broaden the approach to include exponentials and higher-order polymorphism [13]. Adapting the technique of Meijer and Hutton [18] the former extension should be fairly straightforward. Currently, the author is working on the latter extension so that polytypic functions can be defined generically for all datatypes expressible in Haskell. An application of polytypic programming to digital searching is described in a companion paper [6], where we show how to define *tries* and operations on tries generically for arbitrary datatypes of first-order kind. The central insight is that a trie can be considered as a *type-indexed datatype*, which adds an interesting new dimension to polytypic programming.

Acknowledgements

I would like to thank the anonymous referees for many valuable comments.

References

1. M. Abadi, L. Cardelli, B. Pierce, and D. Rémy. Dynamic typing in polymorphic languages. *J. Functional Programming*, 5(1):111–130, January 1995.
2. Richard Bird. *Introduction to Functional Programming using Haskell*. Prentice Hall Europe, London, 2nd edition, 1998.

3. Richard Bird, Oege de Moor, and Paul Hoogendijk. Generic functional programming with types and relations. *J. Functional Programming*, 6(1):1–28, Jan. 1996.
4. Richard Bird and Lambert Meertens. Nested datatypes. In J. Jeuring, editor, *Fourth International Conference on Mathematics of Program Construction, MPC'98*, LNCS 1422, pages 52–67. Springer-Verlag, June 1998.
5. Bruno Courcelle. Fundamental properties of infinite trees. *Theoretical Computer Science*, 25(2):95–169, March 1983.
6. Ralf Hinze. Generalizing generalized tries. *J. Functional Programming*, 1999. Accepted for publication.
7. Ralf Hinze. Polytypic functions over nested datatypes. *Discrete Mathematics and Theoretical Computer Science*, 1999. Accepted for publication.
8. Ralf Hinze. Polytypic programming with ease. Technical Report IAI-TR-99-2, Institut für Informatik III, Universität Bonn, February 1999.
9. P. Jansson and J. Jeuring. Polytypic compact printing and parsing. In S. Doaitse Swierstra, editor, *Proceedings European Symposium on Programming, ESOP'99*, LNCS 1576, pages 273–287. Springer-Verlag, 1999.
10. Patrik Jansson and Johan Jeuring. PolyP—a polytypic programming language extension. In *24th Symposium on Principles of Programming Languages, POPL'97*, pages 470–482. ACM-Press, January 1997.
11. Patrik Jansson and Johan Jeuring. Functional Pearl: Polytypic unification. *J. Functional Programming*, 8(5):527–536, September 1998.
12. Patrik Jansson and Johan Jeuring. PolyLib—A library of polytypic functions. In Roland Backhouse and Tim Sheard, editors, *Informal Proceedings Workshop on Generic Programming, WGP'98*. Department of Computing Science, Chalmers University of Technology and Göteborg University, http://wsinwp01.win.tue.nl:1234/WGPProceedings/index.html, June 1998.
13. Mark P. Jones. Functional programming with overloading and higher-order polymorphism. In *First International Spring School on Advanced Functional Programming Techniques*, LNCS 925, pages 97–136. Springer-Verlag, 1995.
14. M.P. Jones and J.C. Peterson. *Hugs 98 User Manual*, May 1999. Available from http://www.haskell.org/hugs.
15. Nancy Jean McCracken. The typechecking of programs with implicit type structure. In Gilles Kahn, David B. MacQueen, and Gordon D. Plotkin, editors, *Semantics of Data Types*, LNCS 173, pages 301–315. Springer-Verlag, 1984.
16. Lambert Meertens. Calculate polytypically! In H. Kuchen and S.D. Swierstra, editors, *8th International Symposium on Programming Languages: Implementations, Logics, and Programs, PLILP'96*, LNCS 1140, pages 1–16. Springer-Verlag, September 1996.
17. E. Meijer, M. Fokkinga, and R. Paterson. Functional programming with bananas, lenses, envelopes and barbed wire. In *5th Conference on Functional Programming Languages and Computer Architecture, FPCA'91*, LNCS 523, pages 124–144. Springer-Verlag, 1991.
18. Erik Meijer and Graham Hutton. Bananas in space: Extending fold and unfold to exponential types. In *7th Conference on Functional Programming Languages and Computer Architecture, FPCA'95*, pages 324–333. ACM-Press, June 1995.
19. Chris Okasaki. *Purely Functional Data Structures*. Cambridge University Press, 1998.
20. Simon Peyton Jones. Explicit quantification in Haskell, 1998. Available from research.microsoft.com/Users/simonpj/Haskell/quantification.html.

21. Simon Peyton Jones and John Hughes, editors. *Haskell 98 — A Non-strict, Purely Functional Language.* http://www.haskell.org/onlinereport/. February 1999.
22. Zhe Yang. Encoding types in ML-like languages. *SIGPLAN Notices*, 34(1):289–300, January 1999.

Type Inference for Overloading without Restrictions, Declarations or Annotations

Carlos Camarão[1] and Lucília Figueiredo[2]

[1] Universidade Federal de Minas Gerais, DCC-ICEX
Belo Horizonte 31270-010, Brasil
[2] Universidade Federal de Ouro Preto, DECOM-ICEB
Ouro Preto 35400-000, Brasil

Abstract. This article presents a type system based on the Damas-Milner system[DM82], that supports overloading. Types of overloaded symbols are constrained polymorphic types. The work is related to Haskell type classes[Wad89,NP93,HHJW96], System O[OWW95] and other similar type systems[Kae88,Smi91,Jon94,DCO96]. Restrictions imposed in these systems with respect to overloading are eliminated. User-defined global and local overloading is supported without restrictions. There is no need for declarations or annotations of any sort. No language construct is added in order to cope with overloading. The type system uses a context-dependent overloading policy, specified by a predicate used in a single inference rule. Overloading of functions defined over different type constructors is supported, as done with Haskell's constructor classes. No monomorphism restriction is required in order to solve ambiguity problems. The system uses an open-world approach, in which new overloaded definitions can be introduced with types automatically reflecting the new definitions. The article also presents a type inference algorithm for the system, which is proved to be sound and to compute principal typings.

1 Introduction

The problems with the treatment of overloading in languages that provide (parametric) polymorphism and type inference, such as SML[MTH89,Pau96] and Miranda[Tur85], have been discussed for example by Wadler and Blott[Wad89]. For instance, `square x = x * x` cannot be written in SML, the reason being that * is overloaded for integers and reals. Equality is treated in a special way in SML. For example, the type of function `member`, that tests membership in a list, namely `''a list -> ''a -> bool`, involves a special type variable `''a`, constrained so that its instances must admit equality. In Miranda, this type is not constrained in this way; applying `member` to lists whose elements are functions generates a run-time error.

In Haskell[Pe97,Tho96], type classes[NP93,HHJW96] allow overloaded symbols to have different meanings in contexts requiring different types. Type classes

A. Middeldorp, T. Sato (Eds.): FLOPS'99, LNCS 1722, pp. 37–52, 1999.

represented a big step forward, in the direction of providing comprehensive support for overloading, together with polymorphism and type inference. However, the following points can be viewed as disadvantages of type classes:

1. Class declarations, as well as type annotations and type declarations, are not needed for the inference of types of overloaded symbols, as is shown in this paper. Thus, a programmer should not be obliged to make a class declaration or type annotation in order to specify the type of a given symbol (he may still write type annotations for documentation and other purposes).

2. The declaration of type classes involves an issue which is separate from overloading resolution: to group logically related names in the same construct. As pointed out by Odersky, Wadler and Wehr[OWW95], "eliminating class declarations means one needs no longer decide in advance which operations belong together in a class. In many situations, this will be a positive advantage. For instance, if we're dealing with pairs, we want only first and second grouped together, but if we're dealing with triples, we will want third as well. As a further example, consider the difficulties that the Haskell designers had deciding how to group numeric operators into classes. This design is still argued: should + and * be in a 'ring' class?". Grouping logically related symbols together in a language construct involves the definition of a structure of program interfaces; this is intrinsic to modular software development, but overloading resolution is a separate issue.

3. For unrelated definitions of the same name in a program, the programmer is forced to create a class declaration with the type of the overloaded name.

4. For any new definition of any given overloaded name, either its type must be an instance of the type specified in its class declaration, or the class declaration must be modified.

5. The use of classes in type annotations conflicts with data abstraction. If an implementation of (say) x is changed so that an overloaded symbol is no longer used, or a new overloaded symbol is used, the types of all symbols defined by using x may have to be modified.

With respect to specific approaches in implementations[J+98,Jon98a]:

6. Definitions of overloaded symbols must occur in global instance declarations, and overloading is thus restricted to definitions that occur at the outermost level. Local overloading (from bindings occurring inside lambda-abstractions) is not allowed. Local overloading allows a programmer to make definitions where appropriate; he is not forced to make global declarations just because symbols being defined happen to be overloaded.
   Local overloading also allows (as an option for a language designer) the use of symbols defined in an outer level, despite of redefinition in an inner level (with a distinct type).

7. Haskell makes a few restrictions on the form of class and instance declarations, certainly with good reasons, a discussion of these being outside the scope of this paper (see [Jon95,JJM97,Jon98b,Jon94]).

System O[OWW95] is an improvement in relation to type classes with respect to items (1) to (5) above.[1] System O uses universally quantified types, with a constraint on the quantified variable that is a (possibly empty) set of bindings $o :: \alpha \rightarrow \tau$, indicating that there must exist an overloaded operator $o :: p \rightarrow (\tau[p/\alpha])$, for any instance p of α.[2] Although System O was an important step towards the solution to the problem of providing type inference for a language that supports polymorphism and overloading without the need for class declarations, it did not provide a satisfactory solution. Significant limitations of System O are as follows. It supports only context-independent overloading. This means that constants cannot be overloaded, nor function symbols with types like, for example, read : String $\rightarrow$ a, even though they could be used in contexts that resolve the overloading (e.g. read str == "foo"). The type systems presented in [Kae88,Smi91,DCO96] also support only context-independent overloading. System O requires explicit annotation of the type of each overloaded function symbol. Thus, there is no type inference for overloaded symbols. System O requires all type constructors of the arguments of overloaded functions to be pairwise distinct. This restricts even more the set of types of definitions of an overloaded symbol (this restriction is also imposed in the earlier work of Kaes[Kae88]). System O only allows definitions of overloaded symbols at the outermost level (this restriction is also imposed in the works of Kaes[Kae88], Geoffrey Smith[Smi91] and Mark Jones[Jon94]).

2   Overview of System CT

The type system presented in this article, called System CT, allows multiple occurrences of overloaded symbols in a typing context, each occurrence with a distinct type. Typings for overloaded symbols are introduced in the context after corresponding let-bindings for these symbols (which correspond to instance declarations in Haskell, and inst declarations in System O). The overloading policy determines whether or not a given type may be the type of an overloaded symbol in a given context.

System CT uses context-dependent overloading. Overloading of constants is allowed. Consider let one = 1 in let one = 1.0 in ..., for example (we assume that literals 0, 1 etc. have type Int and literals o0.0, 1.0 etc. have type Float). After the let-bindings, the typing context, say Γ_0, contains the typings one : Int and one : Float. The type derived for one in context Γ_0 is $\{one : \alpha\}.\alpha$, indicating a type for which there is a constant one of that type, in Γ_0.

All other type systems use a different approach, as far as we know. The type of a given overloaded symbol is either selected among the set of typings for that symbol in the typing context (e.g. [Kae88,Smi91,OWW95,DCO96]) or, for each overloaded symbol, a fixed typing is used, together with a set of predicates

---

[1] Although System O does not require class and instance declarations, type annotations are required in the definition of overloaded symbols.

[2] The notation $\sigma[\tau/\alpha]$ indicates the usual textual substitution.

(i.e. a set of available type instances) and a constraint elimination rule, for transforming constrained into unconstrained types (e.g. [NP93,Jon94,HHJW96]). With overloading and this context independent constraint elimination, some difficulties arise in detecting ambiguity. A simple example is expression g one in typing context Γ_g with typings one : Int, one : Float, g : Int $\rightarrow$ Int, g : Float $\rightarrow$ Int. The ambiguity in this expression would not be detected without additional rules in the type system, as both $\Gamma_g \vdash$ one : Int and $\Gamma_g \vdash$ g : Int $\rightarrow$ Int could be derived, obtaining $\Gamma_g \vdash$ g one : Int, or $\Gamma_g \vdash$ one : Float and $\Gamma_g \vdash$ g : Float $\rightarrow$ Int, obtaining again $\Gamma_g \vdash$ g one : Int. This is a known problem, of *coherence*[Jon94]. To solve it, restrictions are imposed in order to detect ambiguity.

For example, the type systems of Haskell and Hugs detect this error by means of the following restriction on the syntax of type expressions (called Restriction A for further reference): "If $P \Rightarrow \tau$ is a type, then $tv(P) \subseteq tv(\tau)$", where P specifies a set of constraints, τ is a simple type and tv gives the set of free type variables of its argument. Note that Restriction A must not consider in P type variables that are free in the typing context, so that, for example, g x is not considered ambiguous, in a context as Γ_g above but where x is a lambda-bound variable. In such a context, g x is well typed. Unfortunately, Restriction A prevents the use of expressions which are unambiguous. Consider for example $\Gamma_f = \{$f : Int $\rightarrow$ Float, f : Float $\rightarrow$ Int, one : Int, one : Float$\}$. Expression f one + 1 (in a context such as Γ_f) is a simple example of an unambiguous expression that cannot be written in Haskell, nor in Hugs[Jon98a]. Consider:

```
class F a b where f::a -> b
class O a where one::a
instance F Int Float where ...
instance F Float Int where ...
instance O Int where ...
instance O Float where ...
main = print (f one + (1::Int))
```

In Hugs and GHC 3.02[J+98], which allow multiple parameter type classes, type (F a b, O a) => b (which would be the type of f one) is considered ambiguous (characterizing an overloading that cannot be resolved in any context).

Letting h be defined by h x = True, another example is h one, which has type Bool in System CT and is considered ambiguous in Haskell or Hugs.

System CT adopts a novel approach in the basic rule, (VAR), which gives the type of an overloaded symbol as the least common generalisation of the types of this symbol in a typing context. As a natural consequence, instantiation and constraint elimination are controlled in rule (APPL), by the use of unification.

For example, in Γ_o above (with typings one : Int and one : Float), type $\{$one : $\alpha\}. \alpha$ is derived for one; Int and Float are considered as instances of this type, due to the possible substitutions for unifying α with types of one in Γ_o.

In Γ_f, typing f one : $\{f : \alpha \to \beta, \text{one} : \alpha\}$. β indicates that this expression works like an overloaded constant; it can be used in a context requiring either a value of type Int or Float. Again, this is due to the possible substitutions for unifying types in $\{f : \alpha \to \beta, \text{one} : \alpha\}$ with typings for f and one in Γ_f.

In System CT, the type of any overloaded symbol is computed automatically from the types given by definitions of this symbol that are "visible in the relevant scope" (i.e. that occur in the relevant typing context). The programmer need not anticipate all possible definitions an overloaded symbol might have, something which is needed in order to specify a (least common generalisation) type T for this symbol in a class declaration (so that all definitions of this symbol have types that are instances of T). In System CT, a new definition is not necessarily an instance of the least common generalisation of types given by previous definitions. Instead, any new definition may imply the assignment of a more general type than that computed according to previous definitions (as if a class declaration, if it existed, was automatically modified to reflect the new definition). In this sense, System CT uses in fact an approach that is "more open" than that used with type classes in Haskell.

System CT uses the predicate *ambiguous* for detection of ambiguous overloading (see section 3). With the use of this predicate, expressions with the following types are not considered ambiguous:

1. Types for which $tv(P) \cap tv(\tau) \neq \emptyset$, despite the fact that $tv(P) \not\subseteq tv(\tau)$. This is the case of example f one above. Another example is map f ∘ map g, where the standard map function is overloaded to operate, for example, on lists and trees, and ∘ is the function composition operator.
2. Types for which P has type variables that occur free in the typing context, despite the fact that $tv(P) \cap tv(\tau) = \emptyset$. This is the case of g x above (40).

Constraints that apply to the type of $e\ e'$ are only those that have type variables that occur free in the typing context (e.g. g x), or occur in the "unconstrained part" of the type of $e\ e'$ (e.g. snd (True, one)). In examples for which a component of a value is selected, constraints may not apply to the type of the selected component. For example, fst (True, one) where one is overloaded and fst selects the first component of a pair. In System CT, the type of fst (True, one) is Bool; it is considered ambiguous in Haskell or Hugs.

Another related example (taken from the Haskell mailing list) follows. Suppose that function read is overloaded, having a type that would be written as $\forall\alpha.\ \{\text{read} : \text{String} \to (\alpha, \text{String})\}.$ String $\to (\alpha, \text{String})$ in System CT, and consider: read2 s = let $\{(a, s1) = \text{read } s; (b, s2) = \text{read } s1\}$ in (a, b).   In System CT, the type of s1 is String, irrespective of whether functions fst and snd are used in this example instead of pattern-matching.

System CT supports global and local overloading unrestrictively, without the need for declarations or annotations. Overloaded definitions can occur inside lambda-abstractions, and can use lambda-bound variables. No monomorphism restriction[Pe97,Jon94] is necessary in order to solve ambiguity problems.

System CT also supports overloading of functions defined over different type constructors, as done with Haskell's constructor classes[Jon95]. In System CT this issue has been solely a matter of giving a more informative type, since the original system, without constructor variables, also supported overloading of functions defined over different type constructors. The modifications required in the original system, in order to give such more informative types for overloaded symbols defined over different type constructors, were very simple.

For example, System CT allows the writing of reusable code that works for a variety of essentially similar bulk types (see [Jon96]), in a simple way. Assuming singleton and union to be overloaded to operate on some bulk types (for example List and Queue), we can write:

```
leaves (Leaf a) = singleton a
leaves (Branch t1 t2) = leaves t1 'union' leaves t2
```

Type $\{singleton : a \rightarrow c\, a, union : c\, a \rightarrow c\, a \rightarrow c\, a\}$. Tree $a \rightarrow c\, a$ is infered for leaves. Due to being defined in terms of overloaded functions, function leaves works itself just like an overloaded function. Its constrained polymoprhic type reflects this fact. In the type of leaves, c is a *constructor variable*.

System CT enables a clear separation between the issues of overloading resolution and definition of the structure of program interfaces. The type inference algorithm for System CT is a revised and extended version of a type inference algorithm used for computing *principal pairs* for core-ML[Mit96].

The rest of the paper is organized as follows. Section 3 introduces the type rules of our system. Section 4 presents the type inference algorithm and proves theorems of soundness and computation of principal types. Section 5 concludes.

3   Type System

We use a language similar to core-ML[Mil78,DM82,Mit88,Mit96], but new overloadings can be introduced in let-bindings. Recursive let-bindings are not considered (since they can be replaced by a fix point operator). For simplicity, let-bindings do not introduce nested scopes. Thus: let $x = e_1$ in let $y = e_2$ in e is viewed as in a form let $\{x = e_1; y = e_2\}$ in e, with a list of declarations, as usually found in functional programming languages (in our system allowing $x \equiv y$ for the introduction of new overloadings).

Meta-variables α and β are used for type variables. We include value constructors ($k \in \mathcal{K}$) and type constructors ($C \in \mathcal{C}$). For simplicity, term variables ($x \in X$) are divided into two disjoint groups: let-bound ($o \in O$) and lambda-bound ($u \in U$). Meta-variable κ denotes a set $\{o_i : \tau_i\}^{i=1..n}$, called a set of constraints. A value constructor is considered as a let-bound variable which has a closed type with an empty set of constraints, fixed in a global typing context. Each type constructor C in $C\, \tau_1 \ldots \tau_n$ and each type variable α in $\alpha\, \tau_1 \ldots \tau_n$ has an arity, which is the value of n. It is assumed that there is a function type constructor ($\rightarrow$), which has arity 2 and is used in infix notation. A type variable with an arity greater than zero is called a *constructor variable*. Meta-variable χ is used to denote either a constructor variable or a type constructor.

Figure 1 gives the syntax of pre-terms and types of System CT.

A *typing context* Γ is a set of pairs $x : \sigma$. A let-bound variable can occur more than once in a typing context. A pair $x : \sigma$ is called a *typing for* x; if $\{x : \sigma_i\}^{i=1..n}$ is the set of typings for x in Γ, then $\Gamma(x) = \{\sigma_i\}^{i=1..n}$ is the set of types of x in Γ.

A *type substitution* (or simply substitution) is a function from type variables to simple types or type constructors, that differ from the identity function (id) only on finitely many variables. If σ is a type and S is a substitution, then $S\sigma$ denotes the type obtained by substituting $S(\alpha)$ for each occurrence of free type variable α in σ. Similarly, for a typing context Γ, $S\Gamma$ denotes $\{x : S\sigma \mid x : \sigma \in \Gamma\}$, and for a set of constraints κ, $S\kappa$ denotes $\{o : S\tau \mid o : \tau \in \kappa\}$.

$S|_V$ stands for the restriction of S to type variables in V: $S|_V(\alpha)$ is equal to $S(\alpha)$ if $\alpha \in V$, and to α otherwise.

$tv(\sigma)$ stands for the set of free type variables of σ; $tv(\kappa)$ and $tv(\Gamma)$ are defined similarly, considering types in κ and Γ, respectively. $tv(t_1, \ldots, t_n)$ abbreviates $tv(t_1) \cup \ldots \cup tv(t_n)$. For clarity, we sometimes drop the superscripts in, for example, $\{x_i\}^{i=1..n}$ and $\forall(\alpha_j)^{j=1..m} . \kappa . \tau$, assuming then systematically that i ranges from 1 to n and j ranges from 1 to m (where $m, n \geq 0$).

Types are modified, with respect to the type system of core-ML, to include constrained types. Typing formulas have the form $\Gamma \vdash e : (\kappa . \tau, \Gamma')$, where Γ' contains typings of let-bound variables used for checking satisfiability of constraints in κ (see description of *sat* below).

Quantification is defined over constrained types. Type σ is *closed* if $tv(\sigma) = \emptyset$. Renaming of bound variables in quantified types yield syntactically equal types.

The restriction of a set of constraints κ to a set of type variables V, denoted by $\kappa|_V$, is defined inductively as follows:

$$\emptyset|_V = \emptyset$$
$$\{o : \tau\}|_V = \textbf{if } tv(\tau) \cap V = \emptyset \textbf{ then } \emptyset \textbf{ else } \{o : \tau\}$$
$$(\{o : \tau\} \cup \kappa')|_V = \{o : \tau\}|_V \cup \kappa'|_V$$

The closure of restricting a set of constraints κ to a set of type variables V, denoted by $\kappa|_V^*$, is defined as follows:

$$\kappa|_V^* = \begin{cases} \kappa|_V & \text{if } tv(\kappa|_V) \subseteq V \\ \kappa|_{tv(\kappa|_V)}^* & \text{otherwise} \end{cases}$$

Informally, $\kappa|_V$ is obtained from κ by keeping only typings which have type variables that are in V. $\kappa|_V^*$ keeps typings that have type variables in V or in any typing kept "earlier". $S\kappa|_V^*$ means $(S\kappa)|_V^*$.

The intersection of a set of substitutions $\mathbb{S}$, denoted by $\bigcap \mathbb{S}$, is given by:

$$\bigcap \{S\} = S$$
$$\bigcap(\{S\} \cup \mathbb{S}) = S|_V \text{ where } V = \{\alpha \mid S(\alpha) = S'(\alpha), \text{ and } S' = \bigcap \mathbb{S}\}$$

Terms	$e ::= x \mid \lambda u.\, e \mid e\, e' \mid \text{let } o = e \text{ in } e'$	
Simple Types	$\tau ::= C\, \tau_1 \ldots \tau_n \mid \alpha\, \tau_1 \ldots \tau_n$	$(n \geq 0)$
Constrained Types	$\Delta ::= \{o_i : \tau_i\}.\, \tau$	$(n \geq 0)$
Types	$\sigma ::= \forall \alpha_i.\, \Delta$	$(n \geq 0)$

Figure 1: Abstract Syntax of System CT

The type rules are given in Figure 2.

Overloading is controlled by predicate ρ, in rule (LET). In this rule "$\Gamma, x : \sigma$" is a notation for updating Γ with $x : \sigma$, which requires $\rho(\sigma, \Gamma(x))$.[3] $\rho(\sigma, T)$ basically tests if σ is not unifiable with types in T:

$$\Gamma, x : \sigma = \begin{cases} (\Gamma - \{x : \sigma'\}) \cup \{x : \sigma\} & \text{if } x \in \mathcal{U} \text{ and } x : \sigma' \in \Gamma \\ \Gamma \cup \{x : \sigma\} & \text{if } x \in O \text{ and } (\rho(\sigma, \Gamma(x)) \text{ holds, if } \Gamma(x) \neq \emptyset) \end{cases}$$

$\rho(o : \forall \alpha_i.\, \kappa.\, \tau, T) =$
    $unify(\{\tau = \tau'\})$ fails, for each $\forall \beta_j.\, \kappa'.\, \tau' \in T$,
        where type variables in $\{\alpha_i\}$ and $\{\beta_j\}$ are renamed to be distinct

Rule (VAR) assigns to a given symbol the least common generalisation of the types of this symbol in the given typing context. For overloading resolution, this contrasts with a type system that enables the type of an overloaded symbol to be any of a given set of types in a typing context.

In System CT, instantiation is done on application, where substitution of type variables is determined by unification. The use of unification in rule (APPL) is a fundamental characteristic of the treatment of overloading in System CT. $Unify(E, V)$ is the standard algorithm for computing the most general unifying substitution for the set of type equations E[Rob65,Mit96], but considers that type variables in V are not unifiable (type variables in V are free type variables, originally introduced in types of lambda-bound variables). For reasons of space, we do not present the (slightly modified) unification algorithm.

Function pt, used in rule (VAR), uses function lcg (for *least common generalisation*) to give constrained types for overloaded symbols. In the construction of such types, pt renames term variables to fresh term variables, which are used only internally in the type system (i.e. they do not appear in programs). As an example where this renaming is needed, consider the types of e and e' in $e\, e'$, where $e \equiv (\text{let } x = e_1 \text{ in let } x = e_2 \text{ in } e_3)$ and $e' \equiv (\text{let } x = e_1' \text{ in let } x = e_2' \text{ in } e_3')$. Without renaming, constraints on these types would both include typings for x.

---

[3] Rule (LET) could be modified in order to allow overlapping declarations (for which ρ, as defined, gives false). In this case, there should exist a mechanism for choosing a default implementation (usually the most specific one) for overloading resolution, in cases where overloading should have been resolved. This facility is not discussed in this paper and has been left for future work.

$$\Gamma \vdash x : pt(x, \Gamma) \hspace{4cm} \text{(VAR)}$$

$$\frac{\Gamma \vdash e_1 : (\kappa_1. \tau_1, \Gamma_1) \qquad \Gamma, o : close(\kappa_1. \tau_1, \Gamma) \vdash e_2 : (\kappa_2. \tau_2, \Gamma_2)}{\Gamma \vdash \text{let } o = e_1 \text{ in } e_2 : (\kappa|^*_{tv(\tau,\Gamma)}. \tau, \Gamma')} \quad \mathbf{S} \neq \emptyset \quad \text{(LET)}$$

where $\mathbf{S} = sat\,(\kappa_1 \cup \kappa_2, \Gamma')$, $\quad S_\Delta = \bigcap \mathbf{S}|_{tv(\kappa_1 \cup \kappa_2) - tv(\Gamma)}$
$\tau = S_\Delta \tau_2$, $\Gamma' = \Gamma_1 \cup \Gamma_2$, $\kappa = unresolved\,(S_\Delta(\kappa_1 \cup \kappa_2), \Gamma')$

$$\frac{\Gamma, u : \tau' \vdash e : (\kappa. \tau, \Gamma')}{\Gamma \vdash \lambda u. e : (\kappa. \tau' \to \tau, \Gamma')} \hspace{3cm} \text{(ABS)}$$

$$\frac{\Gamma \vdash e_1 : (\kappa_1. \tau_1, \Gamma_1) \qquad \Gamma \vdash e_2 : (\kappa_2. \tau_2, \Gamma_2)}{\Gamma \vdash e_1\, e_2 : (\kappa|^*_{tv(\tau,\Gamma)}. \tau, \Gamma')} \quad \begin{array}{l} S = Unify(\{\tau_1 = \tau_2 \to \alpha\}, tv(\Gamma)) \\ \mathbf{S} \neq \emptyset \quad not\, ambiguous(tv(S_\Delta S \kappa_1), \\ \kappa, tv(\tau, \Gamma)) \end{array}$$

$$\text{(APPL)}$$

where $\mathbf{S} = sat\,(S(\kappa_1 \cup \kappa_2), \Gamma')$, $\quad S_\Delta = \bigcap \mathbf{S}|_{tv(S(\kappa_1 \cup \kappa_2)) - tv(\Gamma)}$, $\quad \alpha$ is a fresh
type variable
$\tau = S_\Delta S \alpha$, $\Gamma' = \Gamma_1 \cup \Gamma_2$, $\kappa = unresolved\,(S_\Delta S(\kappa_1 \cup \kappa_2), \Gamma')$

Figure 2: Type Rules of System CT

For simplicity, in examples where it is not necessary, renaming of let-bound variables in constraints is not used. $pt(x, \Gamma)$ is given as follows:

$pt(x, \Gamma) =$
    if $\Gamma(x) = \emptyset$ then fail else
    if $\Gamma(x) = \{\forall \alpha_j. \kappa. \tau\}$ then $(\kappa. \tau, \Gamma)$
    else $(\{x' : \tau\}. \tau, \Gamma[x'/x])$, where $\Gamma(x) = \{\forall(\alpha_j)_i. \kappa_i. \tau_i\}^{i=1..n}, n > 1$,
    x' is a fresh term variable and $\tau = lcg(\{\tau_i\})$

$lcg(\{\tau_i\})$ gives the least common generalisation of $\{\tau_i\}$. It takes into account the fact that, for example, $lcg(\{\texttt{Int} \to \texttt{Int}, \texttt{Bool} \to \texttt{Bool}\})$ is $\alpha \to \alpha$, for some α, and not $\alpha \to \alpha'$, for some other type variable $\alpha' \neq \alpha$. Other simple examples: $lcg(\{\texttt{Tree Int}, \texttt{List Int}\}) = \alpha \texttt{ Int}$ and $lcg(\{\texttt{Tree } \beta, \texttt{List } \beta\}) = \alpha\, \alpha'$. Due to reasons of space, we do not present the definition of lcg.

Rule (LET) uses function $close$, to quantify types over type variables that are not free in a typing context: $close(\triangle, \Gamma) = \forall \alpha_j. \triangle$, where $\{\alpha_j\} = tv(\triangle) - tv(\Gamma)$.

Rule (APPL) has a premise with a type that is not in a functional form, and uses a fresh type variable, instead of having the usual premise with a functional type. This occurs because of overloading, as illustrated by the following simple example. Let $\Gamma = \{x : \texttt{Int}, x : \texttt{Int} \to \texttt{Int}, 1 : \texttt{Int}\}$. In this context the type derived for x is not a functional type; we derive instead $\Gamma \vdash x : \{x : \alpha\}.\alpha$. Then $\Gamma \vdash x\,1 : \text{Int}$ is derivable, only with rule (APPL) as presented.

Overloading resolution in rule (APPL) is based on two tests. Consider an application $e\,e'$. The first test guarantees that all constraints occurring in types of both e and e', after unification, are *satisfiable*. This is based on function *sat*, also used in rule (LET) to control overloading resolution.

$sat\,(\kappa, \Gamma)$ returns a set of substitutions that unifies types of overloaded symbols in κ with the corresponding types for these symbols in Γ. It is defined inductively as follows, where we assume that quantified type variables (of types in Γ) are distinct from those in $tv(\kappa, \Gamma)$:

$$sat\,(\emptyset, \Gamma) = \{id\}$$
$$sat\,(\{o : \tau\}, \Gamma) = \bigcup_{\sigma_i \in \Gamma(o)}\{S \mid S = Unify(\{\tau = \tau_i\}, V) \text{ and } sat\,(S\kappa_i, S\Gamma) \neq \emptyset\}$$
$$\text{where } V = tv(\tau_i) - \big(\{(\alpha_j)_i\} \cup tv(\tau)\big) \text{ and } \sigma_i = \forall(\alpha_j)_i.\,\kappa_i.\,\tau_i$$
$$sat\,(\{o : \tau\} \cup \kappa, \Gamma) = \bigcup_{S_i \in sat\,(\{o:\tau\},\Gamma)} \bigcup_{S_{ij} \in sat\,(S_i\kappa, S_i\Gamma)}\{S_{ij} \circ S_i\}$$

To elucidate the meaning of *sat*, let $\Gamma = \{\text{f} : \text{Int} \rightarrow \text{Float}, \text{f} : \text{Float} \rightarrow \text{Int}, \text{one} : \text{Int}, \text{one} : \text{Float}\}$. Then $sat\,(\{\text{f} : \alpha \rightarrow \beta, \text{one} : \alpha\}, \Gamma)$ is a set with two substitutions, say $\{S_1, S_2\}$, where $S_1(\alpha) = \text{Int}$ and $S_1(\beta) = \text{Float}$), and $S_2(\alpha) = \text{Float}$ and $S_2(\beta) = \text{Int}$).

After the first test, any free type variable in constraints of types of e or e' that is mapped (by substitutions given by *sat*) to a single type σ, is replaced by σ, by application of S_Δ. Applying S_Δ thus eliminates constraints when overloading has been resolved.

Function *unresolved* is used to include unresolved constraints, if type σ above is itself the type of an overloaded symbol. For example, if `member` is overloaded for testing membership in lists and trees, having type $\{\text{member} : \alpha \rightarrow \beta\,\alpha \rightarrow \text{Bool}\}.\,\alpha \rightarrow \beta\,\alpha \rightarrow \text{Bool}$ in a context with typings $\text{member} : \forall\alpha\beta.\,\{= : \alpha \rightarrow \alpha \rightarrow \text{Bool}\}.\,\alpha \rightarrow [\alpha] \rightarrow \text{Bool}$ and $\text{member} : \forall\alpha\beta.\,\{= : \alpha \rightarrow \alpha \rightarrow \text{Bool}\}.\,\alpha \rightarrow \text{Tree}\,\alpha \rightarrow \text{Bool}$, then, in a context as above that has also typings $l : [\alpha'], x : \alpha'$, $\text{member}\,x\,l$ has type $\{= : \alpha' \rightarrow \alpha' \rightarrow \text{Bool}\}.\,\text{Bool}$. Function *unresolved* is defined as follows:

$$unresolved\,(\emptyset, \Gamma) = \emptyset$$
$$unresolved\,(\{o : \tau\} \cup \kappa, \Gamma) = \kappa' \cup unresolved(\kappa, \Gamma)$$
$$\text{where } \kappa' = \textbf{if } sat(\{o : \tau\}, \Gamma) = \{S\}, \text{ for some } S,$$
$$\textbf{then } unresolved(S\kappa', \Gamma), \text{ where } \forall\alpha_j.\,\kappa'.\,\tau' \in \Gamma(o),\, S\tau = S\tau'$$
$$\textbf{else } \{o : \tau\}$$

The second test detects ambiguity by looking at the resulting constraint set κ. This includes all constraints for both e and e', after unification and (possibly) constraint elimination. Predicate *ambiguous* issues an error if and only if overloading can no longer be resolved. It is defined as follows:

$$ambiguous(V_1, \kappa, V) = V' \neq \emptyset \text{ and } V' \subseteq V_1$$
$$\text{where } V' = tv(\kappa) - tv(\kappa|_V^*)$$

Type variables in a constraint of a constrained type $\kappa.\tau$ either occur free in τ or in the relevant typing context, or occur in another constraint with this property. Consider, for example, $\Gamma_f \vdash f \text{ one} : \{f : \alpha \to \beta, \text{one} : \alpha\}.\beta$ (cf. section 2). Type variable α does not occur in $tv(\tau, \Gamma) = \{\beta\}$, but constraint $\{\text{one} : \alpha\}$ is captured by operation $\kappa|_{tv(\tau,\Gamma)}^*$ (where $\kappa = \{f : \alpha \to \beta, \text{one} : \alpha\}$). In general, a type variable may occur in $tv(\kappa) - tv(\kappa|_{tv(\tau,\Gamma)}^*)$ if and only if the type variable does not appear in a constraint of the type of the function being applied (i.e. it does not appear in $S_\Delta S \kappa_1$). It may appear though in a constraint of the argument's type. For example, $\Gamma_o \vdash fst \, (\text{True}, \text{one}) : \text{Bool}$, where $\kappa = \{\text{one} : \beta\}$ and $\kappa|_{tv(\text{Bool},\Gamma_o)}^* = \emptyset$ and $ambiguous(\emptyset, \{\text{one} : \beta\}, \emptyset)$ is false.

Example $\Gamma_g \nvdash g \text{ one} : \{g : \alpha \to \text{Int}, \text{one} : \alpha\}.\text{Int}$ (see section 2) illustrates detection of a type error by predicate $ambiguous$. We have that $\kappa = \{g : \alpha \to \text{Int}, \text{one} : \alpha\} \neq \kappa|_\emptyset^*$. There is a constraint in the type of the applied function which should have been resolved (it would never be resolved in a later context).

4   Type Inference

Figure 3 presents the type inference algorithm, PP_c, which gives principal pairs (type and context) for a given term. It allows local overloading only of symbols with closed types.[4] It is proved sound with respect to the version of the type system that uses this overloading policy (i.e. ρ_c below, instead of ρ), and to compute principal typings. The overloading policy is given by:

$$\rho_c(o : \forall \alpha_j. \kappa. \tau, T) = (T = \emptyset) \text{ or}$$
$$tv(\forall \alpha_j. \kappa. \tau) = \emptyset \text{ and for each } \sigma = \forall(\beta_k). \kappa'. \tau' \in T$$
$$unify(\{\tau = \tau'\}) \text{ fails and } tv(\sigma) = \emptyset$$

ρ_c requires closed types only for overloaded symbols ($T = \emptyset$ means no typings for o in the relevant typing context, and in this case $\forall \alpha_j. \kappa. \tau$ may have free type variables). Any core-ML expression is a well-formed expression in System CT.

For simplicity, α-conversions are not considered, following the assumption that if a variable is let-bound, then it is not lambda-bound.

PP_c uses *typing environments* A, which are sets of elements $x : (\sigma, \Gamma)$. Pair (σ, Γ) is called an entry for x in A. We write $A(x)$ for the set of entries of x in A, and $A^t(x)$ for the set of first elements (types) in these entries.

Fresh type variables are assumed to be chosen so as to be different from any other type variable, including any type variable that occurs free in a typing context (in the type system, this assumption is not necessary).

---

[4] Provably sound and complete type inference for local overloading of symbols with non-closed types is, as far as we know, an open problem.

$pt\epsilon(x, A)$ gives both type and context for x in A, as $pt(x, \Gamma)$, but requiring fresh type variables to be introduced for let-bound variables, as defined below:

$pt\epsilon(x, A) =$
    if $A(x) = \emptyset$ **then** $(\alpha, \{x : \alpha\})$, where α is a fresh type variable **else**
    if $A(x) = \{(\forall \alpha_j. \kappa. \tau, \Gamma)\}$ **then** $(\kappa. \tau, \Gamma)$,
        with quantified type variables $\{\alpha_j\}$ renamed as fresh type variables
    else $(\{x' : lcg(\{\tau_i\})\}. \, lcg(\{\tau_i\}), \bigcup \Gamma_i[x'/x])$,
        where $A(x) = \{(\forall (\alpha_j)_i. \kappa_i. \tau_i, \Gamma_i)\}$ and x' is a fresh term variable

---

$PP_c(x, A) = pt\epsilon(x, A)$
$PP_c(\lambda u.e, A) =$
    let $(\kappa. \tau, \Gamma) = PP_c(e, A)$
    in if $u : \tau' \in \Gamma$, for some τ' **then** $(\kappa. \tau' \to \tau, \, \Gamma - \{u : \tau'\})$
        else $(\kappa. \alpha \to \tau, \, \Gamma)$, where α is a fresh type variable
$PP_c(e_1 \, e_2, A) =$
    let $(\kappa_1. \tau_1, \Gamma_1) = PP_c(e_1, A)$, $(\kappa_2. \tau_2, \Gamma_2) = PP_c(e_2, A)$
        $S = unify(\{\tau_u = \tau'_u \mid u : \tau_u \in \Gamma_1 \text{ and } u : \tau'_u \in \Gamma_2\} \cup \{\tau_1 = \tau_2 \to \alpha\})$
                where α is a fresh type variable
        $\Gamma' = S\Gamma_1 \cup S\Gamma_2$, $S = sat(S\kappa_1 \cup S\kappa_2, \Gamma')$
    in if $S = \emptyset$ **then fail**
        else let $S_\Delta = \bigcap S$, $\Gamma = S_\Delta \Gamma'$, $\tau = S_\Delta S\alpha$,
              $V = tv(\tau, \Gamma)$, $\kappa = unresolved(S_\Delta S(\kappa_1 \cup \kappa_2), \Gamma)$
              in if $ambiguous(tv(S_\Delta S\kappa_1), \kappa, V)$ **then fail else** $(\kappa|_V^*. \tau, \Gamma)$
$PP_c(\textbf{let } o = e_1 \textbf{ in } e_2, A) =$
    let $(\kappa_1. \tau_1, \Gamma_1) = PP_c(e_1, A)$, $\sigma = close(\kappa_1. \tau_1, \Gamma_1)$
    in if $\rho_c(\sigma, A^t(o))$ does not hold **then fail**
        else let $A' = A \cup \{o : (\sigma, \Gamma_1)\}$, $(\kappa_2. \tau_2, \Gamma_2) = PP_c(e_2, A')$
              $S = unify(\{\tau_u = \tau'_u \mid u : \tau_u \in \Gamma_1, u : \tau'_u \in \Gamma_2\})$
              $\Gamma' = S\Gamma_1 \cup S\Gamma_2$, $S = sat(S\kappa_1 \cup S\kappa_2, \Gamma')$
        in if $S = \emptyset$ **then fail**
              else let $S_\Delta = \bigcap S$, $\Gamma = S_\Delta \Gamma'$, $\tau = S_\Delta S\tau_2$
                  $V = tv(\tau, \Gamma)$, $\kappa = unresolved(S_\Delta S(\kappa_1 \cup \kappa_2), \Gamma)$
              in $(\kappa|_V^*. \tau, \Gamma)$

Figure 3: Type inference for System CT

PP_c substitutes type variables that occur free in a typing context, reflecting the contexts in which corresponding free term variables are used. sat_c used in PP_c is simplified (with repect to its counterpart sat) due to allowing local overloading only of symbols with closed types:

$$sat_c\,(\emptyset, \Gamma) = \{id\}$$
$$sat_c\,(\{o : \tau\}, \Gamma) = \bigcup_{\sigma_i \in \Gamma(o)} \{S \mid S = unify(\{\tau = \tau_i\}) \text{ and } sat\,(S\kappa_i, \Gamma) \neq \emptyset\}$$
$$\text{where } \sigma_i = \forall(\alpha_j)_i.\,\kappa_i.\,\tau_i$$
$$sat_c\,(\{o : \tau\} \cup \kappa, \Gamma) = \bigcup_{S_i \in sat\,(\{o:\tau\},\Gamma)} \bigcup_{S_{ij} \in sat\,(S_i\kappa,\Gamma)} \{S_{ij} \circ S_i\}$$

4.1   Soundness and Completeness

In this section we prove soundness and completeness of PP_c with respect to the version of System CT that uses the overloading policy given by ρ_c.

Definition 1 A typing context Γ is *valid* if i) $u : \sigma \in \Gamma$ implies that σ is a simple type, ii) $u_1 : \sigma_1 \in \Gamma$, $u_2 : \sigma_2 \in \Gamma$, $\sigma_1 \not\equiv \sigma_2$, implies that $u_1 \not\equiv u_2$, and iii) $o : \sigma \in \Gamma$ implies that $\rho(\sigma, \Gamma(o) - \{\sigma\})$ holds.

Definition 2 An *o-closed* typing context is a valid typing context with the property that $o : \sigma_1, o : \sigma_2 \in \Gamma$, $\sigma_1 \not\equiv \sigma_2$ implies that $tv(\sigma_1, \sigma_2) = \emptyset$.

Definition 3 A typing environment A is *valid* if, for all $x : (\forall \alpha_j.\kappa.\,\tau, \Gamma) \in A$, Γ is o-closed, $\bigcap sat(\kappa, \Gamma) = id$ and $unresolved(\kappa, \Gamma) = \kappa$.

Definition 4 Γ' extends (or is an extension of) Γ if whenever X is the set of all typings for x in Γ, then X is also the set of all typings for x in Γ'.

Definition 5 A_Γ stands for $\{o : (\sigma, \Gamma) \mid o : \sigma \in \Gamma, o \in \mathcal{O}\}$, U_Γ stands for $\{u : \tau \mid u : \tau \in \Gamma, u \in \mathcal{U}\}$ and $O_A = \{o : \sigma \mid o \in \mathcal{O} \text{ and } o : (\sigma, \Gamma) \in A \text{ for some } \Gamma\}$.

Definition 6 $\kappa.\,\tau \preceq_S \kappa'.\,\tau'$ if $S(\kappa.\,\tau) = \kappa'.\,\tau'$, and $\Gamma \preceq_S \Gamma'$ if Γ' extends $S\Gamma$.

Lemma 1 If $\Gamma \vdash e : (\sigma, \Gamma_0)$ is provable and $\Gamma \cup \Gamma'$ is an extension of Γ, then $\Gamma \cup \Gamma' \vdash e : (\sigma, \Gamma'_0)$ is provable, where Γ'_0 is an extension of Γ_0.

Lemma 2 If $PP_c(e, A) = (\kappa.\,\tau, \Gamma)$, where A is valid, then Γ is valid, $tv(\Gamma) = tv(close(\kappa.\,\tau, \Gamma))$, $\bigcap sat(\kappa, \Gamma) = id$ and $unresolved(\kappa, \Gamma) = \kappa$.

Lemma 3 (Substitution Lemma) If $\Gamma \vdash e : (\kappa.\,\tau, \Gamma')$ is provable, where Γ is o-closed, and S, S_Δ are such that $dom(S) \subseteq tv(\Gamma)$, $sat_c(S\kappa, S\Gamma') \neq \emptyset$ and $S_\Delta = \bigcap sat(S\kappa, S\Gamma')$, then $S_\Delta S\Gamma \vdash_e e : (\kappa'.\,\tau', S_\Delta S\Gamma')$ is provable, where $\kappa'.\,\tau' = S_\Delta|_{tv(\Gamma)} S(\kappa.\tau)$ or $\kappa'.\tau' = (S_\Delta S\kappa)|_V^*.S_\Delta S\tau$, where $V = tv(S_\Delta S\tau, S_\Delta S\Gamma)$.

Theorem 1 (Soundness of PP_c) If $PP_c(e, A) = (\kappa. \tau, \Gamma)$, where A is valid, then $O_A \cup U_\Gamma \vdash e : (\kappa. \tau, \Gamma')$ is provable, where $\Gamma' = O_A \cup \Gamma$.

Theorem 2 (Completeness) Let Γ_0 be *o-closed*. If $\Gamma_0 \vdash e : (\kappa_0. \tau_0, \Gamma')$ is provable then either: i) $PP_c(e, A_{\Gamma_0}) = (\kappa. \tau, \Gamma)$ and there is S such that $O_A \cup U_\Gamma \preceq_S \Gamma_0$ and $\kappa. \tau \preceq_S \kappa_0. \tau_0$, or ii) $PP_c(e, A_{\Gamma_0})$ fails and e has a subexpression of the form `let` $o = e_1$ `in` e_2 such that $\Gamma_1 \vdash e_1 : (\kappa_1. \tau_1, \Gamma_1')$ is provable in the derivation of $\Gamma_0 \vdash e : (\kappa_0. \tau_0, \Gamma')$, for some $\Gamma_1, \Gamma_1', \kappa_1. \tau_1$, but $\Gamma_1 \vdash e_1 : (\kappa_1'. \tau_1', \Gamma_1'')$ is also provable, for some $\Gamma_1'', \kappa_1'. \tau_1'$ such that $\kappa_1'. \tau_1' \preceq_{S_1} \kappa_1. \tau_1$, for some S_1, and $\rho_c(close(\kappa_1'. \tau_1', \Gamma_1), \Gamma_1(o))$ does not hold.

An example of item (b) is `let` $f = \lambda x.\, x$ `in` `let` $f = \lambda y.\, y$ `in` ... . Types `Int` $\rightarrow$ `Int` and `Float` $\rightarrow$ `Float` can be derived for $\lambda x.\, x$ and $\lambda y.\, y$, respectively, and overloading of `f` with these two definitions is allowed. PP_c, however, infers the most general type for each of these expressions, namely $\forall \alpha. \alpha \rightarrow \alpha$, and thus does not allow overloading with these two definitions.

Principal Typings

Definition 7 A *typing problem* is a pair (e, Γ_0), where e is an expression and Γ_0 is a valid typing context. A *typing solution* for this typing problem is a pair $(\kappa. \tau, \Gamma)$ such that $\Gamma \preceq_S \Gamma_0$, for some S, and $\Gamma \vdash e : (\kappa. \tau, \Gamma')$ is provable, for some Γ'. It is the *most general* if, for every other typing solution $(\kappa'. \tau', \Gamma')$ to this problem, there exists S such that $\Gamma \preceq_S \Gamma'$ and $\kappa. \tau \preceq_S \kappa'. \tau'$.

Theorem 3 (Principal Typings) If $PP_c(e, A_{\Gamma_0}) = (\kappa. \tau, \Gamma)$, where Γ_0 is *o-closed*, then $(\kappa. \tau, O_A \cup U_\Gamma)$ is the most general solution for (e, Γ_0), and if $PP_c(e, A_{\Gamma_0})$ fails, then (e, Γ_0) does not have a most general solution.

5   Conclusion and Further Work

The type inference algorithm presented in this paper computes most general typings and supports overloading and polymorphism without the need for declarations or annotations, and with the only restriction that types of local overloaded definitions must be closed types. No language construct is introduced for the purpose of coping with overloading. The context-dependent overloading policy, controlled by a single predicate used in let bindings, allows overloading of constants and other similar forms of overloadings. Information provided by the context in which an expression appears is used to detect ambiguity on the use of overloaded symbols. When there is ambiguity, a type error is detected, and when it is possible for overloading to be resolved further on in a later context, this is reflected in the type of the expression.

Our work is a continuation of previous works directed towards a comprehensive support for overloading, together with polymorphism and type inference.

The mechanism of type classes used in Haskell represented a big step forward in this direction. In an upcoming article, a formal semantics of the language of System CT will be presented, together with a type soundness theorem. Further work involves incorporating the type inference algorithm in a modern functional language, and studying support for subtyping and separate compilation. We have a prototype implementation, and are developping it with the aim of exploring further the idea of using overloading to support writing reusable code.

Though we have not discussed the efficiency and time complexity of the type inference algorithm in this article, upon a preliminary evaluation we think that its efficiency should be approximately the same as that of the algorithm used for example for ML. We do not have yet a result on the complexity of the type inference algorithm but we plan to study the subject in detail and perform extensive experimentations with our prototype. We note that the cost of computing sat, as given in this paper, is proportional to m and n, where m is the number of typings on a given constraint set and n is the (average) number of overloadings of a given symbol. Usually, both m and n are small. Moreover, for any given typing $o : \tau$ occurring in a given constraint set k, the number of substitutions obtained as a result of unifying τ with typings for o in a given typing context is "even smaller". If this number is zero, this can eliminate the need to compute all other unifications for the remaining constraints in κ. Other optimizations may be worthwhile. We expect a practical implementation of our type inference algorithm in a language such as Haskell or SML to be efficient.

Acknowledgements

We acknowledge the financial support of FAPEMIG under Project Tec 1243/97.

References

DCO96.   Dominic Duggan, Gordon Cormack, and John Ophel. Kinded type inference for parametric overloading. *Acta Informatica*, 33(1):21–68, 1996.

DM82.   Luís Damas and Robin Milner. Principal type schemes for functional programs. *POPL'82*, pages 207–212, 1982.

HHJW96.   Cordelia Hall, Kevin Hammond, Simon Peyton Jones, and Philip Wadler. Type Classes in Haskell. *ACM TOPLAS*, 18(2):109–138, March 1996.

J+98.   Simon Peyton Jones et al. GHC – The Glasgow Haskell Compiler. Available at http://www.dcs.gla.ac.uk/fp/software/ghc/, 1998.

JJM97.   Simon Peyton Jones, Mark Jones, and Erik Meijer. Type classes: an exploration of the design space. *ACM SIGPLAN Haskell Workshop*, 1997.

Jon94.   Mark Jones. *Qualified Types*. Cambridge University Press, 1994.

Jon95.   Mark Jones. A system of constructor classes: overloading and higher-order polymorphism. *Journal of Functional Programming*, 5:1–36, 1995.

Jon96.   Simon P. Jones. Bulk types with class. In Phil Trinder, ed., *Eletronic Proc. 1996 Glasgow Workshop on Functional Programming*, October 1996. http://ftp.dcs.glasgow.ac.uk/fp/workshops/fpw96/PeytonJones.ps.gz.

Jon98a.   M. Jones. Hugs: The Haskell User's Gofer System. haskell.org/hugs, 1998.

Jon98b.   Simon Peyton Jones. Multi-parameter type classes in GHC. Available at
          http://www.dcs.gla.ac.uk/~simonpj/multi-param.html, 1998.
Kae88.   Stefan Kaes. Parametric overloading in polymorphic programming lan-
          guages. In H. Ganzinger, ed., *ESOP*, LNCS 300, pages 131–144, 1988.
Mil78.   Robin Milner. A theory of type polymorphism in programming. *Journal of
          Computer and System Sciences*, 17:348–375, 1978.
Mit88.   John Mitchell. Polymorphic type inference and containment. *Information
          and Computation*, 76(2/3):211–249, 1988.
Mit96.   John Mitchell. *Foundations for programming languages*. MIT Press, 1996.
MTH89.   Robin Milner, Mads Tofte, and Robert Harper. *The Definition of Standard
          ML*. MIT Press, 1989.
NP93.   Tobias Nipkow and Christian Prehofer. Type Reconstruction for Type
          Classes. *Journal of Functional Programming*, 1(1):1–100, 1993.
OWW95.   Martin Odersky, Philip Wadler, and Martin Wehr. A Second Look at Over-
          loading. In *ACM Conf. Funct. Prog. Comp. Arch.*, pages 135–146, 1995.
Pau96.   L. Paulson. *ML for the Working Programmer, Cambridge Univ. Press, 1996.*
Pe97.   J. Peterson and K. Hammond (eds.). Rep. on the prog. lang. Haskell, a
          non-strict, purely funct. lang. (v1.4). Techn. rep. , Haskell committee, 1997.
Rob65.   J.A. Robinson. A machine oriented logic based on the resolution principle.
          JACM, 12(1):23–41, 1965.
Smi91.   Geoffrey Smith. *Polymorphic Type Inference for Languages with Overload-
          ing and Subtyping*. PhD thesis, Cornell University, 1991.
Tho96.   S. Thompson. *Haskell: The Craft of Funct. Prog.*, Addison-Wesley, 1996.
Tur85.   D. Turner. A non-strict funct. lang. with polymorphic types. In *2nd
          Int. Conf. on Funct. Prog. and Comp. Arch.*, IEEE Comp. Soc. Press, 1985.
Wad89.   P. Wadler. How to make ad-hoc polymorphism less ad hoc. *POPL'89*, 1989.

Partial Evaluation and Non-interference for Object Calculi

Gilles Barthe[1,2] and Bernard P. Serpette[1]

[1] INRIA Sophia-Antipolis, France
[2] Departamento de Informática, Universidade do Minho, Portugal
{Gilles.Barthe,Bernard.Serpette}@sophia.inria.fr

Abstract. We prove the correctness of a multi-level partial evaluator and of an information flow analysis for Abadi and Cardelli's $FOb_{1\leq:}$, a simply typed object calculus with function and object types, object subtyping and subsumption.

1 Introduction

Object calculi, in particular the ς-calculi of Abadi and Cardelli [3], were introduced to provide a foundational paradigm for object-oriented languages in the same way λ-calculi provide a foundational paradigm for functional languages. The work of Abadi and Cardelli was followed by a number of attempts to scale up results from λ-calculi to ς-calculi, including compilation [12], control flow analysis [22] and operational semantics [13].

Partial evaluation [16] is an optimization technique which exploits partial information about a program's input to generate a specialized program with a locally similar behavior. More precisely, a partial evaluator takes as input a program $p(x_1, \ldots, x_{n+m})$ and some fixed partial input for p, say $x_1, \ldots, x_n$, and returns a specialized program $p_{(x_1,\ldots,x_n)}$ such that for all inputs $x_{n+1}, \ldots, x_{n+m}$:

$$p_{(x_1,\ldots,x_n)}(x_{n+1}, \ldots, x_{n+m}) = p(x_1, \ldots, x_{n+m})$$

The specialized program is produced in two phases:[1] first one defines a *binding-time analysis* (BTA) which annotates program points as *static* or known and *dynamic* or unknown. Then the annotated program is fed to a *specializer* which evaluates programs according to the directives provided by the annotations—only known expressions are reduced. A non-standard type system for annotated expressions is used to enforce that all known subexpressions have been eliminated from the specialized program.

Information flow analysis (IFA) is an analysis to establish the absence of information leakage in programs. IFA proceeds by annotating program points as *public* or *secret*. A non-standard type system for annotated expressions is used to enforce a *non-interference* property: secret data cannot be revealed in the public output of a legal program. In other words, a legal program with secret

---

[1] We consider *offline* partial evaluation only.

A. Middeldorp, T. Sato (Eds.): FLOPS'99, LNCS 1722, pp. 53–67, 1999.
© Springer-Verlag Berlin Heidelberg 1999

input and public output must be constant—provided the output is of some base type.

Both BTA and IFA may be generalized to allow for an arbitrary set of binding-times or security levels, possibly with some extra structure, e.g. that of a partial order or of a semi-lattice. This further generality allows to capture a number of situations not allowed by standard BTA and IFA. In particular, *multi-level BTA*, i.e. BTA over an arbitrary set of binding-times, allows to distinguish between run-time, link-time and compile-time [20], or to stage computations in successive steps [11].

It is folklore that BTA and IFA are closely related [2,23,28]. In particular, both may be formalized as a non-standard type system and similar proof techniques may be used to establish the correctness of both analyses. In this paper, we detail the similarities (and differences) between BTA and IFA in the context of $FOb_{1\leq:}$, a first-order typed ς-calculus with object subtyping and subsumption [3, Chapter 8]. In Section 3, we define two non-standard type systems for IFA and BTA. In Section 4, we prove the correctness of both analyses:

1. BTA: this involves defining for each binding-time ϕ a specializer which eliminates all subexpressions known at ϕ and proving (1) a subject reduction theorem for the specializers (2) a progress theorem stating that a specializer never gets stuck, i.e. only terminates when all subexpressions known at ϕ have been eliminated (3) a soundness theorem that specializers preserve the semantics of programs;

2. IFA: this involves defining an operational semantics for the annotated calculus and proving (1) a subject reduction theorem for the operational semantics (2) a non-interference theorem stating that a legal program whose output is of base type and has a level of security ϕ must be constant w.r.t. inputs whose level of security is not inferior or equal to ϕ.

Our proof of correctness of IFA is purely syntactic, as in e.g. [15,26]. Indeed, semantical proofs as in e.g. [2] would require a fair amount of domain-theoretic background (see e.g. [3, Chapter 14]) and models only provide a limited guidance as to the choice of typing rules for the annotated calculi.

Related work

1. [11,14,21] study *multi-level partial evaluation*, but none of these works focuses on the question of correctness. In [28], Thiemann and Klaeren prove the correctness of a multi-level partial evaluator for a first-order language but make the strong assumption that the binding-times form a linear order;

2. *partial evaluation for object-oriented languages* is studied in [7,17,25] while Bertino *et. al.* [5] study *information flow for object-oriented systems*. Building on [19], Myers [18] formalizes information flow for Java (JFlow). However, none of those works address the issue of correctness;

3. *information flow analysis*, which initiates from early work by Bell and La-Padula [4] and by the Dennings [9,10], has since been the subject of much attention, see e.g. [1,2,15,26] for type-based approaches. While these works

have been shown able to handle features such as side-effects and multi-threading, they do not treat objects.

Conventions and notations Throughout the paper, we assume given a fixed set $\mathcal{V}$ of *variables* and a fixed set $\mathcal{L}$ of *labels*; we let $x, x', y, z \ldots$ and $l, l', l_i \ldots$ range over $\mathcal{V}$ and $\mathcal{L}$ respectively. Moreover we assume given a semi-lattice $(D, \sqsubseteq, +)$ of levels—i.e. $(\mathcal{D}, \sqsubseteq)$ is a partial order and $+$ is a binary join operation on $(\mathcal{D}, \sqsubseteq)$.

2 Annotated $FOb_{1\leq:}$

Binding-time and information flow analyses are performed via non-standard type systems. While both systems arise as annotated variants of $FOb_{1\leq:}$ and share the same set of types and expressions, the type system $\vdash_{if}$ for information flow is more liberal than the type system $\vdash_{bt}$ for binding-time analysis. As discussed below, these differences are justified by the respective aims of the systems. In a first stage, we introduce $\vdash_{if}$ and then derive $\vdash_{bt}$ by imposing suitable restrictions on $\vdash_{if}$.

2.1 Information Flow Analysis

Our calculi are annotated variants of the calculus of [3, Chapter 8]. At a syntactic level, the only minor difference is that our calculi contain a base type nat of natural numbers as well as (annotated) numerals—the presence of a non-trivial base type simplifies the statements of our results.

Definition 1 (Types, subtyping).

1. *The set $\mathcal{U}$ of (annotated) types is given by the abstract syntax*

$$
\begin{aligned}
A, B :: = \ &\top^\phi & \textit{(top type)} \\
| \ &\mathsf{nat}^\phi & \textit{(natural numbers)} \\
| \ &A \to^\phi B & \textit{(function type)} \\
| \ &[l_i : A_i \ ^{1\leq i \leq n}]^\phi & \textit{(object type)}
\end{aligned}
$$

   where ϕ ranges over $\mathcal{D}$. By convention, we require that all the labels in an object type are pairwise distinct.
2. *The* top-level annotation *of an annotated type A is denoted by $\mathsf{top}(A)$. Given a type A and $\phi \in \mathcal{D}$, we let $A^{+\phi}$ be the type obtained by replacing the outermost annotation of A by $\mathsf{top}(A) + \phi$.* define
3. *Subtyping $\leq$ on $\mathcal{U}$ is defined by the rules of Figure 1.*

The annotated expressions match the standard expressions, to the exception of the lift operators which apply to elements of arbitrary type and allow to raise the level of an expression.

$$\frac{}{A \leq A} \qquad \frac{A \leq B \quad B \leq C}{A \leq C}$$

$$\frac{\phi \sqsubseteq \phi'}{\mathsf{nat}^\phi \leq \mathsf{nat}^{\phi'}} \qquad \frac{\mathsf{top}(A) \sqsubseteq \phi}{A \leq \mathsf{T}^\phi}$$

$$\frac{A' \leq A \quad B \leq B' \quad \phi \sqsubseteq \phi'}{A \rightarrow^\phi B \leq A' \rightarrow^{\phi'} B'} \qquad \frac{\phi \sqsubseteq \phi'}{[l_i : A_i \ ^{1 \leq i \leq n+m}]^\phi \leq [l_i : A_i \ ^{1 \leq i \leq n}]^{\phi'}}$$

Fig. 1. SUBTYPING

Definition 2 (Annotated expressions, reduction).

1. *The set $\mathcal{W}$ of (annotated) expressions is defined by the abstract syntax*

$$
\begin{array}{lll}
w, w' ::= x & & \textit{(variable)} \\
\quad | \ n^\phi & & \textit{(numeral)} \\
\quad | \ w @^\phi w' & & \textit{(application)} \\
\quad | \ \lambda^\phi x : A.w & & \textit{(abstraction)} \\
\quad | \ [l_i = \varsigma x_i : A.w_i \ ^{1 \leq i \leq n}]^\phi & & \textit{(object)} \\
\quad | \ w.^\phi l & & \textit{(method invocation)} \\
\quad | \ w.^\phi l \Leftarrow \varsigma x : A.w' & & \textit{(method update)} \\
\quad | \ w^{+\phi} & & \textit{(lift)}
\end{array}
$$

   By convention, we require that all the labels in an object are pairwise distinct. Substitution is defined in the usual way and $e\{x := e'\}$ denotes the result of substituting e' for all occurrences of x.
2. *The relation $\rightarrow_{if_0}$ is defined by the rules of Figure 2, where $A = [l_i : B_i \ ^{1 \leq i \leq n}]^\psi$—we do not take the compatible closure of these rules. If $w \rightarrow_{if_0} w'$, we say w is a redex and w' is its reduct.*
3. *An expression w reduces to w', written $w \rightarrow_{if} w'$, if w' is obtained from w by contracting the leftmost outermost redex of w.*

Note that *if*-reduction does not discriminate on security annotations and is sound w.r.t. the operational theory of $FOb_{1\leq:}$; in other words, $w_1 \rightarrow_{if} w_2$ implies $|w_1| \rightarrow_{oc} |w_2|$ where $|w_i|$ is obtained from w_i by removing all annotations and $\rightarrow_{oc}$ is the reduction relation of $FOb_{1\leq:}$.

Definition 3 (Typing).

1. *A context is a sequence of declarations $x_1 : A_1, \ \ldots \ , x_n : A_n$ where $x_1, \ \ldots \ , x_n \in \mathcal{V}$ are pairwise disjoint and $A_1, \ \ldots \ , A_n \in \mathcal{U}$. We write $\mathsf{top}(x_1 : A_1, \ \ldots \ , x_n : A_n) \not\sqsubseteq \phi$ if $\mathsf{top}(A_i) \not\sqsubseteq \phi$ for every $1 \leq i \leq n$. We let $\Gamma, \Gamma', \ldots$ range over contexts.*
2. *A judgment is a statement of the form $\Gamma \vdash_{if} w : A$ where Γ is a context, $w \in \mathcal{W}$ and $A \in \mathcal{U}$.*
3. *The typing relation $\vdash_{if}$ is given by the rules of Figure 3.*

$$(\lambda^\psi x : B.w)@^\phi w' \rightarrow_{if_0} w\{x := w'\}$$

$$[l_i = \varsigma x_i : A.w_i{}^{1 \le i \le n}]^{\psi'}.^{\phi'}l_j \rightarrow_{if_0} w_j\{x_j := [l_i = \varsigma x_i : A.w_i{}^{1 \le i \le n}]^\psi\}$$

$$[l_i = \varsigma x_i : A.w_i{}^{1 \le i \le n}]^{\psi'}.^\phi l_j \Leftarrow \varsigma x : B.w' \rightarrow_{if_0} [l_i = \varsigma x_i : A.w_i{}^{1 \le i \le n}_{i \ne j}, l_j = \varsigma x : A.w']^{\psi'}$$

$$w^{+\psi} \rightarrow_{if_0} w$$

Fig. 2. RULES FOR *if*-REDUCTION

(num) $\Gamma \vdash_{if} n^\phi : \mathsf{nat}^\phi$

(var) $\Gamma \vdash_{if} x : A$ if $(x : A) \in \Gamma$

(abs) $$\dfrac{\Gamma, x : A \vdash_{if} w : B}{\Gamma \vdash_{if} \lambda^\phi x : A.w : A \rightarrow^\phi B}$$

(app) $$\dfrac{\Gamma \vdash_{if} w_0 : A \rightarrow^\phi B \quad \Gamma \vdash_{if} w_1 : A}{\Gamma \vdash_{if} w_0@^\psi w_1 : B^{+\phi+\psi}}$$

(obj) $$\dfrac{\Gamma, x_i : A \vdash_{if} w_i : B_i}{\Gamma \vdash_{if} [l_i = \varsigma x_i : A.w_i{}^{1 \le i \le n}]^\phi : A'}$$ $\begin{aligned}&\text{if } A = [l_i : B_i{}^{1 \le i \le n}]^\psi\\&\text{and } A' = [l_i : B_i{}^{1 \le i \le n}]^\phi\\&\text{and } \psi \sqsubseteq \phi\end{aligned}$

(sel) $$\dfrac{\Gamma \vdash_{if} w : [l_i = B_i{}^{1 \le i \le n}]^\phi}{\Gamma \vdash_{if} w.^\psi l_i : B_i^{+\phi+\psi}}$$

(upd) $$\dfrac{\Gamma \vdash_{if} w : A \quad \Gamma, x : A \vdash_{if} w' : B_i}{\Gamma \vdash_{if} w.^\psi l_i \Leftarrow \varsigma x : A.w' : A^{+\psi}}$$ if $A = [l_i : B_i{}^{1 \le i \le n}]^\phi$

(lift) $$\dfrac{\Gamma \vdash_{if} w : A}{\Gamma \vdash_{if} w^{+\psi} : A^{+\psi}}$$

(sub) $$\dfrac{\Gamma \vdash_{if} w : A}{\Gamma \vdash_{if} w : B}$$ if $A \le B$

Fig. 3. TYPING RULES FOR IFA

The type system is meant to enforce that expressions with a low-level of security (typically public data) do not depend on expressions with a high-level of security (typically secret data). This is achieved by ensuring that the top-level annotation of an expression is always inferior or equal than the top-level annotation of any of its types. Note that the rule for objects does not require that the type of self matches the type of an object: instead, we allow the type of self to be $A = [l_i : B_i {}^{1 \leq i \leq n}]^\psi$ and the type of the object to be $A' = [l_i : B_i {}^{1 \leq i \leq n}]^\phi$ with $\psi \sqsubseteq \phi$. This, together with the slightly unusual reduction rule for object selection, is crucial for subject reduction to hold.

Remarks

1. $\vdash_{if}$ is sound w.r.t. $\vdash$; in other words, $\Gamma \vdash_{if} w : A$ implies $|\Gamma| \vdash |A| : |w|$ where $|\Gamma|, |A|$ are obtained from Γ, A by removing all annotations.
2. Using the techniques of [3], one can establish the soundness and completeness of algorithmic typing—defined in the obvious way. It follows that it is decidable whether any given $\Gamma \vdash_{if} w : A$ is derivable, provided $\sqsubseteq$ and $+$ are decidable.

$$\top^\phi \ \mathsf{wf} \qquad\qquad \frac{A, B \ \mathsf{wf} \quad \rho \sqsubseteq \mathsf{top}(A), \mathsf{top}(B)}{A \rightarrow^\rho B \ \mathsf{wf}}$$

$$\mathsf{nat}^\phi \ \mathsf{wf} \qquad\qquad \frac{A_i \ \mathsf{wf} \quad \psi \sqsubseteq \mathsf{top}(A_i) \quad 1 \leq i \leq n}{[l_i : A_i {}^{1 \leq i \leq n}]^\psi \ \mathsf{wf}}$$

Fig. 4. BT TYPES

2.2 Binding-Time Analysis

The BTA is obtained from that of IFA by imposing suitable restrictions on the typing rules. First, only types whose top-level annotation is smaller than the top-level annotation of its subexpressions are considered, see e.g. [27].

Definition 4. *The set $\mathcal{U}^{bt}$ of BT types is defined by the rules of Figure 4.*

We now turn to the operational semantics. Unlike the system for information flow, we consider a family of reduction strategies $\rightarrow_s^\phi$ for every $\phi \in \mathcal{D}$. Informally, $\rightarrow_s^\phi$ will contract the leftmost outermost redex whose topmost annotation is smaller or equal to ϕ.

Definition 5 (Operational semantics, residual expressions).

1. *The relation $\rightarrow_{s_0}^\phi$ is defined by the rules of Figure 5, where it is assumed $\psi \sqsubseteq \phi$ and $A = [l_i : B_i {}^{1 \leq i \leq n}]^{\psi'}$ —we do not take the compatible closure of these rules. If $w \rightarrow_{s_0}^\phi w'$, we say w is a ϕ-redex and w' is its reduct.*

$$(\lambda^\psi x : B.w)@^\psi w' \to_s^\phi w\{x := (w')^{+\text{top}(B)}\}$$
$$[l_i = \varsigma x_i : A.w_i^{\;1\leq i\leq n}]^\psi.^\psi l_i \to_s^\phi w_i\{x_i := [l_i = \varsigma x_i : A.w_i^{\;1\leq i\leq n}]^{\psi'}\}$$
$$[l_i = \varsigma x_i : A.w_i^{\;1\leq i\leq n}]^\psi.^\psi l_j \Leftarrow \varsigma x : B.w' \to_s^\phi [l_i = \varsigma x_i : A.w_i^{\;1\leq i\leq n}_{\;i\neq j}, l_j = \varsigma x : A.w']^\psi$$
$$(n^\psi)^{+\psi'} \to_s^\phi n^{\psi+\psi'}$$
$$(\lambda^\psi x : B.w)^{+\psi'} \to_s^\phi \lambda^{\psi+\psi'} x : B.w$$
$$([l_i = \varsigma x_i : B.w_i^{\;1\leq i\leq n}]^\psi)^{+\psi'} \to_s^\phi [l_i = \varsigma x_i : B.w_i^{\;1\leq i\leq n}]^{\psi+\psi'}$$

Fig. 5. SPECIALIZATION RULES

2. An expression w ϕ-specializes to w', written $w \to_s^\phi w'$, if w' is obtained from w by contracting the leftmost outermost ϕ-redex of w.
3. An expression w is ϕ-residual, written $w \in \mathcal{R}^\phi$, if all its annotations (except the lift annotations) are $\not\sqsubseteq \phi$ and it does not contain any subexpression of the form $v^{+\psi}$ where $v \in \mathcal{V}$—i.e. v is a numeral, an abstraction or an object.

Equivalently, ϕ-residual terms are those which cannot be specialized at a level lower than ϕ.

Lemma 1. If $w \in \mathcal{R}^\phi$ and $\psi \sqsubseteq \phi$, then there is no $w' \in \mathcal{W}$ such that $w \to_s^\psi w'$.

Proof. By induction on the structure of the expressions.

$$\frac{\Gamma \vdash_{bt} w_0 : A \to^\phi B \quad \Gamma \vdash_{bt} w_1 : A}{\Gamma \vdash_{bt} w_0@^\phi w_1 : B}$$

$$\frac{\Gamma \vdash_{bt} w : [l_i = B_i^{\;1\leq i\leq n}]^\phi}{\Gamma \vdash_{bt} w.^\phi l_i : B_i}$$

$$\frac{\Gamma \vdash_{bt} w : A \quad \Gamma, x : A \vdash_{bt} w' : B_i}{\Gamma \vdash_{bt} w.^\phi l_i \Leftarrow \varsigma x : A.w' : A} \qquad \text{if } A = [l_i : B_i^{\;1\leq i\leq n}]^\phi$$

$$\frac{\Gamma \vdash_{bt} w : A}{\Gamma \vdash_{bt} w^{+\text{top}(B)} : B} \qquad \text{if } A \leq B$$

Fig. 6. TYPING RULES FOR BTA

We finally turn to the typing system. Its aim is to enforce that a closed expression w whose type A satisfies $\text{top}(A) \not\sqsubseteq \phi$ may be ϕ-specialized to a ϕ-residual term, unless ϕ-specialization on w does not terminate. This is achieved by imposing suitable restrictions to the rules of $\vdash_{if}$:

1. the subsumption rule (sub) is modified[2] so that expressions have a unique binding-time, see Subsection 2.3;
2. the (app), (sel) and (upd) rules are restricted so as to avoid stuck redexes such as $(\lambda^\phi x : A.w)@^\psi w'$ with $\psi \neq \phi$.

Definition 6. *The typing relation $\vdash_{bt}$ is defined by the rules of Figure 6.*

Note that $\rightarrow^\phi_s$ is sound w.r.t. the operational theory of $FOb_{1\leq:}$ and $\vdash_{bt}$ is sound w.r.t. $\vdash$.

2.3   Design Choices

In designing an annotated type system for $FOb_{1\leq:}$, we are led to several design choices. The first choice has to do with the treatment of subtyping, as discussed in [27]:

1. one can adopt the subsumption rule (sub) as in $\vdash_{if}$. This is the *inclusion-based approach*;
2. one can adopt a restricted subsumption rule as in $\vdash_{bt}$ so that all the types of an expression have the same top-level. This is the *equational-based approach*.

Note this choice has some impact on the operational semantics of the system, as rules such as $(n^\phi)^{+\psi} \rightarrow_s n^\phi$ would not be sound for $\vdash_{bt}$.

The second choice has to do with lifting. Lifting is often restricted to base types yet better residual programs may be obtained by allowing more general forms of lifting. Here we allow lifting on arbitrary types. The specialization rules for lifting are however rather mild: following e.g. [27], one could envision more aggressive specialization rules which propagate lift annotations. However, the standard rule for lifted products is based on surjective pairing (SP)[3] and, as pointed out in [3, Section 7.6.2], SP is not sound for objects. While we have not checked the details, it may be possible to encounter specialization rules which propagate lift annotations and which do not rely on SP.

The third choice has to do with typing rules for destructors. While we have not checked the details, one could envision more liberal typing rules such as

$$\frac{\Gamma \vdash_{bt} w_0 : A \rightarrow^\phi B \quad \Gamma \vdash_{bt} w_1 : A}{\Gamma \vdash_{bt} w_0@^\psi w_1 : B^{+\psi}} \quad \text{if } \phi \leq \psi$$

However this would require modifying the operational semantics so that redexes of the form $(\lambda^\phi x : A.w)@^\psi w'$ with $\phi \sqsubseteq \psi$ may be specialized at level ϕ and so that subject reduction holds. For example, one would need to adopt the rule

$$(\lambda^\psi x : A.w)@^{\psi'} w' \quad \rightarrow^\phi_s \quad (w\{x := (w')^{+\text{top}(A)}\})^{+\psi'}$$

for $\psi \sqsubseteq \psi'$. The notion of residual expression would also need to be modified so as for correctness results to hold.

---

[2] For the sake of conciseness, we consider a single rule which may introduce unnecessary lifts, namely when $\text{top}(A) = \text{top}(B)$. This may be easily fixed by maintaining the lift rule and restricting subsumption to types having the same top-level annotation.

[3] SP states that two objects o and o' are equal (w.r.t. the equational theory of $FOb_{1\leq:}$) at type $[l_i : B_i \ ^{1\leq i\leq n}]$ iff for $1 \leq i \leq n$, $o.l_i$ is equal to $o'.l_i$ at type B_i.

3   Correctness of the Analyses

In this section, we establish the correctness of IFA by proving a non-interference theorem and of BTA by proving the soundness of partial evaluation.

3.1   Correctness of IFA Analysis

First, one needs to show that if-reduction preserves typing.

Lemma 2 (Subject Reduction). *If $\Gamma \vdash_{if} w : A$ and $w \to_{if} w'$ then $\Gamma \vdash_{if} w' : A$.*

Proof. By induction on the structure of the derivation of $\Gamma \vdash_{if} w : A$.

Second, we need to analyze the possible shapes of legal terms and their behavior. To this end, we begin by classifying expressions into values, reducible expressions and irreducible expressions. Values are λ-abstractions, numerals or objects. Irreducible elements are those whose "heart" is a variable whereas reducible expressions are those whose "heart" is a value. The notion of "heart" can be made precise using the notion of experiment, see e.g. [13]; however we prefer to give an inductive definition of the classes involved.

Definition 7. *The sets $\mathbb{V}$ of values, $\mathbb{I}$ of irreducible expressions and $\mathbb{R}$ of reducible expressions are defined by the abstract syntax*

$$a \in \mathbb{V} = \lambda^{\phi}x : A.w \mid n^{\phi} \mid [l_i = \varsigma x_i : A.w_i \,^{1 \le i \le n}]^{\phi}$$
$$c \in \mathbb{I} = x \mid c@^{\phi}w \mid c.^{\phi}l \mid c.^{\phi}l \Leftarrow \varsigma x : A.w \mid c^{+\psi}$$
$$s \in \mathbb{R} = a@^{\phi}w \mid s@^{\phi}w \mid a.^{\phi}l \mid s.^{\phi}l \mid a.^{\phi}l \Leftarrow \varsigma x : A.w \mid s.^{\phi}l \Leftarrow \varsigma x : A.w \mid a^{+\psi} \mid s^{+\psi}$$

where $e, e_1, \dots, e_n \in \mathcal{W}$.

One easily checks that $\mathcal{W} = \mathbb{V} \sqcup \mathbb{I} \sqcup \mathbb{R}$.

Lemma 3. *If $\Gamma \vdash_{if} w : A$ and $w \in \mathbb{R}$ then $w \to_{if} w'$ for some $w' \in \mathcal{W}$.*

Proof. By induction on $w \in \mathbb{R}$.

Lemma 4. *If $\Gamma, x : C \vdash_{if} w : A$, $\Gamma \vdash_{if} v : C$, $w \in \mathbb{R}$ and $w \to_{if} w'$ then $w\{x := v\} \to_{if} w'\{x := v\}$.*

Proof. By induction on $w \in \mathbb{R}$.

Lemma 5. *If $\Gamma \vdash_{if} w : A$, $\mathsf{top}(\Gamma) \not\sqsubseteq \phi$ and $w \in \mathbb{I}$, then $\mathsf{top}(A) \not\sqsubseteq \phi$.*

Proof. By induction on the derivation of $\Gamma \vdash_{if} w : A$. We treat the case of application so assume $w = w_0@^{\psi}w_1$ and the last rule is

$$\frac{\Gamma \vdash_{if} w_0 : A \to^{\psi'} B \quad \Gamma \vdash_{if} w_1 : A}{\Gamma \vdash_{if} w_0@^{\psi}w_1 : B^{+\psi+\psi'}}$$

Necessarily $w_0 \in \mathbb{I}$ so by induction hypothesis $\psi' \not\sqsubseteq \phi$. Now $\psi' \sqsubseteq \mathsf{top}(B^{+\psi+\psi'})$ hence $\mathsf{top}(B^{+\psi+\psi'}) \not\sqsubseteq \phi$.

Lemma 6. *If $\Gamma \vdash_{if} w : A$ with $\mathrm{top}(\Gamma) \not\sqsubseteq \mathrm{top}(A)$ then $w \in \mathbf{V}$ or $w \to_{if} w'$.*

Proof. By Lemma 5, $w \notin \mathbb{I}$ hence $w \in \mathbf{V}$ or $w \in \mathbb{R}$. In the latter case, $w \to_{if} w'$ by Lemma 3.

Proposition 1. *If $\Gamma \vdash_{if} w : A$ with $\mathrm{top}(\Gamma) \not\sqsubseteq \mathrm{top}(A)$ then $w \twoheadrightarrow_{if} w' \in \mathbf{V}$ or w diverges, i.e. $w \to_{if} w_1 \to_{if} w_2 \to_{if} \ldots$ with $w_i \in \mathbb{R}$ for every $i \geq 1$.*

Proof. By Lemma 6 and Subject Reduction.

The above results can now be used to establish non-interference.

Proposition 2 (Non-interference). *Assume that $\Gamma, x : A \vdash_{if} w : \mathrm{nat}^{\psi}$, $\Gamma \vdash_{if} w' : A$ and $\Gamma \vdash_{if} w'' : A$. If $\mathrm{top}(\Gamma, x : A) \not\sqsubseteq \psi$ then for every $v \in \mathbf{V}$,*

$$w\{x := w'\} \twoheadrightarrow_{if} v \quad \Leftrightarrow \quad w\{x := w''\} \twoheadrightarrow_{if} v$$

Proof. By Proposition 1, there are two possibilities:

1. $w \twoheadrightarrow_{s}^{\phi} w_0 \in \mathbf{V}$ then w_0 must be of the form n^{ψ}. Hence $w\{x := w'\} \twoheadrightarrow_{s}^{\phi} n^{\psi}$ and $w\{x := w''\} \twoheadrightarrow_{s}^{\phi} n^{\psi}$ so we are done;
2. $w \to_{s}^{\phi} w_1 \to_{s}^{\phi} w_2 \ldots$ with $w_i \in \mathbb{R}$ for every $i \geq 1$. By Lemma 4,

$$w\{x := w'\} \to_{s}^{\phi} w_1\{x := w'\} \to_{s}^{\phi} w_2\{x := w'\} \ldots$$
$$w\{x := w''\} \to_{s}^{\phi} w_1\{x := w''\} \to_{s}^{\phi} w_2\{x := w''\} \ldots$$

so we are done.

3.2   Correctness of BTA

Specialization preserves typing; thus we are able to specialize expressions that have been specialized previously. This is the key to staging specialization in successive steps, see e.g. [28].

Lemma 7 (Subject Reduction). *If $\Gamma \vdash_{bt} w : A$ and $w \to_{s}^{\phi} w'$ then $\Gamma \vdash_{bt} w' : A$.*

Proof. By induction on the structure of the derivation of $\Gamma \vdash_{bt} w : A$. We treat somes cases:

1. assume $w = w_0 @^{\psi} w_1$ with $w_0 = \lambda^{\psi} x : A'.w_2$, $w' = w_2\{x := (w_1)^{+\mathrm{top}(A')}\}$ and the last rule is

$$\frac{\Gamma \vdash_{bt} w_0 : A \to^{\psi} B \quad \Gamma \vdash_{bt} w_1 : A}{\Gamma \vdash_{bt} w_0 @^{\psi} w_1 : B}$$

Necessarily $A \leq A'$ and there exists $B' \leq B$ such that $\Gamma, x : A' \vdash_{bt} w_2 : B'$. By subsumption $\Gamma \vdash_{bt} (w_1)^{+\mathrm{top}(A')} : A'$ and by substitution

$$\Gamma \vdash_{bt} w_2\{x := (w_1)^{+\mathrm{top}(A')}\} : B$$

2. assume $w = w_0.{}^\psi l_j$ with $w_0 = [l_i = \varsigma x_i : A.w_i {}^{1 \le i \le n}]^\psi$, $w' = w_j\{x_j := w_0'\}$
   and the last rule is

$$\frac{\Gamma \vdash_{bt} w_0 : [l_i = B_i {}^{1 \le i \le n}]^\psi}{\Gamma \vdash_{bt} w_0.{}^\psi l_j : B_j}$$

Necessarily $A = [l_i = B_i {}^{1 \le i \le n}]^{\psi'}$ with $\psi' \sqsubseteq \psi$ and $\Gamma, x_i : A \vdash_{bt} w_i : B_i$ for $1 \le i \le n$. Set $w_0' = [l_i = \varsigma x_i : A.w_i {}^{1 \le i \le n}]^{\psi'}$. By object, $\Gamma \vdash_{bt} w_0' : [l_i = B_i {}^{1 \le i \le n}]^{\psi'}$ and by substitution $\Gamma \vdash_{bt} w_j\{x_j := w_0'\} : B_j$.

Lemma 8. *If $\Gamma \vdash_{bt} w : A$, $\mathrm{top}(A) \sqsubseteq \phi$ and $w \in \mathbb{R}$ then $w \to_s^\phi w'$.*

Proof. By induction on the derivation of $\Gamma \vdash_{bt} w : A$. We treat some cases:

1. assume that $w = w_0 @^\psi w_1$ and the last rule is application

$$\frac{\Gamma \vdash_{bt} w_0 : A \to^\psi B \quad \Gamma \vdash_{bt} w_1 : A}{\Gamma \vdash_{bt} w_0 @^\psi w_1 : B}$$

with $\psi \sqsubseteq \mathrm{top}(B) \sqsubseteq \phi$. There are two cases to treat:
   (a) if $w_0 \in \mathbb{V}$ then necessarily w_0 is a λ^ψ-abstraction, say $w_0 = \lambda^\psi x : A'.w_2$, and hence $w = w_0 @^\psi w_1 \to_s^\phi w' = w_2\{x := (w_1)^{+\mathrm{top}(A')}\}$.
   (b) if $w_0 \in \mathbb{R}$ then by induction hypothesis $w_0 \to_s^\phi w_0'$ and hence $w_0 @^\psi w_1 \to_s^\phi w_0' @^\psi w_1$.
2. assume $w = w_0^{+\psi}$ and the last rule is lift

$$\frac{\Gamma \vdash_{bt} w_0 : A}{\Gamma \vdash_{bt} w_0^{+\psi} : A^{+\psi}}$$

By hypothesis, $\mathrm{top}(A^{+\psi}) \sqsubseteq \phi$ and hence $\mathrm{top}(A) \sqsubseteq \phi$. There are two cases to treat:
   (a) if $w_0 \in \mathbb{R}$ then by induction hypothesis $w_0 \to_s^\phi w_0'$ and hence $w_0^{+\psi} \to_s^\phi (w_0')^{+\psi}$.
   (b) if $w_0 \in \mathbb{V}$ then necessarily $w_0^{+\psi} \to_s^\phi w'$.

Lemma 9. *If $\Gamma \vdash_{bt} w : A$, $\mathrm{top}(\Gamma) \not\sqsubseteq \phi$ and $w \in \mathbb{I}$, then $\mathrm{top}(A) \not\sqsubseteq \phi$.*

Proof. By induction on the derivation of $\Gamma \vdash_{bt} w : A$. We treat some cases:

1. if $w \in \mathcal{V}$ and the last rule is start, then $(w : A) \in \Gamma$ and we have $\mathrm{top}(A) \not\sqsubseteq \phi$ from the definition of $\mathrm{top}(\Gamma) \not\sqsubseteq \phi$.
2. if $w = w_0 @^\psi w_1$ and the last rule is application

$$\frac{\Gamma \vdash_{bt} w_0 : A \to^\psi B \quad \Gamma \vdash_{bt} w_1 : A}{\Gamma \vdash_{bt} w_0 @^\psi w_1 : B}$$

Then $w_0 \in \mathbb{I}$ so by induction hypothesis $\psi \not\sqsubseteq \phi$. Now $\psi \sqsubseteq \mathrm{top}(B)$ by the definition of annotated types, hence $\mathrm{top}(B) \not\sqsubseteq \phi$.

3. if $w = w'.l$ and the last rule is selection

$$\frac{\Gamma \vdash_{bt} w' : [l_i = B_i {}^{1 \le i \le n}]^\psi}{\Gamma \vdash_{bt} w'.^\psi l_i : B_i}$$

Then $w' \in \mathbb{I}$ so by induction hypothesis $\psi \not\sqsubseteq \phi$. Now $\psi \sqsubseteq \mathrm{top}(B_i)$ by the definition of annotated types, hence $\mathrm{top}(B_i) \not\sqsubseteq \phi$.

4. if $w = w'.^\phi l_i \Leftarrow \varsigma x : A.w_1$ and the last rule is update

$$\frac{\Gamma \vdash_{bt} w' : A \quad \Gamma, x : A \vdash_{bt} w_1 : B_i}{\Gamma \vdash_{bt} w'.^\phi l_i \Leftarrow \varsigma x : A.w_1 : A} \quad \text{with } A = [l_i : B_i {}^{1 \le i \le n}]^\phi$$

Then $w' \in \mathbb{I}$ so by induction hypothesis we got directly $\mathrm{top}(A) \not\sqsubseteq \phi$.

5. if $w = w_0^{+\psi}$ and the last rule is lift

$$\frac{\Gamma \vdash_{bt} w_0 : A}{\Gamma \vdash_{bt} w_0^{+\psi} : A^{+\psi}}$$

Necessarily $w_0 \in \mathbb{I}$. By induction hypothesis, $\mathrm{top}(A) \not\sqsubseteq \phi$. Now $\mathrm{top}(A) \sqsubseteq \mathrm{top}(B)$ and hence $\mathrm{top}(B) \not\sqsubseteq \phi$.

Later we will use the following reformulation of Lemma 9: if $\Gamma \vdash_{bt} w : A$, $\mathrm{top}(\Gamma) \not\sqsubseteq \phi$ and $\mathrm{top}(A) \sqsubseteq \phi$, then $w \notin \mathbb{I}$.

Lemma 10 (No stuck). *If $\Gamma \vdash_{bt} w : B$ with $\mathrm{top}(B), \mathrm{top}(\Gamma) \not\sqsubseteq \phi$, then one of the two properties below holds:*

1. *$w \in \mathcal{R}^\phi$, i.e. w is ϕ-residual;*
2. *$w \to_s^\phi w'$ for some $w' \in \mathcal{W}$.*

Proof. By induction on the derivation of $\Gamma \vdash_{bt} w : A$. We treat some cases:

1. application: assume $w = w_0 @^\psi w_1$ and the last rule is

$$\frac{\Gamma \vdash_{bt} w_0 : A \to^\psi B \quad \Gamma \vdash_{bt} w_1 : A}{\Gamma \vdash_{bt} w_0 @^\psi w_1 : B}$$

By construction, $\psi \sqsubseteq \mathrm{top}(A), \mathrm{top}(B)$. By assumption, $\mathrm{top}(B), \mathrm{top}(\Gamma) \not\sqsubseteq \phi$. There are two possibilities:

(a) if $\psi \sqsubseteq \phi$: by Lemma 9 $w_0 \notin \mathbb{I}$, so $w_0 @^\psi w_1 \notin \mathbb{I}$ and hence $w_0 @^\psi w_1 \in \mathbb{R}$. We conclude by Lemma 8;

(b) if $\psi \not\sqsubseteq \phi$: then $\mathrm{top}(A), \mathrm{top}(B) \not\sqsubseteq \phi$. By induction hypothesis, either $w_0 \to_s^\phi w_0'$ or $w_0 \in \mathcal{R}^\phi$ and either $w_1 \to_s^\phi w_1'$ or $w_1 \in \mathcal{R}^\phi$. There are three cases to treat:
   i. $w_0 \in \mathcal{R}^\phi$ and $w_1 \in \mathcal{R}^\phi$: $w_0 @^\psi w_1 \in \mathcal{R}^\phi$;
   ii. $w_0 \in \mathcal{R}^\phi$ and $w_1 \to_s^\phi w_1'$: $w_0 @^\psi w_1 \to_s^\phi w_0 @^\psi w_1'$;
   iii. $w_0 \to_s^\phi w_0'$: $w_0 @^\psi w_1 \to_s^\phi w_0' @^\psi w_1$.

2. abstraction: assume $w = \lambda^\psi x : A.w_0$ and the last rule is

$$\frac{\Gamma, x : A \vdash_{bt} w_0 : B}{\Gamma \vdash_{bt} \lambda^\psi x : A.w_0 : A \to^\psi B}$$

By construction, $\psi \sqsubseteq \mathrm{top}(A), \mathrm{top}(B)$. By assumption, $\psi, \mathrm{top}(\Gamma) \not\sqsubseteq \phi$. Hence $\mathrm{top}(A), \mathrm{top}(B) \not\sqsubseteq \phi$ and by induction hypothesis, $w_0 \to_s^\phi w'$ or $w_0 \in \mathcal{R}^\phi$. In the first case, $w \to_s^\phi \lambda^\psi x : A.w'$. In the second case, $\lambda^\psi x : A.w_0 \in \mathcal{R}^\phi$.

3. object: assume $w = [l_i = \varsigma x_i : A.w_i {}^{1 \le i \le n}]^\psi$ with $A = [l_i : B_i {}^{1 \le i \le n}]^\psi$ and the last rule is

$$\frac{\Gamma, x_i : A \vdash_{bt} w_i : B_i}{\Gamma \vdash_{bt} [l_i = \varsigma x_i : A.w_i {}^{1 \le i \le n}]^\psi : A}$$

By construction, $\psi \sqsubseteq \mathrm{top}(B_i)$ for $1 \le i \le n$. By assumption, $\mathrm{top}(\Gamma), \psi \not\sqsubseteq \phi$. Hence $\mathrm{top}(B_i) \not\sqsubseteq \phi$ and by induction hypothesis, $w_i \in \mathcal{R}^\phi$ or $w_i \to_s^\phi w_i'$ for $1 \le i \le n$. There are to cases to distinguish:

(a) for all $1 \le i \le n$ we have $w_i \in \mathcal{R}^\phi$ then $w \in \mathcal{R}^\phi$;

(b) for some $1 \le i \le n$ we have $w_i \to_s^\phi w_i'$ then $[l_i = \varsigma x_i : A.w_i {}^{1 \le i \le n}]^\psi \to_s$ $[l_i = \varsigma x_i : A.w_i {}^{1 \le i \le n,\ i \ne j}, l_j = \varsigma x_j : A.w_j']$ where j is the smallest number such that $w_j \notin \mathcal{R}^\phi$.

4. invocation: assume $w = w_0.^\psi l_i$ and the last rule is

$$\frac{\Gamma \vdash_{bt} w_0 : [l_i = B_i {}^{1 \le i \le n}]^\psi}{\Gamma \vdash_{bt} w_0.^\psi l_i : B_i}$$

By construction, $\psi \sqsubseteq \mathrm{top}(B_i)$. By assumption, $\mathrm{top}(\Gamma), \mathrm{top}(B_i) \not\sqsubseteq \phi$. There are two possibilities:

(a) if $\psi \sqsubseteq \phi$: by Lemma 9 $w_0 \notin \mathbb{I}$, so $w_0.^\psi l_i \notin \mathbb{I}$ and hence $w_0.^\psi l_i \in \mathbb{R}$. By Lemma 8 $w_0.^\psi l_i \to_s^\phi w'$.

(b) if $\psi \not\sqsubseteq \phi$: then by induction hypothesis, either $w_0 \to_s^\phi w_0'$ or $w_0 \in \mathcal{R}^\phi$. In the first case $w_0.^\psi l_i \to_s^\phi w_0'.^\psi l_i$ whereas in the second case $w_0.^\psi l_i \in \mathcal{R}^\phi$.

5. lift: assume $w = w_0^{+\psi}$ and the last rule is

$$\frac{\Gamma \vdash_{bt} w_0 : A}{\Gamma \vdash_{bt} w_0^{+\psi} : A^{+\psi}}$$

By assumption $\mathrm{top}(A^{+\psi}) \not\sqsubseteq \phi$. There are two cases to treat:

(a) if $\mathrm{top}(A) \sqsubseteq \phi$ then by Lemma 9, $w_0^{+\psi} \notin \mathbb{I}$. Hence $w_0^{+\psi} \in \mathbb{R}$ and by Lemma 8 $w_0^{+\psi} \to_s^\phi w'$;

(b) if $\mathrm{top}(A) \not\sqsubseteq \phi$: then by induction hypothesis, either $w_0 \to_s^\phi w_0'$ or $w_0 \in \mathcal{R}^\phi$. In the first case, $w_0^{+\psi} \to_s^\phi w'$. In the second case either $w_0 \in \mathbb{V}$ in which case $w_0^{+\psi} \to_s^\phi w'$ or $w_0 \notin \mathbb{V}$ in which case $w_0^{+\psi} \in \mathcal{R}^\phi$.

In the sequel we let $\twoheadrightarrow_s^\phi$ denotes the reflexive-transitive closure of $\to_s^\phi$.

Proposition 3 (Correctness of binding-time analysis). *If $\Gamma \vdash_{bt} w : A$ with $\mathrm{top}(\Gamma), \mathrm{top}(A) \not\sqsubseteq \phi$ then one of the two properties below holds:*

1. $w \twoheadrightarrow_s^\phi w'$ and $w' \in \mathcal{R}^\phi$;
2. $w \to_s^\phi w_1 \to_s^\phi w_2 \to_s^\phi \ldots$

Proof. Follows directly from no stuck and subject reduction.

4   Conclusions and Directions for Future Research

We have defined and shown the correctness of IFA and BTA for $FOb_{1\leq:}$. In the future, it seems worth:

1. extending our results to more powerful and realistic object calculi;
2. scaling up to annotated type systems the existing translations from ς-calculi to λ- and π-calculi, see e.g. [6,24], in particular to reduce non-interference for the former to non-interference for the latter.

Acknowledgements We are grateful to F. van Raamsdonk and the anonymous referees for their constructive comments. Thanks to D. Teller and S. Villemot for implementing the annotated calculi. The first author is partially funded by the FCT grant PRAXIS/P/EEI/14172/1998.

References

1. M. Abadi. Secrecy by typing in security protocols. *Journal of the ACM*. To appear.
2. M. Abadi, A. Banerjee, N. Heintze, and J. Riecke. A core calculus of dependency. In *Proceedings of POPL'99*, pages 147–160. ACM Press, 1999.
3. M. Abadi and L. Cardelli. *A theory of objects*. Springer-Verlag, 1996.
4. D. Bell and L. LaPadula. Secure computer systems: Unified exposition and multics interpretation. Technical Report MTR-2997, MITRE Corporation, July 1975.
5. E. Bertino, E. Ferrari, and P. Samarati. Mandatory security and object-oriented systems: A multilevel entity model and its mapping onto a single-level object model. *Theory and Practice of Object Systems*, 4(3):183–204, 1998.
6. K.B. Bruce, L. Cardelli, and B.C. Pierce. Comparing object encodings. *Information and Computation*, 1999. To appear in a special issue with papers from *Theoretical Aspects of Computer Software (TACS)*.
7. C. Consel, L. Hornof, R. Marlet, G. Muller, S. Thibault, and E.-N. Volanschi. Tempo: Specializing systems applications and beyond. *ACM Computing Surveys*, 30(3), September 1998. Symposium on Partial Evaluation (SOPE '98).
8. O. Danvy, R. Glück, and P. Thiemann, editors. *Partial Evaluation*, volume 1110 of *Lecture Notes in Computer Science*. Springer-Verlag, 1996.
9. D.E. Denning. A lattice model of secure information flow. *Communications of the ACM*, 19(5):236–243, May 1976.
10. D.E. Denning and P.J. Denning. Certification of programs for secure information flow. *Communications of the ACM*, 20(7):504–513, July 1977.
11. R. Glück and J. Jørgensen. An automatic program generator for multi-level specialization. *Lisp and Symbolic Computation*, 10(2):113–158, July 1997.
12. A.D. Gordon, P.D. Hankin, and S.B. Lassen. Compilation and equivalence of imperative objects. In S. Ramesh and G. Sivakumar, editors, *Proceedings of FSTTCS'97*, volume 1346 of *Lecture Notes in Computer Science*, pages 74–87. Springer-Verlag, 1997.
13. A.D. Gordon and G.D. Rees. Bisimilarity for a first-order calculus of objects with subtyping. In *Proceedings of POPL'96*, pages 386–395. ACM Press, 1996.
14. J. Hatcliff and R. Glück. Reasoning about hierarchies of online program specialization systems. In Danvy et al. [8], pages 161–182.

15. N. Heintze and J. Riecke. The SLam calculus: programming with secrecy and integrity. In *Proceedings of POPL'98*, pages 365–377. ACM Press, 1998.
16. N. Jones, C. Gomard, and P. Sestoft. *Partial Evaluation and Automatic Program Generation*. Prenctice Hall, 1993.
17. M. Marquard and B. Steensgaard. Partial evaluation of an object-oriented language. Master's thesis, Department of Computer Science, Copenhagen University (DIKU), 1992.
18. A.C. Myers. Jflow: Practical mostly-static information flow control. In *Proceedings of POPL'99*, pages 228–241. ACM Press, 1999.
19. A.C. Myers and B. Liskov. A decentralized model for information flow control. In *Proceedings of SOSP'97*, pages 129–142. ACM Press, 1997.
20. F. Nielson and H.R. Nielson. *Two-level functional languages*, volume 34 of *Cambridge Tracts In Theoretical Computer Science*. Cambridge University Press, 1992.
21. F. Nielson and H.R. Nielson. Multi-level lambda-calculi: an algebraic description. In Danvy et al. [8], pages 338–354.
22. F. Nielson and H.R. Nielson. Flow analyis for imperative objects. In L. Brim, J. Gruska, and J. Zlatuska, editors, *Proceedings of MFCS'98*, volume 1450 of *Lecture Notes in Computer Science*, pages 220–228. Springer-Verlag, 1998.
23. A. Sabelfeld and D. Sands. A PER model of secure information flow in sequential programs. In D. Swiestra, editor, *Proceedings of ESOP'99*, volume 1576 of *Lecture Notes in Computer Science*, pages 40–58. Springer-Verlag, 1999.
24. D. Sangiorgi. An interpretation of typed objects into typed π-calculus. *Information and Computation*, 143(1):34–73, May 1998.
25. U.P. Schultz, J. Lawall, C. Consel, and G. Muller. Toward Automatic Specialization of Java Programs. In R. Guerraoui, editor, *Proceedings of ECOOP'99*, volume 1628 of *Lecture Notes in Computer Science*, pages 367–390. Springer-Verlag, 1999.
26. G. Smith and D. Volpano. Secure information flow in a multi-threaded imperative language. In *Proceedings of POPL'98*, pages 355–364. ACM Press, 1998.
27. P. Thiemann. A unified framework for binding-time analysis. In M. Bidoit and M. Dauchet, editors, *TAPSOFT'97*, volume 1214 of *Lecture Notes in Computer Science*, pages 742–756. Springer-Verlag, 1997.
28. P. Thiemann and H. Klaeren. What security analysis can do for you or the correctness of a multi-level binding-time analysis. Manuscript, June 1998.

Lazy Lexing is Fast

Manuel M. T. Chakravarty

Institute of Information Sciences and Electronics
University of Tsukuba, Japan
chak@is.tsukuba.ac.jp
www.score.is.tsukuba.ac.jp/~chak/

Abstract This paper introduces a set of combinators for building lexical analysers in a lazy functional language. During lexical analysis, the
combinators generate a deterministic, table-driven analyser on the fly.
Consequently, the presented method combines the efficiency of off-line
scanner generators with the flexibility of the combinator approach. The
method makes essential use of the lazy semantics of the implementation
language Haskell. Finally, the paper discusses benchmarks of a scanner
for the programming language C.

1 Introduction

There are two conceptually different approaches to obtaining a functional implementation of a scanner or parser from a formal lexical or syntactic specification:
(1) the specification is written in a special purpose language and translated into
a functional program by a scanner or parser generator or (2) the specification is
composed from a set of combinators provided by a scanner or parser combinator
library.

Both approaches have their advantages and were pursued in the past. There
are a couple of generators (e.g., [8,2,5]) for widely used languages, such as Haskell
and SML, as well as a number of combinator libraries (e.g., [3,4]). Usually, generators produce more efficient scanners and parsers by implementing table-driven
analysers [1], but this is, in the case of parsers, at the expense of expressiveness,
as generators usually confine the specification to a restricted class of languages,
such as, LALR(1). Furthermore, combinator libraries are easier to handle—no
separate input language and generator program are necessary—and they can
specify analysers for statically unknown grammars, i.e., the grammar can change
during program execution. Recently, Swierstra and Duponcheel [7] introduced
self-optimising parser combinators, which during parsing generate a deterministic analyser for LL(1) grammars, thus, combining the flexibility of combinators
with the efficiency of generators.

The present paper introduces a related technique for lexical analysers (*lexers*,
for short). During application of the lexer, a deterministic, table-driven analyser
is generated on the fly from a combinator-based lexical specification. Tokens are
produced by user-defined *actions*, the standard *principle of the longest match* is
applied [1], and non-regular features, such as nested comments, are supported

A. Middeldorp, T. Sato (Eds.): FLOPS'99, LNCS 1722, pp. 68–84, 1999.

by *meta actions*. The described technique is fully implemented by a Haskell library, called Lexers, and the code is available for public use.[1] The efficiency of the technique was evaluated by benchmarking an implementation of a lexer for the programming language C. Despite the relation to the mentioned work of Swierstra and Duponcheel on parser generators, the presented technique is substantially different from theirs.

An interesting aside is the use made of Haskell's lazy evaluation semantics. The state transition tables generated by the lexer combinators to achieve deterministic behaviour are represented by a cyclic tree structure, which requires either non-strict semantics or impure mutable structures. As an additional advantage of laziness, only those fragments of the table are constructed that are actually needed to accept the input at hand. Thus, we avoid overly high startup costs for short inputs, which would be incurred in non-strict, but eager (= lenient) languages like pH [6].

In summary, the central contributions are the following:

- A new technique for on-line generation of state transition tables from regular expressions in a lazy functional language.
- A combinator library for specifying lexical analysers, including often required non-regular features.
- Experimental evaluation of the proposed table generation technique.

The paper is structured as follows. Section 2 introduces the basic ideas of the combinator library and table generation. Section 3 defines the interface of the combinator library and Section 4 formalises the dynamic table generation. Section 5 presents benchmarks. Finally, Section 6 discusses related work and Section 7 concludes.

2   Combinators and Automata

Specifications of lexers essentially consist of pairs of *regular expressions* and *actions*, where the latter are program fragments that are executed as soon as the associated regular expression matches the current input. Actions usually generate tokens, which are consumed by a parser following the lexer. Regular expressions typically have the following structure [1]:

- ϵ matches the empty word.
- A single character c matches itself.
- $r_1 r_2$ matches a word of which the first part is matched by r_1 and the second part by r_2.
- $r_1 \mid r_2$ matches a word that is either matched by r_1 or by r_2.
- $r*$ matches a word that consists of zero, one, or more successive words matched by r.
- $r+$ matches a word that consists of one or more successive words matched by r.
- $r?$ matches a word that is either empty of matched by r.

---

[1] Download at http://www.score.is.tsukuba.ac.jp/~chak/ctk/

Furthermore, we use $[c_1 \ldots c_n]$ to abbreviate $c_1 \mid \cdots \mid c_n$. For example, integer numbers are matched by $-?[0 \ldots 9]+$, i.e., an optional minus sign is followed by a non-empty sequence of digits. The same regular expression can be expressed in Haskell as follows (we define the used combinators in detail in the next section):

(char '-') 'quest' (alt ['0'..'9']) 'plus' epsilon

or, in this paper with improved typesetting, as $(char\ '-')?\ (alt\ ['0'..'9']) \oplus \epsilon$. In a lexer specification, this regular expression would be paired with an action that, given the string—or, *lexeme*—of a recognised integer, produces the corresponding token.

A well known result from automata theory states that, for each regular expression, there exists a *finite state automaton (FA)* that accepts exactly those words that are matched by the regular expression; more precisely, there even exists a *deterministic finite state automaton (DFA)*, i.e., one where in each state, by looking at the next input symbol, we can decide deterministically into which state the automaton has to go next. This correspondence is exploited in scanner generators to produce a deterministic, table-driven analyser from a lexical specification. The technique presented here builds on the same theory. An additional complication, when handling a full lexical specification, as opposed to a single regular expression, is the requirement to match against a set of regular expressions in a single pass.

By implementing matching of regular expression by a DFA, we get a *table driven lexer*. Such a lexer represents the *state transition graph* of the automaton by a two-dimensional table. During lexical analysis, it traverses the transition graph by repeatedly indexing the table with the current automaton state and input symbol to obtain the next state. In the standard approach, the table is constructed off-line by a scanner generator. More precisely, the regular expressions are either first transformed into a *nondeterministic finite automaton* (NFA), and then, the NFA is converted to an DFA or the DFA is directly obtained from the regular expressions; finally, the number of states of the DFA is minimised and often the table is stored in a compressed format, as it tends to be sparse. This standard technology is described in detail in compiler textbooks [9,1].

As we generate the automaton incrementally during lexing, we cannot use a multi-staged approach and we have to avoid expensive techniques, such as, the subset construction. We essentially build the state transition graph of a DFA directly from the regular expressions and we construct a node of the graph only if we actually reach it during lexing. Representing the graph directly, instead of encoding it in a table, facilitates incremental construction and reduces the storage requirements in comparison to an uncompressed table (the transition table is usually sparse).

3   The Interface

Before we discuss the details of automata construction, we have to fix the combinator set used for the lexical specification. It consists of regular expressions, actions, and meta actions, where regular expressions describe the structure of lexemes, actions specify the transformation of lexemes into tokens, and meta actions keep track of line numbers and implement non-regular features, such as, nested comments.

3.1   Regular Expressions

Sets of lexemes that should trigger the same action (i.e., which usually generate the same sort of token) are specified by regular expressions that are freely constructed from a set of combinators, which resemble the operators on regular expressions discussed in the previous section.

A regular expression is denoted by a Haskell expression of type ($Regexp\ s\ t$). Such a regular expression is, according to its type arguments, used in a lexer, which maintains an internal state of type s and produces tokens of type t—it would be possible to hide the type variables s and t add this point by using the non-standard feature of explicit universal quantification and at the cost of slightly complicating some other definitions. The following combinators[2] are available for constructing regular expressions:

$$
\begin{array}{lll}
\epsilon & :: Regexp\ s\ t & \text{— empty word} \\
char & :: Char \rightarrow Regexp\ s\ t & \text{— single character} \\
(\triangleright) & :: Regexp\ s\ t \rightarrow Regexp\ s\ t \rightarrow Regexp\ s\ t & \text{— concatenation} \\
(\boxplus) & :: Regexp\ s\ t \rightarrow Regexp\ s\ t \rightarrow Regexp\ s\ t & \text{— alternatives} \\
(\circledast) & :: Regexp\ s\ t \rightarrow Regexp\ s\ t \rightarrow Regexp\ s\ t & \text{— zero, one, or more rep.} \\
(\oplus) & :: Regexp\ s\ t \rightarrow Regexp\ s\ t \rightarrow Regexp\ s\ t & \text{— one or more repetitions} \\
(?) & :: Regexp\ s\ t \rightarrow Regexp\ s\ t \rightarrow Regexp\ s\ t & \text{— zero or one occurences}
\end{array}
$$

We can define $(\circledast)$, $(\oplus)$, and $(?)$ in terms of the first four combinators; we shall return to the details of these definitions later. Furthermore, the following two definitions are useful for making regular expressions more concise:

$$
\begin{array}{ll}
alt & :: [Char] \rightarrow Regexp\ s\ t \\
alt\ [c_1, \ldots, c_n] & = char\ c_1 \boxplus \cdots \boxplus char\ c_n
\end{array}
$$

$$
\begin{array}{ll}
string & :: String \rightarrow Regexp\ s\ t \\
string\ [c_1, \ldots, c_n] & = char\ c_1 \triangleright \cdots \triangleright char\ c_n
\end{array}
$$

Finally, the following precedence declarations apply:

$$
\begin{array}{l}
infixl\ 4\ \circledast,\ \oplus,\ ? \\
infixl\ 3\ \triangleright \\
infixl\ 2\ \boxplus
\end{array}
$$

---

[2] This presentation takes the freedom to improve on a purely ASCII-based typesetting of Haskell expressions. In ASCII, ϵ is represented by **epsilon**, $(\triangleright)$ by (**+>**), $(\boxplus)$ by (**>|<**), $(\circledast)$ by **star**, $(\oplus)$ by **plus**, and $(?)$ by **quest**.

Given these combinators, it is straight forward to define familiar token types, e.g., identifiers:

$ident$ :: $Regexp\ s\ t$
$ident$ = $letter \triangleright (letter \boxtimes digit) \circledast \epsilon$
  where
    $letter$ = $alt\ (['a'..'z'] +\!\!+ ['A'..'Z'])$
    $digit$ = $alt\ ['0'..'9']$

In other words, an identifier is composed out of a letter, followed by zero or more letters or digits. Note the use of ϵ at the end of the regular expression; $\circledast$ is an infix operator and requires a second argument. From the point of view of regular expressions, the more natural choice for $\circledast$, $\oplus$, and ? would be the use of (unary) postfix operators. However, Haskell does not have postfix operators and, even if it had, a unary operator would make the implementation more difficult; as we will see in Section 4, the binary nature of these operators allows an important optimization.

3.2 Actions

Whenever the lexer recognises a lexeme matching a given regular expression, it applies an action function to the lexeme and its position to produce a token.

$\textbf{type}\ Action\ t$ = $String \rightarrow Position \rightarrow Maybe\ t$

An action may choose to produce no token (i.e., return $Nothing$); for example, if the lexeme represents white space or a comment. Using the function

$lexaction$ :: $Regexp\ s\ t \rightarrow Action\ t \rightarrow Lexer\ s\ t$

we can bundle a regular expression with an action to form a lexer—the latter are denoted by types $Lexer\ s\ t$ with user-defined state s and tokens t. We can disjunctively combine a collection of such lexers with the following combinator:

$infixl\ 2\ \boxtimes$
$(\boxtimes)$ :: $Lexer\ s\ t \rightarrow Lexer\ s\ t \rightarrow Lexer\ s\ t$

Given these functions, let us continue the above example of lexing identifiers, i.e., the definition of the regular expression $ident$. If tokens are defined as

$\textbf{data}\ Token$ = $IdentTok\ String\ Position$
        | $\cdots$

we can define a lexer that recognises identifiers only by

$lexident$ :: $Lexer\ s\ Token$
$lexident$ = $ident\ `lexaction`\ (\lambda str\ pos \rightarrow Just\ (IdentTok\ str\ pos))$

A compound lexer that recognises sequences of identifiers separated by space characters can be defined as follows:

$$lexer :: Lexer\ s\ Token$$
$$lexer = lexident$$
$$\quad\quad \rhd\!\!\!\rhd char\ '\ '\ 'lexaction'\ (\lambda_{-\ -} \to Nothing)$$

3.3 Meta Actions

In addition to actions that produce tokens, we have meta actions, which alter the internal behaviour of the produced lexer. Like a normal action, a meta action is a function:

$$type\ Meta\ s\ t = Position \to s \to (Position,\ s,\ Maybe\ (Lexer\ s\ t))$$

Given the current position and a user-defined lexer state (of type s), a meta action produces an updated position and an updated user-defined state. Furthermore, it may choose to return a lexer that is used, instead of the current one, to analyse the next token. The user-defined state can, for example, be used to implement a *gensym* routine or to maintain an identifier table during lexical analysis. In combination with the capability of returning a lexer, it can be used to implement non-regular features, such as, nested comments. We can realise the latter as follows:

– The user-defined state keeps track of the current nesting level.
– We use two different lexers: (a) the *standard lexer* recognises tokens outside of comments and (b) the *comment lexer* keeps track of the nesting level while scanning though comments.
– When the lexing process encounters a lexeme starting a comment, it invokes a meta action that increases the nesting count and returns (in the third component of its result) the comment lexer.
– When the lexing process encounters a lexeme ending a comment, it triggers a meta action that decreases the nesting count and returns the standard lexer if the nesting count reached zero; otherwise, it returns the comment lexer.

Note that this technique is a kind of cleaned up, side-effect free variant of the user-defined start states found in parser generators like lex.

Like standard actions, we combine meta actions with regular expressions into lexers:

$$lexmeta :: Regexp\ s\ t \to Meta\ s\ t \to Lexer\ s\ t$$

The library Lexers discussed here internally uses meta actions to keep track of positions in the presence of control characters in the following way (*Position* is a triple composed from a file name, row, and column):

```
ctrlLexer :: Lexer s t
ctrlLexer =
      char '\n' 'lexmeta' newline
  ⊕ char '\r' 'lexmeta' newline
  ⊕ char '\f' 'lexmeta' formfeed
  ⊕ char '\t' 'lexmeta' tab
  where
      newline (fname, row, _ ) s = ((fname, row + 1, 1), s, Nothing)
      formfeed (fname, row, col) s = ((fname, row, col + 1), s, Nothing)
      tab      (fname, row, col) s = ((fname, row, col + 8 − col 'mod' 8),
                                       s, Nothing)
```

3.4 Lexing

While performing lexical analysis, a lexer maintains a lexer state

```
type LexerState s = (String, Position, s)
```

which is composed out of the remaining input string, the current source position, and a user-defined component s—the latter is the same state that is transformed in meta actions. Given a lexer and a lexer state, the following function executes the lexical analysis and yields a token string:[3]

```
execLexer               :: Lexer s t → LexerState s → [t]
execLexer l ([], _, _) = []
execLexer l state      = case lexOne l state of
                            (Nothing, l', state') → execLexer l' state'
                            (Just t  , l', state') → t : execLexer l' state'
```

The definition uses *lexOne* to read a single lexeme from the input stream. If a token is produced, it is added to the resulting token stream. In any case, *execLexer* recurses to process the reminder of the input—in the case, where the just read token triggered a meta action, the lexer l' used in the recursion may differ from l. The signature of *lexOne*, which will be defined in detail later, is

```
lexOne :: Lexer s t → LexerState s → (Maybe t, Lexer s t, LexerState s)
```

4   Table Construction and Lexical Analysis

Given the interface of the previous section, it is not difficult to imagine a standard combinator-based implementation (similar to [3]). The disadvantage of such

---

[3] In the actual implementation of the **Lexers** library, the function also returns the final lexer state as well as a list of error messages.

a naive implementation is, however, its low efficiency (see Section 5). As mentioned, the standard method for making lexers more efficient is to transform the specification into the state transition table of a deterministic finite automaton.

The main contribution of the present paper is a purely functional algorithm that on-the-fly constructs a DFA in a compressed table representation from regular expressions. To improve the execution time for short inputs on big lexical specifications, only those parts of the table that are needed for lexing the input at hand are constructed. We achieve this by implementing the combinators building regular expressions as *smart* constructors of the transition table (instead of regarding a regular expression as a data structure, which is processed by a table construction function). More precisely, an expression of type (*Lexer s t*), which is a combination of regular expressions and actions, evaluates to a state transition table of a DFA that accepts exactly the lexemes specified by the regular expressions and has the actions in the automaton's final states—the table construction algorithm is encoded in the combinators forming regular expressions.

4.1 Table Representation

In imperative algorithms the state transition table may be represented by a two-dimensional array indexed by the current automaton state and the current input symbol. For us, such a representation, however, has two problems: (1) The table tends to be sparse and (2) we like to incrementally refine the table. The sparseness of the table is, of course, also an interesting point in imperative lexers; therefore, the table is often stored in a compressed format after the off-line table construction is completed. However, this approach is not attractive in an on-line approach (i.e., when the table is constructed during lexing). Regarding the second point, our incremental table construction requires frequent updates of the transition table (until, eventually, the table for the whole lexical specification is completed), an operation that is expensive on big arrays in a purely functional programming style.

Using the advanced data structures available in a functional language, we directly represent the state transition graph of the DFA, instead of using a conventional table representation. The state transition graph is a directed, cyclic graph—thus, a direct representation requires either a non-strict functional language or impure operations on mutable structures. Each node in the graph represents a state of the DFA and each edge represents a state transition labelled with the input character triggering the transition. As we represent a DFA (not an NFA), there is at most one outgoing edge for each possible input character from each node. The final states of the DFA are those that are associated with an action and the initial state is the graph node that we use as the root. Overall, we represent a DFA (or lexer) by the following structure:

```
data Lexer s t      = State (LexAction s t) [(Char, Lexer s t)]
data LexAction s t  = Action (Action t)
                    | Meta (Meta s t)
                    | NoAction
```

A *State a c* where *a* is different from *NoAction* represents a final state. The continuation *c* is an association list of admissible transitions—i.e., for each acceptable character in the current state, it contains the node in the graph that is reached after the associated character is read. For example,

$$State\ ac\ [('a', l_1),\ ('c', l_2),\ ('d', l_3)]$$

is a graph node that represents a state with three outgoing edges. On reading 'a', 'c', and 'd' the states l_1, l_2, l_3, respectively, are reached. The action *ac* is executed before the choice between 'a', 'c', and 'd' is made.

The actual implementation of the library **Lexers** uses two different kinds of nodes (instead of only *State*) to represent states: One kind is used for states with only a few outgoing edges and the other for states with many outgoing edges. The former uses an association list, like in the above definition, but the latter uses an array to associate input characters with successor nodes. This increases the efficiency of the lookup in case of many outgoing edges, but does not alter the essence of the actual table construction algorithm.

4.2 Basic Table Construction

Before discussing the table-construction operators, we have to fix the type definition of regular expressions.

$$type\ Regexp\ s\ t\ =\ Lexer\ s\ t\ \rightarrow\ Lexer\ s\ t$$

The essential point is that a regular expression is a lexer that can still be extended by another lexer to form a new lexer. In other words, if we have *re l*, then, if a word matching the regular expression *re* is accepted, the rest of the input is handed to the lexer *l* (which may be a final state associated with an action). In other words, we have to match an arbitrary prefix *re* before the automaton reaches *l* (remember that expressions of type (*Lexer s t*) represent states of the overall automaton), whereas an individual node of the state transition graph specifies the consumption of only a single character, together with the associated transition.

Given this, the definition of ϵ, *char*, and $\triangleright$ is straight forward.

$$\epsilon \qquad ::\ Regexp\ s\ t$$
$$\epsilon \qquad =\ id$$

$$char \quad ::\ Char\ \rightarrow\ Regexp\ s\ t$$
$$char\ c\ =\ \lambda l\ \rightarrow\ State\ NoAction\ [(c,\ l)]$$

$$(\triangleright) \qquad ::\ Regexp\ s\ t\ \rightarrow\ Regexp\ s\ t\ \rightarrow\ Regexp\ s\ t$$
$$(\triangleright) \qquad =\ (\circ)$$

The functions *id* and $(\circ)$ are the identity function and function composition, respectively. Thus, it immediately follows that ϵ is the left and right neutral of

▷, and furthermore, that ▷ is associative. Properties required by formal language theory.

The definition of *lexaction* requires a little more care:

$$lexaction \quad :: Regexp\ s\ t \rightarrow Action\ t \rightarrow Lexer\ s\ t$$
$$lexaction\ re\ a \ = \ re\ (State\ (Action\ a)\ [])$$

It adds a final state containing the given action a and no transitions to the regular expression.

The most interesting combinators are alternatives, because they introduce indeterminism when constructing an NFA; thus, as we directly construct a DFA, we immediately have to resolve this potential indeterminism. To avoid dealing with the same problems in the two combinators ▷⊹ and ⊹, we define ▷⊹ in terms of ⊹:

$$(▷⊹) \quad :: Regexp\ s\ t \rightarrow Regexp\ s\ t \rightarrow Regexp\ s\ t$$
$$re\ ▷⊹\ re' \ = \ \lambda l \rightarrow re\ l\ ⊹\ re'\ l$$

This essentially means that, given a regular expression $(re_1\ ▷⊹\ re_2)▷ re_3$, the continuation of re_1 and re_2 is the same, namely re_3. In other words, in case of an alternative, independent of which branch we take, we reach the same suffix. Given this definition, ▷⊹ is associative and commutative if ⊹ is. The latter we define as

$$(⊹) \qquad\qquad :: Lexer\ s\ t \rightarrow Lexer\ s\ t \rightarrow Lexer\ s\ t$$
$$(State\ a\ c)\ ⊹\ (State\ a'\ c') \ = \ State\ (joinActions\ a\ a')\ (accum\ (⊹)\ (c\ +\!\!+\ c'))$$

The function combines transitions and actions separately. The two transition tables c and c' are combined by $(accum\ (⊹)\ (c\ +\!\!+\ c'))$, which concatenates the association lists c and c' and applies the auxiliary functions *accum* to replace all pairs of conflicting occurrences $(c,\ l)$ and $(c,\ l')$ by a new pair $(c,\ l\ ⊹\ l')$ (we omit the precise definition of *accum*; it is slightly tedious, but does not present new insights). Finally, the following function combines two actions:

$$joinActions :: LexAction\ s\ t \rightarrow LexAction\ s\ t \rightarrow LexAction\ s\ t$$
$$joinActions\ NoAction\ a' \qquad\quad = a'$$
$$joinActions\ a \qquad NoAction = a$$
$$joinActions\ \_ \qquad\quad \_ \qquad = error\ "Lexers:\ Ambiguous\ action!"$$

If both of the two states have an action, *joinActions* raises an error; it implies that there is a lexeme that is associated with two actions, but we can only execute one of them. This indicates an error in the lexical specification. From the definition of *joinActions* and the associativity and commutativity of $+\!\!+$, we can easily deduce the associativity and commutativity of ⊹, and thus, ▷⊹.

As an example for the use of ⊹ consider

$$(char\ 'a'\ `lexaxtion`\ ac_1)\ ⊹\ (char\ 'a'\ ▷\ char\ 'b'\ `lexaxtion`\ ac_2)$$

The two regular expression have a common prefix; thus, the initial state of the resulting lexer only has a single transition for the character a. The following state contains the action ac_1—making it a final state—but also contains a transition for b. The third state contains only the action ac_2, no further transition is possible. Overall, we get the lexer

$$State\ NoAction\ [('a', State\ ac_1\ [('b', State\ ac_2\ [])])]$$

This example illustrates how an action can get in the middle of a more complex lexer. In this example, it may appear as if the choice between ac_1 and ac_2 were indeterministic when accepting ab; however, the principle of the longest match, which we shall discuss in Section 4.4, disambiguates the choice and requires the lexer to execute only ac_2.

At this point, the reason for a design decision made earlier in the definition of the *Lexer* data type also becomes clear. When considering a single regular expression and action, it might seem reasonable to pair the action with the root of the transition graph; instead of allowing an action in every state and putting the initial action at the tips of the structure representing the lexer. As we just saw, when two lexers are disjunctively combined, actions may may move in the middle of the transition graph and the exact location of an action within the graph becomes important—it is not sufficient to collect all actions at the root of the graph.

4.3   Cyclic Graphs

The remaining combinators for regular expressions, ⊛, ⊕, and ?, are build from the basic combinators that we just discussed. The definition of ? is straight forward:

$$(?)\qquad :: Regexp\ s\ t\ \to\ Regexp\ s\ t\ \to\ Regexp\ s\ t$$
$$re1?\ re2\ =\ (re1 \triangleright re2) ⧓ re2$$

The recursive behaviour of ⊛ and ⊕, however, requires some additional thought. In a first attempt, we might define ⊛ as follows:

$$(⊛)\qquad :: Regexp\ s\ t\ \to\ Regexp\ s\ t\ \to\ Regexp\ s\ t$$
$$re1⊛\ re2\ =\ \textbf{let}\ self\ =\ (re1 \triangleright self ⧓ \epsilon)\ \textbf{in}\ self \triangleright re2$$

The recursion is realised by the local definition of *self*, which can either be the empty word ϵ, or it can be a word matched by $re1$ and followed again by *self*, until finally, *self* is followed by $re2$. In other words, we can use $re1$ zero, one, or more times before continuing with $re2$. So, the above definition is correct, but unfortunately, it is operationally awkward. It does not create a cyclic graph, but produces an infinite path, repeating $re1$. As the path is constructed lazily, the definition works, but, for the construction of the state transition graph, it consumes memory and time proportional to the length of the accepted lexeme, rather than the size of the regular expression.

Fortunately, we can turn this inefficient definition by equational reasoning into an efficient, but harder to understand definition:

$$\textbf{let } self \;=\; (re1 \rhd self \,\overline{\divideontimes}\, \epsilon) \textbf{ in } self \rhd re2$$
$$=\quad \{\text{unfold } (\overline{\divideontimes})\}$$
$$\textbf{let } self \; l \;=\; (re1 \rhd self) \; l \,\overline{\divideontimes}\, \epsilon \; l \textbf{ in } self \rhd re2$$
$$=\quad \{\text{unfold } \epsilon \text{ and beta reduction}\}$$
$$\textbf{let } self \; l \;=\; (re1 \rhd self) \; l \,\overline{\divideontimes}\, l \textbf{ in } self \rhd re2$$
$$=\quad \{\text{unfold } (\rhd) \text{ and beta reduction}\}$$
$$\textbf{let } self \; l \;=\; re1 \, (self \; l) \,\overline{\divideontimes}\, l \textbf{ in } self \rhd re2$$
$$=\quad \{\text{unfold } (\rhd)\}$$
$$\textbf{let } self \; l \;=\; re1 \, (self \; l) \,\overline{\divideontimes}\, l \textbf{ in } \lambda l' \;\rightarrow\; self \, (re2 \; l')$$
$$=\quad \{\text{float let inside lambda}\}$$
$$\lambda l' \;\rightarrow\; \textbf{let } self \; l \;=\; re1 \, (self \; l) \,\overline{\divideontimes}\, l \textbf{ in } self \, (re2 \; l')$$
$$=\quad \{\text{lambda dropping}\}$$
$$\lambda l' \;\rightarrow\; \textbf{let } l \;=\; re2 \; l'; \; self \;=\; re1 \, self \,\overline{\divideontimes}\, l \textbf{ in } self$$
$$=\quad \{\text{inlining}\}$$
$$\lambda l' \;\rightarrow\; \textbf{let } self \;=\; re1 \, self \,\overline{\divideontimes}\, (re2 \; l') \textbf{ in } self$$

The reason for the different behaviour of the initial and the derived definition is that in the original definition *self* has type (*Regexp st*), which is a functional, whereas in the derived definition, it has type (*Lexer s t*), which is the datatype in which we want to create the cycle. Note in reference to the remark made at the end of Subsection 3.1 that this calculation depends on ⊛ being a binary operator (and not an unary postfix operator).

It remains the definition of ⊕, which is simple when expressed in terms of ⊛:

$$(\oplus) \qquad :: \; Regexp \; s \; t \;\rightarrow\; Regexp \; s \; t \;\rightarrow\; Regexp \; s \; t$$
$$re1 \oplus re2 \;=\; re1 \rhd (re1 \circledast re2)$$

4.4 Lexing

Given the state transition graph, we have to implement the lexing process by a traversal of the graphical DFA representation. Lazy evaluation of the graph ensures that only those portions of the table that are necessary for lexing the input at hand are actually evaluated and that each part of the graph is evaluated at most once. In Subsection 3.4, the definition of *execLexer* used a function *lexOne*, which reads a single lexeme. In the following, we encode the graph traversal in *lexOne* as a tail recursive function over the input string. The main complication in this function is the implementation of the principle of the longest match, i.e., we cannot take the first action that we encounter, but we have to take the last possible action before the automaton gets stuck. Therefore, during the traversal, we keep track of the last action that we passed along with the lexeme recognised up to this point. When no further transition is possible, we execute the last action on the associated lexeme; if there was no last action, we encountered a lexical error. The concrete definition of *lexOne* makes use of the recursive function *collect*, which collects all characters of the current lexeme. In addition to the current lexer and state, it maintains an accumulator for collecting the lexeme (third argument) and the most recently encountered action (fourth argument). The latter is initially an error, i.e., before the first valid action is encountered during lexing.

> *type OneToken s t = (Maybe t, Lexer s t, LexerState s)*
>
> *lexOne   :: Lexer s t → LexerState s → OneToken s t*
> *lexOne l state = collect l state "" (error "Lexical error!")*

A value of type *OneToken s t* comprises all information associated with a lexeme: possibly a token and the lexer to be applied and state reached after reading the lexeme.

The implementation of *collect* distinguishes three cases, dependent on the next input symbol and the transition table *cls*:

> *collect :: Lexer s t → LexerState s t → String → OneToken s t*
> *   → OneToken s t*
> *collect (State a cls) state@(cs, pos, s) lexeme last =*
>   **let** *last′ = action a state lexeme last*
>   **in**
>   **case** *cs* **of**
>   []   → *last′*
>   (c : cs′) → **case** *lookup c cls* **of**
>   *Nothing* → *last′*
>   *Just l′* → *collect l′ (cs′, pos, s) (lexeme ++ [c]) last′*

We use the auxiliary function *action* to compute the most recent action result *last′*. It applies actions to the current lexer state and the recognised lexeme; we shall return to its definition below. To decide how to react to the current input character *c*, we perform a *lookup* in the transition table *cls*.[4] If the character is not in the transition table (i.e., there is no valid transition in the DFA for the current input symbol), we use the most recent result of an action, namely *last′*. Otherwise, the automaton makes a transition to the state *l′*, which is associated with the current input symbol *c* in the transition table; furthermore, the current lexeme is extended with the character just read.

The function *action* deals with the three possible cases of the data type *LexAction* as follows:

> *action :: LexAction s t → LexerState s t → String → OneToken s t*
> *   → OneToken s t*
> *action NoAction _   _   last = last*
> *action (Action a) (cs, pos, s) lexeme _ =*
>   *(a lexeme, l, (cs, advancePos pos lexeme, s))*

---

[4] The function *lookup :: Eq a ⇒ a → [(a, b)] → Maybe b* is from the Haskell prelude.

$action\ (Meta\ f)\ \ (cs,\ pos,\ s)\ lexeme\ _\ \ =$
$\quad \textbf{let}\ (pos',\ s',\ l') = f\ (advancePos\ pos\ lexeme)\ s$
$\quad \textbf{in}$
$\quad (Nothing,\ fromMaybe\ l\ l',\ (cs,\ pos',\ s'))$

The function *advancePos* adjust the current position by the length of the given lexeme (its definition is not given, as we did not fix a concrete representation for positions). In the third equation of *action* (the case of a meta action), the function of the meta action is applied to yield a new position *pos'*, user-defined state *s'*, and possibly a new lexer *l'*. The function *fromMaybe* selects the new lexer if given; otherwise, it uses the current lexer *l*.[5] It should be clear that keeping track of the last action in the fourth argument of *collect* and *action* realises the principle of the longest match and, by means of lazy evaluation, delays the execution of the candidate actions until it is known which one is the last.

Accumulating the lexeme by appending individual list elements with ++, as in the above definition of *collect* is inefficient. In the Lexers library, difference lists (similar to *ShowS* from the Haskell prelude) are used, which allow constant time appends.

5 Benchmarks

The performance of the presented technique was measured by coding a lexer for the programming language C with the Lexers library as well as implementing a *handcoded* lexer for the same set of regular expressions. The comparison between the two gives an estimate of the overhead incurred when using the more convenient Lexers library. The handcoded lexer implements the DFA using pattern matching on the first character of the remaining input. It carries the same overhead as Lexers for keeping track of token positions; there is still scope for optimisations, but they are not expected to make a big difference. The programs were compiled with the Glasgow Haskell Compiler (GHC), version 4.04, using optimisation level -O. The experiments were conducted on a 300Mhz Celeron processor under Linux. In the Haskell source of the library and the specification of the C lexer, no GHC-specific optimisations or language features were used; the input string was naively represented as a cons list of characters. The benchmark input to the lexer is (a) an artificial code, which contains a struct with 10 fields a 1000 times, and (b) the header file of the GTK+ GUI library after being expanded by a standard C pre-processor. Both files are about 200 kilobyte, i.e., they are real stress tests, not toy examples. The results are summarised in the following table (they do not include I/O time and are the best results from three runs on an unloaded machine):

These results show that for large input, the optimising lexer combinators are in the same ball park as a handcoded lexer, which needs about 70% of the execution time.

---

[5] Haskell's standard library *Maybe* defines *fromMaybe* :: $a \rightarrow Maybe\ a \rightarrow a$.

input	size (byte)	Lexers		handcoded		%
		time (sec)	tokens/sec	time (sec)	tokens/sec	
GTK+	233,406	1.99	16,550	1.52	21,668	76%
structs	207,000	2.36	25,338	1.69	35,384	72%

6 Related Work

In comparison to off-line scanner generators, the added flexibility and ease of use of the presented approach comes for increased startup costs (as the graph has to be build) and the inability to perform some optimisations on the automaton (like computing the minimal automaton). However, lazy evaluation avoids the startup costs partially if the given input requires only some of the regular expressions of the lexical specification.

Regarding related work, the main part of the paper made the relation to the automata theory underlying scanner generators clear. It would be interesting to establish a formal correspondence between the DFA created by the lexer combinators and those produced by the various off-line automata construction algorithms. I do not have a formal result yet, but believe that the automata is the same as the one constructed by the algorithm from the dragonbook [1] that constructs an DFA directly from a set of regular expression. Furthermore, the dragonbook [1, p. 128] mentions a technique called *lazy transition evaluation*. It also constructs a transition table at runtime, but the aim is to avoid the state explosion that can occur during the generation of a DFA from regular expressions—in the worst case, the number of states of the DFA can grow exponentially with the size of the regular expression. In this technique, state transitions are stored in a cache of fixed size. In case of a cache miss, the transition is computed using standard algorithms and stored in the cache; it may later be removed from the cache if it is not used for a while and many other transitions are needed. This technique, however, makes essential use of mutable data structures and is substantially different from the presented one, in both its aim and working principle—it was developed for the use in search routines of text editors.

Swierstra and Duponcheel's [7] parser combinators provided the inspiration for searching for a related technique that works for lexical analysis. Like their approach is based on the theory of SLL(1) stack automata, the present technique is based on the theory of finite state automata. The technique itself, however, is significantly different.

7 Conclusion

We have discussed an approach to lexical analysis in a lazy functional language that combines the ease of use and flexibility of combinator libraries with the efficiency of lexical analyser generators. In this approach, a lexical analyser is specified as a set of pairs of regular expressions and actions using functions from a combinator library. The combinators are smart constructors, building a state transition graph of a deterministic finite state automaton implementing the regular expressions. The graph is lazily constructed during lexing and makes use of cycles to represent the recursive combinators ⊛ and ⊕.

It is worth noting that the discussed technique makes essential use of laziness and can be regarded as a practical example of the usefulness of lazy evaluation. First of all, non-strictness allows to significantly optimise the implementation of recursive combinators by exploiting cyclic structures. Furthermore, the lazy construction of the state transition graph minimises startup costs when the input does not use all regular expressions of the lexical specification. However, the use of cyclic structures is definitely an advanced feature of Haskell, which requires some experience to use; we showed how equational reasoning can help to compute an efficient solution that makes use of cyclic structures from a less efficient, but easier to understand implementation. Furthermore, the implementation of the principle of the longest match is simplified by using lazy evaluation to keep track of the last action.

The use of a lazy list of characters for the input to the lexer is definitely not the most efficient choice. However, it simplifies the presentation and only the function *collect* depends on the representation of the input. It should not be hard to adapt it to a more efficient form of reading the character stream. Furthermore, it might seem attractive to represent lexers as monads; this presents, however, some technical challenges, similar to those reported in [7].

Regarding future work, it would be interesting to investigate whether the whole algorithm could be formally derived from the underlying automata theory, which was only informally described in this paper.

Acknowledgements. I am indebted to Simon Peyton Jones for a number of suggestions that helped to improve this paper and the **Lexers** library considerably. Furthermore, I am grateful to Gabriele Keller and the anonymous referees for their helpful comments and suggestions on the paper. Finally, I like to thank Roman Lechtchinsky for his feedback on the **Lexers** library.

References

1. Alfred V. Aho, Ravi Sethi, and Jeffrey D. Ullman. *Compilers — Principles, Techniques, and Tools.* Addison-Wesley Publishing Company, 1986.
2. Andrew W. Appel, James S. Mattson, and David R. Tardit. A lexical analyzer generator for Standard ML. http://cm.bell-labs.com/cm/cs/what/smlnj/doc/ML-Lex/manual.html, 1994.
3. Graham Hutton. Higher-order functions for parsing. *Journal of Functional Programming*, 2(3):323–343, 1992.
4. Graham Hutton and Erik Meijer. Monadic parsing in Haskell. *Journal of Functional Programming*, 8(4):437–444, 1998.
5. Simon Marlow. Happy user guide. http://www.dcs.gla.ac.uk/fp/software/happy/doc/happy.html, 1997.

6. Rishiyur S. Nikhil, Arvind, James E. Hicks, Shail Aditya, Lennart Augustsson, Jan-Willem Maessen, and Y. Zhou. pH language reference manual, version 1.0. Technical Report CSG-Memo-369, Massachussets Institute of Technology, Laboratory for Computer Science, 1995.

7. S. D. Swierstra and L. Duponcheel. Deterministic, error-correcting combinator parsers. In John Launchbury, Erik Meijer, and Tim Sheard, editors, *Advanced Functional Programming*, volume 1129 of *Lecture Notes in Computer Science*, pages 184–207. Springer-Verlag, 1996.

8. David R. Tarditi and Andrew W. Appel. ML-Yacc user's manual. http://cm.bell-labs.com/cm/cs/what/smlnj/doc/ML-Yacc/manual.html, 1994.

9. William W. Waite and Gerhard Goos. *Compiler Construction*. Springer-Verlag, second edition, 1985.

A Functional-Logic Perspective of Parsing

Rafael Caballero and Francisco J. López-Fraguas *

Departamento de Sistemas Informáticos y Programación
Universidad Complutense de Madrid
{rafa,fraguas}@sip.ucm.es

Abstract. Parsing has been a traditional workbench for showing the virtues of declarative programming. Both logic and functional programming claim the ability of writing parsers in a natural and concise way. We address here the task from a functional-logic perspective. By modelling parsers as non-deterministic functions we achieve a very natural manner of building parsers, which combines the nicest properties of the functional and logic approaches. In particular, we are able to define parsers within our framework in a style very close to that of functional programming parsers, but using simpler concepts. Moreover, we have moved beyond usual declarative approaches to parsers, since the functional-logic parsers presented here can be considered as truly data values. As an example of this feature we define a function that detects ambiguous grammars.

1 Introduction

The problem of syntax analysis or *parsing* has been one of the most thoroughly studied issues in computer science. Its wide range of applications, from compiler development to natural language recognition, is enough to attract the attention of any programming approach. This has also been the case for logic programming (LP, in short) and functional programming (FP, in short), and the parsing problem constitutes in fact one of the favorite fields for exhibiting the virtues of declarative programming, looking for a straightforward way of representing parsers as proper components of the language. This has been achieved by considering *recursive descendent parsers*, usually represented by means of language mechanisms adapted to simulate grammar rules (e.g. BNF rules).

There is a more or less standard approach [19] to the construction of parsers in LP, which is based on a specific representation for grammars, the so-called *Definite Clause Grammars (DCG's)*. DCG's are not logic programs, although they are readily translated to them. With *DCG's*, one can hide the details of handling the input string to be parsed, which is passed from parser to parser using the LP technique of *difference lists*. Parsing in LP benefits from the expressive power of non-determinism, which handles almost effortlessly the non-deterministic essence

* Work partially supported by the Spanish CICYT (project TIC98-0445-C03-02/97 "TREND") and the ESPRIT Working Group 22457 (CCL-II).

A. Middeldorp, T. Sato (Eds.): FLOPS'99, LNCS 1722, pp. 85–99, 1999.

of grammar specifications. In the case of ambiguous grammars this means that multiple solutions are automatically provided where possible. The use of logical variables and unification are also useful in LP parsers. They ease the construction of output representations, which is carried out explicitly by using an input/output extra argument. Moreover, multiple modes of use are allowed, i.e. LP parsers can be regarded as *generators* as well as recognizers of sentences, and parsers for some context sensitive languages can be easily defined.

The main contribution of FP parsers are the so called *higher order* combinators [13,6]. In addition, the use of *monads* (see [20]), specially in combination with the *do notation* [14] gives a very appealing structure to the parsers.

Many efforts have been done in the last decade in order to integrate LP and FP into a single paradigm, *functional-logic programming* (FLP in short, see [10] for a survey). As any other paradigm, FLP should develop its own programming techniques and methodologies, but little work has been done from this point of view. In this paper the problem of developing FLP parsers in a systematic way is addressed, trying to answer the question: can FLP contribute significantly by itself (not just mimicking LP or FP) to the task of writing parsers?

We will show how a suitable combination of LP and FP features leads to parser definitions as expressive as FP parsers, but based on simpler concepts. Moreover, we have moved beyond current FP and LP approaches to parsers, for the FLP parsers presented here can be considered as *truly data values*. Thus, interesting properties of the represented grammar, such as ambiguity, can be easily examined in our purely declarative setting. We stick to a view of FLP whose core notion is that of *non-deterministic function*. A framework for such an approach is given in [7], which is extended to cope with higher-order features in [8], and polymorphic algebraic types in [2].

The rest of the paper is organized as follows. In the next section we will briefly describe the specific functional-logic language we are going to use: $\mathcal{TOY}$. Section 3 examines the main characteristics of parsers in LP and FP, choosing the best features of each paradigm to define our model of FLP parsers. Section 4 is devoted to the definition of some basic parsers and parser combinators. These functions are the basic pieces we will use to build more complicated parsers, like the examples presented in Section 5. In Section 6 we show how the 'intensional' view of functions allows $\mathcal{TOY}$ programs to manipulate parsers as truly data values. In particular, a suitable *fold* function for parsers in $\mathcal{TOY}$ is defined, together with an application of such function used to detect ambiguous grammars. Finally, Section 7 summarizes some conclusions.

2   A Succinct Description of $\mathcal{TOY}$

All the programs in the next sections are written in $\mathcal{TOY}$ [17], a purely declarative functional-logic language with solid theoretical foundations, which can be found in [7,8,2]. We present here the subset of the language relevant to this work (see [3] for a more complete description and a number of representative examples).

A $\mathcal{TOY}$ program consists of *datatype*, *type alias* and *infix operator* definitions, and rules for defining *functions*. Syntax is mostly borrowed from Haskell [12], with the remarkable exception that variables begin with upper-case letters whereas constructor symbols use lower-case, as function symbols do. In particular, functions are *curried* and the usual conventions about associativity of application hold.

Datatype definitions like data nat = zero | suc nat, define new (possibly polymorphic) *constructed types* and determine a set of *data constructors* for each type. The set of all data constructor symbols will be noted as CS (CS^n for all constructors of arity n).

Types $\tau, \tau', \ldots$ can be constructed types, tuples $(\tau_1, \ldots, \tau_n)$, or functional types of the form $\tau \rightarrow \tau'$. As usual, $\rightarrow$ associates to the right. $\mathcal{TOY}$ provides predefined types such as [A] (the type of polymorphic lists, for which Prolog notation is used), bool (with constants true and false), int, real for integer and real numbers, or char (with constants 'a','b', ...). *Type alias* definitions like type parser A = [A] $\rightarrow$ [A] are also allowed. Type alias are simply abbreviations, but they are useful for writing more readable, self-documenting programs. Strings (for which we have the definition type string = [char]) can also be written with double quotes. For instance, "sugar" is the same as ['s','u','g','a','r'].

The purpose of a $\mathcal{TOY}$ program is to define a set FS of functions. Each $f \in FS$ comes with a given *program arity* which expresses the number of arguments that must be given to f in order to make it reducible. We use FS^n for the set of function symbols with program arity n. Each $f \in FS^n$ has an associated principal type of the form $\tau_1 \rightarrow \ldots \rightarrow \tau_m \rightarrow \tau$ (where τ does not contain $\rightarrow$). Number m is called the *type arity* of f and well-typedness implies that $m \geq n$. As usual in functional programming, types are inferred and, optionally, can be declared in the program.

With the symbols in CS and FS, together with a set of variables X, Y, ..., we form more complex expressions. We distinguish two important syntactic domains: *expressions* and *patterns*. *Expressions* are of the form $e ::= X \mid c \mid f \mid (e_1, \ldots, e_n) \mid (e\ e')$, where $c \in CS$, $f \in FS$. As usual, application associates to the left and parentheses can be omitted accordingly. Therefore $e\ e_1 \ldots e_n$ is the same as $((\ldots((e\ e_1)\ e_2)\ldots)e_n)$. Of course expressions are assumed to be well-typed. *Patterns* are a special kind of expressions which can be understood as denoting data values, i.e. values not subject to further evaluation, in contrast with expressions, which can be possibly reduced by means of the rules of the program. They are defined by $t ::= X \mid (t_1, \ldots, t_n) \mid c\ t_1 \ldots t_n \mid f\ t_1 \ldots t_n$, where $c \in CS^m$, $n \leq m$, $f \in FS^m$, $n < m$. Notice that partial applications (i.e., application to less arguments than indicated by the arity) of c and f are allowed as patterns, which are then called *HO patterns*, because they have a functional type. Therefore function symbols, when partially applied, behave as data constructors. HO patterns can be manipulated as any other patterns; in particular, they can be used for matching or checked for equality. With this *intensional* point of view, functions become 'first-class citizens' in a stronger sense that in the case of 'classical' FP. This treatment of HO features is borrowed from [8] and will constitute an useful tool in Sect. 6. Each function $f \in FS^n$ is defined by a set of conditional rules of the form $f\ t_1 \ldots t_n = e \Leftarrow e_1 == e'_1, \ldots, e_k == e'_k$ where $(t_1 \ldots t_n)$ forms a tuple of linear (i.e., with no repeated variable) *patterns*, and e, e_i, e'_i are *expressions*. No other conditions (except well-typedness) are imposed to function definitions. The notation V@pat, with V a variable name and pat a valid pattern, is allowed for the patterns t_i. It represents the so-called *as patterns*: every occurrence of V in the body or the conditions of the rule will be automatically replaced by pat.

Rules have a conditional reading: $f\ t_1 \ldots t_n$ can be reduced to e if all the conditions $e_1 == e'_1, \ldots, e_k == e'_k$ are satisfied. The condition part is omitted if $k = 0$. The symbol == stands for *strict equality*, which is the suitable notion (see e.g. [10]) for equality when non-strict functions are considered. With this notion a condition e == e' can be read as: e and e' can be reduced to the same pattern. When used in the condition of a rule, == is better understood as a constraint (if it is not satisfiable, the computation fails), but the language contemplates also another use of == as a function, returning the value true in the case described above, but false when a clash of constructors is detected while reducing both sides. As a syntactic facility, $\mathcal{TOY}$ allows repeating variables in the head of rules but in this case repetitions are removed by introducing new variables and strict equations in the condition of the rule. As an example, the rule f X X = 0 would be transformed into f X Y = 0 $\Leftarrow$ X == Y.

In addition to ==, $\mathcal{TOY}$ incorporates other predefined functions like the arithmetic functions +,*, ..., or if_then and if_then_else, for which the more usual syntax if _ then _ and if _ then _ else _ is allowed. Symbols ==,+,* are all examples of *infix operators*. New operators can be defined in $\mathcal{TOY}$ by means of *infix* declarations, like infixr 50 ++ which introduces ++ (used for list concatenation, with standard definition) as a right associative operator with priority 50. *Sections*, or partial applications of infix operators, like (==3) or (3==) are also allowed.

Predicates are seen in $\mathcal{TOY}$ as true-valued functions. *Clausal notation* is allowed, according to the syntax $p\ t_1 \ldots t_n :- b_1, \ldots, b_m$ which is simply a syntactic sugar for the functional rule $p\ t_1 .. t_n = true \Leftarrow b_1 == true, \ldots, b_m == true$.

A distinguishing feature of $\mathcal{TOY}$, heavily used throughout this paper, is that no confluence properties are required for programs, and therefore functions can be *non-deterministic*, i.e. return several values for given (even ground) arguments. For example, the rules coin = 0 and coin = 1 constitute a valid definition for the 0-ary non-deterministic function coin. A possible reduction of coin would lead to the value 0, but there is another one giving the value 1. The system will try the first rule first, but if backtracking is required by a later failure or by request of the user, the second one will be tried. Another way of introducing non-determinism is by putting *extra* variables in the right side of the rules, like in z_list = [0|L]. Although in this case z_list reduces only to [0|L], the free variable L can be later on instantiated to any list. Therefore, any list of integers beginning with 0 is a possible value of z_list. Our language adopts the so called *call time choice* semantics for non-deterministic functions. Call-time choice has the following intuitive meaning: given a function call $(f\ e_1 \ldots e_n)$, one chooses some fixed value for each of the e_i before applying the rules for f. As an example, if we consider the function double X = X+X, then the expression (double coin) can be reduced to 0 and 2, but not to 1. As it is shown in [7], call-time choice is perfectly compatible with non-strict semantics and lazy evaluation, provided *sharing* is performed for all the occurrences of a variable in the right-hand side of a rule.

Computing in $\mathcal{TOY}$ means solving *goals*, which take the form $e_1 == e'_1, \ldots, e_k == e'_k$, giving as result a substitution for the variables in the goal making it true. Evaluation of expressions (required for solving the conditions) is done by a variant of lazy narrowing based on the so-called *demand driven strategy* (see [16]). With respect to higher-order functions, a first order translation following [9] is performed.

3   Our Model of Parsers

In declarative programming we aim at defining parsers denoting the structure of the underlying grammar. Consider the following production, written in extended BNF syntax <expr> ::= <term><plus_minus><expr> | <term>.
In order to translate properly this rule into a declarative program, we must come out to some decisions:
(i) How to represent the alternative of parsers, denoted in the rule above by the symbol |.
(ii) How to represent a sequence of parsers like <term><plus_minus><expr>.
(iii) Moreover, the parser expr should not only recognize when a sentence belongs to the underlying formal language. It should also return a suitable representation of the parsed sentence. Hence we must take care of representations when deciding the final structure of parsers.

Before considering these questions in our setting, we will briefly overview the characteristics of parsers in the two main declarative paradigms. In FLP we could remain attached to either the FP or the LP point of view, but we will show how a careful combination of both perspectives leads to the same expressiveness with simpler parser definitions. In the following discussion the LP point of view is represented by Prolog, while functional parsers are those of Haskell as described in [6,20,14].

3.1   Review of LP and FP Parsers

As common ground, both paradigms represent the sentence to be parsed as a list of terminals. This list is provided as an input parameter to the parser, which tries to recognize a prefix returning the non-consumed part. This part, the output sentence, is then supplied as input for the next parser connected in sequence. Now we summarize some of the main differences between both approaches with respect to the points (i), (ii) and (iii) mentioned above.

In **Logic Programming** all the values need to be arguments of some predicate. Thus the input and output sentences and the representation must be parameters of the parser predicate. In addition to that:

(i) The non-deterministic nature of grammar specifications is easily handled in Prolog, just representing different alternatives through different rules for the same predicate. The built-in mechanism of Prolog will initially choose the first rule. If it fails, or more solutions are requested by the user, the next alternative is tried by means of *backtracking*.

(ii) Input and output lists are explicit arguments when writing parsers in sequence, as witnessed by the Prolog definition: `expr(I,O) :- term(I,Aux1)`, `plus_minus(Aux1,Aux2), expr(Aux2,O)`. This notation is rather tedious, and is avoided in Prolog systems by introducing a new formalism which conceals the passing of parameters, namely the DCG's. Using DCG's one can write the more appealing rule `expr ⟶ term, plus_minus, expr`.

(iii) The representation also needs to be an argument, usually used as an output value. However, in this case, it is not a problem but an advantage, as it permits defining explicitly the construction of new representations from those of their components, as in the definition:

$$\text{expr(R)} \longrightarrow \text{term(T) , [+], expr(E), \{R is T+E\}.}$$
$$\text{expr(R)} \longrightarrow \text{term(R).}$$

In **Functional Programming**, input values must be parameters of functions, and output values must be results of evaluating functions. Therefore, the input sentence is the only input parameter of a parser function, while the representation and the output sentence are its result value, usually in the shape of a pair `(repr,sent)`. The solutions provided to the questions of the points (i), (ii) and (iii) mentioned above are:

(i) Since non-determinism is not a built-in mechanism of functional languages, the alternative of parsers need to be 'simulated'. This problem can be solved by collecting in a list the results of trying each alternative, hence representing different alternatives through different elements of the list. In such a context, an empty list means that the parser has failed. Therefore the type of FP parsers is `type Parser rep sym = [sym] → [ (rep,[sym]) ]`. The alternative operator can be defined now as: `(p <|> q) s = (p s) ++ (q s)`.

(ii) The sequence of parsers can be defined by a suitable HO combinator `<*>`, which hides the passing of the output sentence of each parser as input sentence of the next one. However, the definition of `<*>` depends also on the representation, as explained in the following point.

(iii) Often the representation of a parser function must be defined in relation to the representations of its components. In FP this is achieved through the definition of the sequence operator:
`(p <*> q) s = [ (y,s'') | (x,s')← p s, (y,s'')← (q x) s' ]` which has to deal with representations and not only with output sentences. In order to build the parser representation, the operator `<*>` takes out the representation

of the parser p, which is used as input argument for the function q, usually a lambda abstraction.

These operators, together with suitable declarations of priority and associativity, allow us to define

```
expr = term <*> λt.plus_minus <*> λo.expr <*> λe.return (o t e)
       <|> term
```

where t stands for a number representing the evaluation of term, o stands for a functional value ($+$ or $-$) and e denotes the result of evaluating the expression of the right-hand side. Function return can be defined as return x s = [(x,s)]. If we consider parsers as *monads* (see [20]), this notation can be abbreviated by using the *do notation* [14], which is provided as a syntactic sugar to combine monads in sequence:

```
expr = do { t ← term, o ← plus_minus, e ← expr, return (o t e)}
       <|> term
```

3.2   Parsers in $\mathcal{TOY}$

Now we are ready to define our model of parsers. In $\mathcal{TOY}$, we distinguish between parsers without representation, which we will call simply *parsers,* and *parsers with representation.* Parsers in $\mathcal{TOY}$ have the simple type:

```
parser Sym = [Sym] → [Sym]
```

that is, they take a sentence and return the non-consumed part of the sentence. Usually Sym stands for char, but in section 5.3 we will see an example of a language whose sentences are lists of integer numbers.

(i) The solution for the alternative of parsers provided by LP is simpler than that of FP. However, the introduction of the HO combinator <|> in FP permits a more expressive notation. In $\mathcal{TOY}$ we can combine the expressiveness of HO combinators of FP with the simpler definitions allowed by non-deterministic features of logic languages: A suitable non-deterministic HO combinator <|> can be defined in $\mathcal{TOY}$ as

```
(P <|> Q) Sent = P Sent
(P <|> Q) Sent = Q Sent
```

Therefore, parsers in out setting will be non-deterministic functions. This notion reflects the non-deterministic essence of grammar definitions and has been used for theoretical purposes already (see [15]).

(ii) The definition of a sequence combinator <*> in FP avoids the introduction of *ad hoc* mechanisms such as DCG's. However this definition is complicated as it must take care of representations. In $\mathcal{TOY}$ the combinator <*> can be defined as: (P1 <*> P2) I = P2 O1 ⟸ P1 I == O1   that is, the first parser P1 is applied to the input sentence I, and then the second parser is applied to the value O1 returned by P1.

(iii) The solution provided by LP for handling representations is much simpler than the FP solution. Therefore, the representations in $\mathcal{TOY}$ will be extra (usually output) arguments of the parser functions. The type of parsers with representation is: `type parser_rep Rep Sym = Rep → parser Sym` . Observe however that the type of parsers in FP (`type Parser r s = [s] → (r,[s])`) more clearly reflects the usual intended mode of the parameters. Nevertheless we choose the type above because it will lead to simpler parser definitions. It is worth noticing that if P is of type `parser_rep` then P R will be of type `parser`. Hence, we do not need to define an special sequence combinator for parsers with representation: the operator `<*>` can also be used in such situations.

An alternative combinator for parsers with representation is, however, necessary. It can be easily defined as: `(P1 <||> P2) Rep = P1 Rep <|> P2 Rep`, meaning that the alternative of values of type `parser_rep` is converted into an alternative of values of type `parser` as soon as the representation Rep is provided.

As a convenient tool for attaching representations to parsers we define the combinator `>>`, which converts a parser in a parser_rep, as:

$$(\gg) :: \text{parser A} \to \text{B} \to \text{parser\_rep B A}$$
$$(\text{P} \gg \text{Expr}) \text{ R I = O} \Longleftarrow \text{P I == O, Expr == R}$$

That is, the variable R standing for the representation is matched with the expression Expr after applying the parser to the input sentence.

Before ending this section we declare the precedence of the combinators `<*>`, `>>`, `<|>` and `<||>`, together with their associativity. These definitions allow one to omit unnecessary parentheses.

```
infixr 40 <*>          infixr 30 >>          infixr 20 <|>, <||>
```

4   Simple Parsers and Combinators

In this section we introduce a set of simple parsers and parser combinators that we will use to build more complicated parsers later. They are also our first examples of parsers in $\mathcal{TOY}$ and are based on the FP parsers described in [6,13].

The simplest parser, empty, recognizes the empty sentence, which is a prefix of every sentence. Hence, empty always succeeds without consuming any prefix of its input:

```
empty:: parser A
empty S = S
```

Parser `terminal T` recognizes a single symbol T, failing otherwise.

```
terminal:: A → parser A
terminal T [T|L] = L
```

Sometimes it is desirable to recognize not a fixed symbol, but any one fulfilling a given property P. Function `satisfy` accomplishes this aim:

$$\text{satisfy}:: (A \rightarrow \text{bool}) \rightarrow \text{parser\_rep } A \ A$$
$$\text{satisfy P X } [X|L] = \text{if P X then L}$$

Notice that `satisfy P` is a parser with representation, as it returns as representation the recognized terminal X.

In section 3 we introduced some parser combinators: `<*>` , `<|>` and `>>` . Here we introduce two new ones: `star` and `some`. Combinator `star` represents the repetition zero or more times of the parser with representation P. The representation retrieved by `star P` is a list collecting the representations of each repetition of P.

$$\text{star}:: \text{parser\_rep } A \ B \rightarrow \text{parser\_rep } [A] \ B$$
$$\text{star P } = \text{ P X } \texttt{<*>} \text{ (star P) Xs } \texttt{>>} \text{ [X|Xs]}$$
$$\texttt{<|>} \text{ empty} \qquad\qquad \texttt{>>} \text{ []}$$

Function `some` represents the repetition at least once of the same parser, and can be defined easily in terms of `star`: `some P = P X <*> star P Xs  >>  [X|Xs]`.

5   Examples

This section is devoted to present some examples of parsers in $\mathcal{TOY}$. We intend to show how, by means of the simple basic parsers and parser combinators defined before, we achieve the same expressiveness as FP parsers. Furthermore, interesting capabilities of LP parsers, such as the possibility of generating sentences instead of recognizing them are preserved.

5.1   Arithmetic Expressions

The parser shown in figure 1 recognizes arithmetic expressions made from integer numbers, the operators $+$, $-$, $*$, $/$ and parentheses. The main parser is `expression` which returns as representation the numeric value of the expression. The first rule says that an expression is either a term followed by an operator $+$ or - and ended by another expression or simply a term. In the first case the combinator `>>` shows that the representation of the expression is the result of applying the representation of the operator to those of the two other components. In the second case the representation of the expression is the representation of the term. Among the rest of the parsers, we must point out the introduction of a function `numeric_value` which converts a string of digits into its numeric value. The definition of this function relies on the standard functions `foldl1` and `map`: `numeric_value L = foldl1 ((+).(10*)) (map val L)` and constitutes a typical example of how FLP inherits the higher-order machinery usual in FP. For instance, the goal `expression R "(10+5*2)/4" == []` succeeds with R == 5.

```
expression  =  term T <*> plus_minus Op <*> expression E  >> (Op T E)
               <|> term

term        =  factor F <*> prod_div Op <*> term T  >> (Op F T)
               <|> factor

factor      =  terminal '(' <*> expression E <*> terminal ')'  >> E
               <|> num

plus_minus  =  terminal '+'  >> (+)
               <|> terminal '-'  >> (-)
prod_div    =  terminal '*'  >> (*)
               <|> terminal '/'  >> (/)

num         =  some digit L  >> (numeric_value L)
digit       =  satisfy is_digit
```

Fig. 1. Parser for arithmetic expressions

5.2   Parsers as Generators

Owing to the possibility of including logical variables in goals, FLP parsers may
be regarded as generators as well as recognizers. Consider for instance the parser

```
p = empty <|>  a <|>  b <|>  a <*> p <*> a <|>  b <*> p <*> b
a = terminal 'a'
b = terminal 'b'
```

which recognizes the language of the palindrome words over the alphabet $\Sigma = \{a, b\}$. Using this parser we may 'ask' for sentences of length two in the language
recognized by p: p [X,Y] == []. Two answers are retrieved, namely X='a',
Y='a' and X='b', Y='b', meaning that "aa" and "bb" are the only words of
length two in this language.

5.3   Numerical Constraints

The growing interest in languages representing spatial relationships has introduced the study of *numerical constraints* in relation to the parsing problem. Here
we show a very simple but suggestive example of how our parsers can integrate
numerical constraints easily.

Suppose we are interested in a parser for recognizing *boxes*, regarding a box
as a rectangle whose sides are parallel to the X and Y axes. The terminals
of the language will be pairs of integers representing points in the plane, and
a valid sentence will be a sequence of four points standing for the corners of
the box, beginning with the lower-left and following anti-clockwise. The desired

representation is a pair of points representing the lower-left and the upper-right corners of the box.

```
box:: parser_rep ((real,real),(real,real)) (real,real)
box  = point (X1,Y1) <*> point (X2,Y2) <*>
       point (X3,Y3) <*> point (X4,Y4)  >> ((X1,Y1),(X3,Y3))
       <== Y1==Y2, X1==X4, X2==X3,Y4==Y3, Y1<Y4, X1<X2

point:: parser_rep (real,real) (real,real)
point = terminal (X,Y)  >> (X,Y)
```

The conditions assure that the points actually represent a box. Note that these constraints are settled before parsing the point. As a consequence, if the points do not have the shape of a box, the parser can fail as soon as possible. For instance, if the condition Y1==Y2 is not verified, the parser will fail just after parsing the second point. For our example to work properly, the language must be able to handle numerical constraints concerning still uninstantiated variables, and to check incrementally the accumulated constraints whenever new ones are imposed during the computation. Such an extension of the language considered so far is described in [1], and is actually implemented in the system $\mathcal{TOY}$ (with such this example is indeed executable). For example we can fix two points of the box and ask $\mathcal{TOY}$ for the conditions that the other two points must satisfy to form a box: box R [(1,2), (4,2), P, Q] == [] . The goal succeeds, and $\mathcal{TOY}$ returns the answer   R == ((1, 2), (4, _A))   P == (4, _A)   Q == (1, _A)   {_A>2.0 } which are the equations that the variables must satisfy, including an arithmetical constraint.

6 Parsers as Data

In previous sections the advantages of defining parsers in $\mathcal{TOY}$ have been discussed. Here we intend to show how functional-logic languages allowing higher-order patterns can consider parsers as *truly first class data values*, in a broader sense of the term than usual. It is worthwhile to point out that the following discussion is held in a purely declarative framework.

6.1 The Structure of $\mathcal{TOY}$ Parsers

Consider the parser ab defined as: ab = terminal 'a' <*> terminal 'b' Function ab can reduce directly to its right-hand side (terminal 'a' <*> terminal 'b'), while <*> and terminal need to be applied to the input sentence in order to reduce. Therefore we can say that the 'structure' of ab has the shape A <*> B, where both A and B are of the form terminal T. The interesting point is that A <*> B and terminal T are valid HO patterns in $\mathcal{TOY}$ (see Sec. 2). In general, any parser P defined through the *basic components* {<*> , <|>, >> , empty, satisfy, terminal}, can be decomposed by matching it with suitable HO patterns. In this context, the basic components can be effectively considered as *data constructors*, and parsers as *data values*.

6.2 Folding Parsers

Functions *fold* are widely used in FP. They replace the constructors of data structures by given functions. The most usual examples of these constructions are those that handle lists, i.e. the standard functions `foldr`, `foldl`, ..., but the same technique can be applied to other structures (see [18] for many examples). As we have shown above, parsers can be considered data values, and hence we can define a function `foldp` that replaces the constructors of a parser by arbitrary functions. The definition is a little bit tedious, but straightforward:

```
foldp (Emp,_,_,_,_,_)   empty       = Emp
foldp (_,Ter,_,_,_,_)   (terminal T) = Ter T
foldp (_,_,Sat,_,_,_)   (satisfy P R) = Sat P R
foldp F@(_,_,_,Seq,_,_) ((<*>) A B)  = Seq (foldp F A) (foldp F B)
foldp F@(_,_,_,_,Alt,_) ((<|>) A B)  = Alt (foldp F A) (foldp F B)
foldp F@(_,_,_,_,_,Rep) (( >>) A B R) = Rep (foldp F A) B R
```

The first argument of `foldp` is a tuple of the form (`Emp`, `Ter`, `Sat`, `Seq`, `Alt`, `Rep`) with the functions that will replace the 'constructors' `empty`, `terminal`, `satisfy`, `<*>` , `<|>` and `>>` respectively. The second argument is the parser we want to 'fold'. Function `foldp` is recursively applied, replacing each constructor by its correspondent function. At first sight, function `foldp` might seem useless. Indeed, most of the parser definitions are recursive, and hence their basic structures are infinite: function `foldp` would peer into such structures forever, if normal forms were being looked for. Instead we will show that, due to lazy evaluation, function `foldp` allows us to check interesting properties of the represented grammar, such as ambiguity. Observe that (apart from syntactic details) the definition of `foldp` is by no means a valid *Haskell* program, due to the presence of HO patterns.

6.3 Checking Ambiguity

We say that a grammar specification is ambiguous when a sentence exists with more than one parse tree. Consider for instance the grammar represented by the following $\mathcal{TOY}$ parser (we have labelled the productions with P1, P2 and P3):

```
s = terminal 'i' <*> s <*> terminal 'e' <*> s (P1)
    <|> terminal 'i' <*> s                      (P2)
    <|> terminal 'o'                            (P3)
```

This grammar is ambiguous, since the sentence *iioeo* can be derived following either the left derivation *P1, P2, P3, P3* or *P2, P1, P3, P3*. As ambiguity is not a nice property when defining grammars for programming languages, we would like to define a function that look for ambiguous words. A possible solution is to define a parser with representation `s'`, whose representation is the parse tree. By using `s'` we can look for sentences with two different representations. However this means that we need to define a parser P' each time we want to study the ambiguity of a parser P. Obviously, it is much better to mechanize this process by defining a suitable function build_tree that converts a given parser into a new parser that returns as representation parse trees. This function can be defined in terms of foldp as follows:

```
build_tree :: parser A → parser_rep [int] A
build_tree = foldp (empty_t,term_t,sat_t,seq_t,alt_t,rep_t)
```

where

empty_t	= empty	>> []	
term_t T	= terminal T	>> []	
sat_t P RI	= satisfy P RI	>> []	
seq_t P1 P2	= P1 R1 <*> P2 R2	>> R1++R2	
alt_t P1 P2	= P1 R	>> [1|R]	
	<|> P2 R	>> [2|R]	
rep_t P Expr Rep	= (P Tree >> Expr) Rep	>> Tree	

To represent the parse tree we use a list which collects the chosen alternatives as a sequence of 1's (first alternative) and 2's (second alternative). In the case of empty, terminal and satisfy the sequence of alternatives is the empty list. In order to understand the sequence and the alternative we must keep in mind that P1 and P2 have been 'folded' already. The sequence applies each parser and concatenates the two resulting lists, while the alternative includes the number of the chosen option in the current representation. Finally, rep_t takes charge of the parsers with representation. It first applies the parser, getting the list of alternatives. Then the parser is again converted into a parser with representation, in order to keep the initial representation unaffected. For instance, the goal build_tree s L "iioeo" == [] succeeds with R == [1, 2, 1, 2, 2, 2, 2] as well as with R == [2, 1, 1, 2, 2, 2, 2]. Owing to the right associativity of <|>, the sequence 1 means that that the production (P1) was applied, while 2,1 stands for (P2) and 2,2 stands for production (P3).

Now it is easy to define a function that looks for words with two different parse trees:

```
ambi:: parser A → [A]
ambi P = W ⇐ gen_word==W, build_tree P R1 W == [],
              build_tree P R2 W == [], not (R1 == R2)
```

The first condition is used to generate general words in a non-deterministic fashion (see below). The next two conditions try to parse the word twice, while the third condition assures that the two representations returned are different. If they are equal, then backtracking is enforced and a new parse is tried. Otherwise the word W admits two different parse trees (i.e. the grammar is ambiguous) and W is returned. Observe that we are using here the LP capabilities of our language, since R1 and R2 are new (existential) variables. It is also worth noticing that both the fold and the parsing of the input sentence are performed at the same time, avoiding the folding of unsuccessful (and infinite) branches of the parse tree.

Since ambiguity is a semidecidable property, we should only check words in a given range of length. If we find that the parser is ambiguous for any of these words, we have demonstrated that it is ambiguous. Otherwise, we can either try a wider range of lengths, or accept this partial result of non-ambiguity. Owing to this we define a non-deterministic function word_from_to which generates all the general sentences, i.e. lists of variables, whose length is less than or equal to a given number N.

```
all_words N = []
all_words N = [_|all_words (N-1)]  ⟸ N > 0
```

Thus we can define gen_words, for instance, as: gen_words = all_words 10. At this point we can check that s is ambiguous by trying the goal ambi s == W which succeeds with W == "iioeo". Conversely, similar goals for the parsers with representation expression and p, both defined in Sect. 5, will fail, meaning that there is no expression or palindrome word whose length is less than or equal to 10 with two different parse trees.

7   Conclusions

This paper shows how a functional-logic language supporting non-deterministic functions allows defining parsers which combine most of the nicest properties of both functional and logic parsers. Our approach has been presented by means of a concrete language, $\mathcal{TOY}$, but other functional-logic languages supporting non-deterministic functions like Curry [11] could have been used. Specifically, the expressiveness of $\mathcal{TOY}$ parsers is akin to that of FP parsers, but based on simpler concepts and definitions. This is due to the adoption in our model of typical LP characteristics, like the natural way of handling non-determinism provided by non-deterministic computations. Also, parsing in $\mathcal{TOY}$ benefits from the use of logical variables to return representations, thus avoiding the introduction of monads and lambda abstractions. Actually, this technique can be generalized, and represents a simple and natural FLP alternative to monads in many situations (see [5]). Despite their 'functional' shape, parsers in $\mathcal{TOY}$ share with parsers of LP the possibility of multiple modes of use, generating as well as recognizing sentences. We have also investigated further possibilities of our approach to parsers, making use in this case of more specific features of $\mathcal{TOY}$. First, we have briefly indicated how these parsers benefit from the inclusion of arithmetical constraints. In a different direction, $\mathcal{TOY}$'s possibility of using HO patterns in heads of rules has given parsers the role of data values in a very strong sense. We have defined a *fold* function for them, and used this function to check the ambiguity of grammars. Other interesting properties of the underlying grammars, such as the $LL(1)$ property, can be also checked using the same technique, as shown in [4].

Acknowledgements

We thank Mario Rodríguez-Artalejo for many valuable comments about this work.

References

1. P. Arenas-Sánchez , T. Hortalá-González, F.J. López-Fraguas, E. Ullán-Hernández. *Functional Logic programming with Real Numbers*, in M. Chakavrarty, Y. Guo, T. Ida (eds.) *Multiparadigm Logic Programming*, Post-Conference Workshop of the JICLP'96, TU Berlin Report 96-28, 47–58, 1996.
2. P. Arenas-Sánchez, M. Rodríguez-Artalejo. *A Semantic Framework for Functional Logic Programming with Algebraic Polymorphic Types.* Procs. of CAAP'97, Springer LNCS 1214, 453–464, 1997.
3. R. Caballero-Roldán, F.J. López Fraguas, J. Sánchez-Hernández. *User's Manual For TOY .* Technical Report D.I.A. 57/97, Univ. Complutense de Madrid 1997. The system is available at http://mozart.sip.ucm.es/incoming/toy.html
4. R. Caballero-Roldán, F.J. López-Fraguas. *Functional-Logic Parsers in TOY .* Technical Report S.I.P. 74/98. Univ. Complutense de Madrid 1998. Available at http://mozart.sip.ucm.es/papers/1998/trparser.ps.gz
5. R. Caballero, F.J. López-Fraguas. *Extensions: A Technique for Structuring Functional-Logic Programs.* Procs. of PSI'99, Springer LNCS. To appear.
6. J. Fokker. *Functional Parsers.* In J. Jeuring and E. Meijer editors, Lecture Notes on Advanced Functional Programming Techniques, Springer LNCS 925, 1995.
7. J.C. González-Moreno, T. Hortalá-González, F.J. López-Fraguas, M. Rodríguez-Artalejo. *An Approach to Declarative Programming Based on a Rewriting Logic.* Journal of Logic Programming, Vol 40(1), July 1999, pp 47–87.
8. J.C. González-Moreno, T. Hortalá-González, M. Rodríguez-Artalejo. *A Higher Order Rewriting Logic for Functional Logic Programming.* Procs. of ICLP'97, The MIT Press, 153–167, 1997.
9. J.C. González-Moreno. *A Correctness Proof for Warren's HO into FO Translation.* Procs. of GULP'93, 569–585, 1993.
10. M. Hanus. *The Integration of Functions into Logic Programming: A Survey.* J. of Logic Programming 19-20. Special issue *"Ten Years of Logic Programming"*, 583–628, 1994.
11. M. Hanus (ed.). *Curry, an Integrated Functional Logic Language*, Draft, 1998.
12. *Report on the Programming Language Haskell 98: a Non-strict, Purely Functional Language.* Simon Peyton Jones and John Hughes (eds.), February 1999.
13. G. Hutton. *Higher-Order Functions for Parsing.* J. of Functional Programming 2(3):323-343, July 1992.
14. G. Hutton, E. Meijer. *Functional Pearls. Monadic Parsing in Haskell.* Journal of Functional Programming 8 (4), 1998, 437-444.
15. R. Leermakers. *The Functional Treatment of Parsing.* Kluwer Academic Publishers, 1993.
16. R. Loogen, F.J. López-Fraguas, M. Rodríguez-Artalejo. *A Demand Driven Computation Strategy for Lazy Narrowing.* Procs. of PLILP'93, Springer LNCS 714, 184–200, 1993.
17. F.J. López-Fraguas, J. Sánchez-Hérnandez. *TOY: A Multiparadigm Declarative System.* Proc. RTA'99, Springer LNCS 1631, 244–247, 1999.
18. E. Meijer, J. Jeuring. *Merging Monads and Folds for Functional Programming.* Adv. Functional Programming Int. School, Baastad (Sweden). Springer LNCS 925, 228–266, 1995.
19. L. Sterling, E. Shapiro. *The Art of Prolog,* The MIT Press, 1986.
20. P. Wadler. *Monads for functional programming.* In J. Jeuring and E. Meijer editors, Lecture Notes on Advanced Functional Programming Techniques, Springer LNCS 925. 1995.

Implementing Encapsulated Search
for a
Lazy Functional Logic Language

Wolfgang Lux

Universität Münster
wlux@uni-muenster.de

Abstract. A distinguishing feature of logic and functional logic languages is their ability to perform computations with partial data and to search for solutions of a goal. Having a built-in search strategy is convenient but not always sufficient. For many practical applications the built-in search strategy (usually depth-first search via global backtracking) is not well suited. Also the non-deterministic instantiation of unbound logic variables conflicts with the monadic I/O concept, which requires a single-threaded use of the world.
A solution to these problems is to encapsulate search via a primitive operator **try**, which returns all possible solutions to a search goal in a list. In the present paper we develop an abstract machine that aims at an efficient implementation of encapsulated search in a lazy functional logic language.

1 Introduction

A distinguishing feature of logic and functional logic languages is their ability to perform computations with partial data and to search for solutions of a goal. Having a built-in search strategy to explore all possible alternatives of a non-deterministic computation is convenient but not always sufficient. In many cases the default strategy, which is usually a depth-first traversal using global backtracking, is not well suited to the problem domain. In addition, global non-determinism is incompatible with the monadic I/O concept [PW93]. In this concept the outside world is encapsulated in an abstract data type and actions are provided to change the state of the world. These actions ensure that the world is used in a single-threaded way. Global non-determinism would defeat this single-threaded interaction with the world. Encapsulated search [SSW94,HS98] provides a remedy to both of these problems.

In this paper we develop an abstract machine for the functional logic language Curry [Han99]. Curry is a multi-paradigm language that integrates features from functional languages, logic languages and concurrent programming. Curry uses lazy evaluation of expressions and supports the two most important operational principles developed in the area of functional logic programming, narrowing and residuation. Narrowing [Red85] combines unification and reduction. With narrowing unbound logic variables in expressions may be instantiated

A. Middeldorp, T. Sato (Eds.): FLOPS'99, LNCS 1722, pp. 100–113, 1999.
© Springer-Verlag Berlin Heidelberg 1999

non-deterministically. With the residuation strategy [ALN87], on the other hand, the evaluation of expressions containing unbound logic variables may be delayed until these variables are sufficiently instantiated by other parts of the program. Unfortunately this strategy is known to be incomplete [Han92].

Our abstract machine is a stack-based graph reduction machine similar to the G-machine [Joh84] and the Babel abstract machine [KLMR92]. Its novel feature is the implementation of encapsulated search in an efficient manner that is compatible with the overall lazy evaluation strategy of Curry. Due to the lack of space we restrict the presentation of the abstract machine to the implementation of the encapsulated search. The full semantics of the machine can be found in [LK99]. In the rest of the paper we will assume some familiarity with graph reduction machines for functional and functional logic languages [Joh84,KLMR92].

The rest of this paper is organized as follows. In the next section the computation model of Curry is briefly reviewed and the search operator try is introduced. The third section introduces the abstract machine. In section 4 an example is presented, which demonstrates the operation of the abstract machine. The sixth section presents some runtime results for our prototypical implementation. The last two sections present related work and conclude.

2   The Computation Model of Curry

Curry uses a syntax that is similar to Haskell [HPW92], but with a few additions.

The basic computational domain of Curry is a set of data terms. A data term t is either a variable x or constructed from an n-ary data constructor c, which is applied to n argument terms:

$$t ::= x \mid c \, t_1 \, \ldots \, t_n$$

New data constructors can be introduced through data type declarations, e.g. data Nat = Zero | Succ Nat. This declaration defines the nullary data constructor Zero and the unary data constructor Succ.

An expression e is either a variable x, a data constructor c, a defined function f, or the application of an expression e_1 to an argument expression e_2:

$$e ::= x \mid c \mid f \mid e_1 \, e_2$$

Curry provides a predefined type Constraint. Expressions of this type are checked for satisfiability. The predefined nullary function success reduces to a constraint that is always satisfied. An equational constraint $e_1 =:= e_2$ is satisfied, if e_1 and e_2 can be reduced to the same (finite) data term. If e_1 or e_2 contain unbound logic variables, an attempt will be made to unify both terms by instantiating variables to terms. If the unification succeeds, the constraint is satisfied. E.g the constraint Succ m=:=Succ Zero can be solved by binding m to Zero, if m is an unbound variable.

Functions are defined by conditional equations of the form

$$f \, t_1 \, \ldots \, t_n \mid g = e$$

where the so-called guard g is a constraint. A conditional equation for the function f is applicable in an expression $f\ e_1\ \dots\ e_n$, if the arguments $e_1, \dots, e_n$ match the patterns $t_1, \dots, t_n$ and if the guard is satisfied. The guard may be omitted, in which case the equation is always applicable if the arguments match.

A **where** clause can be added to the right hand side of an equation to provide additional local definitions, whose scope is the guard g and the expression e. Unbound logic variables can be introduced by the special syntax[1] **where** $x_1, \dots, x_n$ **free**

A Curry program is a set of data type declarations and function definitions. The following example defines a predicate and an addition function for natural numbers.

```
nat Zero      = success    add Zero      n = n
nat (Succ n) = nat n       add (Succ m) n = add m (Succ n)
```

2.1 Reduction Strategy

An *answer expression* is a pair of an expression e and a substitution σ that describes the bindings for the free variables of the expression e. An answer expression is written as $\sigma\ [\!]\ e$. The computational domain is a set of answer expressions. E.g. the solution of the goal $f\ x$ where x is a free variable and the function f is defined by

```
f 0 = 1
f 1 = 2
```

is the set

$$\{\{x \mapsto 0\}\ [\!]\ 1, \{x \mapsto 1\}\ [\!]\ 2\}$$

A single computation step performs a reduction of exactly one unsolved expression in the set and returns a set of answer expressions for it. If this set has exactly one element, the computation step was deterministic. Otherwise the the computation either failed and the set is empty or a non-deterministic computation step was performed.

An attempt to reduce an expression $f\ e_1 \dots e_n$ triggers the evaluation of $e_1, \dots, e_n$ according to a left-to-right pattern-matching strategy. Thus, in order to reduce the expression nat (add Zero Zero), the argument (add Zero Zero) is reduced to head normal form (i.e., a term without a defined function symbol at the top) in order to select an applicable equation of the function nat.

If an argument is an unbound variable, as e.g. in nat n, the further computations depend on the evaluation mechanism to be used. When narrowing is used, a non-deterministic computation step is performed that yields a set which contains an answer expression for each possible binding of the variable. In the example, the reduction would yield the set

$$\{\{n \mapsto Zero\}\ [\!]\ success, \{n \mapsto Succ\ m\}\ [\!]\ nat\ m\}$$

----

[1] The same syntax is also applicable to **let** expressions.

where m is a fresh, unbound variable. If residuation is used, the evaluation is delayed until the variable has been instantiated by some other concurrent computation. By default, constraint functions use narrowing as their evaluation mechanism, while all other functions use residuation. The user can override these defaults by evaluation annotations.

The concurrent evaluation of subexpressions is introduced by the concurrent conjunction c_1 & c_2 of two constraints, which evaluates the constraints c_1 and c_2 concurrently and is satisfied iff both are satisfiable. For example we might implement the subtraction on natural numbers with two concurrent computations. The second acts as generator of natural numbers, while the first checks if a generated number added to second argument of the subtraction yields the first argument of the subtraction:

```
sub m n | add s n=:=m & nat s = s where s free
```

2.2 Encapsulated Search

The use of monadic I/O, which assumes a single-threaded interaction with the world, conflicts with the non-determinism stemming from the instantiation of unbound variables. For that reason Curry provides the primitive search operator try :: (a->Constraint) -> [a->Constraint] that allows to confine the effects of non-determinism. This operator can also be used to implement find-all predicates in the style of Prolog, but with the possibility to use other strategies than the built-in depth first search [HS98].

The argument of try is the *search goal*. The argument of the search goal can be used to constrain a goal variable by the solutions of the goal. The result of try is either an empty list, denoting that the reduction of the goal has failed, or it is a singleton list containing a function \x -> g, where g is a satisfiable constraint (in solved form), or the result is a list with at least two elements if the goal can be reduced only by a non-deterministic computation step. The elements of this list are search goals that represent the different alternatives for the reduction of the goal immediately after this non-deterministic step.

For instance, the reduction of

```
try (\x -> let s free in add s x=:=Succ Zero & nat s)
```

yields the list

```
[\x -> add Zero x=:=Succ Zero & success,
 \x -> let t free in add (Succ t) x=:=Succ Zero & nat t]
```

3 The Abstract Machine

3.1 Overview

The abstract machine developed in this paper is a stack based graph reduction machine, that implements a lazy evaluation strategy. The concurrent evaluation of expressions is implemented by assigning each concurrent expression to a new thread. The main contribution of the machine is its lazy implementation of encapsulated search, which is described in more detail below.

The state space of the abstract machine is shown in Fig. 1. The state of the abstract machine is described by an 8-tuple $\langle c, ds, es, hp, H, rq, scs, tr \rangle$, where c denotes a pointer to the instruction sequence to be executed. The data stack ds is used to supply the arguments during the construction of data terms and function applications. The environment stack es maintains the environment frames (activation records) for each function call. An environment frame comprises a size field, the return address, where execution continues after the function has been evaluated, the arguments passed to the function, and additional free space for the local variables of the function.

$$
\begin{aligned}
State \in\ & Instr^* \times Adr^* \times EnvFrame^* \times Adr * \times Heap \times ThdState^* \\
& \times SearchContext^* \times Trail \\
Instr =\ & \{\texttt{PushArg}, \texttt{PushInt}, \ldots\} \\
Adr =\ & \mathbb{N} \\
Heap =\ & Adr -\!\!-\!\rightarrow Node \\
Node =\ & \{\texttt{Int}\} \times \mathbb{N} \ \cup\ \{\texttt{Data}\} \times \mathbb{N} \times Adr^* \ \cup\ \{\texttt{Clos}\} \times Instr^* \times \mathbb{N} \times \mathbb{N} \times Adr^* \\
& \cup\ \{\texttt{SrchCont0}\} \times ThdState \times ThdState^* \times SearchSpace \\
& \cup\ \{\texttt{SrchCont1}\} \times ThdState \times ThdState^* \times SearchSpace \times (Adr \cup ?) \\
& \cup\ \{\texttt{Susp}\} \times Adr \ \cup\ \{\texttt{Lock}\} \times ThdState^* \ \cup\ \{\texttt{Var}\} \times ThdState^* \\
& \cup\ \{\texttt{Indir}\} \times Adr \\
EnvFrame =\ & \mathbb{N} \times Instr^* \times (Adr \cup ?)^* \\
ThdState =\ & Instr^* \times Adr^* \times EnvFrame^* \\
SearchContext & Adr \times Instr^* \times Adr^* \times EnvFrame^* \times ThdState^* \times Trail \\
SearchSpace =\ & Adr \times Trail \times Trail \\
Trail =\ & (Adr \times Node)^*
\end{aligned}
$$

Fig. 1. State space

The graph corresponding to the expression that is evaluated, is allocated in the heap H. The register hp serves as an allocation pointer into the heap. We use the notation $H[a/n]$ to denote a variant of the heap H which contains the node n at address a.

$$
H[a/x](a') := \begin{cases} x & \text{if } a = a' \\ H(a') & \text{otherwise} \end{cases}
$$

The graph is composed of tagged nodes. Integer (Int) nodes represent integer numbers. Data nodes are used for data terms and comprise a tag, which enumerates the data constructors of each algebraic data type, and a list of arguments. The arity of a data constructor is fixed and always known to the compiler, for that reason it isn't recorded in the node.

Closure (`Clos`) nodes represent functions and function applications. Besides the code pointer they contain the arity of the function, the number of additional local variables, and the arguments that have been supplied. The closures returned from the encapsulated search are represented by two kinds of search continuation nodes (`SrchCont0` and `SrchCont1`), which will be described in more detail in the next section.

Unbound logic variables are represented by variable (`Var`) nodes. The wait queue field of these nodes is used to collect those threads, that have been suspended due to an access to the unbound variable.

Suspend (`Susp`) nodes are used for the implementation of lazy evaluation. The argument of a suspend node points to the closure or search continuation, whose evaluation has been delayed. Once the evaluation of the function application begins, the node is overwritten by a `Lock` node, in order to prevent other threads from trying to evaluate the suspended application. Those threads will be collected in the wait queue of the lock. If the evaluation of the function application succeeds the node is overwritten again, this time with an indirection (`Indir`) node, that points to the result of the application. Indirection nodes are also used when a logic variable is bound. The variable node is overwritten in that case, too.

The run queue rq maintains the state of those threads, which are runnable, but not active. For each thread the instruction pointer and the thread's data and environment stacks are saved. The search context stack scs is used to save the state of the abstract machine when an encapsulated search is invoked. In each search context the pointer to the instruction, where execution continues after the encapsulated search returns, the data and environment stacks, the run queue, and the trail are saved. In addition the address of the goal variable is saved in a search context.

The final register, tr, holds a pointer to the trail, which is used to save the old values of nodes that have been overwritten, so that they can be restored upon backtracking or when an encapsulated search is left.

The instruction set of the abstract machine is shown in Fig. 2. Many of these instructions operate similarly to the G-machine [Joh87] and the Babel abstract machine [KLMR96]. They are not described in this paper due to lack of space.

3.2   Encapsulated Search

Representation of search goals A search goal that is reduced by the encapsulated search, is a unary function of result type `Constraint`. The encapsulated search returns if the goal either fails, succeeds or can only proceed nondeterministically. The result is a list of closures, where each closure is of the form $x\text{->}x_1\text{:}=e_1\&\ldots\&x_n\text{:}=e_n\&c$. Here $x_1,\ldots,x_n$ denote the logic variables that have already been bound to some value (the parameter x can be a member of this list) and c represents the yet unsolved part of the search goal. This form is not suitable to be used in the abstract machine, however, because we cannot change the code of the search goal dynamically. A more suitable representation is derived from the fact, that the closure represents the continuation of the search

PushArg n	SwitchOnTerm *tags&labels*	TryMeElse *label*
PushInt i	Jmp *label*	RetryMeElse *label*
PushGlobal n	Jmp *Cond label*	TrustMe
PushVar	BindVar	Fail
Pop n	Eval	Succeed
PackData *tag*, n	Return	Solve
SplitData m, n	Fork *label*	
SaveLocal n	Delay	
Apply n	Yield	
Suspend n	Stop	

Fig. 2. Instruction set

goal at the point, where the non-deterministic computation step takes place. Such a continuation is described by the current contents of the machine registers together with the bindings for the logic variables. A search continuation (SrchCont1) node is used to represent this kind of continuation (see Fig. 1).

Local search spaces The different solutions of the search goal may use different bindings for the logic variables and suspended applications contained in the search goal. For instance, in the example given earlier, the local variable s is bound to the constant Zero in the first alternative and to the data term Succ t in the second one.

For efficiency reasons, we do not want to copy the graph corresponding to the search goal for every solution. Instead we share the graph among all solutions and use destructive updates to change the bindings whenever a different search continuation is invoked. Therefore every search continuation is associated with a search space, that contains the list of addresses and values that must be restored, when the search continuation is invoked (the *script* of the search space), and those which must be restored, when the encapsulated search returns (the *trail* of the search space). In addition the search space also contains the address of the logic variable, that was used as an argument to the search goal in order to start its evaluation.

Invocation of search goals A new encapsulated search is started by the Solve instruction. This instruction will save the current machine state in a search context on the search context stack *scs*. If the argument passed to Solve is a closure node, i.e. the search goal is called for the first time, a fresh, unbound variable is allocated and the search goal is applied to it.

$$\langle \text{Solve} : c, ds_1 : ds, es, hp, H, rq, scs, tr \rangle \Longrightarrow$$
$$\langle c', hp : \epsilon, \epsilon, hp + 1, H[hp/(\text{Var}, \epsilon)], \epsilon, (hp, c, ds, es, rq, tr) : scs, \epsilon \rangle$$
where $H[ds_1] = (\text{Clos}, c'', ar, l, a_1, \ldots, a_{ar-1})$
and $c' = \text{Apply } 1 : \text{Suspend} : \text{Eval} : \text{Succeed} : \epsilon$

If instead the argument to the Solve instruction is a search continuation, the bindings from its search space have to be restored before the execution of the goal can continue. No new goal variable needs to be allocated in this case.

$$\langle \text{Solve} : c, ds_1 : ds, es, hp, H, rq, scs, tr \rangle \Longrightarrow$$
$$\langle c', ds', es', hp, restore(H, scr), (g, c, ds, es, rq, tr) : scs, tr' \rangle$$
$$\text{where } H[ds_1] = (\text{SrchCont1}, (c', ds', es'), rq', (g, scr, tr'))$$

The auxiliary function *restore* is defined as follows:

$$restore(H, tr) := \begin{cases} H & \text{if } tr = \epsilon \\ restore(H[a/x], tr') & \text{if } tr = (a, x) : tr' \end{cases}$$

Returning from the encapsulated search There are three different cases to consider here. The easy case is when the search goal fails. In that case, the old heap contents and the top-most context from the search context stack are restored and an empty list is returned into that context.

$$\langle \text{Fail} : c, ds, es, hp, H, rq, (g, c', ds', es', rq', tr') : scs, tr \rangle \Longrightarrow$$
$$\langle c', hp : ds', es', hp + 1, restore(H, tr)[hp/(\text{Data}, [])], rq', scs, tr' \rangle$$

If the search goal succeeds, a singleton list containing the solved search goal must be returned to the context, which invoked the encapsulated search. This is handled by the Succeed instruction, that detects this special case from the presence of an empty return context.

$$\langle \text{Succeed} : c, ds, \epsilon, hp, H, \epsilon, (g, c', ds', es', rq', tr') : scs, tr \rangle \Longrightarrow$$
$$\langle c', hp : ds', es', hp + 3, H'', rq', scs, tr' \rangle$$
$$\text{where } spc = (g, save(H, tr), tr)$$
$$\qquad\quad H' = restore(H, tr)$$
$$\qquad\quad H'' = H'[\, hp/(\text{Data}, :, hp + 1, hp + 2),$$
$$\qquad\qquad\qquad hp + 1/(\text{SrchCont1}, (\text{Succeed} : c, \epsilon, \epsilon), \epsilon, spc, ?),$$
$$\qquad\qquad\qquad hp + 2/(\text{Data}, [])]$$

The *save* function saves the bindings of all variables that have been updated destructively. These are those nodes, which have been recorded on the trail:

$$save(H, tr) := \begin{cases} \epsilon & \text{if } tr = \epsilon \\ (a, H[a]) : save(H, tr') & \text{if } tr = (a, n) : tr' \end{cases}$$

In case of a non-deterministic computation step, a list must be returned as well. However, in this case the tail of that list is not empty. Instead it will contain the search continuations for the remaining alternatives. Due to the lazy evaluation semantics of Curry, this tail has to be a suspended application. We use a second kind of search continuation node (SrchCont0) for that purpose. These search continuations do not accept an argument, as they just jump to the alternative continuation address encoded in the `TryMeElse` and `RetryMeElse` instructions.

$\langle \text{TryMeElse alt} : c, ds, es, hp, H, rq, (g, c', ds', es', rq', tr') : scs, tr \rangle \Longrightarrow$
$\langle c', hp : ds', es', hp + 3, H'', rq', scs, tr' \rangle$
where $spc = (g, save(H, tr), tr)$
$\quad\quad H' = restore(H, tr)$
$\quad\quad H'' = H'[\, hp/(\text{Data}, (:, hp + 1, hp + 2)),$
$\quad\quad\quad\quad\quad\quad hp + 1/(\text{SrchCont1}, (c, ds, es), rq, spc, ?),$
$\quad\quad\quad\quad\quad\quad hp + 2/(\text{SrchCont0}, (alt, ds, es), rq, spc)]$

The `RetryMeElse` and `TrustMe` instructions are handled similarly.

Unpacking the result In order to access the computed solution for a search goal, the (solved) search goal must be applied to an unbound logic variable. This variable will then be unified with the corresponding binding computed in the search goal (if any). The unpack function

```
unpack g | g x = x where x free
```

can be used for that purpose.

In the abstract machine, the `Eval` instruction therefore must also handle suspended applications of search continuations. In that case, the saved search space is merged into the current search space and then execution continues in the solved goal. This will immediately execute the `Succeed` instruction, which unifies the value, that was bound to the goal variable, with the argument applied to the search continuation and then returns into the context where `Eval` was invoked.[2]

$\langle \text{Eval} : c, ds_1 : ds, es, hp, H[ds_1/(\text{Susp}, a)], rq, scs, tr \rangle \Longrightarrow$
$\langle c', ds' \mathbin{+\!\!+} ds', (2 : c : a : g') : es', hp + 1, H', rq' \mathbin{+\!\!+} rq, scs, tr' \mathbin{+\!\!+} tr \rangle$
where $H[a] = (\text{SrchCont1}, (c', ds', es'), rq', (g, scr, tr'), a')$
$\quad\quad H' = restore(H, scr)[hp/(\text{Locked}, \epsilon)]$
$\langle \text{Succeed} : c, ds, es, hp, H, rq, scs, tr \rangle \Longrightarrow$
$\langle c', ds, es, hp, H, rq, scs, tr \rangle$
where $c' = \text{PushArg 1} : \text{PushArg 0} : \text{BindVar} : \text{Return} : \epsilon$
and $es \neq \epsilon$

4 An Example

In order to demonstrate the operation of the abstract machine, we will consider the function

```
sub m n | add s m=:=n & nat s = s where s free
```

again. The code for this function, together with the code for the functions `nat` and `add` introduced earlier, and the code for the primitive function `&` are shown in Fig. 3.

---

[2] For the purpose of the presentation, we assume that the search goal is always applied to an unbound variable, so that the `BindVar` instruction is applicable. The machine in fact allows other arguments to be applied as well.

```
        Fn "sub" sub 2 1              Fn "add" add 2 1
sub: PushVar                   add:   PushArg 0
     SaveLocal 2               add.1: SwitchOnTerm [<Susp>:add.2,<Var>:add.3,
     PushArg 2                                     Zero:add.4,Succ:add.5]
     PushGlobal "nat"          add.2: Eval
     Apply                            Jump add.1
     Suspend                   add.3: Delay
     PushArg 0                        Jump add.1
     PushArg 1                 add.4: Pop 1
     PushArg 2                        PushArg 1
     PushGlobal "add"                 Return
     Apply 2                   add.5: SplitData 2 1
     Suspend                          PushArg 1
     PushGlobal "=:="                 PackData Succ 1
     Apply 2                          PushArg 2
     Suspend                          PushGlobal "add"
     PushGlobal "&"                   Exec 2
     Apply
     Suspend
     Eval                             Fn "nat" nat 1 1
     Pop 1                     nat:   PushArg 0
     PushArg 2                 nat.1: SwitchOnTerm [<Susp>:nat.2,<Var>:nat.3,
     Return                                        Zero:nat.4,Succ:nat.6]
                               nat.2: Eval
                                      Jump nat.1
     Fn "&" 1 2 0              nat.3: TryMeElse nat.5
     Fork 1.1                         PushAtom Zero
     PushArg 1                        BindVar
     Eval                      nat.4: Pop 1
     Pop 1                            PushGlobal "success"
     PushArg 0                        Exec 0
     Eval                      nat.5: TrustMe
     Return                           PushVariables 1
1.1: PushArg 0                        PackData Succ 1
     Eval                             BindVar
     Stop                      nat.6: SplitData 1 1
                                      PushArg 1
                                      PushGlobal "nat"
                                      Exec 2
```

Fig. 3. Sample code

The code for the function sub constructs a suspended application for the guard expression add s m=:=n & nat s. This application is then reduced to weak head normal form with the Eval instruction. If the evaluation of the guard succeeds, the result is discarded (it can only be the solved constraint) and the solution, which is the value bound to the logic variable s, is returned to the caller.

The code for the primitive function &, which implements the concurrent conjunction of two constraints, creates a new thread using the Fork instruction as its first action. The new child thread, which becomes active immediately, shares the current environment frame with its parent, in order to access the arguments passed to the function. The child thread reduces the first argument of & to weak head normal form and then stops. The parent thread, once it becomes active again, reduces the second argument to weak head normal form and invokes Eval for the first argument, too. Because the evaluation of a suspended application replaces the Susp node by a Lock node, this will block the parent thread until the child thread has completed the evaluation of the first argument.

The function add dispatches on the kind of its first argument with the help of the SwitchOnTerm instruction. If the argument is a suspend node, it will be reduced to weak head normal form with the Eval instruction. Otherwise, if the node is an unbound variable, the Delay instruction will suspend the current thread until that variable is instantiated. In both cases the code then redispatches on the result of the evaluation or the instantiated variable, resp. If the node is neither a suspend node nor an unbound variable, then it must be already in weak head normal form and the code jumps directly to the compiled code of the corresponding equation.

The function nat similarly dispatches on the kind of its argument. If the argument is a suspend node it will be evaluated and otherwise, if it is not an unbound variable, the abstract machine will jump directly to the code for the matching equation. If the argument is an unbound variable, the function has to instantiate that variable non-deterministically. This is implemented with the help of the TryMeElse and TrustMe instructions in this example. When the TryMeElse instruction is executed, the abstract machine saves the current machine state into two search continuation nodes. The first of them is a SrchCont1 node whose instruction pointer contains the address of the instruction following the TryMeElse instruction, i.e. in our example the instruction PushAtom Zero. The second search continuation is a SrchCont0 node, that shares the machine state with the former search continuation but has a different continuation address. Its instruction pointer contains the address of the instruction at the label of the TryMeElse instruction, i.e. in our example the TrustMe instruction. Both search continuations are packed into a list node and the abstract machine returns to the top-most context on the search context stack with the the list node on the top of the data stack. The RetryMeElse and TrustMe instructions work similarly, except that for TrustMe the tail of the list node is an empty list instead of a search continuation.

When a SrchCont1 node is used as an argument to the try function, the saved machine state is restored and the execution continues at the addresss following the TryMeElse instruction. The correct local bindings for this search continuation are established with the help of the *script* of the SrchCont1 node. Similarly the SrchCont0 node restores the saved state and continues at the TrustMe instruction.

5 The Implementation

We have implemented a prototype of our abstract machine. Our compiler translates Curry source code into abstract machine code, which is then translated into native machine code using the well-known "C as portable assembler technique" [HCS95,Pey92].

In our implementation we have integrated a few optimizations. Besides using unboxed representations for integer arithmetic like in the G-machine, we were particularly interested in implementing the encapsulated search efficiently. By using destructive updates, we have already minimized the cost for accessing variables and applications. On the other hand we now have an additional overhead on entering and leaving the encapsulated search because the bindings of those nodes have to be updated. However, this update of bindings can be delayed until a search goal is called, that uses a different search space. Because (nearly) all updates affect nodes, that are local to the search space, there is no need to restore those bindings when the encapsulated space is left.[3] If the search goal, that is invoked next, uses the same bindings, as will happen quite often in the case of a depth-first search strategy, then no actions need to be taken and the only overhead, that is caused by the use of the encapsulated search, is due to the creation of the search continuations.

To test the efficiency of our abstract machine, we have run a few benchmarks on it. The results for three of these benchmarks are shown in Fig. 4. The first column lists the execution times for a functional version of the program, the second column shows the same benchmark, but using logical style. The third column shows the results for the benchmarks when translated into Prolog and compiled with Sicstus Prolog. The fourth column contains the execution times for the functional version of the benchmarks compiled with a state-of-the-art Haskell compiler (Glasgow Haskell). All times are given in seconds.

The first benchmark tries to find a solution for the 8-puzzle using a best-first approach. The second benchmark computes the number of solutions for the 8-queens problems. The third benchmark shows the result for naive reverse with a list of 250 elements. The test is repeated 100 times. All benchmarks were run on an otherwise unloaded Ultra Sparc 1 equipped with 128 MBytes of RAM.

---

[3] Any suspended applications that were used as additional arguments for the search goal have to be restored, however. These can easily be identified, if each suspend node is tagged with the search space, in which it was allocated. In practice such nodes seem to occur rarely.

Benchmark	Functional	Logic	Sicstus	ghc
8-puzzle	1.7	4.1	14.4	0.13
queens	2.9	6.5	3.3	0.92
nrev	13.7	33.2	22.7	1.7

Fig. 4. Runtime results

From the figures one can see that our prototype compares well with a mature Prolog implementation. The functional version of the code is always slightly faster than the corresponding Prolog code, while the logical version is a little bit slower, except for the 8-puzzle. However, our implementation is still much slower than the code generated by the Glasgow Haskell compiler.

6 Related Work

The G-machine [Joh87] implements graph reduction for a functional language. The Babel abstract machine [KLMR96] implements graph reduction for a functional language whose operational semantics is based on narrowing. It incorporates ideas from the G-machine and the WAM [War83], which is the standard abstract machine for implementing Prolog. Our abstract machine extends this further by adding concurrent evaluation and encapsulated search.

The encapsulated search in Curry is a generalization of the search operator of Oz [Smo95]. Their abstract machine [MSS95] differs substantially from ours, because of the different computation model employed by Oz. In particular Oz uses eager evaluation instead of lazy evaluation and therefore lacks the possibility to compute only parts of a search tree. E.g. they could not handle a search goal like nats directly.

The implementation of multiple binding environments has been studied in the context of OR-parallel implementations of logic programming languages [GJ93].

7 Conclusion

In this paper we have developed an abstract machine designed for an efficient implementation of Curry. The main contribution of the machine is the integration of encapsulated search into a functional logic language, that employs a lazy reduction strategy. One of the goals of the implementation was to minimize the overhead, that stems from the use of encapsulated search. The prototype, that we have implemented, works reasonably fast compared with the same programs compiled in Prolog. However, we are still at least a magnitude slower than a current state-of-the-art compiler for a functional language. This is due to the fact, that our present compiler does not perform any sensible analysis on the source code. We are currently developing dedicated optimizations in order to include them into the Curry compiler.

References

ALN87.   H. Aït-Kaci, P. Lincoln, and R. Nasr. Le Fun: Logic, Equations, and Functions. *Proc. ILPS'87*, pp. 17–23, 1987.

GJ93.   G. Gupta and B. Jayaraman. Analysis of Or-Parallel Execution Models. *ACM TOPLAS*, 15(4):659–680, Sept. 1993.

Han92.   M. Hanus. On the Completeness of Residuation. *Proc. JICSLP'92*, pp. 192–206. MIT Press, 1992.

Han99.   M. Hanus. Curry: An integrated functional logic language, (version 0.5). http://www-i2.informatik.rwth-aachen.de/~hanus/curry, 1999.

HCS95.   F. Henderson, Th. Conway, and Z. Somogyi. Compiling Logic Programs to C Using GNU C as a Portable Assembler. *Proc. of the ILPS '95 Post-conference Workshop on Sequential Implementation Technologies for Logic Programming Languages*, pp. 1–15, 1995.

HPW92.   P. Hudak, S. Peyton Jones, and P. Wadler. Report on the Programming Language Haskell (version 1.2). *SIGPLAN Notices*, 27(5), 1992.

HS98.   M. Hanus and F. Steiner. Controlling Search in Declarative Programs. *Proc. PLILP'98*, pp. 374–390, 1998.

Joh84.   T. Johnsson. Efficient Compilation of Lazy Evaluation. *Proc. SIGPLAN'84 Symposium on Compiler Construction*, pp. 58–69, 1984.

Joh87.   T. Johnsson. *Compiling Lazy Functional Languages*. PhD thesis, Chalmers Univ. of Technology, 1987.

KLMR92. H. Kuchen, R. Loogen, J. Moreno-Navarro, and M. Rodríguez-Artalejo. Graph-Based Implementation of a Functional Logic Language. *Proc. ALP 1990*, pp. 298–317. Springer LNCS 463, 1992.

KLMR96. H. Kuchen, R. Loogen, J. Moreno-Navarro, and M. Rodríguez-Artalejo. The Functional Logic Language Babel and its Implementation on a Graph Machine. *New Generation Computing*, 14:391–427, 1996.

LK99.   W. Lux and H. Kuchen. An Abstract Machine for Curry. Technical Report, Univerisity of Münster, 1999.

MSS95.   M. Mehl, R. Scheidhauer, and Ch. Schulte. An Abstract Machine for Oz. *Proc. PLILP'95*, pp. 151–168. Springer, LNCS 982, 1995.

Pey92.   S. Peyton Jones. Implementing Lazy Functional Languages on Stock Hardware: The Spineless Tagless G-machine. *Journal of Functional Programming*, 2(1):73–80, Jan 1992.

PW93.   S. Peyton Jones and P. Wadler. Imperative Functional Programming. *Proc. 20th POPL'93*, pp. 123–137, 1993.

Red85.   U. Reddy. Narrowing as the Operational Semantics of Functional Languages. *Proc. ILPS'85*, pp. 138–151, 1985.

Smo95.   G. Smolka. The Oz Programming Model. In J. van Leeuwen (ed.), *Current Trends in Computer Science*. Springer LNCS 1000, 1995.

SSW94.   Ch. Schulte, G. Smolka, and J. Würtz. Encapsulated Search and Constraint Programming in Oz. *Proc. of the Second Workshop on Principles and Practice of Constraint Programming*. Springer, 1994.

War83.   D. Warren. An Abstract Prolog Instruction Set. Technical Report 309, SRI, 1983.

Comparison of Deforestation Techniques for Functional Programs and for Tree Transducers

Armin Kühnemann

Grundlagen der Programmierung,
Institut für Softwaretechnik I, Fakultät Informatik,
Technische Universität Dresden, D–01062 Dresden, Germany,
kuehne@orchid.inf.tu-dresden.de

Abstract. We compare transformations for the elimination of intermediate results in first-order functional programs. We choose the well known deforestation technique of Wadler and composition techniques from the theory of tree transducers, of which the implementation of functional programs yet does not take advantage. We identify syntactic classes of function definitions for which both techniques deliver equally efficient results and for which one technique is more powerful than the other. In particular, this paper offers a technique that eliminates intermediate results for certain kinds of function definitions, for which deforestation fails.

1 Introduction

Functional programs frequently use compositions of functions, where functions produce intermediate results, which are consumed by other functions. On the one hand this modular style of programming simplifies the design and the verification of programs [13]. On the other hand the production and consumption of intermediate results can cause inefficiencies, in particular, if the intermediate results are structured objects like lists or trees.

There are several techniques for transforming programs which use intermediate results into programs which do not. We compare *deforestation* [20,5], which is a well known optimization technique for functional programs, with some *composition techniques* from the theory of tree transducers [7]. The comparison is restricted to the twofold composition of first-order functions, which are defined by an extended scheme of primitive recursion, in which additionally simultaneous definitions of functions and nesting of terms in parameter positions are allowed. This scheme is called *macro tree transducer* [3] (for short *mtt*; cf. also [2,4]).

An mtt m translates trees over a ranked alphabet of input symbols into trees over a ranked alphabet of output symbols. For this translation process, m uses a ranked alphabet of functions which have at least rank 1, and a set of equations. Every function f is defined by a case analysis on the root symbol c of its first argument t. The right-hand side of the equation for f and c may contain recursive function calls, where the first argument of a function call is a variable that refers to a subtree of t. If every function of m has rank 1, then m is called *top-down*

A. Middeldorp, T. Sato (Eds.): FLOPS'99, LNCS 1722, pp. 114–130, 1999.

tree transducer [17,19] (for short *tdtt*). Throughout this paper we will use the following mtts m_{app}, m_{rev}, m_{mir}, and m_{ex} as examples, where m_{ex} is a tdtt.

$$m_{app}: app\ (A\ x_1)\ y_1 = A\ (app\ x_1\ y_1) \qquad m_{mir}: mir\ (A\ x_1)\ y_1 = A\ (mir\ x_1\ (A\ y_1))$$
$$app\ (B\ x_1)\ y_1 = B\ (app\ x_1\ y_1) \qquad\qquad mir\ (B\ x_1)\ y_1 = B\ (mir\ x_1\ (B\ y_1))$$
$$app\ N\ y_1\ \ \ = y_1 \qquad\qquad\qquad\qquad mir\ N\ y_1\ \ \ = y_1$$
$$m_{rev}: rev\ (A\ x_1)\ y_1 = rev\ x_1\ (A\ y_1) \qquad m_{ex}: ex\ (A\ x_1)\ \ \ = B\ (ex\ x_1)$$
$$rev\ (B\ x_1)\ y_1 = rev\ x_1\ (B\ y_1) \qquad\qquad ex\ (B\ x_1)\ \ \ = A\ (ex\ x_1)$$
$$rev\ N\ y_1\ \ \ = y_1 \qquad\qquad\qquad\qquad ex\ N\ \ = N$$

The mtt m_{app} appends two lists containing list elements A and B, where lists are represented by monadic trees. In particular, the empty list is represented by the symbol N with rank 0. In analogy, m_{rev} reverses a list l (starting with an application $rev\ l\ N$) by accumulating the list elements in the second argument of rev. The mtt m_{mir} combines the features of m_{app} and m_{rev} by appending a list l to a list which results from a reversal of l (by starting with an application $mir\ l\ N$). The mtt m_{ex} exchanges list elements A by B and vice versa.

If we evaluate the expression $e = (ex\ (mir\ l_0\ l_1))$, where l_0 and l_1 are lists, then mir produces an intermediate result. In particular, l_0 is traversed *three times* (mir traverses l_0 and ex traverses l_0 and l_0's reversed image). Deforestation can be applied to e and to a program p, which consists of m_{ex} and (a slight syntactic variant of) m_{mir}, and delivers an expression $e_d = (mirex\ l_0\ l_1)$ and a function

$$mirex\ (A\ x_1)\ y_1 = B\ (mirex\ x_1\ (A\ y_1))$$
$$mirex\ (B\ x_1)\ y_1 = A\ (mirex\ x_1\ (B\ y_1))$$
$$mirex\ N\ y_1\ \ \ = ex\ y_1$$

For the evaluation of e_d, the list l_0 is traversed only *twice* ($mirex$ traverses l_0 and ex traverses l_0's reversed image).

In [4] it was shown that for the composition of an mtt with a tdtt (and vice versa) a single mtt can be constructed, which performs the same computation without producing an intermediate result. Since e represents a composition of the mtt m_{mir} with the tdtt m_{ex}, we can get a new expression $e_c = (\overline{mirex}\ l_0\ (ex\ l_1))$ and a function

$$\overline{mirex}\ (A\ x_1)\ y_1 = B\ (\overline{mirex}\ x_1\ (B\ y_1))$$
$$\overline{mirex}\ (B\ x_1)\ y_1 = A\ (\overline{mirex}\ x_1\ (A\ y_1))$$
$$\overline{mirex}\ N\ y_1\ \ \ = y_1$$

The evaluation of e_c requires only *one* traversal of l_0.

We will show that, like in our example, for the composition of an mtt m_1 with a tdtt m_2 (in this order) deforestation successfully eliminates "intermediate symbols" which occur "outside" of the topmost function calls in right-hand sides of equations of m_1, but fails in eliminating symbols "inside" of these function calls. It turns out that the composition technique is more powerful, since it additionally eliminates the latter symbols. For compositions of tdtts with mtts (in this order), the transformation strategies of the composition technique and of deforestation correspond to each other and thus deliver equally efficient programs.

Besides this introduction, the paper contains six further sections. In Section 2 we fix elementary notions and notations. Section 3 introduces our functional language and mtts. Section 4 and Section 5 present deforestation and the composition techniques, respectively. In Section 6 the techniques are compared. Finally, Section 7 contains further research topics.

2   Preliminaries

We denote the set of natural numbers including 0 by $I\!N$. For every $m \in I\!N$, the set $\{1, \ldots, m\}$ is denoted by $[m]$. We will use the sets $X = \{x_0, x_1, x_2, \ldots\}$, $Y = \{y_0, y_1, y_2, \ldots\}$, $Z = \{z_0, z_1, z_2, \ldots\}$, and $V = X \cup Y \cup Z$ of *recursion variables*, *context variables*, *expression variables*, and *variables*, respectively. For a string w and two lists $w_1, \ldots, w_n$ and $w'_1, \ldots, w'_n$ of strings such that no pair w_i and w_j with $i \neq j$ overlaps in w, we denote by $w[w_1/w'_1, \ldots, w_n/w'_n]$ the string which is obtained from w by substituting every occurrence of w_i in w by w'_i. We abbreviate the *substitution* $[w_1/w'_1, \ldots, w_n/w'_n]$ by $[w_i/w'_i \mid w_i \in \{w_1, \ldots, w_n\}]$ or simply by $[w_i/w'_i]$, if the quantification is clear from the context.

Let $\Rightarrow$ be a binary relation on a set K. Then, $\Rightarrow^n$ and $\Rightarrow^*$ denote the n-fold composition and the transitive, reflexive closure, respectively, of $\Rightarrow$. If $k \Rightarrow^* k'$ for $k, k' \in K$ and if there is no $k'' \in K$ such that $k' \Rightarrow k''$, then k' is called a *normal form of k with respect to* $\Rightarrow$, which is denoted by $nf(\Rightarrow, k)$, if it exists and if it is unique. We abbreviate $nf(\Rightarrow, k)$ by $nf(k)$, if $\Rightarrow$ is clear.

A *ranked alphabet* is a pair $(S, rank_S)$ where S is a finite set and $rank_S$ is a mapping which associates with every symbol $s \in S$ a natural number called the *rank* of the symbol. The set of elements of S with rank n is denoted by $S^{(n)}$.

For a ranked alphabet S and a subset V' of V, the set of *trees over S indexed by V'*, denoted by $T_S(V')$, is the smallest subset $T \subseteq (S \cup V' \cup \{(,)\})^*$ such that

- $V' \cup S^{(0)} \subseteq T$ and
- for every $s \in S^{(n)}$ with $n \geq 1$ and $t_1, \ldots, t_n \in T$: $(s\ t_1 \ldots t_n) \in T$.

$T_S(\emptyset)$ is abbreviated by T_S. Let $t \in T_S(V')$. The set of variables that occur in t is denoted by $var(t)$ and the number of occurrences of symbols from a subset $S' \subseteq S$ in t is denoted by $|t|_{S'}$ or simply by $|t|$, if $S = S'$.

3   Functional Programs and Macro Tree Transducers

We consider a simple first-order functional programming language P as source language for our transformations. Every program $p \in P$ consists of several mtts. For simplicity we choose a unique ranked alphabet C of constructor symbols, which is used to build up input trees and output trees of every mtt in p. This fact and the absence of initial functions differ from mtts in the literature. The functions of an mtt are defined by a case analysis on the first argument (*recursion argument*) via pattern matching, where only flat patterns are allowed. The other arguments are called *context arguments*.

Definition 1 Let C and F be ranked alphabets of *constructor symbols* (or *constructors*) and *function symbols* (or *functions*), respectively, such that X, Y, C, and F are pairwise disjoint. We define the classes P, MAC, D, and R of *programs*, *mtts*, *function definitions*, and *right-hand sides*, respectively, by the following grammar. We assume that p, m, d, r, c, and f (also equipped with indices) range over the sets P, MAC, D, R, C, and F, respectively.

$$
\begin{array}{lll}
p & ::= m_1 \ldots m_l & \text{(program)} \\
m & ::= d_1 \ldots d_h & \text{(macro tree transducer)} \\
d & ::= f\,(c_1\,x_1 \ldots x_{k_1})\,y_1 \ldots y_n = r_1 & \text{(function definition)} \\
& \quad\vdots & \\
& \quad f\,(c_q\,x_1 \ldots x_{k_q})\,y_1 \ldots y_n = r_q & \\
r & ::= y_i \mid f\,x_i\,r_1 \ldots r_n \mid c\,r_1 \ldots r_k & \text{(right-hand side)}
\end{array}
$$

The sets of constructors and functions that occur in $p \in P$ are denoted by C_p and F_p, respectively. The set of functions that is defined in $m \in MAC$ is denoted by F_m. In addition to the grammar, the following restrictions have to be fulfilled: For every $i \in [l]$ and $f \in F_{m_i}$, the mtt m_i contains exactly one function definition for f. For every $i, j \in [l]$ with $i \neq j$: $F_{m_i} \cap F_{m_j} = \emptyset$. For every $i \in [l]$, $f \in F_{m_i}^{(n+1)}$, and $c \in C_p^{(k)}$ there is exactly one equation of the form $f\,(c\,x_1 \ldots x_k)\,y_1 \ldots y_n = rhs(f,c)$, where $rhs(f,c) \in T_{C_p \cup F_{m_i}}(\{x_1, \ldots, x_k, y_1, \ldots, y_n\})$.   □

If $F_m = F_m^{(1)}$ for an mtt m, then m is a tdtt. The classes of tdtts and of mtts which are no tdtts are denoted by TOP and by $MAC - TOP$, respectively. A tree t is called *linear*, if every variable occurs at most once in t. An mtt and a program, respectively, is called *linear*, if the right-hand side of each of its equations is linear. We add an index 1 (and l, respectively) to the class MAC and its subclasses, if mtts with only one function (and linear mtts, respectively) are considered. Note that our classes are syntactic classes and no semantic classes (classes of computed functions), which are studied in the theory of tree transducers [7].

Example 2 $m_{ex} \in TOP_{1,l}$ and $m_{app}, m_{rev}, m_{mir} \in (MAC - TOP)_{1,l}$.   □

It turns out that deforestation in general translates a program $p \in P$ into a program p', in which in right-hand sides of an mtt m also applications of the form $f\,r_0\,r_1 \ldots r_n$ with $f \in (F_{p'} - F_m)$ and without restriction "$r_0 = x_i$ for some x_i" can occur. We denote this target language by P^+ and the set of constructors and functions that occur in $p \in P^+$ by C_p and F_p, respectively.

We fix call-by-name semantics, i.e. for every $p \in P^+$ we use a call-by-name reduction relation $\Rightarrow_p$ on $T_{C_p \cup F_p}$. It can be proved that in contrast to general first-order programs, for every $p \in P$ and $e \in T_{C_p \cup F_p}$ the normal form $nf(\Rightarrow_p, e)$ exists. The proof is based on the result in [4], that for every mtt the corresponding (nondeterministic) reduction relation is terminating (and confluent).

In the framework of mtts, a function f_1 produces an intermediate result which is consumed by another function f_2, iff an application of f_1 occurs in the *first* argument of an application of f_2. Thus, in this paper we would like to optimize the evaluation of expressions of the form $(f_2 \; (f_1 \; t_0 \ldots t_{n_1}) \; t_{n_1+1} \ldots t_{n_1+n_2})$, where each t_i is a tree over constructor symbols. Since the particular constructor trees are not relevant for the transformations, we abstract them by expression variables and transform expressions of the form $(f_2 \; (f_1 \; z_0 \ldots z_{n_1}) \; z_{n_1+1} \ldots z_{n_1+n_2})$, which we call *composition expressions*. The transformations will deliver expressions of the form $(f \; z_0 \; z_1 \ldots z_n)$ or $(f \; z_0 \; (f_1 \; z_1)) \ldots (f_n \; z_n))$. All these expressions are special initial expressions for programs, which are defined as follows.

Definition 3 Let $p \in P^+$ and let f range over F_p. The set of *initial expressions for p*, denoted by E_p, is defined as follows, where e (also equipped with indices) ranges over E_p:

$$e ::= f \; e_0 \; e_1 \ldots e_n \mid z_i \quad \text{(initial expression for a program)} \qquad \Box$$

Our transformation techniques take elements of the class $\{(p, e) \mid p \in P, e \in E_p\}$ as input. This class contains the following subclasses with *linear* composition expressions, for which we would like to compare the transformation techniques.

Definition 4 For every $i \in [2]$ let M_i be the class MAC or one of its subclasses. The *composition class* $(M_1; M_2)$ is the set $\{(p, e) \mid p \in P, e \in E_p$, there are mtts m_1 and m_2 in p with $m_1 \in M_1$, $m_2 \in M_2$, and there are $f_1 \in F_{m_1}^{(n_1+1)}$ and $f_2 \in F_{m_2}^{(n_2+1)}$ such that $e = (f_2 \; (f_1 \; z_0 \; z_1 \ldots z_{n_1}) \; z_{n_1+1} \ldots z_{n_1+n_2})\}$. $\qquad \Box$

Example 5 Let p consist of m_{ex} and m_{mir}. Then, $e_1 = (mir \; (ex \; z_0) \; z_1) \in E_p$ and $e_2 = (ex \; (mir \; z_0 \; z_1)) \in E_p$. Moreover, $(p, e_1) \in (TOP_{1,l}; (MAC - TOP)_{1,l})$ and $(p, e_2) \in ((MAC - TOP)_{1,l}; TOP_{1,l})$. Let $t_0, t_1 \in T_{C_p}$ and $\sigma = [z_0/t_0, z_1/t_1]$. Then we have $e_1 \sigma \Rightarrow_p^{2 \cdot |t_0|} nf(e_1 \sigma)$ and $e_2 \sigma \Rightarrow_p^{3 \cdot |t_0| + |t_1| - 2} nf(e_2 \sigma)$. $\qquad \Box$

The transformations should preserve the semantics of pairs in $\{(p, e) \mid p \in P, e \in E_p\}$. This is formalized by the following notion of equivalence.

Definition 6 For every $i \in [2]$ let $(p_i, e_i) \in \{(p, e) \mid p \in P^+, e \in E_p\}$. The pairs (p_1, e_1) and (p_2, e_2) are called *equivalent*, denoted by $(p_1, e_1) \equiv (p_2, e_2)$, if $C_{p_1} = C_{p_2}$ and if for every substitution $\sigma = [v/t_v \mid v \in var(e_1) \cup var(e_2), t_v \in T_{C_{p_1}}]$,

$$nf(\Rightarrow_{p_1}, e_1 \sigma) = nf(\Rightarrow_{p_2}, e_2 \sigma). \qquad \Box$$

4   Deforestation

The (classical) deforestation technique [20,5] can be seen as algorithmic instance of the fold/unfold-technique in [1]. The presentation of deforestation in Transformation 7 obeys the syntax of our language P and is similar to e.g. [18]. Deforestation mimics call-by-name reduction steps (unfold-steps) on expressions with variables, i.e. with "values" which are unknown at transformation time. Therefore, deforestation defines new functions by case analysis, whenever it has to handle an unknown value v in the recursion argument of a function application. Roughly speaking, it uses an expansion of v by every possible constructor.

For *treeless* programs [20], in which essentially every occurrence of a function in the right-hand side of an equation is only applied to variables, the termination of deforestation is ensured by using already defined functions, whenever this is possible (fold-steps). The programs in P are not treeless, since mtts may use nesting of terms in parameter positions. To ensure termination of deforestation also on P, we assume that every context argument of a function application is implicitly abstracted by a let-expression [20,12], i.e. we handle $(f\ x_i\ t_1 \ldots t_n)$ as if it were written like $let\ v_1 = t_1, \ldots, v_n = t_n\ in\ (f\ x_i\ v_1 \ldots v_n)$. We do not choose explicit let-expressions, since this would expand the description of the composition techniques and the comparison in Sections 5 and 6, respectively.

Transformation 7 Let $(p, e) \in (MAC; MAC)$. We define a function $\mathcal{D}$ which takes e (and implicitly p) as input. $\mathcal{D}$ assumes an implicit abstraction with let-expressions and is specialized to handle composition expressions. It can be shown that the five rules for $\mathcal{D}$ perform a complete and disjoint case analysis on the set T of expressions over C_p, F_p, and V, which are encountered starting with a composition expression. In particular, T does not contain expressions of the forms $(f_3\ (f_2\ (f_1 \ldots) \ldots) \ldots)$ and $(f_2\ (f_1\ (c \ldots) \ldots) \ldots)$. The symbols v, c, f, and t (also with indices and apostrophes) range over the sets V, $C_p = \{c_1, \ldots, c_q\}$, F_p, and T, respectively. The notation $\tilde{f}$ and $\widetilde{f_1 f_2}$ in rules (4) and (5), respectively, refers to a function f and $f_1 f_2$, respectively, which either is constructed as specified behind "where" ("where" does not occur in the transformation result), or which was already constructed. In this way $\mathcal{D}[e]$ delivers a new program $p' \in P^+$ and a new initial expression e' for p'. We denote the transformation result (p', e') also by $Def(p, e)$.

(1) $\mathcal{D}[v]$ $\qquad\qquad\qquad\qquad = v$

(2) $\mathcal{D}[c\ t_1 \ldots t_k]$ $\qquad\qquad\quad = c\ \mathcal{D}[t_1] \ldots \mathcal{D}[t_k]$

(3) $\mathcal{D}[f\ (c\ t_1 \ldots t_k)\ t'_1 \ldots t'_n]$ $\quad = \mathcal{D}[rhs(f, c)[x_i/t_i][y_i/t'_i]]$

(4) $\mathcal{D}[f\ v\ t'_1 \ldots t'_n]$ $\qquad\qquad = \tilde{f}\ v\ \mathcal{D}[t'_1] \ldots \mathcal{D}[t'_n]$ where

$\qquad \tilde{f}\ (c_1\ x_1 \ldots x_{k_1})\ y_1 \ldots y_n = \mathcal{D}[rhs(f, c_1)]$

$\qquad\qquad\qquad \vdots$

$\qquad \tilde{f}\ (c_q\ x_1 \ldots x_{k_q})\ y_1 \ldots y_n = \mathcal{D}[rhs(f, c_q)]$

(5) $\mathcal{D}[f_2\ (f_1\ v\ t_1 \ldots t_{n_1})\ t'_1 \ldots t'_{n_2}] = \widetilde{f_1 f_2}\ v\ \mathcal{D}[t_1] \ldots \mathcal{D}[t_{n_1}]\ \mathcal{D}[t'_1] \ldots \mathcal{D}[t'_{n_2}]$

$\quad$ where

$\qquad \widetilde{f_1 f_2}\ (c_1\ x_1 \ldots x_{k_1})\ y_1 \ldots y_{n_1+n_2} = \mathcal{D}[f_2\ (rhs(f_1, c_1))\ y_{n_1+1} \ldots y_{n_1+n_2}]$

$\qquad\qquad\qquad \vdots$

$\qquad \widetilde{f_1 f_2}\ (c_q\ x_1 \ldots x_{k_q})\ y_1 \ldots y_{n_1+n_2} = \mathcal{D}[f_2\ (rhs(f_1, c_q))\ y_{n_1+1} \ldots y_{n_1+n_2}]$ $\qquad$ □

Lemma 8 For every $(p, e) \in (MAC; MAC)$ we have $(p, e) \equiv Def(p, e)$. $\qquad$ □

Instead of proving Lemma 8 formally, we argue by showing the similarities and differences of Transformation 7 and deforestation as it is described e.g. in [18]:

$\mathcal{D}$ terminates, since for the composition of two mtts m_1 and m_2 with h_1 and h_2 functions, respectively, it constructs at most $h_1 h_2 + h_1 + h_2$ functions. The rules (4) and (5) reflect the implicit abstraction of context arguments by let-expressions and differ from the usual presentation (cf. e.g. rule (5) in [18]). In the following we show that rule (4) performs the same transformation as transformation rules in the literature, which can handle explicit let-expressions (cf. e.g. [20]). For rule (5) an analogous argument holds.

$$\mathcal{D}[\![f\ v\ t'_1 \ldots t'_n]\!]$$
$$= \mathcal{D}[\![let\ v_1 = t'_1, \ldots, v_n = t'_n\ in\ (f\ v\ v_1 \ldots v_n)]\!] \qquad \text{(let-abstraction)}$$
$$= let\ v_1 = \mathcal{D}[\![t'_1]\!], \ldots, v_n = \mathcal{D}[\![t'_n]\!]\ in\ \mathcal{D}[\![f\ v\ v_1 \ldots v_n]\!] \qquad \text{($\mathcal{D}$ on let-expr.)}$$
$$= let\ v_1 = \mathcal{D}[\![t'_1]\!], \ldots, v_n = \mathcal{D}[\![t'_n]\!]\ in\ (\tilde{f}\ v\ v_1 \ldots v_n)\ where\ \ldots \qquad \text{($\mathcal{D}$ on function)}$$
$$= \tilde{f}\ v\ \mathcal{D}[\![t'_1]\!] \ldots \mathcal{D}[\![t'_n]\!]\ where\ \ldots \qquad \text{(inlining of let)}$$

Note that in contrast to e.g. [18] we do not introduce a new function in rule (3) for two reasons: On the one hand mtts do not allow *f-functions* in the sense of [18], which are defined without pattern matching. On the other hand, the introduction of f-functions does not contribute to the elimination of intermediate results. The omission of an f-function in rule (3) can cause a later termination of $\mathcal{D}$, but does not affect termination at all, since at the critical steps, where an expansion of variables is performed, new functions are introduced. Note also that f-functions which are not *postunfolded* later [18], increase the number of reduction steps.

For initial expressions like $(app\ z_0\ (app\ z_1\ z_2))$, which are *no composition expressions*, our deforestation algorithm would behave differently from the algorithm described in [20], since $(app\ z_0\ (app\ z_1\ z_2))$ would be treated as if it were the expression $let\ v = (app\ z_1\ z_2)\ in\ (app\ z_0\ v)$.

Example 9 Let $p \in P$ consist of m_{ex} and m_{mir} and let $e_1 = (mir\ (ex\ z_0)\ z_1) \in E_p$. Then, $\mathcal{D}[\![mir\ (ex\ z_0)\ z_1]\!] = (exmir\ z_0\ \mathcal{D}[\![z_1]\!]) = (exmir\ z_0\ z_1)$ where

$$exmir\ (A\ x_1)\ y_1$$
$$= \mathcal{D}[\![mir\ (rhs(ex, A))\ y_1]\!]$$
$$= \mathcal{D}[\![mir\ (B\ (ex\ x_1))\ y_1]\!]$$
$$= \mathcal{D}[\![B\ (mir\ (ex\ x_1)\ (B\ y_1))]\!]$$
$$= B\ \mathcal{D}[\![mir\ (ex\ x_1)\ (B\ y_1)]\!]$$
$$= B\ (exmir\ x_1\ \mathcal{D}[\![B\ y_1]\!])$$
$$= B\ (exmir\ x_1\ (B\ \mathcal{D}[\![y_1]\!]))$$
$$= B\ (exmir\ x_1\ (B\ y_1))$$

$$exmir\ (B\ x_1)\ y_1$$
$$= \ldots = A\ (exmir\ x_1\ (A\ y_1))$$

$$exmir\ N\ y_1$$
$$= \mathcal{D}[\![mir\ (rhs(ex, N))\ y_1]\!]$$
$$= \mathcal{D}[\![mir\ N\ y_1]\!]$$
$$= \mathcal{D}[\![y_1]\!]$$
$$= y_1$$

The new initial expression is $e_{1,d} = (exmir\ z_0\ z_1)$ and the new program $p_{1,d}$ contains the above three equations for the function $exmir$ (where both sides of every equation are underlined). Thus, $Def(p, e_1) = (p_{1,d}, e_{1,d})$. Let $t_0, t_1 \in T_{C_p}$ and $\sigma = [z_0/t_0, z_1/t_1]$. We have $e_{1,d}\sigma \Rightarrow_{p_{1,d}}^{|t_0|} nf(e_{1,d}\sigma)$. □

Example 10 Let $p \in P$ consist of m_{ex} and m_{mir} and let $e_2 = (ex \ (mir \ z_0 \ z_1))$
$\in E_p$. Then, $\mathcal{D}[\![ex \ (mir \ z_0 \ z_1)]\!] = (mirex \ z_0 \ \mathcal{D}[\![z_1]\!]) = (mirex \ z_0 \ z_1)$ where

$$\begin{aligned}
&\underline{mirex \ (A \ x_1) \ y_1} \\
&= \mathcal{D}[\![ex \ (rhs(mir, A))]\!] \\
&= \mathcal{D}[\![ex \ (A \ (mir \ x_1 \ (A \ y_1)))]\!] \\
&= \mathcal{D}[\![B \ (ex \ (mir \ x_1 \ (A \ y_1)))]\!] \quad (+) \\
&= B \ \mathcal{D}[\![ex \ (mir \ x_1 \ (A \ y_1))]\!] \\
&= B \ (mirex \ x_1 \ \mathcal{D}[\![A \ y_1]\!]) \\
&= B \ (mirex \ x_1 \ (A \ \mathcal{D}[\![y_1]\!])) \quad (-) \\
&= \underline{B \ (mirex \ x_1 \ (A \ y_1))}
\end{aligned}$$

$$\begin{aligned}
&\underline{mirex \ (B \ x_1) \ y_1} \\
&= \ldots = \underline{A \ (mirex \ x_1 \ (B \ y_1))} \\
\\
&\underline{mirex \ N \ y_1} \\
&= \mathcal{D}[\![ex \ (rhs(mir, N))]\!] \\
&= \mathcal{D}[\![ex \ y_1]\!] \\
&= \underline{ex \ y_1} \\
&\text{where } ex \text{ is defined as in } m_{ex}.
\end{aligned}$$

The symbols $(+)$ and $(-)$ are explained later. The new initial expression is $e_{2,d} = (mirex \ z_0 \ z_1)$ and the new program $p_{2,d}$ contains the above three equations for the function $mirex$ and the equations from m_{ex}. Thus, $Def(p, e_2) = (p_{2,d}, e_{2,d})$. Note that $p_{2,d} \in (P^+ - P)$, because of the equation $mirex \ N \ y_1 = ex \ y_1$. Let $t_0, t_1 \in T_{C_p}$ and $\sigma = [z_0/t_0, z_1/t_1]$. We have $e_{2,d}\sigma \Rightarrow_{p_{2,d}}^{2 \cdot |t_0| + |t_1| - 1} nf(e_{2,d}\sigma)$. □

5 Composition Techniques

In [17] it was shown that the composition of two tdtts can be simulated by only one tdtt. This result was generalized in [4], where composition techniques are presented which construct an mtt for the composition of a tdtt with an mtt, and of an mtt with a tdtt, respectively. In [4] it was also proved that there is no such construction for the composition of two mtts, since the class of functions which are computed by mtts is not closed under composition. The central idea of the composition techniques for the composition of two tree transducers m_1 and m_2 is the observation that, roughly speaking, intermediate results are built up from right-hand sides of m_1. Thus, instead of translating intermediate results by m_2, right-hand sides of m_1 are translated by m_2 to get the equations of a new tree transducer m. For this purpose, m uses $F_{m_1} \times F_{m_2}$ as function set. In the following, we abbreviate every pair $(f, g) \in F_{m_1} \times F_{m_2}$ by $\overline{fg}$.

The composition technique for the composition class $(TOP; MAC)$ is given by Transformation 11. It will be necessary to extend the call-by-name reduction relation to expressions containing variables (they are handled like 0-ary constructors) and to restrict the call-by-name reduction relation to use only equations of a certain mtt m, which will be denoted by $\Rightarrow_m$.

Transformation 11 Let $(p, e) \in (TOP; MAC)$. Let m_1 be a tdtt in p, let m_2 be an mtt in p, let $f_1 \in F_{m_1}^{(1)}$ and $f_2 \in F_{m_2}^{(n_2+1)}$, such that $e = (f_2 \ (f_1 \ z_0) \ z_1 \ldots z_{n_2})$. We construct a new program p' and a new initial expression e' for p' as follows. The transformation result (p', e') is also denoted by $Com(p, e)$.

1. From m_2 we construct an mtt $\bar{m}_2$ which is able to translate right-hand sides of equations of m_1. Note that $\bar{m}_2$ is not part of p'.

- $\bar{m}_2$ contains the equations of m_2.
- For every $g \in F_{m_2}^{(n+1)}$ and $f \in F_{m_1}^{(1)}$ we add the following equation to $\bar{m}_2$:

$$g\,(f\,x_1)\,y_1\ldots y_n = \overline{fg}\,x_1\,y_1\ldots y_n$$

where every $f \in F_{m_1}^{(1)}$ and $\overline{fg}$ with $f \in F_{m_1}^{(1)}$ and $g \in F_{m_2}^{(n+1)}$ is viewed as additional unary and $(n+1)$-ary constructor, respectively.

2. p' is constructed from p by replacing m_1 and m_2 by the following mtt m with $F_m^{(n+1)} = \{\overline{fg}\,|\,f \in F_{m_1}, g \in F_{m_2}^{(n+1)}\}$: For every $g \in F_{m_2}^{(n+1)}$, $f \in F_{m_1}^{(1)}$, and $c \in C_p^{(k)}$, such that $f\,(c\,x_1\ldots x_k) = rhs(f,c)$ is an equation in m_1, m contains the equation

$$\overline{fg}\,(c\,x_1\ldots x_k)\,y_1\ldots y_n = nf(\Rightarrow_{\bar{m}_2}, g\,(rhs(f,c))\,y_1\ldots y_n)$$

3. $e' = (\overline{f_1 f_2}\,z_0\,z_1\ldots z_{n_2})$ □

Lemma 12 For every $(p,e) \in (TOP; MAC)$ we have $(p,e) \equiv Com(p,e)$.   □

We omit the proof and only mention that in [4] another construction was used, which first splits the mtt into a tdtt and a device for handling parameter substitutions, then composes the two tdtts, and finally composes the resulting tdtt with the substitution device. We get the same transformation result in one step by avoiding the explicit splitting and joining of substitution devices.

Example 13 Let $p \in P$ consist of m_{ex} and m_{mir} and let $e_1 = (mir\,(ex\,z_0)\,z_1) \in E_p$. The mtt $\bar{m}_{mir}$ is given by the following equations:

$$mir\,(A\,x_1)\,y_1 = A\,(mir\,x_1\,(A\,y_1)) \qquad mir\,N\,y_1 \quad\;\; = y_1$$
$$mir\,(B\,x_1)\,y_1 = B\,(mir\,x_1\,(B\,y_1)) \qquad mir\,(ex\,x_1)\,y_1 = \overline{exmir}\,x_1\,y_1$$

The new program $p_{1,c}$ contains only one mtt with the following equations:

$$\overline{exmir}\,(A\,x_1)\,y_1 \qquad\qquad\qquad\qquad \overline{exmir}\,(B\,x_1)\,y_1$$
$$= nf(\Rightarrow_{\bar{m}_{mir}}, mir\,(rhs(ex,A))\,y_1) \qquad = \ldots = A\,(\overline{exmir}\,x_1\,(A\,y_1))$$
$$= nf(\Rightarrow_{\bar{m}_{mir}}, mir\,(B\,(ex\,x_1))\,y_1)$$
$$= nf(\Rightarrow_{\bar{m}_{mir}}, B\,(mir\,(ex\,x_1)\,(B\,y_1))) \qquad \overline{exmir}\,N\,y_1$$
$$= B\,(\overline{exmir}\,x_1\,(B\,y_1)) \qquad\qquad\qquad = \ldots = y_1$$

The new initial expression is $e_{1,c} = (\overline{exmir}\,z_0\,z_1)$. Thus, $Com(p,e_1) = (p_{1,c}, e_{1,c})$. Let $t_0, t_1 \in T_{C_p}$ and $\sigma = [z_0/t_0, z_1/t_1]$. We have $e_{1,c}\sigma \Rightarrow_{p_{1,c}}^{|t_0|} nf(e_{1,c}\sigma)$.   □

The composition class $(MAC - TOP; TOP)$ is handled by Transformation 14. We use the additional observation that for $f_1 \in F_{m_1}$, $f_2 \in F_{m_2}$, and an instance of an initial expression $(f_2\,(f_1\,z_0\,z_1\ldots z_n))$, the results of the instances of $(f_2\,z_1),\ldots,(f_2\,z_n)$ instead of the instances of $z_1,\ldots,z_n$ will occur in the final output. Thus, the context arguments of the functions of the new mtt represent the translations of the context arguments of the functions of m_1 by m_2.

Transformation 14 Let $(p, e) \in (MAC - TOP; TOP)$. Let m_1 be an mtt in p, let m_2 be a tdtt in p, let $f_1 \in F_{m_1}^{(n_1+1)}$ and $f_2 \in F_{m_2}^{(1)}$, such that $e = (f_2 (f_1 z_0 z_1 \ldots z_{n_1}))$. Let $g_1, \ldots, g_h$ be a fixed order of all functions in F_{m_2}. We construct a new program p' and a new initial expression e' for p' as follows. The transformation result (p', e') is also denoted by $Com(p, e)$.

1. From m_2 we construct a tdtt $\bar{m}_2$ which is able to translate right-hand sides of equations of m_1. Note that $\bar{m}_2$ is not part of p'.
   - $\bar{m}_2$ contains the equations of m_2.
   - For every $g \in F_{m_2}^{(1)}$ and $f \in F_{m_1}^{(n+1)}$ we add the following equation to $\bar{m}_2$:

   $$(*_1) \qquad g \, (f \, x_1 \, x_2 \ldots x_{n+1}) \\ = \overline{fg} \, x_1 \, (g_1 \, x_2) \ldots (g_h \, x_2) \ldots \ldots (g_1 \, x_{n+1}) \ldots (g_h \, x_{n+1})$$

   where every $f \in F_{m_1}^{(n+1)}$ and $\overline{fg}$ with $f \in F_{m_1}^{(n+1)}$ and $g \in F_{m_2}^{(1)}$ is viewed as additional $(n + 1)$-ary and $(hn + 1)$-ary constructor, respectively.
   - For every $g \in F_{m_2}^{(1)}$ and for every y_j which occurs in right-hand sides of equations of m_1 add the following equation to $\bar{m}_2$:

   $$(*_2) \qquad g \, y_j = y_{j,g}$$

   where every y_j and every $y_{j,g}$ are viewed as additional 0-ary constructors.
2. p' is constructed from p by keeping m_2 and by replacing m_1 by the following mtt m with $F_m^{(hn+1)} = \{\overline{fg} \mid f \in F_{m_1}^{(n+1)}, g \in F_{m_2}\}$: For every $g \in F_{m_2}^{(1)}$, $f \in F_{m_1}^{(n+1)}$, and $c \in C_p^{(k)}$ such that $f \, (c \, x_1 \ldots x_k) \, y_1 \ldots y_n = rhs(f, c)$ is an equation in m_1, m contains the equation

   $$\overline{fg} \, (c \, x_1 \ldots x_k) \, y_{1,g_1} \ldots y_{1,g_h} \ldots \ldots y_{n,g_1} \ldots y_{n,g_h} = nf(\Rightarrow_{\bar{m}_2}, g \, (rhs(f, c)))$$

3. $e' = (\overline{f_1 f_2} \, z_0 \, (g_1 \, z_1) \ldots (g_h \, z_1) \ldots \ldots (g_1 \, z_{n_1}) \ldots (g_h \, z_{n_1}))$ $\qquad \Box$

Note that e' is no composition expression. The following lemma is a consequence of a result in [4] and will not be proved here:

Lemma 15 For every $(p, e) \in (MAC{-}TOP; TOP)$ we have $(p, e) \equiv Com(p, e)$. $\Box$

Example 16 Let $p \in P$ consist of m_{ex} and m_{mir} and let $e_2 = (ex \, (mir \, z_0 \, z_1)) \in E_p$. The tdtt $\bar{m}_{ex}$ is given by the following equations:

$$ex \, (A \, x_1) = B \, (ex \, x_1) \qquad ex \, N = N \qquad ex \, (mir \, x_1 \, x_2) = \overline{mirex} \, x_1 \, (ex \, x_2)$$
$$ex \, (B \, x_1) = A \, (ex \, x_1) \qquad ex \, y_1 = y_{1,ex}$$

The new program $p_{2,c}$ contains m_{ex} and a new mtt with the following equations:

$\overline{mirex} \, (A \, x_1) \, y_{1,ex}$
$= nf(\Rightarrow_{\bar{m}_{ex}}, ex \, (rhs(mir, A)))$
$= nf(\Rightarrow_{\bar{m}_{ex}}, ex \, (A \, (mir \, x_1 \, (A \, y_1))))$
$= nf(\Rightarrow_{\bar{m}_{ex}}, B \, (ex \, (mir \, x_1 \, (A \, y_1))))$
$= nf(\Rightarrow_{\bar{m}_{ex}}, B \, (\overline{mirex} \, x_1 \, (ex \, (A \, y_1))))$ (!)
$= nf(\Rightarrow_{\bar{m}_{ex}}, B \, (\overline{mirex} \, x_1 \, (B \, (ex \, y_1))))$
$= B \, (\overline{mirex} \, x_1 \, (B \, y_{1,ex}))$

$\overline{mirex} \, (B \, x_1) \, y_{1,ex}$
$= \ldots$
$= A \, (\overline{mirex} \, x_1 \, (A \, y_{1,ex}))$

$\overline{mirex} \, N \, y_{1,ex}$
$= \ldots$
$= y_{1,ex}$

The new initial expression is $e_{2,c} = (\overline{mirex}\ z_0\ (ex\ z_1))$. Thus, $Com(p, e_2) = (p_{2,c}, e_{2,c})$. Let $t_0, t_1 \in T_{C_p}$ and $\sigma = [z_0/t_0, z_1/t_1]$. We have $e_{2,c}\sigma \Rightarrow_{p_{2,c}}^{|t_0|+|t_1|} nf(e_{2,c}\sigma)$.

$\square$

6   Comparison

Although the transformations of Sections 4 and 5 work on nonlinear programs as well, we restrict the following comparison to linear mtts, since nonlinear function definitions can cause a deterioration by deforestation [20] and also by composition. We will use the following notions to compare efficiencies.

Definition 17 For every $i \in [2]$ let $(p_i, e_i) \in \{(p, e) \mid p \in P^+, e \in E_p\}$ such that $(p_1, e_1) \equiv (p_2, e_2)$. We call (p_1, e_1) *as efficient as* (*at least as efficient as*, respectively) (p_2, e_2), denoted by $\mathcal{E}(p_1, e_1) = \mathcal{E}(p_2, e_2)$ ($\mathcal{E}(p_1, e_1) \geq \mathcal{E}(p_2, e_2)$, respectively), if for every $\sigma = [v/t_v \mid v \in var(e_1) \cup var(e_2), t_v \in T_{C_{p_1}}]$ and for every $\alpha_{1,\sigma}, \alpha_{2,\sigma} \in \mathbb{N}$ with $e_i\sigma \Rightarrow_{p_i}^{\alpha_{i,\sigma}} nf(e_i\sigma)$ for every $i \in [2]$,

$$\alpha_{1,\sigma} = \alpha_{2,\sigma}\ (\alpha_{1,\sigma} \leq \alpha_{2,\sigma},\ \text{respectively}).$$

We call (p_1, e_1) *more efficient than* (p_2, e_2), denoted by $\mathcal{E}(p_1, e_1) > \mathcal{E}(p_2, e_2)$, if $\mathcal{E}(p_1, e_1) \geq \mathcal{E}(p_2, e_2)$ and there is $\sigma = [v/t_v \mid v \in var(e_1) \cup var(e_2), t_v \in T_{C_{p_1}}]$ and $\alpha_{1,\sigma}, \alpha_{2,\sigma} \in \mathbb{N}$ with $e_i\sigma \Rightarrow_{p_i}^{\alpha_{i,\sigma}} nf(e_i\sigma)$ for every $i \in [2]$ and

$$\alpha_{1,\sigma} < \alpha_{2,\sigma}.$$

$\square$

We will compare the transformations on the composition class $(MAC_l; MAC_l)$. It turns out that there are different results for its three disjoint subclasses $(TOP_l; MAC_l)$, $((MAC - TOP)_l; TOP_l)$, and $((MAC - TOP)_l; (MAC - TOP)_l)$.

6.1   Where Deforestation and Composition Behave Similarly

Example 18 Let $p \in P$ consist of m_{ex} and m_{mir} and let $e_1 = (mir\ (ex\ z_0)\ z_1)$. Examples 9 and 13 show that deforestation and the composition technique transform (p, e_1), apart from function renaming, into the same program and initial expression. In particular, $\mathcal{E}(Def(p, e_1)) = \mathcal{E}(Com(p, e_1)) > \mathcal{E}(p, e_1)$.

$\square$

This observation can be generalized as follows.

Lemma 19 For every $(p, e) \in (TOP_{1,l}; MAC_{1,l})$: $Def(p, e) = Com(p, e)$ (apart from function renaming).

Proof Idea. Let $(p_d, e_d) = Def(p, e)$ and $(p_c, e_c) = Com(p, e)$. Let m_1 be a tdtt in p, m_2 be an mtt in p, $f_1 \in F_{m_1}^{(1)}$, and $f_2 \in F_{m_2}^{(n+1)}$ such that $e =$

$(f_2 \; (f_1 \; z_0) \; z_1 \ldots z_n)$. Let $c \in C_p^{(k)}$. Deforestation generates in the body of the where-clause in rule (5) the equation

$$f_1 f_2 \; (c \; x_1 \ldots x_k) \; y_1 \ldots y_n = \mathcal{D}[\![f_2 \; (rhs(f_1, c)) \; y_1 \ldots y_n]\!]$$

for p_d and composition generates by 2. in Transformation 11 the equation

$$\overline{f_1 f_2} \; (c \; x_1 \ldots x_k) \; y_1 \ldots y_n = nf(\Rightarrow_{\bar{m}_2}, f_2 \; (rhs(f_1, c)) \; y_1 \ldots y_n)$$

for p_c. Identifying $f_1 f_2$ with $\overline{f_1 f_2}$, these two equations are equal, since

$$\mathcal{D}[\![f_2 \; r \; r_1 \ldots r_n]\!] = nf(\Rightarrow_{\bar{m}_2}, f_2 \; r \; r_1 \ldots r_n),$$

for every right-hand side r of m_1 and for every right-hand sides $r_1, \ldots, r_n$ of m_2 in which recursion variables are instantiated by right-hand sides of m_1, can be proved by an induction on $r \in R$. Additionally, an inner induction proof on the set of in this way instantiated right-hand sides of m_2 has to be performed.   □

If mtts with more than one function are considered, then Lemma 19 remains in principle valid, but the composition technique sometimes constructs new functions which are never used to evaluate instances of the new initial expression. Deforestation prevents the construction of superfluous functions, since it mimics the call-by-name evaluation of an arbitrarily instantiated initial expression.

Lemma 20 For every $(p, e) \in (TOP_l; MAC_l)$: $Def(p, e) = Com(p, e)$ (apart from superfluous functions and apart from function renaming).   □

Since deforestation does not deteriorate the efficiency (cf. e.g.[20,18]), we get:

Corollary 21 For every $(p, e) \in (TOP_l; MAC_l)$:

$$\mathcal{E}(Def(p, e)) = \mathcal{E}(Com(p, e)) \geq \mathcal{E}(p, e).$$

     □

6.2   Where Composition is at Least as Good as Deforestation

Example 22 Let $p \in P$ consist of m_{ex} and m_{mir} and let $e_2 = (ex \; (mir \; z_0 \; z_1))$. We get the result $\mathcal{E}(Com(p, e_2)) > \mathcal{E}(Def(p, e_2)) > \mathcal{E}(p, e_2)$ from Examples 5, 10, and 16.

Example 10 shows that on the one hand deforestation is successful in removing the intermediate constructor "outside" the recursive call of mir by replacing A by B (cf. step marked $(+)$ in Example 10).

On the other hand, deforestation cannot remove the intermediate constructor "inside" the recursive call of mir (cf. step marked $(-)$ in Example 10), since the function ex does not reach the context argument of mir. In contrast to this, the step $(!)$ in Example 16 shows, that ex moves into the context argument of mir, thereby removing also the "inside" intermediate constructor.   □

The different behaviour of the transformations is caused by the different strategies to handle the "meeting" of two functions. Rule (5) in Transformation 7 shows that deforestation generates a new function and simply moves into the context arguments without changing them, whereas equation $(*_1)$ in Transformation 14 shows that composition additionally sends the functions of m_2 into the context arguments. Maybe this observation allows an improvement of deforestation by integrating the behaviour of $(*_1)$ into rule (5). The equation $(*_1)$ also has one negative aspect: Since it copies context arguments according to the number of functions of m_2, the produced program can be nonlinear. We do not know yet, how the efficiency (counting call-by-need reduction steps) of programs, which are constructed in this way, is related to the original programs. Hence, we restrict the statement of the following lemma to tdtts with only one function.

Theorem 23 For every $(p, e) \in ((MAC - TOP)_l; TOP_{1,l})$:

$$\mathcal{E}(Com(p, e)) \geq \mathcal{E}(Def(p, e)) \geq \mathcal{E}(p, e).$$ □

Before we give the proof idea, we would like to discuss, for which composition classes we obtain strict improvements in Theorem 23.

Example 24 Let $p \in P$ consist of m_{ex}, m_{app}, and m_{rev}.

 - For $e = (ex\ (app\ z_0\ z_1))$ we have $\mathcal{E}(Com(p, e)) = \mathcal{E}(Def(p, e)) > \mathcal{E}(p, e)$, since already deforestation completely removes the intermediate result.
 - For $e = (ex\ (rev\ z_0\ z_1))$ we have $\mathcal{E}(Com(p, e)) > \mathcal{E}(Def(p, e)) = \mathcal{E}(p, e)$, since deforestation fails in removing the intermediate result, whereas composition completely removes it.   □

The different results in Example 24 are caused by the different structures of right-hand sides of app and rev. For example, $rhs(app, A)$ has a constructor outside and no constructor inside the recursive function call, whereas in $rhs(rev, A)$ it is vice versa. Roughly speaking, deforestation can only eliminate intermediate constructors, which occur outside the topmost function applications of right-hand sides, whereas composition additionally eliminates intermediate constructors inside the topmost function applications. Following this idea, we define a decomposition of right-hand sides into a top-part and bottom-parts, which will be important to state a refinement of Theorem 23 and to prove Theorem 23.

Definition 25 Let $r \in R$. Define $top(r) \in T_C(y_1, \ldots, y_n, u_1, \ldots, u_m)$, for every $i \in [m]$ define $f_{k_i} \in F^{(n_i+1)}$ and $x_{k_i} \in X$, and for every $j \in [n_i]$ define $bot_{i,j}(r) \in R$, such that $r = top(r)[u_i/(f_{k_i}\ x_{k_i}\ bot_{i,1}(r) \ldots bot_{i,n_i}(r))]$.   □

Example 26 If $r = (A\ (mir\ x_1\ (A\ y_1)))$, then $top(r) = (A\ u_1)$, $f_{k_1} = mir$, $x_{k_1} = x_1$, and $bot_{1,1}(r) = (A\ y_1)$. Thus, $|top(r)|_C = 1$ and $|bot_{1,1}(r)|_C = 1$.   □

Theorem 27 Let $(p, e) \in ((MAC - TOP)_l; TOP_{1,l})$. Let m_1 be an mtt in p, m_2 be a tdtt in p, $f_1 \in F_{m_1}^{(n_1+1)}$, and $f_2 \in F_{m_2}$, such that $e = (f_2\ (f_1\ z_0 \ldots z_{n_1}))$.

- If there is $c \in C_p$ with $|top(rhs(f_1, c))|_{C_p} > 0$, then

$$\mathcal{E}(Def(p, e)) > \mathcal{E}(p, e).$$

- If there are $c \in C_p$, and $i, j > 0$ with $|bot_{i,j}(rhs(f_1, c))|_{C_p} > 0$, and if $var(l) = var(r)$ for every equation $l = r$ of m_1 and m_2 (nondeleting condition), then

$$\mathcal{E}(Com(p, e)) > \mathcal{E}(Def(p, e)). \qquad \square$$

Proof Idea of Theorems 23 and 27. Let $(p, e) \in ((MAC{-}TOP)_l; TOP_{1,l})$, $(p_d, e_d) = Def(p, e)$, and $(p_c, e_c) = Com(p, e)$. Let m_1 be an mtt in p, m_2 be a tdtt in p, $f_1 \in F_{m_1}^{(n_1+1)}$, $g \in F_{m_2}^{(1)}$ such that $e = (g\ (f_1\ z_0 \ldots z_{n_1}))$.

Let $f \in F_{m_1}^{(n+1)}$ and $c \in C_p^{(k)}$. We abbreviate $top(rhs(f, c))$ by top and $bot_{i,j}(rhs(f, c))$ by $bot_{i,j}$. Thus, $rhs(f, c) = top[u_i/(f_{k_i}\ x_{k_i}\ bot_{i,1} \ldots bot_{i,n_i})]$. Deforestation generates (if demanded) the following equation for p_d:

$$
\begin{aligned}
& fg\ (c\ x_1 \ldots x_k)\ y_1 \ldots y_n \\
&= \mathcal{D}[\![g\ (top[u_i/(f_{k_i}\ x_{k_i}\ bot_{i,1} \ldots bot_{i,n_i})])]\!] && \text{(Body of where in (5))} \\
&= nf(\Rightarrow_{m_2}, g\ top)[(g\ y_j)/\mathcal{D}[\![g\ y_j]\!]][(g\ u_i)/\mathcal{D}[\![g\ (f_{k_i}\ x_{k_i}\ bot_{i,1} \ldots bot_{i,n_i})]\!]] \\
& && \text{(Rules (2) and (3))} \\
&= nf(\Rightarrow_{m_2}, g\ top)[(g\ y_j)/(g\ y_j)][(g\ u_i)/\mathcal{D}[\![g\ (f_{k_i}\ x_{k_i}\ bot_{i,1} \ldots bot_{i,n_i})]\!]] \\
& && (\mathcal{D}[\![g\ y_j]\!] = (g\ y_j)) \\
&= nf(\Rightarrow_{m_2}, g\ top)[(g\ u_i)/(f_{k_i}g\ x_{k_i}\ \mathcal{D}[\![bot_{i,1}]\!] \ldots \mathcal{D}[\![bot_{i,n_i}]\!])] \\
& && \text{(Rule (5))} \\
&= nf(\Rightarrow_{m_2}, g\ top)[(g\ u_i)/(f_{k_i}g\ x_{k_i}\ bot_{i,1} \ldots bot_{i,n_i})] && (\mathcal{D}[\![r]\!] = r \text{ for } r \in R)
\end{aligned}
$$

The statements $\mathcal{D}[\![g\ y_j]\!] = (g\ y_j)$ and $\mathcal{D}[\![r]\!] = r$ do not reflect that here functions of m_2 and m_1, respectively, are "reproduced" in general. $\mathcal{D}[\![r]\!] = r$ can be proved by an induction on $r \in R$. Composition generates the following equation for p_c:

$$
\begin{aligned}
& \overline{fg}\ (c\ x_1 \ldots x_k)\ y_{1,g} \ldots y_{n,g} \\
&= nf(\Rightarrow_{\bar{m}_2}, g\ (top[u_i/(f_{k_i}\ x_{k_i}\ bot_{i,1} \ldots bot_{i,n_i})])) && \text{(2. in Transformation 14)} \\
&= nf(\Rightarrow_{\bar{m}_2}, g\ top)[(g\ u_i)/nf(\Rightarrow_{\bar{m}_2}, g\ (f_{k_i}\ x_{k_i}\ bot_{i,1} \ldots bot_{i,n_i}))] \\
& && \text{(Definition of } \bar{m}_2) \\
&= nf(\Rightarrow_{m_2}, g\ top)[(g\ y_j)/y_{j,g}] \\
& \quad [(g\ u_i)/(\overline{f_{k_i}g}\ x_{k_i}\ nf(\Rightarrow_{\bar{m}_2}, g\ bot_{i,1}) \ldots nf(\Rightarrow_{\bar{m}_2}, g\ bot_{i,n_i}))] \\
& && ((*_1) \text{ and } (*_2) \text{ in Tr. 14})
\end{aligned}
$$

Let $t_1, \ldots, t_k, t'_1, \ldots, t'_n \in T_{C_p}$. Let a reduction of p start with the step

$$g\ (f\ (c\ t_1 \ldots t_k)\ t'_1 \ldots t'_n) \Rightarrow_p g\ (top[u_i/(f_{k_i}\ x_{k_i}\ bot_{i,1} \ldots bot_{i,n_i})])[x_l/t_l][y_l/t'_l].$$

The continuation of this reduction will in particular force the evaluation of $(g\ top)$ and of some $(g\ bot_{i,j})$. The corresponding first reduction step of p_d is

$$
\begin{aligned}
& fg\ (c\ t_1 \ldots t_k)\ t'_1 \ldots t'_n \Rightarrow_{p_d} \\
& nf(\Rightarrow_{m_2}, g\ top)[(g\ y_j)/(g\ t'_j)][(g\ u_i)/((f_{k_i}g\ x_{k_i}\ bot_{i,1} \ldots bot_{i,n_i})[x_l/t_l][y_l/t'_l])]
\end{aligned}
$$

It saves the steps for the evaluation of $(g\ top)$. The corresponding first reduction step of p_c also saves the steps for the evaluation of the $(g\ bot_{i,j})$:

$$\overline{fg}\ (c\ t_1\dots t_k)\ (g\ t_1')\dots(g\ t_n') \quad \Rightarrow_{p_c}$$
$$nf(\Rightarrow_{m_2}, g\ top)[(g\ y_j)/(g\ t_j')]$$
$$[(g\ u_i)/((\overline{f_{k_i}g}\ x_{k_i}\ nf(\Rightarrow_{\bar{m}_2}, g\ bot_{i,1})\dots nf(\Rightarrow_{\bar{m}_2}, g\ bot_{i,n_i}))[x_l/t_l][y_{l,g}/(g\ t_l')])]$$

This also holds for corresponding instances of e, e_d, and e_c. The informal explanation can be seen as heart of an induction proof on T_{C_p}, for which additionally an inner induction proof on the set of right-hand sides of m_1 is needed. The proof also shows that, if subtrees are deleted, then this affects the three reductions in the same way. If for some $c \in C_p$ we have $|top(rhs(f_1, c))|_{C_p} > 0$ (and $|bot_{i,j}(rhs(f_1, c))|_{C_p} > 0$ for some $i, j > 0$ such that $bot_{i,j}(rhs(f_1, c))$ is not deleted by $\Rightarrow_p$), then the precomputation of $(g\ top(rhs(f_1, c)))$ (and of $(g\ bot_{i,j}(rhs(f_1, c)))$, respectively) really saves reduction steps. This holds at least for substitutions of z_0 in e by a tree which has the symbol c at its root. □

6.3   Where Deforestation is at Least as Good as Composition

Since for every $(p, e) \in ((MAC-TOP)_l; (MAC-TOP)_l)$ the composition techniques are not applicable, we define $Com(p, e) = (p, e)$ and get as consequence:

Theorem 28 For every $(p, e) \in ((MAC-TOP)_l; (MAC-TOP)_l)$:

$$\mathcal{E}(Def(p, e)) \geq \mathcal{E}(Com(p, e)) = \mathcal{E}(p, e).$$
□

Also here we could distinguish composition classes, which are either improved or not improved by deforestation. Since this leads to an analysis of deforestation and does not contribute to our intended comparison of the two techniques, we only give representative examples for these classes:

Example 29 Let $p \in P$ consist of m_{app} and m_{rev}.

- For $e = (app\ (app\ z_0\ z_1)\ z_2)$ we have $\mathcal{E}(Def(p, e)) > \mathcal{E}(p, e)$.
- For $e = (rev\ (rev\ z_0\ z_1)\ z_2)$ we have $\mathcal{E}(Def(p, e)) = \mathcal{E}(p, e)$.
□

7   Future Work

We have presented qualitative comparisons of deforestation and composition techniques for certain composition classes. A quantitative analysis (also by using more exact efficiency measures) would be useful, in order to calculate speedups, which are realized by the transformations. Moreover, we would like to extend our research to nonlinear programs and to specify composition classes, for which nonlinearity is harmless with respect to deforestation and composition.

Other methods for the elimination of intermediate results should be integrated into the comparison. Therefore, on the one hand we want to analyze

Short Cut (or: *Cheap*) *Deforestation* [11]. In [10] already an informal comparison between classical deforestation and cheap deforestation is performed. On the other hand we would like to inspect composition methods for *attributed tree transducers* [6], which are abstractions of *attribute grammars* [14]. Such composition results were presented e.g. in [6,8,9]. They can also be used for the composition of a restricted class of mtts [15]. For the intended comparison, we consider *macro attributed tree transducers* [16] as suitable integration formalism.

Acknowledgment

I would like to thank Morten Heine Sørensen and Heiko Vogler for stimulating discussions on deforestation and on tree transducers, respectively.

References

1. R. M. Burstall and J. Darlington. A transformation system for developing recursive programs. *J. Assoc. Comput. Mach.*, 24:44–67, 1977.
2. B. Courcelle and P. Franchi–Zannettacci. Attribute grammars and recursive program schemes. *Theoret. Comput. Sci.*, 17:163–191, 235–257, 1982.
3. J. Engelfriet. Some open questions and recent results on tree transducers and tree languages. In R.V. Book, editor, *Formal language theory; perspectives and open problems*, pages 241–286. New York, Academic Press, 1980.
4. J. Engelfriet and H. Vogler. Macro tree transducers. *J. Comput. Syst. Sci.*, 31:71–145, 1985.
5. A.B. Ferguson and P. Wadler. When will deforestation stop? In *1988 Glasgow Workshop on Functional Programming*, pages 39–56, 1988.
6. Z. Fülöp. On attributed tree transducers. *Acta Cybernetica*, 5:261–279, 1981.
7. Z. Fülöp and H. Vogler. *Syntax-directed semantics – Formal models based on tree transducers*. Monographs in Theoretical Computer Science, An EATCS Series. Springer-Verlag, 1998.
8. H. Ganzinger. Increasing modularity and language–independency in automatically generated compilers. *Science of Computer Programming*, 3:223–278, 1983.
9. R. Giegerich. Composition and evaluation of attribute coupled grammars. *Acta Informatica*, 25:355–423, 1988.
10. A. Gill. *Cheap deforestation for non-strict functional languages*. PhD thesis, University of Glasgow, 1996.
11. A. Gill, J. Launchbury, and S.L. Peyton Jones. A short cut to deforestation. In *FPCA'93, Copenhagen, Denmark, Proceedings*, pages 223–231. ACM Press, 1993.
12. G. W. Hamilton and S. B. Jones. Extending deforestation for first order functional programs. In *1991 Glasgow Workshop on Functional Programming*, Series of Workshops in Computing, pages 134–145. Springer-Verlag, 1992.
13. J. Hughes. Why functional programming matters. In D. Turner, editor, *Research Topics in Functional Programming*. Addison-Wesley, 1990.
14. D.E. Knuth. Semantics of context–free languages. *Math. Syst. Th.*, 2:127–145, 1968. Corrections in *Math. Syst. Th.*, 5:95-96, 1971.
15. A. Kühnemann. Benefits of tree transducers for optimizing functional programs. In *FST & TCS'98, Chennai, India, Proceedings*, volume 1530 of *LNCS*, pages 146–157. Springer-Verlag, December 1998.

16. A. Kühnemann and H. Vogler. Synthesized and inherited functions – a new computational model for syntax-directed semantics. *Acta Informatica*,31:431–477, 1994.
17. W.C. Rounds. Mappings and grammars on trees. *Math. Syst. Th.*,4:257–287, 1970.
18. M. H. Sørensen, R. Glück, and N. D. Jones. Towards unifying partial evaluation, deforestation, supercompilation, and GPC. In *ESOP'94, Edinburgh, U.K., Proceedings*, volume 788 of *LNCS*, pages 485–500. Springer–Verlag, 1994.
19. J.W. Thatcher. Generalized^2 sequential machine maps. *J. Comput. Syst. Sci.*, 4:339–367, 1970.
20. P. Wadler. Deforestation: Transforming programs to eliminate trees. *Theor. Comp. Sci.*, 73:231–248, 1990.

Automatic Verification
Based on Abstract Interpretation

Mizuhito Ogawa

NTT Communication Science Laboratories
3-1 Morinosato-Wakamiya Atsugi Kanagawa, 243-0198 Japan
`mizuhito@theory.brl.ntt.co.jp`
`http://www.brl.ntt.co.jp/people/mizuhito/`

Abstract. This paper reconstructs and extends the automatic verification technique of Le Métayer, *Proving properties of programs defined over recursive data structures (ACM PEPM '95)*, based on a backward abstract interpretation.

To show the effectiveness of extensions, we show two examples of the declarative specifications of sorting and formatting programs, which are directly and concisely expressed in our specification language.

1 Introduction

Program errors cause failures during execution that can be classified into three categories.

1. Execution eventually stops as a result of illegal operations.
2. Execution does not terminate.
3. Execution results are not what was intended.

Errors of the first kind are detected by type inference, with such languages as ML. In addition, although termination is in general undecidable, errors of the second kind can be automatically prevented by several techniques, such as simple termination [12,13], termination analysis [16], and dependency pairs [2].

The third kind of error cannot be prevented without a specification language, and there is always a trade-off between expressiveness and feasibility. If the aim is to express everything, it is easy to fall into the trap of undecidability. Moreover, too much expressiveness may make users hard to learn. For compile-time error detection, an automatic verifier that functions without any human guidance is desirable even if it verifies only partial specifications. Then the user can concentrate on what kind of properties, under the limitation of a simple and restricted specification language, properly approximate the program behavior.

By restricting both properties and languages, Le Métayer developed an automatic verification technique [19]. Its target language is a strongly-typed first-order functional language with product types and recursive types. The important restriction is that the conditional part of an if-expression contains only basic predicates (such as *null*, *leq*, *geq*, and *equal*) without any functional symbols.

A. Middeldorp, T. Sato (Eds.): FLOPS'99, LNCS 1722, pp. 131–146, 1999.
© Springer-Verlag Berlin Heidelberg 1999

He defines a language which prescribes a class of *uniform* predicates over recursive types. These predicates are constructed by predicate constructors from basic predicates on base types. As an example, his system expresses that a sort program returns a list of decreasing values (if the sort program terminates) and automatically verifies it. This property is called *orderedness* of the sort program, which is expressed by **true** $\rightarrow \nabla geq(sort\ X)$ in our specification language. Note that the termination of the sort program is not verified; this verification is left to a termination analysis.

Similar ideas to those of uniform predicates are also found in Refs. [15,17,3,21]; however, the significant differences are that

– binary predicates are allowed in constructing predicates, and
– free variables in binary predicates are allowed.

The former extends the expressiveness of target properties from other flow analyses. The latter maintains the power of inter-functional inferences. However, the expressive power of the specification language is still fairly restricted as a verification; for instance, the input-output relation cannot be described.

This paper reconstructs and extends the automatic verification technique of Le Métayer [19] based on a backward abstract interpretation [11,1,7]. The termination and soundness proofs of the verification are naturally derived from the formalization as a backward abstract interpretation.

Extensions are achieved by (1) using the input variable in function properties, (2) introducing new predicate constructors, and (3) using uninterpreted function/predicate symbols. They are demonstrated by verifying the sorting and formatting programs. The first and the second extensions expand the ability of the specification language so that it covers another major specification of the sorting program; namely, *weak preservation*, i.e., the input and the output are the same *set*. This is expressed by **true** $\rightarrow \forall_l \exists_r equal \wedge \forall_r \exists_l equal(sort\ X)$. Note that since our specification language cannot express the number of elements in a list, our algorithm cannot detect the full specification of sort, called *preservation*, i.e., the input and the output are the same *multiset*.

The third extension expands the range of both target programs and the specification language. The expansion of target programs is achieved by loosening the restrictions on the conditional part of an if-expression. The running example is `format`, which formats a given sentence (expressed as a list of strings) to a specified width. The technique behind this extension is the use of *uninterpreted functions*. We also show how partial evaluation will cooperate with the verification. Other major specifications of `format` become expressible by the use of *uninterpreted predicates*. This technique drastically expands the expressive ability, such as the specification that the order of words is preserved by `format`.

This paper is organized as follows: Section 2 defines programming and specification languages. Section 3 provides the verification algorithm based on a backward abstract interpretation. The termination and soundness proofs are also given. Section 4 demonstrates the verification of *orderedness* of the (simple but inefficient) sort program to explain the algorithm. Section 5 presents extensions and demonstrates the verification of major specifications of the sorting and

formatting programs. Section 6 discusses related work and Section 7 concludes
the paper and discusses future work.

2   Preliminaries

2.1   Programming Language

The target language is a strongly-typed first-order functional language with ML-
like syntax, in which product types and recursive types, such as lists $list(A) =$
$\mu\alpha.nil + A \times list(\alpha)$, are allowed. We use :: to mean infix *cons*, @ to mean infix
append, and [ ] to mean a list, namely, $[a_1, a_2, a_3] = a_1 :: (a_2 :: (a_3 :: nil))$. The
semantics of the language is given by an ordinary least fix-point computation.
We assume that the language is strict, but the same technique can be applied
to a lazy language as well. The precise syntax and semantics of the language are
shown in Fig. 1 and Fig. 2. Parentheses in the syntax are used for either making
pairs or clarifying the order of applications of infix operators. Basic concrete
domains D_{Bool} and D_{Int} are flat cpo's (as usual), and the other concrete domains
D_α of type α are constructed by the list and pair constructors. The interpretation
ψ of expressions has the hidden argument, i.e., for simplicity the environment
fve of function variables are omitted in Fig. 2.

The language of expressions

$$E = x \mid C \mid (E_1, E_2) \mid E_1 :: E_2 \mid f\,E \mid op\,E \mid (E) \mid$$
$$\text{if } Cond \text{ then } E_1 \text{ else } E_2 \mid \text{let val } x = E_1 \text{ in } E_2 \text{ end} \mid$$
$$\text{let val } (x,y) = E_1 \text{ in } E_2 \text{ end} \mid \text{let val } x :: xs = E_1 \text{ in } E_2 \text{ end}$$
$$Cond = p_u\,x \mid p_b\,(x,y)$$

where $\begin{cases} E \in Exp & \text{expressions} \\ C \in Const & \text{constants} \\ x \in Bv & \text{bound variables} \end{cases}$ $\begin{aligned} op &\in Prim & \text{primitive functions} \\ p_u, p_b &\in Pred & \text{basic predicates} \\ f &\in Fv & \text{functional variables} \end{aligned}$

The syntax of programs $Prog = \{ \text{ fun } f_i\,x_i = E_i \text{ ; } \}$

The language of types

$$\begin{aligned} T &= T_G \mid T_F & T_F &= T_G \to T_G \\ T_G &= T_U \mid T_P \mid T_R & T_P &= T_G \times T_G \\ T_R &= \mu\alpha.\text{nil} + T_G :: \alpha & T_U &= \tau \quad \text{(basic types)} \end{aligned}$$

Fig. 1. Syntax of Programming Language.

An important restriction is that the conditional part of an if-expression must
consist only of basic predicates without any functional symbols. Section 5 discusses how this requirement can be loosened. Until then, we use only null as the
unary basic predicate on lists, leq, geq, and equal as the binary basic predicates

$$\varphi[\ \{\ \mathbf{fun}\ f_i\ x_i = E_i\ ;\ \}\ ] \qquad = fve\ \mathbf{whererec}$$
$$fve = [(\lambda y_1 \cdots y_n.if\ (bottom?\ y_1 \cdots y_n)$$
$$then\ \bot\ else\ \psi[E_i][y_j/x_j])/f_i]$$

$$\psi[C]bve \qquad = \xi_c[C]$$
$$\psi[x]bve \qquad = bve[x]$$
$$\psi[op\ E]bve \qquad = \xi_f[op](\psi[E]bve)$$
$$\psi[p_u\ x]bve \qquad = \xi_p[p_u](bve[x])$$
$$\psi[p_b\ (x,y)]bve \qquad = \xi_p[p_b](bve[x], bve[y])$$
$$\psi[f\ E]bve \qquad = fve[f](\psi[E]bve)$$
$$\psi[(E_1, E_2)]bve \qquad = (\psi[E_1]bve, \psi[E_2]bve)$$
$$\psi[E_1 :: E_2]bve \qquad = (\psi[E_1]bve) :: (\psi[E_2]bve)$$
$$\psi[\mathbf{if}\ Cond\ \mathbf{then}\ E_1\ \mathbf{else}\ E_2]bve = if\ (bottom?\ (\psi[Cond]bve))\ then\ \bot$$
$$elsif\ \psi[Cond]bve\ then\ \psi[E_1]bve\ else\ \psi[E_2]bve$$
$$\psi[\mathbf{let\ val}\ x = E_1\ \mathbf{in}\ E_2]bve \quad = \psi[E_2](bve[\psi[E_1]bve/x])$$
$$\psi[\mathbf{let\ val}\ (x,y) = E_1\ \mathbf{in}\ E_2]bve = \psi[E_2](bve[\psi[E_1]bve/(x,y)])$$
$$\psi[\mathbf{let\ val}\ x :: xs = E_1\ \mathbf{in}\ E_2]bve = \psi[E_2](bve[\psi[E_1]bve/x :: xs])$$
$$bottom?\ y_1 \cdots y_n \qquad = (y_1 = \bot) \vee \cdots \vee (y_n = \bot)$$

$$\text{where} \begin{cases} \psi : (Fve \to)Exp \to Bve \to D & \xi_f : Prim \to D \to D \\ \psi_p : Prog \to Fve & \xi_p : Pred \to D \to Bool \\ fve \in Fve = Fv \to D \to D & \xi_c : Const \to D \\ bve \in Bve = Bv \to D \end{cases}$$

Fig. 2. Semantics of Programming Language.

on integers, :: as a binary primitive function, and *nil* as a constant. The type description in a program is often omitted if it can be easily deduced by type inference.

For technical simplicity, we also set the following restrictions.

- Basic types are *Int* and *Bool*.
- Product types and recursive types are pairs and lists, respectively.
- Each function is unary, i.e., pairs must be used to compose variables.

The third restriction means that binary functions and predicates are respectively regarded as unary functions and predicates which accept the argument of pair type. This assumption can easily be extended to a more general setting, for instance, with tuple types.

Values are denoted by $a, b, c, \cdots$, lists by $as, bs, cs, \cdots$, and lists of lists by $ass, bss, css, \cdots$.[1] We also assume that variable names of input variables and locally defined variables are different. The following functions present a sorting program with types *sort* : *int list* → *int list* and *max* : *int list* → *int × int list*.

---

[1] *as* is a reserved word of ML, but we ignore it.

$$P_F = P_G^- \ X \rightarrow P_G^- \ (f \ X) \qquad \text{properties of functions}$$
$$P_G^- = \text{predicates in } P_G \text{ without bound variables}$$
$$P_G = P_S \mid P_P \mid \textbf{true} \mid \textbf{false} \qquad \text{ground properties}$$
$$P_S = P_U \mid P_R \qquad \text{unary predicates}$$
$$P_R = \forall P_U \mid \nabla P_G \mid P_P^E \mid P_R \wedge P_R \mid P_R \vee P_R \qquad \text{properties of lists}$$
$$P_P = P_B \mid \bar{P}_P \mid P_S \times P_S \mid \forall_r P_P \mid \forall_l P_P \mid \qquad \text{properties of pairs}$$
$$\qquad P_P \wedge P_P \mid P_P \vee P_P$$
$$P_B = p_b \mid \bar{P}_B \mid P_B \wedge P_B \mid P_B \vee P_B \qquad \text{basic binary predicates}$$
$$P_U = p_u \mid P_B^X \mid P_U \wedge P_U \mid P_U \vee P_U \qquad \text{basic unary predicates}$$
$$E \qquad \text{expressions}$$
$$V \ = X \mid x \mid c \qquad \text{basic expressions}$$
$$X \qquad \text{(finitely many) free variables}$$
$$x \qquad \text{bound variables}$$
$$C \qquad \text{constants}$$

Fig. 3. Language for specification of properties.

```
fun sort as = if null as then nil else
                 let val (b,bs) = max as in b::sort bs end;

fun max cs = let val d::ds = cs in
                if null ds then (d,nil) else
                    let val (e,es) = max ds in
                        if leq(e,d) then (d,e::es) else (e,d::es) end
          end;
```

2.2   Specification Language

The language for specifying properties is constructed by using predicate constructors $\forall, \forall_l, \forall_r$, and ∇ on basic predicates, constants, free variables, and variables appearing in a program. Predicate constructors will be extended in Section 5. A basic unary predicate is denoted by p_U, a basic binary predicate by p_B, a unary predicate by P_U, and a binary predicate by P_B. Indexes U and B are often omitted when they are clear from the context. As convention, bound variables are denoted by $a, b, c, \cdots, x, y, z, \cdots, as, bs, cs, \cdots, xs, ys, zs, \cdots$, free variables by $X, Y, Z, \cdots$, constants by $C, M, \cdots$, and expressions by $E, E_1, E_2, \cdots$.

A binary predicate P is transformed into a unary predicate P^E by substituting an expression E for the second argument. That is, $P^E(E') = P(E', E)$. $\bar{P}$ is defined by $\bar{P}(E_1, E_2) = P(E_2, E_1)$. The grammar of the construction of predicates is shown in Fig. 3. Specification of a function f is expressed with a free variable by $Q(X) \rightarrow P(f \ X)$, which means if input X satisfies Q then output $f \ X$ satisfies P, when $P, Q \in P_G^-$. Each input X is a distinct free variable for each function and property to avoid name crash.

Note that negation is not allowed. The meanings and examples of the predicate constructors $\forall, \forall_l, \forall_r$, and ∇ are given as follows.

- $\forall P_U(xs)$ iff either xs is *nil* or the unary predicate $P_U(x)$ holds for each element x in xs.
- $\nabla P_B(xs)$ iff either xs is *nil* or $\forall \bar{P}_B^y (ys) \wedge \nabla P_B(ys)$ for $xs = y :: ys$.

$\forall_l P_B(xs, y)$ and $\forall_r P_B(x, ys)$ are defined by $\forall P_B^y(xs)$ and $\forall \bar{P}_B^x(ys)$, respectively. The examples are shown in the table below.

predicate	true		false
$geq^3(a)$	4		2
$\forall geq^3(as)$	[3,6,4], nil		[3,6,1]
$\forall_l leq(as, a)$	([3,6,4], 8),	(nil, 8)	([3,6,4], 5)
$\forall_r leq(a, as)$	(3, [3,6,4]),	(3, nil)	(5, [3,6,4])
$\nabla geq(as)$	[6,4,3], nil		[4,6,3]

For instance, the sorting program is fully specified by the following conditions.

1. Output must be ordered (called **orderedness**).
2. Input and output are the same *multiset* (called **preservation**).

Orderedness is expressed as **true** $\rightarrow \nabla geq(sort\ X)$. That is, the output of the sorting program is decreasing if the input satisfies **true** (i.e., empty assumptions). For preservation, the weaker condition called weak preservation, i.e., the input and the output are the same *set*, is expressed by

$$\mathbf{true} \rightarrow (\forall_l \exists_r equal \wedge \forall_r \exists_l equal)^X (sort\ X).$$

with the introduction of additional predicate constructors $\exists, \exists_l,$ and $\exists_r$ (which intuitively mean $\neg\forall\neg, \neg\forall_l\neg,$ and $\neg\forall_r\neg$, respectively), which will be discussed in Section 5. Note that only the input variable of a function remains in the scope when a function call occurs, thus our definition of properties of functions (P_F) is possible (which was neglected in [19]).

3 Automatic Verification as Abstract Interpretation

3.1 Verification Algorithm as Abstract Interpretation

An abstract interpretation consists of an abstract domain, its order, and an interpretation (on an abstract domain) of primitive functions [11,1,7]. Our choice is a backward abstract interpretation with

abstract domain a set of predicates (in Fig. 3) satisfying the type,
order   the entailment relation defined in Fig. 4, and
interpretation   defined in Fig. 5.

Let { **fun** $f_i\ x_i = E_i$; } be a program. The verification algorithm is the least fixed point computation to solve *whererec* equations in Fig. 5. Section 4 explains how this algorithm performs on the sorting program.

The entailment relation $\sqsubseteq$ (in Fig. 4) is intuitively the opposite of the logical implication. That is, $P \sqsubseteq Q$ means that Q implies P. By definition, **true** is

Axioms on basic predicates

$$\overline{equal} \equiv equal \qquad \overline{leq} \equiv geq \qquad null(\text{nil}) \equiv \textbf{true} \qquad null(x :: xs) \equiv \textbf{false}$$

$$equal(x, x) \equiv \textbf{true} \qquad geq(x, x) \equiv \textbf{true} \qquad leq(x, x) \equiv \textbf{true}$$

$$equal \sqsubseteq equal^x \times \overline{equal}^x \qquad geq \sqsubseteq geq^x \times \overline{geq}^x \qquad leq \sqsubseteq leq^x \times \overline{leq}^x$$

$$\frac{P \sqsubseteq P^x \times \bar{P}^x}{\forall P^y \sqsubseteq \forall P^z \wedge P(z, y)} \qquad \frac{P \sqsubseteq P^x \times \bar{P}^x}{\forall_l \forall_r P \sqsubseteq (\forall_l \forall_r P)^{xs} \times (\overline{\forall_l \forall_r P})^{xs}} \; \textbf{Transitivity}$$

Ordinary logical rules on logical connectives

$$P \wedge P \equiv P \qquad\qquad P_1 \sqsubseteq P_1 \wedge P_2 \qquad \textbf{true} \wedge P \equiv P \qquad\qquad \textbf{false} \wedge P \equiv \textbf{false}$$

$$P \vee P \equiv P \qquad\qquad P_1 \vee P_2 \sqsubseteq P_1 \qquad \textbf{true} \vee P \equiv \textbf{true} \qquad \textbf{false} \vee P \equiv P$$

$$\frac{P_1 \sqsubseteq P_2 \quad P_1' \sqsubseteq P_2'}{P_1 \wedge P_1' \sqsubseteq P_2 \wedge P_2'} \qquad\qquad \frac{P_1 \sqsubseteq P_2 \quad P_1' \sqsubseteq P_2'}{P_1 \vee P_1' \sqsubseteq P_2 \vee P_2'}$$

Entailment relation of predicate constructors

$$\frac{P_1 \sqsubseteq P_2}{\bar{P}_1 \sqsubseteq \bar{P}_2} \qquad \frac{P_1 \sqsubseteq P_2}{\dagger P_1 \sqsubseteq \dagger P_2} \; \textbf{list} \qquad \dagger(P_1 \wedge P_2) \equiv \dagger P_1 \wedge \dagger P_2 \quad \text{with } \dagger \in \{\forall, \forall_l, \forall_r, \nabla\}$$

$$\frac{P_1 \sqsubseteq P_1' \quad P_2 \sqsubseteq P_2'}{P_1 \times P_2 \sqsubseteq P_1' \times P_2'} \; \textbf{pair} \qquad (P_1 \times P_2) \wedge (P_1' \times P_2') \equiv (P_1 \wedge P_1') \times (P_2 \wedge P_2')$$

$$\overline{\bar{P}} \equiv P \qquad \overline{P_1 \wedge P_2} \equiv \bar{P}_1 \wedge \bar{P}_2 \qquad \overline{P_1 \vee P_2} \equiv \bar{P}_1 \vee \bar{P}_2 \qquad \overline{P_1 \times P_2} \equiv P_2 \times P_1$$

$$\overline{\forall_l P} \equiv \forall_r \bar{P} \qquad \overline{\forall_r P} \equiv \forall_l \bar{P} \qquad (\forall_l P)^E \equiv \forall(P^E) \qquad \forall_l \forall_r P \equiv \forall_r \forall_l P$$

$$\forall P(a :: as) \equiv P(a) \wedge \forall P(as) \qquad\qquad \forall P(\text{nil}) \equiv \textbf{true}$$

$$\nabla P(a :: as) \equiv \forall \bar{P}^a(as) \wedge \nabla P(as) \qquad \nabla P(\text{nil}) \equiv \textbf{true}$$

Fig. 4. Entailment relation

the least element and **false** is the greatest element in the abstract domain. We denote by $P \equiv Q$ if $P \sqsubseteq Q$ and $P \sqsupseteq Q$. The entailment relation may be used to trim at each step of interpretation Ψ. Formally, the entailment relation consists of axioms on basic predicates/predicate constructors, and ordinary logical rules, and their extensions by predicate constructors, as defined in Fig. 4.

In Fig. 5, let $Formula$ be a set of all formulae constructed from predicates in Fig. 3 and bound variables (in the scope of an expression) with logical connectives $\wedge$ and $\vee$. The disjunction $\vee$ is regarded as composing branches of the verification, i.e., each branch (conjunctive formula) is analyzed independently.

The projection $\downarrow$ extracts a predicate P, in which a bound variable x (in the scope of an expression E) is substituted in a formula. When regarding a conjunctive formula γ as an assignment from bound variables to predicates, $\gamma \downarrow_x$ coincides with the restriction to x. For instance, $(leq(x, y) \wedge \nabla(xs)) \downarrow_x = leq^y(x)$.

$$\Phi[\ \{\ \text{fun}\ f_i\ x_i = E_i\ ;\ \}\ ] \qquad = fvp\ \text{whererec}$$
$$fvp = [\ (\lambda P_1 \cdots P_n.(\Psi[E_i]P_i)\downarrow_{x_i})/f_i\ ]$$

$$\Psi[C]P \qquad = \begin{cases} \textbf{true} & \text{if } P(C) \\ \textbf{false} & \text{otherwise} \end{cases}$$

$$\Psi[x]P \qquad = P(x)$$

$$\Psi[op\ E]P \qquad = \Psi[E](\Xi[op]P)$$

$$\Psi[f\ E]P \qquad = \Psi[E]((fvp[f]P^{\beta\bar\eta})\theta^{\beta\bar\eta})$$

$$\Psi[(E_1,E_2)]P \qquad = \begin{cases} \Psi[E_1]P_1 \wedge \Psi[E_2]P_2 & \text{if } P = P_1 \times P_2 \\ \Psi[E_1]\bar{P}^{E_2} \vee \Psi[E_2]\bar{P}^{E_1} & \text{otherwise} \end{cases}$$

$$\Psi[E_1 :: E_2]P \qquad = \begin{cases} \Psi[E_1]Q \wedge \Psi[E_2]\forall Q & \text{if } P = \forall Q \\ \Psi[(E_1,E_2)]\forall_r Q \wedge \Psi[E_2]\nabla Q & \text{if } P = \nabla Q \end{cases}$$

$$\Psi[\text{if } Cond \text{ then } E_1 \text{ else } E_2]P = \ominus[(Cond \wedge \Psi[E_1]P) \vee (\neg Cond \wedge \Psi[E_2]P)]$$

$$\Psi[\text{let val } x = E_1 \text{ in } E_2]P \quad = \Psi[E_1](\Psi[E_2]P)\downarrow_x$$

$$\Psi[\text{let val } (x,y) = E_1 \text{ in } E_2]P = \Psi[E_1](\Psi[E_2]P)\downarrow_{(x,y)}$$

$$\Psi[\text{let val } x :: xs = E_1 \text{ in } E_2]P = \begin{cases} \Psi[E_1]\nabla Q \text{ if } (\Psi[E_2]P)\downarrow_{(x,xs)} = \forall_r Q \\ \Psi[E_1]\forall Q \text{ if } (\Psi[E_2]P)\downarrow_x = Q \text{ or} \\ \qquad\qquad (\Psi[E_2]P)\downarrow_{xs} = \forall Q \end{cases}$$

$$\text{where} \begin{cases} \Psi : (Fvp \rightarrow)Exp \rightarrow Pred \rightarrow Formula & \Xi : Prim \rightarrow Pred \rightarrow Pred \\ \Phi : Prog \rightarrow Fvp & \downarrow : Formula \rightarrow Bv \rightarrow Pred \\ fvp \in Fvp = Fv \rightarrow Pred \rightarrow Pred & \ominus : Formula \rightarrow Formula \end{cases}$$

Fig. 5. Abstract semantics of verification

Note that the $\downarrow$ operator is used when the local definition of x in a `let`-expression is analyzed, thus $P = \gamma \downarrow_x$ must exclude x. In our specification language, if such case occurs then $P(x)$ can be reduced **true** or **false** using the entailment relation.

The $\neg$-elimination operator $\ominus$ is defined by

$$\ominus[\ (Cond \wedge P) \vee (\neg Cond \wedge P')\ ] = \vee_i Q_i$$

where each Q_i satisfies $Cond \wedge P \sqsubseteq Q_i$ and $\neg Cond \wedge P' \sqsubseteq Q_i$. For instance, $\ominus[\ (leq(e,d) \wedge \forall leq^d(es)) \vee (\neg leq(e,d) \wedge \forall leq^e)\ ] = \forall leq^d(es) \vee \forall leq^e(es)$.

The interpretation of a function call

$$\Psi[f\ E]P = \Psi[E]((fvp[f]P^{\beta\bar\eta})\theta^{\beta\bar\eta})$$

requires another operation, called $\beta\bar\eta$-expansion (similar to the substitution calculus in higher-order rewrite systems [24]). When a function f is called in an expression E, bound variables (except for an input variable to f) become out of the scope. Thus, if a predicate P contains a bound variable, then it must be replaced with a free variable and the substitution to the free variable must be kept. They are $P^{\beta\bar\eta}$ and $\theta^{\beta\bar\eta}$. For instance, $\Psi[f\ E]\forall leq^b$ creates $P^{\beta\bar\eta} = \forall leq^Z$ and $\theta^{\beta\bar\eta} = [Z \leftarrow b]$.

Theorem 1. *The verification algorithm always terminates.*

(Sketch of proof) Basic predicates, variables, and constants appearing in a program are finite. A free variable is introduced as a substitute for a bound variable only when function-calls; thus, only finitely many free variables are used during verifications. Since each predicate constructor enriches types, once types of functions are fixed only finitely many applications of predicate constructors are possible. The finiteness of an input-dependent abstract domain is then guaranteed. The algorithm is therefore formulated as the least fix-point computation on a finite abstract domain, so that it terminates.   □

3.2   Soundness by Domain-Induced Abstract Interpretation

In this section, we will show how the abstract interpretation Φ is obtained as a domain-induced abstract interpretation, i.e., an abstract interpretation induced from domain abstractions. As a consequence, the soundness proof is given. Note that an automatic verification cannot be complete by nature.

Let the domain and codomain of a function f of type $\alpha \to \beta$ be D_α and D_β, respectively. Let the power domain $PD[D_\alpha]$ of D_α be $\{cl^\downarrow_{D_\alpha}(\mathcal{X}) \mid \mathcal{X} \subseteq D_\alpha\}$ with the order $\sqsubseteq_{-1} = \supseteq$, where $cl^\downarrow_{D_\alpha}$ is the downward closure operator in D_α.

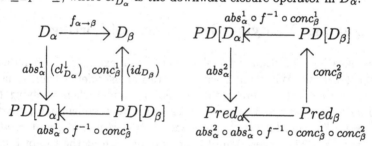

Fig. 6. Two steps of domain-induced abstract interpretation

Φ (in Fig. 5) is expressed as the two-step domain-induced abstract interpretation (as indicated in Fig. 6). The first step is backward and consists of

- the abstract domain $PD[D_\alpha]$
- the concretization map $conc^1_\alpha = id_{D_\alpha}$
- the abstraction map $abs^1_\alpha = cl^\downarrow_{D_\alpha}$

This step precisely detects how much of the input is enough to produce the output satisfying the specification. The next step approximates according to the specification language in order to make the analysis decidable. Let $Pred_\alpha$ be a set of predicates on D_α generated as P^-_G in Fig. 3. The second step is forward and consists of

- the abstract domain $Pred_\alpha$.
- the concretization map $conc^2_\alpha(P) = cl^\downarrow_{D_\alpha}(\{x \in D_\alpha \mid P(x)\})$ for $P \in Pred_\alpha$.

– the abstraction map $abs_\alpha^2(\mathcal{X}) = \sqcap(\{P \in Pred_\alpha \mid conc_\alpha^2(P) \subseteq \mathcal{X}\})$ for $\mathcal{X} \in PD[D_\alpha]$.

Note that the abstract domain $Pred_\alpha$ is a lattice wrt the entailment relation. For instance, $P \sqcup Q$ and $P \sqcap Q$ always exists as $P \wedge Q$ and $P \vee Q$, respectively.

Thus an abstract interpretation Ξ on a primitive function op of type $\alpha \to \beta$ is defined by $\Xi(op) = abs \cdot op^{-1} \cdot conc$, where $abs_\alpha = abs_\alpha^2 \cdot abs_\alpha^1$ and $conc_\beta = conc_\beta^1 \cdot conc_\beta^2$. Similar to Ψ on expressions. The abstract interpretation Φ on recursively defined functions f_i's is obtained by the least fix-point computation.

Definition 1. *For an abstract interpretation Φ, a function f is safe if f satisfies $\Phi(f) \sqsubseteq abs \cdot f^{-1} \cdot conc$. An abstract interpretation Ψ is safe if each primitive function is safe.*

Theorem 2. *The verification algorithm is sound (i.e., the detected property of a program always holds if a program terminates).*

(Sketch of proof) Since the concretization map $conc_\alpha$ and the abstraction map abs_β satisfy $abs_\alpha \cdot conc_\alpha = id_{D_\alpha}$ and $conc_\alpha \cdot abs_\alpha \subseteq cl_{D_\alpha}^\downarrow$, a recursively defined function is safe. Thus the detected property is sound. $\square$

4   Example: Verifying Orderedness of Sorting

The verification algorithm is explained here by an example of orderedness **true** $\to \nabla geq(sort\ X)$. When unknown properties of user-defined functions are required, new conjectures are produced. For instance, when verifying **true** $\to \nabla geq(sort\ X)$, it automatically produces and proves the lemmata; $\forall leq^Z(X) \to \forall leq^Z(sort\ X)$, $\neg null \wedge \forall leq^Z(Y) \to leq^Z \times \forall leq^Z(max\ Y)$, and $\neg null(Y) \to \forall_r geq(max\ Y)$. The generation of lemmata is shown at the top of Fig. 7. The vertical wavy arrow indicates an iterative procedure, the double arrow indicates the creation of a conjecture, and the arrow returns the resulting lemma.

For instance, $\forall leq^Z(X) \to \forall leq^Z(sort\ X)$ means that if an input of $sort$ is *less-than-or-equal-to* any given Z, an output is also *less-than-or-equal-to Z*. This lemma is generated as a conjecture **true** $\to \forall leq^Z(sort\ X)$ at the **else**-branch of the if-expression in $sort$ ($\Psi[\![b::sort\ bs]\!]\nabla geq$) as follows.

$$\nabla geq(b :: sort\ bs) \equiv \forall_r geq(b, sort\ bs) \wedge \nabla geq(sort\ bs)$$
$$\equiv \quad \forall leq^b(sort\ bs) \wedge \nabla geq(sort\ bs)$$

Since there are no conjectures related to $\forall leq^b(sort\ X)$ in the recursion hypothesis, a new conjecture is created. But properties of functions (P_F in Fig. 3) exclude bound variables. Thus, by the $\beta\bar{\eta}$-expansion, $\forall leq^b(sort\ X)$ is transformed to $\forall leq^Z(sort\ X)$ with the substitution $[Z \leftarrow b]$, and **true** $\to \forall leq^Z(sort\ X)$ is created. This means that no local information on b is used during the verification of **true** $\to \forall leq^Z(sort\ X)$. This conjecture does not hold; instead, we obtain $\forall leq^Z(X) \to \forall leq^Z(sort\ X)$ as a lemma.

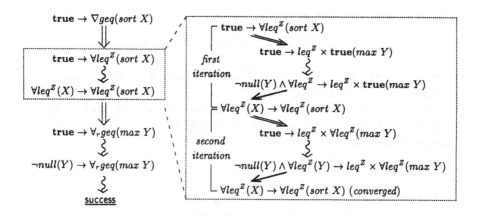

Fig. 7. Generation of lemmata for $\mathbf{true} \rightarrow \nabla geq(sort\ X)$

A typical example of the use of the entailment relation appears in the verification of $\neg null(Y) \rightarrow \forall_r geq(max\ Y)$. At the second if-expression in max, $\Psi[\![\mathtt{if\ leq(e,d)\ then\ (d,e::es)\ else\ (e,d::es)}]\!]\forall_r geq$ is created. Thus, $(leq(e,d) \wedge \forall leq^d(es)) \vee (\neg leq(e,d) \wedge \forall leq^e(es))$ is obtained. From the transitivity of leq, $\overline{leq(e,d) \wedge \forall leq^d(es)} \sqsubseteq leq(e,d) \wedge \forall leq^e(es)$ (see the underlined parts), therefore we obtain $\forall leq^e(es)$ by the $\neg$-elimination. Note that the $\neg$-elimination also creates $\forall leq^d(es)$, but only $\forall leq^e(es)$ branch is successful, i.e., from the recursion hypothesis $\Psi[\![\mathtt{max\ ds}]\!]\forall_r geq$ is reduced to $\neg null(ds)$, as desired. Thus $\forall leq^d(es)$ is omitted.

5   Extensions

5.1   New Predicate Constructors

In this section we introduce new predicate constructors and extend the entailment relation to make it possible to verify weak preservation of sort programs. The new predicate constructors are $\exists, \exists_l, \exists_r$, and $\triangle$. The predicates are extended by updating part of the grammar in Fig. 3 with

$$P_R = \forall P_U \mid \underline{\exists P_U} \mid \nabla P_G \mid \underline{\triangle P_G} \mid P_P^E \mid P_R \wedge P_R \mid P_R \vee P_R \quad \text{properties of lists}$$
$$P_P = P_B \mid \bar{P}_P \mid P_S \times P_S \mid \overline{\forall_r P_B} \mid \forall_l P_B \mid \underline{\exists_l P_B} \mid \exists_r P_B \mid \quad \text{properties of pairs}$$
$$P_P \wedge P_P \mid P_P \vee P_P$$

where the underlined parts are newly added. Their meanings are shown by examples in the table below. The entailment relation is enriched as in Fig. 8.

predicate	true	false
$\exists geq^5(as)$	$[3,6,4]$	$([3,2,4])$, nil
$\exists_l leq(as, a)$	$([3,6,4], 5)$	$([3,6,4], 2)$, $(nil, 5)$
$\exists_r leq(a, as)$	$(5, [3,6,4])$	$(7, [3,6,4])$, $(5, nil)$
$\triangle leq(as)$	$[3,2,4]$	$[3,6,4]$, $[3]$, nil

Then weak preservation of **sort** is expressed by

$$\mathbf{true} \to \overline{\forall_l \exists_r equal \land \forall_r \exists_l equal}^X (sort\ X).$$

During the verification of $\mathbf{true} \to \overline{\forall_l \exists_r equal}^X (sort\ X)$, the key step is at $\forall_l \exists_r equal(as, b :: sort(bs))$ in **sort**. By transitivity $\forall_l \exists_r equal(as, b :: bs) \land \forall_l \exists_r equal(b :: bs, b :: sort(bs))$ is inferred. To solve the second component, the entailment relation $\forall_l \exists_r P(a :: as, b :: bs) \sqsubseteq P(a, b) \land \forall_l \exists_r P(as, bs)$ is used. This is obtained as a transitive closure by

$$\forall_l \exists_r P(a :: as, b :: bs) \equiv \exists_r P(a, b :: bs) \land \underline{\forall_l \exists_r P(as, b :: bs)}$$

$$\sqsubseteq (P(a, b) \lor \exists_r P(a, bs)) \land \forall_l \exists_r P(as, bs)$$

$$\sqsubseteq P(a, b) \land \forall_l \exists_r P(as, bs).$$

Thus $\forall_l \exists_r equal(b :: bs, b :: sort(bs))$ is reduced to $\forall_l \exists_r equal(bs, sort(bs))$ which is a recursion hypothesis. The rest $\forall_l \exists_r equal(as, b :: bs)$ creates the conjecture

$$\mathbf{true} \to \overline{\forall_l (equal \times \mathbf{true} \lor \mathbf{true} \times \exists_r equal)}^Y (max\ Y)$$

at (b,bs) = max as, and similar approximations occur in **max** at expressions (d,e::es) and (e,d::es). $\mathbf{true} \to \overline{\exists_l \forall_r equal}^X (sort\ X)$ is similarly verified.

$$\frac{P_1 \sqsubseteq P_2}{\triangle P_1 \sqsubseteq \triangle P_2} \qquad \frac{P_1 \sqsubseteq P_2}{\dagger P_1 \sqsubseteq \dagger P_2} \text{ list} \qquad \dagger(P_1 \lor P_2) \equiv \dagger P_1 \lor \dagger P_2 \quad \text{with } \dagger \in \{\exists, \exists_l, \exists_r\}$$

$$\overline{\exists_l \bar{P}} \equiv \exists_r \bar{P} \qquad \overline{\exists_r \bar{P}} \equiv \exists_l \bar{P} \qquad (\exists_l P)^E \equiv \exists(P^E) \qquad \exists_l \exists_r P \equiv \exists_r \exists_l P$$

$$\frac{P \sqsubseteq P^x \times \bar{P}^x}{\forall_l \exists_r P \sqsubseteq (\forall_l \exists_r P)^{xs} \times (\overline{\forall_l \exists_r P})^{xs}} \qquad \frac{P \sqsubseteq P^x \times \bar{P}^x}{\exists_l \forall_r P \sqsubseteq (\exists_l \forall_r P)^{xs} \times (\overline{\exists_l \forall_r P})^{xs}} \text{ Transitivity}$$

$$\exists P(a :: as) \equiv P(a) \lor \exists P(as) \qquad \forall_l \exists_r P(as, b :: bs) \sqsubseteq \forall_l \exists_r P(as, bs)$$

$$\exists P(nil) \equiv \mathbf{false} \qquad \forall_r \exists_l P(a :: as, bs) \sqsubseteq \forall_r \exists_l P(as, bs)$$

$$\triangle P(a :: b :: bs) \equiv \exists \bar{P}^a (b :: bs) \land (null(bs) \lor \triangle P(b :: bs))$$

$$\triangle P(a :: nil) \equiv \mathbf{false} \qquad \triangle P(nil) \equiv \mathbf{false}$$

Fig. 8. New entailment relation

5.2   Uninterpreted Functions and Predicates

This section extends the range of conditional expressions that can be included in the programs to be verified. Function symbols (either primitive or user-defined) in the conditional part of an if-expression are allowed. They are left uninterpreted during the verification, and the result will be refined by partial evaluation of these function symbols.

The example is a formatting program **format** that formats a sentence (expressed by a list of strings) as a list of sentences each of which has a width *less-than-or-equal-to* a specified number M. Its specifications are as follows.

- Each sentence of the output must have a width less-than-equal to M.
- The order of each word in the input must be kept in the output.
- Each word of the input must appear in the output, and vice versa.

```
fun format as = f (as,nil);

fun f (bs,cs) = if null bs then [cs] else
                    let val d::ds = bs
                    in if leq (width (cs@[d]),M)
                            then f (ds,cs@[d]))
                            else cs::f (ds,[d]) end;

fun width es = if null es then 0 else
                    let val f::fs=es in
                    if null fs then size f
                                else 1+size f+width fs end;
```

In this example, *string* is added to base types. Basic functions + and constants $0, 1$ also are used in the program, but they are not directly related to the verification. Thus, their interpretation and entailment relations are omitted.

The first specification of **format** states that an output must satisfy $\forall(leq^M \cdot width)$. Note that this predicate allows a function symbol *width* in it. Verification starts with **true** $\rightarrow \forall(leq^M \cdot width)(format\ X)$, which is immediately reduced to **true** $\rightarrow \forall(leq^M \cdot width)(f\ Y)$. The result of the verification is

$$(\forall leq^M \cdot width \cdot [\ ]) \times (leq^M \cdot width)(Y) \rightarrow \forall(leq^M \cdot width)(f\ Y),$$

and this deduces

$$(\forall leq^M \cdot width \cdot [\ ])(X) \wedge (leq^M \cdot width)(nil) \rightarrow \forall(leq^M \cdot width)(format\ X).$$

Note that the result is not affected by whatever *width* is, since *width* is left uninterpreted. The key steps are at if **leq (width (cs@[d]),M) then** .... Since the throughout of **then**-branches $leq(width\ (cs@[d]), M)$ holds, the second argument of $f\ (ds, cs@[d])$ always satisfies $leq^M \cdot width$. These steps depend only on $\vee$-elimination so that the function symbol *width* remains uninterpreted.

With the aid of partial evaluation which leads to $width\ nil = 0$, $width\ [x] = size\ x$, we obtain $\forall(leq^M \cdot size)(X) \wedge leq(0, M) \rightarrow \forall(leq^M \cdot width)(format\ X)$. For the partial evaluation, only the relation between *size* and *width* is important. The information on the function *size* is required only when the final result above is interpreted by a human being. Note that in general a partial evaluation may not terminate. However, this final step is devoted to transforming the detected property into a more intuitive form for a human being, and even if it fails the detected property is correct.

The second and the third specification of format are similar to orderedness and weak preservation of sort, respectively. They require further extensions.

The second specification of format is expressed by a *fresh* binary predicate Rel on pairs of strings as $\nabla Rel\ (X) \rightarrow \forall \nabla Rel \wedge \nabla \square Rel\ (format\ X)$ where $\square$ is an abbreviation of $\forall_l \forall_r$. Note that throughout the verification the predicate Rel is left uninterpreted. This implies that the specification above holds for any binary relation Rel. Finally, the meaning of Rel is assumed by a human being, and in this case it is suitable to be interpreted as the appearance order of strings.

The third specification is expressed by $\mathbf{true} \rightarrow \overline{\forall_l \exists_r \exists_r equal}^X (format\ X)$ and $\mathbf{true} \rightarrow \overline{\forall_r \forall_r \exists_l equal}^X (format\ X)$. Our algorithm detects the latter, but for the former we also need a new transitivity-like entailment relation of type $list(\alpha) \times list(list(\alpha))$, i.e.,

$$\frac{P \sqsubseteq P^x \times \bar{P}^x}{\forall_l \exists_r \exists_r P \sqsubseteq (\forall_l \exists_r P)^{xs} \times (\overline{\forall_l \exists_r \exists_r P})^{xs}.}$$

6   Related Work

Many studies have been undertaken on verification. Most are based on theorem provers, for example, Coq, LCF, Boyer-Moore prover, Larch, and EQP. They require either complex heuristics or strong human guidance (or both), either of which is not easy to learn. However, for huge, complex, and critical systems, this price is worth paying.

The complementary approach uses intelligent compile-time error detection for easy debugging. For imperative programs, Bourdoncle proposed an assertion-based debugging called *Abstract debugging* [5,4]. For logic programs, Comini, et. al. [8] and Bueno, et. al. [6] proposed extensions of declarative diagnosis based on abstract interpretation. Cortesi, et. al. [10,18] proposed the automatic verification based on abstract interpretation. Levi and Volpe proposed the framework based on abstract interpretation to classify various verification methods [20]. Among them, target specifications primarily focus on behavior properties, such as termination, mutual exclusion of clauses, and size/cardinality relation between inputs and outputs.

In contrast, Métayer's [19] and our specification language (for functional programs) directly express the programmer's intention in a concise and declarative description. This point is more desirable for some situation, such as, when a novice programmer writes a relatively small program.

As an abstract interpretation, our framework is similar to *inverse image analysis* [14]. The significant difference is that inverse image analysis determines *how much of the input is needed to produce a certain amount of output* and computes Scott's *open* sets. Our framework, in contrast, determines *how much of the input is enough to produce a certain amount of output* and computes Scott's *closed* sets. In terms of [22], the former is expressed by a HOMT $(id, -, \sqsubseteq_0, min)$, and the latter is expressed by $(id, -, \sqsubseteq_{-1}, max)$.

Similar techniques that treat abstract domain construction as a set of predicates are found in several places. However, predicates are either limited to unary [15,17,3,21] (such as *null* and ¬*null*), or are limited to propositions corresponding to variables appearing in a (logic) program [9].

7 Conclusion

This paper reconstructs and extends the automatic verification technique of Le Métayer [19] based on a backward abstract interpretation. To show the effectiveness, two examples of the declarative specifications of the sorting and formatting programs are demonstrated. Although we adopted the simple and inefficient sorting program here, we also tried efficient sort programs, such as orderedness of *quick-sort* and *merge-sort* (both topdown and bottomup), and weak preservation of the *topdown merge-sort*. These verifications are quite messy by hand [23].

Future work will include the implementation and the exploration of its use on more complex examples. An efficient implementation may require an efficient reachability test algorithm (as well as a congruence-closure algorithm) and a strategy to prune highly-nondeterministic ¬-eliminations and transitivity.

Acknowledgments

The author would like to thank CACA members for their useful comments and discussions.

References

1. S. Abramsky and C. Hankin, editors. *Abstract interpretation of declarative languages.* Ellis Horwood Limited, 1987.
2. T. Arts and J. Gisel. Termination of term rewriting using dependency pairs. *Theoretical Computer Science*, 1999. *to appear.*
3. P.N. Benton. Strictness properties of lazy algebraic datatypes. In *Proc. 3rd WSA*, pages 206–217, 1993. Springer LNCS 724.
4. F. Bourdoncle. Abstract debugging of higher-order imperative programs. In *ACM SIGPLAN PLDI 1993*, pages 46–55, 1993.
5. F. Bourdoncle. Assertion-based debugging of imperative programs by abstract interpretation. In *4th ESEC*, pages 501–516, 1993. Springer LNCS 717.
6. F. Bueno et al. On the role of semantic approximations in validation and diagnosis of constraint logic programs. In *Proc. AADEBUG '97*, pages 155–169, 1997.
7. G.L. Burn. *Lazy Functional Languages: Abstract Interpretation and Compilation.* The MIT Press, 1991.
8. M. Comini, G. Levi, M. C. Meo, and G. Vitiello. Proving properties of logic programs by abstract diagnosis. In M. Dams, editor, *Analysis and Verification of Multiple-Agent Languages, 5th LOMAPS Workshop*, number 1192 in LNCS, pages 22–50. Springer-Verlag, 1996.
9. A. Cortesi, G. Filé, and W. Winsborough. *Prop* revisited: Propositional formula as abstract domain for groundness analysis. In *Proc. 6th LICS*, pages 322–327, 1991.
10. A. Cortesi, B. Le Charlier, and S. Rossi. Specification-based automatic verification of Prolog programs. In *Proc. LOPSTR '96*, pages 38–57, 1996. Springer LNCS 1207.

11. P. Cousot and R. Cousot. Abstract interpretation: A unified lattice model for static analysis of programs by construction of approximation of fixpoints. In *Proc. 4th ACM POPL*, pages 238–252, 1977.
12. N. Dershowitz and J.-P. Jouannaud. Rewrite systems. In J. van Leeuwen, editor, *Handbook of Theoretical Computer Science*, volume B, chapter 6, pages 243–320. Elsevier Science Publishers, 1990.
13. D. Detlefs and R. Forgaard. A procedure for automatically proving the termination of a set of rewrite rules. In *Proc. 1st RTA*, pages 255–270, 1985. Springer LNCS 202.
14. P. Dybjer. Inverse image analysis generalizes strictness analysis. *Information and Computation*, 90(2):194–216, 1991.
15. C. Ernoult and A. Mycroft. Uniform ideals and strictness analysis. In *Proc. 18th ICALP*, pages 47–59, 1991. Springer LNCS 510.
16. J. Gisel. Termination of nested and mutually recursive algorithms. *Journal of Automated Reasoning*, 19:1–29, 1997.
17. T.P. Jensen. Abstract interpretation over algebraic data types. In *Proc. Int. Conf. on Computer Languages*, pages 265–276. IEEE, 1994.
18. B. Le Charlier, C. Leclère, S. Rossi, and A. Cortesi. Automatic verification of behavioral properties of Prolog programs. In *Proc. ASIAN '97*, pages 225–237, 1997. Springer LNCS 1345.
19. D. Le Métayer. Proving properties of programs defined over recursive data structures. In *Proc. ACM PEPM '95*, pages 88–99, 1995.
20. G. Levi and P. Volpe. Derivation of proof methods by abstract interpretation. In *ALP'98*, pages 102–117, 1998. Springer LNCS 1490.
21. M. Ogawa and S. Ono. Deriving inductive properties of recursive programs based on least-fixpoint computation. *Journal of Information Processing*, 32(7):914–923, 1991. *in Japanese*.
22. M. Ogawa and S. Ono. Transformation of strictness-related analyses based on abstract interpretation. *IEICE Trans.*, E 74(2):406–416, 1991.
23. L.C. Paulson. *ML for the working programmer*. Cambridge University Press, 2nd edition, 1996.
24. V. Van Oostrom. *Confluence for Abstract and Higher-Order Rewriting*. PhD thesis, Vrije universiteit, Amsterdam, 1994.

A Transformation System for Lazy Functional Logic Programs[*]

María Alpuente[1], Moreno Falaschi[2], Ginés Moreno[3], and Germán Vidal[1]

[1] DSIC, UPV, Camino de Vera s/n, 46022 Valencia, Spain
{alpuente,gvidal}@dsic.upv.es
[2] Dip. Mat. e Informatica, U. Udine, 33100 Udine, Italy
falaschi@dimi.uniud.it
[3] Dep. Informática, UCLM, 02071 Albacete, Spain
gmoreno@info-ab.uclm.es

Abstract. Needed narrowing is a complete operational principle for modern declarative languages which integrate the best features of (lazy) functional and logic programming. We define a transformation methodology for functional logic programs based on needed narrowing. We provide (strong) correctness results for the transformation system w.r.t. the set of *computed values* and *answer substitutions* and show that the prominent properties of needed narrowing –namely, the optimality w.r.t. the length of derivations and the number of computed solutions– carry over to the transformation process and the transformed programs. We illustrate the power of the system by taking on in our setting two well-known transformation strategies (*composition* and *tupling*). We also provide an implementation of the transformation system which, by means of some experimental results, highlights the benefits of our approach.

1 Introduction

Functional logic programming languages combine the operational principles of the most important declarative programming paradigms, namely functional and logic programming (see [14] for a survey). Efficient demand-driven functional computations are amalgamated with the flexible use of logical variables providing for function inversion and search for solutions. The operational semantics of integrated languages is usually based on narrowing, a combination of variable instantiation and reduction. The instantiation of variables is often computed by unifying a subterm of the goal expression with the left-hand side of some program rule; then narrowing reduces the instantiated goal using that rule. Needed narrowing is currently the best narrowing strategy for first-order, lazy functional logic programs due to its optimality properties [5]. Needed narrowing provides completeness in the sense of logic programming (computation of all solutions) as well as functional programming (computation of values), and it can be efficiently implemented by pattern matching and unification.

[*] This work has been partially supported by CICYT under grant TIC 98-0445-C03-01.

A. Middeldorp, T. Sato (Eds.): FLOPS'99, LNCS 1722, pp. 147–162, 1999.

The fold/unfold transformation approach was first introduced in [8] to optimize functional programs and then used for logic programs [28]. This approach is commonly based on the construction, by means of a *strategy*, of a sequence of equivalent programs each obtained by the preceding ones using an *elementary* transformation rule. The essential rules are *folding* and *unfolding*, i.e., contraction and expansion of subexpressions of a program using the definitions of this program (or of a preceding one). Other rules which have been considered are, for example, instantiation, definition introduction/elimination, and abstraction.

There exists a large class of program optimizations which can be achieved by fold/unfold transformations and are not possible by using a fully automatic method (such as, e.g., partial evaluation). Typical instances of this class are the strategies that perform *tupling* (also known as *pairing*) [8,11], which merges separate (nonnested) function calls with some common arguments into a single call to a (possibly new) recursive function which returns a tuple of the results of the separate calls, thus avoiding either multiple accesses to the same data structures or common subcomputations, similarly to the idea of *sharing* which is used in graph rewriting to improve the efficiency of computations in time and space [6]. A closely related strategy is *composition* [30] (also known as *fusion, deforestation*, or *vertical jamming* [12]), which essentially consists of the merging of nested function calls, where the inner function call builds up a composite object which is used by the outer call, and composing these two calls into one has the effect to avoid the generation of the intermediate data structure. The composition can be made automatically [30], whereas tupling has only been automated to some extent [9,10].

Although a lot of literature has been devoted to proving the correctness of fold/unfold systems w.r.t. the various semantics proposed for logic programs [7,13,20,21,23,28], in functional programming the problem of correctness has received surprisingly little attention [26,27]. Of the very few studies of correctness of fold/unfold transformations in functional programming, the most general and recent work is [26], which defines a simple (syntactic) condition for restricting general fold/unfold transformations and which can be applied to give correctness proofs for several well-known transformation methods, such as the deforestation.

In [2], we investigated fold/unfold rules in the context of a strict (*call-by-value*) functional logic language based on unrestricted (i.e., not optimized) narrowing. The use of narrowing empowers the fold/unfold system by implicitly embedding the instantiation rule (the operation of the Burstall and Darlington framework [8] which introduces an instance of an existing equation) into unfolding by means of unification. However, [2] does not consider a general transformation system (only two rules: fold and unfold), and hence the composition or tupling transformations cannot be achieved. Also, [2] refers to a notion of "reversible" folding, which is strictly weaker than the one which we consider here. On the other hand, the use of unrestricted narrowing to perform unfolding may produce an important increase in the number of program rules.

In this paper we define a transformation methodology for lazy (*call-by-name*) functional logic programs. On the theoretical side, we extend the Tamaki and

Sato transformation rules [28] for logic programs to cope with lazy functional logic programs based on needed narrowing. The transformation process consists of applying an arbitrary number of times the basic transformation rules, which are: definition introduction, definition elimination, unfolding, folding, and abstraction. Needed narrowing is complete for *inductively sequential* programs [4]. Thus, we demonstrate that such a program structure is preserved through the transformation sequence $(\mathcal{R}_0, \ldots, \mathcal{R}_n)$, which is a key point for proving the correctness of the transformation system as well as its effective applicability. For instance, by using other variants of narrowing (e.g., lazy narrowing [22]) the structure of the original program is not preserved, thus seriously restricting the applicability of the resulting system. The major technical result consists of proving strong correctness for the transformation system, namely that the values and answers computed by needed narrowing in the initial and the final program coincide (for goals constructed using the symbols of the initial program). The efficiency improvement of $\mathcal{R}_n$ with regard to $\mathcal{R}_0$ is not ensured by an arbitrary use of the elementary transformation rules but it rather depends on the heuristic which is employed. On the practical side, we investigate how the classical and powerful transformation methodologies of *tupling* and *composition* [24] transfer to our framework. We show the advantages of using needed narrowing to achieve composition and tupling in an integrated setting, and illustrate the power of our transformation system by (automatically) optimizing several significant examples using a prototype implementation [1].

The structure of the paper is as follows. After recalling some basic definitions in the next section, we introduce the basic transformation rules and illustrate them by means of several simple examples in Sec. 3. We also state the correctness of the transformation system and show some results about the structure of transformed programs. Section 4 shows how to achieve the (automatic) composition and tupling strategies in our framework as well as an experimental evaluation of the method on a small set of benchmarks. Section 5 concludes. More details and proofs of all technical results can be found in [3].

2 Preliminaries

We assume familiarity with basic notions of term rewriting [6] and functional logic programming [14]. We consider a *signature* Σ partitioned into a set $\mathcal{C}$ of *constructors* and a set $\mathcal{F}$ of (defined) *functions* or *operations*. We write $c/n \in \mathcal{C}$ and $f/n \in \mathcal{F}$ for n-ary constructor and operation symbols, respectively. There is at least one sort *Bool* containing the 0-ary Boolean constructors *true* and *false*. The set of *terms* and *constructor terms* with *variables* (e.g., x, y, z) from $\mathcal{X}$ are denoted by $\mathcal{T}(\mathcal{C} \cup \mathcal{F}, \mathcal{X})$ and $\mathcal{T}(\mathcal{C}, \mathcal{X})$, respectively. The set of variables occurring in a term t is denoted by $\mathcal{V}ar(t)$. A term is *linear* if it does not contain multiple occurrences of any variable. We write $\overline{o_n}$ for the *list* of objects $o_1, \ldots, o_n$.

A *pattern* is a term of the form $f(\overline{d_n})$ where $f/n \in \mathcal{F}$ and $d_1, \ldots, d_n \in \mathcal{T}(\mathcal{C}, \mathcal{X})$. Note the difference with the usual notion of pattern in functional programming: a constructor term. A term is *operation-rooted* (*constructor-rooted*) if it has an operation (constructor) symbol at the root. A *position* p in a term t is represented by a sequence of natural numbers (Λ denotes the empty sequence, i.e., the root position). Positions are ordered by the *prefix* ordering: $p \leq q$, if $\exists w$ such that $p.w = q$. Positions p, q are *disjoint* if neither $p \leq q$ nor $q \leq p$. Given a term t, we let $\mathcal{P}os(t)$ and $\mathcal{NVP}os(t)$ denote the set of positions and the set of non-variable positions of t, respectively. $t|_p$ denotes the *subterm* of t at position p, and $t[s]_p$ denotes the result of *replacing the subterm* $t|_p$ by the term s.

We denote by $\{x_1 \mapsto t_1, \ldots, x_n \mapsto t_n\}$ the *substitution* σ with $\sigma(x_i) = t_i$ for $i = 1, \ldots, n$ (with $x_i \neq x_j$ if $i \neq j$), and $\sigma(x) = x$ for all other variables x. A substitution σ is *(ground) constructor*, if $\sigma(x)$ is (ground) constructor for all x such that $\sigma(x) \neq x$. The identity substitution is denoted by id. Given a substitution θ and a set of variables $V \subseteq \mathcal{X}$, we denote by $\theta_{\restriction V}$ the substitution obtained from θ by restricting its domain to V. We write $\theta = \sigma \; [V]$ if $\theta_{\restriction V} = \sigma_{\restriction V}$, and $\theta \leq \sigma \; [V]$ denotes the existence of a substitution γ such that $\gamma \circ \theta = \sigma \; [V]$. A *unifier* of two terms s and t is a substitution σ with $\sigma(s) = \sigma(t)$. Two substitutions σ and σ' are *independent* (on a set of variables V) iff there exists some $x \in V$ such that $\sigma(x)$ and $\sigma'(x)$ are not unifiable.

A set of rewrite rules $l \to r$ such that $l \notin \mathcal{X}$, and $Var(r) \subseteq Var(l)$ is called a *term rewriting system* (TRS). The terms l and r are called the *left-hand side* (*lhs*) and the *right-hand side* (*rhs*) of the rule, respectively. A TRS $\mathcal{R}$ is left-linear if l is linear for all $l \to r \in \mathcal{R}$. A TRS is constructor based (CB) if each lhs l is a pattern. In the remainder of this paper, a functional logic *program* is a left-linear CB-TRS. Conditions in program rules are treated by using the predefined functions and, if_then_else, case_of which are reduced by standard defining rules [17,22]. Two (possibly renamed) rules $l \to r$ and $l' \to r'$ overlap, if there is a non-variable position $p \in \mathcal{NVP}os(l)$ and a most-general unifier σ such that $\sigma(l|_p) = \sigma(l')$. A left-linear TRS with no overlapping rules is called *orthogonal*. A *rewrite step* is an application of a rewrite rule to a term, i.e., $t \to_{p,R} s$ if there exists a position p in t, a rewrite rule $R = l \to r$ and a substitution σ with $t|_p = \sigma(l)$ and $s = t[\sigma(r)]_p$ (p and R will often be omitted in the notation of a computation step). The instantiated lhs $\sigma(l)$ is called a *redex*. A term t is called a *normal form* if there is no term s with $t \to s$. $\to^+$ denotes the transitive closure of $\to$ and $\to^*$ denotes the reflexive and transitive closure of $\to$.

To evaluate terms containing variables, narrowing non-deterministically instantiates the variables such that a rewrite step is possible. Formally, $t \rightsquigarrow_{p,R,\sigma} t'$ is a *narrowing step* if p is a non-variable position in t and $\sigma(t) \to_{p,R} t'$. We denote by $t_0 \rightsquigarrow^*_\sigma t_n$ a sequence of narrowing steps $t_0 \rightsquigarrow_{\sigma_1} \cdots \rightsquigarrow_{\sigma_n} t_n$ with $\sigma = \sigma_n \circ \cdots \circ \sigma_1$. Since we are interested in computing *values* (constructor terms) as well as *answers* (substitutions) in functional logic programming, we say that the narrowing derivation $t \rightsquigarrow^*_\sigma c$ computes the result c with answer σ if c is a constructor term. The evaluation to (ground) constructor terms (and not to arbitrary expressions) is the intended semantics of functional languages and also of most functional logic languages. In particular, the equality predicate $\approx$ used in some examples is defined, like in functional languages, as the *strict equality* on terms, i.e., the equation $t_1 \approx t_2$ is satisfied if t_1 and t_2 are reducible to the same ground constructor term. We say that σ is a *computed answer substitution* for an equation e if there is a narrowing derivation $e \leadsto^*_\sigma true$.

Needed Narrowing. A challenge in the design of functional logic languages is the definition of a "good" narrowing strategy, i.e., a restriction λ on the narrowing steps issuing from t, without losing completeness. *Needed narrowing* [5] is currently the best known narrowing strategy due to its optimality properties. It extends the Huet and Lévy's notion of a needed reduction [18]. The definition of needed narrowing [5] uses the notion of *definitional tree* [4]. Roughly speaking, a definitional tree for a function symbol f is a tree whose leaves contain all (and only) the rules used to define f and whose inner nodes contain information to guide the (optimal) pattern matching during the evaluation of expressions. Each inner node contains a pattern and a variable position in this pattern (the *inductive position*) which is further refined in the patterns of its immediate children by using different constructor symbols. The pattern of the root node is simply $f(\overline{x_n})$, where $\overline{x_n}$ are different variables. A defined function is called *inductively sequential* if it has a definitional tree. A rewrite system $\mathcal{R}$ is called *inductively sequential* if all its defined functions are inductively sequential.

To compute needed narrowing steps for an operation-rooted term t, we take a definitional tree $\mathcal{P}$ for the root of t and compute $\lambda(t, \mathcal{P})$. Then, for all $(p, R, \sigma) \in \lambda(t, \mathcal{P})$, $t \leadsto_{p,R,\sigma} t'$ is a *needed narrowing step*. Informally speaking, needed narrowing applies a rule, if possible, or checks the subterm corresponding to the inductive position of the branch: if it is a variable, it is instantiated to the constructor of a child; if it is already a constructor, we proceed with the corresponding child; if it is a function, we evaluate it by recursively applying needed narrowing (see [5] for a detailed definition).

Example 1. Consider the following set of rules for "$\leqslant$" and "$+$":

$$
\begin{aligned}
0 \leqslant N &\rightarrow true & 0 + N &\rightarrow N \\
s(M) \leqslant 0 &\rightarrow false & s(M) + N &\rightarrow s(M + N) \\
s(M) \leqslant s(N) &\rightarrow M \leqslant N
\end{aligned}
$$

Then the function λ computes the following set for the initial term $X \leqslant X + X$:

$$\{(\Lambda, 0 \leqslant N \rightarrow true, \{X \mapsto 0\}),\ (2, s(M) + N \rightarrow s(M + N), \{X \mapsto s(M)\})\}$$

This corresponds to the narrowing steps (the subterm evaluated in the next step is underlined):

$$
\begin{aligned}
\underline{X \leqslant X + X} &\leadsto_{\{X \mapsto 0\}} true \\
X \leqslant \underline{X + X} &\leadsto_{\{X \mapsto s(M)\}} s(M) \leqslant s(M + s(M))
\end{aligned}
$$

Needed narrowing is sound and complete for inductively sequential programs. Moreover, it is *minimal,* i.e., given two distinct needed narrowing derivations $e \leadsto^*_\sigma true$ and $e \leadsto^*_{\sigma'} true$, we have that σ and σ' are independent on $\mathcal{V}ar(e)$.

3   The Transformation Rules

In this section, our aim is to define a set of program transformations which is strongly correct, i.e., sound and complete w.r.t. the semantics of computed values and answer substitutions. Let us first give the rules for the introduction and elimination of function definitions in a similar style to [28], in which the set of definitions is partitioned into "old" and "new" ones. In the following, we consider a fixed transformation sequence $(\mathcal{R}_0, \ldots, \mathcal{R}_k)$, $k \geq 0$.

Definition 1 (Definition introduction). *We may get program $\mathcal{R}_{k+1}$ by adding to $\mathcal{R}_k$ a new rule (the "definition rule") of the form $f(\overline{t_n}) \to r$, such that:*

1. *$f(\overline{t_n})$ is a linear pattern and $Var(f(\overline{t_n})) = Var(r)$ —i.e., it is non-erasing–,*
2. *f does not occur in the sequence $\mathcal{R}_0, \ldots, \mathcal{R}_k$ (f is new), and*
3. *every defined function symbol occurring in r belongs to $\mathcal{R}_0$.*

We say that f is a new function symbol, and every function symbol belonging to $\mathcal{R}_0$ is called an old function symbol.

The introduction of a new definition is virtually always the first step of a transformation sequence. Determining which definitions should be introduced is a task which falls into the realm of *strategies* (see [23] for a survey), which we discuss in Sec. 4.

Definition 2 (Definition elimination). *We may get program $\mathcal{R}_{k+1}$ by deleting from program $\mathcal{R}_k$ all rules defining the function f, say R^f, such that f does not occur in $\mathcal{R}_0$ nor in $(\mathcal{R}_k - R^f)$.*

This rule has been initially proposed with the name of *deletion* (for logic programs) in [21] and also in [7], where it was called *restriction*. Note that the deletion of the rules defining a function f implies that no function calls to f are allowed afterwards. However, subsequent transformation steps (in particular, folding steps) might introduce those deleted functions in the rhs's of the rules, thus producing inconsistencies in the resulting programs. We avoid this encumbrance by the usual requirement [23] not to allow folding steps if a definition elimination step has been performed.

· Now we introduce our unfolding rule, which systematizes a fit combination of instantiation and classical (functional) unfolding into a single transformation rule, thus bearing the capability of narrowing to deal with logical variables.

Definition 3 (Unfolding). *Let $R = (l \to r) \in \mathcal{R}_k$ be a rule (the "unfolded rule") whose rhs is an operation-rooted term. We may get program $\mathcal{R}_{k+1}$ from $\mathcal{R}_k$ by replacing R with $\{\theta(l) \to r' \mid r \rightsquigarrow_\theta r'$ is a needed narrowing step in $\mathcal{R}_k\}$.*

Here it is worth noting that the requirement not to unfold a rule whose rhs is not operation-rooted can be left aside when functions are *totally defined* (which is quite usual in typed languages). The following example shows that the above requirement cannot be dropped in general.

Example 2. Consider the following programs:

$$\mathcal{R} = \left\{ \begin{array}{l} \mathtt{f}(0) \to 0 \\ \mathtt{g}(X) \to \mathtt{s}(\mathtt{f}(X)) \\ \mathtt{h}(\mathtt{s}(X)) \to \mathtt{s}(0) \end{array} \right\} \qquad \mathcal{R}' = \left\{ \begin{array}{l} \mathtt{f}(0) \to 0 \\ \mathtt{g}(0) \to \mathtt{s}(0) \\ \mathtt{h}(\mathtt{s}(X)) \to \mathtt{s}(0) \end{array} \right\}$$

By a needed narrowing step $\mathtt{s}(\mathtt{f}(X)) \leadsto_{\{X \mapsto 0\}} \mathtt{s}(0)$ given from the rhs of the second rule of $\mathcal{R}$, we get (by unfolding) the transformed program $\mathcal{R}'$. Now, the goal $\mathtt{h}(\mathtt{g}(\mathtt{s}(0))) \approx X$ has the successful needed narrowing derivation in $\mathcal{R}$

$$\mathtt{h}(\underline{\mathtt{g}(\mathtt{s}(0))}) \approx X \leadsto \mathtt{h}(\underline{\mathtt{s}(\mathtt{f}(\mathtt{s}(0)))}) \approx X \leadsto \mathtt{s}(0) \approx X \leadsto^*_{\{X \mapsto \mathtt{s}(0)\}} \mathtt{true}$$

whereas it fails in the transformed program. Essentially, completeness is lost because the considered unfolding rule $\mathtt{f}(0) \to 0$ defines a function $\mathtt{f}$ which is not *totally* defined. Hence, by unfolding the call $\mathtt{f}(X)$ we improperly "compile in" an unnecessary restriction in the domain of the function $\mathtt{g}$.

Now, let us introduce the folding rule, which is a counterpart of the previous transformation, i.e., the compression of a piece of code into an equivalent call.

Definition 4 (Folding). *Let $R = (l \to r) \in \mathcal{R}_k$ be a rule (the "folded rule") and let $R' = (l' \to r') \in \mathcal{R}_j$, $0 \le j \le k$, be a rule (the "folding rule") such that $r|_p = \theta(r')$ for some $p \in \mathcal{NVPos}(r)$, fulfilling the following conditions:*

1. *$r|_p$ is not a constructor term;*
2. *either l (the lhs of the folded rule R) is rooted by an old function symbol, or R is the result of at least one unfolding within the sequence $\mathcal{R}_0, \ldots, \mathcal{R}_k$; and*
3. *the folding rule R' is a definition rule.[1]*

Then, we may get program $\mathcal{R}_{k+1}$ from program $\mathcal{R}_k$ by replacing the rule R with the new rule $l \to r[\theta(l')]_p$.

Roughly speaking, the folding operation proceeds in a contrary direction to the usual reduction steps, that is, reductions are performed against the reverse folding rules. Note that the applicability conditions 2 and 3 for the folding rule guarantee that "self folding" (i.e., the possibility to unsafely fold a rule by itself [23]) is disallowed. There are several points regarding our definition of the folding rule which are worth noticing: (i) As a difference w.r.t. the unfolding rule, the subterm which is selected for the folding step needs not be a (needed) narrowing redex. This generality is not only safe but also helpful as it will become apparent in Example 3. (ii) In contrast to [2], the substitution θ of Def. 4 is not a unifier but just a matcher. This is similar to many other folding rules for logic programs, which have been defined in a similar "functional style" (see, e.g., [7,20,24,28]). (iii) Finally, the *non-erasing* condition in Def. 1 can now be fully clarified: it avoids to consider a rule $l \to r$, with $Var(r) \subset Var(l)$, as a folding rule, since it might introduce extra variables in the rhs of the resulting rule.

---

[1] A *definition rule* maintains its status only as long as it remains unchanged, i.e., once a definition rule is transformed it is not considered a *definition rule* anymore.

Many attempts have been also made to define a folding transformation in a (pure) functional context [8,27]. A *marked* folding for a lazy (higher-order) functional language has been presented in [26], which preserves the semantics of (ground constructor) values under applicability conditions which are similar to ours. However, our correctness results are slightly stronger, since we preserve the (non-ground) semantics of computed values and *answers*.

As in our definition of folding, a large number of proposals also allow the folded and the folding rule to belong to different programs (see, e.g., [7,20,23,24,28]), which in general is crucial to achieve an effective optimization. Some other works in the literature have advocated a different style of folding which is *reversible* [13], i.e., a kind of folding which can always be undone by an unfolding step. This greatly simplifies the correctness proofs — correctness of folding follows immediately from the correctness of unfolding—, but usually require too strong applicability conditions, such as requiring that both the folded and the folding rules belong to the same program, which drastically reduces the power of the transformation. The folding rule proposed in [2] for a strict functional logic language is reversible and thus its transformational power is very limited. The folding rule introduced in this paper is more powerful and the applicability conditions are less restrictive.[2] Therefore, its use within a transformation system —when guided by appropriate strategies— is able to produce more effective optimizations for (lazy) functional logic programs.

The set of rules presented so far constitutes the kernel of our transformation system. These rules suffice for automatizing the *composition* strategy. However, the transformation system must be empowered for achieving the *tupling* optimization, which we attain by extending the transformation system with a rule of abstraction [8,26] (often known as *where–abstraction* rule [24]). It essentially consists of replacing the occurrences of some expression e in the rhs of a rule R by a fresh variable z, adding the "local declaration" $z = e$ within a *where* expression in R. For instance, the rule $\texttt{double\_sum}(X, Y) \rightarrow \texttt{sum}(\texttt{sum}(X, Y), \texttt{sum}(X, Y))$ can be transformed into the new rule

$$\texttt{double\_sum}(X, Y) \rightarrow \texttt{sum}(Z, Z) \text{ where } Z = \texttt{sum}(X, Y) .$$

As noted by [24], the use of the where–abstraction rule has the advantage that in the call-by-value mode of execution, the evaluation of the expression e is performed only once. This is also true in a lazy context under an implementation based on *sharing*, which allows us to keep track of variables which occur several times in the expression to be evaluated.

The new rules introduced by the where–abstraction do contain extra variables in the right-hand sides. However, as noted in [26], this can be easily amended by using standard "lambda lifting" techniques (which can be thought of as an appropriate application of a definition introduction step followed by a folding step). For

---

[2] It would be interesting to study a generalization of our folding rule to a *disjunctive* folding rule, i.e., allowing the folding of multiple recursive rules (see [25]).

instance, if we consider again the rule $\texttt{double\_sum}(X, Y) \rightarrow \texttt{sum}(Z, Z)$ where $Z = \texttt{sum}(X, Y)$, we can transform it (by lambda lifting [19]) into the new pair of rules

$$\texttt{double\_sum}(X, Y) \rightarrow \texttt{ds\_aux}(\texttt{sum}(X, Y))$$
$$\texttt{ds\_aux}(Z) \rightarrow \texttt{sum}(Z, Z)$$

Note that these rules can be directly generated from the initial definition by a definition introduction $(\texttt{ds\_aux}(Z) \rightarrow \texttt{sum}(Z, Z))$ and then by folding the original rule at the expression $\texttt{sum}(\texttt{sum}(X, Y), \texttt{sum}(X, Y))$ using as folding rule the newly generated definition for $\texttt{ds\_aux}/1$. The inclusion of an abstraction rule is traditional in functional fold/unfold frameworks [8,24,26,27]. In the case of logic programs, abstraction is only possible by means of the so called *generalization* strategy [24], which generalizes some calls to eliminate the mismatches that prevent a folding step.

Now, we are ready to formalize our abstraction rule, which is inspired by the standard lambda lifting transformation of functional programs. By means of the tuple constructor $\langle \ \rangle$, our definition allows the abstraction of different expressions in one go. For a sequence of (pairwise disjoint) positions $P = \overline{p_n}$, we let $t[\overline{s_n}]_P = (((t[s_1]_{p_1})[s_2]_{p_2}) \ldots [s_n]_{p_n})$. By abuse, we denote $t[\overline{s_n}]_P$ by $t[s]_P$ when $s_1 = \ldots = s_n = s$, as well as $((t[s_1]_{P_1}) \ldots [s_n]_{P_n})$ by $t[\overline{s_n}]_{\overline{P_n}}$.

Definition 5 (Abstraction). *Let $R = (f(\overline{t_n}) \rightarrow r) \in \mathcal{R}_k$ be a rule and let $\overline{P_j}$ be sequences of disjoint positions in $\mathcal{NVPos}(r)$ such that $r|_p = e_i$ for all p in P_i, $i = 1, \ldots, j$, i.e., $r = r[\overline{e_j}]_{\overline{P_j}}$. We may get program $\mathcal{R}_{k+1}$ from $\mathcal{R}_k$ by replacing R with $\{f(\overline{t_n}) \rightarrow f\_aux(\overline{y_m}, \langle e_1, \ldots, e_j \rangle), \ f\_aux(\overline{y_m}, \langle z_1, \ldots, z_j \rangle) \rightarrow r[\overline{z_j}]_{\overline{P_j}}\}$, where $\overline{z_j}$ are fresh variables not occurring in $\overline{t_n}$, f_aux is a fresh function symbol that does not occur in $(\mathcal{R}_0, \ldots, \mathcal{R}_k)$, and $Var(r[\overline{z_j}]_{\overline{P_j}}) = \{\overline{y_m}, \overline{z_j}\}$.*

Informally, the two rules generated by the abstraction transformation can be understood as a syntactic variant of the following rule:

$$f(\overline{t_n}) \rightarrow r[\overline{z_j}]_{\overline{P_j}} \ \text{where} \ \langle z_1, \ldots, z_j \rangle = \langle e_1, \ldots, e_j \rangle \ .$$

Now we state the main theoretical results for the basic transformations introduced in this section. We state the correctness of transformation sequences constructed from an inductively sequential program by applying the following rules: definition introduction, definition elimination, unfolding, folding, and abstraction. In proving this, we assume that no folding step is applied after a definition elimination, which guarantees that no function call to a previously deleted function is introduced along a transformation sequence [23]. First, we state that transformations preserve the inductively sequential structure of programs.

Theorem 1. *Let $(\mathcal{R}_0, \ldots, \mathcal{R}_n)$ be a transformation sequence. If $\mathcal{R}_0$ is inductively sequential, then $\mathcal{R}_i$ is also inductively sequential, for $i = 1, \ldots, n$.*

Sands formalizes a syntactic *improvement* theory [26] which restricts general fold/unfold transformations and can be applied to give correctness proofs for some existing transformation methods (such as deforestation [30]). However, we find it more convenient to stick to the logic programming methods for proving correctness because the narrowing mechanism can be properly seen as a generalization of the SLD-resolution method which implicitly applies instantiation before replacing a call by the corresponding instance of the body. That is, instantiation is computed in a systematic way by the needed narrowing mechanism (as in the unfolding of logic programs), whereas it is not restricted in the Burstall and Darlington's fold/unfold framework considered in [26]. Unrestricted instantiation is problematic since it does not even preserve local equivalence, and for this reason the instantiation rule is not considered explicitly in [26]. As a consequence, the improvement theorem of [26] does not directly apply to our context.

Our demonstration technique for the correctness result is inspired by the original proof scheme of Tamaki and Sato [28] concerning the least Herbrand model semantics of logic programs (and the subsequent extension of Kawamura and Kanamori [20] for the semantics of computed answers). Intuitively, a fold/unfold transformation system is correct if there are "at least as many folds as there are unfolds" or, equivalently, if "going backward in the computation (as folding does) does not prevail over going forward in the computation (as unfolding does)" [23,26]. This essentially means that there must be a kind of "computational cost" measure which is not increased either by folding or by unfolding steps. Several definitions for this measure can be found in the literature: the *rank of a goal* in [28], the *weight of a proof tree* in [20], or the notion of *improvement* in [26]. In our context, we have introduced the notion of *rank of a term* in order to measure the computational cost of a given term. The detailed proof scheme can be found in [3]. The strong correctness of the transformation is stated as follows.

Theorem 2. *Let $(\mathcal{R}_0, \ldots, \mathcal{R}_n)$, $n > 0$, be a transformation sequence. Let e be an equation with no new function symbol and $V \supseteq Var(e)$ a finite set of variables. Then, $e \leadsto_{\sigma}^* true$ in $\mathcal{R}_0$ iff $e \leadsto_{\sigma'}^* true$ in $\mathcal{R}_n$, with $\sigma' = \sigma \, [V]$ (up to renaming).*

4   Some Experiments

The building blocks of strategic program optimizations are transformation tactics (*strategies*), which are used to guide the process and effect some particular kind of change to the program undergoing transformation [12,24].

One of the most relevant quests in applying a transformation strategy is the introduction of new functions, often called in the literature *eureka* definitions. Although there is no general theory of strategies which ensures that derived programs are more efficient than the initial ones, some partial results exist. For instance, in the setting of higher-order (non-strict) functional languages, Sands [26] has recently introduced the theory of *improvement* to provide a syntactic method for guiding and constraining the unfold/fold method in [8] so that total correctness and performance improvement are always guaranteed.

In the following, we illustrate the power of our transformation system by tackling some representative examples regarding the optimizations of composition [30] and tupling [8,11].

4.1   Transformation Strategies

The composition strategy was originally introduced in [8,11] for the optimization of pure functional programs. Variants of this composition strategy are the *internal specialization* technique [27] and the *deforestation* method [30]. By using the composition strategy (or its variants), one may avoid the construction of intermediate data structures that are produced by some function g and consumed as inputs by another function f. In some cases, most of the efficiency improvement of the composition strategy can be simply obtained by lazy evaluation [12]. Nevertheless, the composition strategy often allows the derivation of programs with improved performance also in the context of lazy evaluation [29]. Laziness is decisive when, given a nested function call $f(g(X))$, the intermediate data structure produced by g is infinite but the function f can produce its outcome by knowing only a finite portion of the output of g. The following example illustrates the advantages of our transformation rules w.r.t. those of [2].

Example 3. The function $sum\_prefix(X, Y)$ defined in the following program $\mathcal{R}_0$ returns the sum of the Y consecutive natural numbers, starting from X:

$$sum\_prefix(X, Y) \rightarrow suml(from(X), Y) \ (R_1) \qquad from(X) \rightarrow [X|from(s(X))] \ (R_4)$$
$$suml(L, 0) \rightarrow 0 \qquad\qquad (R_2) \qquad\qquad 0 + X \rightarrow X \qquad\qquad (R_5)$$
$$suml([H|T], s(X)) \rightarrow H + suml(T, X) \quad (R_3) \qquad s(X) + Y \rightarrow s(X + Y) \qquad (R_6)$$

We can improve the efficiency of $\mathcal{R}_0$ by avoiding the creation and subsequent use of the intermediate, partial list generated by the call to the function $from$:

1. Definition introduction:

$$aux(X, Y) \rightarrow suml(from(X), Y) \qquad\qquad (R_7)$$

2. Unfolding of rule R_7 (note that instantiation is automatic):

$$aux(X, 0) \rightarrow 0 \qquad\qquad (R_8)$$
$$aux(X, s(Y)) \rightarrow suml([X|from(s(X))], s(Y)) \quad (R_9)$$

3. Unfolding of rule R_9 (note that this is infeasible with an eager strategy):

$$aux(X, s(Y)) \rightarrow X + suml(from(s(X)), Y) \qquad (R_{10})$$

4. Folding of $suml(from(s(X)), Y)$ in rule R_{10} using R_7:

$$aux(X, s(Y)) \rightarrow X + aux(s(X), Y) \qquad\qquad (R_{11})$$

5. Folding of the rhs of rule R_1 using R_7:

$$sum\_prefix(X, Y) \rightarrow aux(X, Y) \qquad\qquad (R_{12})$$

Then, the transformed program $\mathcal{R}_5$ is formed by the following rules:

$$sum\_prefix(X, Y) \rightarrow aux(X, Y) \qquad\qquad (R_{12})$$
$$aux(X, 0) \rightarrow 0 \qquad\qquad (R_8)$$
$$aux(X, s(Y)) \rightarrow X + aux(s(X), Y) \qquad\qquad (R_{11})$$

(together with the initial definitions for $+$, $from$, and $suml$).

Note that the use of needed narrowing as a basis for our unfolding rule is essential in the above example. It ensures that no redundant rules are produced by unfolding and it also allows the transformation even in the presence of nonterminating functions (as opposed to [2]).

The tupling strategy was introduced in [8,11] to optimize functional programs. The tupling strategy is very effective when several functions require the computation of the same subexpression, in which case we tuple together those functions. By avoiding either multiple accesses to data structures or common subcomputations one often gets linear recursive programs (i.e., programs whose rhs's have at most one recursive call) from nonlinear recursive programs [24]. The following well-known example illustrates the tupling strategy.

Example 4. The fibonacci numbers can be computed by the program $\mathcal{R}_0$:

$$
\begin{array}{ll}
\mathtt{fib(0)} \to \mathtt{s(0)} & (R_1) \\
\mathtt{fib(s(0))} \to \mathtt{s(0)} & (R_2) \\
\mathtt{fib(s(s(X)))} \to \mathtt{fib(s(X))} + \mathtt{fib(X)} & (R_3)
\end{array}
$$

(together with the rules for addition +). Observe that this program has an exponential complexity, which can be reduced to a linear one by applying the tupling strategy as follows:

1. Definition introduction:

$$\mathtt{new(X)} \to \langle \mathtt{fib(s(X))}, \mathtt{fib(X)} \rangle \qquad (R_4)$$

2. Unfolding of rule R_4 (narrowing the needed redex $\mathtt{fib(s(X))}$):

$$
\begin{array}{ll}
\mathtt{new(0)} \to \langle \mathtt{s(0)}, \mathtt{fib(s(0))} \rangle & (R_5) \\
\mathtt{new(s(X))} \to \langle \mathtt{fib(s(X))} + \mathtt{fib(X)}, \mathtt{fib(s(X))} \rangle & (R_6)
\end{array}
$$

3. Unfolding of rule R_5 (narrowing the needed redex $\mathtt{fib(s(0))}$):

$$\mathtt{new(0)} \to \langle \mathtt{s(0)}, \mathtt{s(0)} \rangle \qquad (R_7)$$

4. Abstraction of R_6:

$$
\begin{array}{ll}
\mathtt{new(s(X))} \to \mathtt{new\_aux}(\langle \mathtt{fib(s(X))}, \mathtt{fib(X)} \rangle) & (R_8) \\
\mathtt{new\_aux}(\langle Z_1, Z_2 \rangle) \to \langle Z_1 + Z_2, Z_1 \rangle & (R_9)
\end{array}
$$

5. Folding of $\langle \mathtt{fib(s(X))}, \mathtt{fib(X)} \rangle$ in rule R_8 using R_4:

$$\mathtt{new(s(X))} \to \mathtt{new\_aux(new(X))} \qquad (R_{10})$$

6. Abstraction of R_3:

$$
\begin{array}{ll}
\mathtt{fib(s(s(X)))} \to \mathtt{fib\_aux}(\langle \mathtt{fib(s(X))}, \mathtt{fib(X)} \rangle) & (R_{11}) \\
\mathtt{fib\_aux}(\langle Z_1, Z_2 \rangle) \to Z_1 + Z_2 & (R_{12})
\end{array}
$$

7. Folding of $\langle \mathtt{fib(s(X))}, \mathtt{fib(X)} \rangle$ in rule R_{11} using again rule R_4:

$$\mathtt{fib(s(s(X)))} \to \mathtt{fib\_aux(new(X))} \qquad (R_{13})$$

Now, the (enhanced) transformed program $\mathcal{R}_7$ (with linear complexity thanks to the use of the recursive function new), is the following:

$$
\begin{array}{ll}
\texttt{fib(0)} \rightarrow \texttt{s(0)} & (R_1) \\
\texttt{fib(s(0))} \rightarrow \texttt{s(0)} & (R_2) \\
\texttt{fib(s(s(X)))} \rightarrow Z_1 + Z_2 \text{ where } \langle Z_1, Z_2 \rangle = \texttt{new(X)} & (R_{12}, R_{13}) \\
\texttt{new(0)} \rightarrow \langle \texttt{s(0)}, \texttt{s(0)} \rangle & (R_7) \\
\texttt{new(s(X))} \rightarrow \langle Z_1 + Z_2, Z_1 \rangle \text{ where } \langle Z_1, Z_2 \rangle = \texttt{new(X)} & (R_9, R_{10})
\end{array}
$$

where rules (R_{12}, R_{13}) and (R_9, R_{10}) are expressed by using local declarations for readability.

4.2   Benchmarks

The basic rules presented so far have been implemented by a prototype system SYNTH [1], which is publicly available at http://www.dsic.upv.es/users/elp/soft.html. It is written in SICStus Prolog and includes a parser for the language Curry, a modern multiparadigm declarative language based on needed narrowing which is intended to become a standard in the functional logic community [16,17]. It also includes a fully automatic composition strategy based on some (apparently reasonable) heuristics. The transformation system allows us to choose between two ways to apply the composition strategy. The first way is semi-automatic, since the user has to indicate the rule in which a nested call appears. A second way is completely automatic. It is the transformer which looks for a nested call in one of the rules and introduces a definition rule for a new function to start the process. We are currently extending the system in order to mechanize tupling (e.g., by using the analysis method of [9]).

Table 1 summarizes our benchmark results. The first two columns measure the number of rewrite rules (Rw_1) and the absolute runtimes (RT_1) for the original programs. The next column (*Comp*) shows the execution times of the (automatic) composition algorithm. The other columns show the number of rewrite rules (Rw_2), the absolute runtimes (RT_2), and the speedups achieved for the transformed programs. All the programs have been executed by using Taste-Curry, which is a publicly available interpreter for a subset of Curry [16]. Times are expressed in seconds and are the average of 10 executions. We note that our (automatic) composition strategy performs well w.r.t. the first four benchmarks. They are classical examples in which composition is able to perform an effective optimization (sumprefix is described in Example 3, while doubleappend, lengthapp, and doubleflip are typical functional programs to illustrate deforestation [30]). Regarding the last benchmark fibprefix, which is similar to sumprefix but it sums Fibonacci numbers instead of natural numbers, a slowdown has been produced (due to an incorrect folding, which added a new function call to the recursion). In this case a tupling strategy is mandatory to succeed, as expected.

In general, the transformed programs cannot be guaranteed to be faster than the original ones, since there is a trade-off between the smaller amount of computation needed after the transformation (when guided by appropriate strategies)

Table 1. Benchmark results.

Benchmarks	Rw_1	RT_1	$Comp$	Rw_2	RT_2	Speedup (%)
doubleappend	3	1.77	0.1	6	1.63	10%
sumprefix	8	3.59	0.21	10	3.48	3%
lengthapp	7	1.61	0.17	10	1.51	6%
doubleflip	3	0.95	0.11	5	0.7	26%
fibprefix	11	2.2	0.28	13	2.26	-3%

and the larger number of derived rules. Nevertheless, our experiments seem to substantiate that the smaller computations make up for the overhead of checking the applicability of the larger number of rules in the derived programs.

5   Conclusions

The definition of a fold/unfold framework for the optimization of functional logic programs was an open problem marked in [24] as pending research. We have presented a transformation methodology for lazy functional logic programs preserving the semantics of both values and answers computed by an efficient (currently the best) operational mechanism. For proving correctness, we extensively exploit the existing results from Huet and Levy's theory of needed reductions [18] and the wide literature about completeness of needed narrowing [5] (rather than striving an ad-hoc proof). We have shown that the transformation process keeps the inductively sequential structure of programs. We have also illustrated with several examples that the transformation process can be guided by appropriate strategies which lead to effective improvements. Our experiments show that our transformation framework combines in a useful and effective way the systematic instantiation of calls during unfolding (by virtue of the logic component of the needed narrowing mechanism) with the power of the abstraction transformations (thanks to the functional dimension). We have also presented an implementation which allows us to perform automatically the composition strategy as well as to perform all basic transformations in a semi-automatized way. The multi-paradigm language Curry [15,17] is an extension of Haskell with features for logic and concurrent programming. The results in this paper can be applied to optimize a large class of kernel (i.e., non concurrent) Curry programs.

Acknowledgements

We thank Ivan Ziliotto and Cesar Ferri for having implemented the transformer SYNTH under SICStus Prolog and for the evaluation of the benchmarks.

References

1. M. Alpuente, M. Falaschi, C. Ferri, G. Moreno, G. Vidal, and I. Ziliotto. The Transformation System SYNTH. Technical report DSIC-II/16/99, DSIC, 1999. Available from URL: http://www.dsic.upv.es/users/elp/papers.html.

2. M. Alpuente, M. Falaschi, G. Moreno, and G. Vidal. Safe Folding/Unfolding with Conditional Narrowing. In H. Heering M. Hanus and K. Meinke, editors, *Proc. of ALP'97*, Springer LNCS 1298, pages 1–15, 1997.

3. M. Alpuente, M. Falaschi, G. Moreno, and G. Vidal. A Transformation System for Lazy Functional Logic Programs. Technical report, DSIC, UPV, 1999. Available from URL: http://www.dsic.upv.es/users/elp/papers.html.

4. S. Antoy. Definitional Trees. In *Proc. of ALP'92*, Springer LNCS 632, pages 143–157, 1992.

5. S. Antoy, R. Echahed, and M. Hanus. A Needed Narrowing Strategy. In *Proc. 21st ACM Symp. on Principles of Programming Languages*, pages 268–279, 1994.

6. F. Baader and T. Nipkow. *Term Rewriting and All That*. Cambridge University Press, 1998.

7. A. Bossi and N. Cocco. Basic Transformation Operations which preserve Computed Answer Substitutions of Logic Programs. *JLP*, 16:47–87, 1993.

8. R.M. Burstall and J. Darlington. A Transformation System for Developing Recursive Programs. *Journal of the ACM*, 24(1):44–67, 1977.

9. W. Chin. Towards an Automated Tupling Strategy. In *Proc. of Partial Evaluation and Semantics-Based Program Manipulation*, pages 119–132. ACM, 1993.

10. W. Chin, A. Goh, and S. Khoo. Effective Optimisation of Multiple Traversals in Lazy Languages. In *Proc. of PEPM'99 (Technical Report BRICS-NS-99-1)*, pages 119–130. University of Aarhus, DK, 1999.

11. J. Darlington. Program transformation. In *Functional Programming and its Applications*, pages 193–215. Cambridge University Press, 1982.

12. M. S. Feather. A Survey and Classification of some Program Transformation Approaches and Techniques. In *IFIP'87*, pages 165–195, 1987.

13. P. A. Gardner and J. C. Shepherdson. Unfold/fold Transformation of Logic Programs. In J.L Lassez and G. Plotkin, editors, *Computational Logic, Essays in Honor of Alan Robinson*, pages 565–583. The MIT Press, Cambridge, MA, 1991.

14. M. Hanus. The Integration of Functions into Logic Programming: From Theory to Practice. *Journal of Logic Programming*, 19&20:583–628, 1994.

15. M. Hanus. A Unified Computation Model for Functional and Logic Programming. In *Proc. of the 24th ACM POPL*, pages 80–93. ACM, New York, 1997.

16. M. Hanus, H. Kuchen, and J.J. Moreno-Navarro. Curry: A Truly Functional Logic Language. In *Proc. ILPS'95 Workshop on Visions for the Future of Logic Programming*, pages 95–107, 1995.

17. M. Hanus (ed.). Curry: An Integrated Functional Logic Language. Available at http://www-i2.informatik.rwth-aachen.de/~hanus/curry, 1999.

18. G. Huet and J.J. Lévy. Computations in Orthogonal Rewriting Systems, Part I + II. In J.L. Lassez and G.D. Plotkin, editors, *Computational Logic – Essays in Honor of Alan Robinson*, pages 395–443, 1992.

19. T. Johnsson. Lambda Lifting: Transforming Programs to Recursive Equations. In *FPLCA'85*, pages 190–203. Springer LNCS 201, 1985.

20. T. Kawamura and T. Kanamori. Preservation of Stronger Equivalence in Unfold/Fold Logic Program Transformation. *TCS*, 75:139–156, 1990.

21. M.J. Maher. A Transformation System for Deductive Database Modules with Perfect Model Semantics. *Theoretical Computer Science*, 110(2):377–403, 1993.

22. J.J. Moreno-Navarro and M. Rodríguez-Artalejo. Logic Programming with Functions and Predicates: The language Babel. *JLP*, 12(3):191–224, 1992.

23. A. Pettorossi and M. Proietti. Transformation of Logic Programs: Foundations and Techniques. *Journal of Logic Programming*, 19&20:261–320, 1994.

24. A. Pettorossi and M. Proietti. Rules and Strategies for Transforming Functional and Logic Programs. *ACM Computing Surveys*, 28(2):360–414, 1996.
25. A. Roychoudhury, K. Narayan Kumar, C.R. Ramakrishnan, and I.V. Ramakrishnan. A Parameterized Unfold/Fold Transformation Framework for Definite Logic Programs. In *Proc. of PPDP'99*, Springer LNCS, 1999. To appear.
26. D. Sands. Total Correctness by Local Improvement in the Transformation of Functional Programs. *ACM ToPLaS*, 18(2):175–234, March 1996.
27. W.L. Scherlis. Program Improvement by Internal Specialization. In *Proc. of 8th ACM POPL*, pages 41–49. ACM Press, 1981.
28. H. Tamaki and T. Sato. Unfold/Fold Transformations of Logic Programs. In S. Tärnlund, editor, *Proc. of 2nd ICLP*, pages 127–139, 1984.
29. P.L. Wadler. *Listlessness is better than Laziness*. Computer Science Department, CMU-CS-85-171, Carnegie Mellon Univertsity, Pittsburgh, PA, 1985. Ph.D. Thesis.
30. P.L. Wadler. Deforestation: Transforming programs to eliminate trees. *Theoretical Computer Science*, 73:231–248, 1990.

Termination Analysis of Tabled Logic Programs Using Mode and Type Information

Sofie Verbaeten* and Danny De Schreye**

Department of Computer Science, K.U.Leuven, Belgium
{sofie,dannyd}@cs.kuleuven.ac.be

Abstract. Tabled logic programming is receiving increasing attention in the Logic Programming community. It avoids many of the shortcomings of SLD(NF) execution and provides a more flexible and efficient execution mechanism for logic programs. In particular, tabled execution of logic programs terminates more often than execution based on SLD-resolution. One of the few approaches studying termination of tabled logic programs was developed by Decorte *et al.* They present necessary and sufficient conditions for two notions of universal termination under SLG-resolution, the resolution principle of tabling: quasi-termination and (the stronger notion of) LG-termination. Starting from these necessary and sufficient conditions, we introduce sufficient conditions which are stated fully at the clause level and are easy to automatize. To this end, we use mode and type information: we consider simply moded, well-typed programs and queries. We point out how our termination conditions can be automatized, by extending the recently developed constraint-based automatic termination analysis for SLD-resolution by Decorte and De Schreye.

1 Introduction

Tabled logic programming [5,14], extending standard SLD-resolution with a tabling mechanism, avoids many of the shortcomings of SLD execution and provides a more flexible and often considerably more efficient execution mechanism for logic programs. In particular, tabled execution of logic programs terminates more often than execution based on SLD. So, if a program can be proven to terminate under SLD-resolution (by one of the existing automated techniques surveyed in [6]), then the program will trivially also terminate under SLG-resolution, the resolution principle of tabling [5]. However, since there are programs and queries which terminate under SLG-resolution and not under SLD-resolution, more effective proof techniques can be found. One of the few works studying termination of tabled logic programs is [7], in which necessary and sufficient conditions are

---

* Research Assistant of the Fund for Scientific Research - Flanders (Belgium)(F.W.O.).
** Senior Research Associate of F.W.O. - Flanders (Belgium).

A. Middeldorp, T. Sato (Eds.): FLOPS'99, LNCS 1722, pp. 163–178, 1999.

given for two notions of universal termination under LG-resolution, i.e. SLG-resolution with left-to-right selection rule: namely quasi-termination and (the stronger notion of) LG-termination.

This work is based on [7]. Starting from the necessary and sufficient conditions of [7], we present sufficient conditions for quasi-termination and LG-termination which are stated fully at the clause level. To this end we use mode and type information: we consider simply moded, well-typed programs and queries. Our termination conditions are easy to automatize. In particular, we show how the framework of [8], where a constraint-based automatic termination analysis for LD-resolution (SLD-resolution with left-to-right selection rule) is given, needs to be modified in order to prove quasi-termination and LG-termination in an automatic way.

In the following Section 2 of preliminaries, we first recall the notion of SLG-resolution [5] for definite programs. Next, we define the notions of simply modedness, well-typedness and input safe atoms and we give some definitions and properties of norms and level mappings. In the following Section 3, the notion of quasi-termination and its characterisation of [7], namely quasi-acceptability, are introduced. We present an easy to automatize, sufficient condition for quasi-termination of simply moded well-typed programs and queries in Subsection 3.1. We point out in Subsection 3.2 how this condition can be automatized, by extending the automatic, constraint-based termination analysis for LD-resolution of [8]. By the lack of space, we do not consider the stronger notion of LG-termination in this paper. Instead, we refer to the full version of the paper, [15], where we present an optimizatation of the necessary and sufficient condition of [7] for LG-termination, together with an easy to automatize condition for LG-termination of simply moded well-typed programs and queries. We want to note however that this automatizable condition for LG-termination is obtained from its characterisation in a similar way as the one for quasi-termination. In Section 4 we conclude this paper with a discussion on related works. We refer to the full version of the paper, [15], for more examples and all the proofs.

2 Preliminaries

We refer to [12] for the basic concepts of logic programming. Throughout the paper, P will denote a definite logic program. The *extended Herbrand Universe*, U_P^E, and the *extended Herbrand Base*, B_P^E, associated with a program P are defined as follows. Let $Term_P$ and $Atom_P$ denote the set of respectively all terms and atoms that can be constructed from the alphabet underlying P. The variant relation, denoted $\approx$, defines an equivalence. U_P^E and B_P^E are respectively the quotient sets $Term_P/\approx$ and $Atom_P/\approx$. For any term t (or atom A), we denote its class in U_P^E (B_P^E) as $\tilde{t}$ ($\tilde{A}$). However, when no confusion is possible, we omit the tildes. We use the abbreviation mgu for most general unifier.

We will refer to SLD-derivations following the left-to-right selection rule as LD-derivations. Other concepts will adopt this naming accordingly. Given $S \subseteq B_P^E$, by $Call(P, S)$ we denote the subset of B_P^E such that $\tilde{B} \in Call(P, S)$

whenever an element of $\tilde{B}$ is a selected literal in an LD-derivation for some $P \cup \{\leftarrow A\}$, with $\tilde{A} \in S$. Throughout the paper we assume that in any derivation of a query w.r.t. a program, representatives of equivalence classes are systematically provided with fresh variables, to avoid the necessity of renaming apart.

2.1 SLG-Resolution for Definite Programs

The ideas underlying tabling are very simple. Essentially, under a tabled execution mechanism, answers for selected atoms are stored in a table. When a variant of such an atom is recursively called, the selected atom is not resolved against program clauses, instead, all corresponding answers computed so far are looked up in the table and the corresponding answer substitutions are applied to the atom. This process is repeated for all subsequent computed answer substitutions that correspond to the atom.

We present a non-constructive definition of SLG-resolution, the resolution principle underlying tabling, and refer to [5,14] for more constructive formulations of (variants) of tabled resolution.

Definition 1 (pseudo SLG-tree, pseudo LG-tree). *Let P be a definite program, $\mathcal{R}$ a selection rule and A an atom. A pseudo SLG-tree for $P \cup \{\leftarrow A\}$ under $\mathcal{R}$ is a tree τ_A such that:*

1. *the nodes of τ_A are labeled with queries along with an indication of the selected atom according to $\mathcal{R}$,*
2. *the root of τ_A is $\leftarrow A$,*
3. *the children of the root $\leftarrow A$ are obtained by resolution against all matching program clauses in P, the arcs are labeled with the corresponding mgu used in the resolution step,*
4. *the (possibly infinitely many) children of non-root nodes can only be obtained by resolving the selected (using $\mathcal{R}$) atom B of the node with clauses of the form $B\theta \leftarrow$ (not necessarily in P), the arcs are labeled with the corresponding mgu used in the resolution step (i.e. θ).*

If $\mathcal{R}$ is the leftmost selection rule, τ_A is called a pseudo LG-tree for $P \cup \{\leftarrow A\}$. We say that a pseudo SLG-tree τ_A for $P \cup \{\leftarrow A\}$ is smaller than another pseudo SLG-tree τ'_A for $P \cup \{\leftarrow A\}$ iff τ_A can be obtained from τ_A by attaching new sub-branches to nodes in τ_A.
A (computed) answer clause of a pseudo SLG-tree τ_A for $P \cup \{\leftarrow A\}$ is a clause of the form $A\theta \leftarrow$ where θ is the composition of the substitutions found on a branch of τ_A whose leaf is labeled by the empty query.

Intuitively, a pseudo SLG-tree (in an SLG-forest, see Definition 2 below) represents the tabled computation of all answers for a given subquery labeling the root node of the tree. The trees in the above definition are called *pseudo SLG-trees* because there is no condition yet on which clauses $B\theta \leftarrow$ exactly are to be used for resolution in point 4. These clauses represent the answers found (possibly in another tree of the forest) for the selected atom. This interaction between the trees in an SLG-forest is captured in the following definition.

Definition 2 (SLG-forest, LG-forest). *Let P be a definite program, $\mathcal{R}$ be a selection rule and T be a (possibly infinite) set of atoms such that no two different atoms in T are variants of each other. $\mathcal{F}$ is an SLG-forest for P and T under $\mathcal{R}$ iff $\mathcal{F}$ is a set of minimal pseudo SLG-trees $\{\tau_A \mid A \in T\}$ where*

1. *τ_A is a pseudo SLG-tree for $P \cup \{\leftarrow A\}$ under $\mathcal{R}$,*
2. *every selected atom B of each node in some $\tau_A \in \mathcal{F}$ is a variant of an element B' of T, such that every clause resolved with B is a variant of an answer clause of $\tau_{B'}$ and vice versa, for every answer clause of $\tau_{B'}$ there is a variant of this answer clause which is resolved with B.*

Let S be a set of atoms. An SLG-forest for P and S under $\mathcal{R}$ is an SLG-forest for a minimal set T with $S \subseteq T$. If $S = \{A\}$, then we also talk about the SLG-forest for $P \cup \{\leftarrow A\}$. An LG-forest is an SLG-forest containing only pseudo LG-trees.

Point 2 of Definition 2, together with the imposed minimality of trees in a forest, now uniquely determines these trees. So we can drop the designation "pseudo" and refer to (S)LG-trees in an (S)LG-forest.

Example 1. Let NAT be the following program defining the natural numbers:

$$\begin{cases} nat(0) & \leftarrow \\ nat(s(X)) \leftarrow nat(X) \end{cases}$$

Let $S = \{nat(X)\}$. Then the (unique) (S)LG-forest for P and S, shown in Fig. 1, consists of a single (S)LG-tree. Note that this tree is infinitely branching.

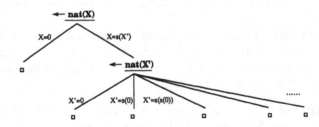

Fig. 1. The SLG-forest for $NAT \cup \{\leftarrow nat(X)\}$.

We want to note that we can use the notions of LD-derivation and LD-computation (as they appear in the definition of the call set $Call(P, S)$) even in the context of SLG-resolution, as the set of call patterns and the set of computed answer substitutions are not influenced by tabling; see e.g. [11, Theorem 2.1].

2.2   Simply Modedness, Well-Typedness and Input Safe Atoms

Definition 3 (mode for a predicate). *Let p be an n-ary predicate symbol. A mode for p is a function $m_p : \{1, \ldots, n\} \to \{In, Out\}$. If $m_p(i) = In$ (resp. Out), then we say that i is an input (resp. output) position of p (w.r.t. m_p).*

We assume that each predicate symbol has a unique mode. Multiple modes can be obtained by simply renaming the predicates. To simplify the notation, when writing an atom as $p(\mathbf{u}, \mathbf{v})$ we assume that $\mathbf{u}$ is the sequence of terms filling in the input positions of p and $\mathbf{v}$ is the sequence of terms filling in the output positions of p. For a term t, we denote by $Var(t)$ the set of variables occurring in t. Similar notation is used for sequences of terms.

We introduce the notion of simply modedness [2]. A family of terms is called *linear* if every variable occurs at most once in it.

Definition 4 (simply modedness). *A clause* $p_0(\mathbf{s_0}, \mathbf{t_{n+1}}) \leftarrow p_1(\mathbf{s_1}, \mathbf{t_1}), \ldots,$ $p_n(\mathbf{s_n}, \mathbf{t_n})$ *is called* simply moded *iff* $\mathbf{t_1}, \ldots, \mathbf{t_n}$ *is a linear family of variables and for* $i \in [1, n]$: $Var(\mathbf{t_i}) \cap (\cup_{j=0}^{i} Var(\mathbf{s_j})) = \emptyset$.
A program is called simply moded *iff every clause of it is simply moded.*
A query $\leftarrow p_1(\mathbf{s_1}, \mathbf{t_1}), \ldots, p_n(\mathbf{s_n}, \mathbf{t_n})$ *is simply moded if the clause* $p \leftarrow p_1(\mathbf{s_1}, \mathbf{t_1}),$ $\ldots, p_n(\mathbf{s_n}, \mathbf{t_n})$ *is simply moded, where* p *is any nullary predicate.*

For instance, with moding $q(In, Out)$, the clause $q(f(X), f(Y)) \leftarrow q(X, Y)$ is simply moded, but the clause $q(X, Y) \leftarrow q(X, f(Y))$ is not. The notion of simply modedness is persistent [2], that is: *An LD-resolvent of a simply moded query and a simply moded clause that is variable-disjoint with it, is simply moded.* An atom is called *input/output disjoint* if the family of terms occurring in its input positions has no variable in common with the family of terms occurring in its output positions. As a corollary to the persistence of the notion of simply modedness, we have that: *For a simply moded program* P *and a simply moded query* Q, *all atoms selected in an LD-derivation of* $P \cup \{\leftarrow Q\}$ *are input/output disjoint and such that each of the output positions is filled in by a distinct variable.* In [2], it is argued that most programs are simply moded, and that often non-simply moded programs can be naturally transformed into simply moded ones.

We next introduce the notion of input-correct atom w.r.t. a set of atoms. This notion will be useful in our termination condition.

Definition 5 (input-correct atom w.r.t. S). *Let* $S \subseteq B_P^E$ *and* $A = p(\mathbf{u}, \mathbf{v})$ *an atom. We call* A input-correct *w.r.t.* S, *denoted by* $A^{In} \in S^{In}$, *iff there is an atom* $B = p(\mathbf{u}, \mathbf{w})$ *such that* $\tilde{B} \in S$.

In the sequel, we also use types. A *type* is defined as a decidable set of terms closed under substitution. A type T is called *ground* if all its elements are ground, and *non-ground* otherwise. A *typed term* is a construct of the form $s : S$, where s is a term and S is a type. Given a sequence $\mathbf{s} : \mathbf{S} = s_1 : S_1, \ldots, s_n : S_n$ of typed terms, we write $\mathbf{s} \in \mathbf{S}$ iff for every $i \in [1, n]$, we have $s_i \in S_i$.

Some examples of types are: U, the set of all terms; $Ground$, the set of all ground terms; $List$, the set of all (possibly non-ground) nil-terminated lists (built on the empty list $[\,]$ and the list constructor $[.|.]$); and NAT, the set of all natural numbers $\{0, s(0), s(s(0)), \ldots\}$. Throughout the paper, we fix a specific set of types, denoted by $Types$. We also associate types with predicates.

Definition 6 (type for a predicate, correctly typed). *Let* p *be an* n-ary *predicate symbol. A type for* p *is a function* $t_p : \{1, \ldots, n\} \to Types$. *If* $t_p(i) = T$,

we call T the type associated with position i of p.
Assuming a type t_p for the predicate p, we say that an atom $p(s_1, \ldots, s_n)$ is correctly typed in position i iff $s_i \in t_p(i)$. We say that $p(s_1, \ldots, s_n)$ is correctly typed iff it is correctly typed in all its positions.

When every considered predicate has a mode and a type associated with it, we can talk about types of input positions and of output positions of an atom. An n-ary predicate p with a mode m_p and type t_p will be denoted by $p(< m_p(1) : t_p(1) >, \ldots, < m_p(n) : t_p(n) >)$. To simplify the notation, when writing an atom as $p(\mathbf{u} : \mathbf{S}, \mathbf{v} : \mathbf{T})$ we assume that $\mathbf{u} : \mathbf{S}$ is a sequence of typed terms filling in the input positions of p and $\mathbf{v} : \mathbf{T}$ is a sequence of typed terms filling in the output positions of p. We call $p(\mathbf{u} : \mathbf{S}, \mathbf{v} : \mathbf{T})$ a *typed atom*.

Next, we introduce the notion of well-typedness [4]. First, we need the following concept of a type judgement.

Definition 7 ((true) type judgement). *A statement of the form $\mathbf{s} : \mathbf{S} \Rightarrow \mathbf{t} : \mathbf{T}$ is called a* type judgement. *A type judgement $\mathbf{s} : \mathbf{S} \Rightarrow \mathbf{t} : \mathbf{T}$ is true, notated $\models \mathbf{s} : \mathbf{S} \Rightarrow \mathbf{t} : \mathbf{T}$, iff for all substitutions θ, $\mathbf{s}\theta \in \mathbf{S}$ implies $\mathbf{t}\theta \in \mathbf{T}$.*

Definition 8 (well-typedness).
A clause $p_0(\mathbf{o_0} : \mathbf{O_0}, \mathbf{i_{n+1}} : \mathbf{I_{n+1}}) \leftarrow p_1(\mathbf{i_1} : \mathbf{I_1}, \mathbf{o_1} : \mathbf{O_1}), \ldots, p_n(\mathbf{i_n} : \mathbf{I_n}, \mathbf{o_n} : \mathbf{O_n})$ is called well-typed *iff for $j \in [1, n+1]$: $\models \mathbf{o_0} : \mathbf{O_0}, \ldots, \mathbf{o_{j-1}} : \mathbf{O_{j-1}} \Rightarrow \mathbf{i_j} : \mathbf{I_j}$.*
A program is called well-typed *iff every clause of it is well-typed.*
A query $\leftarrow p_1(\mathbf{i_1} : \mathbf{I_1}, \mathbf{o_1} : \mathbf{O_1}), \ldots, p_n(\mathbf{i_n} : \mathbf{I_n}, \mathbf{o_n} : \mathbf{O_n})$ is well-typed *if the clause $p \leftarrow p_1(\mathbf{i_1} : \mathbf{I_1}, \mathbf{o_1} : \mathbf{O_1}), \ldots, p_n(\mathbf{i_n} : \mathbf{I_n}, \mathbf{o_n} : \mathbf{O_n})$ is well-typed, where p is any nullary predicate.*

Note that in a well-typed query, the left-most atom is correctly typed in its input positions. We want to note that the notion of *well-modedness* [1], is a special case of the notion of well-typedness. Namely, the definition of well-modedness is an instance of Definition 8, where the types of all positions are (implicitly) defined as *Ground* (see [1, Theorem 3.7] for more details). Hence, the results in this paper obtained for well-typed programs and queries, also hold for well-moded programs and queries.

As for simply modedness, the notion of well-typedness is persistent [4], that is: *An LD-resolvent of a well-typed query and a well-typed clause that is variable-disjoint with it, is well-typed.* Hence, we have that: *For a well-typed program P and a well-typed query Q, all atoms selected in an LD-derivation of $P \cup \{\leftarrow Q\}$ are correctly typed in their input positions.*

In [2] the notion of generic expression for a type was introduced. Intuitively, a term t is a generic expression for a type T if it is more general than all elements of T which unify with t. This notion is the main tool in the approach of [2] towards replacing unification by iterated matching. It turns out that surprisingly often the input positions of the heads of program clauses are filled in by generic expressions for appropriate types (see [2]). We recall the definition.

Definition 9 (generic expression for a type). *Let T be a type. A term t is a generic expression for T iff for every $s \in T$ variable-disjoint with t, if s unifies with t then s is an instance of t.*

For example, $[\ ], [X], [X|Y], [X, Y|Z], \ldots$ are generic expressions for the type *List*; $0, s(X), s(s(s(X))), \ldots$ are generic expressions for the type *NAT*. A term of the form $f(X_1, \ldots, X_m)$ with $X_1, \ldots, X_m$ a sequence of different variables is called a *pure variable term*. In [2, Lemma 3.7], it was shown that: variables are generic expressions for any type; the only generic expressions for type U are variables; if the type T does not contain variables, then every pure variable term is a generic expression for T; and if T is *Ground*, then every term is a generic expression for T. In [2], the notion of input safe atom was introduced as follows.

Definition 10 (input safe atom). *An atom is called* input safe *if (1) each of its input positions is filled in with a generic expression for this positions type, and (2) either the types of all input positions are ground or the terms filling in the input positions are mutually variable-disjoint.*

In particular, an atom is input safe if the types of all input positions are ground. The notion of input safe atom is interesting for the following reason. The parameter passing mechanism in the unification of a simply moded query A, which is correctly typed in its input positions, with an input safe head atom H is as follows: first the input values are passed from the atom A to the head H, then the output values are passed from H to A. The next proposition generalizes this informal argument (we refer to [15] for more details). In the sequel, we abbreviate simply moded well-typed with SMWT.

Proposition 1. *Let P be a SMWT program and $\leftarrow B_1, \ldots, B_n$ be a SMWT query. Suppose that the heads of the clauses of P are input safe.*
If $\sigma = \theta^1 \ldots \theta^k$ is the substitution of a (partial) LD-derivation of $\leftarrow B_1, \ldots, B_n$ in P, then the input arguments of B_1 are equal to the input arguments of $B_1\sigma$ modulo variable renaming.

It follows from Proposition 1 that, if P and $\leftarrow A$ are SMWT and if the heads of the clauses in P are input safe, then in every LD-derivation of $P \cup \{\leftarrow A\}$ the input arguments of A get never instantiated. We will use this in the termination condition for SMWT programs and queries (Theorem 2). Namely, if the heads of the clauses of the program are input safe, we are no longer forced to reason on "calls" in the termination condition, instead, the termination condition can be easily stated at the clause level, which is useful in the context of an automatic termination analysis.

In [2] it was shown that if a program P and query $\leftarrow A$ are SMWT and if the heads of the clauses in P are input safe, $P \cup \{\leftarrow A\}$ is unification free (i.e. unification can be replaced by iterated matching). We refer to the list of program examples in the discussion section of [2], where appropriate modings and typings for the considered predicates are given such that the programs are SMWT and the heads of their clauses are input safe. Note that for surprisingly many programs appropriate modings and typings can be found.

2.3   Norms and Level Mappings

We recall the definitions of norm and level mapping.

Definition 11 (norm, level mapping). *Let P be a definite program. A norm is a function $\| . \| : U_P^E \to \mathbb{N}$. A level mapping is a function $|.| : B_P^E \to \mathbb{N}$.*

We introduce some notation. By $Pred_P$, Fun_P, $Const_P$ and Var_P we denote the sets of predicate, function, constant symbols and variables of P respectively. The set of *predicate coefficients*, $PC(P)$, respectively *functor coefficients*, $FC(P)$, associated to a program P are the sets of symbols $PC(P) = \{p_i \mid p/n \in Pred_P \wedge i \in \{1,\ldots,n\}\}$, and $FC(P) = \{f_i \mid f/m \in Fun_P \wedge i \in \{0,1,\ldots,m\}\}$. Here, all norms and level mappings will be of a specified form (for the norms this is a slight variant of the semi-linear norms [3]).

Definition 12 (symbolic norm and level mapping, symbol mapping). *The symbolic norm $\| . \|^S$ and symbolic level mapping $|.|^S$ are defined as:*

$$\begin{cases} \| X \|^S = \| c \|^S = 0 & \text{for } X \in Var_P, c \in Const_P, \\ \| f(t_1,\ldots,t_m) \|^S = f_0 + \sum_{i=1}^{m} f_i \| t_i \|^S \end{cases}$$

$$|p(t_1,\ldots,t_n)|^S = \sum_{i=1}^{n} p_i \| t_i \|^S$$

with $f_i \in FC(P)$, for $i \in \{0,\ldots,m\}$ and $p_i \in PC(P)$, for $i \in \{1,\ldots,n\}$. A symbol mapping is a mapping $s : FC(P) \cup PC(P) \to \mathbb{N}$.

A symbol mapping s induces in a natural way a norm and a level mapping, by mapping the coefficient symbols in the symbolic norm and level mapping to their actual values under s. The norm, resp. level mapping, induced by the symbol mapping s is denoted by $\| . \|_s$, resp. $|.|_s$. For example, the *term-size norm* is induced by the symbol mapping s with $s(f_i) = 1$, $i = 0,\ldots,n$, for all $f/n \in Fun_P$.

Next, we define the notion of finitely partitioning level mapping. This notion is crucial in the context of a termination analysis for tabled logic programs. In particular, in the termination condition of [7], it is required that the level mapping is finitely partitioning on the call set of the program w.r.t. the set of queries for which one wants to prove termination (see also Theorem 1).

Definition 13 (finitely partitioning level mapping). *Let $|.|$ be a level mapping and $S \subseteq B_P^E$. The level mapping $|.|$ is called finitely partitioning on S iff $\forall n \in \mathbb{N} : \sharp((|.|)^{-1}(n) \cap S) < \infty$, with $\sharp$ the cardinality function.*

It is easy to see that if the set S is finite, all level mappings are finitely partitioning on S (in particular this is the case if the Herbrand Universe is finite). Intuitively it is clear that, for infinite sets S closed under substitutions, a level mapping $|.|_s$ is finitely partitioning on S if it takes into account *enough* argument positions of predicates and functors in S (more precisely, for every atom A in S and every variable X in A, at least one occurrence of X in A is taken into account, i.e. s is not 0 there). We refer to [15] for a formal statement.

In order to automatize termination proofs, and in particular, in order to have a sufficient condition for termination which is stated fully at the clause level (and not on "calls"), most approaches rely on the notion of *rigid* level mapping. In particular, in [8], it is required that the level mapping is rigid on the call set of the program w.r.t. the set of queries for which one wants to prove termination. A level mapping is rigid on a set of atoms, if the value of an atom of the set is invariant under substitutions. As was shown in [3] (see also [15]), a level mapping $|.|_s$ is rigid on a set S if it does *not* take into account *too many* argument positions of predicates and functors in S (more precisely, for every atom A in S and every variable X in A, no occurrence of X in A is taken into account, i.e. s is 0 there).

As follows from the informal argumentation above, the rigidity condition on the level mapping, as it appears in the automated termination analysis of [8], is difficult to combine with the condition on the level mapping to be finitely partitioning, as it appears in the termination condition for tabled logic programs of [7]. In our search for automatizable termination proofs for tabled logic programs, we solve this problem by abandoning the rigidity requirement and using other syntactical conditions on the program and set of queries which allow us to formulate an easy to automatize termination condition which is stated fully at the clause level. In order to find such conditions we use mode and type information. The following concepts will be useful.

Definition 14 (measuring only/all input). *Let $|.|_s$ be a level mapping (induced by the symbol mapping s) and $S \subseteq B_P^E$.*
We say that $|.|_s$ measures only input positions in S iff for every predicate p/n occurring in S: if for $i \in \{1, \ldots, n\}$ $s(p_i) \neq 0$, then $m_p(i) = In$.
We say that $|.|_s$ measures all input positions in S iff (1) for every predicate p/n occurring in S: if $m_p(i) = In$, then $s(p_i) \neq 0$, and (2) for every functor f/m, $m > 0$, occurring in an input position of an atom in S: $s(f_i) \neq 0$ for all $i \in \{0, \ldots, m\}$.

In the case of simply moded programs and queries, a level mapping is finitely partitioning on the call set if it measures *all* input positions in the call set.

Proposition 2. *Let P be a simply moded program and S be a set of simply moded queries. Let $|.|_s$ be a level mapping which measures all input positions in $Call(P, S)$. Then, $|.|_s$ is finitely partitioning on $Call(P, S)$.*

The notion of a level mapping measuring *only* input positions in $Call(P, S)$ will allow us to state the termination conditions fully at the clause level. Note that the conditions on a level mapping to measure all and only input positions in the call set, can be combined without problems.

3   Quasi-Termination

We recall the definition of quasi-termination [7].

Definition 15 (quasi-termination). *Let P be a program and $S \subseteq B_P^E$. P quasi-terminates w.r.t. S iff for all A such that $\tilde{A} \in S$, the LG-forest for $P \cup \{\leftarrow A\}$ consists of a finite number of LG-trees.*

Note that the program NAT of Example 1 quasi-terminates w.r.t. $\{nat(X)\}$. In [7, Lemma 3.1] the following equivalence was proven: *P quasi-terminates w.r.t. S iff for every A in S, $Call(P, \{A\})$ is finite.* It is easy to see that LD-termination of P w.r.t. S (i.e. termination of P w.r.t. S under LD-resolution) implies quasi-termination of P w.r.t. S. Note that when a program is quasi-terminating w.r.t. a query Q, there are a finite number of trees in the LG-forest, all of them have finite branches, but, possibly, they have infinitely branching nodes. The stronger notion of *LG-termination* takes this source of nontermination into account. Namely, a program P is said to LG-terminate w.r.t. S iff for all A such that $\tilde{A} \in S$, the LG-forest for $P \cup \{\leftarrow A\}$ consists of a finite number of finite LG-trees. Note that the program NAT of Example 1 does not LG-terminate w.r.t. $\{nat(X)\}$. By the lack of space, we will not consider LG-termination in this paper. We refer to [15] instead.

In [7], the quasi-acceptability condition was introduced and it was shown to be equivalent with quasi-termination [7, Theorem 3.1].

Theorem 1 (quasi-acceptability w.r.t. S). *Let P be a program and $S \subseteq B_P^E$. P quasi-terminates w.r.t. S iff there is a level mapping $|.|$ which is finitely partitioning on $Call(P, S)$ such that*

- *for every atom A such that $\tilde{A} \in Call(P, S)$,*
- *for every clause $H \leftarrow B_1, \ldots, B_n$ in P such that $mgu(A, H) = \theta$ exists,*
- *for every $i \in \{1, \ldots, n\}$, and every LD-computed answer substitution θ_{i-1} for $\leftarrow (B_1, \ldots, B_{i-1})\theta$,*

$$|A| \geq |B_i \theta \theta_{i-1}|.$$

The aim of this paper is to extend the automatic constraint-based termination analysis for LD-resolution of [8], to prove quasi-termination in an automatic way. In order to do so, we need (1) a termination condition which is stated fully at the clause level (and not on "calls" as in the quasi-acceptability condition of Theorem 1), and (2) a syntactical condition on a level mapping in order to be finitely partitioning on the call set. In the next Subsection 3.1, we present such a condition in the case of SMWT programs and queries. As we will point out in Subsection 3.2, this condition forms the basis for extending the automatic approach of [8], in order to prove quasi-termination of SMWT programs and queries in an automatic way.

3.1 Simply Moded Well-Typed Programs and Queries

Proposition 2 provides us with a syntactical condition on a level mapping to be finitely partitioning on the call set of a simply moded program w.r.t. a set of simply moded queries: the level mapping has to measure all input positions in the call set. In order to be able to state a condition for quasi-termination which reasons fully at the clause level, we use Proposition 1. In Proposition 1, we proved that for a SMWT program P and query $\leftarrow A$, such that the heads of the clauses of P are input safe, the input arguments of A get never instantiated during an LD-derivation. This allows us to state a condition at the clause level, if we require in addition that the level mapping measures only input positions in the call set.

Theorem 2. *Let P be a SMWT program and $S \subseteq B_P^E$ be a set of SMWT queries. Suppose that the heads of the clauses in P are input safe. If there is a model M for P and a level mapping $|.|_s$ which measures all and only the input positions in $Call(P, S)$, such that*

– for every clause $H \leftarrow B_1, \ldots, B_n$ in P,
– for $i \in \{1, .., n\}$ and every substitution ψ such that $M \models (B_1 \wedge \ldots \wedge B_{i-1})\psi$ and $(H\psi)^{In}, (B_1\psi)^{In}, \ldots, (B_i\psi)^{In} \in Call(P, S)^{In}$,

$$|H\psi|_s \geq |B_i\psi|_s,$$

then P is quasi-acceptable w.r.t. S. Hence, P quasi-terminates w.r.t. S.

Note that, because P and S are well-typed, it follows that, if the conditions of the theorem are satisfied, i.e. if ψ is a substitution such that $M \models (B_1 \wedge \ldots \wedge B_{i-1})\psi$ and $(H\psi)^{In}, (B_1\psi)^{In}, \ldots, (B_i\psi)^{In} \in Call(P, S)^{In}$, then $H\psi$ is correctly typed in its input positions, $(B_1, \ldots, B_{i-1})\psi$ is correctly typed and $B_i\psi$ is correctly typed in its input positions.

We want to note that Theorem 2 can also be applied in the case of *simply moded well-moded* programs and queries. We already noted in Subsection 2.2 that the notion of well-modedness [1] is a special case of the notion of well-typedness: namely, well-typedness collapses to well-modedness if the types of all predicate positions are defined as *Ground*. Recall also from Subsection 2.2 that all terms are generic expressions for the *Ground* type, so the heads of all clauses of a well-moded program (in which we defined the types of all predicate positions as *Ground*) are trivially input safe. Finally, note that in the case of a well-moded program and set of queries, the condition on the level mapping to measure only input positions in the call set, has as a consequence that the level mapping is rigid on the call set. We refer to [15] for more details.

Example 2. Let P be the following program computing the cyclic permutations of a list.

$$
\begin{aligned}
&splitlast([X], [\,], X) &&\leftarrow \\
&splitlast([X|L], [X|R], Y) &&\leftarrow splitlast(L, R, Y) \\
&cycperm(L, L) &&\leftarrow \\
&cycperm(L, R) &&\leftarrow splitlast(L, T, X), cycperm([X|T], R)
\end{aligned}
$$

with $splitlast(< In : List >, < Out : List >, < Out : U >)$ and $cycperm(< In : List >, < Out : List >)$. Let S be the set of queries $\{cycperm(l, X) \mid l \in List\}$. We prove that P quasi-terminates w.r.t. S by applying Theorem 2 (note that P even LG-terminates w.r.t. S, a proof can be found in [15]; note however that P does not LD-terminate w.r.t. S). Let's abbreviate $splitlast$ to sp and $cycperm$ to cyc.

P and S are well-typed. This is trivial to see for the set S. The program P is well-typed because the following type judgements are true:

$$\begin{aligned}
[X] : List &\Rightarrow [\,] : List \wedge X : U \\
[X|L] : List &\Rightarrow L : List \\
[X|L] : List \wedge R : List \wedge Y : U &\Rightarrow [X|R] : List \wedge Y : U \\
L : List &\Rightarrow L : List \\
L : List \wedge T : List \wedge X : U &\Rightarrow [X|T] : List \\
L : List \wedge T : List \wedge X : U \wedge R : List &\Rightarrow R : List
\end{aligned}$$

Also, P and S are simply moded and the heads of the clauses in P are input safe. Let $|.|_s$ be the following level mapping (measuring all and only the input positions in $Call(P, S)$):

$$\begin{aligned}
|sp(t_1, t_2, t_3)|_s &= \| t_1 \|_s, \\
|cyc(t_1, t_2)|_s &= \| t_1 \|_s,
\end{aligned}$$

with $\| . \|_s$ the term-size norm.

Consider the recursive clause for $splitlast$. For every ψ, $|sp([X|L], [X|R], Y)\psi|_s = \| [X|L]\psi \|_s = 1 + \| L\psi \|_s \geq \| L\psi \|_s = |sp(L, R, Y)\psi|_s$. Consider the recursive clause for $cycperm$. Again, for every ψ, $|cyc(L, R)\psi|_s = \| L\psi \|_s \geq \| L\psi \|_s = |sp(L, T, X)\psi|_s$. Let ψ be a substitution such that $sp(L, T, X)\psi$ is a consequence of the program and such that $cyc(L, R)\psi$, $sp(L, T, X)\psi$ and $cyc([X|T], R)\psi$ are input-correct w.r.t. $Call(P, S)$. Note that then, $\| L\psi \|_s \geq 1 + \| X\psi \|_s + \| T\psi \|_s = \| [X|T]\psi \|_s$. Thus, $|cyc(L, R)\psi|_s = \| L\psi \|_s \geq \| [X|T]\psi \|_s = |cyc([X|T], R)\psi|_s$. Hence, by Theorem 2, P quasi-terminates w.r.t. S.

3.2 Constraint-Based Approach for Automatically Proving Quasi-Termination

In this subsection, we point out how the constraint-based approach of [8] for automatically proving LD-termination of definite programs w.r.t. sets of queries needs to be changed in order to prove quasi-termination in an automatic way. We restrict ourselves to SMWT programs and queries such that the heads of the program clauses are input safe. The basis of the automatic approach towards quasi-termination is Theorem 2 of the previous subsection.

We first recall the main ideas of [8]. In [8], a new strategy for automatically proving LD-termination of logic programs w.r.t. sets of queries is developed. A symbolic termination condition is introduced, called rigid acceptability, by parametrising the concepts of norm, level mapping and model. In order to symbolize the notion of model, symbolic versions of interargument relations are introduced. Interargument relations are abstractions of interpretations by specifying relations which hold between the norms of certain arguments of their member atoms. In [8], interargument relations express an inequality relation. The rigid acceptability condition is translated into a system of constraints on the values of the introduced symbols only. A system of constraints identifies sets of suitable norms, level mappings and interarguments relations which can be used in the termination condition. In other words, if a solution for the constraint system exists, termination can be proved. The solving of constraint sets enables the different components of a termination proof to communicate with one another and to direct the proof towards success (if there is). The method of [8] is both efficient and precise.

We adapt the approach of [8] to prove quasi-termination of SMWT programs w.r.t. sets of SMWT queries, such that the clauses of the programs have input safe heads, by using Theorem 2. Note that this theorem is stated fully at the clause level. As can be seen from Theorem 2, quasi-termination is implied by the following conditions on the introduced symbols for norm, level mapping and interargument relations.

(i) The level mapping has to measure all and only input positions in $Call(P, S)$.

(ii) Every introduced interargument relation must be valid (meaning that the induced interpretation is a model of P).

(iii) For every clause $H \leftarrow B_1, \ldots, B_n$ in P, for $i \in \{1, .., n\}$, and for every substitution ψ such that $B_1\psi, \ldots, B_{i-1}\psi$ belong to their valid interargument relations and such that $(H\psi)^{In}, (B_1\psi)^{In}, \ldots, (B_i\psi)^{In} \in Call(P, S)^{In}$, the weak inequality $|H\psi| \geq |B_i\psi|$ must hold.

Except maybe for condition (i), the modifications needed to transform the constraints of [8] into the constraints for quasi-termination, are straightforward, and we will not elaborate on them (we refer to [15] and [8]). We show in the following example how the first condition (i) is translated into symbolic constraints.

Example 3. Recall the SMWT program P and set S of Example 2. Note that $Call(P, S) = \{cyc(l, X), sp(l, R, Y) \mid l \in List\}$. We introduce symbolic versions for the norm and level mapping (see Definition 12). Let $t \in U_P^E$, then the symbolic norm on t is defined as:

$$\begin{cases} \| X \|^S = \| [\,] \|^S = 0 & \text{for } X \in Var_P, [\,] \in Const_P \\ \| t \|^S = [.|.]_0 + [.|.]_1 \| t_1 \|^S + [.|.]_2 \| t_2 \|^S & \text{for } t = [t_1|t_2], \end{cases}$$

with $\{[.|.]_0, [.|.]_1, [.|.]_2\} = FC(P)$. Let $sp(t_1, t_2, t_3), cyc(t_1, t_2) \in B_P^E$, then the symbolic level mapping is defined as:

$$|sp(t_1, t_2, t_3)|^S = sp_1\| t_1 \|^S + sp_2\| t_2 \|^S + sp_3\| t_3 \|^S,$$
$$|cyc(t_1, t_2)|^S = cyc_1\| t_1 \|^S + cyc_2\| t_2 \|^S$$

with $\{sp_1, sp_2, sp_3, cyc_1, cyc_2\} = PC(P)$.
The condition on the level mapping to measure only input positions in $Call(P, S)$

is expressed in the following constraints: $s(cyc_2) = 0$, $s(sp_2) = 0$ and $s(sp_3) = 0$. Condition (i) also requires that the level mapping measures all input positions. This gives rise to the following constraints: $s(cyc_1) \neq 0$, $s(sp_1) \neq 0$, $s([.|.]_0) \neq 0$, $s([.|.]_1) \neq 0$ and $s([.|.]_2) \neq 0$.

Note that the level mapping proposed in Example 2 is a solution for the set of 8 constraints above and indeed, that level mapping measures all and only input positions in $Call(P, S)$.

4   Conclusions and Related Works

In this paper, we investigated the problem of automatically proving termination of logic programs under a tabled execution mechanism. Two works form the basis of this paper: [7], where the notion of quasi-termination is introduced and a necessary and sufficient condition (quasi-acceptability) is given, and [8], where an automatic approach towards LD-termination is developed. It turned out that the rigidity condition on the level mapping, as it appears in the automated termination analysis of [8], is difficult to combine with the condition on the level mapping to be finitely partitioning, as it appears in the quasi-acceptability condition of [7]. In this paper, we showed that for simply moded well-typed programs such that the heads of the clauses are input safe, a sufficient condition for quasi-termination can be given, which is formulated fully at the clause level and which is easy to automatize. We pointed out how this sufficient condition can be automatized by extending the approach of [8]. Due to space limitations, we did not include our results on the stronger notion of LG-termination. We refer to [15] instead.

Since all programs that terminate under LD-resolution, are quasi-terminating and LG-terminating as well, verification of termination under LD-resolution using an existing automated termination analysis (such as those surveyed in e.g. [6]) is a sufficient proof of the programs quasi-termination and LG-termination. In the recent paper [9], Etalle *et al* study how mode information can be used for characterizing properties of LD-termination. They define and study the class of well-terminating programs, i.e. programs for which all well-moded queries have finite LD-derivations. They introduce the notion of well-acceptability and show that for well-moded programs, well-acceptability implies well-termination.

Termination proofs for (S)LD-resolution are sufficient to prove termination under a tabled execution mechanism, but, since there are quasi-terminating and LG-terminating programs, which are not LD-terminating, more effective proof techniques can be found. There are only relatively few works studying termination under a tabled execution mechanism. We already discussed the work of [7], which forms the basis of this paper. In [13], in the context of well-moded programs, a sufficient condition is given for the bounded term-size property, which implies LG-termination. [10] provides another sufficient condition for quasi-termination in the context of functional programming. In parallel with the work reported on in this paper, in [16] the authors of this paper together with K. Sagonas, investigated an orthogonal extension of the work of [7]. Namely, in [16], termination under a mix of tabled and Prolog execution is considered and, besides a characterisation of the two notions of universal termination under such a mixed execution, modular termination conditions are given. An integration of [16] with the results of this paper is straightforward.

We plan to implement the constraint-based technique for automatically proving quasi-termination and LG-termination (note that a prototype implementation for automatically proving LD-termination [8] exists and is available at our site). Also, it remains to be studied how our results can be extended to automatically prove quasi-termination and LG-termination for a larger class of programs and queries (i.e. for programs and queries which are not simply moded well-typed). Finally, the study of termination of normal logic programs under tabled execution mechanism is an interesting topic for future research.

References

1. K.R. Apt and E. Marchiori. Reasoning about Prolog programs: from modes through types to assertions. *Formal Aspects of Computing*, 6(6A):743–765, 1994.
2. K.R. Apt and S. Etalle. On the unification free Prolog programs. In A. Borzyszkowski and S. Sokolowski, editors, *Proc. MFCS*, pages 1–19. number 771 in LNCS, Springer-Verlag, 1993.
3. A. Bossi, N. Cocco, and M. Fabris. Norms on terms and their use in proving universal termination of a logic program. *Theoretical Computer Science*, 124(2):297–328, 1994.
4. F. Bronsard, T. Lakshman, and U. Reddy. A framework of directionality for proving termination of logic programs. In K.R. Apt, editor, *Proc. JICSLP*, pages 321–335. MIT Press, 1992.
5. W. Chen and D. S. Warren. Tabled Evaluation with Delaying for General Logic Programs. *J. ACM*, 43(1):20–74, 1996.
6. D. De Schreye and S. Decorte. Termination of logic programs: the never-ending story. *Journal of Logic Programming*, 19 & 20:199–260, 1994.
7. S. Decorte, D. De Schreye, M. Leuschel, B. Martens, and K. Sagonas. Termination Analysis for Tabled Logic Programming. In N. Fuchs, editor, *Proc. LOPSTR*, number 1463 in LNCS, pages 107–123. Springer-Verlag, 1997.
8. S. Decorte, D. De Schreye, and H. Vandecasteele. Constraint-based automatic termination analysis for logic programs. *ACM TOPLAS*. to appear.
9. S. Etalle, A. Bossi, and N. Cocco. Termination of well-moded programs. *Journal of Logic Programming*, 38(2):243–257, 1998.
10. C. K. Holst. Finiteness Analysis. In J. Hughes, editor, *Proc. of the 5th ACM Conference on FPCA*, number 523 in LNCS, pages 473–495. Springer-Verlag, 1991.
11. T. Kanamori and T. Kawamura. OLDT-based abstract interpretation. *Journal of Logic Programming*, 15(1 & 2):1–30, 1993.
12. J. Lloyd. *Foundations of logic programming*. Springer-Verlag, 1987.
13. L. Plümer. *Termination proofs for logic programs*. Number 446 in LNAI. Springer-Verlag, 1990.
14. H. Tamaki and T. Sato. OLD Resolution with Tabulation. In *Proc. ICLP*, number 225 in LNCS, pages 84–98. Springer Verlag, 1986.
15. S. Verbaeten and D. De Schreye. Termination analysis of tabled logic programs using mode and type information. Technical Report 277, Department of Computer Science, K.U.Leuven. Available at http://www.cs.kuleuven.ac.be/~sofie.

16. S. Verbaeten, K. Sagonas, and D. De Schreye. Modular termination proofs for Prolog with tabling. Technical report, Department of Computer Science, K.U.Leuven, 1999. Available at http://www.cs.kuleuven.ac.be/~sofie (accepted for PPDP'99).

On Quasi-Reductive and Quasi-Simplifying Deterministic Conditional Rewrite Systems

Enno Ohlebusch

University of Bielefeld, Faculty of Technology,
P.O. Box 10 01 31, 33501 Bielefeld, Germany,
enno@TechFak.Uni-Bielefeld.DE

Abstract. Deterministic conditional rewrite systems permit extra variables on the right-hand sides of the rules. If such a system is quasi-reductive or quasi-simplifying, then it is terminating and has a computable rewrite relation. This paper provides new criteria for showing quasi-reductivity and quasi-simplifyingness. In this context, another criterion from [ALS94] will be rectified and a claim in [Mar96] will be refuted. Moreover, we will investigate under which conditions the properties exhibit a modular behavior.

1 Introduction

Conditional term rewriting systems (CTRSs) are the basis for the integration of the functional and logic programming paradigms; see [Han94] for an overview of this field. In these systems variables on the right-hand side of a rewrite rule which do not occur on the left-hand side are problematic because it is in general not clear how to instantiate them. On the other hand, a restricted use of these extra variables enables a more natural and efficient way of writing programs. A paradigmatic example is the Fibonacci system $\mathcal{R}_{fib}$

$$fib(0) \rightarrow \langle 0, s(0) \rangle$$
$$fib(s(x)) \rightarrow \langle z, y + z \rangle \Leftarrow fib(x) \rightarrow \langle y, z \rangle$$

which has extra variables on the right-hand side of the last rule. The rewrite relation induced by the above CTRS is effectively terminating (that is, computable and terminating) because the system is a *quasi-reductive deterministic* CTRS. This class of CTRSs was introduced by Ganzinger [Gan91] in order to efficiently translate order-sorted specifications into conditional many-sorted equations. Quasi-reductivity is in general undecidable but sufficient criteria to check quasi-reductivity are known [Gan91,ALS94]. The criterion in [ALS94] contains a flaw which will be rectified and the rectified criterion shows in fact *quasi-simplifyingness* (a stronger property than quasi-reductivity).

Similar to the approach of Marchiori [Mar96], we will show how every deterministic CTRS $\mathcal{R}$ can be transformed into an unconditional TRS $U(\mathcal{R})$ such that (simple) termination of $U(\mathcal{R})$ implies quasi-reductivity (quasi-simplifyingness) of $\mathcal{R}$. (A counterexample will show that quasi-reductivity of $\mathcal{R}$ does not imply

A. Middeldorp, T. Sato (Eds.): FLOPS'99, LNCS 1722, pp. 179–193, 1999.

termination of $U(\mathcal{R})$, even if $\mathcal{R}$ is left-linear and confluent.) By means of this transformational approach, standard methods for proving (simple) termination of TRSs can now be employed to infer quasi-reductivity (quasi-simplifyingness). Due to the fact that powerful techniques for showing termination like simplification orderings [Der87] and dependency pairs [AG99] are amenable to automation, our new criteria now allow us to infer quasi-reductivity (quasi-simplifyingness) automatically. This is a major improvement on the known criteria.

Since both simple termination of $U(\mathcal{R})$ and the rectified criterion of [ALS94] prove quasi-simplifyingness of $\mathcal{R}$, we will investigate the relationship between the two criteria. It will be shown that none of the criteria is subsumed by the other. En passant, a claim in [Mar96] will be refuted: Simplifyingness of a join CTRS $\mathcal{R}$ without extra variables does *not* imply simple termination of its transformed unconditional TRS.

Finally, we will address the problem of modularity. We will show that quasi-simplifyingness is not modular, whereas quasi-reductivity is modular for non-overlapping syntactically deterministic CTRSs. Under certain (natural) conditions, it is modular even for hierarchical combinations of these systems.

The material presented in this paper complements results reported in [Ohl99].

2   Preliminaries

The reader is assumed to be familiar with the basic concepts of term rewriting which can for instance be found in the textbook of Baader and Nipkow [BN98]. Here we will only recall the definitions which are crucial to this paper.

A *rewrite relation* R is a binary relation on terms which is *closed under contexts* (i.e., if $s \, R \, t$, then $C[s] \, R \, C[t]$ for all contexts $C[\ ]$) and *closed under substitutions* (i.e., if $s \, R \, t$, then $s\sigma \, R \, t\sigma$ for all substitutions σ). A *rewrite order* is a rewrite relation which is also a partial order. A well-founded rewrite order is called *reduction order*. A *simplification order* $\succ$ is a reduction order which contains the proper subterm relation $\rhd$, i.e., $C[t] \succ t$ for all contexts $C[\ ] \neq \square$ and terms t.

In a CTRS $(\mathcal{F}, \mathcal{R})$ rules have the form $l \rightarrow r \Leftarrow s_1 = t_1, \ldots, s_k = t_k$ with $l, r, s_1, \ldots, s_k, t_1, \ldots, t_k \in \mathcal{T}(\mathcal{F}, \mathcal{V})$. l may not be a variable. We frequently abbreviate the conditional part of the rule by c. If a rule has no conditions, we write $l \rightarrow r$, demand that $Var(r) \subseteq Var(l)$, and call $l \rightarrow r$ an unconditional rule. The = symbol in the conditions can be interpreted in different ways which lead to different rewrite relations associated with $\mathcal{R}$. For instance, in a *join* CTRS the = symbol stands for joinability ($\downarrow_\mathcal{R}$). This paper deals with finite *oriented* CTRSs in which the equality signs are interpreted as reachability ($\rightarrow^*_\mathcal{R}$). A *normal* CTRS $(\mathcal{F}, \mathcal{R})$ is an oriented CTRS in which the rewrite rules are subject to the additional constraint that every t_j is a ground normal form with respect to $\mathcal{R}_u$, where $\mathcal{R}_u = \{l \rightarrow r \mid l \rightarrow r \Leftarrow c \in \mathcal{R}\}$.

For every rule $\rho : l \rightarrow r \Leftarrow c$, the set of variables occurring in ρ is denoted by $Var(\rho)$ and the set of extra variables in ρ is $\mathcal{E}Var(\rho) = Var(\rho) \setminus Var(l)$. A 1-CTRS has no extra variables, a 2-CTRS has no extra variables on the right-hand sides of the rules, and a 3-CTRS may contain extra variables on the right-hand sides of the rules provided that these also occur in the corresponding conditional part (i.e., $Var(r) \subseteq Var(l) \cup Var(c)$).

3 Quasi-Reductive Deterministic 3-CTRSs

First of all, we will review the definition of deterministic systems from [Gan91].

Definition 1. *An oriented 3-CTRS $\mathcal{R}$ is called* deterministic *if (after appropriately changing the order of the conditions in the rewrite rules) for every $l \rightarrow r \Leftarrow s_1 \rightarrow t_1, \ldots, s_k \rightarrow t_k$ in $\mathcal{R}$ and every $1 \leq i \leq k$, we have $Var(s_i) \subseteq Var(l) \cup \bigcup_{j=1}^{i-1} Var(t_j)$. In the following, we will frequently use the notation $\mathcal{E}Var(t_i) = Var(t_i) \setminus (Var(l) \cup \bigcup_{j=1}^{i-1} Var(t_j))$.*

The rewrite relation $\rightarrow_{\mathcal{R}}$ associated with an oriented deterministic 3-CTRS $\mathcal{R}$ is defined by: $s \rightarrow_{\mathcal{R}} t$ if and only if there exists a rewrite rule $\rho : l \rightarrow r \Leftarrow s_1 \rightarrow t_1, \ldots, s_k \rightarrow t_k$ in $\mathcal{R}$, a substitution $\sigma : Var(\rho) \rightarrow \mathcal{T}(\mathcal{F}, \mathcal{V})$, and a context $C[\ ]$ such that $s = C[l\sigma], t = C[r\sigma]$, and $s_i\sigma \rightarrow_{\mathcal{R}}^* t_i\sigma$ for all $1 \leq i \leq k$. We stress the fact that σ instantiates every variable in ρ and not only those variables occurring in l; for an extra variable x, $x\sigma$ is determined as follows. The conditions are evaluated from left-to-right. Since s_1 contains only variables from $Var(l)$, the variables in $Var(s_1)$ have a binding. Then $s_1\sigma$ is rewritten until $t_1\sigma$ matches a reduct. The term $t_1\sigma$ may contain extra variables but all of these are bound during the match. Now s_2 contains only variables which already occurred to its left (in l and t_1) and are thus bound. The instantiated term s_2 is then reduced until the (partially) instantiated term t_2 matches a reduct and so on. If all the conditions are satisfied, then all variables in the conditions are bound in the process of evaluating the conditions. Hence the reduct of $l\sigma$ is well-defined (but in general not unique) because r contains only variables which also appear in the conditions or in l.

The next definition is based on the well-known fact that if $\succ$ is a well-founded partial order which is closed under contexts, then the order $\succ_{st} = (\succ \cup \rhd)^+$ is also well-founded ($\rhd$ denotes the proper subterm relation).

Definition 2. *A deterministic 3-CTRS $(\mathcal{F}, \mathcal{R})$ is called* quasi-reductive *if there is an extension $\mathcal{F}'$ of the signature $\mathcal{F}$ (so $\mathcal{F} \subseteq \mathcal{F}'$) and a reduction order $\succ$ on $\mathcal{T}(\mathcal{F}', \mathcal{V})$ which, for every rule $l \rightarrow r \Leftarrow s_1 \rightarrow t_1, \ldots, s_k \rightarrow t_k \in \mathcal{R}$, every substitution $\sigma : \mathcal{V} \rightarrow \mathcal{T}(\mathcal{F}', \mathcal{V})$, and every $0 \leq i < k$ satisfies:*

1. *if $s_j\sigma \succeq t_j\sigma$ for every $1 \leq j \leq i$, then $l\sigma \succ_{st} s_{i+1}\sigma$,*
2. *if $s_j\sigma \succeq t_j\sigma$ for every $1 \leq j \leq k$, then $l\sigma \succ r\sigma$.*

Quasi-reductive deterministic 3-CTRSs were introduced by Ganzinger [Gan91, Def. 4.2] without mentioning that the original signature can be extended. This, however, is crucial because otherwise Propositions 4.3 and 4.4 in [Gan91] would be incorrect. Finite quasi-reductive deterministic 3-CTRSs have a terminating and computable rewrite relation [Gan91,ALS94].

To start with, there is the following sufficient condition for quasi-reductivity.

Definition 3. *Given a deterministic 3-CTRS $\mathcal{R}$, we define a deterministic 3-CTRS $\mathcal{R}_q$ with $\mathcal{R} \subseteq \mathcal{R}_q$ as follows: $\mathcal{R}_q = \bigcup_{\rho \in \mathcal{R}} q(\rho)$, where the transformation q on a rule $\rho : l \to r \Leftarrow s_1 \to t_1, \ldots, s_k \to t_k$ is defined by*

$$q(\rho) = \{\, l \to s_1$$
$$l \to s_2 \Leftarrow s_1 \to t_1$$
$$\ldots$$
$$l \to s_k \Leftarrow s_1 \to t_1, \ldots, s_{k-1} \to t_{k-1}$$
$$l \to r \Leftarrow s_1 \to t_1, \ldots, s_{k-1} \to t_{k-1}, s_k \to t_k\}$$

Proposition 4. *A deterministic 3-CTRS $\mathcal{R}$ is quasi-reductive if the deterministic 3-CTRS $\mathcal{R}_q$ is terminating.*

Proof. Since $\mathcal{R}_q$ is terminating, the relation $\to^+_{\mathcal{R}_q}$ is a reduction order and it is easy to see that $\mathcal{R}$ is quasi-reductive w.r.t. this order.

The following example taken from [Mar95] shows that the converse of Proposition 4 does not hold.

Example 5. The normal 1-CTRS $\mathcal{R}$

$$
\begin{array}{ll}
a \to c & a \to d \\
b \to c & b \to d \\
c \to e & c \to l \\
k \to l & k \to m \\
d \to m & \\
A \to h(f(a), f(b)) & \\
h(x, x) \to g(x, x, f(k)) & \\
g(d, x, x) \to A & \\
f(x) \to x & \Leftarrow x \to e
\end{array}
$$

can be shown quasi-reductive. The system $\mathcal{R}_q = \mathcal{R} \cup \{f(x) \to x\}$, however, is not terminating because there is the following cyclic derivation

$$A \to_{\mathcal{R}_q} h(f(a), f(b)) \to^+_{\mathcal{R}_q} h(f(d), f(d)) \to_{\mathcal{R}_q} g(f(d), f(d), f(k))$$
$$\to_{\mathcal{R}_q} g(d, f(d), f(k)) \to^+_{\mathcal{R}_q} g(d, f(m), f(m)) \to_{\mathcal{R}_q} A.$$

Ganzinger [Gan91, Prop. 4.3] provided the following sufficient condition for quasi-reductivity: Let $\mathcal{F}'$ be an enrichment of the original signature $\mathcal{F}$ such that the order $\succ$ can be extended to a reduction order over $T(\mathcal{F}', \mathcal{V})$. A deterministic rule $l \to r \Leftarrow s_1 \to t_1, \ldots, s_k \to t_k$ is quasi-reductive if there exists a sequence $h_i(x)$ of terms in $T(\mathcal{F}', \mathcal{V})$, where $x \in \mathcal{V}$, such that $l \succ h_1(s_1), h_i(t_i) \succeq h_{i+1}(s_{i+1})$ for every $1 \le i < k$, and $h_k(t_k) \succeq r$.

This criterion, however, does not tell us how the terms $h_i(x)$ should be chosen. A systematic way of showing quasi-reductivity consists of transforming a deterministic 3-CTRS $\mathcal{R}$ into an unconditional TRS $U(\mathcal{R})$ and showing termination of $U(\mathcal{R})$. For normal 1-CTRSs, a similar transformation was already given in [BK86, Def. 2.5.1]. Marchiori [Mar96,Mar95] studied such transformations of 1-CTRSs (which he called *unravelings*) in detail.

Definition 6. *Let $\mathcal{R}$ be a deterministic 3-CTRS over the signature $\mathcal{F}$. For every rewrite rule $\rho : l \to r \Leftarrow c \in \mathcal{R}$, let $|\rho|$ denote the number of conditions in ρ. In the transformation, we need $|\rho|$ fresh function symbols $U_1^\rho, \ldots, U_{|\rho|}^\rho$ for every conditional rule $\rho \in \mathcal{R}$. Moreover, by abuse of notation, $\mathcal{V}ar$ (resp. $\mathcal{E}\mathcal{V}ar$) denotes a function which assigns the sequence of the variables (in some fixed order) in the set $\mathcal{V}ar(t)$ (resp. $\mathcal{E}\mathcal{V}ar(t)$; cf. Def. 1) to a term t. We transform $\rho : l \to r \Leftarrow s_1 \to t_1, \ldots, s_{|\rho|} \to t_{|\rho|}$ into a set $U(\rho)$ of $|\rho| + 1$ unconditional rewrite rules as follows:*

$$l \to U_1^\rho(s_1, \mathcal{V}ar(l))$$
$$U_1^\rho(t_1, \mathcal{V}ar(l)) \to U_2^\rho(s_2, \mathcal{V}ar(l), \mathcal{E}\mathcal{V}ar(t_1))$$
$$U_2^\rho(t_2, \mathcal{V}ar(l), \mathcal{E}\mathcal{V}ar(t_1)) \to U_3^\rho(s_3, \mathcal{V}ar(l), \mathcal{E}\mathcal{V}ar(t_1), \mathcal{E}\mathcal{V}ar(t_2))$$
$$\cdots$$
$$U_{|\rho|}^\rho(t_{|\rho|}, \mathcal{V}ar(l), \mathcal{E}\mathcal{V}ar(t_1), \ldots, \mathcal{E}\mathcal{V}ar(t_{|\rho|-1})) \to r$$

Since $\mathcal{R}$ is deterministic, the system $U(\mathcal{R}) = \bigcup_{\rho \in \mathcal{R}} \{U(\rho)\}$ is an unconditional TRS over the extended signature $\mathcal{F}' = \mathcal{F} \cup \bigcup_{\rho \in \mathcal{R}, 1 \leq i \leq |\rho|} U_i^\rho$ (that is, $\mathcal{V}ar(r') \subseteq \mathcal{V}ar(l')$ holds for every rewrite rule $l' \to r' \in U(\mathcal{R})$).

For example, the transformation of the system $\mathcal{R}_{fib}$ yields the TRS

$$fib(0) \to \langle 0, s(0) \rangle$$
$$fib(s(x)) \to U_1(fib(x), x)$$
$$U_1(\langle y, z \rangle, x) \to \langle z, y + z \rangle$$

It turns out that termination of $U(\mathcal{R})$ is a sufficient but not a necessary condition for quasi-reductivity of $\mathcal{R}$.

Proposition 7. *If $U(\mathcal{R})$ is terminating, then $\mathcal{R}$ is quasi-reductive.*

The proof of the proposition can be found in [Ohl99] and a similar result for normal 1-CTRSs appeared in [Mar96]. In our Fibonacci example, termination of the transformed system $U(\mathcal{R}_{fib})$ can be shown by rpo. Thus the system $\mathcal{R}_{fib}$ is quasi-reductive by Proposition 7.

Example 5 can be used to show that the converse of Proposition 7 does not hold. To be precise, it can be shown that $h(f(a), f(b)) \to_{U(\mathcal{R})}^+ A$ and hence $U(\mathcal{R})$ is not terminating; see [Mar95]. In Example 5, however, the CTRS $\mathcal{R}$ is neither left-linear nor confluent and one might wonder whether this is essential (for 1-CTRSs non-left-linearity is crucial; see [Mar96, Thm. 6.12]). The following example shows that left-linearity and confluence of a quasi-reductive 3-CTRS $\mathcal{R}$ are not sufficient to ensure termination of $U(\mathcal{R})$.

Example 8. Let $\mathcal{R}$ contain the rule $g(x) \to k(y) \Leftarrow h(x) \to d, h(x) \to c(y)$ and the following unconditional rules

$$h(d) \to c(a) \qquad\qquad h(d) \to c(b)$$
$$a \to e \qquad\qquad b \to e$$
$$f(k(a), k(b), x) \to f(x, x, x) \qquad f(x, y, z) \to e$$

We have $\mathcal{R}_q = \mathcal{R} \cup \{g(x) \to h(x), g(x) \to h(x) \Leftarrow h(x) \to d\}$. Let $\mathcal{R}'$ contain the rule $g(x) \to h(x)$ and the unconditional rules of $\mathcal{R}$. The rewrite relations $\to_{\mathcal{R}'}$ and $\to_{\mathcal{R}_q}$ coincide because the rules $g(x) \to k(y) \Leftarrow h(x) \to d, h(x) \to c(y)$ and $g(x) \to h(x) \Leftarrow h(x) \to d$ are never applicable (there is no term t such that $h(t) \to_{\mathcal{R}}^* d$). It can be shown that $\mathcal{R}'$ is terminating. Hence $\mathcal{R}$ is quasi-reductive by Proposition 4. $\mathcal{R}$ is also confluent because every critical pair is joinable. The transformed system $U(\mathcal{R})$ consists of

$$g(x) \to U_1(h(x), x)$$
$$U_1(d, x) \to U_2(h(x), x)$$
$$U_2(c(y), x) \to k(y)$$

and the unconditional rules of $\mathcal{R}$. $U(\mathcal{R})$ is not terminating because of the following cyclic derivation

$$f(k(a), k(b), U_2(h(d), d)) \to_{U(\mathcal{R})} f(U_2(h(d), d), U_2(h(d), d), U_2(h(d), d))$$
$$\to_{U(\mathcal{R})}^+ f(U_2(c(a), d), U_2(c(b), d), U_2(h(d), d))$$
$$\to_{U(\mathcal{R})}^+ f(k(a), k(b), U_2(h(d), d)).$$

Observe that the preceding derivation is not innermost and it has been shown in [Ohl99] that this is essential.

Theorem 9. *If $\mathcal{R}$ is a quasi-reductive deterministic 3-CTRS, then $U(\mathcal{R})$ is innermost terminating.*

Another sufficient criterion for quasi-reductivity is given in [ALS94, Lemma 3.1]. In order to formulate it (claim below), we need the following definition.

Definition 10. *Let $\rho : l \to r \Leftarrow s_1 \to t_1, \ldots, s_k \to t_k$ be a conditional rule of the deterministic 3-CTRS $\mathcal{R}$. The transformed rule $\bar{\rho}$ is defined as follows. For $x \in \mathcal{E}Var(\rho)$ let $\alpha(x)$ be the smallest i, $1 \le i \le k$, such that $x \in Var(t_i)$ and define*

$$\varphi_1 = id$$
$$\varphi_{i+1} = \{x \leftarrow \bar{s}_{\alpha(x)} \mid x \in Var(t_1, \ldots, t_i) \cap \mathcal{E}Var(\rho)\} \text{ for } 1 \le i \le k$$
$$\bar{s}_i = \varphi_i(s_i)$$

Then the backward substituted rule $\bar{\rho}$ is $l \to \bar{r} \Leftarrow \bar{s}_1 \to c, \ldots, \bar{s}_k \to c$, where c is a new constant and $\bar{r} = \varphi_{k+1}(r)$.

Claim: Let $\succ$ be a reduction order and let $\mathcal{R}$ be a deterministic 3-CTRS. If, for every rule ρ in $\mathcal{R}$, the backward substituted rule $\bar{\rho}$ satisfies $l \succ_{st} \bar{s}_i$ for $1 \le i \le k$ and $l \succ \bar{r}$, then $\mathcal{R}$ is quasi-reductive w.r.t. $\succ$.

The next example, however, refutes the claim.

Example 11. Consider the deterministic 3-CTRS

$$\mathcal{R} = \begin{cases} b \to g(d) \\ f(d) \to f(a) \\ a \to y \quad \Leftarrow b \to g(y) \end{cases}$$

Its backward substituted system $\overline{\mathcal{R}}$ consists of the two unconditional rules of $\mathcal{R}$ and the conditional rule $a \to b \Leftarrow b \to c$. The unconditional TRS $\overline{\mathcal{R}}_u$ obtained from $\overline{\mathcal{R}}$ by dropping the conditions is terminating. Hence the order $\succ \; = \; \to_{\overline{\mathcal{R}}_u}^+$ is a reduction order which satisfies the above claim. The original system $\mathcal{R}$, however, is not even terminating because there is the infinite rewrite sequence $f(d) \to_{\mathcal{R}} f(a) \to_{\mathcal{R}} f(d) \to_{\mathcal{R}} \cdots$.

The criterion will be rectified in the next section.

4 Quasi-Simplifying Deterministic 3-CTRSs

Definition 12. *We call $\mathcal{R}$ quasi-simplifying if it is quasi-reductive w.r.t. a simplification order $\succ$ (note that in this case $\succ \; = \; \succ_{st}$).*

By definition, quasi-simplifyingness implies quasi-reductivity. We shall see later that the converse is not true. In contrast to quasi-reductivity, quasi-simplifyingness is independent of signature extensions in the following sense: if a deterministic 3-CTRS $(\mathcal{F}, \mathcal{R})$ is quasi-simplifying w.r.t. a simplification order $\succ$ on $\mathcal{T}(\mathcal{F}', \mathcal{V})$, where $\mathcal{F} \subseteq \mathcal{F}'$, then $(\mathcal{F}, \mathcal{R})$ is quasi-simplifying w.r.t. the restriction of $\succ$ on $\mathcal{T}(\mathcal{F}, \mathcal{V})$. The simple proof of this fact is left to the reader.

Quasi-simplifyingness is closely related to simplifyingness. A join 1-CTRS $\mathcal{R}$ is *simplifying* if there is a simplification order $\succ$ such that $l \succ r$, $l \succ s_j$ and $l \succ t_j$ for every $l \to r \Leftarrow s_1 \downarrow t_1, \ldots, s_k \downarrow t_k \in \mathcal{R}$; see [Kap87]. For oriented 1-CTRSs, the condition $l \succ t_j$ can be dropped because the term t_j is never reduced. Thus an oriented 1-CTRS $\mathcal{R}$ is *simplifying* if there is a simplification order $\succ$ such that $l \succ r$ and $l \succ s_j$ for every $l \to r \Leftarrow s_1 \to t_1, \ldots, s_k \to t_k$ in $\mathcal{R}$. Obviously, every simplifying oriented 1-CTRS is quasi-simplifying.

Next we will provide several criteria which guarantee quasi-simplifyingness. To this end, we need the following lemmata.

Lemma 13. *An unconditional TRS $\mathcal{R}$ over the (finite) signature $\mathcal{F}$ is simply terminating if and only if $\mathcal{R} \cup \mathcal{E}mb(\mathcal{F})$ is terminating. The TRS $\mathcal{E}mb(\mathcal{F})$ consists of all rules $f(x_1, \ldots, x_n) \to x_j$ where $f \in \mathcal{F}$ has arity $n \geq 1$, $j \in \{1, \ldots, n\}$, and the variables $x_1, \ldots, x_n$ are pairwise distinct.*

A proof of the preceding lemma can be found in [Zan94] and the proof of the next lemma is straightforward; cf. [Ohl94, Lemma 8.1.9].

Lemma 14. *An oriented 1-CTRS $\mathcal{R}$ is simplifying if and only if the TRS*

$$\mathcal{R}_s = \mathcal{R}_u \cup \{l \to s_j \mid l \to r \Leftarrow s_1 \to t_1, \ldots, s_k \to t_k \in \mathcal{R}; \; 1 \leq j \leq k\}$$

is simply terminating. Analogously, a join 1-CTRS $\mathcal{R}$ is simplifying if and only if the following TRS is simply terminating:

$$\mathcal{R}_u \cup \{l \to s_j \mid l \to r \Leftarrow s_1 \downarrow t_1, \ldots, s_k \downarrow t_k \in \mathcal{R}; \; 1 \leq j \leq k\}$$
$$\cup \{l \to t_j \mid l \to r \Leftarrow s_1 \downarrow t_1, \ldots, s_k \downarrow t_k \in \mathcal{R}; \; 1 \leq j \leq k\}.$$

The first sufficient criterion uses the CTRS $\mathcal{R}_q$ from Definition 3. It is actually a characterization of quasi-simplifyingness.

Proposition 15. *A deterministic 3-CTRS $\mathcal{R}$ over a (finite) signature $\mathcal{F}$ is quasi-simplifying if and only if the deterministic 3-CTRS $\mathcal{R}_q \cup \mathcal{E}mb(\mathcal{F})$ is terminating.*

Proof. "if": It is not difficult to prove that $\to^+_{\mathcal{R}_q \cup \mathcal{E}mb(\mathcal{F})}$ is a simplification order[1] and that $\mathcal{R}$ is quasi-simplifying w.r.t. that order.
"only-if": Let $\mathcal{R}$ be quasi-simplifying w.r.t. the simplification order $\succ$. We show $\to^+_{\mathcal{R}_q \cup \mathcal{E}mb(\mathcal{F})} \subseteq \succ$. Clearly, it is sufficient to show that $s \to_{\mathcal{R}_q \cup \mathcal{E}mb(\mathcal{F})} t$ implies $s \succ t$. If $s \to_{\mathcal{E}mb(\mathcal{F})} t$, that is, $s = C[f(u_1, \ldots, u_n)]$ and $t = C[u_j]$ for some $f \in \mathcal{F}$, then the assertion follows from the fact that $\succ$ has the subterm property and is closed under contexts. We prove by induction on the depth of the rewrite step that $s \to_{\mathcal{R}_q \cup \mathcal{E}mb(\mathcal{F})} t$ also implies $s \succ t$. Consider the reduction step $s = C[l\sigma] \to_{\mathcal{R}_q \cup \mathcal{E}mb(\mathcal{F})} C[s_{i+1}\sigma] = t$, where the rewrite rule $l \to s_{i+1} \Leftarrow s_1 \to t_1,$ $\ldots, s_i \to t_i$ is used (let $s_{k+1} = r$), so $s_j\sigma \to^*_{\mathcal{R}_q \cup \mathcal{E}mb(\mathcal{F})} t_j\sigma$ for $1 \leq j \leq i$. One has $s_j\sigma \succeq t_j\sigma$ by the inductive hypothesis. It then follows from quasi-simplifyingness that $l\sigma \succ s_{i+1}\sigma$. We eventually infer $s \succ t$ because $\succ$ is closed under contexts.

The second sufficient criterion uses the transformation of Definition 6.

Proposition 16. *If $U(\mathcal{R})$ is simply terminating, then $\mathcal{R}$ is quasi-simplifying.*

Proof. By Lemma 13, $U(\mathcal{R}) \cup \mathcal{E}mb(\mathcal{F}')$ is terminating. We show $\to_{\mathcal{R}_q \cup \mathcal{E}mb(\mathcal{F})} \subseteq \to^+_{U(\mathcal{R}) \cup \mathcal{E}mb(\mathcal{F}')}$. The proposition then follows from Proposition 15. If $s \to_{\mathcal{E}mb(\mathcal{F})} t$, then we have $s \to_{\mathcal{E}mb(\mathcal{F}')} t$ because $\mathcal{F} \subseteq \mathcal{F}'$. We prove by induction on the depth of the rewrite step that $s \to_{\mathcal{R}_q \cup \mathcal{E}mb(\mathcal{F})} t$ implies $s \to^+_{U(\mathcal{R}) \cup \mathcal{E}mb(\mathcal{F}')} t$. Consider the reduction step $s = C[l\sigma] \to_{\mathcal{R}_q \cup \mathcal{E}mb(\mathcal{F})} C[s_{i+1}\sigma] = t$, where the rewrite rule $l \to s_{i+1} \Leftarrow s_1 \to t_1, \ldots, s_i \to t_i$ is used, so $s_j\sigma \to^*_{\mathcal{R}_q \cup \mathcal{E}mb(\mathcal{F})} t_j\sigma$ for $1 \leq j \leq i$. One has $s_j\sigma \to^*_{U(\mathcal{R}) \cup \mathcal{E}mb(\mathcal{F}')} t_j\sigma$ by the inductive hypothesis. Thus,

$$
\begin{aligned}
l\sigma &\to_{U(\mathcal{R})} & U_1^\rho(s_1, Var(l))\sigma \\
&\to^*_{U(\mathcal{R}) \cup \mathcal{E}mb(\mathcal{F}')} & U_1^\rho(t_1, Var(l))\sigma \\
&\to_{U(\mathcal{R})} & U_2^\rho(s_2, Var(l), \mathcal{E}Var(t_1))\sigma \\
&\ldots \\
&\to^*_{U(\mathcal{R}) \cup \mathcal{E}mb(\mathcal{F}')} & U_i^\rho(t_i, Var(l), \mathcal{E}Var(t_1), \ldots, \mathcal{E}Var(t_{i-1}))\sigma \\
&\to_{U(\mathcal{R})} & U_{i+1}^\rho(s_{i+1}, Var(l), \mathcal{E}Var(t_1), \ldots, \mathcal{E}Var(t_i))\sigma \\
&\to_{\mathcal{E}mb(\mathcal{F}')} & s_{i+1}\sigma.
\end{aligned}
$$

We have already seen that $U(\mathcal{R}_{fib})$ is simply terminating, hence $\mathcal{R}_{fib}$ is quasi-simplifying according to Proposition 16.

In order to rectify [ALS94, Lemma 3.1], it is sufficient to replace "reduction order" with "simplification order". This yields the third sufficient condition for quasi-simplifyingness.

---

[1] This is true because we consider finite signatures only; see [MZ97] for details on infinite signatures.

Proposition 17. *Let $(\mathcal{F}, \mathcal{R})$ be a deterministic 3-CTRS. If its backward substituted system $(\mathcal{F} \cup \{c\}, \overline{\mathcal{R}})$ is simplifying, then $(\mathcal{F}, \mathcal{R})$ is quasi-simplifying.*

Proof. If $(\mathcal{F} \cup \{c\}, \overline{\mathcal{R}})$ is simplifying, then there is a simplification order $\succ$ such that $l \succ \overline{r}$ and $l \succ \overline{s}_i$ for $1 \le i \le k$ for every backward substituted rule $\overline{\rho}$ of a rule $\rho = l \to r \Leftarrow s_1 \to t_1, \ldots, s_k \to t_k$ from $\mathcal{R}$.

We will only show that the first condition of Definition 12 (if $s_j\sigma \succeq t_j\sigma$ for every $1 \le j \le i$, then $l\sigma \succ s_{i+1}\sigma$) is satisfied. The second condition (if $s_j\sigma \succeq t_j\sigma$ for every $1 \le j \le k$, then $l\sigma \succ r\sigma$) follows by similar reasoning. It will be shown by induction on i that $s_j\sigma \succeq t_j\sigma$ for every $1 \le j \le i$ implies $\overline{s}_{i+1}\sigma \succeq s_{i+1}\sigma$. This is sufficient because $l \succ \overline{s}_{i+1}$ further implies $l\sigma \succ \overline{s}_{i+1}\sigma \succeq s_{i+1}\sigma$. The base case $i = 0$ holds as $\overline{s}_1 = s_1$. In order to show the inductive step, note that $\overline{s}_{i+1}\sigma = \varphi_{i+1}(s_{i+1})\sigma$. Let $y \in \mathcal{V}ar(t_1, \ldots, t_i) \cap \mathcal{E}\mathcal{V}ar(\rho)$. According to the inductive hypothesis, $\overline{s}_{\alpha(y)}\sigma \succeq s_{\alpha(y)}\sigma$. Therefore, $\overline{s}_{\alpha(y)}\sigma \succeq s_{\alpha(y)}\sigma \succeq t_{\alpha(y)}\sigma \succeq y\sigma$ and hence $\varphi_{i+1}(y)\sigma = \overline{s}_{\alpha(y)}\sigma \succeq y\sigma$. Now $\overline{s}_{i+1}\sigma \succeq s_{i+1}\sigma$ is a consequence of the following observation: If $u_1 \succeq v_1, \ldots, u_n \succeq v_n$, then $C[u_1, u_2, \ldots, u_n] \succeq C[v_1, u_2, \ldots, u_n] \succeq \cdots \succeq C[v_1, \ldots, v_n]$ since $\succ$ is closed under contexts. $\qquad \square$

Proposition 17 can also be used to show quasi-simplifyingness of $\mathcal{R}_{fib}$. This can be seen as follows. $\overline{\mathcal{R}}_{fib}$ consists of the rules

$$fib(0) \to \langle 0, s(0)\rangle$$
$$fib(s(x)) \to \langle fib(x), fib(x) + fib(x)\rangle \Leftarrow fib(x) \to c$$

By Lemma 14, simplifyingness of $\overline{\mathcal{R}}_{fib}$ is equivalent to simple termination of the TRS $(\overline{\mathcal{R}}_{fib})_s$ and simple termination of this TRS can easily be shown by rpo.

Since both Proposition 16 and Proposition 17 are sufficient conditions for proving quasi-simplifyingness, it is natural to ask whether one is subsumed by the other. This is not the case as the following examples will show.

Example 18. Let $\mathcal{R} = \{f(s(x)) \to f(s(y)) \Leftarrow f(x) \to f(s(y))\}$. It is fairly simple to show that $U(\mathcal{R})$ is simply terminating. To verify that Proposition 17 is not applicable is equally simple; see [ALS94].

Example 19. Consider the oriented 1-CTRS $(\mathcal{F}, \mathcal{R})$ consisting of the rules

$$
\begin{array}{ll}
a \to d & a \to e \\
b \to d & b \to e \\
A \to h(f(a), f(b)) & \\
h(x, x) \to g(x, x) & \\
g(d, e) \to A & \\
f(x) \to x & \Leftarrow x \to d
\end{array}
$$

Its backward substituted system $\overline{\mathcal{R}}$ over $\overline{\mathcal{F}} = \mathcal{F} \cup \{c\}$ is obtained from $\mathcal{R}$ by replacing its last rule with $f(x) \to x \Leftarrow x \to c$. We claim that $\overline{\mathcal{R}}$ is simplifying. By Lemmata 13 and 14, it suffices to show that $\overline{\mathcal{R}}_s \cup \mathcal{E}mb(\overline{\mathcal{F}})$ is terminating. For an indirect proof of the claim, suppose that there is an infinite $\overline{\mathcal{R}}_s \cup \mathcal{E}mb(\overline{\mathcal{F}})$

reduction sequence. It is not difficult to see that in this case there must be a cycle $A \to_{\mathcal{R}_s \cup \mathcal{E}mb(\mathcal{F})} h(f(a), f(b)) \to^+_{\mathcal{R}_s \cup \mathcal{E}mb(\mathcal{F})} A$. If $h(f(a), f(b)) \to^+_{\mathcal{R}_s \cup \mathcal{E}mb(\mathcal{F})} A$, then there must be a term t such that

$$h(f(a), f(b)) \to^+_{\mathcal{R}_s \cup \mathcal{E}mb(\mathcal{F})} h(t, t) \to_{\mathcal{R}_s} g(t, t) \to^+_{\mathcal{R}_s \cup \mathcal{E}mb(\mathcal{F})} g(d, e) \to_{\mathcal{R}_s \cup \mathcal{E}mb(\mathcal{F})} A.$$

So t must be a common reduct of $f(a)$ and $f(b)$ and t must rewrite to d and e. The common reducts of $f(a)$ and $f(b)$ are $f(d)$, $f(e)$, d, and e. Neither of them reduces to both d and e. We conclude that $\mathcal{R}_s \cup \mathcal{E}mb(\mathcal{F})$ is terminating. Thus $\overline{\mathcal{R}}$ is simplifying and, according to Proposition 17, $\mathcal{R}$ is quasi-simplifying.

$U(\mathcal{R})$ is obtained from $\mathcal{R}$ by replacing the conditional rewrite rule with the unconditional rewrite rules $f(x) \to U(x, x)$ and $U(d, x) \to x$. The following cyclic derivation shows that $U(\mathcal{R})$ is not simply terminating.

$$A \to_{U(\mathcal{R})} h(f(a), f(b)) \to^+_{U(\mathcal{R})} h(U(a, a), U(b, b)) \to^+_{U(\mathcal{R})} h(U(d, e), U(d, e))$$
$$\to_{U(\mathcal{R})} g(U(d, e), U(d, e)) \to^+_{\mathcal{E}mb(\mathcal{F}')} g(d, e) \to_{U(\mathcal{R})} A.$$

The preceding example is also interesting because it refutes the claim below which is a reformulation of [Mar96, Lemma 5.6]. Let us first review the definition of the transformation $\mathbb{U}$ as given in [Mar96, Def. 4.1]. Given a join 1-CTRS $\mathcal{R}$ and a rule $\rho : l \to r \Leftarrow s_1 \downarrow t_1, \ldots, s_k \downarrow t_k \in \mathcal{R}$, the transformation $\mathbb{U}(\rho)$ yields the set which contains the two unconditional rules

$$l \to U_\rho(s_1, t_1, \ldots, s_k, t_k, Var(l))$$
$$U_\rho(x_1, x_1, \ldots, x_k, x_k, Var(l)) \to r$$

where $x_1, \ldots, x_k$ are fresh and pairwise distinct variables. Moreover, $\mathbb{U}(\mathcal{R})$ is defined as usual: $\mathbb{U}(\mathcal{R}) = \bigcup_{\rho \in \mathcal{R}} \mathbb{U}(\rho)$.

Claim: If a join 1-CTRS $\mathcal{R}$ is simplifying, then the transformed TRS $\mathbb{U}(\mathcal{R})$ is simply terminating.

If we view the system $\mathcal{R}$ from Example 19 as a join CTRS, then $\mathbb{U}(\mathcal{R}) = \mathcal{R}' \cup \{f(x) \to U(x, d, x), U(x_1, x_1, x) \to x\}$, where $\mathcal{R}'$ consists of the unconditional rules of $\mathcal{R}$. As in Example 19, it can be shown that the system $\mathcal{R}' \cup \{f(x) \to x, f(x) \to d\}$ is simply terminating. Thus the join 1-CTRS $\mathcal{R}$ is simplifying according to Lemma 14. On the other hand, the transformed system $\mathbb{U}(\mathcal{R})$ is not simply terminating because there is a cyclic derivation as in Example 19.

5   Modularity

In this section, we will investigate under which conditions quasi-reductivity and quasi-simplifyingness are modular. The reader is assumed to be familiar with the concepts of the field of modularity. Details can be found e.g. in [Ohl94,KR95]. Let $\mathcal{R}$ be a CTRS over the signature $\mathcal{F}$. A function symbol $f \in \mathcal{F}$ is called a *defined symbol* if there is a rewrite rule $l \to r \Leftarrow c \in \mathcal{R}$ such that $f = root(l)$.

Function symbols from $\mathcal{F}$ which are not defined symbols are called *constructors*. If $\mathcal{R}_1$ and $\mathcal{R}_2$ are CTRSs over the signatures $\mathcal{F}_1$ and $\mathcal{F}_2$, respectively, then their *combined system* is their union $\mathcal{R} = \mathcal{R}_1 \cup \mathcal{R}_2$ over the signature $\mathcal{F} = \mathcal{F}_1 \cup \mathcal{F}_2$. Its set of defined symbols is $\mathcal{D} = \mathcal{D}_1 \cup \mathcal{D}_2$ and its set of constructors is $\mathcal{C} = \mathcal{F} \setminus \mathcal{D}$, where $\mathcal{D}_i$ ($\mathcal{C}_i$) denotes the defined symbols (constructors) in $\mathcal{R}_i$.

(1) $\mathcal{R}_1$ and $\mathcal{R}_2$ are *disjoint* if $\mathcal{F}_1 \cap \mathcal{F}_2 = \emptyset$.
(2) $\mathcal{R}_1$ and $\mathcal{R}_2$ are *constructor-sharing* if $\mathcal{F}_1 \cap \mathcal{F}_2 = \mathcal{C}_1 \cap \mathcal{C}_2$ ($\subseteq \mathcal{C}$).
(3) $\mathcal{R}_1$ and $\mathcal{R}_2$ form a *hierarchical combination* of base $\mathcal{R}_1$ and extension $\mathcal{R}_2$ if $\mathcal{C}_1 \cap \mathcal{D}_2 = \mathcal{D}_1 \cap \mathcal{D}_2 = \emptyset$.

A property $\mathcal{P}$ is *modular* for a certain class of CTRSs if, for all CTRSs $(\mathcal{F}_1, \mathcal{R}_1)$ and $(\mathcal{F}_2, \mathcal{R}_2)$ belonging to that class and having property $\mathcal{P}$, their union $(\mathcal{F}_1 \cup \mathcal{F}_2, \mathcal{R}_1 \cup \mathcal{R}_2)$ also belongs to that class and has the property $\mathcal{P}$.

It is well known that simple termination is modular for constructor-sharing TRSs; see [KO92,MZ97]. It readily follows from Lemma 14 that simplifyingness is also modular for finite constructor-sharing 1-CTRSs. Therefore, if quasi-simplifyingness of two constructor-sharing 3-CTRSs $\mathcal{R}_1$ and $\mathcal{R}_2$ can be shown by Proposition 17, then $\mathcal{R}_1 \cup \mathcal{R}_2$ is also quasi-simplifying. This is because the simplifying backward substituted 1-CTRSs $\overline{\mathcal{R}}_1$ and $\overline{\mathcal{R}}_2$ are also constructor-sharing. Hence it is a bit surprising that quasi-simplifyingness is in general *not* modular for disjoint deterministic 3-CTRSs. The next example which is taken from [Mid93] is a counterexample.

Example 20. Consider the 1-CTRS

$$\mathcal{R}_1 = \{f(x) \to f(x) \Leftarrow x \to a, x \to b\}$$

over the signature $\mathcal{F}_1 = \{f, a, b\}$. It is not difficult to show that the system $\{f(x) \to x, f(x) \to x \Leftarrow x \to a, f(x) \to f(x) \Leftarrow x \to a, x \to b\}$ is terminating because the last rule can never be applied. Hence $\mathcal{R}_1$ is quasi-simplifying by Proposition 15. The TRS

$$\mathcal{R}_2 = \begin{cases} or(x, y) \to x \\ or(x, y) \to y \end{cases}$$

is obviously quasi-simplifying, too. The combined system $\mathcal{R}_1 \cup \mathcal{R}_2$, however, is not even terminating: $f(or(a, b)) \to_{\mathcal{R}_1 \cup \mathcal{R}_2} f(or(a, b))$ is a cyclic derivation because $or(a, b) \to_{\mathcal{R}_2} a$ and $or(a, b) \to_{\mathcal{R}_2} b$.

Quasi-simplifyingness of $\mathcal{R}_1$ cannot be proven by Proposition 16 because

$$U(\mathcal{R}_1) = \begin{cases} f(x) & \to U_1(x, x) \\ U_1(a, x) \to U_2(x, x) \\ U_2(b, x) \to f(x) \end{cases}$$

is not simply terminating as the following cyclic derivation shows:

$$
\begin{aligned}
f(U_1(a, b)) &\to_{U(\mathcal{R}_1)} U_1(U_1(a, b), U_1(a, b)) \to_{\mathcal{E}mb(\mathcal{F}')} U_1(a, U_1(a, b)) \\
&\to_{U(\mathcal{R}_1)} U_2(U_1(a, b), U_1(a, b)) \to_{\mathcal{E}mb(\mathcal{F}')} U_2(b, U_1(a, b)) \\
&\to_{U(\mathcal{R}_1)} f(U_1(a, b)).
\end{aligned}
$$

This is not surprising because the combined system of two constructor-sharing deterministic 3-CTRSs $\mathcal{R}_1$ and $\mathcal{R}_2$ is quasi-simplifying if both $U(\mathcal{R}_1)$ and $U(\mathcal{R}_2)$ are simply terminating. This fact is an easy consequence of the following simple generic proposition.

Proposition 21. *Let $\mathcal{R}_1$ and $\mathcal{R}_2$ be deterministic 3-CTRSs. Their combined system $\mathcal{R}_1 \cup \mathcal{R}_2$ is quasi-simplifying if*

1. *both $U(\mathcal{R}_1)$ and $U(\mathcal{R}_2)$ are simply terminating, and*
2. *$U(\mathcal{R}_1)$ and $U(\mathcal{R}_2)$ belong to a class of TRSs for which simple termination is modular.*

Proof. Since simple termination is a modular property, the combined system $U(\mathcal{R}_1) \cup U(\mathcal{R}_2)$ is simply terminating. Now the proposition follows from $U(\mathcal{R}_1 \cup \mathcal{R}_2) = U(\mathcal{R}_1) \cup U(\mathcal{R}_2)$ in conjunction with Proposition 16.

A similar result can of course be stated for quasi-reductivity (just replace simple termination with termination). However, better results can be obtained by taking advantage of the implications $U(\mathcal{R})$ is terminating $\Rightarrow$ $\mathcal{R}$ is quasi-reductive (Proposition 7), $\mathcal{R}$ is quasi-reductive $\Rightarrow$ $U(\mathcal{R})$ is innermost terminating (Theorem 9), and the fact that termination and innermost termination coincide for non-overlapping TRSs; see [Gra95, Thm. 3.23].

Proposition 22. *Let $\mathcal{R}_1$ and $\mathcal{R}_2$ be quasi-reductive deterministic 3-CTRSs. Their combined system $\mathcal{R}_1 \cup \mathcal{R}_2$ is quasi-reductive if*

1. *$U(\mathcal{R}_1)$ and $U(\mathcal{R}_2)$ belong to a class of TRSs for which innermost termination is modular, and*
2. *$U(\mathcal{R}_1 \cup \mathcal{R}_2)$ is non-overlapping.*

Proof. Since $\mathcal{R}_1$ and $\mathcal{R}_2$ are quasi-reductive, the transformed TRSs $U(\mathcal{R}_1)$ and $U(\mathcal{R}_2)$ are innermost terminating according to Theorem 9. Their combination $U(\mathcal{R}_1) \cup U(\mathcal{R}_2) = U(\mathcal{R}_1 \cup \mathcal{R}_2)$ is also innermost terminating because innermost termination is modular. Therefore, termination of $U(\mathcal{R}_1 \cup \mathcal{R}_2)$ is a consequence of its non-overlappingness; see [Gra95, Thm. 3.23]. Now the assertion follows from Proposition 7.

However, non-overlappingness of $U(\mathcal{R})$ is not implied by non-overlappingness of $\mathcal{R}$. For example, the system $\mathcal{R} = \{a \to b \Leftarrow b \to a\}$ is non-overlapping but $U(\mathcal{R}) = \{a \to U(b), U(a) \to b\}$ is not. The situation is different for syntactically deterministic 3-CTRSs.

Definition 23. *A deterministic 3-CTRS $\mathcal{R}$ is called* syntactically deterministic *if, for every $l \to r \Leftarrow s_1 \to t_1, \ldots, s_k \to t_k$ in $\mathcal{R}$, every term t_i, $1 \le i \le k$, is a constructor term[2] or a ground $\mathcal{R}_u$-normal form.*

Syntactically deterministic CTRSs are a natural generalization of normal CTRSs. For example, the Fibonacci system $\mathcal{R}_{fib}$ is syntactically deterministic. The proof of the next lemma is straightforward; see [Ohl99].

---

[2] A *constructor term* is a term without defined symbols.

Lemma 24. *The transformed system $U(\mathcal{R})$ of a syntactically deterministic 3-CTRS $\mathcal{R}$ is non-overlapping if $\mathcal{R}$ is non-overlapping.*

Lemma 24 can be refined to demand only exactly what is required by the proof. For instance, the 3-CTRS $\mathcal{R}$ need not be syntactically deterministic; it is sufficient to demand that no left-hand side l_1 of a rule from $\mathcal{R}$ overlaps a term t_i of another rule $l_2 \rightarrow r_2 \Leftarrow s_1 \rightarrow t_1, \ldots, s_k \rightarrow t_k$ from $\mathcal{R}$. On the other hand, the example before Def. 23 shows that the lemma does not hold for strongly deterministic CTRSs (see [ALS94] for a definition of this notion).

Next we will prove a modularity result for hierarchical combinations of CTRSs with extra variables on the right-hand sides of the rules. Let us first review some formal definitions. Let $\mathcal{R}$ be a CTRS and $\mathcal{D}$ be the set of its defined symbols. As defined in [KR95,Mar95], the dependency relation $\succeq_d$ on $\mathcal{D}$ is the smallest quasi-order satisfying $f \succeq_d g$ whenever there is a rule $l \rightarrow r \Leftarrow s_1 \rightarrow t_1, \ldots, s_k \rightarrow t_k \in \mathcal{R}$ such that $root(l) = f$ and $g \in \mathcal{D}$ occurs in one of the terms $s_1, \ldots, s_k, r$. If $\mathcal{R}_1$ and $\mathcal{R}_2$ form a hierarchical combination, then the set of defined symbols $\mathcal{D}_2$ of $\mathcal{R}_2$ is split into two sets $\mathcal{D}_2^1 = \{f \mid f \in \mathcal{D}_2, f \succeq_d g \text{ for some } g \in \mathcal{D}_1\}$ and $\mathcal{D}_2^2 = \mathcal{D} \setminus \mathcal{D}_2^1$. Krishna Rao [KR95] proved the following theorem.

Theorem 25. *Let $\mathcal{R}_1$ and $\mathcal{R}_2$ form a hierarchical combination of unconditional TRSs. Suppose $\mathcal{R}_2$ is a proper extension of $\mathcal{R}_1$, i.e., every rule $l \rightarrow r \in \mathcal{R}_2$ satisfies the following condition: For every subterm t of r, if $root(t) \in \mathcal{D}_2^1$ and $root(t) \succeq_d root(l)$, then t does not contain symbols from $\mathcal{D}_1 \cup \mathcal{D}_2^1$ except at the root position. If both $\mathcal{R}_1$ and $\mathcal{R}_2$ are innermost terminating, then $\mathcal{R}_1 \cup \mathcal{R}_2$ is innermost terminating as well.*

The combination of Lemma 24, Proposition 22, and Theorem 25 yields the following theorem.

Theorem 26. *Let $\mathcal{R}_1$ and $\mathcal{R}_2$ be quasi-reductive non-overlapping syntactically deterministic 3-CTRSs. Their hierarchical combination $\mathcal{R}_1 \cup \mathcal{R}_2$ is a quasi-reductive non-overlapping syntactically deterministic 3-CTRS as well provided that every rule $l \rightarrow r \Leftarrow s_1 \rightarrow t_1, \ldots, s_k \rightarrow t_k$ in $\mathcal{R}_2$ satisfies:*

1. *neither l nor one of the terms $t_1, \ldots, t_k$ contains a symbol from $\mathcal{D}_1$,*

If some s_j, $1 \leq j \leq k+1$, where $s_{k+1} = r$, contains a symbol from $\mathcal{D}_1 \cup \mathcal{D}_2^1$,

2. *then every subterm t of s_j with $root(t) \in \mathcal{D}_2^1$ and $root(t) \succeq_d root(l)$ does not contain symbols from $\mathcal{D}_1 \cup \mathcal{D}_2^1$ except at the root position, and*
3. *none of the terms $s_{j+1}, \ldots, s_k, s_{k+1}$ contain an $f \in \mathcal{D}_2^1$ with $f \succeq_d root(l)$.*

Proof. The combined system $U(\mathcal{R}_1) \cup U(\mathcal{R}_2) = U(\mathcal{R}_1 \cup \mathcal{R}_2)$ is non-overlapping because the TRSs $U(\mathcal{R}_1)$ and $U(\mathcal{R}_2)$ are non-overlapping by Lemma 24 and every rule $l \rightarrow r \Leftarrow s_1 \rightarrow t_1, \ldots, s_k \rightarrow t_k$ in $\mathcal{R}_2$ satisfies: neither l nor one of the terms $t_1, \ldots t_k$ contains a symbol from $\mathcal{D}_1$. For the same reason, $\mathcal{R}_1 \cup \mathcal{R}_2$ is non-overlapping and syntactically deterministic. We claim that $U(\mathcal{R}_2)$ is a proper extension of $U(\mathcal{R}_1)$. Since innermost termination is modular for proper extensions by Theorem 25, it then follows from Proposition 22 that $\mathcal{R}_1 \cup \mathcal{R}_2$ is quasi-reductive.

In order to prove the claim, consider $\rho : l \rightarrow r \Leftarrow s_1 \rightarrow t_1, \ldots, s_k \rightarrow t_k \in \mathcal{R}_2$ and its transformation $U(\rho)$. If $root(l) \in \mathcal{D}_2^2$, then none of the terms $s_1, \ldots, s_k, s_{k+1}(= r)$ contain a symbol from $\mathcal{D}_1 \cup \mathcal{D}_2^1$ and every rule in $U(\rho)$ satisfies the proper extension condition. Thus, suppose $root(l) \in \mathcal{D}_2^1$ and let j, $1 \leq j \leq k+1$, be the smallest index such that s_j contains a symbol from $\mathcal{D}_1 \cup \mathcal{D}_2^1$. Every rule $l \rightarrow U_1^\rho(s_1, \ldots), U_1^\rho(t_1, \ldots) \rightarrow U_2^\rho(s_2, \ldots), \ldots, U_{j-2}^\rho(t_{j-2}, \ldots) \rightarrow U_{j-1}^\rho(s_{j-1}, \ldots)$ vacuously satisfies the proper extension condition. Observe that $U_j^\rho \succeq_d root(l)$ can only hold if one of the terms $s_{j+1}, \ldots, s_k, s_{k+1}$ contains a symbol f with $f \succeq_d root(l)$ (which further implies $f \in \mathcal{D}_2^1$). This, however, is impossible because of assumption (3). Now the rewrite rule $U_{j-1}^\rho(t_{j-1}, \ldots) \rightarrow U_j^\rho(s_j, \ldots)$ satisfies the proper extension condition by assumption (2) because for every subterm t of $U_j^\rho(s_j, \ldots)$ with $root(t) \in \mathcal{D}_2^1$ and $root(t) \succeq_d U_{j-1}^\rho$ we have $root(t) \succeq_d root(l)$. The remaining rules $U_j^\rho(t_j, \ldots) \rightarrow U_{j+1}^\rho(s_{j+1}, \ldots), \ldots, U_k^\rho(t_k, \ldots) \rightarrow r$ satisfy the proper extension condition because of assumption (3) and the resultant fact that $U_i^\rho \not\succeq_d root(l)$ for every $j + 1 \leq i \leq k$.

As an example, consider the quasi-reductive systems $\mathcal{R}_+ = \{0+y \rightarrow y, s(x)+y \rightarrow s(x+y)\}$ and $\mathcal{R}_{fib}$. Since $\mathcal{R}_+$ and $\mathcal{R}_{fib}$ meet the requirements of Theorem 26, their hierarchical combination $\mathcal{R}_+ \cup \mathcal{R}_{fib}$ is quasi-reductive as well.

Condition (1) in Theorem 26 guarantees that the system $U(\mathcal{R}_1) \cup U(\mathcal{R}_2)$ is non-overlapping. The following example shows that condition (2) is necessary. The quasi-reductive non-overlapping syntactically deterministic 3-CTRSs $\mathcal{R}_1 = \{a \rightarrow b\}$ and $\mathcal{R}_2 = \{f(x,x) \rightarrow c \Leftarrow f(a,b) \rightarrow c\}$ form a hierarchical combination. If $\mathcal{R}_1 \cup \mathcal{R}_2$ were quasi-reductive w.r.t. an order $\succ$, then $f(b,b) \succ_{st} f(a,b) \succ f(b,b)$ would hold, but this contradicts the irreflexivity of $\succ_{st}$. Finally, we exemplify the necessity of condition (3). $\mathcal{R}_1$ and $\mathcal{R}_3 = \{c \rightarrow d \Leftarrow a \rightarrow b, c \rightarrow d\}$ form a hierarchical combination. Here $s_1 = a$ contains a symbol from $\mathcal{D}_1$ and $s_2 = c$ contains $c \in \mathcal{D}_2^1$ with $c \succeq_d root(l)$. If $\mathcal{R}_1 \cup \mathcal{R}_3$ were quasi-reductive w.r.t. an order $\succ$, then $c \succ_{st} c$ would hold, but $\succ_{st}$ is irreflexive.

6   Related Work

One of the anonymous referees pointed out that a transformation similar to the one from Definition 6 was independently found by Marchiori [Mar97, Def. 4.1]. Our transformation differs only slightly from Marchiori's: in the sequence $Var(l)$, $\mathcal{E}Var(t_1), \ldots, \mathcal{E}Var(t_i)$ every variable occurs exactly once which is not the case in the sequence $VAR(l, t_1, \ldots, t_i)$ from [Mar97, Def. 4.1]. The results of the paper at hand, however, are completely different from the ones reported in the technical report [Mar97], except for one: Proposition 7 is akin to [Mar97, Lemma 4.6].

Acknowledgements: I thank Michael Hanus for the (email) discussion which led to the development of the transformation U. I am also grateful to Aart Middeldorp and the anonymous referees for their comments.

References

AG99.   T. Arts and J. Giesl. Termination of term rewriting using dependency pairs. *Theoretical Computer Science*, 1999. To appear.

ALS94. J. Avenhaus and C. Loría-Sáenz. On conditional rewrite systems with extra variables and deterministic logic programs. In *Proceedings of the 5th International Conference on Logic Programming and Automated Reasoning*, volume 822 of *Lecture Notes in Artificial Intelligence*, pages 215–229, Berlin, 1994. Springer-Verlag.

BK86.   J.A. Bergstra and J.W. Klop. Conditional rewrite rules: Confluence and termination. *Journal of Computer and System Sciences*, 32(3):323–362, 1986.

BN98.   F. Baader and T. Nipkow. *Term Rewriting and All That*. Cambridge University Press, 1998.

Der87. N. Dershowitz. Termination of rewriting. *Journal of Symbolic Computation*, 3(1):69–116, 1987.

Gan91. H. Ganzinger. Order-sorted completion: The many-sorted way. *Theoretical Computer Science*, 89:3–32, 1991.

Gra95. B. Gramlich. Abstract relations between restricted termination and confluence properties of rewrite systems. *Fundamenta Informaticae*, 24:3–23, 1995.

Han94. M. Hanus. The integration of functions into logic programming: From theory to practice. *The Journal of Logic Programming*, 19&20:583–628, 1994.

Kap87. S. Kaplan. Simplifying conditional term rewriting systems: Unification, termination and confluence. *Journal of Symbolic Computation*, 4(3):295–334, 1987.

KO92.   M. Kurihara and A. Ohuchi. Modularity of simple termination of term rewriting systems with shared constructors. *Theoretical Computer Science*, 103:273–282, 1992.

KR95.   M.R.K. Krishna Rao. Modular proofs for completeness of hierarchical term rewriting systems. *Theoretical Computer Science*, 151:487–512, 1995.

Mar95. M. Marchiori. Unravelings and ultra-properties. Technical Report 8, Dept. of Pure and Applied Mathematics, University of Padova, Italy, 1995.

Mar96. M. Marchiori. Unravelings and ultra-properties. In *Proceedings of the 5th International Conference on Algebraic and Logic Programming*, volume 1139 of *Lecture Notes in Computer Science*, pages 107–121, Berlin, 1996. Springer-Verlag.

Mar97. M. Marchiori. On deterministic conditional rewriting. Computation Structures Group, Memo 405, MIT Laboratory for Computer Science, 1997.

Mid93. A. Middeldorp. Modular properties of conditional term rewriting systems. *Information and Computation*, 104(1):110–158, 1993.

MZ97.   A. Middeldorp and H. Zantema. Simple termination of rewrite systems. *Theoretical Computer Science*, 175(1):127–158, 1997.

Ohl94. E. Ohlebusch. *Modular Properties of Composable Term Rewriting Systems*. PhD thesis, Universität Bielefeld, 1994.

Ohl99. E. Ohlebusch. Transforming conditional rewrite systems with extra variables into unconditional systems. In *Proceedings of the 6th International Conference on Logic for Programming and Automated Reasoning*, Lecture Notes in Artificial Intelligence, Berlin, 1999. Springer-Verlag. To appear.

Zan94. H. Zantema. Termination of term rewriting: Interpretation and type elimination. *Journal of Symbolic Computation*, 17:23–50, 1994.

An Interval Lattice-Based Constraint Solving Framework for Lattices

Antonio J. Fernández[1]* and Patricia M. Hill[2]

[1] Departamento de Lenguajes y Ciencias de la Computación,
E.T.S.I.I., 29071 Teatinos, Málaga, Spain
afdez@lcc.uma.es
[2] School of Computer Studies, University of Leeds,
Leeds, LS2 9JT, England
hill@scs.leeds.ac.uk

Abstract. We present a simple generic framework to solve constraints on any domain (finite or infinite) which has a lattice structure. The approach is based on the use of a single constraint similar to the indexicals used by CLP over finite domains and on a particular definition of an interval lattice built from the computation domain. We provide the theoretical foundations for this framework, a schematic procedure for the operational semantics, and numerous examples illustrating how it can be used both over classical and new domains. We also show how lattice combinators can be used to generate new domains and hence new constraint solvers for these domains from existing domains.

Keywords: Lattice, constraint solving, constraint propagation, indexicals.

1 Introduction

Constraint Logic Programming (CLP) systems support many different domains such as finite ranges of integers, reals, finite sets of elements or the Booleans. The type of the domain determines the nature of the constraints and the solvers used to solve them. Existing constraint solvers (with the exception of the CHR approach [7]), only support specified domains. In particular, the cardinality of the domain determines the constraint solving procedure so that existing CLP systems have distinct constraint solving methods for the finite and the infinite domains. On the other hand, CHR [7] is very expressive, allowing for user-defined domains. Unfortunately this flexibility has a cost and CHR solvers have not been able to compete with the other solvers that employ the more traditional approach. In this paper we explore an alternative approach for a flexible constraint solver that allows for user and system defined domains with interaction between them.

---

* This work was partly supported by EPSRC grants GR/L19515 and GR/M05645 and by CICYT grant TIC98-0445-C03-03.

A. Middeldorp, T. Sato (Eds.): FLOPS'99, LNCS 1722, pp. 194–208, 1999.
© Springer-Verlag Berlin Heidelberg 1999

Normally, for any given domain, a solver has many constraints, each with its own bespoke implementation. The exception to this rule is CLP(FD) [4] which is designed for the finite domain of integers and based on a single generic constraint often referred to as an *indexical*. The implementation of indexicals uses a simple interval narrowing technique which can be smoothly integrated into the WAM [2,6]. This approach has been shown to be adaptable and very efficient and now integrated into mainstream CLP systems such as SICStus Prolog.

This paper has two contributions. First, we provide a theoretical framework for the indexical approach to constraint solvers. This is formulated for any ordered domain that is a lattice. We have observed that most of the existing constraint solvers are for domains that are lattices. Thus our second contribution is to provide a theoretical foundation for more generic constraint solvers where a single solver can support any system or user-defined domain (even if its cardinality is infinite) provided it is a lattice. One advantage of our framework is that, as it is based on lattice theory, it is straightforward to construct new domains and new constraint solvers for these domains from existing ones. In this paper, we describe different ways of performing these constructions and illustrate them by means of examples.

The paper is structured as follows. Section 2 recalls algebraic concepts used in the paper. In Section 3 the computation domain, the execution model and a schema of an operational semantics are described. Section 4 shows the genericity of the theoretical framework by providing several instances which include both the common well-supported domains as well as new domains. Section 5 describes with examples how the framework can be used on the combination of domains. The paper ends with some considerations about related work and the conclusions.

2 Preliminaries

2.1 Ordered Sets

Definition 1. *(Ordering) Let C be a set with equality. A binary relation $\preceq$ on C is an* ordering *relation if it is reflexive, antisymmetric and transitive. The relation $\prec$ can be defined in terms of $\preceq$*

$$c \prec c' \Leftrightarrow c \preceq c' \wedge c \neq c',$$
$$c \preceq c' \Leftrightarrow c \prec c' \vee c = c'.$$

We write $c \preceq_C c'$ (when necessary) to express that $c \preceq c'$ where $c, c' \in C$. Let C be a set with ordering relation $\preceq$ and $c, c' \in C$. Then we write $c \sim c'$ if either $c \preceq c'$ or $c' \preceq c$ and $c \not\sim c'$ otherwise. Any set C which has an ordering relation is said to be ordered. *Evidently any subset of an ordered set is ordered.*

Definition 2. *(Dual of an ordered set) Given any ordered set C we can form a new ordered set $\hat{C}$ (called the* dual *of C) which contains the same elements as C and $b \preceq_{\hat{C}} a$ if and only if $a \preceq_C b$. In general, given any statement Φ about ordered sets, the dual statement $\hat{\Phi}$ may be obtained by replacing each expression of the form $x \preceq y$ by $y \preceq x$.*

Definition 3. *(Bounds) Let C be an ordered set. An element s in C is a* lower (upper) bound *of a subset $E \subseteq C$ if and only if $\forall x \in E$: $s \preceq x$ ($x \preceq s$). If the set of lower (upper) bounds of E has a greatest (least) element, then that element is called the* greatest lower bound *(least upper bound) of E and denoted by $glb_C(E)$ ($lub_C(E)$). For simplicity, we adopt the notation $glb_C(x,y)$ and $lub_C(x,y)$ when E contains only two elements x and y.*

Definition 4. *(Predecessor and successor) Let C be an ordered set and let $c, c' \in C$. Then c is called a* predecessor *of c' and c' a* successor *of c if $c \preceq c'$. We say c is the* immediate predecessor *of c' if $c \prec c'$ and for any $c'' \in C$ such that $c \preceq c'' \prec c'$ implies $c = c''$. The* immediate successor *of c is defined dually.*

Definition 5. *(Direct product) Let C_1 and C_2 be ordered sets. The* direct product *$C = \langle C_1, C_2 \rangle$ is an ordered set with domain the Cartesian product of C_1 and C_2 and ordering defined by: $\langle x_1, x_2 \rangle \preceq_C \langle y_1, y_2 \rangle \iff x_1 \preceq_{C_1} y_1$ and $x_2 \preceq_{C_2} y_2$*

Definition 6. *(Lexicographic product) Let C_1 and C_2 be ordered sets. The* lexicographic product *$C = (C_1, C_2)$ is an ordered set with domain the Cartesian product of C_1 and C_2 and ordering defined by:*

$$(x_1, x_2) \preceq_C (y_1, y_2) \iff x_1 \prec_{C_1} y_1 \text{ or } x_1 = y_1 \text{ and } x_2 \preceq_{C_2} y_2$$

2.2 Lattices

Definition 7. *(Lattice) Let L be an ordered set. L is a* lattice *if $lub_L(x,y)$ and $glb_L(x,y)$ exist for any two elements $x, y \in L$. If $lub_L(S)$ and $glb_L(S)$ exist for all $S \subseteq L$, then L is a* complete lattice.

Definition 8. *(Top and bottom elements) Let L be a lattice. $glb_L(L)$, if it exists, is called the* bottom element *of L and written $\perp_L$. Similarly, $lub_L(L)$, if it exists, is called the* top element *of L and written $\top_L$. The lack of a bottom or top element can be remedied by adding a fictitious one. Thus, we define the* lifted lattice of *L to be $L \cup \{\perp_L, \top_L\}$ where, if $glb_L(L)$ does not exist, $\perp_L$ is a new element not in L such that $\forall a \in L, \perp_L \prec a$ and similarly, if $lub_L(L)$ does not exist, $\top_L$ is a new element not in L such that $\forall a \in L, a \prec \top_L$.*

Proposition 1. *(Products of lattices) Let L_1 and L_2 be two (lifted) lattices. Then the direct product $\langle L_1, L_2 \rangle$ and the lexicographic product (L_1, L_2) are lattices when we define:*

$$glb(\langle x_1, x_2 \rangle, \langle y_1, y_2 \rangle) = \langle glb_{L_1}(x_1, y_1), glb_{L_2}(x_2, y_2) \rangle$$

$$glb((x_1, x_2), (y_1, y_2)) = \text{if } x_1 = y_1 \text{ then } (x_1, glb_{L_2}(x_2, y_2))$$
$$\text{elsif } x_1 \prec y_1 \text{ then } (x_1, x_2)$$
$$\text{elsif } x_1 \succ y_1 \text{ then } (y_1, y_2)$$
$$\text{else } (glb_{L_1}(x_1, y_1), \top_{L_2})$$

lub is defined dually to glb[1].

Proofs and more information about lattices can be found in [5].

---

[1] Note that $\top_{L_2}$ must be also changed to its dual $\perp_{L_2}$.

3   The Constraint Domains

3.1   The Computation Domain

The underlying domain for the constraints, denoted here by D_0, is a lattice called the *computation domain*. It is assumed that D_0 has been lifted to include top and bottom elements, $\top_{D_0}$ and $\bot_{D_0}$ respectively.

   The domain that is actually used for the constraint solving is a set of intervals on the computation domain and called the *interval domain*. We allow for the bounds of the interval to be either open or closed and denote these bounds with open and closed brackets, respectively. Thus, we first need to define an ordering between the open and closed right brackets ')', ']' so that the domain of right brackets is itself a lattice.

Definition 9. *(Bracket domain) The bracket domain B is the lattice of two elements ')' and ']' with ordering ')' $\prec_B$ ']'. Any element of B is denoted by '}'.*

Definition 10. *(Simple bounded computation domain) The simple bounded computation domain D is the lexicographic product (D_0, B).*

By Proposition 1, D is a lattice. For clarity we write a} to express (a,'}') in D. For example, if D_0 is the integer domain, then in $D = (D_0, B)$, 3) $\preceq_D$ 3], 4] $\preceq_D$ 7], $glb_D(3], 5]) = 3]$ and $lub_D(3], 3)) = 3]$. Note that $\bot_D = \bot_{D_0})$ and that $\top_D = \top_{D_0}]$.

Definition 11. *(Mirror of D) The mirror of D is the lexicographic product $(\hat{D}_0, B)$ and is denoted by $\overline{D}$. The mirror of an element $t \in D$ is denoted by $\overline{t}$. By Proposition 1, $\overline{D}$ is a lattice. For convenience, we write $\{a$ to express $\overline{a}\}$.*

   Note that if $t_1 = a_1\}_1, t_2 = a_2\}_2 \in D$ where $a_1 \neq a_2$ we have:
(1) $\overline{t_2} \preceq_{\overline{D}} \overline{t_1} \Leftrightarrow t_1 \preceq_D t_2$;
(2) $glb_{\overline{D}}(\overline{t_1}, \overline{t_2}) = \overline{lub_D(t_1, t_2)}$ and $lub_{\overline{D}}(\overline{t_1}, \overline{t_2}) = \overline{glb_D(t_1, t_2)}$;
(3) $\bot_{\overline{D}} = \overline{\top_{D_0}}) = (\top_{D_0}, \top_{\overline{D}} = \overline{\bot_{D_0}}] = [\bot_{D_0}$.
   For example, if $D_0 = \Re$, $\overline{3.1]} = [3.1$ and $\overline{6.7)} = (6.7$, $[5.2 \preceq_{\overline{D}} (3.1 \preceq_{\overline{D}} [3.1 \preceq_{\overline{D}} [2.2$, $glb_{\overline{D}}([5.0, [7.2) = [7.2$ and $lub_{\overline{D}}([5.0, [7.2) = [5.0$.

3.2   Constraint Operators

Let $D = (D_0, B)$ be the simple bounded computation domain for D_0.

Definition 12. *(Constraint operators) A constraint operator (for D) is a function $\circ :: D_1 \times D_2 \to D$ where $D_1, D_2 \in \{D, \overline{D}\}$. Given a constraint operator $\circ$, the mirror operator $\overline{\circ} :: \overline{D_1} \times \overline{D_2} \to \overline{D}$ is defined, for each $t_1 \in D_1$ and $t_2 \in D_2$, to be $\overline{t_1 \circ t_2} = \overline{t_1} \circ \overline{t_2}$.*

Definition 13. *(Monotonicity of operators) Suppose $D_1, D_2 \in \{D, \overline{D}\}$ and $\circ ::$ $D_1 \times D_2 \to D$ is a constraint operator. Then, $\circ$ is monotonic if, for all $t_1, t_1' \in D_1$ and $t_2, t_2' \in D_2$ such that $t_1 \preceq_{D_1} t_1'$ and $t_2 \preceq_{D_2} t_2'$ we have*

$$(t_1 \circ t_2) \preceq_D (t_1' \circ t_2)$$
$$(t_1 \circ t_2) \preceq_D (t_1 \circ t_2').$$

Lemma 1. *The constraint operator $\circ$ is monotonic if and only if the mirror operator $\overline{\circ}$ is monotonic.*

We impose the following restriction on the constraint operators.

Law of monotonicity for constraint operators.

- Each constraint operator must be monotonic.

Normally, a constraint operator $\circ :: D_1 \times D_2 \to D$ where $D_1, D_2 \in \{D, \overline{D}\}$ will be defined by the user or system on D_0 and B separately. The value of $\circ$ on D is then inferred from its value on D_0 and B so that, if $t_1 = a_1\}_1, t_2 = a_2\}_2$ are terms in D_1, D_2, respectively, then $t_1 \circ t_2 = (a_1 \circ a_2)(\}_1 \circ \}_2)$. Then, if the law of monotonicity is to hold in D, it has to hold for the definitions of $\circ$ on each of D_0 and B.

For example, if $D_0 = \Re, 3.0) + 4.0] = 7.0)$ where $)+] =)$ and $3.0 + 4.0 = 7.0$.

3.3   Indexicals

We now add indexicals to the domains D and $\overline{D}$. To distinguish between the simple bounded computation domain already defined and the same domain but augmented with indexicals, we denote the simple bounded computation domain for D_0 as D^s. We assume that there is both a set O_D of constraint operators defined on D^s and a set V_{D_0} of variables associated with the domain D_0.

Definition 14. *(Bounded computation domain) If D^s is a simple bounded computation domain for D_0, then the bounded computation domain D for D_0 and its mirror $\overline{D}$ are defined*

$$D = D^s \cup \{max(x) \mid x \in V_{D_0}\} \cup \{t_1 \circ t_2 \mid \circ :: D_1^s \times D_2^s \to D^s \in O_D, t_1 \in D_1, t_2 \in D_2\},$$
$$\overline{D} = \overline{D^s} \cup \{min(x) \mid x \in V_{D_0}\} \cup \{\overline{t_1 \circ t_2} \mid \circ :: D_1^s \times D_2^s \to D^s \in O_D, t_1 \in D_1, t_2 \in D_2\}.$$

where, if $t \in D \setminus D^s$

$$\overline{max(x)} = min(x),$$
$$\overline{t_1 \circ t_2} = \overline{t_1} \overline{\circ} \overline{t_2}.$$

The expressions $max(x), min(x)$ are called indexicals. *Elements of $D \setminus D^s$ and $\overline{D} \setminus \overline{D^s}$ are called* indexical terms

The bounded computation domain D is also a lattice inheriting its ordering from D^s. Thus, if $t_1, t_2 \in D$, then $t_1 \preceq_D t_2$ if and only if $t_1, t_2 \in D^s$ and $t_1 \preceq_{D^s} t_2$ or $t_1 = t_1' \circ t_1'', t_2 = t_2' \circ t_2''$ and $t_1' \preceq_D t_2', t_1'' \preceq_D t_2''$.

3.4   Interval Domain

Definition 15. *(Interval domain) We define the* interval domain R_D *over* D_0 *as the lattice resulting from the direct product* $\langle \overline{D}, D \rangle$. *The* simple interval domain R_D^s *is the lattice* $\langle \overline{D^s}, D^s \rangle$.

Therefore, for any $r_1 = \langle \overline{s_1}, t_1 \rangle$ *and* $r_2 = \langle \overline{s_2}, t_2 \rangle$, *where* $s_1, s_2, t_1, t_2 \in D$ *and* $r_1, r_2 \in R_D$,

$$r_1 \preceq_{R_D} r_2 \iff (\overline{s_1} \preceq_{\overline{D}} \overline{s_2}) \text{ and } (t_1 \preceq_D t_2),$$
$$glb_{R_D}(r_1, r_2) = \langle glb_{\overline{D}}(\overline{s_1}, \overline{s_2}), glb_D(t_1, t_2) \rangle,$$
$$lub_{R_D}(r_1, r_2) = \langle lub_{\overline{D}}(\overline{s_1}, \overline{s_2}), lub_D(t_1, t_2) \rangle,$$
$$\top_{R_D} = [\bot_{D_0}, \top_{D_0}],$$
$$\bot_{R_D} = (\top_{D_0}, \bot_{D_0}).$$

An element $\langle \overline{s}, t \rangle$ *in* R_D *is* inconsistent *if*
(1) $s \not\preceq_D t$ *(note that this means the range is inconsistent if* $s \not\prec_D t$*) or*
(2) $s = a\}$ *and* $t = a\}$.
Otherwise $\langle \overline{s}, t \rangle$ *in* R_D *is* consistent. *Note that this means that* $\bot_{R_D}$ *is inconsistent.*

A range *is an element of* R_D^s. *A* range expression *is an element of* $R_D \setminus R_D^s$.

For simplicity, $\langle \overline{s}, t \rangle$ will be written as $\overline{s}, t$ for both ranges and range expressions. Thus an element $\langle a\}, b \rangle \rangle$ is written as $\{a, b\}$. As examples of the definitions shown above and considering the real domain we have that $[2.3, 8.9)$ is a range, $[1.4, max(x) + 4.9]$ is a range expression, $[3.0, 4.0) \preceq_{R_D} (1.8, 4.5]$, $glb_{R_D}([3.2, 6.7], (1.8, 4.5]) = [3.2, 4.5]$ and $lub_{R_D}([3.2, 6.7], (1.8, 4.5]) = (1.8, 6.7]$. It is important to note that $\preceq_{R_D}$ simulates the interval inclusion.

3.5   Interval Constraints

Let R_D denote the interval domain over D_0 and let V_{D_0} be a set of variables associated with the domain D_0. An interval constraint for D_0 assigns an element in R_D to a variable in V_{D_0}.

Definition 16. *(Interval constraint) Suppose* $r \in R_D$ *and* $x \in V_{D_0}$. *Then*

$$x \sqsubseteq r$$

is called an interval constraint *for* D_0. x *is called the* constrained variable. *If* r *is a range (resp. range expression), then* $x \sqsubseteq r$ *is called a* simple *(resp. non-simple) interval constraint. The interval constraint* $x \sqsubseteq \top_{R_D}$ *is called a* type constraint *and denoted by* $x ::' D_0$. *A simple interval constraint* $x \sqsubseteq r$ *is* consistent *(resp. inconsistent) if* r *is consistent (resp. inconsistent).*

To illustrate these definitions: $y, x ::' Integer$, $b ::' Bool$, $w, t ::' Real$, and $n ::' Natural$ are examples of type constraints; $y \sqsubseteq [1, 4)$, $b \sqsubseteq [True, True]$, and $n \sqsubseteq [zero, suc(suc(zero))]$ are examples of simple interval constraints; $x \sqsubseteq min(y), max(y) + 3]$ and $t \sqsubseteq (1.21\overline{*}min(w), 4.56)$ are examples of non-simple interval constraints where $+$ and $*$ are constraint operators for the *Integer* and *Real* domains.

Definition 17. *(A partial ordering on interval constraints) Suppose $x \in V_{D_0}$. Let C_D^x be the set of all interval constraints over D_0 with constrained variable x. Suppose $c_1 = x \sqsubseteq r_1, c_2 = x \sqsubseteq r_2 \in C_D^x$. Then $c_1 \preceq_{C_D^x} c_2$ if and only if $r_1 \preceq_{R_D} r_2$. As R_D is a lattice, C_D^x is also a lattice. Note that $glb_{C_D^x}(c_1, c_2) = x \sqsubseteq glb_{R_D}(r_1, r_2)$.*

Definition 18. *(Constraint store) A constraint store for D_0 is a finite set of interval constraints for D_0. The set of all variables constrained in a store S is denoted by X_S. A constraint store S is in a stable form (or is stable) wrt a set of variables $X \subseteq X_S$ if for each $x \in X$ there is exactly one simple constraint $x \sqsubseteq r$ in S. If no set of variables is specified, we say that the store S is in a stable form if it is stable wrt X_S. A store is inconsistent if it contains at least one inconsistent interval constraint.*

Definition 19. *(Evaluating Indexical Terms) For each stable constraint store S for D_0, we define the (overloaded) evaluation functions*

$$eval_S :: D \to D^s, \qquad eval_S :: \overline{D} \to \overline{D^s}$$

$$
\begin{aligned}
eval_S(t) &= t & &\text{if } t \in D^s \cup \overline{D^s}, \\
eval_S(max(x)) &= t & &\text{if } x \sqsubseteq \overline{s}, t \in C^s, \\
eval_S(max(x)) &= \top_D & &\text{if } C^s \text{ has no constraint for } x, \\
eval_S(min(x)) &= \overline{s} & &\text{if } x \sqsubseteq \overline{s}, t \in C^s, \\
eval_S(min(x)) &= \bot_D & &\text{if } C^s \text{ has no constraint for } x, \\
eval_S(t_1 \circ t_2) &= eval_S(t_1) \circ eval_S(t_2),
\end{aligned}
$$

where C^s is the set of all simple constraints in S.

An indexical term is a generalisation of the indexical terms provided by CLP finite domain languages [4] and allow for infinite as well as finite ranges.

Remark 1. (Monotonicity of interval constraints) Note that with our definition of interval constraint we disallow a constraint such as[2] $x \sqsubseteq [10, 20] - max(y)$ by declaring the operator '$-$' as $-::D \times \overline{D} \to D$ since $20] - max(y) \notin D$. This constraint is non-monotonic since, as the range of y decreases (so that $max(y)$ decreases), the term $20] - max(y)$ increases in D (so that the range of x increases). Observe that a range such as $[10, 20] - max(y)$ could not contribute to constraint propagation.

3.6   Execution Model

The execution model is based on a particular intersection of simple interval constraints and on two processes: the stabilisation of a constraint store and the constraint propagation.

---

[2] It is easier to understand this constraint when written as $x \sqsubseteq [10, -max(y) + 20]$.

Intersection of simple interval constraints

Definition 20. $(\cap_D)$ *The intersection in the domain D of two simple interval constraints $c_1 = x \sqsubseteq r_1$ and $c_2 = x \sqsubseteq r_2$ for the same* constrained *variable x is defined as follows:*

$$c_1 \cap_D c_2 = glb_{C_D}(c_1, c_2)$$

Note that this can be expressed in terms of ranges as follows:

$$(x \sqsubseteq r_1) \cap_D (x \sqsubseteq r_2) = x \sqsubseteq glb_{R_D}(r_1, r_2)$$

The following properties of $\cap_D$ are direct consequences of the definition.

Proposition 2. $(\cap_D$ *Properties) Suppose $x \in V_{D_0}$ and c_1, c_2, c_3 are consistent constraints defined on the variable x where $c_3 = c_1 \cap_D c_2$. Then $\cap_D$ has the following properties:*

(1) Contractance: $c_3 \preceq_{C_D} c_1$ and $c_3 \preceq_{C_D} c_2$.

(2) Correctness: Only values which can't be part of any feasible solution, are removed. If $c \preceq_{C_D} c_1$ and $c \preceq_{C_D} c_2$, then $c \preceq_{C_D} c_3$.

(3) Commutativity: $(c_1 \cap_D c_2) = (c_2 \cap_D c_1)$.

(4) Idempotence: The final constraint c_3 has to be computed once: $(c_1 \cap_D c_3) = c_3$ and $(c_3 \cap_D c_2) = c_3$.

If C^s is a set of simple constraints with the same constrained variable, then we define $\cap_D C^s = glb_{C_D}(C^s)$. As a result of the contractance property (1) in Proposition 2 we have $\cap_D C^s \preceq c^s$, for each $c^s \in C^s$.

Definition 21. *(Stabilised store) Let S be a constraint store and, for each $x \in X_S$, C_x^s the set of simple interval constraints constraining x in S. Then, the stabilised store S' of S is defined as follows:*

$$S' = (S \setminus \bigcup_{x \in X_S} C_x^s) \cup \{\cap_D(C_x^s) \mid x \in X_S\}$$

Note that, by Definition 17, if $C_x^s = \emptyset$ then $\cap_{C_D}(C_x^s) = x \sqsubseteq \top_{R_D}$. This ensures that the stabilised store S' of S has exactly one simple interval constraint for each $x \in X_S$.

We write $S \mapsto S'$ to express that S' is the stabilised store of S.

Definition 22. *(Propagation of a constraint) Let c^{ns} be a non-simple interval constraint $x \sqsubseteq \overline{s}, t$ and S a stable constraint store. We say that c^{ns} is propagated (using S) to the simple interval constraint $x \sqsubseteq \overline{s_1}, t_1$ (denoted by c') if $eval_S(\overline{s}) = \overline{s_1}$ and $eval_S(t) = t_1$. We write $c^{ns} \rightsquigarrow^S c'$ to express that constraint c^{ns} has been propagated using S to c'.*

Definition 23. *(Store propagation) Let S be a stable store and C a set (possibly empty) of simple interval constraints. We say that S is propagated to C and write $S \rightsquigarrow C$ if $C = \{c \mid \exists c^{ns} \in S \wedge c^{ns} \rightsquigarrow^S c\}$.*

3.7 Operational Schema

In this section we present as a schema an outline procedure for the execution model. Let C be a set of interval constraints to be solved and let V be the set of all the variables constrained or indexed in C. Suppose $C = C^s \cup C^{ns}$ where C^s is the set of simple constraints in C and C^{ns} is the set of non-simple constraints in C.

Definition 24. *(Solution) A solution for C is a constraint store R that is stable with respect to V and containing only simple constraints where,*

(1) $\forall c^s \in C^s \; \exists c \in R.c \preceq_{C_D} c^s$,

(2) $\forall c^{ns} \in C^{ns} \; \exists c \in R.c \preceq_{C_D} c^s$, *where* $c^{ns} \rightsquigarrow^{C'} c^s$ *and* $C \mapsto C'$.

We provide here a schema for computing a solution for C. Suppose $C \mapsto S$ and $S' = \emptyset$. The *operational schema* is as follows:

(1) *while* $S \neq S'$ *do*

(2) $\quad S \rightsquigarrow C^s$ %% Constraint Propagation

(3) $\quad S' := S$;

(4) $\quad S' \cup C^s \mapsto S$; %% Store stabilisation

(5) $\quad$ *if* S is inconsistent then exit with fail *endif*

(6) *endwhile*

We do not discuss possible efficiency improvements here since the main aim here is to provide the basic methodology, showing how the execution method of CLP(FD) may be generalised for constraint solving on any domain with a lattice structure. If a solution exists, the solution is the set of all the simple interval constraints belonging to S.

Precision. New constraints, created by the propagation step (line 2), are added to the set of constraints before the stabilisation step (line 4). Thus, with infinite domains, the algorithm may not terminate (note that the constraints can be indefinitely contracted in the stabilisation step). To avoid it, we introduce the overloaded function *precision*/1 which is declared as $precision :: R_D^s \rightarrow \Re$. This function must satisfy the following properties:

(i) $precision(r) = 0.0$ if $r = \bar{s}, s$.

(ii) $precision(r_2) \leq precision(r_1)$ if $r_2 \preceq_{R_D} r_1$ (*Monotonicity*)

To allow for the lifted bounds for infinite domains, let Hr be the highest representable real in the computation machine. Then *precision* must also satisfy $precision(\top_{\overline{D}}, \top_D) = Hr$. The actual definition of *precision* depends on the computation domain. For Example:

- On the integer and $\Re$ domains: $precision(\{a, b\}) \Leftrightarrow |b-a|$.
- On the $\Re^2$ domain:

$$precision(\{(x_1, y_1), (x_2, y_2)\}) \Leftrightarrow \sqrt{(x_1 - x_2)^2 + (y_1 - y_2)^2}.$$

- On the set domain: $precision(\{s_1, s_2\}) \Leftrightarrow \#(s_2 \setminus s_1)$.

We overload *precision*/1 and define the precision of a simple interval constraint $c^s = x \sqsubseteq r$ as $precision(c^s) = precision(r)$ and the precision of a store S, which is stable wrt V, as $precision(S) = \sum_{x \in V, c^s \in S} precision(c^s)$.

By defining a computable[3] bound $\varepsilon \in \Re$, we can check if the precision of ranges for the simple constraints in a constraint store S were reduced by a significant amount in the stabilisation process. If the change is large enough then the propagation procedure continues. Otherwise the set of simple constraints in the store S is considered a "good enough" solution and the procedure terminates. The function *precision*/1 and bound ε are user or system defined for each computational domain.

To use *precision*/1 and ε, the operational schema needs to be extended with an extra test by replacing line (1) as follows:

(1) *while* $(S \neq S')$ and $(precision(S') - precision(S) \geq \varepsilon)$ *do*

As ranges in S and S' are contracted, $precision(S)$ and $precision(S')$ decrease by more than ε times the number of iterations of the loop *while*. Thus, there is a maximum number of possible iterations, depending on ε and the initial stabilised constraint store S.

Remark 2. (Some remarks on the precision map)

(1) A range can be contracted whereas its precision does not decrease (i.e. in the real domain, a range $r_1 = [-\infty, +\infty]$ can be contracted to a range $r_2 = [0, Hr]$ whereas $precision(r_1) = precision(r_2)$). To avoid an early termination, an additional test to check a change on the bounds of the ranges must also be added to the while loop condition.

(2) The bound ε allows a direct control over the accuracy of the results[4]. For example, $\varepsilon = 0.0$ for integers, $\varepsilon = 10^{-8}$ for reals and $\varepsilon = 0.0$ for sets. This provides the facility to obtain an *approximate solution* when an accurate solution may not be computable.

We show in the appendix that the extended operational schema has the following two properties.

1. *Termination.* The procedure shown above always terminates returning a fail or a solution.
2. *Correctness.* If it exists, the algorithm reaches a solution and this solution does not depend on the order in which constraints are chosen.

3.8   Improving Constraint Solving on Discrete Domains

We introduce two rules to improve our generic framework on discrete domains in which the *immediate predecessor pre(K)* and *immediate successor suc(K)* of every value K in the domain can be computed. It is possible to eliminate the '(',')' brackets in favour of the '[',']' ones using the following two *range rules*:

$$\{a, K) \equiv \{a, pre(K)] \qquad \textbf{rleft}$$
$$(K, a\} \equiv [suc(K), a\} \qquad \textbf{rright}$$

---

[3] That is, representable in the machine which is being used - the computation machine.
[4] [9] provided a similar idea but only over reals.

If $\perp_D$ and $\top_D$ elements were added as fictitious bounds, we define: (1) $pre(\top_D) \equiv \top_D$ and (2) $suc(\perp_D) \equiv \perp_D$.

As an example, consider the Boolean domain with the ordering $false < true$ and the constraint $x \sqsubseteq [false, true)$. This constraint provides enough information to know the value of x must be $false$. Thus, given $suc(false) = true$ and $pre(true) = false$ and by applying **rleft**, the constraint $x \sqsubseteq [false, true)$ is transformed to $x \sqsubseteq [false, false]$.

As this domain is finite, the constraints could have been solved using an enumeration strategy[5] as is done in the existing finite domain constraint languages. However, by using immediate predecessors and successors, further constraint propagation may be generated without enumeration.

4   Instances of Our Framework

The framework can be used on many different domains. In this section, we present some examples. In the following, $(D_0, \preceq_{D_0}, glb_{D_0}, lub_{D_0}, \perp_{D_0}, \top_{D_0})$ denotes a lattice on D_0.

4.1   Classical Domains

Most classical constraint domains are lattices: $(Integer, \leq, min, max, -\infty, +\infty)$, $(\Re, \leq, min, max, -\infty, +\infty)$, $(Bool, \leq, \wedge, \vee, false, true)$ and $(Natural, \preceq, min, max, zero, \infty)$ are lattices under their usual orders and $false < true$. min and max functions return, respectively, the minimum and maximum element of any two elements in the computation domain. Here are examples of constraint intersection in the interval domain over these domains:

(1) $i \sqsubseteq [1, 8) \cap_D i \sqsubseteq (0, 5] = i \sqsubseteq [1, 5]$

(2) $r \sqsubseteq [1.12, 5.67) \cap_D r \sqsubseteq [2.34, 5.95) = r \sqsubseteq [2.34, 5.67)$

(3) $b \sqsubseteq (false, true] \cap_D b \sqsubseteq [false, true] = b \sqsubseteq (false, true]$

(4) $n \sqsubseteq [zero, suc(suc(zero))] \cap_D n \sqsubseteq [zero, suc(zero)] = n \sqsubseteq [zero, suc(zero)]$

4.2   Reasoning about Sets

$(Set\ D, \subseteq, \cap, \cup, \emptyset, \top_{Set\ D})$ is a lattice over which it is possible to solve set constraints. For example, consider $\{s ::' Set\ Integer, s \sqsubseteq [\{1\}, \{1, 2, 3, 4\}], s \sqsubseteq [\{3\}, \{1, 2, 3, 5\}]\}$ for solving. By applying $\cap_D$ twice, it is solved as follows:

$$s \sqsubseteq [\emptyset, \top_{Set\ Integer}] \cap_D s \sqsubseteq [\{1\}, \{1, 2, 3, 4\}] = s \sqsubseteq [\{1\}, \{1, 2, 3, 4\}]$$
$$s \sqsubseteq [\{1\}, \{1, 2, 3, 4\}] \cap_D s \sqsubseteq [\{3\}, \{1, 2, 3, 5\}] = s \sqsubseteq [\{1, 3\}, \{1, 2, 3\}]$$

---

[5] Possible values are assigned to the constrained variables and the constraints checked for consistency.

4.3   User Defined Domains

Binary Strings. The domain of binary strings $\sum^*$ is the set of all sequences (possibly infinite) of zeros and ones together with $\top_{\sum^*}$. The empty sequence is $\perp_{\sum^*}$. We define $x \preceq_{\sum^*} y$ if and only if x is a prefix (finite initial substring) of y. Note that, in the case, $x \not\sim y$, $glb_{\sum^*}(x, y)$ is the largest common prefix of x and y (i.e. $glb_{\sum^*}(00010, 00111) = 00$, $glb_{\sum^*}(01, 00101) = 0$) and $lub_{\sum^*}(x, y)$ is $\top_{\sum^*}$. Then $(\sum^*, \preceq_{\sum^*}, glb_{\sum^*}, lub_{\sum^*}, \perp_{\sum^*}, \top_{\sum^*})$ is a lattice. This means is possible to define constraints on an interval lattice $\langle \overline{D}, D \rangle$ (with $D = \sum^* \times B$) i.e. $x, y ::' \sum^*, x \sqsubseteq [001 \mp min(y), \top_{\sum^*}]$ defines the interval of all strings which start with the substring 001. $+$ denotes the concatenation of strings.

Non Negative Integers Ordered by Division. Consider $(\mathcal{N}_d, \preceq_{\mathcal{N}_d})$ as the set of non negative integers (plus value 0) ordered by division, that is, for all $n, m \in \mathcal{N}_d$, $m \preceq_{\mathcal{N}_d} n$ iff $\exists k \in \mathcal{N}_d$ such that $km = n$ (that is, m divides n). This defines a partial order. Then any number) $(\mathcal{N}_d, \preceq_{\mathcal{N}_d}, gcd, lcm, 1, 0)$ is a lattice where gcd denotes the greatest common divisor function and lcm the least common multiple function. Thus our framework will solve constraints on this domain as follows: $x \sqsubseteq [2, 24] \cap_D x \sqsubseteq [3, 36] = x \sqsubseteq [6, 12]$.

Numeric Intervals We consider $Interv$ as the domain of the numeric intervals. We define $a \preceq_{Interv} b$ if and only if $a \subseteq b$. Thus glb_{Interv} and lub_{Interv} are the intersection and union of intervals respectively. Our framework solves constraints for the $Interv$ computational domain as follows:

$$i \sqsubseteq [[5, 6], [2, 10]] \cap_D i \sqsubseteq [(7, 9], [4, 15]] = i \sqsubseteq [[5, 6] \cup (7, 9], [4, 10]]$$

5   Combinations of Domains

Our lattice-based framework allows for new computation domains to be constructed from previously defined domains.

5.1   Product of Domains

As already observed, the direct and lexicographic products of lattices are lattices.

As an example, consider $\mathcal{N}_0 = \mathcal{N} \cup 0$ the domain of naturals plus 0. Then $\mathcal{N}_0$ is a lattice under the usual ordering. Note that $\perp_{\mathcal{N}_0} = 0$ and $\top_{\mathcal{N}_0}$ is lifted.
(1) Let $Point$ be the direct product domain $\mathcal{N}_0 \times \mathcal{N}_0$. Then, $Point$ is a lattice. Note that $\perp_{Point} = (0, 0)$ and $\top_{Point} = (\top_{\mathcal{N}_0}, \top_{\mathcal{N}_0})$.
(2) A rectangle can be defined by two points in a plane: its lower left corner and its upper right corner. Let $\Box$ be the direct product domain $Point \times Point$. Then, $\Box$ is a lattice. Note that $\perp_\Box = ((0, 0), (0, 0))$ and $\top_\Box = (\top_{Point}, \top_{Point})$

5.2   Sum of Domains

A lattice can be also constructed as a linear sum of other lattices.

Definition 25. *(Sum) Let $L_1, \ldots, L_n$ be lattices. Then their linear sum $L_1 \oplus \ldots \oplus L_n$ is the lattice L_S where:*
(1) $L_S = L_1 \cup \ldots \cup L_n$
(2) the ordering relation $\preceq_{L_S}$ is defined by:

$$x \preceq_{L_S} y \iff \quad x, y \in L_i \text{ and } x \preceq_{L_i} y$$
$$\text{or } x \in L_i, \ y \in L_j \text{ and } i \prec j$$

(3) glb_{L_S} and lub_{L_S} are defined as follows:

$$glb_{L_S}(x,y) = glb_{L_i}(x,y) \text{ and } lub_{L_S}(x,y) = lub_{L_i}(x,y) \text{ if } x,y \in L_i$$
$$glb_{L_S}(x,y) = \ x \text{ and } lub_{L_S}(x,y) = y \text{ if } x \in L_i, \ y \in L_j \text{ and } i \prec j$$
$$glb_{L_S}(x,y) = \ y \text{ and } lub_{L_S}(x,y) = x \text{ if } x \in L_i, \ y \in L_j \text{ and } j \prec i$$

and (4) $\perp_{L_S} = \perp_{L_1}$ and $\top_{L_S} = \top_{L_n}$.

It is routine to check that the linear sum of lattices is a lattice. As an example, consider the lattice *AtoF* containing all the (uppercase) alphabetic characters between 'A' and 'F' with the usual alphabetical ordering and *0to9* the numeric characters from '0' to '9'. Then the lattice of hexadecimal digits can be defined as the lattice *0to9* $\oplus$ *AtoF*.

6   Related Work

In addition to related work already discussed earlier in the paper, there are two other approaches to the provision of a general framework for constraint satisfaction. These are described in [3] and [1]. We discuss these here.

Bistarelli et al. [3] describe, for finite domains, a general framework based on a finite semiring structure (called c-semirings). They show that c-semirings can also be assimilated into finite complete lattices. This framework is shown to be adequate for classical domains and for domains which use a level of preference (i.e. cost or degree). However, unlike our proposal, they require the computational domain to be finite. Moreover, our framework does not require a level of confidence and, although they extended the approach of c-semirings to finite complete lattices and, in particular, for distributive lattices, they did not consider, as we have done, arbitrary lattices.

One important part of the definition of a constraint solver is the algorithm for constraint propagation and we have provided a simple schematic algorithm suitable for our constraint solving framework. In contrast, in [1], Apt focusses on just the algorithms and describes a generalisation for constraint propagation algorithms based on chaotic iterations. He shows how most of the constraint propagation algorithms presented in the literature can be expressed as instances of this general framework. Further work is needed to investigate the relationship between our algorithm and this framework.

7 Conclusions

In this paper we have defined a theoretical framework for constraint solving on domains with a lattice structure. Using such a domain, we have shown how to construct an interval lattice which allows the use of open, semi-open, semi-closed and closed intervals as well as infinite intervals. Variables, constraint operators and indexicals for each domain provide the tools for constructing interval constraints. We have shown that these constraints are a natural generalisation of the indexical constraints used in [4]. A schema for the operational semantics which is a modified form of the procedure proposed in [8] is also given and the main properties derived from it are studied. This schema is only partially specified making the incorporation of efficiency optimisations easier. To ensure termination, an idea from [9] for controlling accuracy in the processing of disjoint intervals over the reals has been generalised for our interval lattices.

Since the only requirement for our framework is that the computational domain must be a lattice, new domains can be obtained from previously defined domains using standard combinators (such as direct product and sum). We have provided examples to highlight the potential here.

To demonstrate the feasibility of our approach we have implemented a prototype (built using CHRs [7]). This is still being improved and extended but the latest version may be obtained from $http://www.lcc.uma.es/\sim afdez/generic$.

References

1. Apt K.R., From Chaotic Iteration to Constraint Propagation. In Proc. of the *24th International Colloquium on Automata, Languages and Programming (ICALP'97)* (invited lecture), LNCS 1256, pp:36-55, 1997.
2. Ait-kaci H., Warren's Abstract Machine: A Tutorial Reconstruction. The MIT Press, Cambridge, Massachusetts, London, England,1991
3. Bistarelli S., Montanari U. and Rossi F., Semiring-Based Constraint Satisfaction and Optimization. In *Journal of the ACM*, 44(2), pp:201-236, 1997.
4. Codognet P. and Diaz D., Compiling Constraints in *clp(FD)*. In *The Journal of Logic Programming*, 27, pp:185-226, 1996.
5. Davey B.A. and Priestley H.A., Introduction to Lattices and Order. Cambridge University Press, England, 1990.
6. Diaz D. and Codognet P., A minimal extension of the WAM for clp(FD). In Proc. of the *10th International Conference on Logic Programming (ICLP'93)*, pp:774-790,1993.
7. Frühwirth T., Theory and practice of constraint handling rules. In *The Journal of Logic Programming*, 37, pp:95-138, 1998.
8. Fernández A.J. and Hill P.M., A Design for a Generic Constraint Solver for Ordered Domains. In Proc. of *TCLP'98:Types for Constraint Logic Programming*, a JICSLP'98 Post Conference Workshop, Manchester, 1998.
9. Sidebottom G. and Havens, W.S., Hierarchical Arc Consistency for Disjoint Real Intervals in Constraint logic programming. In Computational Intelligence 8(4), 1992.

Proofs of Properties of the Operational Schema

(1) Termination. Let S_i and S'_i denote the constraint stores S and S', respectively, at the start of the of the $i + 1$ iteration of the *while* loop. Then, S_0 is obtained by the initial stabilisation step for C and, for $i \geq 1$, S_i is obtained by the stabilisation step (4) in the $i - 1$'st iteration. Also, $S'_0 = \emptyset$ and, for $i \geq 1$, $S'_i = S_{i-1}$, by step (3). Since both S_i and S'_i are stable wrt V, for each variable $x \in V$, there are unique simple constraints $c^s_x \in S_i$ and $c'^s_x \in S'_i$. By the contractance property (1) of Theorem 2, $c^s_x \preceq c'^s_x$, for each $x \in V$. Thus, at the start of the $i + 1$'st iterations of the while loop, because of the monotonicity condition (ii) for the *precision/1* function, $precision(S_{i-1}) \geq precision(S_i)$. Thus using the extended version of step (1) that allows for a precision test, if there is an $i + 1$ iteration, $precision(S_{i-1}) \geq precision(S_i) + \varepsilon$. Thus, $precision(S_0) \geq precision(S_i) + i \times \varepsilon$. However, for some $k \geq 0$, $precision(S_0) < k \times \varepsilon$, so that the procedure must terminate after no more than k iterations of the while loop.

(2) Correctness. Suppose the procedure terminates after k iterations. (If there are no iterations, then $C = \emptyset$ and the result is trivial.) We denote by S^s_i the set of all simple constraints in S_i, $0 \leq i \leq k$. Suppose S^s_i is propagated to C^s_i so that C^s_i is the set of simple constraints obtained in step (2) of the i'th iteration of the procedure. We need to show that if the procedure does not fail, then S^s_k is a solution for C. We show, by induction on i that S^s_i is stable wrt V and
(A) for $j \leq i$ and each $c^s_j \in S^s_j$, there exists $c^s_i \in S^s_i$ with the same constrained variable and $c^s_i \preceq_{R_D} c^s_j$.

When $i = 0$, then $C \mapsto S_0$ and, trivially $c^s_0 \preceq_{R_D} c^s_0$. Suppose next that $i > 0$. Then $S_{i-1} \cup C^s_{i-1} \mapsto S^s_i$ so that S^s_i is stable wrt V. Moreover, by Definition 21 for each $c^s_{i-1} \in S^s_{i-1}$ there exists $c^s_i \in S^s_i$ with the same constrained variable and $c^s_i \preceq_{R_D} c^s_{i-1}$. However, by the induction hypothesis, if $j \leq i - 1$ and $c^s_j \in C^s_j$ there is $c^s_{i-1} \in S^s_{i-1}$ with the same constrained variable and $c^s_{i-1} \preceq_{R_D} c^s_j$. Hence, for each $j \leq i$ and each $c^s_j \in C^s_j$, there exists $c^s_i \in S^s_i$ with the same constrained variable and $c^s_i \preceq_{R_D} c^s_j$. Letting $j = 0$ in (A), and using the fact that in the initialisation of the algorithm $C \mapsto S_0$, we obtain condition (1) in Definition 24.

We next prove that condition (2) in Definition 24 holds:
(B) for each $c^{ns} \in C^{ns}$ there is $c^s_k \in S^s_k$ with the same constrained variable and $c^s_k \preceq_{R_D} c^s$, where $c^{ns} \rightsquigarrow^{S_0} c^s$.

In the initialisation step for the algorithm, we have $C \mapsto S_0$. Then, in step (2), $S_0 \rightsquigarrow C^s_1$. Thus, by Definition 22, for each $c^{ns} \in C^{ns}$ (and hence also in S_0), there exists $c^s_1 \in C^s_1$ and $c^{ns} \rightsquigarrow^{S_0} c^s_1$. Now, by step (4), $S_0 \cup C^s_1 \mapsto S_1$ so that, by Definition 23, for each $c^s_1 \in C^s_1$ there is $c^s \in S^s_1$ with the same constrained variable and $c^s_1 \preceq_{R_D} c^s$. By (A) we have, for each $c^s_1 \in S^s_1$ there is $c^s_k \in S^s_k$ with the same constrained variable and $c^s_k \preceq_{R_D} c^s_1$. Hence (B) holds.

By commutativity property of $\cap_D$ (see Subsection 3.6), for each $0 \leq i \leq k$, S_i is independent of the order in which the constraints in $S_{i-1} \cup C_{i-1} \mapsto S_i$ were intersected. Thus the solution S^s_k does not depend on the order in which the constraints were chosen.

Higher Order Matching for Program Transformation

Oege de Moor and Ganesh Sittampalam

Programming Research Group, Oxford University Computing Laboratory
Wolfson Building, Parks Road, Oxford OX1 3QD, United Kingdom

Abstract. We present a simple, practical algorithm for higher order matching in the context of automatic program transformation. Our algorithm finds more matches than the standard *second order matching* algorithm of Huet and Lang, but it has an equally simple specification, and it is better suited to the transformation of programs in modern programming languages such as Haskell or ML. The algorithm has been implemented as part of the MAG system for transforming functional programs.

1 Background and Motivation

1.1 Program Transformation

Many program transformations are conveniently expressed as higher order rewrite rules. For example, consider the well-known transformation that turns a tail recursive function into an imperative loop. The pattern

$$f\,x = \text{if } p\,x$$
$$\text{then } g\,x$$
$$\text{else } f\,(h\,x)$$

is rewritten to the term

$$f\,x = |[\ \text{var } r;$$
$$r := x;$$
$$\text{while } \neg(p\,r) \text{ do}$$
$$r := h\,r;$$
$$r := g\,r;$$
$$\text{return } r$$
$$]|$$

Carefully consider the pattern in this rule: it involves two bound variables, namely f and x, and three free variables, namely p, g and h. When we match the pattern against a concrete program, we will have to find instantiations for these three free variables. Finding such instantiations involves the 'invention' of

A. Middeldorp, T. Sato (Eds.): FLOPS'99, LNCS 1722, pp. 209–224, 1999.
© Springer-Verlag Berlin Heidelberg 1999

new function definitions. For example, here is the function that sums the digits of a number, in tail recursive form:

$$sumdigs\,(x, s) = \text{if } x < 10$$
$$\text{then } s + x$$
$$\text{else } sumdigs\,(x \text{ div } 10, s + x \bmod 10)$$

Matching this recursive definition against the above pattern should result in the substitution:

$$p\,(x, s) = x < 10$$
$$g\,(x, s) = s + x$$
$$h\,(x, s) = (x \text{ div } 10, s + x \bmod 10)\ .$$

This paper is concerned with an algorithm for finding such substitutions. Because the construction of these substitutions involves the synthesis of new functions, it is sometimes called *higher order matching*. This contrasts with ordinary *first order matching*, where we only solve for variables of base types such as *Int* or *Bool*.

1.2   Higher Order Matching

Abstracting from the particular programming language in hand, we are led to consider the following problem. Given λ-expressions P (the pattern) and T (the term), find a substitution ϕ such that

$$\phi\,P = T\ .$$

Here equality is taken modulo renaming (α-conversion), elimination of redundant abstractions (η-conversion), and substitution of arguments for parameters (β-conversion). A substitution ϕ that satisfies the above equation is said to be a *match*. Later on, we shall refine the notion of a match.

Unlike ordinary first order matching, there is no canonical choice for ϕ. For example, let

$$P = f\,x \text{ and } T = 0\ .$$

Possible choices for ϕ include:

$$f := (\lambda a.a) \text{ and } x := 0,$$
$$f := (\lambda a.0),$$
$$f := (\lambda g.g\,0) \text{ and } x := (\lambda a.a),$$
$$f := (\lambda g.g\,(g\,0)) \text{ and } x := (\lambda a.a),$$

$$\cdots$$

All these matches are *incomparable* in the sense that they are not substitution instances of each other.

1.3 Second Order Matching

Clearly a potentially infinite set of matches is undesirable in the context of automatic program transformation. In a trail-blazing paper [14], Huet and Lang suggested restricting attention to matching of *second order* terms.

This is a condition on types: a base type (for example *Int*) is *first* order. The order of a derived type is calculated by adding one to the order of the argument type and taking the maximum of this value and the order of the result type. So for example *Int* → *Bool* is second order. The order of a term is simply the order of its type.

This simple restriction guarantees that there are only a finite number of incomparable matches. Huet and Lang's algorithm is the de facto standard for higher order matching in program transformation. In the example shown above, we have to give simple types to our variables to apply Huet and Lang's algorithm, for example

$f :: Int \rightarrow Int$ and $x :: Int$.

Now the only matches found are

$f := (\lambda a.a)$ and $x := 0$,

$f := (\lambda a.0)$.

Note that we do not apply evaluation rules for constants; so for example

$f := (\lambda a.a \times a)$ and $x := 0$

is not a match. Of course there are other second order matches, such as

$f := (\lambda a.0)$ and $x := 1$,

but all of these are specialisations (substitution instances) of the matches returned by Huet and Lang's algorithm. Note that none of the other matches we quoted before qualifies as second order, because there the variable f has type $(Int \rightarrow Int) \rightarrow Int$.

Despite its success, Huet and Lang's algorithm suffers from a number of disadvantages:

- The restriction to second order terms is not reasonable in modern programming languages that feature functions as first-class values. For example, the *fusion* transformation [3] is routinely applied to higher order arguments: implementing that rule via Huet and Lang's algorithm would severely limit its use (see Section 5 for an example).
- Huet and Lang's algorithm only applies to simply typed terms: it needs to be modified for polymorphically typed terms. For example, if we allowed type variables, it would be natural to assign the following types in the example above:

$f :: \alpha \rightarrow Int$ and $x :: \alpha$.

We now have to complicate the definition of allowable matches to prevent α being instantiated to function types such as $Int \to Int$. (It is not impossible however: in [17], it is shown how Huet's higher order unification algorithm may be adapted to polymorphic typing. The same techniques apply to matching.)

- The Huet and Lang algorithm requires all terms to be in η-expanded, uncurried form, which means we are forced to work with typed terms.

The purpose of this paper is to present a new matching algorithm that does not suffer these drawbacks. In particular, our algorithm shares the property that it returns a well-defined, finite set of incomparable matches. It furthermore is guaranteed to give at least the second order matches, but possibly more. Finally, its implementation is simple and efficient.

This paper is an abridged version of a full report [10]. That full report contains detailed proofs of all major claims in this paper, and it also reports on computational experiments.

2   Preliminaries and Specification

We start by introducing some notation, and then pin down the matching problem that we intend to solve. Users of our algorithm (for instance those who wish to understand the operation of the MAG.system [9]) need to know only about this section of the paper.

2.1   Expressions

An *expression* is a constant, a variable, a λ-abstraction or an application. There are two types of variables: bound ("local") variables and free ("pattern") variables. We shall write a, b, c for constants, x, y, z for local variables, p, q, r for pattern variables, and use capital identifiers for expressions. Furthermore, function applications are written $F E$, and lambda abstractions are written $\lambda x.E$. As usual, application associates to the left, so that $E_1 E_2 E_3 = (E_1 E_2) E_3$.

It is admittedly unattractive to make a notational distinction between local and pattern variables, but the alternatives (De Bruijn numbering or explicit environments) would unduly clutter the presentation. In the same vein, we shall ignore all problems involving renaming and variable capture, implicitly assuming that identifiers are chosen to be fresh, or that they are renamed as needed. Equality is modulo renaming of bound variables. For example, we have the identity

$$(\lambda x.\lambda y.a\,x\,(b\,x\,y)) = (\lambda y.\lambda z.a\,y\,(b\,y\,z))\,.$$

Besides renaming, we also consider equality modulo the elimination of superfluous arguments. The η-conversion rule states that $(\lambda x.E\,x)$ can be written as E, provided x is not free in E. An expression of this form is known as an η-redex. We shall write

$$E_1 \simeq E_2$$

to indicate that E_1 and E_2 can be converted into each other by repeated application of η-conversion and renaming. For example,

$$(\lambda x.\lambda y.a\,x\,y) \simeq a \ ,$$

but it is *not* the case that

$$(\lambda x.\lambda y.a\,y\,x) \simeq a \ .$$

Since reduction with the η-conversion rule is guaranteed to terminate (the argument becomes smaller at each step), we have a total function *etaNormalise* which removes all η-redexes from its argument. It follows that

$$E_1 \simeq E_2 \ \equiv \ etaNormalise\ E_1 = etaNormalise\ E_2 \ .$$

The *β-conversion* rule states how arguments are substituted for parameters: $(\lambda x.E_1)\,E_2$ is converted to $(x := E_2)E_1$. A subexpression of this form is known as a *β-redex*. The application of this rule in a left-to-right direction is known as *β-reduction*. Unlike η-reduction, repeated application of β-reduction is not guaranteed to terminate.

An expression is said to be *normal* if it does not contain any η-redex or β-redex as a subexpression. An expression is *closed* if all the variables it contains are bound by an enclosing λ-abstraction.

Some readers may find it surprising that we have chosen to work with untyped λ-expressions, instead of committing ourselves to a particular type system. Our response is that types could be represented explicitly in expressions (as in Girard's second order λ-calculus, which forms the core language of the Haskell compiler ghc [20]). Our algorithm can be adapted accordingly to expressions in which types are explicit in the syntax. However, as with the unification algorithm presented in [16], it does not depend on a particular typing discipline for its correctness.

2.2   Parallel β-Reduction

We now introduce the operation that is the key both to the specification and implementation of our matching algorithm.

The function *step* performs a bottom-up sweep of an expression, applying β-reduction wherever possible. Intuitively, we can think of *step* as applying one *parallel* reduction step to its argument. Formally, *step* is defined by

$$
\begin{aligned}
step\ c &= c \\
step\ x &= x \\
step\ p &= p \\
step\ (\lambda x.E) &= \lambda x.(step\ E) \\
step\ (E_1\ E_2) &= \text{case } E_1'\text{ of} \\
&\qquad\quad (\lambda x.B) \rightarrow (x := E_2')B \\
&\qquad\quad \ \ - \quad\ \ \rightarrow (E_1'\ E_2') \\
&\qquad \text{where } E_1' = step\ E_1 \\
&\qquad\qquad\quad\ \ E_2' = step\ E_2
\end{aligned}
$$

Clearly *step* always terminates, as it proceeds by recursion on the structure of terms. It is not quite the same, therefore, as the operation that applies β-reduction exhaustively, until no more redexes remain. To appreciate the difference, consider

$$step \ ((\lambda x.\lambda y.a\,(x\,b)\,y)\,(\lambda z.c\,z\,z)\,d) = a\,((\lambda z.c\,z\,z)\,b)\,d \ .$$

It is worthwhile to note that our definition of *step* does not coincide with similar notions in the literature. A more common approach is to define a parallel reduction step by underlining all β-redexes in the original term, and reducing all underlined β-redexes. According to that definition, we have for example

$$((\lambda x.x)\,(\lambda x.x))\,((\lambda x.x)\,(\lambda x.x))$$
$$\rightarrow (\lambda x.x)\,(\lambda x.x)$$
$$\rightarrow \lambda x.x \ .$$

in two parallel steps. By contrast, with our definition of *step*, we have

$$step \ [((\lambda x.x)\,(\lambda x.x))\,((\lambda x.x)\,(\lambda x.x))] = \lambda x.x$$

in one step. We are grateful to Mike Spivey and Zena Ariola who independently pointed out this subtlety.

The operation of *step* can be a little difficult to understand. In a certain sense, it represents an approximation of *betanormalise*, the function that exhaustively applies β-reduction: if *betanormalise* E exists then there exists some positive integer n such that $step^n\,E = betanormalise\,E$. However it is not always the case that *betanormalise* E exists, since in the untyped lambda-calculus, exhaustive β-reduction is not guaranteed to terminate.

If E does not contain a λ-abstraction applied to a term containing another λ-abstraction, then $step\,E = betanormalise\,E$. In particular, this condition will be satisfied in a typed setting by all terms which only contain subterms of second order or below. This claim will be further articulated in Section 5, where it is shown that our matching algorithm returns all second order matches.

2.3   Substitutions

A *substitution* is a total function mapping pattern variables to expressions. Substitutions are denoted by Greek identifiers. We shall sometimes specify a substitution by listing those assignments to variables that are not the identity. For instance,

$$\phi = \{\,p := (a\,r), \quad q := (\lambda y.b\,y\,x)\,\}$$

makes the indicated assignments to p and q, but leaves all other variables unchanged.

Substitutions are applied to expressions in the obvious manner. Composition of substitutions ϕ and ψ is defined by first applying ψ and then ϕ:

$$(\phi \circ \psi)\,E = \phi(\psi\,E) \ .$$

We say that one substitution ϕ is *more general* than another substitution ψ if there exists a third substitution δ such that

$$\psi = \delta \circ \phi \ .$$

When ϕ is more general than ψ, we write $\phi \leq \psi$. Intuitively, when $\phi \leq \psi$, the larger substitution ψ substitutes for variables that ϕ leaves alone, or it makes more specific substitutions for the same variables. For example, with ϕ as above and ψ specified by

$$\psi = \{ \, p := (a \, (b \, c)), \quad q := (\lambda y. b \, y \, x), \quad r := (b \, c) \, \}$$

we have $\phi \leq \psi$ because $\psi = \delta \circ \phi$ where

$$\delta = \{ \, r := (b \, c) \, \} \ .$$

If two substitutions ϕ and ψ are equally general, they only differ by renaming: that is, we can find a substitution δ that only renames variables so that $\phi = \delta \circ \psi$.

A substitution is said to be *normal* if all expressions in its range are normal, and *closed* if any variables that it changes are mapped to closed expressions.

2.4   Rules

A *rule* is a pair of expressions, written $(P \rightarrow T)$, where P does not contain any η-redexes, and T is normal, with all variables in T being local variables, *i.e.* they occur under an enclosing λ-abstraction. The matching process starts off with T closed, but because it proceeds by structural recursion it can generate new rules which do not have T closed. In such a rule, a variable is still regarded as being local if it occurred under an enclosing λ-abstraction in the original rule. We call P the *pattern* and T the *term* of the rule. Rules are denoted by variables X, Y and Z. Sets of rules are denoted by Xs, Ys and Zs.

The *measure* of a rule is a pair of numbers: the first component is the number of pattern variables in the pattern, and the second component is the total number of symbols in the pattern (where the space representing function application is taken to be a symbol). The *measure* of a set of rules is defined by pairwise summing of the measures of its elements. When Xs and Ys are sets of rules, we shall write $Xs \ll Ys$ to indicate that in the lexicographic comparison of pairs, the measure of Xs is strictly less than the measure of Ys. Note that $\ll$ is a well-founded transitive relation. We can use this fact to prove termination of our matching algorithm, and also in an inductive proof about its result.

A substitution ϕ is said to be *pertinent* to a rule $(P \rightarrow T)$ if all variables it changes are contained in P. Similarly, a substitution is pertinent to a set of rules if all variables it changes are contained in the pattern of one of the rules.

A rule $(P \rightarrow T)$ is *satisfied* by a normal substitution ϕ if

$$step(\phi \, P) \simeq T \ .$$

The substitution ϕ is then said to be a *one-step match*. Note that we take equality not only modulo renaming, but also modulo η-conversion. A normal substitution *satisfies* a set of rules if it satisfies all elements of that set. We write $\phi \vdash X$ to indicate that ϕ satisfies a rule X, and also $\phi \vdash Xs$ to indicate that ϕ satisfies a set of rules Xs.

The notion of a one-step match contrasts with that of a *general* match in that it restricts the notion of equality somewhat; a normal substitution ϕ is said to be a general match if $betanormalise(\phi\, P) \simeq T$. For convenience we shall refer to a one-step match simply as a *match*.

The application of a substitution to a rule is defined by $\sigma(P \to T) = \sigma P \to T$ (since T is closed there is no point in applying a substitution to it). The obvious extension of this definition to a set of rules applies.

2.5 Match Sets

Let Xs be a set of rules. A *match set* of Xs is a set $\mathcal{M}$ of normal substitutions such that:

- For all normal ϕ: $\phi \vdash Xs$ if and only if there exists $\psi \in \mathcal{M}$ such that $\psi \leq \phi$.
- For all $\phi_1, \phi_2 \in \mathcal{M}$: if $\phi_1 \leq \phi_2$, then $\phi_1 = \phi_2$.

The first condition is a soundness and completeness property. The backwards direction is soundness; it says that all substitutions in a match set satisfy the rules. The forwards implication is completeness; it says that every match is represented. The second condition states that there are no redundant elements in a match set.

For example, if $Xs = \{p\, q \to a\}$, then

$$\{\, \{p := (\lambda x.a)\},$$
$$\{p := (\lambda x.x),\ \ q := a\}\ \}$$

is a match set.

Note that since

$$betanormalise((\lambda f.f\ a)\ (\lambda x.x)) = a$$

we have that

$$\{p := (\lambda f.f\ a),\ \ q := (\lambda x.x)\}$$

is a general match. However since

$$step((\lambda f.f\ a)\ (\lambda x.x)) \neq a\ ,$$

it is not a member of the match set.

In general, match sets are unique up to pattern variable renaming, and consequently we shall speak of *the* match set of a set of rules.

In the remainder of this paper, we present an algorithm that computes match sets. Although it is not part of the definition, the matches returned by our algorithm are in fact pertinent to the relevant set of rules. Furthermore, it can be shown that match sets include all second order matches.

3   Outline of an Algorithm

Our matching algorithm operates by progressively breaking down a set of rules until there are none left to solve. This section does not spell out the algorithm in full detail. Instead, we outline its structure, and give a specification for the function *resolve* that provides the means of breaking down an individual rule. If that specification is met, the algorithm produces a match set. Then, in the next section, we set about deriving the function *resolve* that was left unimplemented.

3.1   Matching

The function *matches* takes a set of rules and returns a match set. It is defined recursively (using the notation of Haskell [4]):

$$matches :: [Rule] \rightarrow [Subst]$$
$$matches\,[\,] = [idSubst]$$
$$matches\,(X : Xs) = [(\phi \circ \sigma) \mid (\sigma, Ys) \leftarrow resolve\,X,$$
$$\phi \leftarrow matches(\sigma(Ys + Xs)))]$$

That is, the empty set of rules has the singleton set containing the identity substitution as a match set. For a non-empty set of rules $(X : Xs)$, we take the first rule X and break it down into a (possibly empty) set of smaller rules Ys together with a substitution σ which makes Ys equivalent to X. We then combine the Ys with Xs, the remainder of the original rules, apply σ, and return the results of a recursive call to *matches* combined with σ.

The function that breaks up X into smaller rules is called *resolve*. Readers who are familiar with the logic programming paradigm will recognise it as being analogous to the concept of "resolution".

Clearly it would be advantageous to arrange the rules in such a manner that we first consider rules where *resolve* X is small, perhaps only a singleton. There is no particular reason why we should take the union of Ys and Xs by list concatenation: we could place 'cheap' rules at the front, and 'expensive' rules at the back.

We shall not implement

$$resolve :: Rule \rightarrow [(Subst, [Rule])]$$

as yet, because that involves quite a long and tricky case analysis. Instead, we specify its behaviour through three properties. Let

$$[(\sigma_0, Ys_0), (\sigma_1, Ys_1), \ldots, (\sigma_k, Ys_k)] = resolve\,X .$$

We require that

− For all normal substitutions ϕ:

$$(\phi \vdash X) \equiv \bigvee_i (\phi \vdash Ys_i \wedge \sigma_i \leq \phi) .$$

- For all normal substitutions ϕ and indices i and j:

$$(\phi \vdash Ys_i) \wedge (\phi \vdash Ys_j) \Rightarrow i = j \ .$$

- For each index i, σ_i is pertinent to X, closed and normal.
- The pattern variables in Ys_i are contained in the pattern variables of X.
- For each index i:

$$Ys_i \ll X \ .$$

The first of these is a soundness and completeness condition: it says that all relevant matches can be reached via *resolve*, and that *resolve* stays true to the original set of rules. The second condition states that *resolve* should not return any superfluous results. The third and fourth conditions are technical requirements we need to prove the non-redundancy of *matches*. Finally, the last condition states that we make progress by applying *resolve*; i.e. that the process of breaking down the set of rules will eventually terminate.

4   Implementing *resolve*

The function *resolve* breaks down a rule into smaller rules, recording substitutions along the way. It does so by syntactic analysis of the shape of the argument rule. In all there are seven cases to consider, and these are summarised in the table below. The intention is that the first applicable clause is applied. The reader is reminded of the notational distinction we make between variables: x and y represent local variables, a and b constants, and p a pattern variable.

X	*resolve* X
$x \to y$	$[(id, [])]$, if $x = y$ $[]$, otherwise
$p \to T$	$[(p := T, [])]$, if T is closed $[]$, otherwise
$a \to b$	$[(id, [])]$, if $a = b$ $[]$, otherwise
$(\lambda x.P) \to (\lambda x.T)$	$[(id, [P \to T])]$
$(\lambda x.P) \to T$	$[(id, [P \to (T\ x)])]$
$(F\ E) \to T$	$[(id, [(F \to T_0), (E \to T_1)]) \mid (T_0\ T_1) = T]\ +\!\!+$ $[(id, [(F \to T_0), (E \to T_1)]) \mid (T_0, T_1) \leftarrow apps\ T]\ +\!\!+$ $[(id, [F \to (\lambda x.T)])]$, x fresh
$P \to T$	$[]$

Let us now examine each of these clauses in turn.

The first clause says that two local variables match only if they are equal.

The second clause says that we can solve a rule $(p \to T)$ where the pattern is a pattern variable by making an appropriate substitution. Such a substitution can only be made, however, if T does not contain any local variables occurring without their enclosing λ: since the original term cannot contain any pattern variables, any variables in T must have been bound in the original term and so the substitution would move these variables out of scope.

The third clause deals with matching of constants a and b. These only match when they are equal.

Next, we consider matching of λ-abstractions $(\lambda x.P)$ and $(\lambda x.T)$. Here it is assumed that the clauses are applied modulo renaming, so that the bound variable on both sides is the same, namely x. To match the λ-abstractions is to match their bodies.

Recall, however, that we took equality in the definition of matching not only modulo renaming, but also modulo η-conversion. We therefore have to cater for the possibility that the pattern contains a λ-abstraction, but the term (which was assumed to be normal) does not. This is the purpose of the clause for matching $(\lambda x.P)$ against a term T that is not an abstraction: we simply expand T to $(\lambda x.T\,x)$ and then apply the previous clause.

The sixth clause deals with matching where the pattern is an application $(F\,E)$. This is by far the most complicated clause, and in fact the only case where *resolve* may return a list with more than one element. It subsumes the projection and imitation steps of Huet's algorithm; in essence, it attempts to write the term T as an application in three different ways. The first and simplest way is to leave T unchanged: of course this only gives an application if $T = T_0\,T_1$ (for some T_0 and T_1) in the first place. If that condition is satisfied, we match F against T_0, and E against T_1.

Another way of writing T as an application is to take (T_0, T_1) from *apps T*. This function returns all pairs of normal expressions (T_0, T_1) such that:

$$\exists B : (\quad T_0 = \lambda x.B$$
$$\wedge\,(x := T_1)B = T$$
$$\wedge\,x \text{ occurs in } B,\, x \text{ fresh}) .$$

For example, a correct implementation of *apps* would return

$$apps\,(a + a) = [\;(\lambda x.x + x, a)$$
$$(\lambda x.x + a, a)$$
$$(\lambda x.a + x, a)$$
$$(\lambda x.x, a + a)$$
$$(\lambda x.x\,a, ((+)a))$$
$$(\lambda x.x\,a\,a, (+))\;] .$$

We require that x occurs in B because otherwise the value of T_1 would not matter: it could be absolutely anything. The most general choice for T_1 would then be a fresh free variable — but introducing such a variable would go against our dictum that the term in a rule must be closed: substitutions are applied to the pattern, but not to the term. We therefore deal with the case of x not occurring in B separately: in that case, all we need to do is match F against $(\lambda x.T)$, and the argument E in the pattern is ignored.

The final clause in the definition of *resolve* says that if none of the earlier clauses apply, the pattern does not match the term, and the empty list is returned.

To implement *resolve*, all that is needed is an effective definition of *apps*. The function *apps* T can in fact be implemented by abstracting subexpressions from T, in all possible ways. This is fairly easy to program, and we omit details.

5   Inclusion of All Second Order Matches

As remarked earlier, our algorithm does not depend on a particular typing discipline for its correctness. However, if we use the simply typed lambda calculus (and run the algorithm ignoring the type information), the algorithm does return all matches of second order or lower, so long as the pattern does not contain any β-redexes. For the purpose of this section, we regard a substitution as a finite set of (variable, term) pairs. The order of a substitution (or a match) is the maximum of the order of the terms it contains.

To show that our algorithm returns all matches of second order or lower, consider a rule $P \rightarrow E$, where P does not contain any β-redexes. (Recall that in a rule, the term E is always normal and therefore free of β-redexes.) Let ϕ be a match between P and E:

$$betanormalise\,(\phi\,P) \simeq E \ .$$

Furthermore assume that ϕ does not contain any terms of order greater than 2. We claim that there exists a ψ in the match set of $P \rightarrow E$ such that $\psi \leq \phi$. The detailed proof can be found in [10].

As we stated earlier, our algorithm also returns some matches which have an order greater than two. We see a rather trivial example of this if we match $p\,(\lambda x.x + 1)$ against $\lambda x.x + 1$; we get the match $p := \lambda y.y$, which is of type $(Int \rightarrow Int) \rightarrow Int \rightarrow Int$ and therefore a third order function.

A more practically relevant example comes from using term rewriting to transform functional programs. The naive quadratic time program for reversing a list can be expressed as a "fold":

$$reverse = foldr\,(\lambda x.\lambda xs.xs \mathbin{+\!\!+} [x])\,[]$$
$$foldr\,(\oplus)\,e\,[] = e$$
$$foldr\,(\oplus)\,e\,(x:xs) = x \oplus (foldr\,(\oplus)\,e\,xs)$$

We can then define *fastrev* $xs\ ys = reverse\ xs \mathbin{+\!\!+} ys$ and transform this to a more efficient linear time program using the "fold fusion" law:

$$f\,(foldr\,(\oplus)\,e\,xs) = foldr\,(\otimes)\,(f\,e)\,xs \text{ if } \lambda x\,y.x \otimes (f\,y) = \lambda x\,y.f\,(x \oplus y)$$

Application of this law proceeds as follows. First the left-hand side is matched with the expanded definition of *fastrev*, giving the substitutions

$$\{ f := (+\!\!+), \; (\oplus) := (\lambda x.\lambda xs.xs +\!\!+ [x]), \; e := [\,] \}$$

We apply this substitution to the right-hand side of the side condition, and rewrite it as far as possible, using the associativity of concatenation. We now need to solve the rule

$$\lambda x\, y.x \otimes (f\, y) \rightarrow \lambda\, x\, y\, ys.y +\!\!+ (x : ys) \; .$$

This is where higher order matching comes in. The definition that needs to be generated is $(\otimes) = \lambda x.\lambda g.\lambda ys.g\,(x : ys)$, which is a third order function (since g is a function). We have applied our algorithm to many similar examples with the MAG system [9]; that paper gives a much more detailed account of the way higher order matching is applied in the context of program transformation. In particular it shows how the above transformation can be done without first needing to express *reverse* as a fold.

Finally, we stress that the algorithm does not find all third order matches. For example, when matching $p\, q$ against 0, we do not get the match $p := \lambda g.g\, 0, q := \lambda a.a$. As we remarked in the introduction, the set of third order matches is potentially infinite.

6 Discussion

Higher order matching allows many program transformations to be concisely expressed as rewrite rules. Two examples of systems that have incorporated its use are KORSO [15] and MAG [9]. The Ergo system is based on higher order unification [21]. Despite the conceptual advantages offered by higher order matching, there also exist very successful transformation systems that do not incorporate its use, for example Kids [23] and APTS [19]. There are two significant objections to the use of higher order matching. First, even second order matching is known to be NP-hard [7,25], so a truly efficient implementation is out of the question. Second, higher order matching algorithms are restrictive, in particular in the typing discipline that they require. In this paper, we have demonstrated how that second objection can be eliminated, by giving an algorithm that operates on untyped terms.

Although there is a clear specification for the set of matches the algorithm returns, it is sometimes not quite obvious why a particular match was not produced. This contrasts with Huet and Lang's algorithm, where the reason for failed matches is crystal clear: it takes some time to gain an intuition of what the function *step* does, whereas it is easy to see whether a function is second order or not. In our experience with the MAG system [9] there seem to be a handful of techniques to deal with failed matches (for instance 'raising' a rule by introducing explicit abstractions), so we feel that the disadvantage is not too serious.

There is a wealth of related work on higher order matching and unification [5,7,11,12,13,16,18,24,25], to name just a few. One important concept identified in some of these works (in particular [16,18]) is that of a restricted notion of higher order pattern. To wit, a *restricted pattern* is a normal term where every occurrence of a free function variable is applied to a list of distinct local variables, and nothing else. For such restricted patterns, much simpler and more efficient matching and unification algorithms are possible. Our algorithm returns all higher order matches for rules where the pattern satisfies the above restriction; in fact there is at most one such match. We have not yet investigated the efficiency of our algorithm in this important special case.

There are a number of specialised *pattern languages* for the purpose of program inspection and transformation *e.g.* [1,2,8]. Often these do not include higher order patterns, and it would be interesting to see what primitives suggested in these languages can be profitably combined with higher order matching.

It remains to be seen whether we can overcome the second objection to higher order matching in program transformation, namely its inherent inefficiency. We are currently investigating to what extent techniques for fast implementation of first order matching [6] can be applied here. Preliminary experiments show that the efficiency of our algorithm is comparable to that of the algorithm by Huet and Lang.

Acknowledgements

Ganesh Sittampalam would like to thank Microsoft Research for its generous financial support. This work is part of a larger effort to realise the Intentional Programming (IP) system at Microsoft research [22]. We would like to thank Charles Simonyi and Will Aitken (both of Microsoft Research) for helpful discussions on the topic of this paper, and its relation to other work on IP. Zena Ariola, Henk Barendregt, and David Wolfram kindly answered our questions, and pointed us to related work. Richard Bird, Tobias Nipkow, and Luke Ong commented on an earlier draft.

References

1. M. Alt, C. Fecht, C. Ferdinand, and R. Wilhelm. The TrafoLa-H subsystem. In B. Hoffmann and B. Krieg-Brückner, editors, *Program Development by Specification and Transformation*, volume 680 of *Lecture Notes in Computer Science*, pages 539–576. Springer-Verlag, 1993.
2. T. Biggerstaff. Pattern matching for program generation: A user manual. Technical Report MSR TR-98-55, Microsoft Research, 1998. Available from URL: http://www.research.microsoft.com/~tedb/Publications.htm.
3. R. S Bird. The promotion and accumulation strategies in functional programming. *ACM Transactions on Programming Languages and Systems*, 6(4):487–504, 1984.
4. R. S Bird. *Introduction to Functional Programming in Haskell*. International Series in Computer Science. Prentice Hall, 1998.

5. R. J. Boulton. A restricted form of higher-order rewriting applied to an HDL semantics. In J. Hsiang, editor, *Rewriting Techniques and Applications: 6th International Conference*, volume 914 of *Lecture Notes in Computer Science*, pages 309–323. Springer-Verlag, 1995.

6. J. Cai, R. Paige, and R. E. Tarjan. More efficient bottom-up multi-pattern matching in trees. *Theoretical Computer Science*, 106(1):21–60, 1992.

7. H. Comon. Higher-order matching and tree automata. In M. Nielsen and W. Thomas, editors, *Proc. Conf. on Computer Science Logic*, volume 1414 of *Lecture Notes in Computer Science*, pages 157–176. Springer-Verlag, 1997.

8. R. F. Crew. A language for examining abstract syntax trees. In C. Ramming, editor, *Proc. of the Conf. on Domain-Specific Languages*. Usenix, 1997.

9. O. de Moor and G. Sittampalam. Generic program transformation. In *Third International Summer School on Advanced Functional Programming*, Lecture Notes in Computer Science. Springer-Verlag, 1998.

10. O. de Moor and G. Sittampalam. Higher-order matching for program transformation (full report). Available from URL:http://www.comlab.ox.ac.uk/oucl/users/oege.demoor/pubs.htm, March 1999.

11. D. J. Dougherty. Higher-order unification via combinators. *Theoretical Computer Science*, 114:273–298, 1993.

12. G. Dowek. A second-order pattern matching algorithm for the cube of typed lambda calculi. In A. Tarlecki, editor, *Mathematical Foundations of Computer Science*, volume 520 of *Lecture Notes in Computer Science*, pages 151–160. Springer-Verlag, 1991.

13. G. Dowek. Third order matching is decidable. In M. Nielsen and W. Thomas, editors, *Logic in Computer Science (LICS)*, pages 2–10. IEEE, 1992.

14. G. Huet and B. Lang. Proving and applying program transformations expressed with second-order patterns. *Acta Informatica*, 11:31–55, 1978.

15. B. Krieg-Brückner, J. Liu, H. Shi, and B. Wolff. Towards correct, efficient and reusable transformational developments. In *KORSO: Methods, Languages, and Tools for the Construction of Correct Software*, volume 1009 of *Lecture Notes in Computer Science*, pages 270–284. Springer-Verlag, 1995.

16. D. Miller. A logic programming language with lambda-abstraction, function variables, and simple unification. *Journal of Logic and Computation*, 1:479–536, 1991.

17. T. Nipkow. Higher-order unification, polymorphism, and subsorts. In S. Kaplan and M. Okada, editors, *Proc. 2nd International Workshop on Conditional and Typed Rewriting Systems*, volume 516 of *Lecture Notes in Computer Science*, pages 436–447. Springer-Verlag, 1990.

18. T. Nipkow. Functional unification of higher-order patterns. In *8th IEEE Symposium on Logic in Computer Science*, pages 64–74. IEEE Computer Society Press, 1993.

19. R. Paige. Viewing a program transformation system at work. In M. Hermenegildo and J. Penjam, editors, *Joint 6th Intl. Conf. on Programming Language Implementation and Logic Programming, and 4th Intl. Conf. on Algebraic and Logic Programming*, volume 844 of *Lecture Notes in Computer Science*, pages 5–24. Springer-Verlag, 1994.

20. S. L. Peyton-Jones and A. L. M. Santos. A transformation-based optimiser for Haskell. *Science of Computer Programming*, 32(1–3):3–48, 1998.

21. F. Pfenning and C. Elliott. Higher-order abstract syntax. In *Proc. SIGPLAN '88 Conf. on Programming Language Design and Implementation*, pages 199–208. ACM, 1988.

22. C. Simonyi. Intentional programming: Innovation in the legacy age. Presented at IFIP Working group 2.1. Available from URL http://www.research.microsoft.com/research/ip/, 1996.

23. D. R. Smith. KIDS: A semiautomatic program development system. *IEEE Transactions on Software Engineering*, 16(9):1024–1043, 1990.

24. J. Springintveld. Third-order matching in the presence of type constructors. In M. Dezani-Ciancaglini and G. D. Plotkin, editors, *Typed Lambda Calculi and Applications*, volume 902 of *Lecture Notes in Computer Science*, pages 428–442. Springer-Verlag, 1995.

25. D. A. Wolfram. *The Clausal Theory of Types*, volume 21 of *Cambridge Tracts in Theoretical Computer Science*. Cambridge University Press, 1993.

Automated Generalisation of Function Definitions

Adam Bakewell and Colin Runciman

Department of Computer Science, University of York,
York Y010 5DD, England.
{ajb,colin}@cs.york.ac.uk

Abstract. We address the problem of finding the common generalisation of a set of Haskell function definitions so that each function can be defined by partial application of the generalisation. By analogy with unification, which derives the *most general* common specialisation of two terms, we aim to infer the *least general* common generalisation. This problem has a unique solution in a first-order setting, but not in a higher-order language. We define a smallest minimal common generalisation which is unique and consider how it might be used for automated program improvement. The same function can have many definitions; we risk over-generalisation if equality is not recognised. A normalising rewrite system is used before generalisation, so many equivalent definitions become identical. The generalisation system we describe has been implemented in Haskell.

1 Introduction

In functional programming we often use general-purpose functions from a library to make our definitions simpler and more concise. Conversely, if we recognise a common evaluation pattern in our own definitions we may wish to add a new general-purpose library function to realise that pattern. This paper is about the automatic creation of general functions. Given a set of Haskell function definitions we find their common generalisation g and a set of embedding equations which redefine each function as a partial application of g.

Example 1.
```
omnivores [] = []
omnivores (a:as) = if eatsMeat a && eatsVeg a then a:oas else oas
                   where oas = omnivores as
teens [] = []
teens (n:ns) = if 13 <= n && 19 >= n then n:tns else tns
               where tns = teens ns
```

We define omnivores to select animals which eat meat and vegetables from a list. It looks similar to teens which finds all numbers in its argument list in the range 13–19. We can define a new function dFilter by keeping the common

A. Middeldorp, T. Sato (Eds.): FLOPS'99, LNCS 1722, pp. 225–240, 1999.

parts of omnivores and teens and introducing new variables p and q where they differ. Now omnivores and teens can be given simpler definitions as partial applications of dFilter.

```
dFilter p q [] = []
dFilter p q (x:xs) = if p x && q x then x:dfxs else dfxs
                       where dfxs = dFilter p q xs
omnivores = dFilter eatsVeg eatsMeat
teens = dFilter (19 >=) (13 <=)
```

Generalisation is a routine part of programming, the original motivation for this work was to provide a tool to assist programmers. Other possible applications include selective generalisation in optimising compilers. This work raises qualitative issues like which generalisation is most useful, as well as quantitative ones such as which generalisation gives the most compact code.

We want a generalisation that is minimal in some sense. In first-order logic a *least-general generalisation* is found by *co-unification (anti-unification)* [13,12]. In a higher-order functional setting we can say g is less general than g' if there is a partial application of g' specialising it to g. The problem with this is g may also specialise to g', neither is less general, let alone least general.

Example 2. We could use the prelude function filter as the generalisation of omnivores and teens. It is less general, filter = dFilter (const True); it is also more general, dFilter p q = filter (\x -> p x && q x).

```
filter p [] = []
filter p (x:xs) = if p x then x:xs' else xs'
                    where xs' = filter p xs
omnivores = filter (\x -> eatsMeat x && eatsVeg x)
teens = filter (\x -> 13 <= x && 19 >= x)
```

1.1 Structure of the Paper

A Core language in which generalisations are inferred is defined in Sect. 2. This restricted syntax makes equivalences easier to identify, so there is less risk of over-generalisation. Further, even within the core language, distinct definitions can be recognised as equivalent by normalisation, Sect. 3 explains the rewrite system used for this purpose and its properties. In Sect. 4 the idea of a smallest minimal common generalisation is developed: Its inference rules are given and its properties are discussed. In Sect. 5 the generalisations produced are evaluated and potential applications for automated generalisation are considered. Related work and extensions to generalisation are discussed in Sect. 6.

2 The Core Language

Core is a subset of Haskell used for generalisation to reduce the number of ways a function can be written. It is similar to Haskell Kernel [5] but lambda or let abstractions are not allowed in arbitrary positions and features to simplify generalisation are included.

$$
\begin{array}{llll}
d \in \mathit{Def} & ::= f\,x_a \cdots x_1 = e \text{ where } \mathcal{L} & \text{function definition} \\
\mathcal{L} \in \mathit{Locs} & ::= \{f_{i,j}\,y_1 \cdots y_a = e\} & \text{local function definitions} \\
e \in \mathit{Exp} & ::= k \mid v & \text{constructor, variable} \\
& \mid\; e\,e & \text{application} \\
& \mid\; \text{case } e \text{ of}\{p_i \to e_i\}[;\, c_j \to e] & \text{case expression} \\
u, v \in \mathit{Var} & ::= f_i \mid f_{i,j} & \text{constant, local function} \\
& \mid\; r \mid y_i & \text{recursive call, local function parameter} \\
& \mid\; x_i \mid c_i & \text{function parameter, pattern variable} \\
p \in \mathit{Pat} & ::= k\,c_1 \cdots c_a & \text{constructor pattern}
\end{array}
$$

Fig. 1. Core language grammar

2.1 Core Language Definition

Core is defined in Fig. 1. Function definitions include *local definition sets*. This allows partial applications, local recursion and higher-order substitutions to be written, whilst simplifying local definition naming and positioning.

Case expressions with simple patterns are included, as in Haskell Kernel. They include a set of constructor-pattern alternatives possibly followed by a default alternative with a variable pattern. This simplifies matters because the ordering of constructor alternatives is immaterial. To convert a standard case expression with a sequence of alternatives we remove any alternatives that can never match. For example, (case x of $\langle 1 \to y, 1 \to z, v \to u, 2 \to w\rangle$) becomes (case x of $\{1 \to y\}; v \to u$).

A sequence of zero or more expressions $(e_1 \cdots e_n)$ may be written $\bar{e}$. A set of constructor-pattern alternatives may be abbreviated A and all the alternatives of a case as AS. So $(f\,\bar{x} = \text{case } k\,\bar{e} \text{ of } \{k\,\bar{c} \to e\} \cup A)$ is a schematic function definition, the body is a case expression with constructor k applied to some expressions as its subject and a set of constructor-pattern alternatives including and whose alternatives include one with constructor k binding the variables $\bar{c}$ as its pattern, there may be any number of other alternatives.

Recursive occurrences of f_i are named r: They will become calls of the generalisation. Other free variables, including mutual recursions, are not affected by generalisation. *Reverse indexing* of function-bound variables makes adding arguments during generalisation simpler: They are added to the start of the argument list so the original can be recreated by partial application. Different kinds of bound variable are clearly distinguished. Case-bound variables and local definitions are uniquely named in a script. Function and local definition parameters are named by position.

Example 3. The Core translation of **omnivores** has case expressions instead of if-expressions and multiple equations. The variable naming and list notation are standardised. The lifted local definition requires the parameter y_1. The recursive call is replaced by r.

$$size(k) = 0 \qquad \text{constructor}$$
$$size(v) = 0 \qquad \text{variable}$$
$$size(e_l\ e_r) = 1 + size(e_l) + size(e_r) \qquad \text{application}$$
$$size(\text{case } e \text{ of } \{a_i\}_{i=1}^{n}; a) = 1 + size(e) + \sum_{i=1}^{n}(1 + size(a_i)) + size(a) \qquad \text{case}$$
$$size(p \rightarrow e) = 1 + size(p) + size(e) \qquad \text{alternative}$$
$$size(f_{i,j}\ y_1 \cdots y_a = e)) = 1 + a + size(e) \qquad \text{local definition}$$
$$size(f\ x_a \cdots x_1 = e \text{ where } \{l_i\}_{i=1}^{n}) = 1 + a + size(e) + \sum_{i=1}^{n}(1 + size(l_i)) \ \text{definition}$$
$$size(\{d_i\}_{i=1}^{n}) = \sum_{i=1}^{n}(1 + size(d_i)) \qquad \text{definitions}$$

Fig. 2. Expression and definition sizes

$$omnivores\ x_1 = \text{case } x_1 \text{ of}$$
$$\left\{ \begin{array}{l} [] \rightarrow [], (:)\ c_1\ c_2 \rightarrow \text{case } (\&\&)\ (eatsMeat\ c_1)\ (eatsVeg\ c_1) \text{ of} \\ \qquad\qquad\qquad\qquad \{False \rightarrow f_{1,1}\ c_2, True \rightarrow (:)\ c_1\ (f_{1,1}\ c_2)\} \end{array} \right\}$$
$$\text{where } \{f_{1,1}\ y_1 = r\ y_1\}$$

2.2   Expression and Definition Size

To provide an abstract measure of the complexity of an expression or definition, its *size* is defined in Fig. 2 as the number of internal nodes needed to represent it as a binary tree. This is useful for comparing generalisations and deciding if generalisation is worthwhile.

2.3   Equality

Core variable naming ensures that corresponding function arguments and recursive calls are identical. Case-bound variables and local functions are uniquely named across all definitions, $e_a =_\alpha e_b$ means e_a and e_b are *equal up to renaming* of case-bound variables. We also assume that where there is no default alternative, (case e of A) $=_\alpha$ (case e of $A; v \rightarrow error$). We need to consider partial equality of case expressions so we define *equality modulo case splitting*, (case e of $A \cup A'; v \rightarrow e'$) = (case e of $A; u \rightarrow$ case u of $A'; v \rightarrow e'$), as $e_a =_{\alpha c} e_b$. For example, (case x_1 of $\{1 \rightarrow x_2, 2 \rightarrow x_3\}; v \rightarrow error$) $=_{\alpha c}$ (case x_1 of $\{2 \rightarrow x_3\}; u \rightarrow$ case u of $\{1 \rightarrow x_2\}$). Equality by definition or *extensional equality* is written $e_a = e_b$.

3   Function Normalisation

There are still many ways to define a function in Core. Showing equivalence is an undecidable problem but we can improve the chances of equivalent expressions having the same definition – and therefore becoming part of the generalisation – by using a normalising rewrite system to eliminate differences of style.

3.1 Normalisation Rules

Normalisation makes distinct definitions identical if they are equal under a set of equivalences. We use local equivalences – no knowledge of free variables is assumed. Obvious extensions to this scheme could make use of axioms about primitive functions or established prelude function definitions.

The rules (see Appendix) are based on β,η and Case reduction [2,5], they are divided into two systems. A rule $l \to_R r$ rewrites a definition (or expression) matching l to r. Side-conditions are used to constrain the definitions that may match l.

The first normalisation system in-lines non-recursive local definitions to expose common structure, partial applications are saturated if possible or specialised (*rules $\beta1$–$\beta4$*). Eta-reduction (*rules $\eta1, \eta2$*) is applied to local definitions, it is defined inductively because an outermost application can be disguised as a case by the equivalence used in rule Case6. Case expressions are reduced to a specialisation of an alternative right-hand side if possible; if not, they are rewritten into a normal form where dead subexpressions can be identified. The merging and floating rules improve the likelihood of similar expressions being kept in the generalisation (*rules Case1–Case9*).

The second normalisation system cleans up the result of the first by removing dead local definitions, η-reducing function definitions and merging case alternatives where possible.

Example 4. The normal forms of **omnivores** and **teens** are shown here. Local definition in-lining and removal have been applied.

$$omnivores\ x_1 = \text{case } x_1 \text{ of}$$
$$\left\{ [] \to [], (:)\ c_1\ c_2 \to \begin{array}{l} \text{case } (\&\&)\ (eatsMeat\ c_1)\ (eatsVeg\ c_1) \text{ of} \\ \{\text{False} \to r\ c_2, \text{True} \to (:)\ c_1\ (r\ c_2)\} \end{array} \right\}$$
$$teens\ x_1 = \text{case } x_1 \text{ of}$$
$$\left\{ [] \to [], (:)\ c_3\ c_4 \to \begin{array}{l} \text{case } (\&\&)\ ((\le)\ 13\ c_3)\ ((\ge)\ 19\ c_3) \text{ of} \\ \{\text{False} \to r\ c_4, \text{True} \to (:)\ c_3\ (r\ c_4)\} \end{array} \right\}$$

3.2 Properties of Normalisation

Proposition 1. *Core normalisation terminates.*

Termination is demonstrated using a well-founded ordering over the expressions. The right-hand side of each rule is lower in the ordering than the left-hand side. The ordering is monotonic – reducing a subexpression reduces its context. A simplification ordering [3] proves termination where rules remove arguments, definitions or alternatives. For the in-lining rules, replacing a (non-recursive) function by its definition is strictly reducing in the ordering, this follows from the typed lambda calculus strong normalisation property.

Proposition 2. *Core normalisation is confluent. The normal form of an expression is the same regardless of the order in which the rules are applied.*

As normalisation is terminating, it is sufficient to show *local* confluence [4]: For all critical pairs of rules (those with overlapping left-hand sides), the result of applying either rule first has a common descendant. For example, specialisation and in-lining overlap. Full in-lining gives the same result as partial specialisation followed by in-lining, once the specialisation is removed.

4   Generalisation by Co-unification

In this section we define a unique minimal generalisation of a set of Core function definitions using a form of *co-unification*. We consider why the usual method for comparing generality is inadequate, then by restricting the kind of generalisation we are willing to allow we develop an alternative definition of a minimum that meets our expectations and is equivalent to the usual minimum in the first order case. This idea is extended to full Core by defining a smallest minimal generalisation.

Definition 1. *Expression Context.*
An expression context E of arity $h \geq 0$ is an expression containing h holes written $[\cdot]$. Such a context is instantiated by applying it to a vector V of h expressions, $[e_1, \ldots, e_h]$, which fill the holes left to right. Expression vectors may be appended by writing $V \oplus V'$.

Example 5.

$$((\&\&) ((\leq) 13\, c_1) ((\geq) 19\, c_1)) = ((\&\&) ([\cdot]\, c_1) ([\cdot]\, c_1))[(\leq) 13, (\geq) 19]$$
$$= ((\&\&) ([\cdot]\, c_1) ([\cdot]\, c_1))[(\leq) 13] \oplus [(\geq) 19]$$

Definition 2. *Generalisation.*
A generalisation of an indexed set of m function definitions, $\langle f_i\, \overline{x_i} = e_i \rangle_{i=1}^m$ (abbreviated $\langle f_i\, \overline{x_i} = e_i \rangle$) is a definition of a general function g and an indexed set of m embedding equation definitions which redefine each f_i in terms of g: $(g\, \overline{x_g} = e_g, \langle f_i = g\, \overline{e'_i} \rangle)$.

4.1   Minimal Common Generalisation (MCG)

The generality of generalisations in first-order logic is compared using the restricted instantiation preorder [1]. In the first-order case there is always a unique minimum common generalisation of a set of terms which is least in this ordering. The ordering can be adapted to a functional setting to give a generalisation ordering that places g' above g when g' can be specialised to g.

Definition 3. *Generalisation ordering.*
$(g \cdots, \langle f_i \cdots \rangle) \leq (g' \cdots, \langle f'_i \cdots \rangle) \iff \exists h \cdot (h\, \overline{x} = g'\, \overline{e}) \wedge h = g.$

Example 6. The functions $\langle f_1 = 1 + 2, f_2 = 3 + 4 \rangle$ can be generalised to $(g'x = x, \langle f_1 = g'(1+2), f_2 = g'(3+4) \rangle)$ or $(gyz = y+z, \langle f_1 = g12, f_2 = g34 \rangle)$. We can define $h\,y\,z = g'(y + z)$ and use h in place of g, therefore $g \leq g'$.

This ordering is consistent with the intuition that g' is more general than g if g' has a variable where g has some other expression. In first-order logic it can be formalised using the lattice structure of first-order terms [10], there is always a unique least generalisation which is the least upper bound of the terms. Analogously, we can define a least-general generalisation, this ought to be the one we choose to infer – intuitively it is just general enough.

Definition 4. *Least-general generalisation.*
$(g \cdots, \langle f_i \cdots \rangle)$ *is a least-general generalisation of a set of functions F if for all other generalisations $(g' \cdots, \langle f_i' \cdots \rangle)$ of F, $(g \cdots, \langle f_i \cdots \rangle) \leq (g' \cdots, \langle f_i' \cdots \rangle)$.*

In a higher-order functional setting, where we can apply the generalisation to functions, there is no unique least-general generalisation. We saw this in the introduction, `filter` and `dFilter` are instances of each other so neither is a unique minimum. We develop a minimal common generalisation (MCG) for a first-order subset of Core where there are no local functions. Generalisations are restricted so that the specialised generalisation must be *identical* to the original definitions – not merely equal. A unique minimum is defined using the idea that all parts common to the original definitions should be kept by the generalisation (and therefore not substituted by the embedding equations). We also need to rule out generalisations that include unneccesary arguments.

Definition 5. *Simple generalisation.*
$(g\,\overline{x} = E[x_1, \ldots, x_n], \langle f_i = g\,e_{1_i} \cdots e_{n_i} \rangle)$ *is a simple generalisation of the definitions $\langle f_i\,\overline{x_i} = e_i \rangle$ if $\forall i \cdot E[e_{1_i}, \ldots, e_{n_i}] =_{ac} e_i$.*

Definition 6. *Common part.*
The common part of a set of expressions, $cp\,\langle e_i \rangle$ is an expression context and a set of substitutions, $(E, \langle V_i \rangle)$ such that $e_i =_{ac} EV_i$. It is defined in Fig. 3. The expressions have nothing in common if their common part is $([\cdot], \langle [e_i] \rangle)$.

When all the expressions are equal up to bound-variable renaming they are the common part (1). When they are all applications 2), the common part is formed as the application of the left common part to the right common part. When they are all case expressions and there are some common constructor patterns (3), the common part is a case expression with the common part of the subject expressions as its subject and the common part of the alternatives as its alternatives. In any other case the expressions have nothing in common and a single hole is returned (4).

The common part of a set of case alternatives is found by cp'. If all the alternatives include a common constructor pattern then a new alternative is formed by finding the common part of the corresponding right-hand sides. A substitution ϕ is needed to make the corresponding pattern-bound variables

$$cp \langle e_i \rangle = (e, \langle [] \rangle), \text{if } \forall i \cdot e =_\alpha e_i \tag{1}$$

$$cp \langle e_{l_i} \ e_{r_i} \rangle = (E_l \ E_r, \langle V_{l_i} \oplus V_{r_i} \rangle) \tag{2}$$

$$cp \langle \text{case } e_{s_i} \text{ of } AS_i \rangle = (\text{case } E_s \text{ of } AS, \langle V_{s_i} \oplus V_{AS_i} \rangle), \text{if } AS \neq (\emptyset; v \to [\cdot]) \tag{3}$$

$$cp \langle e_i \rangle = ([\cdot], \langle [e_i] \rangle), \text{otherwise} \tag{4}$$

$$\text{where } (E_l, \langle V_{l_i} \rangle) = cp \langle e_{l_i} \rangle, \ (E_r, \langle V_{r_i} \rangle) = cp \langle e_{r_i} \rangle$$
$$(E_s, \langle \theta_{s_i} \rangle) = cp \langle e_{s_i} \rangle, \ (AS, \langle V_{AS_i} \rangle) = cp' \langle AS_i \rangle$$

$$cp' \langle A_i; v_i \to e_i \rangle$$
$$= \begin{cases} (\{p \to E_p\} \cup A; v \to E, \langle V_{p_i} \oplus V_{A_i} \rangle), \text{if } \forall i \cdot \exists (p_i \to e_{p_i}) \in A_i \cdot p = p_i \phi \\ (\emptyset; u \to E', \langle V_{e_i} \rangle), \text{otherwise} \end{cases}$$

$$\text{where } (E_p, \langle V_{p_i} \rangle) = cp \langle e_{p_i} \phi \rangle$$
$$(A; v \to E, \langle V_{A_i} \rangle) = cp' \langle A_i - \{p_i \to e_{p_i}\}; v_i \to e_i \rangle$$
$$(E', \langle V_{e_i} \rangle) = \begin{cases} cp \langle e_i[u/v_i] \rangle, \text{if } \forall i \cdot A_i = \emptyset \\ ([\cdot], \langle rhs_i \rangle), \text{otherwise} \end{cases}$$
$$rhs_i = \begin{cases} e_i[u/v_i], \text{if } A_i = \emptyset \\ \text{case } u \text{ of } A_i; v_i \to e_i, \text{otherwise} \end{cases}$$

Fig. 3. Common part of a set of expressions

---

identical. When there are no common constructor patterns, a variable pattern alternative is returned. Its right-hand side is the common part of the expressions $\langle e_i \rangle$ if there are no constructor-pattern alternatives left, otherwise it is a hole and rhs_i is an expression built from the remaining alternatives.

Example 7. Here we find the common part of two case expressions. The common pattern 0 is kept, the common part of False and 0 is a hole. There are no more common patterns so a new variable-pattern alternative is given with a hole as its right-hand side. The first equation is reconstructed by putting a case expression containing the remaining alternative in the second hole, the second equation just puts the expression (x_2/x_1) in the second hole.

$$cp \langle \text{case } x_1 \text{ of } \{0 \to \text{False}, 1 \to \text{True}\}, \text{case } x_1 \text{ of } \{0 \to 0\}; c_1 \to x_2/x_1 \rangle =$$
$$((\text{case } x_1 \text{ of } \{0 \to [\cdot]\}; c_2 \to [\cdot]), \langle [\text{False}, \text{case } c_2 \text{ of } \{1 \to \text{True}\}], [0, x_2/x_1] \rangle)$$

We formalise generalisation by co-unification of a set of function definitions by equilizing their arities then taking the common part of their bodies. The generalisation is formed by dropping a new variable into each hole. For the generalisation to be minimal we need to use the same variable in two holes that are always filled by the same expression for each function. We achieve this by labelling the holes, labelling repeatedly applies *merging* which gives two holes the same label if they always have the same substitution. If the set of vectors $\langle V_i \rangle$ in the common part are viewed as a matrix with a column for each function, merging eliminates any repeated rows. For example, $label((\&\&)([\cdot][\cdot])([\cdot][\cdot]), \langle [((\leq)13), c_1, ((\geq)19), c_1]\rangle) = ((\&\&) \ ([\cdot]_1 \ [\cdot]_2) \ ([\cdot]_3 \ [\cdot]_2), \langle \{((\leq) \ 13)/[\cdot]_1, c_1/[\cdot]_2, ((\geq) \ 19)/[\cdot]_3\} \rangle)$.

Definition 7. *Labelled Expression Context.*
A labelled expression context E of arity n contains h labelled holes, $[\cdot]_L$. It is instantiated by applying it to a hole substitution set $\{e_1/[\cdot]_1, \ldots, e_n/[\cdot]_n\}$.

Definition 8. *Labelling and Merging.*

$$label(E, \langle [e_{1_i}, \ldots, e_{h_i}] \rangle) = (E', \langle \theta_i \rangle)$$
$$\text{where } (E[[\cdot]_1, \ldots, [\cdot]_h], \langle \{e_{j_i}\}_{j=1}^h \rangle) \Longrightarrow_{merge} (E', \langle \theta_i \rangle)$$
$$(E, \langle \{e_{j_i}/[\cdot]_j\} \cup \theta_i \rangle) \longrightarrow_{merge} (E\{[\cdot]_k/[\cdot]_j\}, \langle \theta_i \rangle), \text{if } \forall i \cdot e_{j_i} =_\alpha \theta_i([\cdot]_k)$$

Definition 9. *Minimum common generalisation (MCG).*
The simple generalisation $(g\,\overline{x} = E\{x_j/[\cdot]_j\}_{j=1}^n, \langle f_i = g\,e_{1_i} \cdots e_{n_i} \rangle)$ is an MCG of $\langle f_i\,\overline{x_i} = e_i \rangle$ iff $label(cp\,\langle e_i \rangle) = (E, \langle \{e_{j_i}\}_{j=1}^n \rangle)$. This implies $\forall j \cdot cp\,\langle e_{j_i} \rangle = ([\cdot], \langle [e_{j_i}] \rangle)$.

Proposition 3. *The MCG is the least-general simple generalisation.*

In the first-order case – where we can substitute expressions but not functions – the arity of a simple generalisation can be reduced by merging or the expressions substituted for the same variable by the embedding equations have a common part iff there is a less general simple generalisation.

4.2 Smallest MCG of Higher-Order Functions

Extending the MCG definition to full Core – where local definitions may have parameters (necessary for substituting expressions that include variables) – allows us to compare generalisations that are indistinguishable under the generalisation ordering. For example, filter is not an MCG of omnivores and teens because the embedding equations have a common part – both apply && – dFilter is an MCG . An MCG is not unique. We may need to substitute functions so the holes will be filled with expressions of the form $(x_j\,\overline{v_j})$ and the embedding equations will substitute a function of the variables $\overline{v_j}$ for x_j. Because the parameters to x_j may be reordered or added to without compromising the minimality of the context we define a *smallest* MCG – the generalisation we choose to infer.

Definition 10. *Smallest minimum common generalisation (SMCG).*
The SMCG of $\langle f_i\,\overline{x_i} = e_i$ where $\mathcal{L}_i \rangle$ is the smallest least-general generalisation of the form $(g\,\overline{x} = E\{x_j\,\overline{v_j}/[\cdot]_j\}_{j=1}^n, \langle f_i = g\,f_{1_i} \cdots f_{n_i}$ where $\{f_{j_i}\,\overline{v_j} = e_{j_i}\}_{j=1}^n \rangle)$ where $\forall i \cdot (E\{e_{j_i}/[\cdot]_j\}_{j=1}^n =_{\alpha c} e_i)$.

Proposition 4. *The SMCG is unique up to variable renaming.*

$$smcg\langle f_i\, x_{a_i} \cdots x_1 = e_i \text{ where } \mathcal{L}_i\rangle = \langle g\, x_{a+n} \cdots x_1 = e_g[g\, x_{a+n} \cdots x_{a+1}/r], \tag{5}$$
$$\langle f_i = (r \perp_a \cdots \perp_{a_i+1} \text{ where } \{f_{i,j}\, \overline{v_j} = e_{j_i}\}_{j=1}^n)[g\, f_{i,n} \cdots f_{i,1}/r]\rangle)$$

where

$$a = \max_i(a_i), (e_i' \text{ where } \mathcal{L}_i') = (e_i \text{ where } \mathcal{L}_i)[r\, x_a \cdots x_{a_i+1}/r] \tag{6}$$

$$(E, \langle \theta_i \rangle) = label(cp\, \langle e_i' \rangle) \tag{7}$$

$$(E \text{ where } \cup_i \mathcal{L}_i, \langle \theta_i \rangle, \emptyset) \Longrightarrow_{cpb} (E' \text{ where } \mathcal{L}, \langle \{e_{j_i}\}_{j=1}^n \rangle, \phi) \tag{8}$$

$$\overline{v_j} = sort(\cup_i(x_k, y_k, c_k, f_{k,l} \in FV(e_{j_i}))) \tag{9}$$

$$e_g = (E' \text{ where } \mathcal{L})\{x_{a+j}\, \overline{v_j}/[\cdot]_j\}_{j=1}^n \tag{10}$$

$$(E \text{ where } \mathcal{L}, \langle \{f_{i,j_i}/[\cdot]_k\} \cup \theta_i \rangle, \phi)$$
$$\longrightarrow_{cpb} \begin{cases} ((E \text{ where } \mathcal{L})[f/[\cdot]_k], \langle \theta_i \rangle, \phi), \text{ if } (f/\langle f_{i,j_i} \rangle) \in \phi \\ (E'', \langle \theta_i'' \rangle, \phi \cup \{f_{new}/\langle f_{i,j_i} \rangle\}), \text{ otherwise} \end{cases}$$
$$\text{where } \{f_{i,j_i}\, y_1 \cdots y_a = e_i\} \subseteq \mathcal{L}, (E', \langle \theta_i' \rangle) = label(cp\, \langle e_i \rangle)$$
$$(E \text{ where } \mathcal{L} \cup \{f_{new}\, y_1 \cdots y_a = E'\}, \langle \theta_i \cup \theta_i' \rangle) \Longrightarrow_{merge} (E'', \langle \theta_i'' \rangle)$$

Fig. 4. SMCG inference rules

The SMCG is uniquely determined up to the ordering and naming of new variables x_j and the ordering of their parameters $\overline{v_j}$.

SMCG inference (Fig. 4) is defined in terms of the common part and redundancy removal. First any recursive calls are modified to assumes all the functions have arity a – the maximum of their arities (6). Then the common part of the defining equations is found (7), the labelled common part of the bodies is found by $cp b$ (8) which creates a new local definition from any local definitions with the same arity which are called at the same position. This labelled context is turned into the generalisation body (10) by putting a new variable applied to any variables needed by the corresponding substitutions (9). Any recursive calls in g must include these new variables; the embedding equations substitute a function for each new variable, recursive calls become calls of g (5).

Example 8. The SMCG of normalised *teens* and *omnivores* is g. It is a version of dFilter with the local definition in-lined.

$$g\, x_3\, x_2\, x_1 = \text{case } x_1 \text{ of}$$
$$\left\{ \begin{array}{l} [] \to [], (:)\, c_5\, c_6 \to \text{ case } (\&\&)\, (x_2\, c_5)\, (x_3\, c_5) \text{ of} \\ \qquad\qquad \{\text{False} \to g\, x_3\, x_2\, c_6, \text{True} \to (:)\, c_5\, (g\, x_3\, x_2\, c_6)\} \end{array} \right\}$$
$$omnivores = g\, eatsVeg\, eatsMeat, \; teens = g\, ((\geq)\, 19)\, ((\leq)\, 13)$$

4.3   Properties of SMCG Inference

Proposition 5. SMCG *inference is sound (up to type inference). The embedding equations are exact replacements for the original functions.*

By induction on the *cp* rules, the instantiated context yields the original expression. The treatment of recursive calls in the *smcg* rule ensures the generalisation process is sound. Merging may cause type errors though. The system is not currently safe in this respect, hole merging only when type-safe is left as further work.

Proposition 6. SMCG *inference terminates.*

The presence of local definitions means that the generalisation will not necessarily be smaller than the original definitions as in first-order logic [12]. Without local definitions the complexity of the rules is quadratic in the size of the input, owing to the union and sorting operations needed. Where local definition calls are in the common part, new local definitions are formed from their definitions. Termination is demonstrated by induction on the number of local definition calls in the common part.

5 Evaluation

The generalisation system is capable of *generating new library functions* from examples, we have already seen an example of this with dFilter. We are also able to generate well-known prelude functions from instances, e.g. foldr from list summation and multiplication functions. The SMCG might not always be the generalisation a programmer would like though, even with some normalisation, co-unification is susceptible to differences in style.

Example 9.
```
omnivores [] = []
omnivores (a:as) = if eatsMeat a && eatsVeg a then a:oas else oas
                 where oas = omnivores as
teens [] = []
teens (n:ns) = if n >= 13 && 19 >= n then n:tns else tns
             where tns = teens ns
```

The SMCG of these definitions is different to dFilter because a and n occur at different positions, it seems more difficult to use than dFilter did.

```
g q f h [] = []
g q f h (x:xs) = if (h x (f x) && q x)
                 then x:g q f h xs else g q f h xs
omnivores = g eatsVeg id (const eatsMeat)
teens = g ((>=) 19) (const 13) (>=)
```

Automated generalisation is a *reliable* way of creating new functions, but programmers may be less interested in strictly minimal functions like g in the previous example and prefer generalisations defined in terms of functions they are familiar with. Indeed, as programs are usually written assuming certain primitive and library functions, the generalisations should be much better if the generaliser could work from the same background knowledge. A generalisation system incorporating more heuristics and rewriting its output in terms of prelude functions may be more appealing in this application.

If using an instance of a general-purpose function produces smaller compiled code then automatic generalisation can be used for *code storage-space optimisation*. As a compiler optimisation, our worries about the legibility of the output would not be an issue. Certainly introducing new library functions can make programs more compact. For example, the abstract size of omnivores and teens is 44, the size of their SMCG and the embedding equations is 37. Another set of tests we did looked at finding generalisations of groups of standard prelude function definitions.

Example 10.
```
sinh x = (exp x - exp (-x)) / 2; cosh x = (exp x + exp (-x)) / 2
```

These definitions are taken from the Haskell 1.4 standard prelude. Their abstract size is 20. The size of their SMCG (below) is 17. In a simple application compiled with the Glasgow Haskell Compiler on our machine, the object code size using the original definitions was 332 bytes larger than when the generalised definitions were used. With full optimisation on, the saving was 4,888 bytes. Note that a simple common subexpression analysis could not save any space in this example.

```
g x2 x1 = x2 (exp x1) (exp (-x1)) / 2
sinh = g (-); cosh = g (+)
```

The ad-hoc construction of existing libraries suggests they may contain opportunities for space and structural improvement by generalisation, our tests reinforce this view. Alternatively, libraries could be *tailored* for particular applications. The difficulty in large programs is choosing which functions to generalise. The module system may be helpful in that functions working over the same data type are likely to have something in common. Functions with similar types are also likely to have some common content.

If an interactive editor could *recognise instances* of existing library functions (by generalisation the instance with suitable functions to find one that allows the instance to be defined as a simple embedding), it could give useful hints to trainee programmers. *Finding a library function* by this method would be more reliable than simply using the polymorphic type, as in [14]. Again, we have the problem of selecting which library functions to try.

6   Related Work and Further Work

Generalisation in first-order logic was investigated by Reynolds and Plotkin [13,12] who defined a unique *least-general generalisation* of any two terms, obtained by *co-unification*. Generalisation is the basis for *program synthesis* [16] where rules are inferred from examples. Hagiya [7] uses higher-order and semantic unification to synthesize programs by generalising first-order terms. A *higher-order unification* algorithm is given by Huet [8] which finds a higher-order unifier whenever one exists. A common generalisation always exists, SMCG inference provides a meaningful way to choose a generalisation.

There are many possible improvements to the generalisation system. Recognising more equivalences and using additional rewriting to suit the application have been mentioned. A normal form for mutually recursive local definitions would also be useful; *partial evaluation* [] could be used to specialise such definitions, the call graph could be normalised by selective inlining.

Type safety of generalisation should be investigated so we can guarantee that the type of an embedding equation is the same as the type of the function it replaces. Another potential problem with the current system is that normalisation can change the complexity of definitions. Some other useful improvements are outlines below, they all have the drawback of not giving a unique minimal generalisation.

Repeating generalisation the MCG definition could be interpreted to mean there should be as few new variables as possible. The SMCG is a first approximation to this true minimum. We only replace two new variables by one if one is redundant. In general, one variable will suffice where their substitutions can be co-unified. Repeating co-unification will give a higher approximation to the minimum. In an untyped language we can always find a generalisation that only needs one new variable, in the typed case we are more restricted.

Example 11.
```
mean x y = (x + y) / 2; avg x y = (y + x) / 2

g f h x y = (h x y + f x y) / 2
mean = g (\x y -> x) (\x y -> y); avg = g (\x y -> y) (\x y -> x)
```

By co-unifying the expressions substituted for x3 and x4 in the SMCG of mean and avg we get the generalisation below which needs only one new variable.
```
g f x y = (f x y + f y x) / 2
mean = g (\x y -> x); avg = g (\x y -> y)
```

Generalisation modulo theory E could give better generalisations. In the previous example we could recognise that mean *is* avg modulo commutativity. Equality modulo theory E cannot always be shown by normalisation, so the generalisation rules need extending, though where possible normalisation appears to be a better solution. Unification modulo E has been studied for many theories. Stickel's algorithm for associative-commutative functions is a good example [15]. Generalisation relative to a background theory for atomic formulas has also been studied [11]. Baader [1] defines E-generalisation in the same framework as E-unification.

Promoting embedding equations to be more than passive suppliers of substitutions could give smaller generalisations. Yet another way to generalise mean and avg is to swap the arguments and define mean x y = avg y x.

Unused parameters (for which embedding equations substitute $\perp$) could be used to substitute expressions. This idea is used by Furtado [6] where the co-unification of the terms $\langle x, t \rangle$ is $(x, \langle \{x/x\}, \{t/x\} \rangle)$.

Generalisation is a powerful transformation. Using ideas about program improvement, such as size reduction, seems a suitable way to utilise some of its untapped potential in a controlled way.

References

1. F Baader. Unification, weak unification, upper bound, lower bound, and generalization problems. *Lecture Notes in Computer Science*, 488:86–97, 1991.
2. H P Barendregt. *The Lambda Calculus: its syntax and semantics*. Elsevier Science Publishers BV, 1984.
3. N Dershowitz. Termination of rewriting. *J. Sym. Comp.*, 3(1-2):69–116, 1987.
4. N Dershowitz and J P Jouannaud. *Handbook of Theoretical Computer Science*, volume B, chapter 6: Rewrite Systems, pages 243–320. Elsevier, 1990.
5. J Peterson et al. *Haskell 1.4: A Non-Strict, Purely Functional Language*, 1997.
6. A I Furtado. Analogy by generalization — and the quest for the grail. *ACM SIGPLAN Notices*, 27(1):105–113, January 1992.
7. M Hagiya. Synthesis of rewrite programs by higher-order unification and semantic unification. *New Generation Computing*, 8(4):403–420, 1991.
8. G P Huet. A unification algorithm for typed $\overline{\lambda}$-calculus. *Theor. Comp. Sci.*, 1:27–57, 1975.
9. N D Jones, C K Gomard, and P Sestoft. *Partial Evaluation and Automatic Program Generation*. Prentice-Hall International, 1993.
10. K Knight. Unification: A multidisciplinary survey. *ACM Computing Surveys*, 21(1):93–124, March 1989.
11. C D Page and A M Frisch. *Inductive Logic Programming*, chapter 2: Generalization and Learnability: A Study of Constrained Atoms. London Academic Press, 1992.
12. G D Plotkin. A note on inductive generalization. In B Meltzer and D Mitchie, editors, *Machine Intelligence 5*, pages 153–163. Edinburgh University Press, 1969.
13. J C Reynolds. Transformational systems and the algebraic structure of atomic formulas. In B Meltzer and D Mitchie, editors, *Machine Intelligence 5*, pages 135–151. Edinburgh University Press, 1970.
14. C Runciman and I Toyn. Retrieving reusable software components by polymorphic type. *Journal of Functional Programming*, 1(2):191–211, 1991.
15. M E Stickel. A unification algorithm for associative-commutative functions. *JACM*, 28(3):423–434, July 1981.
16. P D Summers. A methodology for lisp program construction from examples. *JACM*, 24(1):161–175, 1977.

Appendix: Normalisation Rules

Normalisation system 1 rules based on β, η-reduction

$reachable(e) = fix\,(\lambda F. F \cup \{f' \mid f \in F, f\,\overline{y} = e', f' \in FV(e')\})\,(FV(e))$

Assume $f'\,y'_1 \cdots y'_{a'} = e'$ where $f' \notin reachable(e')$ for rules $\beta 1$ to $\beta 4$.

$\beta 1$(**saturated application inlining**)

$\left(f'\,e_1 \cdots e_l\right) \longrightarrow_{\beta 1} \left(e'[e_1/y'_1, \ldots, e'_a/y'_{a'}]\,e_{(a'+1)} \cdots e_l\right)$, if $l \geq a'$

$\beta 2$(**arity-raising base case**)

$\left(f\,\overline{v} = f'\,\overline{e}\right) \longrightarrow_{\beta 2} \left(f\,\overline{v}\,\overline{u} = e\right)$, if $l < a' \wedge \left(f'\,\overline{e}\,\overline{u}\right) \longrightarrow_{\beta 1} (e)$

$\beta 3$(**arity-raising induction step**)

$\left(f\,\overline{v} = \text{case } e \text{ of } \{p_i \rightarrow e_i\}; c \rightarrow e_0\right) \longrightarrow_{\beta 3} \left(f\,\overline{v}\,\overline{u} = \text{case } e \text{ of } \{p_i \rightarrow e'_i\}; c \rightarrow e'_0\right)$

if $\exists j \cdot \left(f\,\overline{v} = e_j\right) \longrightarrow_{\beta 2, \beta 3} \left(f\,\overline{v}\,\overline{u} = e'_j\right) \wedge k \neq j \iff (e'_k = e_k\,\overline{u})$

$\beta 4$(**partial application specialisation**)

$\left(f\,\overline{v} = E[f'\,e_1 \cdots e_l]\right) \longrightarrow_{\beta 4} \left(f\,\overline{v} = E[f''\,u_1 \cdots u_k]\right)$, if $l < a'$

where $\langle u_1, \ldots, u_k \rangle = sort(y_i, c_i \in FV(\{e_1, \ldots, e_l\}))$

$\qquad f''\,u_1 \cdots u_k\,y_{l+1} \cdots y_a = e'[e_1/y_1, \ldots, e_l/y_l]$

$\eta 1$(**eta reduction base case**)

$\left(f\,\overline{u}\,v = e\,v\right) \longrightarrow_{\eta 1} \left(f\,\overline{u} = e\right)$, if $v \notin FV(e)$

$\eta 2$(**eta reduction induction step**)

$\left(f\,\overline{u}\,v = \text{case } e \text{ of } \{p_i \rightarrow e_i\}; c \rightarrow e_0\right) \longrightarrow_{\eta 2} \left(f\,\overline{u} = \text{case } e \text{ of } \{p_i \rightarrow e'_i\}; c \rightarrow e'_0\right)$

if $v \notin FV(e) \wedge \forall j \cdot \left(f\,\overline{u}\,v = e_j\right) \longrightarrow_{\eta 1, \eta 2} \left(f\,\overline{u} = e'_j\right)$

Normalisation system 1 rules based on case reduction

Case1(variable pattern case reduction)

$\left(\text{case } e_s \text{ of } \emptyset; v \rightarrow e\right) \longrightarrow_{Case1} \left(e[e_s/v]\right)$

Case2(case variable specialisation)

$\left(\text{case } e_s \text{ of } A; v \rightarrow e\right) \longrightarrow_{Case2} \left(\text{case } e_s \text{ of } A; v \rightarrow e[e_s/v]\right)$

Case3(case merging)

$\left(\text{case } e_s \text{ of } A; v \rightarrow \text{case } e_s \text{ of } \{k_i\,\overline{c_i} \rightarrow e_i\}; u \rightarrow e\right)$

$\longrightarrow_{Case3} \left(\left(\text{case } e_s \text{ of } A \cup \{k_i\,\overline{c_i} \rightarrow e_i \mid k_i\,\overline{c'_i} \rightarrow e'_i \notin A\}; u \rightarrow e\right)[e_s/v]\right)$

Case4(pattern matching case reduction)

$\left(\text{case } k\,\overline{e} \text{ of } \{k_i\,\overline{c_i} \rightarrow e_i\}; v \rightarrow e\right) \longrightarrow_{Case4} \begin{cases} e_j[\overline{e}/\overline{c_j}], & \text{if } k = k_j \\ e[k\,\overline{e}/v], & \text{if } \forall i,\, k \neq k_i \end{cases}$

Case5(floating case out of case)

$\left(\text{case }(\text{case } e_s \text{ of } \{p_i \rightarrow e_i\}; v \rightarrow e) \text{ of } AS\right)$

$\longrightarrow_{Case5} \left(\text{case } e_s \text{ of } \{p_i \rightarrow \text{case } e_i \text{ of } AS\}; v \rightarrow \text{case } e \text{ of } AS\right)$

Case6(floating apply into case)

$\left((\text{case } e_s \text{ of } \{p_i \rightarrow e_i\}; v \rightarrow e)\,\overline{e}\right) \longrightarrow_{Case6} \left(\text{case } e_s \text{ of } \{p_i \rightarrow e_i\,\overline{e}\}; v \rightarrow e\,\overline{e}\right)$

Case7(dead alternative elimination)

$\left(\text{case } e_s \text{ of } \{k\,\overline{v} \rightarrow e\} \cup A; v \rightarrow E\left[\text{case } e'_s \text{ of } \{k\,\overline{u} \rightarrow e''\} \cup A'; a\right]\right)$

$\longrightarrow_{Case7} \left(\text{case } e_s \text{ of } \{k\,\overline{v} \rightarrow e\} \cup A; v \rightarrow E\left[\text{case } e'_s \text{ of } A'; a\right]\right)$, if $e_s =_\alpha e'_s$

Case8(repeated computation elimination)

$\left(\text{case } e_s \text{ of } \{p \rightarrow e\} \cup A; a\right) \longrightarrow_{Case8} \left(\text{case } e_s \text{ of } \{p \rightarrow e[p/e_s]\} \cup A; a\right)$

Case9(variable pattern simplification)

$$\left(\text{case } e_s \text{ of } A; v \to e\right) \longrightarrow_{Case9} \begin{cases} \text{case } e_s \text{ of } A \cup \{k\,\bar{c} \to e[k\,\bar{c}/v]\}, \text{ if } U = \{k\} \\ \text{case } e_s \text{ of } A, \text{ if } U = \emptyset \end{cases}$$

where $U = \{\text{constructors } k \text{ of type } \tau(e_s) \mid (k\,\bar{c} \to e) \notin A\}$

Normalisation system 2 rules

$\beta5$(local definition elimination)

$(e \text{ where } \mathcal{L}) \longrightarrow_{\beta5} (e \text{ where } \{(f \cdots) \in \mathcal{L} \mid f \in \text{reachable}(e)\})$

Case10(redundant alternative elimination)

$(\text{case } e_s \text{ of } \{p \to e\} \cup A; v \to e')$

$$\longrightarrow_{Case10} \begin{cases} \text{case } e_s \text{ of } A; v \to e', \text{ if } e =_\alpha e' \wedge A \neq \emptyset \\ \text{case } e_s \text{ of } \{p_0 \to e\}; v \to e', \text{ if } e =_\alpha e' \wedge A = \emptyset \end{cases}$$

where p_0 is the least constructor of type $\tau(e_s)$

An Extensional Characterization
of Lambda-Lifting and Lambda-Dropping

Olivier Danvy

BRICS - Centre of the Danish National Research Foundation
Department of Computer Science, University of Aarhus
Building 540, Ny Munkegade, DK-8000 Aarhus C, Denmark
danvy@brics.dk
www.brics.dk

Abstract. Lambda-lifting and lambda-dropping respectively transform
a block-structured functional program into recursive equations and vice
versa. Lambda-lifting was developed in the early 80's, whereas lambda-
dropping is more recent. Both are split into an analysis and a transformation. Published work, however, has only concentrated on the analysis
parts. We focus here on the transformation parts and more precisely on
their correctness, which appears never to have been proven. To this end,
we define extensional versions of lambda-lifting and lambda-dropping
and establish their correctness with respect to a least fixed-point semantics.

1   Introduction and Motivation

If procedural programming languages are out of the Turing tar pit today, it
is largely due to the expressive power induced by block structure and lexical
scope. However block structure and lexical scope are not essential: in the mid
80's, Hughes, Johnsson, and Peyton Jones showed how to *lambda-lift* any block-
structured program into recursive equations, which can then be efficiently compiled on the G-machine [5,6,9]. Since then, lambda-lifting has had its ups and
downs: it is used for example in at least one compiler and two partial eval-
uators for the Scheme programming language [1,2,3]; in an unpublished note,
"Down with Lambda-Lifting" [7], Meijer severely criticizes it; and it is no longer
systematically used to compile Haskell programs today [8]. In all cases, lambda-
lifting is considered as an intermediate transformation in a compiler or a partial
evaluator.

Our own stab at lambda-lifting is linguistic. We are interested in programming and in the expressive power induced by block structure and lexical scope,
which lambda-lifting eliminates. This led us to devise an inverse transformation to *lambda-drop* recursive equations into a block-structured, lexically scoped
program. Lambda-dropping was reported at PEPM'97 jointly with Schultz and
implemented as the back-end of a partial evaluator [4,10]. In that joint work,
we tried to emphasize the symmetric aspects of lambda-lifting and lambda-
dropping:

A. Middeldorp, T. Sato (Eds.): FLOPS'99, LNCS 1722, pp. 241–250, 1999.
© Springer-Verlag Berlin Heidelberg 1999

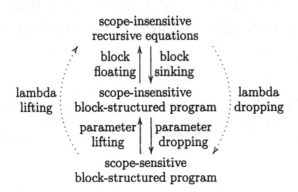

Let us start from a block-structured program. A priori, this program contains free variables and is thus scope-sensitive. To make it scope-insensitive, we pass extra parameters to each of its locally defined functions. These extra parameters account for the free variables of each function. Once the program is scope-insensitive, we globalize each block by making it float to the top level and defining each of its locally defined functions as a global recursive equation.[1] Conversely, lambda-dropping requires us to group recursive equations into blocks and make these blocks sink in the corresponding recursive equation, following the edges of the source call graph. The resulting program is block-structured but scope insensitive, except for the names of the (ex-)recursive equations, of course. We make it scope sensitive by preventing each function from passing variables whose end use is lexically visible.

A simple example: Figure 1 displays the power function in ML. Many other examples exist [2,4,5,6,9,10] but this one is simple and illustrative enough. One of its parameters is "inert," i.e., it does not change through the recursive calls. The lambda-lifted version carries the inert argument through each recursive call. The lambda-dropped version does not, making it instead a free variable in the actual traversal of the other argument. Lambda-lifting and lambda-dropping transform one definition into the other and vice-versa.

The anatomy of lambda-lifting and lambda-dropping: Both naturally split into an *analysis* and a *transformation*. Leaving aside block-sinking, which is specific to lambda-dropping, the analysis determines which parameters can be lifted and which parameters can be dropped.

It is however a fact that most of the work in lambda-lifting and lambda-dropping has concentrated on its analysis and neglected its transformation. Both at PEPM'97 and at a meeting of the IFIP Working Group on Functional Programming in June 1997, we ventured that the correctness of lambda-lifting was still an open problem and there was a general agreement that it was so.

---

[1] Incidentally, we favor Johnsson's style of lambda-lifting [6], where recursive equations are named and names of recursive equations are free in their bodies. This makes it possible to see them as mutually recursive top-level functions in a functional programming language.

```
fun power_l (base, 0) = 1
  | power_l (base, expo) = base * (power_l (base, expo - 1))
(* power_l : int * int -> int *)

fun power_d (base, expo)
    = let fun loop 0 = 1
            | loop expo = base * (loop (expo - 1))
      in loop expo
      end (* loop : int -> int *)
(* power_d : int * int -> int *)
```

Fig. 1. λ-lifted and λ-dropped versions of the power function

Our goal: We address parameter lifting and dropping and their formal correctness. More precisely, we want to know whether a lambda-lifted program and the corresponding lambda-dropped program compute the same function.

Our means: We consider the meanings of the lambda-lifted and the lambda-dropped programs in a least-fixed point semantics [11]. Using fixed-point induction, we prove that the lambda-lifted version and the lambda-dropped version of **power** compute the same function.

Our point: We generalize this example and introduce *extensional versions* of lambda-lifting and lambda-dropping, i.e.,

Extensional lambda-lifting: a type-indexed mapping from the functional associated to a lambda-dropped function to the functional associated to the corresponding lambda-lifted function; and

Extensional lambda-dropping: a type-indexed mapping from the functional associated to a lambda-lifted function to the functional associated to the corresponding lambda-dropped function.

Overview: In Section 2, we present two extensional, type-indexed transformations respectively lambda-lifting and lambda-dropping a functional, and we show that the input and the output functionals share the same fixed point. These extensional transformations assume that one knows which parameter(s) to lift or to drop. In Section 3, we scale up extensional lambda-lifting and lambda-dropping to mutually recursive functions. Section 4 concludes.

2   Extensional Lambda-Lifting and Lambda-Dropping

Lambda-lifting and lambda-dropping are defined intensionally, i.e., they are textual transformations. Could we define their extensional counterparts, that we could apply to the corresponding meanings instead of to their text? We answer positively to this question by exhibiting two mappings between the functional corresponding to the lambda-dropped version of a function and the functional corresponding to its lambda-lifted counterpart.

2.1   Extensional Lambda-Lifting

Let us define an extensional lambda-lifter for unary functionals abstracted by a dropped parameter. The lambda-lifter lifts the abstracted parameter in first position in the resulting uncurried binary functional.

Definition 1. *Let A, B, and X denote pointed CPOs.*

$$\text{lift}_1 : (X \to (A \to B) \to A \to B) \to (X \times A \to B) \to X \times A \to B$$
$$\text{lift}_1 \, F \, f \, \langle x, a \rangle = F \, x \, (\lambda a'.f \, \langle x, a' \rangle) \, a$$

This extensional version makes it possible to lambda-lift a functional prior to taking its fixed point.

Theorem 1 (lambda-lifting). *Let A, B, and X denote pointed CPOs and let $F \in X \to (A \to B) \to A \to B$. Then for any $x \in X$ and $a \in A$,*

$$\textit{fix}_{A \to B} \, (F \, x) \, a = \textit{fix}_{X \times A \to B} \, (\text{lift}_1 \, F) \, \langle x, a \rangle.$$

Proof. By fixed-point induction. Let us define R_x as an X-indexed family of admissible relations between $A \to B$ and $X \times A \to B$:

$$R_x = \{(d, \ell) \mid \forall a \in A.d \, a = \ell \, \langle x, a \rangle\}$$

Each R_x is pointed (contains $(\perp_{A \to B}, \perp_{X \times A \to B})$) and admissible (it is defined as an intersection of inverse images by (continuous) application functions of the admissible equality relation). Now $\forall x \in X$ and $\forall (d, \ell) \in R_x$,

$$(F \, x \, d, \text{lift}_1 \, F \, \ell) \in R_x$$

since $\forall a \in A$, $\text{lift}_1 \, F \, \ell \, \langle x, a \rangle = F \, x \, (\lambda a'.\ell \, \langle x, a' \rangle) \, a$
$$= F \, x \, (\lambda a'.d \, a') \, a$$
$$= F \, x \, d \, a$$

Therefore, by fixed-point induction, the least fixed points of the two functions are also related, i.e.,

$$(\text{fix}_{A \to B} \, F \, x, \text{fix}_{X \times A \to B} \, (\text{lift}_1 \, F)) \in R_x$$

which, expanding the definition of R_x, is precisely what we wanted to prove. $\square$

Similarly, we can define an extensional lambda-lifter that lifts the abstracted parameter in second position in the resulting uncurried binary functional.

Definition 2. *Let A, B, and X denote pointed CPOs.*

$$\text{lift}_2 : (X \to (A \to B) \to A \to B) \to (A \times X \to B) \to A \times X \to B$$
$$\text{lift}_2 \, F \, f \, \langle a, x \rangle = F \, x \, (\lambda a'.f \, \langle a', x \rangle) \, a$$

2.2   Extensional Lambda-Dropping

We now turn to defining an extensional lambda-dropper for uncurried binary functionals. The lambda-dropper drops the first parameter of the functional, assuming it to be inert.

Definition 3. $F : (A \times X \to B) \to A \times X \to B$ *is inert in* X *if and only if* $\forall f \in A \times X \to B$, $\forall x \in X$, *and* $\forall a \in A$,

$$F\left(\lambda\langle x', a'\rangle.f\left\langle x, a'\right\rangle\right)\langle x, a\rangle = F\left(\lambda\langle x', a'\rangle.f\left\langle x', a'\right\rangle\right)\langle x, a\rangle$$

Definition 4. *Let* A, B, *and* X *denote pointed CPOs.*

$$\mathrm{drop}_1 : ((X \times A \to B) \to X \times A \to B) \to X \to (A \to B) \to A \to B$$
$$\mathrm{drop}_1\, F\, x\, f\, a = F\left(\lambda\langle x, a'\rangle.f\, a'\right)\langle x, a\rangle$$

This extensional version makes it possible to lambda-drop a functional prior to taking its fixed point.

Theorem 2 (lambda-dropping). *Let* A, B, *and* X *denote pointed CPOs and let* $F \in (X \times A \to B) \to X \times A \to B$ *be inert in* X. *Then for any* $x \in X$ *and* $a \in A$,

$$\mathit{fix}_{X \times A \to B}\, F\, \langle x, a\rangle = \mathit{fix}_{A \to B}\, (\mathrm{drop}_1\, F\, x)\, a.$$

Proof. By fixed-point induction. Let us define R_x as an X-indexed family of admissible relations between $X \times A \to B$ and $A \to B$:

$$R_x = \{(\ell, d) \mid \forall a \in A.\ell\,\langle x, a\rangle = d\,a\}$$

Each R_x is pointed and admissible. Now $\forall x \in X$ and $\forall(\ell, d) \in R_x$,

$$(F\,\ell,\, \mathrm{drop}_1\, F\, x\, d) \in R_x$$

since $\forall a \in A$, $\mathrm{drop}_1\, F\, x\, d\, a = F\left(\lambda\langle x', a'\rangle.d\,a'\right)\langle x, a\rangle$

$$\begin{aligned}
&= F\left(\lambda\langle x', a'\rangle.\ell\,(x, a')\right)\langle x, a\rangle\\
&= F\left(\lambda\langle x', a'\rangle.\ell\,(x', a')\right)\langle x, a\rangle \text{ since } F \text{ is inert in } X\\
&= F\,\ell\,\langle x, a\rangle
\end{aligned}$$

Therefore, by fixed-point induction, the least fixed points of the two functions are also related, i.e.,

$$(\mathit{fix}_{X \times A \to B}\, F,\, \mathit{fix}_{A \to B}\, (\mathrm{drop}_1\, F\, x)) \in R_x$$

which is what we wanted to prove.   □

Similarly, we can define an extensional lambda-dropper that drops the second parameter of an uncurried binary functional, assuming it to be inert.

Definition 5. *Let* A, B, *and* X *denote pointed CPOs.*

$$\mathrm{drop}_1 : ((A \times X \to B) \to A \times X \to B) \to X \to (A \to B) \to A \to B$$
$$\mathrm{drop}_1\, F\, x\, f\, a = F\left(\lambda\langle a', x\rangle.f\, a'\right)\langle a, x\rangle$$

```
signature LIFT2
= sig
    val lift1 : ('e -> (('a -> 'b) * ('c -> 'd) -> 'a -> 'b) *
                        (('a -> 'b) * ('c -> 'd) -> 'c -> 'd)) ->
                (('e * 'a -> 'b) * ('e * 'c -> 'd) ->
                 'e * 'a -> 'b) *
                (('e * 'a -> 'b) * ('e * 'c -> 'd) ->
                 'e * 'c -> 'd)
  end
structure Lift2 : LIFT2
= struct
    fun lift1 F
        = (fn (f,g) => fn (x1, x2) => let val (F1,F2) = F x1
                                      in F1 (fn a2 => f (x1, a2),
                                             fn a2 => g (x1, a2)) x2
                                      end,
           fn (f,g) => fn (x1, x2) => let val (F1,F2) = F x1
                                      in F2 (fn a2 => f (x1, a2),
                                             fn a2 => g (x1, a2)) x2
                                      end)
  end
```

Fig. 2. Extensional lambda-lifting for mutually recursive functions

```
signature DROP2
= sig
    val drop1 : (('e * 'a -> 'b) * ('e * 'c -> 'd) ->
                 'e * 'a -> 'b) *
                (('e * 'a -> 'b) * ('e * 'c -> 'd) ->
                 'e * 'c -> 'd) ->
                'e -> (('a -> 'b) * ('c -> 'd) -> 'a -> 'b) *
                      (('a -> 'b) * ('c -> 'd) -> 'c -> 'd)
  end
structure Drop2 : DROP2
= struct
    fun drop1 (F1, F2) x1
        = (fn (f, g) => fn x2 => F1 (fn (a1, a2) => f a2,
                                     fn (a1, a2) => g a2) (x1, x2),
           fn (f, g) => fn x2 => F2 (fn (a1, a2) => f a2,
                                     fn (a1, a2) => g a2) (x1, x2))
  end
```

Fig. 3. Extensional lambda-dropping for mutually recursive functions

```
signature FIX2
= sig
    val fix : (('a -> 'b) * ('c -> 'd) -> 'a -> 'b) *
              (('a -> 'b) * ('c -> 'd) -> 'c -> 'd) ->
              ('a -> 'b) * ('c -> 'd)
  end
structure Fix2 : FIX2
= struct
    fun fix (f1, f2)
        = (fn a1 => f1 (fix (f1, f2)) a1,
           fn a2 => f2 (fix (f1, f2)) a2)
  end
```

Fig. 4. Applicative-order fixed-point operator for pairs of functionals

2.3   Inverseness Properties

It is a simple matter to check that $drop_1 \circ lift_1 = $ identity and that $lift_1 \circ drop_1 =$ identity over functionals that are inert in their first parameter.

3   Scaling up to Mutual Recursion

Extensional lambda-lifting and lambda-dropping scale up to mutual recursion, along the lines of Section 2.

For the record, Figure 2 displays an extensional lambda-lifter for a pair of unary functionals abstracted by a dropped parameter, using ML as a meta-language. The lambda-lifter lifts the abstracted parameter in first position in the resulting pair of uncurried binary functionals. Similarly, Figure 3 displays an extensional lambda-dropper for a pair of uncurried binary functionals. The lambda-dropper drops the first parameter of the two functionals. The dropped parameter is assumed to be inert.

These pairs of functionals require a fixed-point operator such as the one in Figure 4.

For example, here is a lambda-dropped pair of functionals computing the parity of a non-negative integer. Their fixed point is the pair of mutually recursive functions **even** and **odd**, parameterized with the value to test for the base case.

```
val mkFodd_even_d
    = fn b => (fn (ev, od) => fn n => (n = b) orelse od (n - 1),
               fn (ev, od) => fn n => (n > b) andalso ev (n - 1))
(*
  mkFodd_even_d : int -> ('a * (int -> bool) -> int -> bool) *
                         ((int -> bool) * 'b -> int -> bool)
*)
```

The corresponding two lambda-dropped parity functions are obtained by instantiating the base value and taking the fixed point of the result:

```
val (even_d, odd_d)
    = Fix2.fix (mkFodd_even_d 0)
(*
  even_d : int -> bool
  odd_d : int -> bool
*)
```

Applying `Lift2.lift1` to the lambda-dropped pair of functionals yields the corresponding lambda-lifted pair of functionals:

```
val Fodd_even_1
    = Lift2.lift1 mkFodd_even_d
(*
  Fodd_even_1 : ((int * int -> bool) * (int * int -> bool) ->
                    int * int -> bool) *
                ((int * int -> bool) * (int * int -> bool) ->
                    int * int -> bool)
*)
```

And indeed, simplifying `Lift2.lift1 Fodd_even_d` yields:

```
(fn (ev, od) => fn (b, n) => (n = b) orelse od (b, n - 1),
 fn (ev, od) => fn (b, n) => (n > b) andalso ev (b, n - 1))
```

which is lambda-lifted.

We obtain two mutually recursive lambda-lifted functions by taking the fixed point of this pair. Instantiating their first argument yields the parity functions:

```
val (even_1, odd_1)
    = let val (even_aux, odd_aux) = Fix2.fix Fodd_even_1
      in (fn n => even_aux (0, n), fn n => odd_aux (0, n))
      end
(*
  even_1 : int -> bool
  odd_1 : int -> bool
*)
```

Finally, applying `Drop2.drop1` to the lambda-lifted pair of functionals yields a lambda-dropped pair of functionals which is extensionally equivalent to the original lambda-dropped pair of functionals.

```
val mkFodd_even_d'
    = Drop2.drop1 Fodd_even_1
(*
  mkFodd_even_d' : int -> ((int -> bool) * (int -> bool) ->
                              int -> bool) *
                          ((int -> bool) * (int -> bool) ->
                              int -> bool)
*)
```

4 Conclusion

Over the last ten years, only the analysis part of lambda-lifting and lambda-dropping have been investigated. Establishing the formal correctness of their transformation appeared to be still an open problem. We have introduced extensional versions of lambda-lifting and lambda-dropping to address this problem. For the sake of expository concision, we have concentrated on single recursive functions and only informally outlined how the approach scales up to mutually recursive functions.

Concentrating on single recursive functions makes it clear how both lambda-lifting and lambda-dropping connect to the static-argument transformation in Haskell [4,8]. One thing we have not reported here (because it is a little tedious) is that lambda-lifting and lambda-dropping are correct both in a call-by-name language and in a call-by-value language. To this end, we defined the denotational semantics of two functional languages, one following call-by-name and one following call-by-value, and we considered the denotations of a lambda-dropped function and of a lambda-lifted function such as the power function of Figure 1: $lift_1$ and $drop_1$ respectively map one into the other and vice-versa.

On the other hand, experimenting with mutually recursive functions reveals the practical limitations of extensional, type-directed lambda-lifting and lambda-dropping: handling block structure becomes daunting rather quickly. Some automated support is needed here to study extensional lambda-lifting and lambda-dropping further.

Acknowledgements

Glynn Winskel suggested that the equation of Theorem 1 should be a foundation for extensional lambda-lifting. I am also grateful to Ulrik Schultz for our enjoyable joint work and for many discussions about possible ways of formalizing lambda-dropping, to Belmina Dzafic and Karoline Malmkjær for comments on an earlier draft, and to Daniel Damian, Andrzej Filinski and Lasse R. Nielsen for further comments and suggestions. Thanks are also due to the anonymous referees.

References

1. Anders Bondorf. Similix manual, system version 3.0. Technical Report 91/9, DIKU, Computer Science Department, University of Copenhagen, Copenhagen, Denmark, 1991.
2. William Clinger and Lars Thomas Hansen. Lambda, the ultimate label, or a simple optimizing compiler for Scheme. In Carolyn L. Talcott, editor, *Proceedings of the 1994 ACM Conference on Lisp and Functional Programming*, LISP Pointers, Vol. VII, No. 3, pages 128–139, Orlando, Florida, June 1994. ACM Press.
3. Charles Consel. A tour of Schism: A partial evaluation system for higher-order applicative languages. In David A. Schmidt, editor, *Proceedings of the Second ACM SIGPLAN Symposium on Partial Evaluation and Semantics-Based Program Manipulation*, pages 145–154, Copenhagen, Denmark, June 1993. ACM Press.

4. Olivier Danvy and Ulrik Pagh Schultz. Lambda-dropping: transforming recursive equations into programs with block structure. In Charles Consel, editor, *Proceedings of the ACM SIGPLAN Symposium on Partial Evaluation and Semantics-Based Program Manipulation*, pages 90–106, Amsterdam, The Netherlands, June 1997. ACM Press. Extended version available as the technical report BRICS-RS-97-6.
5. John Hughes. Super combinators: A new implementation method for applicative languages. In Daniel P. Friedman and David S. Wise, editors, *Conference Record of the 1982 ACM Symposium on Lisp and Functional Programming*, pages 1–10, Pittsburgh, Pennsylvania, August 1982. ACM Press.
6. Thomas Johnsson. Lambda lifting: Transforming programs to recursive equations. In Jean-Pierre Jouannaud, editor, *Functional Programming Languages and Computer Architecture*, number 201 in Lecture Notes in Computer Science, pages 190–203, Nancy, France, September 1985. Springer-Verlag.
7. Erik Meijer. Down with lambda-lifting. Unpublished note, April 1992.
8. Simon Peyton Jones, Will Partain, and André Santos. Let-floating: moving bindings to give faster programs. In R. Kent Dybvig, editor, *Proceedings of the 1996 ACM SIGPLAN International Conference on Functional Programming*, pages 1–12, Philadelphia, Pennsylvania, May 1996. ACM Press.
9. Simon L. Peyton Jones. *The Implementation of Functional Programming Languages*. Prentice Hall International Series in Computer Science. Prentice-Hall International, 1987.
10. Ulrik P. Schultz. Implicit and explicit aspects of scope and block structure. Master's thesis, DAIMI, Department of Computer Science, University of Aarhus, Aarhus, Denmark, June 1997.
11. Glynn Winskel. *The Formal Semantics of Programming Languages*. Foundation of Computing Series. The MIT Press, 1993.

Using Types as Approximations for Type Checking Prolog Programs

Christoph Beierle[1] and Gregor Meyer[2]

[1] FernUniversität Hagen, FB Informatik,
58084 Hagen, Germany
beierle@fernuni-hagen.de
[2] IBM Germany, SWSD,
71003 Böblingen, Germany
grmeyer@de.ibm.com

Abstract. Subtyping tends to undermine the effects of parametric polymorphism as far as the static detection of type errors is concerned. Starting with this observation we present a new approach for type checking
logic programs to overcome these difficulties. The two basic ideas are,
first, to interpret a predicate type declaration as an approximation for
the success set of the predicate. Second, declarations are extended with
type constraints such that they can be more refined than in other conventional type systems. The type system has been implemented in a
system called Typical which provides a type checker for Standard Prolog
enriched with type annotations.

1 Introduction

There are quite a few approaches to typed logic programming. Several type systems support parametric polymorphism and subtypes e.g. [28,12,8], see also the
collection in [24]. In [18] a classification scheme for the various uses of types
in logic programming is developed. It distinguishes three almost independent
dimensions of using types in logic programming: *types for proving partial correctness*, *types as constraints*, and *types as approximations* used in consistency
annotations. Another aspect for the comparison of typed logic languages is how
the semantics of typed predicates is defined, depending either on the clauses *and*
the type declarations (called *prescriptive typing* [15]) or independent from type
declarations (*descriptive typing*).

While there are many motivations for introducing types (naturalness of the
representation, efficiency when using types as active constraints, etc.) the software engineering point of view seems to be the most important one: The aim
is to detect as many programming errors as possible by static program analysis
before running the program. In this paper, we argue that in logic programming
subtyping tends to undermine the effects of parametric polymorphism as far as
the (static) detection of type errors is concerned. To overcome these difficulties
we use powerful type constraints in predicate type declarations which are interpreted as approximations of the intended model. Here, we present an overview
of the Typical system in which these ideas have been implemented.

A. Middeldorp, T. Sato (Eds.): FLOPS'99, LNCS 1722, pp. 251–266, 1999.

In Sec. 2 we motivate our approach by showing shortcomings of polymorphic type systems with subtypes. In Sec. 3 we tailor the "types as approximations" dimension of [18] towards Prolog clauses. Sec. 4 describes the Typical system and shows how predicate declarations with constraints are used as approximations of the intended model. Typical has been applied successfully to various programs, including its own source code in Standard Prolog enriched with type annotations. In Sec. 5 we argue why the descriptive approach is useful for Prolog type checking. Finally, we give some conclusions and point out further work.

2   Problems of Polymorphic Type Systems with Subtypes

An ML-like type system for logic programming was proposed and used by Mycroft and O'Keefe [21]. It includes explicit type declarations and parametric polymorphism but no subtypes. Most prominently the languages Gödel [11] and Mercury [29] are based on this kind of type system. But it is not possible to model often needed type hierarchies as in 'integers are numbers and numbers are expressions'.

There are many different proposals for combining a logical programming language with a type system comprising parametric polymorphisms as well as subtyping. Smolka uses type rewriting [28], partial order on type symbols is used by [3,12], Hanus proposes more general equational type specifications [10] and also Horn clauses for the subtype relation [9]. Naish uses Prolog clauses to define polymorphic predicates [22]; the predicate type is specified by some general constraint expression in [13], and so on. However, these approaches have a serious shortcoming when it comes to detect obviously ill-typed expressions involving subtypes.

Example 1.

```
:- type male --> peter; paul.      %      person
:- type female --> anne; mary.     %     /      \
:- type person.                    %  female    male
:- subtype male < person.          %
:- subtype female < person.        %

:- pred father(male,person).
   father(peter,paul).
:- pred mother(female,person).
   mother(anne,peter).
   mother(mary,paul).
```

The program defines a small type hierarchy with type **person** having (disjoint) subtypes **female** and **male**. By and large we follow the syntactical style used in [21]. Function symbols and their argument types are given by enumeration. Predicate declarations define the expected types of arguments. If we add

```
:- pred q1(person).
   q1(X) :- father(X,Y), mother(X,Z).
```

the clause for q1 can be detected as ill-typed. The type constraints for the variable X, i.e., X:male and X:female are not simultaneously satisfiable. However, using the common parametric type declaration for equality, i.e., '=': T x T, the clause for q2 in

```
:- pred q2(person).
   q2(X) :- father(X,Y), X = Xm, mother(Xm,Z).
```

is usually not detected as ill-typed (see e.g. [28,12]) although it is logically equivalent to q1! If the type parameter T in the declaration '=': T x T is substituted by person, then X = Xm is not ill-typed, because the variable X has type male which is a subtype of person, and the same applies to the type female of the variable Xm.

Note that the problem illustrated here does not depend on the equality predicate; as we will show in the next sections similar problems occur with many often-used polymorphic predicates like append, member etc.

Subtyping tends to undermine the effects of parametric polymorphism in the conventional approaches as far as the detection of type errors is concerned. This anomaly seems to be generally neglected in the literature; [30] is an exception mentioning the weakness in type-checking, which is caused by the generally used method for combining subtypes and parametric polymorphism. We will present a new type system which enables static type checking and type inferencing to spot such errors.

Logic programming in general has no modes for input/output. One way to attack the difficulties for type systems is to restrict logic programming towards a functional or directional style with fixed modes and then apply ideas known from typed functional programing (c.f. Sec. 6). Our approach instead is to extend the type system and make it suitable for general logic programming.

3   Types as Approximations

In this section, by tailoring the "types as approximations" dimension of [18] towards Prolog clauses, we develop a general method of static program analysis for finding programming errors like the ones illustrated in the examples above. We interpret predicate declarations as consistency annotations and take these annotations as approximations of a set of atoms intended to be true. We will discuss the applicability of consistency annotations and show how they can reasonably be used to find erroneous expressions. Specific instances of the general scheme we present here can be found as part of many proposed type systems (e.g. [22]), although mostly it is used only indirectly.

3.1   Consistency Annotations

For the beginning we will allow a rather general form of predicate declarations. For each predicate p we assume that there is a function tc_p which generates an appropriate constraint over some theory. The function tc_p is directly or indirectly defined by the type declaration for the predicate p. Given a syntactically well-formed atom $A = p(\ldots)$, then $tc_p(A)$ yields a constraint which is wanted to be satisfiable, otherwise A is called ill-typed.

Intuitively, the declaration is an approximation of the set of atoms $p(\ldots)$ which should be true. I.e., a model intended by the programmer is described in two ways: first by the logical clauses and second by the predicate type declarations. Of course, in practice the predicate declarations are much simpler than the clauses and they only roughly approximate the intended meaning of a predicate. Thus, for any program we can distinguish the following three models whose possible interrelationships are illustrated as in the following diagram:

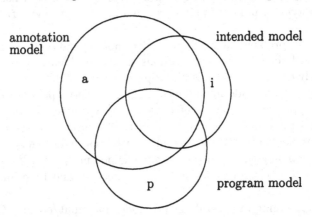

p) The program clauses alone define some model shown as region p; this model is of central importance. Based on the formal semantics of the programming language in general this model exactly represents the meaning of the program, i.e., which facts are true and which are false.

a) The predicate types also define a model that may be different from the program model. With 'types as approximations' the model of the predicate declarations, or annotations in general, should be a superset of the model of the program clauses.

i) Last but not least, the intended model, i.e., what the program should compute as required by the application domain, is just another model. In an ideal program the program model should be the same as the intended model.

We do not use the annotation model a in a specification of a program. This differs from the equation "Specification = Program + Types" in [22]. A consequence of the approach in [22] would be to further include modes and other implicit or explicit assumptions in the specification for a program.

Let us now discuss various cases where the model of the program clauses p coincides or differs from the other models:

p = i) In the optimal case the program model coincides with the intended model. I.e., the set of inferred solutions is exactly the set wanted by the programmer. Formal annotations describe some superset of the intended and inferred model.

a \ p ≠ ∅) There is no problem if the model of annotations a is a strict superset of the program model p. Annotations are not required and are not even intended to describe the model as exactly as the program clauses. They can only provide an approximation as far as it can be described using the type language alone.

$p \setminus a \neq \emptyset$) A program may happen to have solutions which are not consistent with the type annotations, i.e., these solutions are ill-typed and they are marked as being errors. Such an error may also be due to an inappropriate type declaration. If an inconsistency between a program solution and the annotations is detected, it is not possible to decide automatically whether the program clauses or the annotations are not correct; this decision depends on the intended model.

$i \setminus p \neq \emptyset$) If a solution in the intended model is not computed by the program then this corresponds to an error because an intended answer is missing.

$p \setminus i \neq \emptyset$) The difference of the program model and the model intended by the programmer marks inferred solutions which are 'not wanted' by the programmer. E.g., 'append([],3,3)' is true w.r.t. the usual untyped implementation of append.

Of course, if we do not have a formal description of the intended model i, we do not have a chance to automatically analyze the cases involving i. Since in this paper we do not want to deal with formal program specifications other than the discussed annotations we will therefore use the annotations as a specification of a superset of the intended model and assume $i \subseteq a$. As a consequence, the declarations can be used for static type checking purposes in the following way: each program clause is inspected statically if it contains expressions, possibly the whole clause, that do not fit with the semantics given by the predicate declarations. If the checking procedure finds that some expression is inconsistent with the declaration then probably a programming error is detected. In all cases the semantics of the clauses remain unaffected and well-defined. This is similar to the detection of redundant code, e.g., unreachable statements in a procedural program, which is done by many state-of-the-art compilers.

3.2   Inconsistent Atoms

For any atom $A = p(t_1, \cdots, t_n)$ the type-constraint is given by $tc_p(A)$. For simplicity we often write $tc(A)$. If there is no type declaration for p in the type part, by default we take the type constraint to be *true*.

Clauses that conflict with the predicate declaration will be called *type-inconsistent* or *ill-typed*. We argue that such clauses are useless in the program because they contain subexpressions which are not satisfiable in the intended model. A sound but not necessarily complete algorithm for detecting ill-typed clauses will point out clauses which conflict with the type declaration of the head atom, or which can be eliminated without affecting the semantics of the specification. These two cases can be illustrated by the following specification:

```
:- pred p(male).          % type declaration
   p(peter) :- p(1).      % body is always false
   p(2).                  % conflict with the type declaration
```

In the intended semantics implied by the type declarations, the body of the first clause is not true. If the body of a clause is known to be unsatisfiable due to its inconsistency with the type declarations, then such a clause can be called useless: it is logically redundant. Also the second clause is inconsistent. Usually there is no reason for a programmer to write such a clause having an unsatisfiable type constraint, in this case 2:male.

For every atom A that has an instance which is true in the intended model, we assume that $tc(A)$ is satisfiable. This is a very important assumption, because it gives the programmer a device to describe properties of the intended model. If for some atom A we can show that the type constraint $tc(A)$ is not satisfiable, then we have found an atom that has no instance in the intended model. This simple correspondence is the basis for an automated type checking method where unsatisfiable type constraints indicate programming errors.

3.3   Consistency Checks for Clauses

In a program we could translate each clause into a formula where every atom A is replaced by the type constraint $tc(A)$. If the transformed formula is not satisfiable, we have shown, using our basic assumption, that the original clause is not satisfiable in the intended model of the program. Hence, the original clause probably contains an error (at least, it is inconsistent with the annotation model). As we will show in the following, in practice we can make a more detailed analysis of program clauses exploiting predicate declarations.

Horn Clauses: First consider a program which is given by Horn clauses. If there is a simple fact $p(\ldots)$ and $tc_p(p(\ldots))$ is not satisfiable, then the fact contradicts with the intended model as specified by the predicate declaration. Hence this fact can be marked as erroneous, it contains a programming error with respect to the predicate declaration. A similar line of reasoning applies to clauses

$$A \leftarrow B_1, \ldots, B_n.$$

where A and B_i are atoms. If the conjunction of type constraints $tc(B_1) \wedge \ldots \wedge tc(B_n)$ is not satisfiable, we know that the body of the rule is not satisfiable (in the intended model). Formally, the complete clause together with the type constraints is a tautology, but practically we can say that the clause is useless. I.e., if such a clause appears in a logic program, this clause can be marked as containing a type error. A similar view is generally taken in type inferencing frameworks for Prolog, starting with [19]. Furthermore, it is reasonable to require the type constraint

$$tc(A) \wedge tc(B_1) \wedge \ldots \wedge tc(B_n)$$

to be satisfiable. Otherwise the body of the rule would imply an atom A that contradicts the consistency requirement as given by its declaration.

Clauses with Negation: In the general scheme we develop here we want to be independent of specific semantics for negation. We assume that for an atom C

such that a model does not contain any instance of it, with any reasonable semantics of negation not C is true in the model. If in the extended Horn clause

$$A \leftarrow B_1, \ldots, B_n, \text{not } C$$

$tc(C)$ is not satisfiable then not C will thus be true in the intended model, and therefore this subexpression can be seen as practically useless. Also, if $tc(B_1) \wedge \ldots \wedge tc(B_n) \wedge tc(C)$ is not satisfiable, then we either know that the conjunction $B_1, \ldots, B_n$ always fails or not C is always true when the conjunction $B_1, \ldots, B_n$ succeeds. In both cases we can argue that the body of the rule contains a programming error. As before, we will also require the type constraint of the head atom to be satisfiable simultaneously. I.e., if the type constraint expression

$$tc(A) \wedge tc(B_1) \wedge \ldots \wedge tc(B_n) \wedge tc(C)$$

is not satisfiable, we argue that the clause contains a type error. If there is more than one negated atom in an extended Horn clause, i.e. we have

$$A \leftarrow B_1, \ldots, B_n, \text{not } C_1, \ldots, \text{not } C_k$$

we require

$$tc(A) \wedge tc(B_1) \wedge \ldots \wedge tc(B_n) \wedge tc(C_i)$$

to be satisfiable for each atom C_i. We will take a closer look at the following rule, referring to Example 1:

```
:- pred p(person).
   p(P) :- not mother(P,X), not father(P,Y).
```

Intuitively, p is true for persons that are neither mother nor father of someone. If we required the variable P to be of type female, due to its occurrence in mother(P,X), and also to be of type male, due to its occurrence in father(P,Y), then these constraints would not be simultaneously satisfiable, because the types female and male are disjoint. Instead, with our condition the rule for p has no type error. It is interesting to note that there are other proposals such as [12], which view this clause as not being well-typed. The reason is that the variable P is required to have a unique type such that all atoms are well-typed, including both negated atoms. We think that this requirement is appropriate for pure Horn clauses but that in general it is too strong for predicate logic formulas or their variants with negation as failure as the given example illustrates.

4 The Typical System

The aim of Typical is to do static type checking on logic programs. The software will check Standard Prolog programs that are extended with type declarations. The type system includes subtyping and parametric polymorphism. In addition to the usual Prolog clauses, Typical expects type definitions and predicate declarations. No type declarations for variables are needed; variable types are inferred automatically by Typical.

4.1 The Type Language

Here we give an overview on the language for defining types in Typical. The basic form of monomorphic type definitions are the same as already used in Example 1. If a function symbol has arguments, then the corresponding types must be given in the definition

```
:- type machine --> fastm(int,string); slowm(int,string).
```

Parametric types are defined by using type variables and they can be ordered in the same way as other types. However, the parameters of parametric types that have a subtype relation must be the same. E.g., a complete type definition for the ubiquitous list and for binary trees modelled as a subtype of trees in general could look like

```
:- type list(T) --> [] ; [ T | list(T) ].
:- type bintree(T) --> leaf(T) ; bnode(T,bintree(T),bintree(T)).
:- type tree(T) --> node(T,list(tree(T))).
:- subtype bintree(T) < tree(T).
```

Note that infix notation for operators and types mix well.

There are various technical conditions the defined type hierarchy must fulfill, e.g. the existence of greatest lower bounds for non-disjoint types required for the existence of principal types as needed in Sec. 4.3. For technical simplicity we assume that each function symbol has a unique declared type. Subtype relationships must be given explicitly, we do not automatically detect subtyping between types if the set of terms in one type is a subset of the terms in another type. A precise description of these conditions is given in [17].

4.2 Predicate Declarations

Predicate declarations specify the types which are expected for the actual arguments when a predicated is called. E.g., if the first argument of a predicate sumlist must be a list of integers and the second argument must be an integer, the declaration is

```
:- pred sumlist(list(int), int)).
```

Declarations may also contain (implicitly existentially quantified) type parameters, written as Prolog variables, e.g., for append

```
:- pred append(list(T), list(T), list(T)).
```

More specific type declarations are possible by using *type constraints* over type variables occurring in the declaration. In order to identify this new form of declarations syntactically, we prefix type parameters within formal argument types with '@' [16]:

```
:- pred sublist(list(@T1), list(@T2)) |> T1 =< T2.
```

The expressions on the right of |> describe type constraints where =< stands for the subtype relationship. Syntactically similar type declarations have been used independently for type dependencies in [7] and in [23].

4.3 Approximations and Type Consistency

We first illustrate the use of the new form of type declarations for predicates by means of an example. Intuitively, in Typical a type declaration for a predicate describes a superset of the predicate solutions (cf. Section 3). E.g., the conventional declaration

    :- pred append_old(list(T), list(T), list(T)).

defines that for any (ground) atom append(L1,L2,L3), which is true in some model, there is a type substitution Θ for the type parameter T such that each argument is of type $\Theta(\text{list}(T))$. With type hierarchies, possibly being rather deep or even containing a most general type, this semantics leads to anomalies as pointed out in Section 2. As part of our solution we allow for more exact declarations using type constraints:

    :- pred append_new(list(@T1), list(@T2), list(@T3))
                     |> T1 =< T3, T2 =< T3.

Now an atom append(L1,L2,L3), where the arguments L1, L2, and L3 have the *principal* (or *least*) *types* list(A), list(B), and list(C) respectively, is well-typed (also called type consistent) if the conjunction of type constraints A =< C, B =< C is satisfied.

We can easily transform the declaration for append_old into an equivalent one using the new framework, yielding

    :- pred append_old(list(@T1), list(@T2), list(@T3))
                     |> T1 =< T, T2 =< T, T3 =< T.

which is obviously weaker than the append_new declaration. (Note that type variables occurring only in the constraint part of a predicate declaration - like T here - are implicitly existentially quantified.) The following figure illustrates the type constraints imposed by append_old and append_new, respectively:

Now consider the append_new declaration. Since predicate declarations are seen as annotations that approximate the intended semantics of the program, the atom append([1],[-1],L) is well-typed with the variable L having the (least) type list(int). Given the least type of the first argument [1] as list(nat) and the least type of [-1] as list(negint), the type constraints nat =< int and negint =< int are satisfied.

On the other hand, if the variable L is constrained to the type list(nat) the same atom is not well-typed, because there is no type T2' such that [-1] has (least) type list(T2') and also T2' =< nat. This indicates that the atom as a goal literal will always fail, because with the intended meaning there is no list of natural numbers that contains a negative number.

Similarly, the atom append(L2, [-1], [1]) is not well-typed under the declaration for append_new although it is considered well-typed w.r.t. the conventional typing for append_old.

4.4 Principal Types

One of the central notions within the Typical type system is the *principal type* of a term, which is the most specific type of a term. A principal type π of the term t has the property: t has type π (denoted as $t : \pi$) and if t has type τ then there is a type substitution Θ such that $\Theta(\pi) \leq \tau$, i.e.,

$$\pi \text{ is principal type of } t \quad \Leftrightarrow \quad t : \pi \text{ and } (\forall \tau)\, (t : \tau \Rightarrow (\exists \Theta)\, \Theta(\pi) \leq \tau).$$

The principal type is as minimal as possible with respect to the type order, but it is also as polymorphic as possible.

Example 2. Given the type declaration

    :- type pair(T, S) --> mkpair(T, S).

and usual declarations for int and list then the term mkpair([1],[]) has type pair(list(int),list(int)), as well as pair(list(nat),list(nat)), pair(list(nat),list(T)), etc. The latter is the principal type of the term.

The notion of principal types is well-known from typed functional programming. Our definition is somewhat different because in our framework we don't have λ-abstraction and the principal type does not depend on type constraints.[1]

The syntactical appearance of type constraints in declarations is similar to declarations in functional programming with parametric types and subsumption [20,6], commonly known as $F_{\leq}$. However, their impact within Typical is rather different. As an important factor we will see that a type parameter with an @-prefix matches with the principal type of an argument term. Therefore, a declaration for append_new should *not* be seen as a simple 'logical variant' of functional declarations such as

    func app: list(T1)×list(T2)×list(T3) → bool with T1≤T3, T2≤T3.
    func app: list(T1)×list(T2) → list(T3) with T1≤T3, T2≤T3.

because of the following observations: The first function declaration is similar to append_old because the expression app([1],[-1],L) is well-typed even if L has type list(nat). The type parameter T3 can be instantiated with int. The second function declaration is closer to the declaration append_new in Typical. An equation L = app([1],[-1]) is detected as ill-typed when L has type list(nat). However, this requires a fixed partitioning of input and output arguments which is not appropriate in logic programming.

---

[1] A similar definition of principal types is used in [12]. Neglecting technical problems in [12] (see [2]) our approach is rather different in the way how principal types are used for checks of type consistency.

4.5   Procedure for Type Consistency Checks

In general, a predicate declaration has the form

p : pattern$_1$ ... pattern$_n$ $\triangleright$ Constraint.

Given some atom $p(\ldots)$, for each argument we will determine the most specific instance of each pattern$_i$ that matches the type of the corresponding argument and the constraint part is checked for satisfiability. Thus, in order to check if an atom $p(t_1, \ldots, t_n)$ is type-consistent with respect to a declaration $p : \pi_1 \ldots \pi_n \triangleright C$ the following steps are performed (where the whole procedure fails if any of the steps fails):

1. compute the principal type τ_i of every argument t_i,
2. for each τ_i determine the least instance $\Theta_i(\pi_i)$ with $\tau_i \leq \Theta_i(\pi_i)$,
3. check if there is a substitution Θ such that $\Theta(\pi_i) = \Theta_i(\pi_i)$ for each i.
4. check if $\Theta(C)$ is satisfiable.

The first three steps implement the abstract function tc_p as used in Section 3.1. As usual, a clause is type-consistent if every atom in it is type-consistent w.r.t. the same variable typing.

Example 3. The steps to compute type consistency are illustrated by checking the atom append([],[-1],[1]) with respect to the declaration

    :- pred append_new(list(@T1), list(@T2), list(@T3))
                       |> T1 =< T3, T2 =< T3.

In the first step the principal types for the argument terms are computed. The empty list [] has the principal type $\tau_1 =$ list(α), For [-1] and [1] the principal types are $\tau_2 =$ list(negint) and $\tau_3 =$ list(nat), respectively. If there was any argument term which is not type correct, e.g., [1|2] does not conform to the declaration of [_|_] because 2 is not a list, then the atom would not be type consistent.

Second, the principal types τ_i are matched against the formal types π_i in the predicate declaration. The least instances $\Theta_i(\pi_i)$ are given by $\Theta_1 = \{T1 \leftarrow \alpha\}$, $\Theta_2 = \{T2 \leftarrow$ negint$\}$, and $\Theta_3 = \{T3 \leftarrow$ nat$\}$. If there is no least instance of a formal type π_i, e.g., if an integer occurs where a list is expected, then the atom would not be type consistent.

Third, all substitutions are combined into a single substitution $\Theta = \{T1 \leftarrow \alpha, T2 \leftarrow$ negint$, T3 \leftarrow$ nat$\}$. In case of conflicts between the single substitutions Θ_i, e.g., if Θ_3 was $\{T2 \leftarrow$ nat$\}$ then the atom would not be type consistent.

In the last step we determine that the constraint set $\Theta(\{T1 \leq T3, T2 \leq T3\}) = \{\alpha \leq$ nat, negint $\leq$ nat$\}$ is not satisfiable. Hence, append([],[-1],[1]) is not type consistent. For the atom append([],[1],[1]), however, we would get the set of constraints $\{\alpha \leq$ nat, nat $\leq$ nat$\}$ which is satisfiable with the substitution $\{\alpha \leftarrow$ posint$\}$, i.e., the modified atom is type consistent.

Consider the Typical type declaration

    :- pred '=': @T x @T.

With this declaration for '=' the type error in the clause (from Section 2)

    q2(X) :- father(X,Y), X = Xm, mother(Xm,Z).

is detected since the atom X = Xm with X of type male and Xm of type female is illtyped.

Example 4. Using the declarations

    :- pred abs(int, nat).
    :- pred member(@T1, list(@T2)) |> T1 =< T2.

the expression

    member(X,[-1,-2]), abs(Z,X)

is found to be not type consistent: The principal type of X in the first subgoal is inferred to be negint which is incompatible with the type nat required for X in the second subgoal.

Further examples of type declarations in Typical are:

:- pred reverse(list(@T), list(@T)).
% principal types of arguments must be identical
:- pred intersection(list(@T1),list(@T2),list(@T)) |> T=<T1, T=<T2.
% intersection(L1,L2,L) :- elements of L are in both L1 and L2.
:- pred overlap(list(@T), list(@U)) |> V =< T, V =<U.
% overlap(L1,L2) :- lists L1 and L2 have members in common.

Our notion of ill-typing does not preclude standard Prolog idioms, such as the failure driven loop. For instance, consider

    q :- p(X), side_effect(X), fail.
    q :- succeed.

where we assume that p and side_effect constrain their arguments to be of the same type and the type constraints of the nullary predicates are always true. Although in a purely declarative setting the body of the first clause is not satisfiable (assuming fail to be always false), i.e. the whole clause is trivially true, it is not rejected as ill-typed because we use the constant *true* as type constraint for the atom fail.

In [17] typing rules are given that precisely define well-typedness for a program and clauses by a set of logical inference rules. A complete type inferencing algorithm together with a description of the involved (finite domain) constraint solving over a partially ordered set of type symbols is also given in [17].

5 Why Syntactical Type Checking is Useful for Prolog

By writing type declarations for predicates, the programmer gives hints on the intended semantics for that predicate. Every atom intended to be true shall be well-typed with respect to the declaration. Nevertheless, our type system presented so far remains purely syntactical. While a corresponding semantics for well-typed models could be defined, e.g. using results from [9], we believe that it is reasonable to consider syntactical type checking for its own. Assume a programmer wants to define the absolute difference of numbers by the (erroneous) clauses

```
:- pred absdist(int, int, nat).
    absdist(X,Y,D) :- X < Y, D is Y - X.
    absdist(X,Y,D) :- X >= Y, D is Y - X.
```

Of course, the second clause should have 'D is X-Y' instead of 'D is Y-X'. Both clauses are well-typed under the variable typing {X:int, Y:int, D:nat}. Nevertheless, using normal Prolog-resolution, the goal absdist(5,4,D) gives the result D = -1, which is not intended and, even more, does not correspond to the type declaration of the predicate absdist. With respect to the type system the usual reaction is to reject such an approach for typed logic programming and require the resolution and its unification to obey the type constraints on variables. In that case, i.e. using an inference calculus implementing the correct order-sorted unification as in e.g. [3], the goal absdist(5,4,D) fails. With respect to detecting the programming error in this example, the practical consequences of using or leaving out order-sorted unification are essentially the same: the program is well-typed but it does not produce the intended results. Type-correct inference calculi tend to (correctly) produce a logical failure instead of reporting a type-error. Here a difference between our approach and [22] becomes apparent. While [22] uses checks for type consistency to find clauses which would produce a type incorrect answer, we use type consistency also to find clauses which produce no answer at all.

Thus, rephrasing Millner's slogan *Well-typed [functional] programs don't go wrong* yields *Well-typed logic programs fail instead of going wrong*. On the other hand, for our types-as-approximations approach whose purpose is to detect useless atoms and clauses we get the slogan *Type inconsistent clauses don't succeed [in the intended model]*.

Is it reasonable to allow the logic inference calculus to produce results that do not conform to type declarations? On the positive side there are strong practical arguments: We have a type system that allows natural modeling of data structures and also enables detailed static program analysis proceeding incrementally clause by clause. At the same time the runtime execution of the program can still be done by any (efficient, commercially available) Prolog system that does not have to provide any form of typed unification. Other approaches to define an expressive type system and a new typed inference calculus in combination sometimes have to cope with severe undecidability problems, or they restrict the language or impose a run-time overhead that is not accepted by most programmers.

6   Conclusions and Further Work

Generally used type systems for logic programming with parametric polymorphism and subtyping have an anomaly which weakens the ability to detect type errors as shown in Sec. 2. Our new type system Typical overcomes this anomaly.

It provides type checking at a very detailed level without restricting common programming practice.

The Typical typing approach is independent of any mode system for specifying an input/output behavior for predicates. In this way it differs from other proposals e.g., using so-called implication types [26,25] or type dependencies (e.g. [14]). An example for a type dependency is $append\langle list(T), list(T), list(T)/1, 2 \rightarrow 3; 3 \rightarrow 1, 2\rangle$. Its meaning is: For all τ, if the first two arguments of *append* have the type $list(\tau)$ then so does the third argument, and vice-versa. This type dependency has a similar effect for append as our declaration with type constraints. But there are other declarations, e.g. for `overlap`, that are not expressible with type dependencies. Typical does not impose a functional or directional view on logic programs as it is done by further systems with 'directional types' and variants thereof (see e.g. [5,27,1,4]). It doesn't matter if the inference calculus is top-down as in Prolog or bottom-up as it can be in a deductive database system. In [7] and similarly in [23] mode declarations are used which are syntactically similar to our type declarations. However, in Typical the declarations are exploited for checking clauses for logical consistency with the model of the declarations instead of checking input/output correctness.

Here, we could only present an overview of the complete type checking and inferencing algorithms underlying Typical; they are spelled out in detail in [17]. Apart from providing a method for dealing with negation, Typical contains several extensions for higher-order programming and extra-logical built-ins (e.g. a built-in type `goal` which is used in declarations like `:- pred call(goal).`) such that the system could be applied successfully to its own source code of about 4000 lines of Prolog code [16,17]. A more refined treatment of such higher order features within the types-as-approximations approach is subject of our current work.

Acknowledgements

We thank the anonymous referees for helpful comments.

References

1. A. Aiken and T. K. Lakshman. Directional type checking of logic programs. In *Static Analysis Symposium*, LNCS. Springer Verlag, 1994.
2. C. Beierle. Type inferencing for polymorphic order-sorted logic programs. In L. Sterling, editor, *Proc. of the 12th Int. Conf. on Logic Programming*, Tokyo, June 1995.
3. C. Beierle and G. Meyer. Run-time type computations in the Warren Abstract Machine. *The Journal of Logic Programming*, 18(2):123–148, Feb. 1994.
4. J. Boye and J. Małuszyński. Two aspects of directional types. In L. Sterling, editor, *Logic Programming, Proceedings of the Twelfth International Conference on Logic Programming*, pages 747–761, Tokio, 1995. The MIT Press.

5. F. Bronsard, T. Lakshman, and U. S. Reddy. A framework of directionality for proving termination of logic programs. In K. R. Apt, editor, *Logic Programming: Proceedings of 1992 Joint International Conference and Symposium*, pages 321–335. The MIT Press, 1992.

6. L. Cardelli and P. Wegner. On understanding types, data abstraction, and polymorphism. *ACM Computing Surveys*, 17:471–522, Dec. 1986.

7. M. Codish and B. Demoen. Deriving polymorphic type dependencies for logic programs using multiple incarnations of Prop. In B. L. Charlier, editor, *Static Analysis, First International Symposium, SAS'94*, volume 864 of *LNCS*, pages 281–296, Namur, Belgium, Sept. 1994. Springer Verlag.

8. M. Hanus. Horn clause programs with polymorphic types: Semantics and resolution. *Theoretical Computer Science*, 89:63–106, 1991.

9. M. Hanus. Parametric order-sorted types in logic programming. In *Proc. TAPSOFT'91*, volume 494 of *LNCS*, pages 181–200, Brighton, Apr. 1991. Springer Verlag.

10. M. Hanus. Logic programming with type specifications. In Pfenning [24], chapter 3, pages 91–140.

11. P. Hill and J. Lloyd. *The Gödel Programming Language*. Logic programming series. The MIT Press, 1994.

12. P. M. Hill and R. W. Topor. A semantics for typed logic programs. In Pfenning [24], chapter 1, pages 1–62.

13. M. Höhfeld and G. Smolka. Definite relations over constraint languages. IWBS Report 53, IBM Scientific Center, Stuttgart, Germany, Oct. 1988.

14. M. Kifer and J. Wu. A first-order theory of types and polymorphism in logic programming. Techn.Rep. 90/23, SUNY, New York, July 1990.

15. T. K. Lakshman and U. S. Reddy. Typed Prolog: A semantic reconstruction of the Mycroft-O'Keefe type system. In Saraswat and Ueda, editors, *Int. Symp. on Logic Programming, ILPS 91*, pages 202–217, San Diego, 1991.

16. G. Meyer. Type checking and type inferencing for logic programs with subtypes and parametric polymorphism. Informatik Berichte 200, FernUniversität Hagen, June 1996. available via http://www.fernuni-hagen.de/pi8/typical/.

17. G. Meyer. *On Types and Type Consistency in Logic Programming*. PhD thesis, FernUniversität Hagen, Germany, 1999. (to appear).

18. G. Meyer and C. Beierle. Dimensions of types in logic programming. In W. Bibel and P. H. Schmitt, editors, *Automated Deduction - A Basis for Applications*, chapter 10. Kluwer Academic Publishers, Netherlands, 1998.

19. P. Mishra. Towards a theory of types in Prolog. In *Proceedings of the 1984 Symposium on Logic Programming*, pages 289–298, Atlantic City, New Jersey, 1984.

20. J. Mitchell. Type inference and type containment. In G. Kahn, D. B. MacQueen, and G. Plotkin, editors, *International Symposium Semantics of Data Types*, number 173 in LNCS, pages 257–277, Sophia-Antipolis, France, June 1984. Springer Verlag.

21. A. Mycroft and R. A. O'Keefe. A polymorphic type system for Prolog. *Artificial Intelligence*, 23:295–307, 1984.

22. L. Naish. Types and intended meaning. In Pfenning [24], chapter 6, pages 189–216.

23. L. Naish. A declarative view of modes. In M. Maher, editor, *Proc. of the 1996 Joint International Conference and Symposium on Logic Programming*, pages 185–199, Bonn, Sept. 1996. The MIT Press.

24. F. Pfenning, editor. *Types in Logic Programming*. Logic Programming Series. The MIT Press, 1992.

25. C. Pyo and U. S. Reddy. Inference of polymorphic types for logic programs. In E. Lusk and R. Overbeck, editors, *Logic Programming, Proc. of the North American Conference*, pages 1115–1132, 1989.
26. U. S. Reddy. Notions of polymorphism for predicate logic programs. In *Int. Conf. on Logic Programming*, pages 17–34, (addendum, distributed at conference). The MIT Press, Aug. 1988.
27. Y. Rouzaud and L. Nguyen-Phuong. Integrating modes and subtypes into a prolog type-checker. In K. Apt, editor, *Logic Programming, Proc. of JICSLP*, pages 85–97. Cambridge, Mass., 1992.
28. G. Smolka. *Logic Programming over Polymorphically Order-Sorted Types*. PhD thesis, Universität Kaiserslautern, Germany, 1989.
29. Z. Somogyi. The Mercury project. http://www.cs.mu.oz.au/~zs/mercury.html, 1995.
30. J. J. Wu. *A First-order Theory of Types and Polymorphism in Logic Programming*. PhD thesis, State University of New York at Stony Brook, 1992.

Typed Static Analysis: Application to Groundness Analysis of PROLOG and λPROLOG

Olivier Ridoux[1], Patrice Boizumault[2], and Frédéric Malésieux[2*]

[1] IRISA, Campus universitaire de Beaulieu
F-35042 RENNES cedex, FRANCE
Olivier.Ridoux@irisa.fr
[2] École des Mines de Nantes, 4, rue Alfred Kastler, BP 20722
F-44307 NANTES cedex03, FRANCE
Patrice.Boizumault@emn.fr

Abstract. We enrich the domain $\mathcal{P}os$ by combining it with types. This makes static analysis more precise, since deduced properties concern both terms considered as a whole, and the details of their structure, as it is defined by types. We use this enriched domain to redefine first-order groundness analysis (PROLOG terms) as it is formalized by Codish and Demoen [CD95] and higher-order groundness analysis (λPROLOG terms) as defined by the authors [MRB98].

1 Introduction

The works presented in this article as been stimulated by the study of static analysis for λPROLOG [Mal99], but applies equally well to typed versions of PROLOG.

Our purpose is not to define a new type analysis for PROLOG or for λPROLOG; there are already several proposals, and in facts, PROLOG and λPROLOG do not diverge too much as far as *prescriptive* typing is considered [MO84,Han89,LR91,NP92,LR96]. The prescriptive point of view considers well-typing as a property of programs, and relates it to the semantics of program *via* a *semantic soundness* theorem which says roughly that "Well-typed programs cannot go wrong" [Mil78]. In the prescriptive view, one can consider as ill-typed programs and goals with a perfectly well-defined (but undesired) semantics. For instance, one can reject every program where a call to the classical predicate *append* has arguments that are not lists (though $append([], 3, 3)$ is a logical consequence of the standard semantics). In a sense, the prescriptive view bridges the gap between the intended semantics of a program and its actual semantics.

Our purpose is to combine existing informations about types with informations that can be expressed in a domain like $\mathcal{P}os$ [CFW91,MS93]. So doing, we expect a better precision as illustrated in the following example. In a non-typed groundness analysis using $\mathcal{P}os$, if an element of a list is non-ground, all the list is said to be non-ground (e.g., $[A, 2, 3]$). An incomplete list is deemed non-ground

---

* This work was done while the author was at École des Mines de Nantes.

A. Middeldorp, T. Sato (Eds.): FLOPS'99, LNCS 1722, pp. 267–283, 1999.

as well (e.g., $[1, 2, 3|Z]$), so that groundness analysis with domain $\mathcal{P}os$ does not make a difference between these two cases. However, predicates such as *append* see the difference because they have only to do with the structure of lists. If the length of an input list is unknown, they try to complete it by unification and backtracking, but if it is known, these predicates are deterministic. So, it is important to formalize the difference between a proper[1] list of ground elements (which we will write[2] $(list_a\ true)$ or, equivalently, $true$), a proper list of not-all-ground elements (written $(list_a\ false)$) and an improper list (written $false$).

Predicates like *append* are especially interested in the structure of lists because they are generic; i.e., they are defined for lists in general, without considering the types of elements. This is what the type declarations of these predicates indicate formally; they are polymorphic, e.g., **type** *append* $(list\ A)$ $\rightarrow (list\ A) \rightarrow (list\ A) \rightarrow o$. This suggests to model the expression of abstract properties on the expression of polymorphism. So, we will derive from the presence of type variables in declarations (e.g., A in $(list\ A)$) abstract domains which are more refined than the ordinary $\mathcal{P}os$ domain (i.e., a two-value domain: $true$ and $false$). Thus, in the case of lists, the abstract domain contains values $true$, $(list_a\ false)$, $(list_a\ (list_a\ false))$, etc.

In the sequel, we first analyze the case of a typed variant of PROLOG in Section 2, and then the case of λPROLOG in Section 3. Section 2 also briefly presents the domain $\mathcal{P}os$ and the abstract compilation of groundness for PROLOG, while Section 3 contains an introduction to λPROLOG and to the abstract compilation of groundness for λPROLOG. We discuss correctness and termination of our proposal in Section 4.

2   Typed Properties for PROLOG

We combine $\mathcal{P}os$ with simple types in the static analysis of PROLOG programs. We first recall the principles of abstract compilation, and then we expose our technique.

2.1   Abstract Compilation

The principle of abstract compilation is to translate a source program into an abstract program whose denotation is computed according to its concrete semantics. This can be seen as a way of implementing abstract interpretation by partially evaluating it for a given program. This technique is called abstract compilation by Hermenegildo *et al.* [HWD92] and originated from works by Debray

---

[1] Proper/partial/incomplete are used here as in [O'K90]. I.e., A "proper" *Thing* is a non-variable *Thing* each of whose *Thing* arguments is a proper *Thing*; A "partial" *Thing* is either a variable or a *Thing* at least one of whose *Thing* arguments is a partial *Thing*; Partial *Things* are sometimes called "incomplete" *Things*.

[2] Everywhere in this article, when a program symbol is reused to express an abstraction, we write its abstract version with a subscripted a.

and Warren [DW86]. Codish and Demoen apply it to the analysis of groundness for PROLOG programs [CD95].

The analysis proceeds in several phases, but we only focus on the translation of a program P into a program P_a whose denotation approximates the non-ground minimal model of P (e.g., as defined in the S-semantics [FLMP89]).

All programs must be normalized before being translated. Normalization is independent from the analyzed property. The purpose of normalization is to make every unification step explicit, and to make sure that every goal corresponds to a single unification step. So, there must be at most one constant in every goal, and all variables of a goal must be different. More precisely, PROLOG programs are normalized in a way such that every atom occurring in a program clause is either of the form $X = Y$, $p(X_1, \ldots, X_k)$, or $X_0 = f(X_1, \ldots, X_k)$ where all the X_i are distinct variables.

The abstraction of a normalized program is obtained by replacing every atom by an abstract atom that depends on the analyzed property because it describes the relation that exists between the arguments of a successful call to the atom. In this article, we only consider the groundness property: a ground term is a term with no free variable.

2.2   Abstract Compilation for Groundness

Atoms of the form $p(X_1, \ldots, X_k)$ are abstracted into $p_a(X_1, \ldots, X_k)$. Atoms of the form $X_0 = f(X_1, \ldots, X_k)$ are abstracted into $iff(X_0, [X_1, \ldots, X_k])$, which[3] is true if and only if $X_0 \Leftrightarrow (X_1 \wedge \ldots \wedge X_k)$. In particular, $iff(X_0, [])$ is logically equivalent to $X_0 = true$. For groundness analysis, $iff(X_0, [X_1, \ldots, X_k])$ can be read as "X_0 is bound to a ground term if and only if $X_1, \ldots, X_k$ are bound to ground terms". Atoms of the form $X = Y$ are abstracted into $iff(X, [Y])$

The abstracted program is a DATALOG program [RU95] with propositional constants $true$ and $false$ as computation domain. Computing all the answers of a DATALOG program is a decidable problem. This property is crucial for the abstract compilation technique; the language of the abstract programs must be a decidable language.

The abstracted program can be seen as defining formulas in $\mathcal{P}os$ [CFW91,MS93]. $\mathcal{P}os$ consists of positive propositional formulas. Here, positive means that when all variables of a propositional formula are instantiated to $true$, the formula is equivalent to $true$. An alternative definition is that positive propositional formulas are built with connectives $\wedge$, $\vee$, and $\leftrightarrow$.

---

[3] Actually, other authors do not use a list as second argument of iff. They rely on the ability of concrete PROLOG systems to use the same identifier for functors with different arities: e.g., $iff/1$, $iff/2$, $iff/3$, etc. Since this form of overloading is not generally handled in typed variants of Prolog, we aggregate the optional arguments in a list. Note that these lists do not change the computation domain. In particular, there is no variable of type list.

Example 1. Let P be the following Prolog program:

$append([], L, L)$. $append([X|Xs1], Ys, [X|Zs1]) \Leftarrow append(Xs1, Ys, Zs1)$.
$reverse([], [])$.
$reverse([X|Xs1], Ys) \Leftarrow reverse(Xs1, Ys1) \wedge append(Ys1, [X], Ys)$.

P is normalized (left column) and abstracted in P_a (right column).

$append(Xs, Ys, Zs) \Leftarrow$ $append_a(Xs, Ys, Zs) \Leftarrow$
    $Xs = [] \wedge Ys = Zs$. $iff(Xs, []) \wedge iff(Ys, [Zs])$.
$append(Xs, Ys, Zs) \Leftarrow$ $append_a(Xs, Ys, Zs) \Leftarrow$
    $Xs = [X|Xs1] \wedge$ $iff(Xs, [X, Xs1]) \wedge$
    $Zs = [X|Zs1] \wedge$ $iff(Zs, [X, Zs1]) \wedge$
    $append(Xs1, Ys, Zs1)$. $append_a(Xs1, Ys, Zs1)$.

$reverse(Xs, Ys) \Leftarrow$ $reverse_a(Xs, Ys) \Leftarrow$
    $Xs = [] \wedge Ys = []$. $iff(Xs, []) \wedge iff(Ys, [])$.
$reverse(Xs, Ys) \Leftarrow$ $reverse_a(Xs, Ys) \Leftarrow$
    $Xs = [X|Xs1] \wedge$ $iff(Xs, [X, Xs1]) \wedge$
    $reverse(Xs1, Ys1) \wedge$ $reverse_a(Xs1, Ys1) \wedge$
    $A = [X|A1] \wedge A1 = [] \wedge$ $iff(A, [X, A1]) \wedge iff(A1, []) \wedge$
    $append(Ys1, A, Ys)$. $append_a(Ys1, A, Ys)$.

The minimal model of P_a gives the following set of facts, $M(P_a)$:

{ $append_a(true, true, true)$, $append_a(true, false, false)$,
    $append_a(false, true, false)$, $append_a(false, false, false)$,
    $reverse_a(true, true)$, $reverse_a(false, false)$ }.

This says in particular that the first argument of an answer to *append* is either ground or not, which is a trivial fact, and misses an important point. Namely, the first argument of an answer to *append* is always a proper list, which is not true of the other arguments. Note that though prescriptive typing forces all three arguments to be seen as lists, it does not force them to be proper list in all answers. This shows that typed analysis is not a trivial combination of typing and static analysis.

Let B be the goal $reverse([1], L)$. Its normal form is

$X = [Y|Z] \wedge Y = 1 \wedge Z = [] \wedge reverse_a(X, L)$

and its abstraction B_a is $iff(X, [Y, Z]) \wedge iff(Y, []) \wedge iff(Z, []) \wedge reverse_a(X, L)$.

An approximation of the answer set results from executing B_a on $M(P_a)$: $\{reverse_a(true, true)\}$. It says that all answers to goal $reverse([1], L)$ are ground.

For the sake of the combination with types, we give a slightly different view on the previous abstraction. The abstraction of an atom $X_0 = f(X_1, \ldots, X_k)$ into a goal $iff(X_0, [X_1, \ldots, X_k])$ corresponds to the following deduction rule:

$$\frac{X_1 : P_1 \quad \cdots \quad X_k : P_k}{f(X_1, \ldots, X_k) : \bigwedge_{i \in [1,k]} P_i}$$

In the case of lists, one can specialize this rule into the two following rules:

$$\frac{X_1 : P_1 \quad X_2 : P_2}{[X_1|X_2] : P_1 \wedge P_2} \qquad\qquad \frac{}{[] : true}$$

2.3 PROLOG Terms with Simple Types

We describe λPROLOG types and a part of λPROLOG term formation rules as a way of building a typed version of PROLOG. This allows a progressive introduction to the typed analysis of λPROLOG.

Simple types are generated by the following grammar:

$$\mathcal{T} ::= \mathcal{W} \mid (\mathcal{K}_i \underbrace{\mathcal{T} \ldots \mathcal{T}}_{i}) \mid (\mathcal{T} \rightarrow \mathcal{T})$$

where $\mathcal{W}$ and $\mathcal{K}_i$ are respectively type variables and type constants of arity i. We suppose that $\mathcal{K}_0$ contains the constant o for the type of truth values. The arrow associates to the right. The rightmost type is called the *result type*. Type constants are declared as follows: **kind** τ *type* $\rightarrow \ldots \rightarrow$ *type* $\rightarrow$ *type*. The number of arrows defines the arity of the type constant τ.

Simply typed first-order terms are defined as follows[4]:

$$\mathcal{FOT}_t ::= \mathcal{C}_t \mid \mathcal{U}_t$$
$$\mathcal{FOT}_t ::= (\mathcal{FOT}_{t' \rightarrow t} \;\; \mathcal{FOT}_{t'})$$

where $\mathcal{C}_t$ and $\mathcal{U}_t$ are respectively term constants and logical variables, all being of type t. The second rule generates *applications*. Application is considered left-associative. Every logical variable X has a type inferred by a typing system. Every constant f has a type defined by a type declaration: e.g., **type** *nil* (*list A*). A constant is called a *predicate constant* if its result type is o: e.g., **type** *nilp* (*list A*) $\rightarrow o$.

The inference of types of variables is decidable when types of all constants (especially predicate constants) are known [MO84]. The inference of types of predicate constants is also decidable if clauses are not subject to the *head condition* (i.e., *definitional genericity*) [LR91]. According to this condition every predicate constant must occur under the same type in the head of every clause that defines it. When the head condition is assumed, the inference of the types of predicates is undecidable in general.

In this article, we assume that all types are available, either via inference or via declaration, and we also assume that definitional genericity is enforced; this will help in proving the termination of the analysis (see Section 4). Brisset and Ridoux adopt these conventions in their λPROLOG compiler [BR93], though Nadathur and Pfenning propose a typing scheme that rejects the head-condition [NP92].

2.4 Domain $\mathcal{P}os$ with Types

For typed analysis, we combine the domain $\mathcal{P}os$ with types. We call this new domain $\mathcal{P}os_T$. The constants of this domain are built with values *true* and *false* and with type constants (defined in the program). We define a partial order relation, $<$, and an equivalence relation, $=$, on $\mathcal{P}os_T$.

---

[4] This is not the standard notation for Prolog. This Lisp-like notation has been chosen for compatibility with the λPROLOG part of this article. Moreover, the expression of the discipline of simple types is easier with this syntax because only one application is considered at a time.

Definition 1. $(\mathcal{P}os_T)$ *true* $\in \mathcal{P}os_T$, *false* $\in \mathcal{P}os_T$, *and for every type constant* $\tau \in \mathcal{K}_i$, *if all* $x_j \in \mathcal{P}os_T$, $(\tau\ x_1\ \dots\ x_i) \in \mathcal{P}os_T$.
(Equivalence relation, $=$**)** $(\tau_a\ true\ \dots\ true) = true$.
   $(\tau_a\ P_1\ \dots\ P_n) = (\tau_a\ Q_1\ \dots\ Q_n)$ *if and only if* $P_i = Q_i$ *for every* i.
(Partial order relation, $<$**)** *false* $< (\tau_a\ P_1\ \dots\ P_n)$ *for all* $P_1\ \dots\ P_n$.
   $(\tau_a\ P_1\ \dots\ P_n) < (\tau_a\ Q_1\ \dots\ Q_n)$ *if and only if* $P_i < Q_i$ *for at least one* i, *and* $P_i \leq Q_i$ *for others (product order).*

Example 2. If there is a declaration **kind** *pair type* $\rightarrow$ *type* $\rightarrow$ *type* in the program, values $(pair_a\ true\ true)$, $(pair_a\ true\ false)$, etc, are in $\mathcal{P}os_T$. And if both *pair* and *list* are declared, then $(list_a\ (pair_a\ true\ false))$ and $(pair_a\ true\ (list_a\ false))$, etc, are in $\mathcal{P}os_T$ as well.

$\mathcal{P}os_T$ with these relations forms a lattice whose least value is *false* and greatest value is *true*. Every time there is a type constant of arity greater than 0, $\mathcal{P}os_T$ is a lattice with an infinite height. We we will see in section 4 that it does not impede termination. More precisely, there are infinite increasing chains (e.g., *false*, $(list_a\ false)$, $(list_a\ (list_a\ false))$, $\dots$, $(list_a^n\ false)$, $\dots$), but all decreasing chains are finite.

Definition 2 (Lattice operations in typed $\mathcal{P}os$).
   $v_1 \sqcap v_2$ *is the greatest* v *such that* $(v \leq v_1) \wedge (v \leq v_2)$.
   $v_1 \sqcup v_2$ *is the least* v *such that* $(v_1 \leq v) \wedge (v_2 \leq v)$.

Formulas of $\mathcal{P}os_T$ are built with $\mathcal{P}os_T$ constants, variables, and operators $\sqcap$ and $\sqcup$. They are positive formulas in the sense that if all variables of a formula are set to *true*, the formula is never equivalent to *false*. Since $\mathcal{P}os_T$ is not a complemented lattice, there is no simple definition of a $\leftrightarrow$ operation.

Predicate *iff* must be redefined to take into account the domain $\mathcal{P}os_T$.

Definition 3. $(iff\ X_0\ [X_1, \dots, X_k]) \stackrel{def}{=} X_0 = \bigsqcap_{i \in [1,k]} X_i$

2.5   First Order Typed Groundness Analysis

Let us first study the case of lists. The data type *list* is defined as follows:
   kind *list type* $\rightarrow$ *type* .
   type $[]$ $(list\ \_)$.   **type** '.' $A \rightarrow (list\ A) \rightarrow (list\ A)$.
These declarations represent the following deduction rules:

$$\frac{}{[] : (list\ \_)} \qquad \frac{X_1 : A \qquad X_2 : (list\ A)}{[X_1|X_2] : (list\ A)}$$

Now, we combine typing rules with deduction rules for groundness (see Section 3) such that the conclusions of new rules are lower ($<$ order) than or equal to conclusions of typing rules, and if one of the groundness premises is strictly lower than a typing one, as well is the conclusion.

$$\frac{}{[] : (list_a\ true)} \qquad \frac{X_1 : A_1 \qquad X_2 : (list_a\ A_2)}{[X_1|X_2] : (list_a\ A_1 \sqcap A_2)}$$

$$\frac{X_1 : P_1 \quad X_2 : P_2}{[X_1|X_2] : false} \qquad if\ \forall P[P_1 < P] \vee \forall P[P_2 < (list_a\ P)]$$

Since $false$ is the least value of $\mathcal{P}os_T$, we can replace the last rule with:

$$\frac{X_1 : P_1 \quad X_2 : P_2}{[X_1|X_2] : false} \qquad if\ P_1 < false \vee P_2 < (list_a\ false)$$

Constraint $P_1 < false$ cannot be satisfied, and the second one simply says $P_2 = false$. However, in the sequel, we prefer to use forms similar to $P_1 < false$ and $P_2 < (list_a\ false)$ for the sake of generalization.

We can easily generalize these deduction rules to all the first-order constants, **type** $c\ \tau_1 \to \ldots \to \tau_k \to (\tau\ T_1\ \ldots\ T_n)$, where $\tau_1, \ldots, \tau_k$ and $(\tau\ T_1\ \ldots\ T_n)$ are either basic types (int, $float$, $string$, etc), or constructed types $((list\ A)$, $(pair\ A\ B)$, etc). Every declaration of a term constant corresponds to three deduction rules: the usual typing rule, a static analysis rule that propagates groundness, and a static analysis rule that propagates non-groundness. These rules are as follows:

$$\frac{X_1 : \tau_1 \quad \ldots \quad X_k : \tau_k}{(c\ X_1\ \ldots\ X_k) : (\tau\ T_1\ \ldots\ T_n)} \qquad \text{typing}$$

$$\frac{X_1 : \tau'_1 \quad \ldots \quad X_k : \tau'_k}{(c\ X_1\ \ldots\ X_k) : (\tau_a\ (\sqcap R_1)\ \ldots\ (\sqcap R_n))} \qquad \text{groundness}$$

where τ'_j (j from 1 to k) are copies of types τ_j where all occurrences of all variables are renamed apart. R_i is a list of all the renaming variables of T_i in the τ'_j's (j from 1 to k). In the example of lists, the list of renaming variables of A is $[A_1, A_2]$.

Non-groundness propagation rules are as follow:

$$\frac{X_1 : P_1 \quad \ldots \quad X_k : P_k}{(c\ X_1\ \ldots\ X_k) : false} \qquad if\ \bigvee_{i \in [1,k]} (P_i < \tau''_i) \qquad \text{non-groundness}$$

where P_i are new variables, one per argument of c, and τ''_j are instances of τ_j where all variables are replaced with $false$. The general scheme can produce unsatisfiable constraints $P_i < false$; and this allows in practice to forget rules if none of their premises can be satisfied.

Note that concrete programs are supposed to be well-typed, so all occurrences of a constant have types which are instances of its type scheme. So, the reason why a constraint like $P_i < \tau''_i$ fails cannot be that P_i is not comparable with τ''_i. The only reason $P_i < \tau''_i$ can fail is that $P_i \geq \tau''_i$.

Abstraction procedures for declarations of type and term constants are as follows:

Definition 4. (Abstraction of type constant) *For each type constant τ:*

$$Abstr_{kind}[\![\textbf{kind}\ \tau\ \underbrace{\textbf{type} \to \ldots \textbf{type}}_{n}]\!] \equiv \textbf{type}\ \tau_a\ \underbrace{\mathcal{P}os_T \to \ldots \mathcal{P}os_T}_{n}.$$

(Abstraction of term constant) *For each term constant c:*

$$Abstr_{type}[\![\textbf{type}\ c\ \tau_1 \to \ldots \to \tau_k \to (\tau\ T_1\ \ldots\ T_n)]\!] \equiv$$
$$\textbf{type}\ iff\_\tau\_c\ \mathcal{P}os_T \to (list\ \mathcal{P}os_T) \to o.$$

$$iff\_\tau\_c \ (\tau_a \ T_1 \ \ldots \ T_n) \ [\tau_1', \ldots, \tau_k'] \ \Leftarrow \ iff \ T_1 \ R_1 \wedge \ldots \wedge iff \ T_n \ R_n \ .$$
$$iff\_\tau\_c \ false \ [P_1, \ldots, P_k] \ \Leftarrow \ P_1 < \tau_k'' \vee \ldots \vee P_k < \tau_k'' \ .$$

The following example shows one application of this method to a more complex type (trees with varisized nodes).

Example 3. Concrete declarations:
   kind $ntree \ type \rightarrow type \rightarrow type$.
   type $leaf \ L \rightarrow (ntree \ N \ L)$.
   type $node \ (list \ (ntree \ N \ L)) \rightarrow N \rightarrow (ntree \ N \ L)$.
Their abstractions (where unsatisfiable premisses are underlined):
   $iff\_ntree\_leaf \ (ntree_a \ N_0 \ L_0) \ [L_1] \ \Leftarrow \ iff \ L_0 \ [L_1]$.
   $iff\_ntree\_leaf \ false \ [P_1] \ \Leftarrow \ \underline{P_1 < false}$.
   $iff\_ntree\_node \ (ntree_a \ N_0 \ L_0) \ [((list_a \ (ntree_a \ N_1 \ L_1)), N_2] \ \Leftarrow$
      $iff \ L_0 \ [L_1] \wedge iff \ N_0 \ [N_1, N_2]$.
   $iff\_ntree\_node \ false \ [P_1, P_2] \ \Leftarrow$
      $(\underline{P_1 < (list_a \ (ntree_a \ false \ false))} \vee \underline{P_2 < false})$.

The abstraction procedure for first-order terms is given below (Φ is a term constant).

Definition 5. (Abstraction of equalities with term constants)
   $Abstr_{goal} [\![F = (\Phi \ X_1 \ldots X_k)]\!] \ \equiv \ iff\_\tau\_\Phi \ F \ [X_1, \ldots, X_k]$
   where Φ is the term constant of result type $(\tau \ T_1 \ \ldots \ T_n)$.
(Abstraction of equalities without term constants)
   $Abstr_{goal} [\![F = X]\!] \ \equiv \ iff \ F \ [X]$ *where X is a variable.*

The definition of $Abstr_{goal}$ must be completed to handle connectives, and an $Abstr_{clause}$ procedure must also be defined. They are straightforward, and we lack of space for presenting them in more details.

Example 4. Let us apply this method to program *append* (see definition and normal form in Example 1). The abstraction of this program gives the following result:
   type $append_a \ \mathcal{P}os_T \rightarrow \mathcal{P}os_T \rightarrow \mathcal{P}os_T \rightarrow o$.
   $append_a \ Xs \ Ys \ Zs \ \Leftarrow \ iff\_list\_nil \ Xs \ [] \wedge iff \ Ys \ [Zs]$.
   $append_a \ Xs \ Ys \ Zs \ \Leftarrow$
      $iff\_list\_cons \ Xs \ [X|Xs1] \wedge iff\_list\_cons \ Zs \ [X|Zs1] \wedge append_a \ Xs1 \ Ys \ Zs1$.
The set of success patterns of program $append_a$ is as follows:
   { $append_a \ true \ true \ true, \ append_a \ (list_a \ false) \ (list_a \ false) \ (list_a \ false),$
      $append_a \ true \ (list_a \ false) \ (list_a \ false)$,
      $append_a \ (list_a \ false) \ true \ (list_a \ false)$,
      $append_a \ (list_a \ false) \ false \ false \ , \ append_a \ true \ false \ false$ }
Note that this set does not contain atoms like $(append_a \ false \ \ldots \ \ldots)$. This is because predicate *append* either goes through or constructs an entire list in its first argument. Hence, the first argument of every answer to *append* is a proper list. Note that typed analysis is not merely a product of type inference/checking and static analysis in $\mathcal{P}os$. For instance, an argument can be a list, and still have property *false* (e.g., second and third arguments of *append*).

3 Typed Properties for λPROLOG

The study of static analysis for λPROLOG programs was our original motivation for elaborating a typed static analysis simply because types are there. We show in this section what typed analysis of groundness looks like for λPROLOG.

3.1 λPROLOG

λPROLOG terms are *simply typed λ-terms*. Simple types are generated as written above (see Section 2.3). Simply typed λ-terms are defined as follows:

$$\Lambda_t \quad ::= \quad \mathcal{C}_t \mid \mathcal{V}_t \mid \mathcal{U}_t \mid (\Lambda_{t' \to t} \quad \Lambda_{t'})$$
$$\Lambda_{t' \to t} \quad ::= \quad \lambda \mathcal{V}_{t'} \Lambda_t$$

where the notations are as for simply typed first-order terms (see Section 2.3), and $\mathcal{V}_t$ is a set of λ-variables of type t for all t. The novelty is essentially in the second rule, which generates λ-*abstractions*. An occurrence of a λ-variable x is called *bound* if and only if it occurs in a λ-abstraction $\lambda x(E)$; otherwise, it is called *free*.

The leftmost component in nested applications is called the *head* of the outermost application. The notion of head is extended to non-applications as follows: the head of either a constant, a logical variable or of a λ-variable is itself, and the head of a λ-abstraction is the head of its body (recursively, if the body is itself a λ-abstraction).

An equivalence relation on λ-terms, the λ-equivalence, is defined by three axioms:

α: $\lambda x(M)$ is α-equivalent to $\lambda y(M[x \leftarrow y])$, if y has no occurrence in M. This formalizes the safe renaming of the λ-variables of a term.

β: $(\lambda x(M) \; N)$ is β-equivalent to $M[x \leftarrow N]$, if no free variable of N is bound in M. This formalizes the safe substitution of an effective parameter N to a formal parameter x.

η: $\lambda x(M \; x)$ is η-equivalent to M, if x has no free occurrence in M. This formalizes functional extensionality for λ-terms: two functions are equivalent if they yield equivalent results.

When oriented left-to-right, axiom β forms a rewriting rule called β-reduction. Oriented right-to-left, axiom η forms a rewriting rule called η-expansion. Terms that match the left-hand side of the β-reduction rule are called β-redexes. A term with no occurrence of a β-redex is called β-normal. In the simply typed λ-calculus, every term has a unique β-normal form, which can be computed by applying the rules in any order.

λPROLOG formulas (called *hereditary Harrop formulas*) are based on three hierarchical levels (like PROLOG): definite clauses ($\mathcal{D}$), goals ($\mathcal{G}$) and atomic formulas ($\mathcal{A}$). A λPROLOG program is a set of declarations and an ordered set of clauses. Clauses and goals are generated by the following grammar:

$$\mathcal{D} ::= \mathcal{A} \mid \mathcal{A} \Leftarrow \mathcal{G} \mid \forall x.\mathcal{D} \mid \mathcal{D} \wedge \mathcal{D}$$
$$\mathcal{G} ::= \mathcal{A} \mid \mathcal{G} \wedge \mathcal{G} \mid \mathcal{G} \vee \mathcal{G} \mid \exists x.\mathcal{G} \mid \forall x.\mathcal{G} \mid \mathcal{D} \Rightarrow \mathcal{G}$$
$$\mathcal{A} ::= atomic \; formula$$

The novelty of Harrop formulas is in the goal language: universal quantifications and implications may occur in goals, which is forbidden with Horn formulas.

In λPROLOG, there are three different notions of scope: λ-abstraction limits the scope of variables in terms, quantifications limit the scope of variables in formulas, and the deduction rules (see below) for universal quantification and implication limit the scope of constants and clauses, respectively, in the proof process.

$$\frac{P, D \vdash G}{P \vdash D \Rightarrow G} \qquad \frac{P \vdash G[x \leftarrow c]}{P \vdash \forall x.G} \qquad c \text{ occurs neither in } P \text{ nor in } G$$

In the implication rule a clause D is added to a program P for the proof of a goal G, and in the universal quantification rule, a *new* constant c is added for the proof of $G[x \leftarrow c]$.

The following example illustrates an application of λ-terms for representing data-structures. It defines the reversal of functional lists (lists represented by functions so that nil, $[1, 2]$ and $[A|B]$ correspond to $\lambda x(x)$, $\lambda x[1, 2|x]$ and $\lambda x[A|(B\ x)]$).

   type $fnrev\ ((list\ A) \rightarrow (list\ A)) \rightarrow ((list\ A) \rightarrow (list\ A)) \rightarrow o$.

   $fnrev\ \lambda z(z)\ \lambda z(z)$. $fnrev\ \lambda z[A|(L\ z)]\ \lambda z(R\ [A|z])\ \Leftarrow\ fnrev\ L\ R$.

The first clause reverses empty lists, represented by the identity function. The second one uses higher-order unification to split a list and to construct another one.

3.2   Groundness Analysis for λPROLOG Programs

The normal form of λPROLOG programs extends the normal form for PROLOG programs with additional rules for normalizing the new structures of λPROLOG: λ-terms, quantifications and implication. Normalization for λPROLOG has the same goal as for PROLOG programs. In particular, it makes unification steps explicit.

The most important feature of normalized λPROLOG programs is that equalities have the form $F = \lambda x_1 \ldots x_l(\Phi\ (X_1\ x_1\ \ldots\ x_l) \ldots (X_k\ x_1\ \ldots\ x_l))$ where Φ can be either a constant (e.g., add), a bound λ-variable (e.g., x_i, with $i \in [1, l]$), or a logical variable. Moreover, all terms are η-expanded, so that the number of arguments of Φ reflects its type. In PROLOG/MALI (a λPROLOG system), type checking/inferring and η-expansion are done anyway [BR93]. Every λPROLOG program can be transformed into an equivalent normalized form [MRB98].

Example 5. A normalized form of predicate $fnrev$ is as follows:
   $fnrev\ U0\ U1\ \Leftarrow\ U0 = \lambda x(x) \wedge U1 = \lambda x(x)$.
   $fnrev\ U0\ U1\ \Leftarrow$
         $U0 = \lambda x[(E0\ x)|(E1\ x)] \wedge E0 = \lambda x(A)\ \wedge$
         $E1 = \lambda x(L\ (E2\ x)) \wedge E2 = \lambda x(x)\ \wedge$
         $U1 = \lambda x(R\ (E3\ x)) \wedge E3 = \lambda x[(E4\ x)|(E5\ x)]\ \wedge$
         $E4 = \lambda x(A) \wedge E5 = \lambda x(x) \wedge fnrev\ L\ R$.

The aim of groundness analysis for λPROLOG is to determine which arguments of which atoms are instantiated to terms that are β-equivalent[5] to ground terms when the program is executed. The main difference with PROLOG is the handling of λ-terms. A λ-term has two roles with respect to groundness: it may be ground, and it may propagates the non-groundness of its arguments to its β-normal form.

Example 6. Let $First = \lambda xy(x)$ be a λ-term: $First$ is ground. Now, let $G = (First\ 1\ X)$ and $H = (First\ X\ 1)$: G and H are ground terms if and only if X is ground. However, G β-reduces to a ground term whereas H β-reduces to a ground term if and only if X does so. So, the behaviors of G and H are different.

The way a λ-term propagates the analyzed property must be represented somehow. We call it the *transfer function* of a λ-term. So, we associate with $First$ a transfer function which says that the first argument is propagated but not the second. Such a transfer function can be represented by a boolean vector that indicates which arguments are actually used. For reasons of convenience, we will code these boolean vectors as boolean lists. So, the transfer function of term $First$ is represented by $[t, f]$.

The transfer function of a given term is also used to compute the transfer functions of other terms in which it occurs. It is done by the means of a disjunction of transfer functions. Given a term $F = \lambda x_1 \ldots x_l(\Phi\ (X_1\ x_1\ \ldots\ x_l) \ldots (X_k\ x_1\ \ldots\ x_l))$, the transfer function of F is a function of the transfer functions of Φ and the X_i's. Roughly, F needs its ith argument if either Φ is its ith bound variable (i.e., x_i), or if it is needed by an X_j that is itself needed by Φ.

Definition 6 (Disjunction of transfer functions).

$$(ho\_disj\ F_{tf}\ \Phi_v\ \Phi_{tf}\ [X_{1_{tf}}, \ldots, X_{k_{tf}}]) \overset{def}{=} F_{tf} = \Phi_v \vee \bigvee_{j \in [1,k] || \Phi_{tf_j} = t} X_{j_{tf}}$$

where $\vee$ is bitwise disjunction of boolean vectors.

We define a predicate *ho_iff* that plays the same role as predicate *iff*, except that it uses a transfer function for filtering out the properties of useless arguments. Roughly, a term $F = \lambda x_1 \ldots x_l(\Phi\ (X_1\ x_1\ \ldots\ x_l) \ldots (X_k\ x_1\ \ldots\ x_l))$ β-normalizes into a ground term if Φ is not a logical variable, and if all the X_j's that Φ needs also β-normalize into ground terms.

Definition 7 (Relation *ho_iff*).

$$(ho\_iff\ F_a\ \Phi_a\ \Phi_{tf}\ [X_{1_a}, \ldots, X_{k_a}]) \overset{def}{=} F_a = \Phi_a \wedge \bigwedge_{j \in [1,k] || \Phi_{tf_j} = t} X_{j_a}$$

The heart of abstraction is described by the abstraction of equalities.

---

[5] Only β-equivalence matters since η-equivalence only concerns occurrences of λ-variables ($\lambda x(M\ x) \equiv_\eta M$). β-Equivalence matters because the argument N may either occur or not in the β-reduced term according to whether the λ-variable x occurs in the body M of the function $((\lambda x(M)\ N) \equiv_\beta M[x \leftarrow N])$.

Definition 8 (Abstraction of equalities).
$Abstr_{goal}[\![F = \lambda x_1 \ldots x_l(\Phi \ (X_1 \ x_1 \ \ldots \ x_l) \ldots (X_k \ x_1 \ \ldots \ x_l))]\!] \equiv$
$\quad ho\_iff \ F_a \ \Phi_a \ \Phi_{tf}[X_{1_a}, \ldots, X_{k_a}] \wedge ho\_disj \ F_{tf} \ \Phi_v \ \Phi_{tf} \ [X_{1_{tf}}, \ldots, X_{k_{tf}}]$

If Φ is a constant: $\Phi_a = true, \ \Phi_{tf} = \underbrace{[t, \ldots, t]}_{k} \ and \ \Phi_v = \underbrace{[f, \ldots, f]}_{l}.$

If Φ is a λ-variable: $\Phi_a = true, \ \Phi_{tf} = \underbrace{[t, \ldots, t]}_{k} \ and \ \Phi_v = [\underbrace{f, \ldots, f}_{i-1}, t, \underbrace{f, \ldots, f}_{l-i}].$

If Φ is an unknown: $\Phi_a, \ \Phi_{tf} \ are \ unknowns, \ and \ \Phi_v = \underbrace{[f, \ldots, f]}_{l}.$

Example 7. If we apply this method to predicate *fnrev* (see normalized form in Example 5), we obtain the following abstract program for the property of groundness,

$\quad fnrev_a \ U0_a \ U0_{tf} \ U1_a \ U1_{tf} \ \Leftarrow$
$\qquad ho\_iff \ U0_a \ true \ [] \ [] \wedge \ ho\_disj \ U0_{tf} \ [t] \ [] \ [] \ \wedge$
$\qquad ho\_iff \ U1_a \ true \ [] \ [] \wedge ho\_disj \ U1_{tf} \ [t] \ [] \ [] \ .$
$\quad fnrev_a \ U0_a \ U0_{tf} \ U1_a \ U1_{tf} \ \Leftarrow$
$\qquad ho\_iff \ U0_a \ true \ [t,t] \ [E0_a, E1_a] \wedge ho\_disj \ U0_{tf} \ [f] \ [t,t] \ [E0_{tf}, \ E1_{tf}] \ \wedge$
$\qquad ho\_iff \ E0_a \ A_a \ [] \ [] \ \wedge \ ho\_disj \ E0_{tf} \ [f] \ [] \ [] \ \wedge$
$\qquad ho\_iff \ E1_a \ L_a \ L_{tf} \ [E2_a] \wedge ho\_disj \ E1_{tf} \ [f] \ L_{tf} \ [E2_{tf}] \ \wedge$
$\qquad ho\_iff \ E2_a \ true \ [] \ [] \wedge ho\_disj \ E2_{tf} \ [t] \ [] \ [] \ \wedge$
$\qquad ho\_iff \ U1_a \ R_a \ R_{tf} \ [E3_a] \wedge ho\_disj \ U1_{tf} \ [f] \ R_{tf} \ [E3_{tf}] \ \wedge$
$\qquad ho\_iff \ E3_a \ true \ [t,t] \ [E4_a, E5_a] \wedge ho\_disj \ E3_{tf} \ [f] \ [t,t] \ [E4_{tf}, \ E5_{tf}] \ \wedge$
$\qquad ho\_iff \ E4_a \ A_a \ [] \ [] \wedge ho\_disj \ E4_{tf} \ [f] \ [] \ [] \ \wedge$
$\qquad ho\_iff \ E5_a \ true \ [] \ [] \wedge ho\_disj \ E5_{tf} \ [t] \ [] \ [] \wedge fnrev_a \ L_a \ L_{tf} \ R_a \ R_{tf} \ .$

and finally a set of abstract answers,
$\quad \{ \ fnrev_a \ true \ [t] \ true \ [t], \ fnrev_a \ false \ [t] \ false \ [t] \ \}.$

This result shows that both arguments of *fnrev* are unary functions that use their argument, and that an argument of *fnrev* is ground whenever the other is also ground.

3.3   Higher Order Typed Groundness Analysis

Let us consider the case of lists and then generalize as in Section 2.5, but in a higher-order context.

In a normalized program, the form of every goal with an occurrence of a list constant is either $F = \lambda x_1 \ldots x_l[]$ or $F = \lambda x_1 \ldots x_l[(X_1 \ x_1 \ \ldots \ x_l)|(X_2 \ x_1 \ \ldots \ x_l)]$. All equalities whose right member does not contain a list constant are abstracted by *ho_iff* and equalities with list constants are abstracted with specialized predicates.

To compute groundness, we need the transfer function of F and the transfer function of the head of the application (which, in this case, is either *nil* or *cons*). The transfer function of *nil* is [] whereas the transfer function of *cons* is $[t,t]$ because *cons* uses its two arguments. The transfer function of $\lambda x_1 \ldots x_l[]$

is $[\underbrace{f,\ldots,f}_{l}]$ because none of the x_i's occurs in the body of the abstraction.

The transfer function of $\lambda x_1 \ldots x_l[(X_1 \ x_1 \ \ldots \ x_l)|(X_2 \ x_1 \ \ldots \ x_l)]$ is a disjunction between the transfer function of X_1 and the transfer function of X_2; i.e., a λ-variable x_i occurs in the β-normal form of this term only if it occurs in the β-normal form of either $(X_1 \ x_1 \ \ldots \ x_l)$ or $(X_2 \ x_1 \ \ldots \ x_l)$. The non-typed analysis presented in Section 3.2 needs also know whether the head of the application is ground or not. In the present case, the head is ground since it is a term constant. To summarize, the abstraction of equality goals where the head is a constant falls in the first case of definition 8. I.e., transfer functions play no role in these goals, so we will use iff_list_Φ predicates instead of the expected $ho\_iff\_list\_\Phi$. Then, the procedure for abstracting equalities is as follows:

Definition 9 (Abstraction of equalities).
If Φ is a term constant of result type $(\tau \ T_1 \ldots T_n)$:
$$Abstr_{goal}[\![F = \lambda x_1 \ldots x_l(\Phi \ (X_1 \ x_1 \ \ldots \ x_l)\ldots(X_k \ x_1 \ \ldots \ x_l))]\!] \equiv$$
$$iff\_\tau\_\Phi \ F_a \ [X_{1_a},\ldots,X_{k_a}] \wedge ho\_disj \ F_{tf} \ \underbrace{[f,\ldots,f]}_{l} \ \underbrace{[t,\ldots,t]}_{k} \ [X_{1_{tf}},\ldots,X_{k_{tf}}]$$

Otherwise, and with the same conditions on Φ, Φ_v and Φ_{tf} as in definition 8:
$$Abstr_{goal}[\![F = \lambda x_1 \ldots x_l(\Phi \ (X_1 \ x_1 \ \ldots \ x_l)\ldots(X_k \ x_1 \ \ldots \ x_l))]\!] \equiv$$
$$ho\_iff \ F_a \ \Phi_a \ \Phi_{tf} \ [X_{1_a},\ldots,X_{k_a}] \wedge ho\_disj \ F_{tf} \ \Phi_v \ \Phi_{tf} \ [X_{1_{tf}},\ldots,X_{k_{tf}}]$$

Predicate ho_iff is still used to abstract equalities whose head is not a constant. We give its definition with respect to $\mathcal{P}os_T$.

Definition 10. $(ho\_iff \ F_a \ \Phi_a \ \Phi_{tf} \ [X_{1_p},\ldots,X_{k_p}]) \overset{def}{=} F_a = \Phi_a \ \sqcap \ \underset{i \in [1,k]|\Phi_{tf_i}=t}{\sqcap} X_{i_p}$

Example 8. Let us analyze program $fnrev$ with our new definition: the normalized program is as in Example 7, and the abstracted program is as follows:
type $fnrev_a \ \mathcal{P}os_T \rightarrow (list \ bool) \rightarrow \mathcal{P}os_T \rightarrow (list \ bool) \rightarrow o$.
$fnrev_a \ U0_a \ U0_{tf} \ U1_a \ U1_{tf} \Leftarrow$
　　$ho\_iff \ U0_a \ true \ [] \ [] \wedge ho\_disj \ U0_{tf} \ [t] \ [] \ [] \wedge$
　　$ho\_iff \ U1_a \ true \ [] \ [] \wedge ho\_disj \ U1_{tf} \ [t] \ [] \ []$.
$fnrev_a \ U0_a \ U0_{tf} \ U1_a \ U1_{tf} \Leftarrow$
　　$iff\_list\_cons \ U0_a \ [E0_a, E1_a] \wedge ho\_disj \ U0_{tf} \ [f] \ [t,t] \ [E0_{tf}, E1_{tf}] \wedge$
　　$ho\_iff \ E0_a \ A_a \ [] \ [] \wedge ho\_disj E \ 0_{tf} \ [f] \ [] \ [] \wedge$
　　$ho\_iff \ E1_a \ L_a \ L_{tf} \ [E2_a] \wedge ho\_disj \ E1_{tf} \ [f] \ L_{tf}[E2_{tf}] \wedge$
　　$ho\_iff \ E2_a \ true \ [] \ [] \wedge ho\_disj \ E2_{tf} \ [t] \ [] \ [] \wedge$
　　$ho\_iff \ U1_a \ R_a \ R_{tf} \ [E3_a] \wedge ho\_disj \ U1_{tf} \ [f] \ R_{tf} \ [E3_{tf}] \wedge$
　　$iff\_list\_cons \ E3_a \ [E4_a, E5_a] \wedge ho\_disj \ E3_{tf} \ [f] \ [t,t] \ [E4_{tf}, E5_{tf}] \wedge$
　　$ho\_iff \ E4_a \ A_a \ [] \ [] \wedge ho\_disj \ E4_{tf} \ [f] \ [] \ [] \wedge$
　　$ho\_iff \ E5_a \ true \ [] \ [] \wedge ho\_disj \ E5_{tf} \ [t] \ [] \ [] \wedge fnrev_a \ L_a \ L_{tf} \ R_a \ R_{tf}$.
We obtain a set of success patterns which takes into account the structure of lists:
$\{fnrev_a \ true \ [t] \ true \ [t], fnrev_a \ (list_a \ false) \ [t] \ (list_a \ false) \ [t]\}$.

We can compare these results with those obtained with the non-typed groundness analysis (Example 7). With typed analysis, $(fnrev_a \ false \ [t] \ false \ [t])$ is not a solution. This is because all the answers will be proper lists, even if the arguments passed to predicate $fnrev$ are improper lists.

4   Termination and Correctness

The lattice Pos_T has an infinite height in all non-degenerated cases. In this section, we show that it does not impede the termination of the analysis.

The reason comes from the hypothesis that programs are type-checked before being analyzed, that they follow the discipline of simple types and the polymorphism discipline of definitional genericity [LR91] (related to the so-called *head-condition* [HT92]), and that all decreasing chains in Pos_T are finite.

The first hypothesis essentially implies that a type is associated to every component (constants or variables) of a clause. The second hypothesis implies that all occurrences in clause heads of a predicate constant have equivalent types, and that all other occurrences (i.e., in clause bodies) have types that are either equivalent to or more instantiated than the types of head occurrences. This condition implies among other things that no type information goes from a called predicate to a calling goal.

Example 9. Let the following predicates p and q:

$p \ X \ \Leftarrow \ p \ [X] \ .$ $q \ [X] \ \Leftarrow \ q \ X \ .$

p is definitionally generic (e.g., give type $A \rightarrow o$ to p), but q is not. Indeed, whichever type is given to q, the type of the head occurrence is either not compatible or is strictly more instantiated than the type of the body occurrence.

Thus, every component of a clause is equipped with a simple type that may contain type variables as a trace of polymorphic declarations. The head-condition insures that the types of most-general answers, like those computed by the S-semantics [FLMP89] for PROLOG, or by a similar semantics defined for λPROLOG [Mal99], are not more instantiated than the type of their predicate.

Finally, conclusions of typed analysis rules are either *true*, or lower than or equal (in the $<$ order of Definition 1) to conclusions of the type rules from which they are derived. The typed analysis rules being applied to the same terms as the typing rules, they associate to terms properties that are either *true*, or are lower than or equal to their types. So, the answers computed by the S-semantics applied to the abstract program are on chains descending from the types of the clause heads.

So, the effective domain of typed analysis is the set of type instances obtained by substituting *true* or *false* to type variables in types of all program components, plus all lower properties. It is a finite set, that could be represented as a set of constants, though this would not be suitable for comparing properties. Then, the domain of abstract programs can be assimilated with DATALOG (DATALOG$_\Rightarrow$ for λPROLOG[6]).

Proof of correctness derives from the observation that typed analysis rules are a refinement of non-typed analysis rules. In particular, one can prove by induction on typed and non-typed analysis rules that an abstract answer in the typed analysis is *true* only if it is also *true* in the non-typed analysis.

Bonner has shown that DATALOG$_\Rightarrow$ is decidable, but he has also shown that answering queries in DATALOG$_\Rightarrow$ is in PSPACE [Bon90]. We do not know yet if this is an obstacle for the method we propose.

5   Conclusion and Further Works

Codish and Demoen have proposed a method for static analysis of PROLOG programs which is based on abstract compilation. They apply their method to the analysis of the groundness property. In preceding works [MRB98], we have proposed an extension of this method for the static analysis of λPROLOG programs. In this article, we augment the precision of informations obtained with analysis by combining the types of terms with the expression of the analyzed property.

Our typed analysis is not a type inference. It is also different from Codish and Demoen's analysis on types dependencies [CD94], which, in fact, is a form a type inference. More generally, as types are only a special kind of properties, it may seem vain to discriminate type inference and static analysis. However, a clear difference arises when one considers prescriptive types (which are not consequences of a program semantics), and semantic properties. This is what we are doing in supposing that polymorphic types are given, either via declarations or via inference, and we use them to build a property domain that is more refined than $\mathcal{P}os$. It is also important for the termination of evaluation of the abstract program that definitional genericity is enforced (see Section 4).

To summarize, let us say that groundness analysis has to do with groundness, type inference/checking has to do with well-typing, and typed groundness analysis has to do with typed terms forming *proper* structures [O'K90]. Typed groundness analysis meets simple groundness analysis when a term and all its subterms are proper structures.

The result of abstracting a λPROLOG program with respect to the typed groundness property is a DATALOG$_\Rightarrow$ program in which a finite set of constants is represented by complex terms. This language is decidable, so it makes sense to use it as the target of an abstract compilation method. In fact, the inferred/verified types form an envelop for the properties which can be reached in typed static analysis.

The present work can be continued on different ways. First, one can apply it to other properties of PROLOG and of λPROLOG: e.g., sharing. A list whose

---

[6] The $\Rightarrow$ comes from implications in goals. For groundness analysis, universal quantifiers in goals do not remain in the abstract program, but implication connectives do [MRB98].

elements share a subterm could be distinguished from a list that shares with a sublist. The second direction is to implement the method completely. At the present time, a prototype implements the normalization, the abstraction, and the evaluation when the abstract program contains no ⇒. Another direction is to handle function types directly in the abstract domain rather than via the transfer functions. This could lead to a smoother handling of higher-order terms. Finally, a more thorough analysis of $\mathcal{P}os_T$ is also necessary.

References

Bon90.   A.J. Bonner. Hypothetical datalog: Complexity and expressibility. *Theoretical Computer Science*, 76:3–51, 1990.

BR93.   P. Brisset and O. Ridoux. The compilation of λProlog and its execution with MALI. Rapport de recherche 1831, INRIA, 1993.

CD94.   M. Codish and B. Demoen. Deriving polymorphic type dependencies for logic programs using multiple incarnations of Prop. In *First Symp. Static Analysis*, volume 864 of *LNCS*, pages 281–297. Springer-Verlag, 1994.

CD95.   M. Codish and B. Demoen. Analyzing logic programs using "Prop"-ositional logic programs and a magic wand. *J. Logic Programming*, 25(3):249–274, 1995.

CFW91.   A. Cortesi, G. Filé, and W. Winsborough. Prop revisited: Propositional formula as abstract domain for groundness analysis. In *SLCS*, volume CH3025-4, pages 322–327. IEEE, 1991.

DW86.   S. K. Debray and D. S. Warren. Detection and optimization of functional computations in prolog. In E.Y. Shapiro, editor, *Third Int. Conf. Logic Programming*, volume 225 of *LNCS*, pages 490–504. Springer, 1986.

FLMP89.   M. Falaschi, G. Levi, M. Martelli, and C. Palamidessi. Declarative modeling of the operational behavior of logic languages. *Theoretical Computer Science*, 69(3):289–318, 1989.

Han89.   M. Hanus. Horn clause programs with polymorphic types: Semantics and resolution. In *TAPSOFT'89*, LNCS 352, pages 225–240. Springer-Verlag, 1989.

HT92.   P.M. Hill and R.W. Topor. A semantics for typed logic programs. In F. Pfenning, editor, *Types in Logic Programming*, pages 1–62. MIT Press, 1992.

HWD92.   M. V. Hermenegildo, R. Warren, and S. K. Debray. Global flow analysis as a practical compilation tool. *J. Logic Programming*, 13(4):349–366, 1992. preliminary version: ICLP 1988: 684-699.

LR91.   T.K. Lakshman and U.S. Reddy. Typed Prolog: A semantic reconstruction of the Mycroft-O'Keefe type system. In V. Saraswat and K. Ueda, editors, *8th Int. Logic Programming Symp.*, pages 202–217. MIT Press, 1991.

LR96.   P. Louvet and O. Ridoux. Parametric polymorphism for Typed Prolog and λProlog. In *8th Int. Symp. Programming Languages Implementation and Logic Programming*, LNCS 1140, pages 47–61. Springer-Verlag, 1996.

Mal99.   F. Malésieux. *Contribution à l'analyse statique de programmes λProlog*. PhD thesis, Université de Nantes, 1999.

Mil78.   R. Milner. A theory of type polymorphism in programming. *J. Computer and System Sciences*, 17:348–375, 1978.

MO84.   A. Mycroft and R.A. O'Keefe. A polymorphic type system for Prolog. *Artificial Intelligence*, 23:295–307, 1984.

MRB98. F. Malésieux, O. Ridoux, and P. Boizumault. Abstract compilation of
        λProlog. In J. Jaffar, editor, *Joint Int. Conf. and Symp. Logic Program-
        ming*, pages 130–144. MIT Press, 1998.
MS93.   K. Marriott and H. Søndergaard. Precise and efficient groundness analysis
        for logic programs. *ACM Letters on Programming Languages and Systems*,
        2(1–4):181–196, 1993.
NP92.   G. Nadathur and F. Pfenning. The type system of a higher-order logic
        programming language. In F. Pfenning, editor, *Types in Logic Programming*,
        pages 245–283. MIT Press, 1992.
O'K90. R.A. O'Keefe. *The Craft of Prolog*. MIT Press, 1990.
RU95.   R. Ramakrishnan and J. Ullman. A survey of deductive database systems.
        J. Logic Programming, 23(2):125–149, 1995.

A Space Efficient Engine for Subsumption-Based Tabled Evaluation of Logic Programs*

Ernie Johnson, C. R. Ramakrishnan, I. V. Ramakrishnan, and Prasad Rao**

Department of Computer Science, State University of New York at Stony Brook
Stony Brook, New York 11794-4400
{ejohnson,cram,ram}@cs.sunysb.edu

Abstract. Tabled resolution improves efficiency as well as termination properties of logic programs by sharing answer computations across "similar" subgoals. Similarity based on subsumption of subgoals rather than variance (i.e., identity modulo variable renaming) promotes more aggressive sharing, but requires mechanisms to *index* answers from dynamically growing sets. Earlier we proposed Dynamic Threaded Sequential Automata (DTSA) as the data structure for organizing answer tables in subsumption-based tabling. Using a DTSA, we can retrieve answers one at a time from the table, strictly in the order of their insertion. Although DTSA performed very well, its space usage was high. Here we present an alternative data structure called *Time-Stamped Trie* (TST) that relaxes the retrieval order, and yet ensures that all answers will be eventually retrieved. We show that TST has superior space performance to DTSA in theory as well as practice, without sacrificing time performance.

1 Introduction

Tabled resolution methods in logic programming (LP), beginning with OLDT resolution pioneered by Tamaki and Sato [10], address the well-known shortcomings of the SLD evaluation mechanism of Prolog, namely, susceptibility to infinite looping, redundant subcomputations, and inadequate semantics for negation. Using tabled resolution we can finitely compute the minimal model for datalog programs. More recent methods [1,2] compute well-founded semantics [11] for normal logic programs. Due to this added power, tabled evaluation enables us to combine LP, deductive databases, and nonmonotonic reasoning, and develop complex applications requiring efficient fixed point computations (e.g., see [7,6]).

The power of tabled resolution stems from one simple notion: avoid redundant computation by permitting the use of proven instances, or answers, from past computation for satisfying new subgoals. This is achieved by maintaining a *table* of the called subgoals paired with the set of answers derived for each such subgoal

---

* This work was supported in part by NSF grants C-CR 9711386, C-CR 9876242, and EIA 9705998.
** Currently at Telcordia Technologies (prasadr@research.telcordia.com); work done while at Stony Brook.

A. Middeldorp, T. Sato (Eds.): FLOPS'99, LNCS 1722, pp. 284–299, 1999.

(known as answer tables). When a subgoal is selected for resolution, it is first checked against the entries maintained in the call table. If there exists a "similar-enough subgoal", then its associated answers are used for resolving this subgoal (*answer resolution*). Otherwise the subgoal is entered in the call table, and its answers, computed by resolving the subgoal against program clauses (*program resolution*) are entered in the corresponding answer table.

There are two approaches to locate a "similar-enough" goal. One approach, used by the XSB system [8], is to look for an entry that is a variant of the current goal, i.e., identical modulo variable renaming. Although variant-based tabling has been highly successful, this approach permits only limited sharing of answer computations.

The second alternative, called *subsumption-based* tabling, permits greater reuse of computed results. Notice that, given a goal G, any entry in the table, say G', which *subsumes* G will contain in its final answer set all the instances to satisfy G.[1] Using the answers of G' to resolve G avoids computationally-expensive program resolution, and thereby can lead to superior time performance. Space performance may also improve as fewer calls and their associated answer sets need be stored in the tables. However, the mechanisms for efficiently representing and accessing the call and answer tables are more complex. In particular, answer resolution now involves indexing, since not all answers in a selected answer table (say, that of G') may be applicable to the given goal (say, G). This process is especially challenging since all answers to G' may not yet be present in the table when the call to G is made.

In an earlier work [9], we proposed a data structure called Dynamic Threaded Sequential Automaton (DTSA) for representing and retrieving terms from dynamic answer sets. Answer resolution is performed one tuple at a time by backtracking through a DTSA. To ensure that every relevant answer is visited, answers are retrieved strictly in the order of their insertion into the table. Although an implementation based on this strategy shows improvement in time performance on queries where the subsumption of calls is possible, it performs poorly in space when compared to the variant-based tabling engine: potentially quadratic in the size of corresponding tables constructed in a variant-based tabling engine. Moreover, the incremental traversal of the DTSA for resolving each answer forces us to maintain complex state information, thereby increasing choice point space.

In this paper we describe an alternative approach for answer resolution. We tag each answer with a time stamp and store them in *Time-Stamped Tries* (*TST*) which provides indexing based on the symbols in terms as well as the time stamp. Answers relevant to a call are periodically collected from the subsuming call's answer set and cached locally (by the subsumed call) for later consumption. The local cache is updated whenever all answers currently held in the cache have already been resolved against the goal. Each collection phase completely searches the set for answers which have been entered since the previous phase, selecting only those answers which unify with the subsumed goal. Since a complete search

---

[1] A term t_1 *subsumes* a term t_2 if t_2 is an instance of t_1. Further, t_1 *properly subsumes* t_2 if t_1 subsumes t_2 and t_1 is not a variant of t_2.

is done in each phase, only minimal state information— the time stamp of the
last update— is needed between collection phases. The tables stored as TSTs are
at most twice as large as the tables in the variant engine, and at most as large
as the tables in our earlier DTSA-based engine. Moreover, the space efficiency
comes with little or no time penalty.

The rest of the paper is organized as follows. In Section 2, we present an
operational overview of tabling operations and answer resolution in subsumption-
based tabling. The design and implementation of TSTs appears in Section 3.
Comparisons between DTSA, TST and variant-based tabling engines appear in
Section 4. In Section 5 we provide performance results of a subsumption-based
tabling engine implemented using TSTs.

2   Answer Clause Resolution via Time Stamps

Below we give an overview of the time-stamp-based subsumptive tabling engine.
We begin with an abstract description of the operations of a tabling system.

2.1   An Overview of Tabling Operations

We can view top-down tabled evaluation of a program in terms of four abstract table operations: *call-check-insert*, *answer-check-insert*, *retrieve-answer*
and *pending-answers*. Below, we describe each of these operations in the context
of subsumptive tabling.

Call-check-insert. Given a call c, the *call-check-insert* operation finds a call c'
in the call table that subsumes c. If there is no such c', then c is inserted into
the call table. Note that *call-check-insert* is independent of the data structures
used to represent answer tables.

A subgoal that is resolved using program creates answers to be inserted into
the corresponding answer table, say T, and is known as the *producer* of T.
A subgoal that is resolved using answer resolution with respect to an answer
table T is known as a *consumer* of T.

Answer-check-insert. This operation is used to add the answers computed for a
call1 into its corresponding answer table. The operation ensures that the answer
tables contain only unique answers. Note that, while the data structures used
to represent answer tables may be different between subsumptive and variant
tabling, the requirements on *answer-check-insert* remain the same.

Retrieve-answer. Answer clause resolution of a call c against a set of terms
$T = \{t_1, t_2, \ldots, t_n\}$ in an answer table produces a set R such that $r \in R$ iff
$r = t_i\theta_i$ for some t_i, where $\theta_i = mgu(c, t_i)$. This resolution is performed using
retrieve-answer operations. In a tuple-at-a-time resolution engine, a *consumer
choice point* is placed so that the answers can be retrieved one by one using
backtracking. To ensure that an answer is returned at most once, we maintain an

answer continuation in the choice point, which represents the set of all answers remaining to be retrieved. Hence the arguments supplied to a *retrieve-answer* operation is split naturally into:

- *first_answer:* Given an answer table T and a call c, return an answer from T that unifies with c, and an answer continuation.
- *next_answer:* Given an answer table T, a call c, and an answer continuation γ, return the next answer a from T that unifies with c as specified by γ, and a modified answer continuation γ' that represents the remaining answers.

Pending-answers. Answer continuation $\perp$ denotes that there are no more remaining answers. When a *retrieve-answer* operation for a call c on an incomplete table T returns $\perp$, the call c will be suspended. The suspended call is later resumed when new answers have been added to T, or when T is known to be complete. Suspension and resumption of calls are performed by the answer scheduler which invokes *pending-answers* to determine whether a suspended call needs to be resumed. Given an answer continuation, *pending-answers* succeeds iff the continuation represents a non-empty set of answers.

2.2 Answer Retrieval in Subsumptive Tabling

The DTSA, proposed as a data structure for answer tables in [9], directly supports the *first-answer* and *next-answer* operations. In this paper, we describe an alternate, two-tier mechanism to realize these operations. At the fundamental level, we decouple the operation of *identifying* the answers relevant to a given goal in an answer set from the operation of *unifying* one of these answers with the goal. This separation frees the identification process from tuple-at-a-time execution. We hence propose an efficient mechanism to identify *all* relevant answers that have been added since the last time the table was inspected. We associate a time stamp with each answer and maintain, as part of the answer continuation, the maximum time stamp of any answer in the set. These answers are stored in a TST and accessed using *identify_relevant_answers* which, given a table T, time stamp τ and goal G, identifies the set of all answers in T with time stamps *greater than* τ that unify with G. It returns this set as a list (with some internal order) as well as the maximum time stamp of any answer in T.

Recall that answers are consumed from a table by a *first_answer* operation followed by a sequence of *next_answer* operations. We can implement these tuple-at-a-time operations based on time stamps as follows. We assume that time stamps are positive (non zero) integers. To compute *first_answer*, we use *identify_relevant_answers* with a time stamp of zero (thereby qualifying all available answers), select one answer from the returned set as the current answer, and store those remaining in an internal data structure called an *answer list*. The answer list, together with the maximum time stamp returned by *identify_relevant_answers*, form the answer continuation. On subsequent invocations of *next_answer*, we simply manipulate the answer list component of the continuation, as long as the answer list is not empty. Should the answer list be empty, we "refresh" the continuation by another call to *identify_relevant_answers*, using the time stamp component of the continuation to restrict identification to only those answers that have been inserted since the last call to *identify_relevant_answers*.

Let τ be the time stamp returned by an invocation of the access function *identify_relevant_answers*. Since this operation identifies *all* relevant answers, $\langle [\,], \tau \rangle$ represents the empty continuation, $\bot$. Note that the continuation, $\langle [\,], 0 \rangle$, that represents all answers in a table. Thus, *first_answer*(T, c) can be realized simply as *next_answer*$(T, c, \langle [\,], 0 \rangle)$.

The method described above can be formalized readily; see [5] for details. We now state the requirement on *identify_relevant_answers* that is needed to show the correctness of *first_answer* and *next_answer*:

Requirement 1 *Given an answer table T representing a set of answers S, a goal G and a time stamp τ, identify_relevant_answers(T, G, τ) returns a permutation of the set $\{a \in S \mid a$ unifies with G and timestamp$(a) > \tau\}$.*

The correctness of operation *retrieve-answer* is then ensured by the following proposition:

Proposition 1. *Given a goal G and answer table T representing a set of answers S, let $\langle a_1, \gamma_1 \rangle, \ldots, \langle a_n, \gamma_n \rangle$ be a sequence of values such that $\langle a_1, \gamma_1 \rangle = $ first_answer(T, G) and $\langle a_{i+1}, \gamma_{i+1} \rangle = $ next_answer(T, G, γ_i), where $1 \leq i < n$ and $\gamma_n = \bot = \langle [\,], \tau \rangle$. Further, let B be the set $\{b \in S \mid b$ unifies with G and timestamp$(b) > \tau\}$. Then, provided identify_relevant_answers satisfies Requirement 1, the sequence $\langle a_1, \ldots, a_n \rangle$ is a permutation of the set $\{b\theta \mid b \in B$, where $\theta = mgu(b, G)\}$.*

3   Time-Stamped Tries

In this section we describe Time-Stamped Trie, which permits indexing on term symbols as well as time stamps. A TST represents a set of terms T and supports two operations: (1) Insert a term t into set T if not already present, and (2) Given a term t, determine the set of all terms $t' \in T$ that unify with t. Below we describe these operations formally. We begin by defining notational conventions and terminology and review answer tries described in [8].

A *position* in a term is either the empty string Λ that reaches the root of the term, or $\pi.i$, where π is a position and i is an integer, that reaches the ith child of the term reached by π. By $t|_\pi$ we denote the symbol at position π in t. For example, $p(a, f(X))|_{2.1} = X$. Terms are built from a finite set of function symbols $\mathcal{F}$ and a countable set of variables $\mathcal{V} \cup \hat{\mathcal{V}}$, where $\mathcal{V}$ is a set of *normal* variables and $\hat{\mathcal{V}}$ is a set of *position* variables. The variables in the set $\hat{\mathcal{V}}$ are of the form X_π, where π is a position, and are used to mark certain positions of interest in a term. We denote the elements of $\mathcal{F} \cup \mathcal{V}$ by α.

A *trie* is a tree-structured automaton used for representing a set of terms $T = \{t_1, t_2, \ldots, t_n\}$. A trie for T has a unique leaf state s_i for every t_i, $1 \leq i \leq n$, such that the sequence of symbols on the transitions from the root to s_i

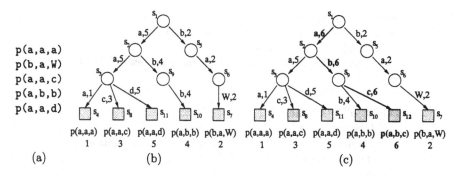

Fig. 1. Set of terms (a), its corresponding TST representation (b), and effect of inserting p(a,b,c) to the TST (c)

correspond to the sequence of symbols encountered in a preorder traversal of t_i. Moreover, for every state in a trie, all outgoing transitions have unique labels. With each state s is associated a skeleton, denoted by $Skel_s$, that represents the set of unification operations that must be performed to reach that state. The fringe of $Skel_s$ represents positions where further unification operations need to be performed before unifying a goal term with a term in T. The position in the goal term inspected at s is represented by the first position variable encountered in a preorder traversal of the skeleton. We denote this position by $\pi(s)$. Each outgoing transition from s represents a unification operation involving position $\pi(s)$ in the goal and the symbol labeling this transition. We label transitions by α, where α is a variable or a function symbol. Let the position examined at the current state be π. Then the skeleton of the destination state reached by a transition labeled by α is $Skel_s[t/X_\pi]$, where $t = f(X_{\pi.1}, \dots, X_{\pi.n})$ if α is a n-ary function symbol f and $t = \alpha$ otherwise. Note that for a leaf state s in the trie, $fringe(Skel_s)$ is empty and that $Skel_s \in T$ is the term represented by s.

A Time-Stamped Trie (see Figure 1) is a trie augmented with information about the relative time its terms were inserted. The time of insertion of each term is called its *time stamp*, and is represented by a positive (non zero) integer. Each transition in a TST is additionally labeled with the maximum time stamp of any leaf reachable using that transition. Hence, all transitions in a TST will be of the form $s \xrightarrow{\langle \alpha, \tau \rangle} d$, where s and d are states in the TST, α is the symbol, and τ is the time stamp. We refer to these attributes of a transition δ as *symbol(δ)* and *timestamp(δ)*, respectively. Since *identify_relevant_answers* looks only for answers with time stamps greater than a given value, the *maximum* time stamp information on transitions is necessary to restrict the search on portions of the TST that correspond to answers with such time stamp values.

3.1   Term Insertion into a TST

Terms are inserted into a TST in a manner analogous to the single-pass check-insert for the trie representation described in [8]. The TST is traversed recursively

```
algorithm insert(s, t, τ)
(* returns true iff t was successfully inserted *)
  if ( fringe(Skelₛ) = {} ) then
    return ( false ) (* term already exists, hence insert fails *)
  endif
  let G|π(s) = f/n = α
  if ( ∃δ : s ⟨α,τ'⟩→ d ) then
    if ( insert(d, t, τ) ) then
      timestamp(δ) = τ (* insert successful, so update time stamp *)
      return ( true )
    else
      return ( false ) (* insert failed; propagate failure up *)
    endif
  else (* match fails at s, so add a new path *)
    create new state d and add transition δ : s ⟨α,τ⟩→ d
    Skel_d = Skelₛ [f(X_{π(s).1}, ... , X_{π(s).n})/X_{π(s)}]
    insert(d, t, τ)
    return ( true )
  endif
```

Fig. 2. Term Insertion into a Time-Stamped Trie

starting at the root. A transition from states s to d, $s \xrightarrow{\langle \alpha, \tau \rangle} d$, is taken if the symbol α matches the symbol in the goal term at the position specified by s. If a leaf state is reached, then the term already exists in the set, and hence the TST is left unchanged. On the other hand, if a match operation fails at a state s, then a new path is added to the TST corresponding to the given term. All time stamps on the transitions along the root-to-leaf path corresponding to this term are updated with a value greater than any other time stamp in the TST. This recursive procedure is specified in Figure 2. The TST obtained from the one in Figure 1(b) by adding the term p(a,b,c) is given in Figure 1(c). The new transitions and states, as well as the transitions whose time stamps were modified by the addition, appear in bold face in the figure.

3.2   Identifying Relevant Answers Using a TST

We now describe how TST supports *identify_relevant_answers*. Given a goal G and a time stamp τ, answers in a TST, T, are identified by recursively traversing T from the root, at each state exploring all transitions that meet the term indexing as well as the time stamp constraints. The set of transitions to be explored can be formally specified as follows.

Definition 1 (Set of Applicable Destinations). *Given a Time-Stamped Trie T, the set of all destination states that are applicable upon reaching a state s in T with an initial goal G and time stamp τ, denoted dest(s, G, τ), is such that*

$d \in \text{dest}(s, G, \tau)$ iff (i) $Skel_d$ is unifiable with G, and (ii) $s \xrightarrow{\langle \alpha, \tau' \rangle} d$ is a transition in T with $\tau' > \tau$.

In the above definition, condition (i) corresponds to indexing on *terms* while (ii) corresponds to indexing on *time stamps*.

Given a state s in a TST, a goal G, and time stamp τ, the set of all terms represented by the leaves reachable from s with time stamps greater than τ and unifiable with G is given by:

$$
relevant(s, G, \tau) = \begin{cases} \{Skel_s\} & \text{if } s \text{ is a leaf} \\ \bigcup_{d \in \text{dest}(s,G,\tau)} relevant(d, G, \tau) & \text{otherwise} \end{cases}
$$

Finally, let T be a TST. Then,

$$
identify\_relevant\_answers(T, G, \tau) = relevant(root(T), G, \tau) \; .
$$

We can establish that the above definition of *identify_relevant_answers* meets Requirement 1.

Proposition 2 (Correctness). *Given a Time-Stamped Trie T representing a set of terms S, a goal G and a time stamp τ, identify_relevant_answers(T, G, τ) computes the set $\{a \in S \mid a$ unifies with G and timestamp$(a) > \tau\}$.*

Although one can readily derive a computation based on the above definition of *identify_relevant_answers*, its effectiveness depends on the efficient implementation of *dest*. It should be noted that the condition in *dest* for indexing on terms is identical to the one with which transitions to be traversed are selected in a (non time-stamped) trie [8]. The indexing on time stamps, however, is unique to TSTs. We can show that *identify_relevant_answers* can be efficiently computed given an efficient technique to index on time stamps at *each state* in a TST, as formally stated below.

Requirement 2 *Given a Time-Stamped Trie T, $\Delta = \text{dest}(s, G, \tau)$ is computed in time proportional to $|\Delta|$.*

Proposition 3 (Efficiency). *Let G be an open goal – i.e., a term whose immediate subterms are all distinct variables – T be a Time-Stamped Trie, and identify_relevant_answers(T, G, τ) be a non-empty set of terms S for some given value of τ. Then, if dest satisfies Requirement 2, the set S can be computed in time proportional to the sum of the sizes of the terms in S.*

The structure of TSTs do provide at each state, in addition to the normal index on symbols present in tries, an index on time stamps. Each time index can be maintained as a doubly-linked list of outgoing transitions *in reverse time-stamp order*. This organization allows us to select transitions based on time stamps alone, at constant time per selected transition, thereby satisfying Requirement 2. Moreover, by cross-linking the time and term indices, the time index can be updated in constant time as new transitions are created. Finally, note that TSTs support answer retrieval from *incomplete* answer sets the time index can be deleted when the answer table is complete.

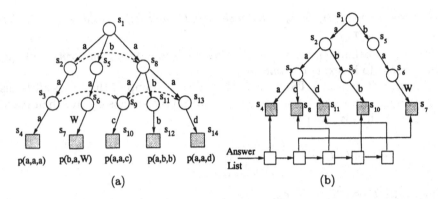

Fig. 3. DTSA (a) and Trie (b) representation of terms in Figure 1(a)

4 Comparison of Tabling Approaches

We now compare variant- , TST-, and DTSA-based tabling engines. To provide
the context for comparisons, we now briefly review the data structure called
Dynamic Threaded Sequential Automaton (DTSA) that was used in our earlier
implementation of a subsumption based tabling engine.

The DTSA Structure. DTSA is a trie-like automaton for representing a set of
ordered terms $\{t_1, t_2, \dots, t_n\}$. A DTSA is constructed such that, in a preorder
traversal, the leaf representing term t_i is visited before the leaf representing
term t_{i+1} (Figure 3(a)). Since transitions from a state s preserve the order of
terms represented by the final states reachable from s, there may be multiple
transitions with the same label. The loss of indexing due to this duplication
is offset by using *threads* which link states that share prefixes. For instance,
using the DTSA in Figure 3(a) to find terms unifiable with a given goal term
p(a,a,V), after finding the first term (at state s_4), the next term, p(a,a,c), can
be retrieved by backtracking to s_3, following the thread to s_9, and making the
transition to s_{10}. Observe that both s_3 and s_9 have p(a,a,X_3) as their skeleton.

4.1 Shared Features

The variant, DTSA- and TST-based subsumption engines share many common
features. For instance all engines distinguish between *complete* and *incomplete*
table entries. Completed answer tables are organized as *compiled trie code* in
all of them (see [8] for details). Although incomplete tables are organized differently they all use substitution factoring whereby only the substitutions for
the variables of the call are stored in the answer tries [8]. Once a table entry
has completed, all structures created to support answer resolution from the incomplete table are reclaimed. These include the leaf node pointers, the auxiliary
structures for indexing on time in the TST-based subsumption engine, and the
entire DTSA itself in the DTSA-based subsumption engine.

In the following, we focus on the differences between the three engines.

4.2   Variant- vs. TST-Based Engine

Subsumption engines have a more complex call-check-insert operation than the variant engine. However, this adds very little (constant factor) overhead to the evaluation time. Due to sharing of answer computations, subsumption engines can show arbitrary gains in time performance. The interesting result is that the table space used by a TST-based engine is always within a constant factor of that used by the variant engine. In fact,

Proposition 4 (Space Complexity of TST-Based Engine). *The maximum table space used during computation in a TST-based engine is at most twice that of the variant engine.*

This bound follows from the observation that a TST is structured like a trie with respect to the representation of the answers as sequences of symbols – i.e., a trie and a TST representing the same set of answers have the same number of nodes (states) – and that the size of a TST node is twice that of a trie node (including space for the time index).

4.3   DTSA- vs. TST-Based Engine

The subsumptive engines can be distinguished by their approaches to performing answer retrieval. Subsumption using Time-Stamped Tries divides this operation into two processes: (i) identifying answers relevant to a particular goal, and (ii) unifying a selected relevant answer with that goal. Identification of relevant answers is achieved by a complete search of the TST, yielding a *set* of answers, as discussed in Section 3.2. In contrast, DTSA directly supports the primitive operations of answer retrieval, providing for simultaneous identification and consumption of a *single* answer.

Consequently, DTSAs have more complex continuations, requiring enough state information to resume the traversal; a continuation consists of a *set* of choice points, one for each level in the DTSA. On the other hand, since complete traversals of a TST are performed during each identification phase, only the maximum time stamp of all answers contained in the TST is required for subsequent processing.

DTSA also consumes more table space than TST. In contrast to Proposition 4, the maximum size of a table in the DTSA-based engine is *at least* double that of the representation in the variant engine, as an answer trie (Figure 3(b)) is created in addition to the DTSA. Moreover, the number of nodes in a DTSA may be quadratic in the number of nodes in a corresponding TST. For example, consider the program depicted in Figure 4(a). Answers to the query a(X,Y) are discovered in such an order that no sharing of nodes is possible in the DTSA (Figure 4(b)). However, since answers are simply marked with the insertion time in a TST, rather than stored in derivation order, the resulting sharing makes the corresponding TST more compact (Figure 4(c)). It can be shown that the number of nodes required to represent the set of answers to the query a(X,Y) in the TST is $n(n-1)/2 + 2k$, whereas in the DTSA, the number of nodes required

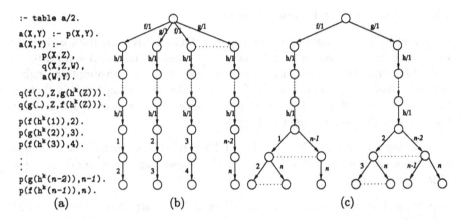

```
:- table a/2.

a(X,Y) :- p(X,Y).
a(X,Y) :-
     p(X,Z),
     q(X,Z,W),
     a(W,Y).

q(f(_),Z,g(h^k(Z))).
q(g(_),Z,f(h^k(Z))).

p(f(h^k(1)),2).
p(g(h^k(2)),3).
p(f(h^k(3)),4).
  ⋮

p(g(h^k(n-2)),n-1).
p(f(h^k(n-1)),n).
```

    (a)   (b)   (c)

Fig. 4. Program (a) and two organizations of the answer set for the query a(X,Y): That which would be produced for a DTSA (b) and a (Time-Stamped) Trie (c)

is $n(n-1)(2+k)$. As can be seen from both the diagram and these expressions, the size of k adds but a constant factor to the size of the TST, whereas in the DTSA, its effect is multiplicative.

5   Experimental Results

We now present experimental results to compare the performance of the TST engine with that of the variant and DTSA engines. All measurements were taken on a SparcStation 20 with 64MB of main memory running Solaris 5.6. We present the results using the benchmarks presented in [8], derived from the programs: left-, right-, and double-recursive versions of transitive closure (lrtc/2, rrtc/2, drtc/2), and the same generation program (sg/2). We note that both the TST and DTSA engines were constructed from different base versions of XSB – the TST engine from version 1.7.2, and the DTSA engine from version 1.4.3. The measurements were made so as to minimize the impact of this difference during each experiment, as discussed below. Because the changes between to two versions did not grossly affect the method of evaluation— in particular, XSB's scheduler— we feel that the following results accurately reflect the relative performance of the systems.

Time Efficiency. The TST engine shows little overhead when the evaluation does not lead to subsumed calls. The overheads result only from the subsumption-checking *call-check-insert* operation. As time-stamp indexes are lazily created, no penalty is incurred due to their maintenance. In addition, updating of time stamps along the path of insertion is avoided by assigning a time stamp value of 1 to all answers entered before the first subsumed call is made. These optimizations enable the TST engine to perform performing within 2% of the speed of the variant engine (see [5] for details).

Table 1. Speedups of DTSA and TST engines in evaluations involving subsumption

Query	Graph Size		XSB 1.4.3			XSB 1.7.2		
			Variant	DTSA	Speedup	Variant	TST	Speedup
`rrtc(X,Y)`	Chain	512	3.36	3.44	0.97	3.05	2.16	1.41
		1024	16.8	13.8	1.21	14.6	8.74	1.68
	Tree	2048	0.48	0.77	0.62	0.45	0.37	1.21
		4096	1.06	2.08	0.51	1.00	0.83	1.20
`drtc(X,Y)`	Chain	128	6.54	4.60	1.43	5.88	3.09	1.90
		256	52.0	38.7	1.35	51.5	24.1	2.14
	Tree	2048	1.87	1.91	0.98	1.72	1.25	1.38
		4096	4.57	4.86	0.94	4.24	3.00	1.41
`sg(X,Y)`	Chain	512	0.68	0.06	11.3	0.64	0.04	15.8
		1024	2.73	0.12	22.5	2.58	0.09	27.5
	Tree	128	0.12	0.14	0.89	0.11	0.10	1.10
		256	0.49	0.50	0.97	0.43	0.43	1.01
`lrtc(1,X),`	Chain	2048	29.4	0.13	219	27.5	0.10	277
`lrtc(2,X)`		4096	118	0.30	392	110	0.20	574
	Tree	2048	17.6	0.10	176	17.3	0.09	190
		4096	71.1	0.20	351	69.7	0.18	388

The performances of variant and TST engines differ when subsuming valls are made. Table 5 shows the execution times of the TST and DTSA engines relative to their base variant engines on examples with this behavior. We compare the performance of each engine using the speedups achieved over their base variant engines, thereby removing the noise in the results caused by differences in their base implementations. As each subsumptive engine merely extends the tabling subsystem to support subsumption, this method measures the performance gain achievable by each tabling approach. Notice that in all cases, the TST engine performs at least as well as the DTSA engine.

Table Space Usage. In Table 5 we report on the memory utilized in representing the tables for some of the benchmarks described earlier. This *table space* consists of the call and answer tables, where the latter consists of answer tries, TSTs, DTSA, and answer lists as present in a particular engine. We report the maximum space consumed *during* evaluation, as well as the space consumed by the *completed* tables. Table 5 is divided into three sections: the upper portion shows results for benches that do not make use of subsumption; the middle section shows results for benches for which properly subsumed calls consume answers only from incomplete tables; and the bottom portion shows results for a bench whose subsumed calls consume answers from completed tables only. The space used by the DTSA engine for completed tables is identical to that of TST, and therefore is not repeated.

Table 2. Space usage for tables in variant and subsumptive engines

Query	Graph Size		Maximum Table Space			Completed Table Space	
			Variant	DTSA	TST	Variant	TST
lrtc(1,Y)	Chain	4096	128 KB	144 KB	144 KB	96.1 KB	112 KB
		8192	256 KB	288 KB	288 KB	192 KB	224 KB
rrtc(1,Y)	Chain	512	4.23 MB	4.75 MB	4.75 MB	3.23 MB	3.75 MB
		1024	16.8 MB	18.8 MB	18.8 MB	12.8 MB	14.8 MB
rrtc(X,Y)	Chain	512	7.41 MB	9.89 MB	7.73 MB	6.41 MB	3.73 MB
		1024	29.5 MB	39.1 MB	30.8 MB	25.5 MB	14.8 MB
	Tree	2048	1.23 MB	1.64 MB	1.23 MB	1.09 MB	702 KB
		4096	2.68 MB	3.58 MB	2.69 MB	2.36 MB	1.48 MB
drtc(X,Y)	Chain	128	492 KB	826 KB	508 KB	429 KB	252 KB
		256	1.87 MB	3.19 MB	1.95 MB	1.62 MB	971 KB
	Tree	2048	1.23 MB	1.71 MB	1.23 MB	1.09 MB	702 KB
		4096	2.68 MB	3.73 MB	2.69 MB	2.36 MB	1.48 MB
sg(X,Y)	Chain	512	88.1 KB	110 KB	84.1 KB	84.1 KB	60.1 KB
		1024	176 KB	220 KB	168 KB	168 KB	120 KB
	Tree	128	231 KB	430 KB	309 KB	188 KB	168 KB
		256	855 KB	1602 KB	1190 KB	685 KB	629 KB
lrtc(1,X),	Chain	2048	320 KB	128 KB	128 KB	304 KB	112 KB
lrtc(2,X)		4096	640 KB	256 KB	256 KB	608 KB	224 KB
	Tree	2048	276 KB	100 KB	100 KB	260 KB	84.4 KB
		4096	522 KB	200 KB	200 KB	520 KB	168 KB

As mentioned earlier, the subsumptive engines exhibit a 20% overhead in the representation of answer tries as compared to the variant engine. For the benches which do not exhibit subsumption, observe that the actual increase appears lower due to the presence of the call table and answer lists in this measure, which are present in all engines. When answer lists are reclaimed upon completion, the space overhead approaches 20%.

The query lrtc(1,X),lrtc(2,X) exhibits behavior similar to nonsubsumptive evaluations during construction of the tables as subsumed calls do not occur until the tables complete. This allows both subsumptive engines to avoid constructing their respective subsumption-supporting data structures. Since answer tables are shared, the subsumption makes the subsumption engines consume less maximum and final spaces than the variant engine.

For those queries which utilize subsumption from incomplete tables, only a single table is constructed under subsumptive evaluation – that of the original query. This table expands throughout the computation until it completes, terminating the evaluation. Under variant evaluation, however, several tables are constructed in addition to the one for the query itself, but are completed incrementally during the computation. Therefore, memory usage is somewhat amortized as space is periodically freed by the tables as they complete. The rel-

Table 3. Maximum choice point space usage for various tabling engines

Query	Graph Size		Variant	DTSA	TST
lrtc(1,Y)	Chain	4096	0.61 KB	0.61 KB	0.61 KB
		8192	0.66 KB	0.66 KB	0.66 KB
rrtc(1,Y)	Chain	512	36.5 KB	36.5 KB	36.5 KB
		1024	72.5 KB	72.5 KB	72.5 KB
rrtc(X,Y)	Chain	512	36.5 KB	100 KB	30.5 KB
		1024	72.6 KB	208 KB	60.5 KB
	Tree	2048	1.64 KB	288 KB	120 KB
		4096	1.81 KB	592 KB	240 KB
drtc(X,Y)	Chain	128	16.4 KB	494 KB	477 KB
		256	32.5 KB	1950 KB	1913 KB
	Tree	2048	1.76 KB	1.22 MB	1.06 MB
		4096	1.94 KB	2.69 MB	2.34 MB
sg(X,Y)	Chain	512	0.71 KB	100 KB	30.5 KB
		1024	0.77 KB	208 KB	60.6 KB
	Tree	128	0.76 KB	16.5 KB	7.93 KB
		256	0.82 KB	33.7 KB	15.5 KB
lrtc(1,X),	Chain	2048	0.74 KB	0.74 KB	0.74 KB
lrtc(2,X)		4096	0.80 KB	0.80 KB	0.80 KB
	Tree	2048	0.78 KB	0.78 KB	0.78 KB
		4096	0.84 KB	0.84 KB	0.84 KB

ative performance in maximum space usage between the two tabling paradigms, then, depends not only on the amount of answer sharing that is possible – and so the extent to which duplicity can be avoided – but also on the pattern of table completion. For these queries, only sg(X,Y) on chains exhibits conditions during the evaluation which are conducive to savings under subsumption, and that by using TSTs only. However, as Table 5 also shows, in *all* subsumptive cases (middle and lower portions of the table) the TST engine yields a more compact representation of the *completed tables*, even though each TST consumes more space than the corresponding answer trie in the variant engine.

Finally, for all queries where subsumed calls are resolved only with incomplete tables, the TST engine outperforms the DTSA engine in maximum space required as predicted (Sect 4.3). The results show that the amount of savings can be significant, in absolute (see rrtc(X,Y)) or relative terms (see drtc(X,Y)).

Choice Point Creation. In Table 5 we present maximum choice point stack usage which, together with table space usage, accounts for most of the total memory used during query evaluation with subsumption. As the sizes of producer and consumer choice point frames differ between the versions of XSB, we have added padding to these structures to normalize the values and enable a direct comparison. For this reason, only results from one version of a variant engine is shown in this table.

As compared to a variant based evaluation, choice point space is likely to increase as subsumed calls are dependent upon the more general goal, and therefore cannot complete before the general goal itself is completed. Hence, the corresponding consumer choice points must remain active on the choice point stack. In contrast, under variant evaluation, the more specific goals are resolved by program resolution, independent of the more general call, and hence have the opportunity to complete earlier and free stack space for reuse. Note that the former condition is a characteristic of subsumption-based query evaluation rather than any particular implementation of the tables. In particular, for the query drtc(X,Y) executed on trees of depth k, it can be shown that the maximum number of concurrently active choice points is equal to the number of calls to drtc/2, which is proportional to $k2^k$, whereas under variant evaluation, the maximum number of active choice points is only $2k$. However, there are cases, such as occurs in the evaluation of rrtc(X,Y), where the initial call pattern is identical under either evaluation strategy. Here, the use of subsumption actually saves space as the representation of a consuming call on the choice point stack is more compact than that of a producer. Note that, even in the worst case, the choice point stack expansion is tied to the number of interdependent calls, and hence proportional to the table space.

As discussed in Section 4.3, the DTSA engine uses more stack space than the TST due to the addition of specialized choice points for performing answer resolution from the DTSA. As the data in Table 5 shows, the TST engine outperforms the DTSA engine in terms of choice point space usage in all examples. Moreover, the overhead is significant, sometimes resulting in usage that is more than triple that of the TST engine. Finally, recall that the table space of the TST engine is proportional to that of the variant engine, and that its choice point space usage is proportional to its table space usage. Therefore, the TST engine's total usage is proportional to that of the variant engine.

6   Discussion

We presented a new organization of tables based on time-stamped tries for subsumption based tabling. We showed from a theoretical as well as practical perspective that it is superior to a tabling engine based on DTSA. Further we have shown that the space performance of such an implementation is no worse than a constant factor away from a variant implementation.

Existence of an efficient subsumption based tabling engine opens up interesting new opportunities for expanding the applicability of top-down evaluation strategies. For instance, programs exist for which top-down, goal-directed query evaluations impose a high factor of overhead during the computation when compared to semi-naive bottom-up evaluation. Preliminary evidence suggests that the performance of our TST-based tabling engine augmented with *call abstraction* is competitive with semi-naive bottom-up evaluation methods (see [5] for details). In general, abstraction of a call c is performed by first making a more general call, c', and allowing c to consume answers from c'. Observe that doing call abstraction within a subsumptive engine on a call c amounts to losing goal directedness as far as the evaluation of c is concerned. Thus by selectively abstracting calls we can vary the degree of goal directness employed during an evaluation without changing the core evaluation strategy.

References

1. R. Bol and L. Degerstadt. Tabulated resolution for well-founded semantics. In *Proc. of the Symp. on Logic Programming*, 1993.
2. W. Chen and D. S. Warren. Tabled evaluation with delaying for general logic programs. *JACM*, 43(1), 1996.
3. S. Dawson, C. R. Ramakrishnan, I. V. Ramakrishnan, and T. Swift. Optimizing clause resolution: Beyond unification factoring. In *ICLP*, 1995.
4. Y. Dong, et al. Fighting livelock in the i-protocol: A comparative study of verification tools. In *Tools and Algorithms for the Construction and Analysis of Systems, (TACAS '99)*. Springer Verlag, 1999.
5. E. Johnson, C. R. Ramakrishnan, I. V. Ramakrishnan, and P. Rao. A space-efficient engine for subsumption-based tabled evaluation of logic programs. Technical report. Available from http://www.cs.sunysb.edu/~ejohnson.
6. Y. S. Ramakrishna, et al. Efficient model checking using tabled resolution. In *Proceedings of the 9th International Conference on Computer-Aided Verification (CAV '97)*, Haifa, Israel, July 1997. Springer-Verlag.
7. C. R. Ramakrishnan, S. Dawson, and D. S. Warren. Practical program analysis using general purpose logic programming systems - a case study. In *ACM Symposium on Programming Language Design and Implementation*, 1996.
8. I. V. Ramakrishnan, P. Rao, K. Sagonas, T. Swift, and D. S. Warren. Efficient access mechanisms for tabled logic programs. *JLP*, January 1999.
9. P. Rao, C. R. Ramakrishnan, and I. V. Ramakrishnan. A thread in time saves tabling time. In *JICSLP*. MIT Press, 1996.
10. H. Tamaki and T. Sato. OLDT resolution with tabulation. In *ICLP*, pages 84–98. MIT Press, 1986.
11. A. van Gelder, K. A. Ross, and J. S. Schlipf. The well-founded semantics for general logic programs. *JACM*, 38(3), July 1991.
12. The XSB Group. The XSB programmer's manual, Version 1.8, 1998. Available from http://www.cs.sunysb.edu/~sbprolog.

The Logical Abstract Machine: A Curry-Howard Isomorphism for Machine Code

Atsushi Ohori

Research Institute for Mathematical Sciences
Kyoto University, Kyoto 606-8502, Japan
ohori@kurims.kyoto-u.ac.jp

Abstract. This paper presents a logical framework for low-level machine code and code generation. We first define a calculus, called *sequential sequent calculus*, of intuitionistic propositional logic. A proof of the calculus only contains left rules and has a linear (non-branching) structure, which reflects the properties of sequential machine code. We then establish a Curry-Howard isomorphism between this proof system and machine code based on the following observation. An ordinary machine instruction corresponds to a polymorphic proof transformer that extends a given proof with one inference step. A return instruction, which turns a sequence of instructions into a program, corresponds to a logical axiom (an initial proof tree). Sequential execution of code corresponds to transforming a proof to a smaller one by successively eliminating the last inference step. This logical correspondence enables us to present and analyze various low-level implementation processes of a functional language within the logical framework. For example, a code generation algorithm for the lambda calculus is extracted from a proof of the equivalence theorem between the natural deduction and the sequential sequent calculus.

1 Introduction

Theoretical foundations of syntax and semantics of functional languages have been well established through extensive studies of typed lambda calculi. (See [14,6] for surveys in this area.) Unfortunately, however, those theoretical results are not directly applicable to implementation of a functional language on a low-level sequential machine because of the mismatch between models of typed lambda calculi and actual computer hardware. For example, consider a very simple program $(\lambda x.\lambda y.(x, y))$ 1 2. In the typed lambda calculus with products, this itself is a term and denotes an element in a domain of integer products. In an actual language implementation, however, this program is transformed to an intermediate expression and then compiled to a sequence of machine instructions. The details of the compiled code depend on the target computer architecture. Fig. 1 shows pseudo codes we consider in this paper for a stack-based machine and for a register based machine. The properties of these codes are radically different from those of existing semantic models of the lambda calculus. As a result, theoretical analysis of a programming language based on typed lambda calculi does not directly extend to implementation of a programming language.

A. Middeldorp, T. Sato (Eds.): FLOPS'99, LNCS 1722, pp. 300–318, 1999.

```
        Code(label1)
        Const(1)
        Const(2)                      r0 <- Code(label1)
        Call(2)                       r1 <- Const(1)
        Return                        r2 <- Const(2)
                                      r0 <- call r0 with (r1,r2)
label1: Acc(0)                        Return(r0)
        Acc(1)
        Pair                   label1: r2 <- Pair(r1,r0)
        Return                        Return(r2)
```

In a stack-based machine.   In a register-based machine.

Fig. 1. Machine codes for $(\lambda x.\lambda y.(x,y))\ 1\ 2$

The general motivation of this study is to establish logical foundations for implementing a functional language on conventional computer hardware. To achieve this goal, we need to find a constructive logic appropriate for machine code, and to establish a logical interpretation of a compilation process from a high-level language to machine code, possibly using an intermediate language. In a previous work [17], the author has shown that the process of translating the typed lambda calculus into an intermediate language called "A-normal forms" [4] is characterized as a proof transformation from the natural deduction proof system to a variant of Gentzen's intuitionistic sequent calculus (Kleene's G3a proof system [9]). However, A-normal forms are still high-level expressions, which must be compiled to machine code. A remaining technical challenge is to establish a logical framework for machine code and code generation. An attempt is made in the present paper to develop such a framework.

We first define a proof system, called *sequential sequent calculus*, of intuitionistic propositional logic, whose proofs closely reflect the properties of low-level machine code. By applying the idea of Curry-Howard isomorphism, the *logical abstract machine* (LAM for short) is derived from the calculus. When we regard the set of assumptions in a sequent as a list of formulas, then the derived machine corresponds to a stack-based abstract machine similar to those used, for example, in Java [13] and Camllight [12] implementation. We call this machine the stack-based logical abstract machine (SLAM). When we regard the set of assumptions as an association list of variables and formulas, then the derived machine corresponds to a "register transfer language" which is used as an abstract description of machine code in a native code compiler. We call this machine the register-based logical abstract machine (RLAM).

We prove that the sequential sequent calculus is equivalent to existing proof systems of intuitionistic propositional logic. From the proofs of the equivalence, we can extract code generation algorithms. The choice of the source proof system determines the source language, and the choice of the representation of an assumption set determines the target machine code. For example, if we choose the natural deduction as the source proof system and the association list representation of an assumption set, then the extracted algorithm generates RLAM code for a register machine from a lambda term. Other combinations are equally possible. This framework enables us to analyze compilation process and to represent various optimization methods within a logical framework.

Backgrounds and related works. There have been a number of approaches to systematic implementation of a functional programming language using an abstract machine. Notable results include Landin's SECD machine [11], Turner's SK-reduction machine [20], and the categorical abstract machine of Cousineauet et. al. [2]. In a general perspective, all those approaches are source of inspiration of this work. The new contribution of our approach is to provide a formal account for low-level machine code based on the principle of Curry-Howard isomorphism [3,7]. In [2], it is emphasized that the categorical abstract machine is a law-level machine manipulating a stack or registers. However, its stack based sequential machine is ad-hoc in the sense that it is outside the categorical model on which it is based. In contrast, our LAM is directly derived from a logic that models sequential execution of primitive instructions using stack or registers, and therefore its sequential control structure is an essential part of our formal framework. We establish that a LAM program is isomorphic to a proof in our sequential sequent calculus, and that a code generation algorithm is isomorphic to a proof of a theorem stating that any formula provable in the natural deduction (or a sequent calculus) is also provable in the sequential sequent calculus. This will enable us to extend various high-level logical analyses to low-level machine code and code generation process.

With regard to this logical correspondence, the SK-reduction machine [20] deserves special comments. The core of this approach is the translation from the lambda calculus to the combinatory logic [3]. As observed in [3,10], in the typed setting, this translation algorithm corresponds exactly to a proof of a well know theorem in propositional logic stating that any formula provable in the natural deduction is also probable in the Hilbert system. The bracket abstraction used in the translation algorithm (to simulate lambda abstraction in the combinatory logic) is isomorphic to a proof of the deduction theorem in Hilbert system stating that if τ_1 is provable from $\Delta \cup \tau_2$ then $\tau_2 \supset \tau_1$ is provable from Δ. Although this connection does not appear to be well appreciated in literature, this can be regarded as the first example of Curry-Howard isomorphism for compilation of a functional language to an abstract machine. However, the SK-reduction machine is based on the notion of functions (primitive combinators) and does not directly model computer hardware. We achieve the same rigorous logical correspondence for machine code and code generation.

Another inspiration of our work comes from recent active researches on defining a type system for low-level machine languages. Morrisett et. al. [16,15] define a "typed assembly language." Stata and Abadi [19] define a type system for Java byte-code. In those works, a type system is successfully used to prove soundness of code execution. However, the type system is defined by considering each instruction's effect on the state of memory (registers or stack), and its logical foundations have not been investigated. In our approach, the logical abstract machine is derived from a logic. This enables us to present various implementation processes such as code generation entirely within a logical framework.

Paper Organization. Section 2 analyzes the nature of machine code and defines the sequential sequent calculus. Section 3 extracts the logical abstract machine from the proof system of the sequential sequent calculus and establish a Curry-Howard isomorphism between the calculus and the machine. Section 4 shows that the sequential sequent calculus is equivalent to other formalisms for intuitionistic propositional logic, and extracts compilation algorithms. Section 5 discusses some issues in implementation of a functional language.

Limitations of space make it difficult to present the framework fully; the author intends to present a more detailed description in another paper.

2   The Sequential Sequent Calculus

The first step in establishing logical foundations for machine code and code generation is to find a constructive logic that reflects the essential natures of conventional sequential machines.

By examining machine code such as those shown in Fig. 1, we observe the following general properties.

1. Machine code is constructed by sequential composition of instructions, each of which performs an action on machine memory. The machine is run by mechanically executing the first instruction of the code.
2. An instruction is polymorphic in the sense that it may be a part of various different programs computing difference values. The result of the entire code is determined by a special instruction that returns a value to the caller.
3. To represent arbitrary computation, the machine supports an operation to call a pre-compiled code.

In the following discussion, we write $\Delta \triangleright \tau$ for a logical sequent with a set Δ of assumptions and a conclusion τ.

Logical inference rules that reflect item 1 are those of the form

$$\frac{\Delta_2 \triangleright \tau}{\Delta_1 \triangleright \tau}$$

which have only one premise and do not change the conclusion τ. By interpreting an assumption set as a description of the state of machine memory, a proof composed by this form of rules would yields a sequence of primitive instructions, each of which operates on machine memory. This is in contrast with the natural deduction where rules combine arbitrary large proofs. Moreover, sequential execution of machine is modeled by the (trivial) transformation of a proof to a smaller one by successively eliminating the last inference step.

In the context of proof system, the item 2 is understood as the property that each instruction corresponds not to a complete proof but to an inference step that extends a proof. This observation leads us to interpret each machine instruction I as a polymorphic function that transforms a proof of the form

$$\vdots$$

$$\Delta_1 \triangleright \tau$$

to a proof of the form

$$\vdots$$

$$\frac{\Delta_1 \triangleright \tau}{\Delta_2 \triangleright \tau} \; R_I$$

for *arbitrary result type* τ. At run-time, the instruction corresponding to this rule transforms the memory state represented by Δ_2 to the one represented by Δ_1. Note that the direction in which machine performs the memory state transformation is the opposite to the direction in logical inference. For example, an instruction that creates a pair of integer is modeled by the following inference step.

$$\frac{\Delta; \tau_1 \wedge \tau_2 \triangleright \tau}{\Delta; \tau_1; \tau_2 \triangleright \tau} \; (pair)$$

A return instruction in a program computing a value of type τ corresponds to an axiom $\Delta \triangleright \tau$ such that $\tau \in \Delta$.

The logical interpretation of item 3 of the ability to call a pre-compiled code is the availability of a proof of a sequent, and it can be modeled by a rule to assume an already proved formula as an axiom.

The above analysis leads us to define the sequential sequent calculus of intuitionistic propositional logic. We first consider the calculus for stack-based machines where an assumption set is a list of formulas.

We write $\langle \tau_1; \ldots; \tau_n \rangle$ for the list containing $\tau_1, \ldots, \tau_n$, and write $\Delta; \tau$ for the list obtained from Δ by appending τ to Δ. We also use the notation $\Delta(n)$ for the nth element in the list Δ (counting from the left starting with 0,) and $|\Delta|$ for the length of Δ. The empty list is denoted by ϕ. A list of assumptions describes the type of a stack. We adopt the convention that the right-most formula in a list corresponds to the top of the stack. We assume that there is a given set of non-logical axioms (ranged over by b), and consider the following set of formulas (ranged over by τ).

$$\tau ::= b \mid \tau \wedge \tau \mid \tau \vee \tau \mid (\Delta \Rightarrow \tau)$$

$\tau_1 \wedge \tau_2$ and $\tau_1 \vee \tau_2$ are conjunction and disjunction, corresponding to product and disjoint union, respectively. A formula $(\Delta \Rightarrow \tau)$ intuitively denotes the fact that τ is derived from Δ. Its constructive interpretation is the availability of a proof of the sequent $\Delta \triangleright \tau$. This serves as an alternative to implication formula. The set of proof rules is given in Fig. 2. The rationale behind the rather unusual names of the rules will become clear later when we show a correspondence between this logic and an abstract machine. We write S_S for this proof system, and write $S_S \vdash \Delta \triangleright \tau$ if $\Delta \triangleright \tau$ is provable in this proof system.

The sequential sequent calculus suitable for register-based machines is obtained by changing the representation of an assumption list Δ to a named assumption set. We let Γ range over functions representing named assumption

The axiom:

(return) $\Delta; \tau \triangleright \tau$

Inference rules.

(acc) $\dfrac{\Delta; \tau_1 \triangleright \tau}{\Delta \triangleright \tau}$ $(\tau_1 \in \Delta)$ (const) $\dfrac{\Delta; b \triangleright \tau}{\Delta \triangleright \tau}$ (if b is a non-logical axiom)

(pair) $\dfrac{\Delta; \tau_1 \wedge \tau_2 \triangleright \tau}{\Delta; \tau_1; \tau_2 \triangleright \tau}$ (fst) $\dfrac{\Delta; \tau_1 \triangleright \tau}{\Delta; \tau_1 \wedge \tau_2 \triangleright \tau}$

(snd) $\dfrac{\Delta; \tau_2 \triangleright \tau}{\Delta; \tau_1 \wedge \tau_2 \triangleright \tau}$ (inl) $\dfrac{\Delta; \tau_1 \vee \tau_2 \triangleright \tau}{\Delta; \tau_1 \triangleright \tau}$

(inr) $\dfrac{\Delta; \tau_1 \vee \tau_2 \triangleright \tau}{\Delta; \tau_2 \triangleright \tau}$ (case) $\dfrac{\Delta; \tau_3 \triangleright \tau}{\Delta; \tau_1 \vee \tau_2 \triangleright \tau}$ (if $\vdash \Delta; \tau_1 \triangleright \tau_3$ and $\vdash \Delta; \tau_2 \triangleright \tau_3$)

(code) $\dfrac{\Delta; (\Delta_0 \Rightarrow \tau_0) \triangleright \tau}{\Delta \triangleright \tau}$ (if $\Delta_0 \triangleright \tau_0$)   (call) $\dfrac{\Delta; \tau_0 \triangleright \tau}{\Delta; (\Delta_0 \Rightarrow \tau_0); \Delta_0 \triangleright \tau}$

(app) $\dfrac{\Delta; (\Delta_1 \Rightarrow \tau_0) \triangleright \tau}{\Delta; (\Delta_0; \Delta_1 \Rightarrow \tau_0); \Delta_0 \triangleright \tau}$

Fig. 2. $\mathcal{S}_S$: the Sequential Sequent Calculus for Stack Machines

---

sets, and write $\Gamma, x : \tau$ for the function Γ' such that $dom(\Gamma') = dom(\Gamma) \cup \{x\}$, $\Gamma'(x) = \tau$, and $\Gamma'(y) = \Gamma(y)$ for any $y \in dom(\Gamma), y \neq x$. The set of proof rules is given in Fig. 3. We write $\mathcal{S}_R$ for this proof system, and write $\mathcal{S}_R \vdash \Gamma \triangleright \tau$ if $\Gamma \triangleright \tau$ is provable in this proof system.

3 The Logical Abstract Machines

Guided by the notion of Curry-Howard isomorphism [3,7], machine instructions are extracted from the sequential sequent calculi.

3.1 SLAM: The Stack Based LAM

The stack-based logical abstract machine, SLAM, is obtained from the calculus $\mathcal{S}_S$. The set of instructions (ranged over by I) is given as follows

$$I ::= \mathsf{Return} \mid \mathsf{Acc}(n) \mid \mathsf{Const}(c^b) \mid \mathsf{Pair} \mid \mathsf{Fst} \mid \mathsf{Snd}$$
$$\mid \mathsf{Inl} \mid \mathsf{Inr} \mid \mathsf{Case} \mid \mathsf{Code}(C) \mid \mathsf{Call}(n) \mid \mathsf{App}(n)$$

where C ranges over lists of instructions. We adopt the convention that the leftmost instruction of C is the first one to execute, and write $I; C$ (and $C'; C$) for the list obtained by appending an instruction I (a list C' of instructions) at the front of C. The type system of these instruction is obtained by decorating each rule of $\mathcal{S}_S$ with the corresponding instruction. Fig. 4 shows the typing rule for SLAM, which is the term calculus of $\mathcal{S}_S$.

The axiom:

(return) $\Gamma, x : \tau \triangleright \tau$

Inference rules.

(acc) $\dfrac{\Gamma, x : \tau_1, y : \tau_1 \triangleright \tau}{\Gamma, x : \tau_1 \triangleright \tau}$ (const) $\dfrac{\Gamma, x : b \triangleright \tau}{\Gamma \triangleright \tau}$ (if b is a non-logical axiom)

(pair) $\dfrac{\Gamma, x : \tau_1, y : \tau_2, z : \tau_1 \wedge \tau_2 \triangleright \tau}{\Gamma, x : \tau_1, y : \tau_2 \triangleright \tau}$ (fst) $\dfrac{\Gamma, x : \tau_1 \wedge \tau_2, y : \tau_1 \triangleright \tau}{\Gamma, x : \tau_1 \wedge \tau_2 \triangleright \tau}$

(snd) $\dfrac{\Gamma, x : \tau_1 \wedge \tau_2, y : \tau_2 \triangleright \tau}{\Gamma, x : \tau_1 \wedge \tau_2 \triangleright \tau}$ (inl) $\dfrac{\Gamma, x : \tau_1, y : \tau_1 \vee \tau_2 \triangleright \tau}{\Gamma, x : \tau_1 \triangleright \tau}$

(inr) $\dfrac{\Gamma, x : \tau_2, y : \tau_1 \vee \tau_2 \triangleright \tau}{\Gamma, x : \tau_2 \triangleright \tau}$

(case) $\dfrac{\Gamma, x : \tau_1 \vee \tau_2, y : \tau_3 \triangleright \tau}{\Gamma, x : \tau_1 \vee \tau_2 \triangleright \tau}$ (if $\Gamma, z_1 : \tau_1 \triangleright \tau_3$, $\Gamma, z_2 : \tau_2 \triangleright \tau_3$)

(code) $\dfrac{\Gamma, x : (\Gamma_0 \Rightarrow \tau_0) \triangleright \tau}{\Gamma \triangleright \tau}$ (if $\vdash \Gamma_0 \triangleright \tau_0$)

(call) $\dfrac{\Gamma_1, x : (\Gamma_2 \Rightarrow \tau_0), y : \tau_0 \triangleright \tau}{\Gamma_1, x : (\Gamma_2 \Rightarrow \tau_0) \triangleright \tau}$

$\quad\quad (\Gamma_2 = \{y_1 : \tau_1; \cdots; y_n : \tau_n\}, \Gamma_1(x_i) = \tau_i, 1 \le i \le n)$

(app) $\dfrac{\Gamma_1, x : (\Gamma_2, \Gamma_3 \Rightarrow \tau_0); y : (\Gamma_3 \Rightarrow \tau_0) \triangleright \tau}{\Gamma_1, x : (\Gamma_2, \Gamma_3 \Rightarrow \tau_0) \triangleright \tau}$

$\quad\quad (\Gamma_2 = \{y_1 : \tau_1; \cdots; y_n : \tau_n\}, \Gamma_1(x_i) = \tau_i, 1 \le i \le n)$

Fig. 3. $\mathcal{S}_R$: the Sequential Sequent Calculus for Register Machines

Each instruction "pops" arguments (if any) from the top of the stack and pushes the result on top of the stack. Code(C) pushes a pointer to code C. Call(n) pops n arguments and a function, calls the function with the arguments, and pushes the result. App(n) pops n arguments and a function closure and pushes the function closure obtained by extending the closure's stack with the n arguments. The meanings of the other instructions are obvious from their typing rules. Their precise behavior is defined by an operational semantics, given below.

The set of run-time values (ranged over by v) is defined as follows

$$v ::= c^b \mid (v, v) \mid inl(v) \mid inr(v) \mid cls(S, C)$$

where $cls(S, C)$ is a function closure consisting of stack S, which is a list of values, and code C. The operational semantics is defined as a set of rules to transform a configuration

$$(S, C, D)$$

where D is a "dump," which is a list of pairs of S and C. Fig. 5 gives the set of transformation rules. The reflexive, transitive closure of the relation $\longrightarrow$ is denoted by $\overset{*}{\longrightarrow}$.

(return) $\Delta; \tau \triangleright \mathsf{Return} : \tau$ (acc) $\dfrac{\Delta; \tau_1 \triangleright C : \tau}{\Delta \triangleright \mathsf{Acc}(n); C : \tau}$ $(\Delta(n) = \tau_1)$

(const) $\dfrac{\Delta; b \triangleright C : \tau}{\Delta \triangleright \mathsf{Const}(c^b); C : \tau}$ (pair) $\dfrac{\Delta; \tau_1 \wedge \tau_2 \triangleright C : \tau}{\Delta; \tau_1; \tau_2 \triangleright \mathsf{Pair}; C : \tau}$

(fst) $\dfrac{\Delta; \tau_1 \triangleright C : \tau}{\Delta; \tau_1 \wedge \tau_2 \triangleright \mathsf{Fst}; C : \tau}$ (snd) $\dfrac{\Delta; \tau_2 \triangleright C : \tau}{\Delta; \tau_1 \wedge \tau_2 \triangleright \mathsf{Snd}; C : \tau}$

(inl) $\dfrac{\Delta; \tau_1 \vee \tau_2 \triangleright C : \tau}{\Delta; \tau_1 \triangleright \mathsf{Inl}; C : \tau}$ (inr) $\dfrac{\Delta; \tau_1 \vee \tau_2 \triangleright C : \tau}{\Delta; \tau_2 \triangleright \mathsf{Inr}; C : \tau}$

(case) $\dfrac{\Delta; \tau_3 \triangleright C : \tau}{\Delta; \tau_1 \vee \tau_2 \triangleright \mathsf{Case}(C_1, C_2); C : \tau}$ (if $\vdash \Delta; \tau_1 \triangleright C_1 : \tau_3$ and $\vdash \Delta; \tau_2 \triangleright C_2 : \tau_3$)

(code) $\dfrac{\Delta; (\Delta_0 \Rightarrow \tau_0) \triangleright C : \tau}{\Delta \triangleright \mathsf{Code}(C_0); C : \tau}$ (if $\vdash \Delta_0 \triangleright C_0 : \tau_0$)

(call) $\dfrac{\Delta; \tau_0 \triangleright C : \tau}{\Delta; (\Delta_1 \Rightarrow \tau_0); \Delta_1 \triangleright \mathsf{Call}(n); C : \tau}$ $(|\Delta_1| = n)$

(app) $\dfrac{\Delta; (\Delta_1 \Rightarrow \tau_0) \triangleright C : \tau}{\Delta; (\Delta_2; \Delta_1 \Rightarrow \tau_0); \Delta_2 \triangleright \mathsf{App}(n); C : \tau}$ $(|\Delta_2| = n)$

Fig. 4. Type System of SLAM

$$(S; v, \mathsf{Return}, \phi) \longrightarrow (v, \phi, \phi)$$
$$(S; v, \mathsf{Return}, D; (S_0, C_0)) \longrightarrow (S_0; v, C_0, D)$$
$$(S, \mathsf{Acc}(n); C, D) \longrightarrow (S; S(n), C, D)$$
$$(S, \mathsf{Const}(c); C, D) \longrightarrow (S; c, C, D)$$
$$(S; v_1; v_2, \mathsf{Pair}; C, D) \longrightarrow (S; (v_1, v_2), C, D)$$
$$(S; (v_1, v_2), \mathsf{Fst}; C, D) \longrightarrow (S; v_1, C, D)$$
$$(S; (v_1, v_2), \mathsf{Snd}; C, D) \longrightarrow (S; v_2, C, D)$$
$$(S; v, \mathsf{Inl}; C, D) \longrightarrow (S; inl(v), C, D)$$
$$(S; v, \mathsf{Inr}; C, D) \longrightarrow (S; inr(v), C, D)$$
$$(S; inl(v), \mathsf{Case}(C_1, C_2); C, D) \longrightarrow (S; v, C_1, D; (S, C))$$
$$(S; inr(v), \mathsf{Case}(C_1, C_2); C, D) \longrightarrow (S; v, C_2, D; (S, C))$$
$$(S, \mathsf{Code}(C_0); C, D) \longrightarrow (S; cls(\phi, C_0), C, D)$$
$$(S; cls(S_0, C_0); v_1; \cdots; v_m, \mathsf{Call}(m); C, D) \longrightarrow (S_0; v_1; \cdots; v_m, C_0, D; (S, C))$$
$$(S; cls(S_0, C_0); v_1; \cdots; v_m, \mathsf{App}(m); C, D) \longrightarrow (S; cls(S_0; v_1; \cdots; v_m, C_0), C, D)$$

Fig. 5. Operational Semantics of SLAM

Evaluation of code under this operational semantics corresponds to the trivial proof transformation by successively eliminating the last inference step. To formally establish this relation, we define the typing relations for values and for stack (written $\models v : \tau$ and $\models S : \Delta$ respectively) as follows.

- $\models c^b : b$.
- $\models (v_1, v_2) : \tau_1 \wedge \tau_2$ if $\models v_1 : \tau_1$ and $\models v_2 : \tau_2$.
- $\models inl(v) : \tau_1 \vee \tau_2$ if $\models v : \tau_1$
- $\models inr(v) : \tau_1 \vee \tau_2$ if $\models v : \tau_2$.
- $\models cls(S, C) : (\Delta \Rightarrow \tau)$ if $\models S : \Delta_1$ and $\Delta_1; \Delta \triangleright C : \tau$ for some Δ_1.
- $\models S : \Delta$ if $S = \langle v_1; \ldots; v_n \rangle, \Delta = \langle \tau_1; \ldots; \tau_n \rangle$ such that $\models v_i : \tau_i (1 \leq i \leq n)$.

We can then show the following.

Theorem 1. *If there is a proof of the form*

$$
\vdots
$$
$$
\frac{\Delta_2 \triangleright C_2 : \tau}{}
$$
$$
\vdots
$$
$$
\overline{\Delta_1 \triangleright C_1; C_2 : \tau}
$$

$S_1 \models \Delta_1$, *and* $(S_1, C_1; C_2, D) \xrightarrow{*} (S_2, C_2, D)$ *then* $S_2 \models \Delta_2$.

Proof. This is shown by induction on the number of reduction steps of the machine. The proof proceeds by cases in terms of the first instruction of C. For the instructions other than $\mathsf{Case}(C_1, C_2)$ and $\mathsf{Call}(n)$, the property is show by checking the rule of the instruction against the proof rule and then applying the induction hypothesis. The cases for $\mathsf{Case}(C_1, C_2)$ and $\mathsf{Call}(n)$ can be shown by using the fact that the only instruction that decreases (pops) the dump D is Return.   □

We can also show that the machine does not halt unexpectedly. To show this property, we need to define the type correctness of a dump. We write $\models D : \tau$ to represent the property that D is a type correct dump expecting a return value of type τ. This relation is given below.

- $\models \phi : \tau$.
- $\models D; (S, C) : \tau$ if there are some Δ and τ' such that $S \models \Delta, \Delta; \tau \triangleright C : \tau'$ and $\models D : \tau'$.

Theorem 2. *If $\Delta \triangleright C : \tau$, $S \models \Delta$ and $\models D : \tau$ then $(S, C, D) \longrightarrow (S', C', D')$ and if $C' \neq \phi$ then there are some Δ', τ' such that $S' \models \Delta', \Delta' \triangleright C' : \tau'$ and $\models D' : \tau'$.*

Proof. By cases in terms of the first instruction of C.

Combining the two theorems, we have the following.

Corollary 1. *If* $\Delta \triangleright C : \tau$, $S \models \Delta$, $(S, C, \phi) \xrightarrow{*} (S', C', D)$ *and there is no* (S'', C'', D') *such that* $(S', C', D) \longrightarrow (S'', C'', D')$ *then* $(S', C', D) = (v, \phi, \phi)$ *such that* $\models v : \tau$.

Proof. By the property of the proof system, there are Δ', C_0 such tha $C = C_0$; Return and Δ'; $\tau \triangleright$ Return : τ. It is easily checked that if $D \neq \phi$ then $C \neq \phi$. Then by Theorem 2, the property that $(S, C, \phi) \xrightarrow{*} (S', C', D)$ and there is no (S'', C'', D') such that $(S', C', D) \longrightarrow (S'', C'', D')$ implies that $(S, C_0; \text{Return}, \phi) \xrightarrow{*} (S_1, \text{Return}, \phi)$ for some S_1. By Theorem 1, $\models S_1 : \Delta'$; τ. Thus $S_1 = S_1'$; v such that $\models v : \tau$. Then $(S_1'; v, \text{Return}, \phi) \longrightarrow (v, \phi, \phi)$. □

3.2 RLAM: The Register-Based LAM

Parallel to the stack-based logical abstract machine, SLAM, we can also construct the register based machine, RLAM, from the sequential sequent calculus, $\mathcal{S}_R$, and we can show the properties analogous to those of SLAM. Here we only give the set of instructions and the typing rules in Fig. 6, where $x \leftarrow I$ intuitively means that the value denoted by I is assigned to register x. The intuitive meaning of each instruction can then be understood analogously to the corresponding instruction of SLAM.

4 Code Generation as Proof Transformation

The sequential sequent calculus is shown to be equivalent to existing intuitionistic propositional calculi with conjunction and disjunction. Moreover, the proof of the equivalence is effective. For example, any proof in the natural deduction of intuitionistic propositional logic can be transformed to a proof in the sequential sequent calculus, and vice versa. The same also holds for the intuitionistic propositional sequent calculus. Through Curry-Howard isomorphism, these results immediately yield compilation algorithms from the lambda calculus or the A-normal forms to the logical abstract machine.

Here we only consider the typed lambda calculus (with products and sums.) The set of types is given by the following grammar.

$$\tau ::= b \mid \tau \supset \tau \mid \tau \wedge \tau \mid \tau \vee \tau$$

The set of typing rules of the lambda calculus is given in Fig. 7. We denote this proof system by $\mathcal{N}$ and write $\mathcal{N} \vdash \Gamma \triangleright M : \tau$ if $\Gamma \triangleright M : \tau$ is provable in this proof system.

We identify implication type $\tau_1 \supset \tau_2$ of $\mathcal{N}$ with code type $(\langle \tau_1 \rangle \Rightarrow \tau_2)$ of $\mathcal{S}_S$. For a type assignment Γ in $\mathcal{N}$ we let Δ_Γ be the corresponding assumption list in $\mathcal{S}_S$ obtained by a linear ordering on variables, i.e., if $\Gamma = \{x_1 : \tau_1, \ldots, x_n : \tau_n\}$ such that $x_i < x_j$ for any $1 \leq i < j \leq n$, then $\Delta_\Gamma = \langle \tau_1; \ldots; \tau_n \rangle$. If $x \in dom(\Gamma)$ then we write $lookup(\Gamma, x)$ for the position in Δ_Γ corresponding to x.

$$I ::= \mathsf{Return}(x) \mid x{\leftarrow}y \mid x{\leftarrow}\mathsf{Const}(c^b) \mid x{\leftarrow}\mathsf{Pair}(y,z) \mid x{\leftarrow}\mathsf{Fst}(y) \mid x{\leftarrow}\mathsf{Snd}(y)$$
$$\mid x{\leftarrow}\mathsf{Inl}(y) \mid x{\leftarrow}\mathsf{Inr}(y) \mid x{\leftarrow}\mathsf{Case}(y,(x).C_1,(x).C_2) \mid x{\leftarrow}\mathsf{Code}(C)$$
$$\mid y{\leftarrow}\mathsf{Call}\ x\ \text{with}\ (y_1{\leftarrow}x_1,\ldots,y_n{\leftarrow}x_n)$$
$$\mid y{\leftarrow}\mathsf{App}\ x\ \text{to}\ (y_1{\leftarrow}x_1,\ldots,y_n{\leftarrow}x_n)$$

(return) $\quad \Gamma, x : \tau \triangleright \mathsf{Return}(x) : \tau$

(acc) $\quad \dfrac{\Gamma, x : \tau_1; y : \tau_1 \triangleright C : \tau}{\Gamma, x : \tau_1 \triangleright y{\leftarrow}x; C : \tau}$

(const) $\quad \dfrac{\Gamma, x : b \triangleright C : \tau}{\Gamma \triangleright x{\leftarrow}c^b; C : \tau}$

(pair) $\quad \dfrac{\Gamma, x : \tau_1; y : \tau_2; z : \tau_1{\wedge}\tau_2 \triangleright C : \tau}{\Gamma, x : \tau_1; y : \tau_2 \triangleright z{\leftarrow}\mathsf{Pair}(x,y); C : \tau}$

(fst) $\quad \dfrac{\Gamma, x : \tau_1{\wedge}\tau_2; y : \tau_1 \triangleright C : \tau}{\Gamma, x : \tau_1{\wedge}\tau_2 \triangleright y{\leftarrow}\mathsf{Fst}(x); C : \tau}$

(snd) $\quad \dfrac{\Gamma, x : \tau_1{\wedge}\tau_2; y : \tau_2 \triangleright C : \tau}{\Gamma, x : \tau_1{\wedge}\tau_2 \triangleright y{\leftarrow}\mathsf{Snd}(x); C : \tau}$

(inl) $\quad \dfrac{\Gamma, x : \tau_1; y : \tau_1{\vee}\tau_2 \triangleright C : \tau}{\Gamma, x : \tau_1 \triangleright y{\leftarrow}\mathsf{Inl}(x); C : \tau}$

(inr) $\quad \dfrac{\Gamma, x : \tau_2; y : \tau_1{\vee}\tau_2 \triangleright C : \tau}{\Gamma, x : \tau_2 \triangleright y{\leftarrow}\mathsf{Inr}(x); C : \tau}$

(case) $\quad \dfrac{\Gamma, x : \tau_1{\vee}\tau_2; y : \tau_3 \triangleright C : \tau}{\Gamma, x : \tau_1{\vee}\tau_2 \triangleright y{\leftarrow}\mathsf{Case}(x, (z_1).C_1, (z_2).C_2); C : \tau}$
$$(\text{if } \Gamma, z_1 : \tau_1 \triangleright C_1 : \tau_3,\ \Gamma, z_2 : \tau_2 \triangleright C_2 : \tau_3)$$

(code) $\quad \dfrac{\Gamma, x : (\Gamma_0 \Rightarrow \tau_0) \triangleright C : \tau}{\Gamma \triangleright x{\leftarrow}\mathsf{Code}(C'); C : \tau}\quad (\text{if } \vdash \Gamma_0 \triangleright C' : \tau_0)$

(call) $\quad \dfrac{\Gamma_1, x : (\Gamma_2 \Rightarrow \tau_0); y : \tau_0 \triangleright C : \tau}{\Gamma_1, x : (\Gamma_2 \Rightarrow \tau_0) \triangleright y{\leftarrow}\mathsf{Call}\ x\ \text{with}\ (y_1{\leftarrow}x_1,\ldots,y_n{\leftarrow}x_n); C : \tau}$
$$(\Gamma_2 = \{y_1 : \tau_1; \cdots; y_n : \tau_n\}, \Gamma_1(x_i) = \tau_i, 1 \le i \le n)$$

(app) $\quad \dfrac{\Gamma_1, x : (\Gamma_2, \Gamma_3 \Rightarrow \tau_0); y : (\Gamma_3 \Rightarrow \tau_0) \triangleright C : \tau}{\Gamma_1, x : (\Gamma_2, \Gamma_3 \Rightarrow \tau_0) \triangleright y{\leftarrow}\mathsf{Appl}\ x\ \text{to}\ (y_1{\leftarrow}x_1,\ldots,y_n{\leftarrow}x_n); C : \tau}$
$$(\Gamma_2 = \{y_1 : \tau_1; \cdots; y_n : \tau_n\}, \Gamma_1(x_i) = \tau_i, 1 \le i \le n)$$

Fig. 6. The Register-Based Logical Abstract Machine, RLAM

(taut) $\quad \Gamma, x : \tau \triangleright x : \tau$ 　　(axiom) $\quad \Gamma \triangleright c^\tau : \tau$ 　　($\supset$:I) $\quad \dfrac{\Gamma, x : \tau_1 \triangleright M : \tau_1}{\Gamma \triangleright \lambda x.M : \tau_1{\supset}\tau_2}$

($\supset$:E) $\quad \dfrac{\Gamma \triangleright M_1 : \tau_1{\supset}\tau_2 \quad \Gamma \triangleright M_2 : \tau_1}{\Gamma \triangleright M_1\, M_2 : \tau_2}$

($\wedge$:I) $\quad \dfrac{\Gamma \triangleright M_1 : \tau_1 \quad \Gamma \triangleright M_2 : \tau_2}{\Gamma \triangleright (M_1, M_2) : \tau_1{\wedge}\tau_2}$

($\wedge$:E1) $\quad \dfrac{\Gamma \triangleright M : \tau_1{\wedge}\tau_2}{\Gamma \triangleright M.1 : \tau_1}$

($\wedge$:E2) $\quad \dfrac{\Gamma \triangleright M : \tau_1{\wedge}\tau_2}{\Gamma \triangleright M.2 : \tau_2}$

($\vee$:I1) $\quad \dfrac{\Gamma \triangleright M : \tau_1}{\Gamma \triangleright inl(M) : \tau_1{\vee}\tau_2}$

($\vee$:I2) $\quad \dfrac{\Gamma \triangleright M : \tau_2}{\Gamma \triangleright inr(M) : \tau_1{\vee}\tau_2}$

($\vee$:E) $\quad \dfrac{\Gamma \triangleright M_1 : \tau_1{\vee}\tau_2 \quad \Gamma, x : \tau_1 \triangleright M_2 : \tau_3 \quad \Gamma, y : \tau_2 \triangleright M_3 : \tau_3}{\Gamma \triangleright case\ M_1\ of\ x.M_2, y.M_3 : \tau_3}$

Fig. 7. $\mathcal{N}$: Typed Lambda Calculus with Products and Sums

We first show that any lambda term M can be translated to SLAM code $[\![M]\!]$ that extends a given stack with the value denoted by M. To establish this connection, we define the following relation for SLAM code.

$$C : \Delta_1 \Rightarrow \Delta_2 \Longleftrightarrow \text{ for any } C', \tau \text{ if } \mathcal{S}_S \vdash \Delta_2 \rhd C' : \tau \text{ then } \mathcal{S}_S \vdash \Delta_1 \rhd C; C' : \tau.$$

From this definition, it is immediate that each inference rule of SLAM of the form $\quad (R_I) \quad \dfrac{\Delta_2 \rhd C : \tau}{\Delta_1 \rhd I; C : \tau}$ is regarded as the relation $I : \Delta_1 \Rightarrow \Delta_2$, and that this relation is "transitive", i.e., if $C_1 : \Delta_1 \Rightarrow \Delta_2$ and $C_2 : \Delta_2 \Rightarrow \Delta_3$ then $C_1; C_2 : \Delta_1 \Rightarrow \Delta_3$.

The following lemma plays a central role in establishing the logical correspondence. Since a proof of this lemma gives a code generation algorithm and its type correctness proof, we show it in some detail.

Lemma 1. *If $\mathcal{N} \vdash \Gamma \rhd M : \tau$ then there is SLAM code $[\![M]\!]$ such that $[\![M]\!] : \Delta_\Gamma \Rightarrow \Delta_\Gamma; \tau$.*

Proof. By induction on M.

Case x. Since $x : \tau \in \Gamma$, by rule (acc), $\mathsf{Acc}(lookup(\Gamma, x)) : \Delta_\Gamma \Rightarrow \Delta_\Gamma; \tau$.

Case c^b. By rule (const), $\mathsf{Push}(c^b) : \Delta_\Gamma \Rightarrow \Delta_\Gamma; b$.

Case $\lambda x.M'$. By the typing rule, there are some τ_1, τ_2 such that $\tau = \tau_1 \supset \tau_2$, and $\mathcal{N} \vdash \Gamma, x : \tau_1 \rhd M' : \tau_2$. By the induction hypothesis, $[\![M']\!] : \Delta_{\Gamma, x:\tau_1} \Rightarrow \Delta_{\Gamma, x:\tau_1}; \tau_2$. Since $\mathcal{S}_S \vdash \Delta_{\Gamma, x:\tau_1}; \tau_2 \rhd \mathsf{Return} : \tau_2$, by definition, $\mathcal{S}_S \vdash \Delta_{\Gamma, x:\tau_1} \rhd [\![M']\!]; \mathsf{Return} : \tau_2$. By the bound variable convention in $\mathcal{N}$ we can assume that x is larger than any variables in $dom(\Gamma)$ and therefore $\Delta_{\Gamma, x:\tau_1} = \Delta_\Gamma; \tau_1$. Thus we have $\mathsf{Code}([\![M']\!]; \mathsf{Return}) : \Delta_\Gamma \Rightarrow \Delta_\Gamma; (\Delta_\Gamma; \tau_1 \Rightarrow \tau_2)$. Let $n = |\Delta_\Gamma|$. By repeated applications of rule (acc),

$$\mathsf{Code}([\![M']\!]; \mathsf{Return}); \mathsf{Acc}(0); \cdots; \mathsf{Acc}(n-1) : \Delta_\Gamma \Rightarrow \Delta_\Gamma; (\Delta_\Gamma; \tau_1 \Rightarrow \tau_2); \Delta_\Gamma$$

By rule (app), we have

$$\mathsf{Code}([\![M']\!]; \mathsf{Return})); \mathsf{Acc}(0); \cdots; \mathsf{Acc}(n-1); \mathsf{App}(n) : \Delta_\Gamma \Rightarrow \Delta_\Gamma; (\langle \tau_1 \rangle \Rightarrow \tau_2)$$

Case $M_1\, M_2$. By the type system of $\mathcal{N}$, there is some τ_1 such that $\mathcal{N} \vdash \Gamma \rhd M_1 : \tau_1 \supset \tau$ and $\mathcal{N} \vdash \Gamma \rhd M_2 : \tau_1$. By the induction hypothesis for M_1, $[\![M_1]\!] : \Delta_\Gamma \Rightarrow \Delta_\Gamma; (\langle \tau_1 \rangle \Rightarrow \tau)$. Let x be a variable larger than any variables in $dom(\Gamma)$. By the property of $\mathcal{N}$, $\mathcal{N} \vdash \Gamma, x : \tau_1 \supset \tau \rhd M_2 : \tau_1$. By the choice of x, $\Delta_{\Gamma, x:(\langle \tau_1 \rangle \Rightarrow \tau)} = \Delta_\Gamma; (\langle \tau_1 \rangle \Rightarrow \tau)$. Then by the induction hypothesis for M_2, $[\![M_2]\!] : \Delta_\Gamma; (\langle \tau_1 \rangle \Rightarrow \tau) \Rightarrow \Delta_\Gamma; (\langle \tau_1 \rangle \Rightarrow \tau); \tau_1$ Then we have

$$[\![M_1]\!]; [\![M_2]\!]; \mathsf{Call}(1) : \Delta_\Gamma \Rightarrow \Delta_\Gamma; \tau$$

Case (M_1, M_2). By the type system of $\mathcal{N}$, there are some τ_1, τ_2 such that $\tau = \tau_1 \wedge \tau_2$, $\mathcal{N} \vdash \Gamma \rhd M_1 : \tau_1$ and $\mathcal{N} \vdash \Gamma \rhd M_2 : \tau_2$. By the induction hypothesis for M_1, $[M_1] : \Delta_\Gamma \Rightarrow \Delta_\Gamma; \tau_1$. Let x be a variable larger than any variables in $dom(\Gamma)$. By the property of $\mathcal{N}$, $\mathcal{N} \vdash \Gamma, x : \tau_1 \triangleright M_2 : \tau_2$. By the choice of x, $\Delta_{\Gamma, x:\tau_1} = \Delta_\Gamma; \tau_1$. Then by the induction hypothesis for M_2, $[M_2] : \Delta_\Gamma; \tau_1 \Rightarrow \Delta_\Gamma; \tau_1; \tau_2$ Thus we have

$$[M_1]; [M_2]; \text{Pair} : \Delta_\Gamma \Rightarrow \Delta_\Gamma; \tau_1 \wedge \tau_2$$

Case $M.1$. By the type system of $\mathcal{N}$, there is some τ_1 such that $\mathcal{N} \vdash \Gamma \triangleright M_1 : \tau \wedge \tau_1$. By the induction hypothesis, $[M_1] : \Delta_\Gamma \Rightarrow \Delta_\Gamma; \tau \wedge \tau_1$. Thus we have $[M_1]; \text{Fst} : \Delta_\Gamma \Rightarrow \Delta_\Gamma; \tau$
The case for $M.2$ is similar.

Case $inl(M_1)$. By the type system of $\mathcal{N}$, there are some τ_1, τ_2 such that $\tau = \tau_1 \vee \tau_2$ and $\mathcal{N} \vdash \Gamma \triangleright M_1 : \tau_1$. By the induction hypothesis, $[M_1] : \Delta_\Gamma \Rightarrow \Delta_\Gamma; \tau_1$. Then we have $[M_1]; \text{Inl} : \Delta_\Gamma \Rightarrow \Delta_\Gamma; \tau_1 \vee \tau_2$
The case for $inr(M)$ is similar.

Case $case\ M_1\ of\ x.M_2, y.M_3$. There are some τ_1, τ_2 such that $\Gamma \triangleright M_1 : \tau_1 \vee \tau_2$, $\Gamma, x : \tau_1 \triangleright M_2 : \tau$, and $\Gamma, y : \tau_2 \triangleright M_3 : \tau$. By the induction hypothesis for M_1, $[M_1] : \Delta_\Gamma \Rightarrow \Delta_\Gamma; \tau_1 \vee \tau_2$. By the bound variable convention in the lambda calculus, we can assume that x, y are larger than any variables in $dom(\Gamma)$. Thus $\Delta_{\Gamma, x:\tau_1} = \Delta_\Gamma; \tau_1$ and $\Delta_{\Gamma, y:\tau_2} = \Delta_\Gamma; \tau_2$. Then by the induction hypotheses for M_2 and M_3, $[M_2] : \Delta_\Gamma; \tau_1 \Rightarrow \Delta_\Gamma; \tau_1; \tau$ and $[M_3] : \Delta_\Gamma; \tau_2 \Rightarrow \Delta_\Gamma; \tau_2; \tau$ Then by definition $\mathcal{S}_S \vdash \Delta_\Gamma; \tau_1 \triangleright [M_2]; \text{Return} : \tau$ and $\mathcal{S}_S \vdash \Delta_\Gamma; \tau_2 \triangleright [M_3]; \text{Return} : \tau$, and therefore

$$[M_1]; \text{Case}([M_2]; \text{Return}, [M_3]; \text{Return}) : \Delta_\Gamma \Rightarrow \Delta_\Gamma; \tau$$

$\square$

Theorem 3. *If $\mathcal{N} \vdash \Gamma \triangleright M : \tau$ then there is some SLAM program C_M such that $\mathcal{S}_S \vdash \Delta_\Gamma \triangleright C_M : \tau$.*

Proof. By Lemma 1, there is some $[M]$ such that $[M] : \Delta_\Gamma \Rightarrow \Delta_\Gamma; \tau$. Take C_M to be $[M]; \text{Return}$. Since $\mathcal{S}_S \vdash \Delta_\Gamma; \tau \triangleright \text{Return} : \tau$, we have $\mathcal{S}_S \vdash \Delta_\Gamma \triangleright C_M : \tau$.
$\square$

Those who have written a byte-code compiler would immediately recognize the similarity between this proof and a compilation algorithm; but they would also recognize some redundancy this translation produces. This point will be taken up in Section 5 when we discuss implementation issues.

The sequential sequent calculus is sound with respect to the intuitionistic propositional logic, and any sequent provable in the sequential sequent calculus is also provable in other proof systems including the natural deduction and a sequent calculus. Under our Curry-Howard isomorphism, this means that the above theorem is reversible. To formally state this connection, we define the type $\bar{\tau}$ of $\mathcal{N}$ corresponding to a type τ of $\mathcal{S}_S$ as follows.

$$\overline{b} = b$$

$$\overline{(\langle \tau_1; \ldots; \tau_n \rangle \Rightarrow \tau)} = \overline{\tau_1} \supset \cdots \overline{\tau_n} \supset \overline{\tau}$$

$$\overline{\tau_1 \wedge \tau_2} = \overline{\tau_1} \wedge \overline{\tau_2}$$

$$\overline{\tau_1 \vee \tau_2} = \overline{\tau_1} \vee \overline{\tau_2}$$

Let Δ be an assumption set of $\mathcal{S}_S$ and let $n = |\Delta|$. We write Γ_Δ for the type assignment of $\mathcal{N}$ such that $dom(\Gamma) = \{x_1, \ldots, x_n\}$ and $\Gamma_\Delta(x_i) = \overline{\Delta(i)}$, where $x_1, \ldots, x_n$ are distinct variables chosen in some arbitrary but fix way (we can use integer i itself for x_i.) We can then show the following.

Theorem 4. *If $\mathcal{S}_S \vdash \Delta \triangleright C : \tau$ then there is a lambda term M_C such that $\mathcal{N} \vdash \Gamma_\Delta \triangleright M_C : \overline{\tau}$.*

Proof. By induction on the derivation of $\mathcal{S}_S \vdash \Delta \triangleright C : \tau$ using the substitution lemma in the lambda calculus. □

Different from the relationship between the lambda calculus (natural deduction) and the combinatory logic (Hilbert system), the term obtained by a proof of this theorem is not a trivial one, but reflects the logical structure of the program realized by the code. This has the important implication of opening up the possibility of high-level code analysis. This topic is outside the scope of the current paper. In near future, we shall report on this topic elsewhere.

The above two theorems are proved for the natural deduction. The same results can be proved for Kleene's G3a, yielding translation algorithms between A-normal forms and LAM code.

5 Implementing a Functional Language Using LAM

In this section, we consider some issues in implementing a functional language based on a logical framework presented in this paper.

A typical implementation of a functional language consists of the following steps.

1. A-norm transformation.
2. Lambda lifting and closure optimization.
3. Pseudo code generation.
4. Register allocation and native code generation.

These processes are usually thought of as those required for converting a heigh-level programming language into a low-level machine language. A machine language is indeed low-level for the programmer in the sense that it consists of simple and primitive operations. However, this does not means that code generation and optimization are inevitably "low-level" and ad-hoc. As we have demonstrated, a machine language is understood as a proof system, and code generation process is a proof transformation. These results enables us to analyze various implementation issues in a rigorous logical framework.

In a logical perspective, A-normal transformation is to transform the elimination rules in the natural deduction system to combinations of left rules and cut rules in a sequent calculus. The resulting sequent calculus (Kleene's G3a) is much closer to the sequential sequent calculus, and therefore the subsequent code generation process become much simpler. This topic is outside the scope of the present paper. The interested reader is referred to [17] for Curry-Howard isomorphism for A-normal translation. In the rest of this section, we consider some issues in the context of direct-style compilation for the lambda calculus.

5.1   Lambda Lifting and Closure Optimization

Lambda lifting and associated closure optimization are the processes of absorbing the difference between functions and machine code. (See [18,1] for the details.) In the lambda calculus, one-argument function abstraction and function application are the primitives. On the other hand, in computer hardware, the unit of execution is a pre-compiled code requiring multiple arguments. Our logical abstract machine properly reflects this situation, and is therefore a suitable formalism to analyze the efficiency of these processes.

Examining the code generation algorithm given in the proof of theorem 3 reveals the redundancy in treating nested lambda abstractions and nested lambda applications. For example, consider the lambda term $(\lambda x.\lambda y.(x,y))$ 1 2. A straightforward application of the algorithm yields the following code in SLAM (written in a linear fashion using labels).

```
          Code(label1);Const(1);Call(1);Const(2);Call(1);Return
label1:   Code(label2);Acc(0);App(1);Return
label2:   Acc(0);Acc(1);Pair;Return
```

Apparently, the intermediate closure creation is redundant. One way of eliminating this redundancy is to translate the lambda calculus to an intermediate language that is closer to the logical abstract machine. We show one possible definition of an intermediate language below.

$$P ::= decl\ D\ in\ M$$
$$D ::= \phi \mid D; L = \lambda\langle x_1, \ldots, x_n\rangle.M$$
$$M ::= x \mid L \mid (MM\ \cdots\ M) \mid (M,M) \mid M.1 \mid M.2$$
$$\mid inl(M) \mid inr(M) \mid case\ M_1\ of\ \lambda x.M_2, \lambda x.M_3$$

In this definition, a program P consists of a sequence of declarations D and a program body. A declaration is an association list of a label (denoted by L) and a multi-argument function $\lambda\langle x_1, \ldots, x_n\rangle.M$ such that $FV(M) = \{x_1, \ldots, x_n\}$, and corresponds to a "super combinator" which is a target expression of lambda lifting [18]. Instead of lambda abstraction and lambda application, the set of terms contains a label L referring to a code, and a function call with multiple arguments.

A type system for this language and a compilation algorithm from this language to the logical abstract machine are easily given. However, a non-trivial static analysis is needed to translate the lambda calculus to this language. This is outside the scope of the present paper. We plan to present a detailed account for the type-directed translation from the lambda calculus to LAM code using this intermediate language elsewhere. Here we only show an example of the compilation process using this intermediate language. Fig. 8 is an actual output of a prototype compiler the author has implemented based on the logical approach presented in this paper. In this example, $1 is a label and [$1 1 2] is function application to multiple arguments. One can see that the generated code does not contain the redundancy mentioned above. Also note that the compiler calculates the maximum height of the stack needed for each code.

```
Source expr:
 (fn x=>fn y=>(x,y)) 1 2

Typecheked and transformed to:
 decls
    $1 = (fn <x,y> => (x,y)) : ('a.'b.<'a;'b> => 'a * 'b)
 in
    [|$1| 1 2]
 end
  : int * int

Compiled to SLAM code:
Start at :label0

Max stack size : 3          Max stack size : 4
label0: Code(label1)        label1: Acc(0)
        Const(1)                    Acc(1)
        Const(2)                    Pair
        App(2)                      Return
        Return
```

Fig. 8. Compilation process for $(\lambda x.\lambda y.(x,y))$ 1 2

5.2   Generating Efficient RLAM Code

We have explained our logic-based approach using the stack-based machine SLAM, which is suitable for a byte-code interpreter. However, some inefficiency is inevitable in a stack-based code mainly because its restricted memory access through the stack-top pointer. For example, accessing and pushing two arguments Acc(0) and Acc(1) in the code shown in Fig. 8 for (x,y) is redundant if arguments can be passed through registers. By choosing a register-based machine RLAM we defined in Section 3.2 we can solve this problem. As already mentioned, all the major results so far presented hold for RLAM. Our prototype compiler also generate RLAM machine code. Fig. 9 shows the RLAM code generated for $(\lambda x.\lambda y.(x,y))\ 1\ 2$.

Compiled to RLAM code:
Start at :label0

```
label0: r0 <- Code(label1)              label1: r5<- Pair(r3,r4)
        r1 <- Const(1)                          Return(r5)
        r2 <- Const(2)
        r0 <- Call r0 with (r3<-r1, r4<-r2)
        Return(r0)
```

Fig. 9. RLAM code for $(\lambda x.\lambda y.(x,y))\ 1\ 2$

In RLAM, an assumption list Γ in each sequent $\Gamma \triangleright C : \tau$ is a mapping from variable names to formula, and models the registers used at the time when the first instruction of C is executed. By this interpretation, RLAM is regarded as a register transfer language where an inference step of the form $\dfrac{\Gamma_2 \triangleright C : \tau}{\Gamma_1 \triangleright I; C : \tau}$ indicates that the instruction I modifies the set of registers indicated by Γ_1 to those of Γ_2. In particular, if Γ_2 extends Γ_1 then I "loads" an empty register with a value. Note that the notation $\Gamma, x : \tau$ may override x in Γ. This corresponds to re-using a register which is no longer "live," i.e. if x is not free in the premise.

By the above simple analysis, it is expected that RLAM can serve as a formal basis to analyze and design register allocation. Katsumata's recent result [8] indicates that this is indeed the case; he have shown that by incorporating the mechanism of linear logic, a calculus similar to RLAM is used to perform precise analysis on register liveness.

6   Conclusions and Further Investigations

We have developed a logical framework for machine code and code generation. As a logic for machine code, we have define the *sequential sequent calculus*, which is a variant of a sequent calculus whose proof only involves left rules and has a linear (non-branching) structure. We have established a Curry-Howard isomorphism between this proof system and a sequential machine language. We have then shown that code generation algorithm is extracted from a proof of the equivalence theorem between the natural deduction and the sequential sequent calculus. We have also demonstrated that various implementation issues can be analyzed and expressed in our logical framework.

This is a first step towards a logical approach to implementation of a high-level programming language, and there are a number of interesting issues remain to be investigated. Here we briefly mention some of them.

- Various language extensions.
  In order to apply the framework presented in this paper to actual language implementation, we need to extend it with various features of practical programming languages. Adding recursion is relatively straightforward (though the resulting proof system no longer corresponds to the intuitionistic propositional logic.) A more challenging issue would be to extend the framework to classical logic for representing various control structures such as those investigated in [5]. Another interesting issue in this direction is to consider higher-order logic to represent polymorphism.
- Static analysis of machine code.
  As we have mentioned, we are developing a method to reconstruct the logical structure of a program from machine code. Other possibility would be to develop a framework for type inference and abstract interpretation for machine code. These static analyses would be particularly important in ensuring security in mobile and network programming.
- Development of a practical compiler.
  Another important topic is to consider proof reduction and equational theory for machine code. They will provide a firm basis for code optimization.

We believe that with further research for optimizations, the logical framework presented in this paper will serve as a basis for efficient and robust implementation of high-level programming languages.

Acknowledgments

The author would like to thank Shin'ya Katsumata for stimulating discussion on logic and computer hardware, and for comments on a draft of this paper.

References

1. Andrew W. Appel. *Compiling with Continuations*. Cambridge University Press, 1992.
2. G. Cousineau, P-L. Curien, and M. Mauny. The categorical abstract machine. *Science of Computer Programming*, 8(2), 1987.
3. H. B. Curry and R. Feys. *Combinatory Logic*, volume 1. North-Holland, Amsterdam, 1968.
4. C. Flanagan, A. Sabry, B.F. Duba, and M. Felleisen. The essence of compiling with continuation. In *Proc. ACM PLDI Conference*, pages 237–247, 1993.
5. T. Griffin. A formulae-as-types notion of control. In *Conference Record of the Seventeenth Annual ACM Symposium on Principles of Programming Languages*, pages 47–58, 1990.
6. C.A. Gunter. *Semantics of Programming Languages – Structures and Techniques*. The MIT Press, 1992.
7. W. Howard. The formulae-as-types notion of construction. In *To H. B. Curry: Essays on Combinatory Logic, Lambda-Calculus and Formalism*, pages 476–490. Academic Press, 1980.

8. S. Katsumata, 1999. Personal communication.

9. S. Kleene. *Introduction to Metamathematics*. North-Holland, 1952. 7th edition.

10. J. Lambek. From λ-calculus to cartesian closed categories. In *To H. B. Curry: Essays on Combinatory Logic, Lambda-Calculus and Formalism*, pages 375–402. Academic Press, 1980.

11. P. J. Landin. The mechanical evaluation of expressions. *Computer Journal*, 6:308–320, 1964.

12. X. Leroy. The ZINC experiment: an economical implementation of the ML language. Technical Report 117, INRIA, 1992.

13. T. Lindholm and F. Yellin. *The Java virtual machine specification*. Addison-Wesley, 1996.

14. J.C. Mitchell. *Foundations for Programming Languages*. MIT Press, 1996.

15. G. Morrisett, K. Crary, N. Glew, and D. Walker. Stack-based typed assembly language. In *Proc. International Workshop on Types in Compilation, Springer LNCS 1478*, 1998.

16. G. Morrisett, D. Walker, K. Crary, and N. Glew. From system F to typed assembly language. In *Proc. ACM Symposium on Principles of Programming Languages*, 1998.

17. A Ohori. A Curry-Howard isomorphism for compilation and program execution. In *Proc. Typed Lambda Calculi and Applications, Springer LNCS 1581*, pages 258–179, 1999.

18. Simon L. Peyton Jones. *The Implementation of Functional Programming Languages*. Series in Computer Science. Prentice-Hall, 1987.

19. B. Stata and M. Abadi. A type system for java bytecode subroutines. In *Proc. ACM Symposium on Principles of Programming Languages*, pages 149–160, 1998.

20. D.A. Turner. A new implementation technique for applicative languages. *Software Practice and Experience*, 9:31–49, 1979.

On Reducing the Search Space of Higher-Order Lazy Narrowing[*]

Mircea Marin[1], Tetsuo Ida[2], and Taro Suzuki[3]

[1] Institute RISC-Linz
Johannes Kepler University, A-4232 Linz, Austria
Mircea.Marin@risc.uni-linz.ac.at
[2] Institute of Information Sciences and Electronics
University of Tsukuba, Tsukuba 305-8573, Japan
ida@score.is.tsukuba.ac.jp
[3] School of Information Science,
JAIST Hokuriku, 923-1292, Japan
t_suzuki@jaist.ac.jp

Abstract. Higher-order lazy narrowing is a general method for solving E-unification problems in theories presented as sets of rewrite rules. In this paper we study the possibility of improving the search for normalized solutions of a higher-order lazy narrowing calculus LN. We introduce a new calculus, LN_{ff}, obtained by extending LN and define an equation selection strategy S_n such that LN_{ff} with strategy S_n is complete. The main advantages of using LN_{ff} with strategy S_n instead of LN include the possibility of restricting the application of outermost narrowing at variable position, and the computation of more specific solutions because of additional inference rules for solving flex-flex equations. We also show that for orthogonal pattern rewrite systems we can adopt an eager variable elimination strategy that makes the calculus LN_{ff} with strategy S_n even more deterministic.

1 Introduction

Lazy narrowing is a method for solving E-unification problems in equational theories represented as sets of rewrite rules. It has been shown [2] that the lazy narrowing calculus forms a basis of functional logic programming. In recent years, various extensions of the lazy narrowing calculus to higher order equational theories have been proposed [3,4,14] in an attempt to define a suitable model for the design of an equational programming language. One such calculus is the calculus HLNC (Higher-order Lazy Narrowing Calculus) proposed by Suzuki, Nakagawa and Ida [14]. HLNC is based on the idea of combining the β-reduction

---

[*] This work is partially supported by Grant-in-Aid for Scientific Research on Priority Areas "Research on the Principles for Constructing Software with Evolutionary Mechanisms", Grant-in-Aid for Scientific Research (B) 10480053, and Grant-in-Aid for Encouragement of Young Scientists 11780204, Ministry of Education, Science, Sports and Culture, Government of Japan.

A. Middeldorp, T. Sato (Eds.): FLOPS'99, LNCS 1722, pp. 319–334, 1999.
© Springer-Verlag Berlin Heidelberg 1999

of the lambda calculus and the first-order narrowing calculus LNC [6]. Based on HLNC, a programming system called CFLP (Constraint Functional Logic Programming) has been designed and implemented [5]. Independently, Prehofer studied higher-order lazy narrowing based on the higher-order rewrite system of Nipkow [9] and introduced the calculus LN [11].

Both calculi HLNC and LN are highly nondeterministic and they create a huge search space for solutions. In order to guarantee completeness, we must take into account all possible choices of (1) the equation in the current goal to be solved, (2) the inference rule of the calculus to be applied, and (3) the rewrite rule to be considered for outermost narrowing. For first-order lazy narrowing, research in reducing this non-determinism has brought important results [6,7,1] and gives an insight to how to eliminate some sources of the non-determinism in higher-order lazy narrowing.

In this paper we tackle the problem of reducing the non-determinism of computing substitutions that subsume all the normalized solutions of a given higher-order goal. Our main contribution in this paper is the following.

(a) We present a new higher-order lazy narrowing calculus LN_{ff} by extending LN.
(b) We introduce an equation selection strategy S_n that restricts the application of outermost narrowing at variable position and enables the application of the inference rules that can solve certain flex-flex equations.
(c) We prove that LN_{ff} with strategy S_n is complete (with respect to normalized solutions).
(d) We show that an eager variable elimination strategy makes our calculus even more deterministic for orthogonal pattern rewrite systems.

As a result we successfully reduce the search space of normalized solutions and compute more specific solutions than with LN.

The rest of this paper is structured as follows. In Sect. 2 we introduce some preliminary notions and notations. In Sect. 3 we recall some theoretical results about preunification and pattern unification. In Sect. 4 we introduce the un-oriented higher-order lazy narrowing calculus LN and state the completeness result. In Sect. 5 we define our main calculus LN_{ff}. In Sect. 6 we define the equation strategy S_n and the class of normal LN_{ff}-refutations, and prove that all the normalized solutions of a goal are subsumed by substitutions computable with normal LN_{ff}-refutations. In Sect. 7 we extend our completeness result with an eager variable elimination strategy for solving parameter-passing equations. Finally we draw some conclusions and directions for further research.

2   Preliminaries

We employ the notation $a_{m,n}$ for a sequence $a_m, a_{m+1}, \ldots, a_n$. We write $\mathbf{a}_n$ instead of $\mathbf{a}_{1,n}$. If the length of a sequence is irrelevant then we may omit the indices and write, e.g., $\mathbf{a}$ for an arbitrary (including the empty) sequence of a's. We sometimes denote an empty sequence by the symbol $\square$.

A *term* is a simply typed lambda-term over a signature $\mathcal{F}$. We distinguish bound and free variables at the syntax level; we use uppercase letters X, Y, Z, H for free variables, lowercase letters x, y for bound variables, and letters l, r, s, t, u, v, w for terms if not stated otherwise. We extend this convention to sequences; For instance, $\mathbf{x}$ denotes a sequence of bound variables, whereas $\mathbf{s}_n$ denotes the sequence of terms $s_1, \ldots, s_n$. We denote by $\mathcal{FV}$ the set of free variables, and by $\mathcal{V}(t)$ the set of free variables occurring in a term t. A *flex term* is a term of the form $\lambda\mathbf{x}.X(\mathbf{s})$. A *rigid term* is a term which is not flex. A *pattern* is a term with the property that all its flex sub-terms are of the form $\lambda\mathbf{x}.X(\mathbf{y})$ with $\mathbf{y}$ distinct bound variables. We consider two terms s and t equal, notation $s = t$, if they are $\alpha\beta\eta$-equivalent. This notion of equality is extended to substitutions. In the sequel we represent terms in long $\beta\eta$-normal form.

Definition 1 (pattern rewrite system) A *pattern rewrite system* (PRS for short) is a set of rewrite rules of the form $f(\mathbf{l}) \to r$ with $f \in \mathcal{F}$, $f(\mathbf{l})$, r terms of the same base type, $\mathcal{V}(f(\mathbf{l})) \supseteq \mathcal{V}(r)$ and $f(\mathbf{l})$ a pattern.

Given a PRS $\mathcal{R}$, we denote by $\to$ the rewrite relation induced by $\mathcal{R}$. The relations $\to^*$, $\leftrightarrow^*$ and $\downarrow$ are defined as usual.

Definition 2 (equation) An *unoriented equation* is a pair $s \approx t$ of terms s and t of the same type. An *oriented equation* is a pair $s \rhd t$ of terms s and t of the same type. An *equation* is either an unoriented or an oriented equation. A *flex-flex equation* is an equation between flex terms. A *flex-rigid equation* is an equation between a flex and a rigid term. A *pattern equation* is an equation between patterns. A *goal* is a finite sequence of equations. A *flex-flex goal* is a goal consisting of flex-flex equations.

Let θ be a substitution. We define the *domain* of θ as $\mathcal{D}(\theta) \overset{\text{def}}{=} \{X \in \mathcal{FV} \mid X\theta \neq X\}$ and the *codomain* of θ as $\mathcal{I}(\theta) \overset{\text{def}}{=} \{X\theta \mid X \in \mathcal{D}(\theta)\}$. If θ_1, θ_2 are substitutions and V is a set of variables, we write $\theta_1 \leq \theta_2 \, [V]$ if $\theta_1\delta \restriction_V = \theta_2 \restriction_V$ for some δ.

Definition 3 (unifier and solution) A substitution θ is a *unifier of two terms* s and t if $s\theta = t\theta$. A substitution θ is a *unifier of a goal* G if $s\theta = t\theta$ for every equation $s \approx t$ or $s \rhd t$ in G. θ is a solution of an equation $s \approx t$ if $s\theta \leftrightarrow^* t\theta$. θ is a *solution of an equation* $s \rhd t$ if $s\theta \to^* t\theta$. θ is a *solution of a goal* G if θ is a solution of all equations in G.

We will make use of the following important property of patterns. Given a PRS $\mathcal{R}$ and a substitution θ, we say that θ is $\mathcal{R}$-*normalized* if every term in $\mathcal{I}(\theta)$ is $\mathcal{R}$-normalized.

Lemma 1 If $\mathcal{R}$ is a PRS, X a free variable, $\mathbf{y}_m$ distinct bound variables and θ a substitution then $\lambda\mathbf{x}_k.X\theta(\mathbf{y}_m)$ is $\mathcal{R}$-normalized iff $X\theta$ is $\mathcal{R}$-normalized.

In the sequel, if not stated otherwise, $\mathcal{R}$ is a confluent PRS. We will often omit the prefix $\mathcal{R}$- when $\mathcal{R}$ is understood from the context. We denote by $\mathcal{R}_+$ the PRS $\mathcal{R}$ extended with the rules $\{X \approx X \to \mathbf{true}, X \rhd X \to \mathbf{true}\}$. $s \simeq t$ stands for either $s \approx t$ or $t \approx s$. We extend the notation of the binary relations between terms to componentwise relations between sequences of terms. For example, $s_n \triangleright t_n$ stands for $s_1 \triangleright t_1, \ldots, s_n \triangleright t_n$. We denote sequences of equations by E, F and G, possibly subscripted.

3 Higher-Order Unification

We start our discussion with the general higher-order unification system PT.

The system PT. PT is a version of the preunification system proposed by Snyder and Gallier [12]. We omit the variable elimination rule in PT since it is not necessary for our completeness results. The inference rules for higher-order unification are:

$[\text{del}]_{\approx}$ Deletion

$$\frac{E_1, t \approx t, E_2}{E_1, E_2}$$

$[\text{dec}]_{\approx}$ Decomposition

$$\frac{E_1, \lambda \mathbf{x}.v(\mathbf{s}_n) \approx \lambda \mathbf{x}.v(\mathbf{t}_n), E_2}{E_1, \lambda \mathbf{x}.\mathbf{s}_n \approx \lambda \mathbf{x}.\mathbf{t}_n, E_2}$$

where $v \in \mathcal{F} \cup \{\mathbf{x}\}$.

$[\text{i}]_{\approx}$ Imitation

$$\frac{E_1, \lambda \mathbf{x}.X(\mathbf{s}_n) \approx \lambda \mathbf{x}.f(\mathbf{t}_m), E_2}{E_1\delta, \lambda \mathbf{x}.\mathbf{H}_m(\mathbf{s}_n\delta) \approx \lambda \mathbf{x}.\mathbf{t}_m\delta, E_2\delta} \quad \frac{E_1, \lambda \mathbf{x}.f(\mathbf{t}_m) \approx \lambda \mathbf{x}.X(\mathbf{s}_n), E_2}{E_1\delta, \lambda \mathbf{x}.\mathbf{t}_m\delta \approx \lambda \mathbf{x}.\mathbf{H}_m(\mathbf{s}_n\delta), E_2\delta}$$

if $f \in \mathcal{F}$ where $\delta = \{X \mapsto \lambda \mathbf{x}_n.f(\mathbf{H}_m(\mathbf{x}_n))\}$.

$[\text{p}]_{\approx}$ Projection

$$\frac{E_1, \lambda \mathbf{x}.X(\mathbf{s}_n) \approx \lambda \mathbf{x}.t, E_2}{E_1\delta, \lambda \mathbf{x}.(s_i\delta)(\mathbf{H}_p(\mathbf{s}_n\delta)) \approx \lambda \mathbf{x}.t\delta, E_2\delta} \quad \frac{E_1, \lambda \mathbf{x}.t \approx \lambda \mathbf{x}.X(\mathbf{s}_n), E_2}{E_1\delta, \lambda \mathbf{x}.t\delta \approx \lambda \mathbf{x}.(s_i\delta)(\mathbf{H}_p(\mathbf{s}_n\delta)), E_2\delta}$$

if $\lambda \mathbf{x}.t$ is rigid, where $\delta = \{X \mapsto \lambda \mathbf{x}_n.x_i(\mathbf{H}_p(\mathbf{x}_n))\}$.

In the inference rules $[\text{i}]_{\approx}$ and $[\text{p}]_{\approx}$, H_i are distinct fresh variables.

Notation. We write $G_1 \Rightarrow_{\alpha,\delta} G_2$ whenever $\dfrac{G_1}{G_2}$ is an instance of a PT inference rule α which computes δ. The label can be omitted if it is not relevant or it is clear from the context. We sometimes distinguish the selected equation in a PT-step by underlining it. The same conventions will be used later when we introduce other calculi.

The following completeness result is known for PT:

Theorem 1 (Completeness of PT) Let θ be a unifier of a goal G and $V \supseteq \mathcal{V}(G) \cup \mathcal{D}(\theta)$. There exist substitutions δ, θ' and a PT-derivation $G \Rightarrow_\delta^* F$ such that: (a) F is a flex-flex goal, and (b) $\delta\theta' = \theta$ $[V]$.

A proof of this theorem can be found in [11]. We note here that PT is strongly complete, i.e. Theorem 1 holds regardless of the order of selecting equations in the goal.

The system PU. It is well-known that two unifiable patterns have a unique (modulo variable renaming) most general unifier. PU is a transformation system for pattern unification. It consists of all the inference rules of the system PT and the following two inference rules:

[ffs]$_\approx$ Flex-flex same equation

$$\frac{E_1, \lambda\mathbf{x}.X(\mathbf{y}_m) \approx \lambda\mathbf{x}.X(\mathbf{y}'_m), E_2}{(E_1, E_2)\delta}$$

where $\delta = \{X \mapsto \lambda\mathbf{y}_m.H(\mathbf{z}_p)\}$ with $\{\mathbf{z}_p\} = \{y_i \mid 1 \leq i \leq m \text{ and } y_i = y'_i\}$.

[ffd]$_\approx$ Flex-flex different equation

$$\frac{E_1, \lambda\mathbf{x}.X(\mathbf{y}_m) \approx \lambda\mathbf{x}.Y(\mathbf{y}'_n), E_2}{(E_1, E_2)\delta}$$

where $\delta = \{X \mapsto \lambda\mathbf{x}_m.H(\mathbf{z}_p), Y \mapsto \lambda\mathbf{y}_n.H(\mathbf{z}_p)\}$ with $\{\mathbf{z}_p\} = \{\mathbf{y}_m\} \cap \{\mathbf{y}'_n\}$.

H is here a fresh variable, and $\mathbf{y}, \mathbf{y}'$ are sequences of distinct bound variables.

We denote by PU$_d$ the system consisting of the inference rules of PU with $E_1 = \square$. PU$_d$ is of interest because of the following property (cf.[8]):

Theorem 2 (Completeness of PU$_d$) Let s, t be two unifiable patterns. Then there exists a PU$_d$-derivation of the form $s \approx t \Rightarrow^*_\theta \square$ with θ a most general unifier of s and t.

4 Higher-Order Lazy Narrowing

Lazy narrowing is a goal-directed method for solving goals in equational theories presented by a confluent term rewriting system. In the first-order case a calculus called LNC [7] has been defined. LNC is sound and complete with respect to the leftmost equation selection strategy and several refinements have been proposed to reduce its non-determinism. The calculus LN introduced by Prehofer [11] is an approach for solving higher-order equations with respect to confluent PRSs. Since the calculus LN restricted to first-order terms has many similarities with LNC, one could expect that some of the deterministic refinements of LNC can be carried over to LN. Our starting point of investigation is the calculus LN defined below. It is a generalization of Prehofer's calculus LN in that we allow both unoriented and oriented equations in goals.

In order to handle oriented equations, we will introduce the following inference rules for oriented equations: [dec]$_\triangleright$, [del]$_\triangleright$, [i]$_\triangleright$, [p]$_\triangleright$, [ffs]$_\triangleright$ and [ffd]$_\triangleright$. They are distinguished from the corresponding rules of PU for unoriented equations by subscripting them with the equality symbol $\triangleright$. Each new rule differs from the corresponding one only in that it treats oriented equations. For instance, the decomposition rule $[\text{dec}]_{\triangleright}$ is the same as $[\text{dec}]_{\approx}$ except that all the occurrences of $\approx$ in the inference rule of $[\text{dec}]_{\approx}$ are replaced by $\triangleright$.

The Calculus LN. LN consists of the inference rules $[\text{dec}]_{\approx}$, $[\text{del}]_{\approx}$, $[\text{i}]_{\approx}$, $[\text{p}]_{\approx}$, $[\text{dec}]_{\triangleright}$, $[\text{del}]_{\triangleright}$, $[\text{i}]_{\triangleright}$, $[\text{p}]_{\triangleright}$, plus the narrowing rules $[\text{of}]_{\simeq}$, $[\text{ov}]_{\simeq}$, $[\text{of}]_{\triangleright}$, $[\text{ov}]_{\triangleright}$ defined below:

$[\text{of}]_{\simeq}$ outermost narrowing for unoriented equations

$$\frac{E_1, \lambda\mathbf{x}.f(\mathbf{s}_n) \simeq \lambda\mathbf{x}.t, E_2}{E_1, \lambda\mathbf{x}.\mathbf{s}_n \triangleright \lambda\mathbf{x}.\mathbf{l}_n, \lambda\mathbf{x}.r \approx \lambda\mathbf{x}.t, E_2}$$

$[\text{ov}]_{\simeq}$ outermost narrowing at variable position for unoriented equations

$$\frac{E_1, \lambda\mathbf{x}.H(\mathbf{s}_n) \simeq \lambda\mathbf{x}.t, E_2}{E_1\delta, \lambda\mathbf{x}.\mathbf{H}_m(\mathbf{s}_n\delta) \triangleright \lambda\mathbf{x}.\mathbf{l}_n, \lambda\mathbf{x}.r \approx \lambda\mathbf{x}.t\delta, E_2\delta}$$

if $\lambda\mathbf{x}.t$ is rigid, where $\delta = \{H \mapsto \lambda\mathbf{x}_n.f(\mathbf{H}_m(\mathbf{x}_n))\}$.
$[\text{of}]_{\triangleright}$ outermost narrowing for oriented equations

$$\frac{E_1, \lambda\mathbf{x}.f(\mathbf{s}_n) \triangleright \lambda\mathbf{x}.t, E_2}{E_1, \lambda\mathbf{x}.\mathbf{s}_n \triangleright \lambda\mathbf{x}.\mathbf{l}_n, \lambda\mathbf{x}.r \triangleright \lambda\mathbf{x}.t, E_2}$$

$[\text{ov}]_{\triangleright}$ outermost narrowing at variable position for oriented equations

$$\frac{E_1, \lambda\mathbf{x}.H(\mathbf{s}_n) \triangleright \lambda\mathbf{x}.t, E_2}{E_1\delta, \lambda\mathbf{x}.\mathbf{H}_m(\mathbf{s}_n\delta) \triangleright \lambda\mathbf{x}.\mathbf{l}_n, \lambda\mathbf{x}.r \triangleright \lambda\mathbf{x}.t\delta, E_2\delta}$$

if $\lambda\mathbf{x}.t$ is rigid, where $\delta = \{H \mapsto \lambda\mathbf{x}_n.f(\mathbf{H}_m(\mathbf{x}_n))\}$.

In these inference rules $\mathbf{H}_m$ are distinct fresh variables and $f(\mathbf{l}_m) \to r$ is a fresh variant of an x-lifted rule (see [11] for the definition of x-lifting). We write $[\text{of}]$ to denote $[\text{of}]_{\simeq}$ or $[\text{of}]_{\triangleright}$, and $[\text{ov}]$ to denote $[\text{ov}]_{\simeq}$ or $[\text{ov}]_{\triangleright}$. $[\text{o}]$ denotes $[\text{of}]$ or $[\text{ov}]$. We use letter π to denote an LN-step and Π to denote an LN-derivation.

It can be easily verified that the calculus LN is sound, i.e. if $G_1 \Rightarrow_{\alpha,\delta} G_2$ and θ is a solution of G_2 then $\delta\theta$ is a solution of G_1.

In the sequel we use $\{\ldots\}$ to denote multisets and $>_{mul}$ for the multiset ordering on sets of non-negative integers. The expression $|e|$ may denote: (a) the length of e if e is a derivation, or (b) the size of e if e is an equation or a term.

The use of LN in solving higher-order goals is justified by the following completeness result:

Theorem 3 (Completeness of LN) Let $\mathcal{R}$ be a confluent PRS and G a goal with solution θ. Then there exists an LN-derivation $\Pi : G \Rightarrow_{\delta}^* F$ such that $\delta \leq \theta \; [\mathcal{V}(G)]$ and F is a flex-flex goal.

Proof. (Sketch) The proof of this theorem is along the following lines. We first define a suitable well-founded ordering on some structures that encode the fact that a substitution is a solution of a goal.

Definition 4 Let $G = \mathbf{e}_n$ be a goal. We define $\mathrm{Repr}(G)$ as the set of triples of the form $\langle G, \theta, \mathbf{R}_n \rangle$ with θ solution of G and $\mathbf{R}_n$ a sequence of reduction derivations of the form $R_j : e_j\theta \to^*_{\mathcal{R}_+} \mathrm{true}$.

On such triples we define the following well-founded orderings:

- $\langle \mathbf{e}_n, \theta, \mathbf{R}_n \rangle >_A \langle \mathbf{e}'_m, \theta', \mathbf{R}'_m \rangle$ if $\{|R_1|, \ldots, |R_n|\} >_{mul} \{|R'_1|, \ldots, |R'_m|\}$,
- $\langle \mathbf{e}_n, \theta, \mathbf{R}_n \rangle >_B \langle \mathbf{e}'_m, \theta', \mathbf{R}'_m \rangle$ if $\{|t| \mid t \in \mathcal{I}(\theta{\upharpoonright}_{\mathcal{V}(\mathbf{e}_n)})\} >_{mul} \{|t'| \mid t' \in \mathcal{I}(\theta'{\upharpoonright}_{\mathcal{V}(\mathbf{e}'_m)})\}$,
- $\langle \mathbf{e}_n, \theta, \mathbf{R}_n \rangle >_C \langle \mathbf{e}'_m, \theta', \mathbf{R}'_m \rangle$ if $\{|e_1|, \ldots, |e_n|\} >_{mul} \{|e'_1|, \ldots, |e'_m|\}$,
- $\succ$ is the lexicographic combination of $>_A, >_B, >_C$.

Next we prove the following lemma, which is also used in the proof of Lemma 4:

Lemma 2 Let $G_0 = E_1, e, E_2$ be a goal with solution θ_0 and non-flex-flex equation e. Assume $V \supseteq \mathcal{V}(G_0) \cup \mathcal{D}(\theta_0)$. Then for any triple $\langle G_0, \theta_0, \mathbf{R}^0 \rangle \in \mathrm{Repr}(G_0)$ there exists an LN-step $\pi : G_0 = E_1, \underline{e}, E_2 \Rightarrow_{\alpha,\delta} G_1$ and a triple $\langle G_1, \theta_1, \mathbf{R}^1 \rangle \in \mathrm{Repr}(G_1)$ such that: (a) $\langle G_0, \theta_0, \mathbf{R}^0 \rangle \succ \langle G_1, \theta_1, \mathbf{R}^1 \rangle$, and (b) $\theta_0 = \delta\theta_1 [V]$.

We omit the proof of this lemma since it is similar to the proof of Theorem 6.1.1 in [11].

Finally, we note that repeated applications of Lemma 2 starting from a triple $\langle G_0, \theta_0, \mathbf{R}^0 \rangle \in \mathrm{Repr}(G_0)$ produces the desired LN-derivation.   □

Remark 1 1. The substitution δ in Theorem 3 is a pattern substitution[1], since it is a composition of pattern substitutions.

2. LN is strongly complete, namely it does not depend on the order of selecting the non-flex-flex equations in the goal.

5 The Calculus LN$_\mathit{ff}$

In this section we introduce our main calculus.

The calculus LN$_\mathit{ff}$. LN$_\mathit{ff}$ consists of the inference rules of LN and the rules $[\mathrm{ffs}]_\approx, [\mathrm{ffs}]_\rhd, [\mathrm{ffd}]_\approx, [\mathrm{ffd}]_\rhd$.

In the sequel we omit the subscripts $\approx$ and $\rhd$ of inference rules $\alpha_\approx$ and $\alpha_\rhd$ and write α when we treat the inference rules collectively.

We now obtain a more powerful calculus since all the rules for pattern unification are available. Unfortunately the calculus LN$_\mathit{ff}$ is no longer strongly complete as we can see from the example below:

Example 1. Let $\mathcal{R} = \{f(X, a) \to b\}$ and the goal

$$G_0 = f(X, a) \rhd Z, Z \approx Y, b \rhd Y, Z \rhd f(X, a)$$

---

[1] A substitution θ is a *pattern substitution* if every term in $\mathcal{I}(\theta)$ is a pattern.

with solution $\theta = \{Z \mapsto f(X, a), Y \mapsto b\}$. If we select the equation $Z \approx Y$ to solve the goal G_0 then the only applicable rule is $[\text{ffd}]_{\approx}$. Hence we have the following derivation:

$$G_0 \Rightarrow_{[\text{ffd}]_{\approx}, \{Z \mapsto H, Y \mapsto H\}} G_1 = f(X, a) \rhd H, b \rhd H, H \rhd f(X, a)$$

It can be easily seen that the goal G_1 has no solution. Hence, LN_{ff} is not strongly complete. $\square$

Note that the previous example does not refute the strong completeness of LN because no rule of LN can act on the flex-flex equation $Z \approx Y$.

In the following we show that there exists an equation selection strategy $\mathcal{S}_n$ with respect to which the calculus LN_{ff} is complete. Actually we show a stronger result: by adopting the calculus LN_{ff} with strategy $\mathcal{S}_n$ we achieve two important desiderata:

1. We eliminate the nondeterminism due to the choice of the equation in a goal to be solved next,
2. We restrict the application of outermost narrowing at variable position; as a consequence, a smaller search space for solutions is created.

The steps of our investigation can be summarized as follows:

1. We first observe that if we know that the solution of a goal is normalized with respect to certain variables then we can apply the rules [ffs] and [ffd] to certain pattern equations and safely avoid the application of [ov] to certain flex-rigid or rigid-flex equations (Lemma 3 and Lemma 4).
2. We identify sufficient conditions which guarantee that the solution of a goal is normalized with respect to certain variables (Lemma 5).
3. Based on 2., we define a strategy $\mathcal{S}_n$. For the calculus LN_{ff} with the strategy $\mathcal{S}_n$ we identify the class of normal LN_{ff}-refutations and prove that any normalized solution of a goal G is subsumed by a substitution which is computable with a normal LN_{ff}-refutation that starts from G (Theorem 4).

Before starting to describe in detail the steps mentioned above, we note some similarities between the calculi LNC and LN_{ff} when we restrict ourselves to first-order terms:

1. It can be verified that LN_{ff} subsumes LNC with the rule [v] restricted to equations between variables.
2. A [v]-step in LNC can be simulated in LN_{ff} by a sequence of [i]-, [p]-,[ffs]-, and [ffd]-steps. Since LNC with leftmost equation selection strategy $\mathcal{S}_{\text{left}}$ is complete [7], we conclude that the calculus LN_{ff} without [ov]-rules is complete if we adopt the strategy $\mathcal{S}_{\text{left}}$.
3. Middeldorp *et al.* [7] conjecture that LNC is complete with respect to any strategy that never selects descendants of an equation created by an outermost narrowing step before all descendants of the corresponding parameter-passing equations created in that step have been selected. If this conjecture holds then we can replace $\mathcal{S}_{\text{left}}$ with such a strategy and retain the completeness of LN_{ff} without [ov]-rules.

Note that the substitution θ in Example 1 is not normalized. We noticed that the normalization of substitutions restricted to the so called *critical variables* is crucial to restore completeness of LN_{ff}.

Definition 5 (critical variable) The set $\mathcal{V}_c(e)$ of *critical variables* of an equation e is $\mathcal{V}(s) \cup \mathcal{V}(t)$ if $e = s \approx t$ and $\mathcal{V}(s)$ if $e = s \triangleright t$.

We first prove the following technical lemma.

Lemma 3 If $G_0 = E_1, \underline{e}, E_2 \Rightarrow_{[\text{ff}], \delta_0} G_1$, and $\theta_0 \lceil_{\mathcal{V}_c(e)}$ is normalized then for any $\langle G_0, \theta_0, \mathbf{R}^0 \rangle \in \text{Repr}(G_0)$ there exists a solution θ_1 of G_1 and $\langle G_1, \theta_1, \mathbf{R}^1 \rangle \in \text{Repr}(G_1)$ such that: (a) $\langle G_0, \theta_0, \mathbf{R}^0 \rangle \succ \langle G_1, \theta_1, \mathbf{R}^1 \rangle$, and (b) $\theta_0 = \delta_0 \theta_1$.

Proof. Let $\langle G_0, \theta_0, \mathbf{R}^0 \rangle \in \text{Repr}(G_0)$. The proof is by case distinction on the shape of e.

(i) If $e = \lambda \mathbf{x}.X(\mathbf{y}_m) \approx \lambda \mathbf{x}.Y(\mathbf{y}'_n)$ then $\lambda \mathbf{x}.X(\mathbf{y}_m)\theta_0 \downarrow \lambda \mathbf{x}.Y(\mathbf{y}'_n)\theta_0$ because θ_0 is a solution of e. In this case $\mathcal{V}_c(e) = \{X, Y\}$ and therefore the terms $X\theta_0$ and $Y\theta_0$ are normalized. By Lemma 1 the terms $\lambda \mathbf{x}.X(\mathbf{y}_m)\theta_0$ and $\lambda \mathbf{x}.Y(\mathbf{y}'_n)\theta_0$ are also normalized. Hence the equality $\lambda \mathbf{x}.X(\mathbf{y}_m)\theta_0 = \lambda \mathbf{x}.Y(\mathbf{y}'_n)\theta_0$ holds, i.e. θ_0 is a unifier of $\lambda \mathbf{x}.X(\mathbf{y}_m), \lambda \mathbf{x}.Y(\mathbf{y}'_n)$. Since δ_0 is a most general unifier of $\lambda \mathbf{x}.X(\mathbf{y}_m)$ and $\lambda \mathbf{x}.Y(\mathbf{y}'_n)$ there exists a solution θ_1 of G_1 such that $\theta_0 = \delta_0 \theta_1$. The construction of $\mathbf{R}^1$ such that $\langle G_0, \theta_0, \mathbf{R}^0 \rangle =_A \langle G_1, \theta_1, \mathbf{R}^1 \rangle$ and $\langle G_0, \theta_0, \mathbf{R}^0 \rangle >_B \langle G_1, \theta_1, \mathbf{R}^1 \rangle$ is straightforward. Therefore, (a) holds as well.

(ii) The case when $e = \lambda \mathbf{x}.X(\mathbf{y}_m) \approx \lambda \mathbf{x}.X(\mathbf{y}'_m)$ can be proved in a similar way.

(iii) Let $e = \lambda \mathbf{x}.X(\mathbf{y}_m) \triangleright \lambda \mathbf{x}.Y(\mathbf{y}'_n)$. Because θ_0 is a solution of $\lambda \mathbf{x}.X(\mathbf{y}_m) \triangleright \lambda \mathbf{x}.Y(\mathbf{y}'_n)$, we have $\lambda \mathbf{x}.X(\mathbf{y}_m)\theta_0 \rightarrow^* \lambda \mathbf{x}.Y(\mathbf{y}'_n)\theta_0$. In this case we have $\mathcal{V}_c(e) = \{X\}$ and thus $X\theta_0$ is normalized. By Lemma 1 the term $\lambda \mathbf{x}.X(\mathbf{y}_m)\theta_0$ is also normalized. Therefore θ_0 is a unifier of the terms $\lambda \mathbf{x}.X(\mathbf{y}_m)\theta_0$ and $\lambda \mathbf{x}.Y(\mathbf{y}'_n)\theta_0$. Since δ_0 is a most general unifier of $\lambda \mathbf{x}.X(\mathbf{y}_m)$ and $\lambda \mathbf{x}.Y(\mathbf{y}'_n)$ there exists a solution θ_1 of G_1 such that $\theta_0 = \delta_0 \theta_1$. The construction of $\mathbf{R}^1$ such that $\langle G_0, \theta_0, \mathbf{R}^0 \rangle =_A \langle G_1, \theta_1, \mathbf{R}^1 \rangle$ and $\langle G_0, \theta_0, \mathbf{R}^0 \rangle >_B \langle G_1, \theta_1, \mathbf{R}^1 \rangle$ is straightforward. Therefore, (a) holds as well.

(iv) The case when $e = \lambda \mathbf{x}.X(\mathbf{y}_m) \triangleright \lambda \mathbf{x}.X(\mathbf{y}'_m)$ can be proved in a similar way.

We next investigate restrictions under which the rules $[\text{ov}]_{\approx}$, $[\text{ov}]_{\triangleright}$ can be eliminated without losing the completeness of LN_{ff}. The next example illustrates that in general we can not drop $[\text{ov}]$ without loss of completeness.

Example 2. Consider the PRS $\mathcal{R} = \{f(g(X)) \rightarrow X\}$ and the goal $Z(g(a)) \approx a$. Obviously the normalized answer $\{Z \mapsto \lambda x.f(x)\}$ could not be computed by LN_{ff} if we dropped the $[\text{ov}]$-rule. □

Lemma 4 Let θ_0 be a solution of a goal $G_0 = E_1, e, E_2$ with $e = \lambda \mathbf{x}.X(\mathbf{y}) \simeq t$ or $e = \lambda \mathbf{x}.X(\mathbf{y}) \triangleright t$, where t is a rigid term and $\lambda \mathbf{x}.X(\mathbf{y})$ is a pattern. Assume $V \supseteq \mathcal{V}(G_0) \cup \mathcal{D}(\theta_0)$. If $X\theta_0$ is normalized then for any $\langle G_0, \theta_0, \mathbf{R}^0 \rangle \in \text{Repr}(G_0)$ there exists an LN_{ff}-step $\pi : G_0 = E_1, \underline{e}, E_2 \Rightarrow_{\alpha, \delta_0} G_1$ with $\alpha \neq [\text{ov}]$ such that: (a) $\langle G_0, \theta_0, \mathbf{R}^0 \rangle \succ \langle G_1, \theta_1, \mathbf{R}^1 \rangle$, and (b) $\theta_0 = \delta_0 \theta_1$ $[V]$.

Proof. By Lemma 2, there exists an LN-step π which satisfies conditions (a) and (b). If $\alpha = [\text{ov}]$ then the term $\lambda\mathbf{x}.X(\mathbf{y})\theta_0$ is reducible. This implies that $X\theta_0$ is reducible, which contradicts our hypothesis. Hence $\alpha \neq [\text{ov}]$. $\square$

6   Normal LN$_\mathrm{ff}$-Refutations

We will use the results of Lemmata 3 and 4 in order to define a suitable equation selection strategy S_n with respect to which the calculus LN$_\mathrm{ff}$ is complete. The success of defining such a strategy depends on the possibility to determine whether the solution of an equation is normalized with respect to certain variables. In the sequel we look for such normalization criteria.

The notions of *immediate linear descendant* (ILD for short) and of *immediate descendant* of the selected equation in an LN$_\mathrm{ff}$-step are defined as shown in the table below. In the table, the symbol $=^?$ stands for either $\approx$ or $\rhd$ (but the same in the same row). The superscripts 1 and 2 on [i] and [p] distinguish the first and the second case of the corresponding inference rule.

rule	ILD	immediate descendant
[of]	$\lambda\mathbf{x}.r =^? \lambda\mathbf{x}.t$	$\lambda\mathbf{x}.s_n \rhd \lambda\mathbf{x}.l_n, \lambda\mathbf{x}.r =^? \lambda\mathbf{x}.t$
[ov]	$\lambda\mathbf{x}.r =^? \lambda\mathbf{x}.t$	$\lambda\mathbf{x}.H_m(s_n\delta) \rhd \lambda\mathbf{x}.l_n, \lambda\mathbf{x}.r =^? \lambda\mathbf{x}.t\delta$
[dec]	$\lambda\mathbf{x}.s_n =^? \lambda\mathbf{x}.t_n$	$\lambda\mathbf{x}.s_n =^? \lambda\mathbf{x}.t_n$
[i]^1	$\lambda\mathbf{x}.H_m(s_n\delta) =^? \lambda\mathbf{x}.t_m\delta$	$\lambda\mathbf{x}.H_m(s_n\delta) =^? \lambda\mathbf{x}.t_m\delta$
[i]^2	$\lambda\mathbf{x}.t_m\delta =^? \lambda\mathbf{x}.H_m(s_n\delta)$	$\lambda\mathbf{x}.t_m\delta =^? \lambda\mathbf{x}.H_m(s_n\delta)$
[p]^1	$\lambda\mathbf{x}.(s_i\delta)(H_p(s_n\delta)) =^? \lambda\mathbf{x}.v(t_m\delta)$	$\lambda\mathbf{x}.(s_i\delta)(H_p(s_n\delta)) =^? \lambda\mathbf{x}.v(t_m\delta)$
[p]^2	$\lambda\mathbf{x}.v(t_m\delta) =^? \lambda\mathbf{x}.(s_i\delta)(H_p(s_n\delta))$	$\lambda\mathbf{x}.v(t_m\delta) =^? \lambda\mathbf{x}.(s_i\delta)(H_p(s_n\delta))$
[del]	-	-
[ffs], [ffd]		

Descendants and ILDs of non-selected equations are defined as expected. The equations $\lambda\mathbf{x}.s_n \rhd \lambda\mathbf{x}.l_n$ and $\lambda\mathbf{x}.H_m(s_n\delta) \rhd \lambda\mathbf{x}.l_n$ created in an [of]-step and [ov]-step respectively, are called *parameter passing equations* created by that step.

The notion of *descendant* is obtained from that of immediate descendant by reflexivity and transitivity. The *ancestor* relation is defined as the inverse of the descendant relation.

Definition 6 (precursor) Let $\Pi : G_0 \Rightarrow^* E_1, e_1, E_2, e_2, E_3$ be an LN$_\mathrm{ff}$-derivation. e_1 is a *precursor* of e_2 in Π if there exists an equation e which is subjected to an [o]-step π in Π such that (a) e_1 is a descendant of a parameter passing-equation created by π, and (b) e_2 is a descendant of the ILD of e in π.

Given an LN$_\mathrm{ff}$-derivation $\Pi : G_0 \Rightarrow^N G_N = E_1, e, E_2$, we denote by $\text{prec}_\Pi(e)$ the sub-sequence of equations of G_N that are precursors of e in Π.

Definition 7 (regular transformation) Let G_0, G_1 be goals with $\langle G_0, \theta_0, \mathbf{R}^0 \rangle$ $\in \text{Repr}(G_0)$, $G_0 = E_1, e, E_2$ and $\langle G_1, \theta_1, \mathbf{R}^1 \rangle \in \text{Repr}(G_1)$. Assume $V \supseteq \mathcal{V}(G_0) \cup \mathcal{D}(\theta_0)$. A transformation step $\langle G_0, \theta_0, \mathbf{R}^0 \rangle \Rightarrow \langle G_1, \theta_1, \mathbf{R}^1 \rangle$ is *regular* if:

- e is a non-flex-flex equation and there exists an LN-step $\pi : E_1, \underline{e}, E_2 \Rightarrow_{\alpha, \delta} G_1$ such that the conditions (a) and (b) of Lemma 2 hold, or
- $\theta_0 \lceil_{\mathcal{V}_c(e)}$ is normalized, $G_0 = E_1, \underline{e}, E_2 \Rightarrow_{[ff], \delta} G_1$ and the conditions (a) and (b) of Lemma 3 hold.

Lemma 5 Let G_0 be a goal with normalized solution θ_0 and $\langle G_0, \theta_0, \mathbf{R}^0 \rangle \in \mathrm{Repr}(G_0)$. If $\langle G_0, \theta_0, \mathbf{R}^0 \rangle \Rightarrow \ldots \Rightarrow \langle G_N, \theta_N, \mathbf{R}^N \rangle$ is a sequence of regular transformation steps and $\Pi : G_0 \Rightarrow_{\delta_0} G_1 \Rightarrow_{\delta_1} \cdots \Rightarrow_{\delta_{N-1}} G_N$ is the corresponding LN$_{ff}$-derivation then for any $e \in G_N$ with $\mathrm{prec}_\Pi(e) = \square$ we have that $\theta_N \lceil_{\mathcal{V}_c(e)}$ is normalized.

Proof. Let e_i be the ancestor of e in G_i and $\gamma_i = \delta_i \delta_{i+1} \ldots \delta_{N-1}$ $(0 \leq i \leq N)$. We prove a slightly stronger result: $\theta_N \lceil_{\mathcal{V}_c(e_i \gamma_i)}$ is normalized for any $0 \leq i \leq N$. It is easy to see that this implies the normalization of $\theta_N \lceil_{\mathcal{V}_c(e)}$.

We first introduce the notion of [o]-ancestor. We say that an ancestor e' of e is an [o]-*ancestor* of e if we have

$$\Pi : G \Rightarrow^* E_1, \underline{e'}, E_2 \Rightarrow_{[o], \sigma} E_1 \sigma, E_3, e'', E_2 \sigma \Rightarrow^* E_1', e, E_2'.$$

(That is, an [o]-step is applied to e' and e descends from the ILD of e'.) We prove by induction on i $(0 \leq i \leq N)$ that $\theta_N \lceil_{\mathcal{V}_c(e_i \gamma_i)}$ is normalized. Let π_i be the i-th step of Π.

If $i = 0$ then $\theta_N \lceil_{\mathcal{V}_c(e_0 \gamma_0)}$ is normalized because $\gamma_0 \theta_N = \theta_0$ $[\mathcal{V}_c(e_0)]$ and θ_0 is normalized.

We next show that $\theta_N \lceil_{\mathcal{V}_c(e_{i+1} \gamma_{i+1})}$ is normalized if $\theta_N \lceil_{\mathcal{V}_c(e_i \gamma_i)}$ is normalized.

Suppose e_i is not an [o]-ancestor. We show $\mathcal{V}_c(e_{i+1}) \subseteq \mathcal{V}_c(e_i \delta_i)$ by the following case distinction.

(a) π_i is an [o]-step. Since e_i is not an [o]-ancestor, we have that e_{i+1} is a parameter-passing equation created by the i-th step of Π and therefore $\mathcal{V}_c(e_{i+1}) \subseteq \mathcal{V}_c(e_i \delta_i)$.

(b) π_i is not an [o]-step. If e_i is unoriented then $\mathcal{V}_c(e_{i+1}) = \mathcal{V}(e_{i+1}) \subseteq \mathcal{V}(e_i \delta_i) = \mathcal{V}_c(e_i \delta_i)$. If e_i is of the form $s \triangleright t$ then it can be shown by case distinction on π_i that $\mathcal{V}_c(e_{i+1}) \subseteq \mathcal{V}(s \delta) = \mathcal{V}_c(e_i \delta)$.

The induction hypothesis yields the normalization of $\theta_N \lceil_{\mathcal{V}_c(e_i \delta_i \gamma_{i+1})}$. Hence the above inclusion implies the normalization of $\theta_N \lceil_{\mathcal{V}_c(e_{i+1} \gamma_{i+1})}$.

Suppose e_i is an [o]-ancestor. Then $e_i = \lambda \mathbf{x}.h(\mathbf{s}_n) =^? \lambda \mathbf{x}.t$ or $e_i = \lambda \mathbf{x}.t \approx \lambda \mathbf{x}.h(\mathbf{s}_n)$ and Π is of the form

$$\Pi : G_0 \Rightarrow^i_{\delta_0 \ldots \delta_{i-1}} \quad G_i = E_1, \underline{e}, E_2$$
$$\Rightarrow_{[o], f(\mathbf{l}_m) \to r, \delta_i} G_{i+1} = E_1 \delta_i, \lambda \mathbf{x}.\mathbf{w}_m \triangleright \lambda \mathbf{x}.\mathbf{l}_m, \lambda \mathbf{x}.r =^? \lambda \mathbf{x}.t \delta_i, E_2 \delta_i$$
$$\Rightarrow^*_{\delta_{i+1} \ldots \delta_{N-1}} \quad G_N = E_1', e, E_2'.$$

Since $\mathrm{prec}_\Pi(e) = \square$ we have

$$(\lambda \mathbf{x}.\mathbf{w}_m \triangleright \lambda \mathbf{x}.\mathbf{l}_m) \delta_{i+1} \ldots \delta_{N-1} \to^* \top.$$

We show that the following relation holds:

$$e\gamma_i \to^* (\lambda\mathbf{x}.r =^? \lambda\mathbf{x}.t\delta_i)\gamma_{i+1}. \tag{1}$$

If $h = f$ then we have $\delta_i = \varepsilon$, $n = m$ and $\lambda\mathbf{x}.\mathbf{w}_n = \lambda\mathbf{x}.\mathbf{s}_n$. Since $\delta_{i+1}\ldots\delta_{N-1}$ is a solution of $\lambda\mathbf{x}.\mathbf{s}_n \rhd \lambda\mathbf{x}.\mathbf{l}_n$ we learn that $\lambda\mathbf{x}.s_j\gamma_{i+1} \to^* \mathbf{x}.l_j\gamma_{i+1}$ for $1 \le j \le n$ and therefore $\lambda\mathbf{x}.h(\mathbf{s}_n)\gamma_i \to^* \lambda\mathbf{x}.f(\mathbf{l}_n\gamma_{i+1}) \to \lambda\mathbf{x}.r\gamma_{i+1}$.

Otherwise $h \in \mathcal{FV}$ and in this case we have $\delta_i = \{h \mapsto \lambda\mathbf{x}_n.f(\mathbf{H}_m(\mathbf{x}_n))\}$ and $\lambda\mathbf{x}.\mathbf{w}_m = \lambda\mathbf{x}.\mathbf{H}_m(\mathbf{s}_n\delta_i)$. Because γ_{i+1} is a solution of $\lambda\mathbf{x}.\mathbf{w}_m \rhd \lambda\mathbf{x}.\mathbf{l}_m$ we have $\lambda\mathbf{x}.h(\mathbf{s}_n)\gamma_i =_\beta \lambda\mathbf{x}.f(\mathbf{H}_m(\mathbf{s}_n\delta_i)\gamma_{i+1}) \to^* \lambda\mathbf{x}.f(\mathbf{l}_m\gamma_{i+1}) = \lambda\mathbf{x}.f(\mathbf{l}_m)\gamma_{i+1} \to \lambda\mathbf{x}.r\gamma_{i+1}$.

Thus in both situations we have $\lambda\mathbf{x}.h(\mathbf{s}_n)\gamma_i \to^* \lambda\mathbf{x}.r\gamma_{i+1}$ and hence (1) holds.

It follows that $\mathcal{V}_c(e_{i+1}\gamma_{i+1}) \subseteq \mathcal{V}_c(e_i\gamma_i)$. Since $\theta_N \restriction_{\mathcal{V}_c(e_i\gamma_i)}$ is normalized, the substitution $\theta_N \restriction_{\mathcal{V}_c(e_{i+1}\gamma_{i+1})}$ is normalized as well. $\square$

We are ready now to define our equation selection strategy for $\mathrm{LN}_{\mathrm{ff}}$.

Definition 8 (strategy $\mathcal{S}_n$) An $\mathrm{LN}_{\mathrm{ff}}$-derivation Π respects the strategy $\mathcal{S}_n$ if for any subderivation $\Pi' : G_0 \Rightarrow^* G_m = E_1, \underline{e}, E_2$ of Π we have:

(c1) If [ffs] or [ffd] is applicable to e then $\mathrm{prec}_{\Pi'}(e) = \square$.

(c2) If e is of the form $\lambda\mathbf{x}.X(\mathbf{s}) \simeq t$ or $\lambda\mathbf{x}.X(\mathbf{s}) \rhd t$, with t rigid and $\mathrm{prec}_{\Pi'}(e) \ne \square$ then all the selectable equations of G_m satisfy condition (c2).

Condition (c1) enables the selection of an equation e to which [ffs]- or [ffd]-rules are applicable only when e has no precursor. Condition (c2) enables the selection of equations to which [ov]-rules are applicable only when there is no other choice.

Definition 9 (normal $\mathrm{LN}_{\mathrm{ff}}$-refutation) An $\mathrm{LN}_{\mathrm{ff}}$-derivation $\Pi : G_0 \Rightarrow^* F$ is a *normal $\mathrm{LN}_{\mathrm{ff}}$-refutation* if

1. Π respects $\mathcal{S}_n$, and
2. F does not contain equations which are selectable with $\mathcal{S}_n$.

Completeness. We will prove that $\mathrm{LN}_{\mathrm{ff}}$ with strategy $\mathcal{S}_n$ is complete with respect to normalized solutions.

Theorem 4 For any normalized solution θ_0 of a goal G_0 such that $\mathcal{V}(G_0) \cup \mathcal{D}(\theta) \subseteq V$ there exists a normal $\mathrm{LN}_{\mathrm{ff}}$-refutation $\Pi : G_0 \Rightarrow^*_\delta F$ with $\delta \le \theta$ [V].

Proof. Assume $\langle G_0, \theta_0, \mathbf{R}^0 \rangle \in \mathrm{Repr}(G_0)$. Let

$$A : \langle G_0, \theta_0, \mathbf{R}^0 \rangle \Rightarrow \langle G_1, \theta_1, \mathbf{R}^1 \rangle \Rightarrow \ldots \Rightarrow \langle G_N, \theta_N, \mathbf{R}^N \rangle$$

be a maximal sequence of transformation steps starting from $\langle G_1, \theta_1, \mathbf{R}^1 \rangle$ such that the corresponding $\mathrm{LN}_{\mathrm{ff}}$-step $\pi_i : G_i \Rightarrow G_{i+1}$ satisfies strategy $\mathcal{S}_n$. The existence of the sequence A is a consequence of the fact that $\Rightarrow_{\subseteq} \succ$ and $\succ$ is terminating. It suffices to show that the $\mathrm{LN}_{\mathrm{ff}}$-derivation $\pi_0 \cdots \pi_{N-1}$ is a normal $\mathrm{LN}_{\mathrm{ff}}$-refutation, which is obvious. $\square$

7   Eager Variable Elimination

We address here the eager variable elimination problem for LN_{ff} with respect to normal LN_{ff}-refutations. In the first-order case this problem is related to the possibility to apply the variable elimination rule prior to other applicable inference rules. In [6] it is shown that an eager variable elimination strategy for parameter-passing equations is complete for left-linear confluent TRSs.

The proof is mainly due to the standardization theorem for left-linear confluent TRSs, which roughly states that if a term s is reachable to a term t then an outside-in reduction derivation from s to t exists.

We will generalize the first-order eager variable elimination strategy to LN_{ff} with the help of outside-in reduction derivations.

Definition 10 An LN_{ff} refutation Π *respects the eager variable elimination strategy* if $[o]_{\triangleright}$ is never applied to rigid-flex equations of the form $\lambda\mathbf{x}.s \triangleright \lambda\mathbf{x}.X(\mathbf{t})$ in Π.

We say that *LN_{ff} with eager variable elimination strategy is complete for a class of PRSs* if for any goal G with a solution θ there exists an LN_{ff} refutation $G \Rightarrow_{\sigma}^{*} \square$ that respects the eager variable elimination strategy with $\sigma \leq_{\mathcal{R}} \theta$, when $\mathcal{R}$ belongs to the class of PRSs.

The notion of outside-in reduction derivations for orthogonal PRSs is carried over from that of first order TRSs [13] except for the definition of anti-standard pairs stated below.

Definition 11 (outside-in reduction derivation for orthogonal PRSs)
An $\mathcal{R}_{+}$-reduction derivation by an orthogonal PRS is called *outside-in* if every subderivation $e \to_p e_0 \to_{p_1} \cdots \to_{p_n} e_n \to_{q,l\to r} e'$ satisfies the following condition: if $p > q > \varepsilon$ and all p_i $(1 \leq i \leq n)$ are disjoint from p then p/q is above or disjoint from any free variable position in l. Here p/q is a position satisfying $p = q \cdot (p/q)$.

The only difference from the first-order case given in [6] is disregard for the bound variables below the free variables. The definition above states that the subterms headed by free variables in a higher-order pattern, called the *binding holes* after Oostrom [10], are regarded as mere variables.

In [10] Oostrom claimed that the following statement holds, which allows us to concentrate on only the outside-in reduction derivations.

Theorem 5 For any rewrite derivation $s \to_{\mathcal{R}}^{*} t$ by an orthogonal PRS $\mathcal{R}$, there exists an outside-in rewrite derivation from s to t. $\square$

We follow the same line of reasoning as in [7] to show that the eager variable elimination strategy for parameter-passing equations preserves completeness of LN_{ff}: first we introduce a property of reduction derivations which holds for any outside-in reduction derivation starting from a goal consisting of unoriented equations. Next we show that regular transformations preserve this property.

This result motivates the possibility to inhibit the application of [o] to equations of the form $\lambda x.s \triangleright \lambda x.X(\mathbf{y})$.

First we introduce a class of restricted outside-in reduction derivations.

Definition 12 Let $\mathcal{R}$ be an orthogonal PRS and $s \triangleright t\theta \rightarrow^*$ **true** an outside-in $\mathcal{R}_+$-reduction derivation. Then we say the derivation has property $\mathcal{P}_{HO}$ if every reduction step in it satisfies the following condition: if a position $1 \cdot p$ is rewritten in the reduction step and later steps except the final step do not take place above $1 \cdot p$, then p is above or disjoint from any free variable position in t.

Let $\langle G, \theta, \mathbf{R} \rangle \in \text{Repr}(G)$ such that every reduction derivation in R is outside-in. It is obvious that all the outside-in reduction derivations in $\mathbf{R}$ have property $\mathcal{P}_{HO}$ if the goal G consists only of unoriented equations. The following lemma establishes the preservation of the property $\mathcal{P}_{HO}$ during regular transformations.

Lemma 6 Let $\langle G, \theta, \mathbf{R} \rangle \in \text{Repr}(G)$ and suppose $\langle G', \theta', \mathbf{R'} \rangle$ is obtained by a regular transformation from $\langle G, \theta, \mathbf{R} \rangle$. If $\mathbf{R}$ only consists of outside-in derivations with property $\mathcal{P}_{HO}$, then the same holds for $\mathbf{R'}$. $\square$

The proof is done by an easy but tedious case analysis on the regular transformations.

Theorem 6 LN_{ff} with eager variable elimination strategy is complete for orthogonal PRSs with respect to normalized solutions for goals consisting of unoriented equations.

Proof. Let $\langle G, \theta, \mathbf{R} \rangle \in \text{Repr}(G)$, where G consists of unoriented equations, θ is a normalized substitution, and $\mathbf{R}$ contains an outside-in reduction derivation R. Note that R has no extended anti-standard pairs. For any $\langle G', \theta', \mathbf{R'} \rangle$ obtained by the repeated applications of regular transformations, from Lemma 6 we learn that if G' includes an equation e of the form $\lambda x.s\theta' \triangleright \lambda x.X\theta'(t\theta')$ then the corresponding reduction derivation in $\mathbf{R'}$ should be $e \rightarrow_\varepsilon$ **true**; otherwise $\mathbf{R'}$ has an extended anti-standard pair. The regular transformation applied to the equation e never produces an [o]-step. $\square$

Note that once we get outside-in reduction derivations, we no longer need the restriction on terms to patterns. The restriction, however, becomes crucial for further eager variable elimination. For instance, $[ov]_\triangleright$ may be applied to a flex-rigid parameter-passing equation with non-pattern in the left-hand side. On the other hand, from Lemma 5 and Lemma 6 we infer that normal LN_{ff}-refutations never contain applications of $[ov]_\triangleright$-steps to flex-rigid parameter-passing equations with pattern in the left-hand side provided we are interested only in normalized solutions and the precursors of the equation were completely solved. In practice, we expect that most terms occurring in LN_{ff} derivations are patterns and hence $[ov]_\triangleright$ is rarely employed.

The above remark assures that normal LN_{ff} refutations that respect eager variable elimination strategy enjoy a generalization of the eager variable elimination strategy in the first order case. Recall that eager variable elimination is also applicable to parameter-passing equations of the form $X \triangleright t$ in the first order case [6]. Since X is obviously a pattern, we can prohibit the application of [ov] to this equation.

8   Conclusions and Further Research

We identified an equation selection strategy class with respect to which the calculus LN_{ff} is complete. Note that S_n does not identify the equation which must be selected next but specifies a condition which must be satisfied by the selected equation. Therefore it is possible to define more specific equation selection strategies for LN_{ff}. Such a strategy is the one that always selects an equation which satisfies S_n and has small nondeterminism due to the selection of the applicable inference rule. Also, our result confirms the validity of the conjecture of Middeldorp which we mentioned in Sect. 5.

In Sect. 7 we proved that if we restrict ourselves to an orthogonal PRS then we can make the calculus LN_{ff} even more deterministic by adopting an eager-variable elimination strategy.

We mention here the result of Prehofer [11] about the possibility to completely drop the [ov]-rules from LN if we restrict to convergent PRS. The proof is based on the existence of innermost derivations for such rewriting systems. However, the termination condition is very strong in practice.

References

1. M. Hamada, T. Ida. *Deterministic and Non-deterministic Lazy Conditional Narrowing and their Implementations.* Transactions of Information Processing Society of Japan, Vol. 39, No. 3, pp. 656–663, March 1998.
2. M. Hanus. *The Integration of Functions into Logic Programming: From Theory to Practice.* Journal of Logic Programming, 19&20:583-628, 1994.
3. K. Nakahara, A. Middeldorp, T. Ida. A Complete Narrowing Calculus for Higher-order Functional Logic Programming. In *Proceedings of the Seventh International Conference on Programming Languages: Implementations, Logics and Programs 95 (PLILP'95), LNCS 982,* 97-114, 1995.
4. M. Marin, A. Middeldorp, T. Ida, T. Yanagi. *LNCA: A Lazy Narrowing Calculus for Applicative Term Rewriting Systems.* Technical Report ISE-TR-99-158, University of Tsukuba, 1999.
5. M. Marin, T. Ida, W. Schreiner. CFLP: a Mathematica Implementation of a Distributed Constraint Solving System. *Third International Mathematica Symposium (IMS'99),* Hagenberg, Austria, August 23-25, 1999. Computational Mechanics Publications, WIT Press, Southampton, UK.
6. A. Middeldorp, S. Okui. A Deterministic Lazy Narrowing Calculus. *Journal of Symbolic Computation* 25(6), pp. 733-757, 1998.
7. A. Middeldorp, S. Okui, T. Ida. Lazy Narrowing: Strong Completeness and Eager Variable Elimination. *Theoretical Computer Science* 167(1,2), pp. 95-130, 1996.
8. T. Nipkow. Functional Unification of Higher-order Patterns. In *Proceedings of 8th IEEE Symposium on Logic in Computer Science,* pp. 64-74, 1993.

9. T. Nipkow, C. Prehofer. Higher-Order Rewriting and Equational Reasoning. In *Automated Deduction - A Basis for Applications*. Volume I. Kluwer, 1998, 399-430.

10. V. van Oostrom. Higher-order Families. In *International Conference on Rewriting Techniques and Applications '96, LNCS*, 1996.

11. C. Prehofer. *Solving Higher-Order Equations. From Logic to Programming.* Birkhäuser Boston, 1998.

12. W. Snyder, J. Gallier. Higher-order unification revisited: Complete sets of transformations. *Journal of Symbolic Computation*, 8:101-140, 1989.

13. T. Suzuki. Standardization Theorem Revisited. In *Proceedings of 5th International Conference, ALP'96, LNCS* 1139, pp.122-134, 1996.

14. T. Suzuki, K. Nakagawa, T. Ida. Higher-Order Lazy Narrowing Calculus: A Computation Model for a Higher-order Functional Logic Language. In *Proceedings of Sixth International Joint Conference, ALP '97 - HOA '97, LNCS* 1298, pp. 99–113, September 1997, Southampton.

Typed Higher-Order Narrowing without Higher-Order Strategies [*]

Sergio Antoy and Andrew Tolmach

Department of Computer Science, Portland State University,
P.O. Box 751, Portland, OR 97207, USA,
{antoy,apt}@cs.pdx.edu

Abstract. We describe a new approach to higher-order narrowing computations in a class of systems suitable for functional logic programming. Our approach is based on a translation of these systems into ordinary (first-order) rewrite systems and the subsequent application of conventional narrowing strategies. Our translation is an adaptation to narrowing of Warren's translation, but unlike similar previous work, we preserve static type information, which has a dramatic effect on the size of the narrowing space. Our approach supports sound, complete, and efficient higher-order narrowing computations in classes of systems larger than those previously proposed.

1 Introduction

Functional logic languages generalize functional languages by supporting the evaluation of expressions containing (possibly uninstantiated) logic variables. Narrowing is an essential component of the underlying computational mechanism of an internationally supported unified functional logic language [4]. In recent years a considerable effort has been invested in the development of narrowing strategies. The results of this effort are satisfactory for first-order computations. Higher-order narrowing, the situation in which a computation may instantiate a variable of functional type, is still evolving.

The most fundamental question is what universe of functions should be considered as possible instantiations for variables of functional type. One attractive answer is to consider just those functions (perhaps partially applied) that are explicitly defined in the program already, or a user-specified subset of these functions. For example, consider the program

```
data nat = z | s nat
data list = [] | nat:list
compose (F,G) X = F (G X)
map F [] = []
map F (H:T) = (F H):(map F T)
```

[*] This work has been supported in part by the National Science Foundation under grant CCR-9503383.

A. Middeldorp, T. Sato (Eds.): FLOPS'99, LNCS 1722, pp. 335–352, 1999.
© Springer-Verlag Berlin Heidelberg 1999

and abbreviate s z with 1, s 1 with 2, etc. The goal map G [1,2] == [2,3] would have the solution {G ↦ s}, the goal map G [1,2] == [3,4] would have the solution {G ↦ compose (s,s)}, but the goal map G [1,2] == [2,4] would have no solutions.

This approach is quite expressive, and also relatively easy for the programmer to understand. Moreover, there is a very reasonable approach to solving higher-order problems of this kind by translating them into equivalent first-order problems, in which unapplied and partially applied functions are represented by constructors and implicit higher-order applications are made into explicit first-order applications. This idea dates back to Warren [13] for logic programs and to Reynolds [11] for functional programs. Hanus [7,8] shows how this idea works for dynamically typed languages. González-Moreno [5] adapts the same idea to untyped narrowing.

Our contribution is to define this transformation for *statically typed* source and target languages. We give a rigorous presentation for monomorphic programs and sketch an extension to polymorphic programs. The benefits of a typed source language are well known. The benefits of maintaining types during program transformation and compilation are becoming increasingly recognized in the functional programming community (e.g., [14,15]); these include the ability to use efficient, type-specific data representations, the ability to perform optimizations based on type information, and enhanced confidence in compiler correctness obtained by type-checking compiler output. In functional logic programming, typing the target language has additional dramatic, immediate effects on the narrowing space; in particular, typing allows possibly infinite, extraneous branches of the narrowing space to be avoided. This obviously improves the efficiency of the language, and avoids run-time behaviors, especially for sequential implementations, that would be unintelligible to the programmer.

2   Background

The most recent and comprehensive proposals of higher-order narrowing strategies differ in both the domain and the computation of the strategy. González-Moreno [5] considers *SFL-programs*. Rules in these systems are constructor-based, left-linear, non-overlapping, conditional, and allow extra variables in the conditional part. A translation inspired by Warren [13] removes higher-order constructs from these systems and allows the use of (first-order) narrowing strategies for higher-order narrowing computations

Nakahara et al. [10] consider first-order *applicative* constructor-based orthogonal rewrite systems. A rule's left-hand side in these systems allows variables of functional type, but prohibits both the application of a variable to subterms and the presence of a function symbol in a pattern. The strategy proposed for these systems is computed by a handful of small inference steps, where "small" characterizes the fact that several inferences may be necessary to compute an ordinary narrowing step.

Hanus and Prehofer [6] consider *higher-order* inductively sequential systems. An operation in these systems has a definitional tree in which the patterns may contain higher-order patterns [9] as subterms and the application of variables to subterms. The strategy proposed for these systems is again computed by a handful of small inference rules that, when concatenated together, for the most part simulate a needed narrowing computation.

The domains of these strategies have a large intersection, but none is contained in any other. For example, applicative orthogonal systems include Berry's system, which is excluded from inductively sequential systems; higher-order inductively sequential systems allow higher-order patterns in left-hand sides, which are banned in SFL programs; and SFL programs use conditional rules with extra variables, which are excluded from applicative systems. All the above strategies are sound and complete for the classes of systems to which they are applied.

While first-order narrowing is becoming commonplace in functional logic programming, the benefits and costs of higher-order narrowing are still being debated. Factors limiting the acceptance of higher-order narrowing are the potential inefficiency of computations and the difficulty of implementations. In this paper we describe a new approach to higher-order narrowing that addresses both problems. Our approach is based on a program translation, similar to [3,5,11,12,13], that replaces higher-order narrowing computations in a source program with first-order narrowing computations in the corresponding target program. Our approach expands previous work in three directions.

(1) We use a translation [12] that preserves type information of the source program. Type information dramatically affects the size of the narrowing space of a computation.

(2) We present our technical results for the same class of systems discussed in [10]. We will argue later that our approach extends the systems considered in [5] and with minor syntactic changes extends the systems considered in [6], too.

(3) For a large class of source programs of practical interest [4], our approach supports optimal, possibly non-deterministic, higher-order functional logic computations [1] without the need for a higher-order narrowing strategy.

3 Language

3.1 Basics

We describe our approach with reference to a monomorphically typed functional logic language L, whose abstract syntax is specified in Figure 1. For ease of presentation, we explicitly type all functions, constructors, and variables, but types could be inferred (and we therefore omit some typing information in the concrete examples in this paper). The abstract syntax is something of a compromise among the conventional notations for functional programs, logic programs, and rewrite systems. The concrete syntax of functional logic languages that could benefit from our approach could be much richer, e.g., it could allow infix operators, ad-hoc notation for numeric types and lists, nested blocks with locally scoped identifiers, anonymous functions, etc. Programs in languages with these features are easily mapped to programs in our language during the early phases of compilation. Thus, our approach is perfectly suited for contemporary functional logic languages, too.

(algebraic types)	$d := identifier$	
(types)	$t := d$	(algebraic types)
	$\mid (t_1, \ldots, t_n)$	(tuples; $n \geq 0$)
	$\mid (t \rightarrow t)$	(functions)

(variables)	$v := identifier\ beginning\ with\ upper\text{-}case\ letter$	
(constructors)	$c := identifier$	
(functions)	$f := identifier$	
(symbols)	$s := c \mid f$	

(problems)	$problem := (program, goal)$	

(programs)	$program := dec_1 \ldots dec_m\ rule_1 \ldots rule_n$	$(m, n \geq 0)$

(goals)	$goal := (v_1 : t_1, \ldots, v_n : t_n)\ e_1 \mathrel{=\mkern-4mu=} e_2$	$(v_i\ disjoint)$	(1)

(constr. decl.)	$dec := c : t_1 \rightarrow \ldots \rightarrow t_n \rightarrow d$	$(n = ar(c))$

(function rules)	$rule := f\ p_1 \ldots p_n \mathrel{\blacksquare} e$	$(n = ar(f))$

(patterns)	$p := (v : t)$	(variable)
	$\mid (c\ p_1 \ldots p_n)$	(constructor; $n \leq ar(c)$)
	$\mid (f\ p_1 \ldots p_n)$	(function; $n < ar(f)$)
	$\mid (p_1, \ldots, p_n)$	($n \geq 0$)(tuple)

(expressions)	$e := v$	(variable)
	$\mid s$	(constructor or function)
	$\mid (e_1, \ldots, e_n)$	(tuple)
	$\mid (e_1\ e_2)$	(application)

Fig. 1. Abstract syntax of functional logic language L. By convention, type arrows associate to the right and expression applications associate to the left. Each symbol s has a fixed associated arity, given by $ar(s)$. Only partially-applied function symbols are allowed in a pattern.

A *program* is a collection of *constructor* declarations and *function* definitions. Constructors and functions are collectively called *symbols*; we use identifiers not beginning with upper-case letters for symbol names. Each symbol s has a unique associated non-negative arity, given by $ar(s)$. A function definition consists of one or more *rules* (not necessarily contiguously presented); each rule has a left-hand side which is a sequence of *patterns* and a right-hand side which is an *expression*. All the rules for a function of arity n must have n patterns. The patterns control which right-hand side(s) should be invoked when the function is applied; they serve both to match against actual arguments and to bind local variables mentioned in the right-hand side. Patterns are *applicative terms*, i.e., they are built from *variables*, fully-applied constructors, partially-applied functions, and *tuples*. This definition of *"applicative"* generalizes the one in [10], in that it permits partially-applied functions. In the logic programming tradition, we reserve identifiers beginning with upper-case letters for variables. Expressions are built from symbols, variables, tuples and binary application denoted by juxtaposition. Intuitively, function applications evaluate to the right-hand side of a matching rule, and constructor applications evaluate to themselves. Parentheses in expressions are avoided under the convention that application is left associative.

Functions (and constructors) are *curried*; that is, a function f of arity $ar(f) > 1$ is applied to only one argument at a time. This permits the manipulation of partially-applied functions, which is fundamental to expressing higher-order algorithms involving non-local variables. Unlike conventional functional and functional logic languages, which treat functions as black boxes, we permit matching against unapplied or partially-applied functions (or constructors). We delay the discussion of this feature until Section 6 when we compare our approach with [6]. It is often useful (particularly in presenting the result of our translation system) to describe uncurried functions that take their arguments "all at once;" this is done by specifying an arity-1 function taking a tuple argument.

A *problem* (p, g) consists of a program p and a goal g. A *goal* consists of a sequence of variable declarations followed by an *equation*, an expression of the form $e_1 == e_2$. Any variables appearing in e_1 or e_2 must appear in a declaration. There is no loss of generality in restricting goals to equations. A problem *solution* is a substitution θ (see Sect. 3.4) from the variables declared in the goal to applicative terms, such that $\theta(e_1)$ and $\theta(e_2)$ reduce to the same applicative term.

3.2   Typing

L is an explicitly typed, monomorphic language. Types include algebraic types, whose values are generated by constructors; tuple types; and function types. The typing rules are specified in Figure 2 as a collection of judgments for the various syntactic classes. The judgment $E \vdash_{class} phrase : t \Rightarrow E'$ asserts that *phrase* of syntactic category *class* is well-typed with type t in environment E, and generates an environment E'; judgments for specific classes may omit one or more of these components. Environments map symbols and variables to types. Note that all functions are potentially mutually recursive.

Each variable declaration (in rules or goals) has an explicit type annotation; together with the typing rules these allow us to assume the existence of a well-defined function $typeof()$, mapping each (well-typed) expression or pattern to its type. A solution substitution $\{v_i \mapsto e_i\}$ is well-typed if and only

$$\frac{\vdash_{program} program \Rightarrow E \quad E \vdash_{goal} goal}{\vdash_{problem} (program, goal)}$$

$$\frac{\vdash_{dec} dec_1 \Rightarrow E_1 \quad \ldots \quad \vdash_{dec} dec_m \Rightarrow E_m}{E \vdash_{rule} rule_1 \Rightarrow E_{m+1} \quad \ldots \quad E \vdash_{rule} rule_n \Rightarrow E_{m+n}}{E = E_1 + \ldots + E_{m+n}}{\vdash_{program} dec_1 \ldots dec_m \; rule_1 \ldots rule_n \Rightarrow E}$$

$$\frac{E + \{v_1 \mapsto t_1, \ldots, v_n \mapsto t_n\} \vdash_e e_i : t(i=1,2)}{E \vdash_{goal} (v_1 : t_1, \ldots, v_n : t_n) \; e_1 \mathbin{\texttt{==}} e_2}$$

$$\frac{}{\vdash_{dec} c : t_1 \to \ldots \to t_n \to d \Rightarrow \{c \mapsto t_1 \to \ldots \to t_n \to d\}}$$

$$\frac{E(f) = t_1 \to \ldots \to t_n \to t \quad E \vdash_p p_i : t_i \Rightarrow E_i (1 \le i \le n) \quad E + E_1 + \ldots + E_n \vdash_e e : t}{E \vdash_{rule} f \; p_1 \ldots p_n = e \Rightarrow \{f \mapsto t_1 \to \ldots \to t_n \to t\}}$$

$$\frac{}{E \vdash_p (v : t) : t \Rightarrow \{v \mapsto t\}}$$

$$\frac{E(c) = t_1 \to \ldots \to t_n \to d \quad E \vdash_p p_i : t_i \Rightarrow E_i (1 \le i \le n)}{E \vdash_p (c \; p_1 \ldots p_n) : d \Rightarrow E_1 + \ldots + E_n}$$

$$\frac{E(f) = t_1 \to \ldots \to t_n \to t \quad E \vdash_p p_i : t_i \Rightarrow E_i (1 \le i \le m)}{E \vdash_p (f \; p_1 \ldots p_m) : t_{m+1} \to \ldots \to t_n \to t \Rightarrow E_1 + \ldots + E_m}$$

$$\frac{E \vdash_p p_i : t_i \Rightarrow E_i (1 \le i \le n)}{E \vdash_p (p_1, \ldots, p_n) : (t_1, \ldots, t_n) \Rightarrow E_1 + \ldots + E_n}$$

$$\frac{E(v) = t}{E \vdash_e v : t} \qquad\qquad \frac{E(s) = t}{E \vdash_e s : t}$$

$$\frac{E \vdash_e e_i : t_i (1 \le i \le n)}{E \vdash_e (e_1, \ldots, e_n) : (t_1, \ldots, t_n)} \qquad \frac{E \vdash_e e_1 : t_2 \to t \quad E \vdash_e e_2 : t_2}{E \vdash_e (e_1 e_2) : t}$$

Fig. 2. Typing rules for language L. The environment union operator $E_1 + E_2$ is defined only when E_1 and E_2 agree on any elements in the intersection of their domains.

if $\forall i, typeof(v_i) = typeof(e_i)$. In practice, we could generate the type annotations for L automatically by inference from a source program with missing or incomplete type annotations.

3.3 Relationship to Term Rewriting

A program p may be viewed as a rewrite system $(\Sigma, \mathcal{R})$ where

- Σ is a *signature*, i.e., a set of symbols (partitioned into functions and constructors), with associated types, consisting of those symbols that appear in p;
- $\mathcal{R}$ is the set of *rewrite rules* consisting of the function rules in p.

In the terminology of [10], our system is an *applicative term rewriting system* ($\mathcal{A}$TRS) using our slightly generalized notion of *applicative term*. We do not specify other fundamental properties, such as left-linearity, or non-overlapping of rules, though each of these may be useful in practice. For simplicity of presentation, we prohibit extra variables on the right-hand sides of rules, but these could be added similarly to goal variables without fundamental difficulty, as could conditions to the rules.

3.4 Evaluation

This view of programs as rewrite systems defines the notion of evaluation for our system. We define the evaluation of variable-free expressions as ordinary rewriting. An expression is in normal form if it cannot be further rewritten. Orthogonal (left-linear and non-overlapping) programs will be confluent, but not necessarily terminating. Well-typed expressions enjoy the *subject reduction* property, which says that their type is invariant under reduction.

As noted above, a problem solution is a substitution from the variables declared in the goal to applicative terms. This definition doesn't indicate how a solution might be found. To be more concrete, we define the evaluation of a problem to mean the computation of a solution substitution by a sequence of *narrowing* steps. Formally, a *substitution* is a mapping from variables to terms which is the identity almost everywhere. Substitutions are extended to homomorphisms from terms to terms. The narrowing relation on $\mathcal{R}$, denoted $\underset{\mathcal{R}}{\rightsquigarrow}$, is defined as follows: $e \underset{\mathcal{R}}{\rightsquigarrow}_{\theta,p,l=r} e'$, iff θ unifies $e_{|p}$ (the subterm of e at position p) with the left-hand side l of some rule $l=r$ (with fresh variables), and $e' = \theta(e[r]_p)$ (where $e[r]_p$ is the result of replacing the subterm at position p of e by r). We will drop θ, p, or $l=r$ from this notation when they are irrelevant. When presented, the representation of θ will be restricted to the variables of a goal.

As habitual in functional logic languages with a lazy operational semantics, we define the validity of an equation as a strict equality on terms denoted by the infix operator ==. Because of the applicative nature of our systems, strict equality is defined by the families of rules

$$c == c = \mathit{true}, \qquad\qquad\qquad\qquad\qquad\qquad\qquad\qquad \forall c$$
$$c\, X_1 \ldots X_n == c\, Y_1 \ldots Y_n = X_1 == Y_1 \wedge \ldots \wedge X_n == Y_n, \quad \forall c, ar(c) \geqslant n > 0$$
$$(X_1, \ldots, X_n) == (Y_1, \ldots, Y_n) = X_1 == Y_1 \wedge \ldots \wedge X_n == Y_n, \forall n > 0$$
$$f == f = \mathit{true}, \qquad\qquad\qquad\qquad\qquad\qquad\qquad\qquad \forall f, ar(f) > 0$$
$$f\, X_1 \ldots X_n == f\, Y_1 \ldots Y_n = X_1 == Y_1 \wedge \ldots \wedge X_n == Y_n, \quad \forall f, ar(f) > n \geqslant 0$$
$$\mathit{true} \wedge X = X$$

where c is a constructor and f is a function. (Recall that our language allows only partially-applied function symbols in a pattern.)

A sequence of narrowing steps $g \overset{*}{\underset{\mathcal{R}}{\leadsto}}_\theta$ *true*, where $\mathcal{R}$ is the set of rules of p, is called an *evaluation* of (p, g) producing *solution* θ.

As a very simple example, consider the following problem, taken from [5, Ex. 1] (originally from [13]).

```
z : nat
s : nat -> nat
twice (F:nat->nat) (X:nat) = F (F X)
(G:(nat->nat)->(nat->nat)) G s z == s (s z)
```

A solution of this problem is the substitution $\{G \mapsto \texttt{twice}\}$. It is computed by the following evaluation.

$$G \; s \; z \; == \; s \; (s \; z) \leadsto_{\{G \mapsto \texttt{twice}\}} s \; (s \; z) \; == \; s \; (s \; z) \overset{+}{\leadsto}_{\{\}} \; true$$

Note that we still haven't suggested a strategy for choosing the appropriate sequence of narrowing steps. In fact, while a great deal is known about efficient strategies for first-order programs, we understand much less about higher-order ones. We will show shortly, however, that typing information can be a valuable guide to computing an efficient strategy. The main idea of this paper is to reduce the higher-order case to the first-order one while maintaining typability, as described in the next section.

4 Translation

The idea behind the translation is to encode all unapplied or partially-applied symbols[1] as constructors (called *closure constructors*), grouped into new algebraic data types (*closure types*), and replace all applications in the original program by applications of special new *dispatch functions*. As its name suggests, a dispatch function takes a closure constructor as argument, and, based on the value of that argument, dispatches control to (a translation of) the appropriate original function. The resulting program is well-typed in the strict first-order subset of the original language, so ordinary first-order narrowing strategies can be used to find solutions.

The main novelty introduced by the presence of types is that the translation constructs type-specific dispatch functions and associated closure-constructor types, one for each different function type encountered in the source program. (The obvious alternative—using a single dispatch function that operates over all closure constructors—is unattractive, because such a function could not be given a conventional static polymorphic type; some form of dependent typing would be required, and this would in general require dynamic type checking.) The translation essentially consists of two parts:

---

[1] Because constructors in the source program can be treated just like first-class functions (e.g., as arguments to higher-order functions), they are encoded just like functions.

$$[\![d]\!] = d$$
$$[\![(t_1, \ldots, t_n)]\!] = ([\![t_1]\!], \ldots, [\![t_n]\!])$$
$$[\![t_1 \rightarrow t_2]\!] = \$_{[\![t_1]\!] \rightarrow [\![t_2]\!]}$$

$$[\![dec_1 \ldots dec_m \; rule_1 \ldots rule_n]\!] = [\![dec_1]\!] \ldots [\![dec_m]\!] \; newsigs$$
$$[\![rule_1]\!] \ldots [\![rule_n]\!] \; newrules$$
$$\text{where } newsigs = nsigs(dec_1) \ldots nsigs(dec_m)$$
$$nsigs'(rule_1) \ldots nsigs'(rule_n)$$
$$\text{and } newrules = nrules(dec_1) \ldots nrules(dec_m)$$
$$nrules'(rule_1) \ldots nrules'(rule_n)$$
$$[\![(v_1 : t_1, \ldots, v_n : t_n) \; e_1 \; == \; e_2]\!] = (v_1 : [\![t_1]\!], \ldots, v_n : [\![t_n]\!]) \; [\![e_1]\!] \; == \; [\![e_2]\!]$$

$$[\![c : t_1 \rightarrow \ldots \rightarrow t_n \rightarrow d]\!] = c : ([\![t_1]\!], \ldots, [\![t_n]\!]) \rightarrow d \qquad (\text{if } ar(c) = n > 0)$$
$$= c : d \qquad\qquad\qquad\quad (\text{if } ar(c) = n = 0)$$

$$[\![f \; p_1 \ldots p_n \; = \; e]\!] = f([\![p_1]\!], \ldots, [\![p_n]\!]) = [\![e]\!]$$

(patterns)
$$[\![(v : t)]\!] = (v : [\![t]\!])$$
$$[\![(c \; p_1 \ldots p_n)]\!] = (c([\![p_1]\!], \ldots, [\![p_n]\!]))$$
$$[\![f]\!] = \#f_0$$
$$[\![(f \; p_1 \ldots p_n)]\!] = (\#f_n([\![p_1]\!], \ldots, [\![p_n]\!]))$$
$$[\![(p_1, \ldots, p_n)]\!] = ([\![p_1]\!], \ldots, [\![p_n]\!])$$

(expressions)
$$[\![v]\!] = v$$
$$[\![s]\!] = \#s_0 \qquad\qquad\qquad (\text{if } ar(s) > 0)$$
$$[\![s]\!] = s \qquad\qquad\qquad\quad (\text{if } ar(s) = 0)$$
$$[\![(e_1, \ldots, e_n)]\!] = ([\![e_1]\!], \ldots, [\![e_n]\!])$$
$$[\![(e_1 \; e_2)]\!] = @_{[\![typeof(e_1)]\!]}([\![e_1]\!], [\![e_2]\!])$$

Fig. 3. Translation Rules. The notation for translation is overloaded to work on each syntactic class. The definitions of $nsigs()$, $nsigs'()$, $nrules()$, and $nrules'()$ are given in Figure 4.

- generation of a set of new nullary or unary *closure constructors*, corresponding to partially applied functions and constructors in the source program, and a set of new unary *dispatch functions*;
- a syntax-directed transformation of the original program and goal, which replaces original constructor and function names by closure constructor names, original applications by dispatch function applications and original function definitions by equivalent uncurried function definitions.

The closure constructors and dispatch functions are then integrated with the translated program to produce the complete translated problem. Details of the translation are specified in Figures 3 and 4. Borrowing from [5], we denote closure constructors with identifiers prefixed by "#," closure types with the symbol "$"

indexed by an (arrow) type, and dispatch functions with the symbol "@" indexed by a type.

$$nsigs(s : d) = \{\}$$

$$nsigs(s : t_1 \to \ldots \to t_n \to d) = \left\{ \begin{array}{l} \#s_0 : [\![t_1 \to \ldots \to t_n \to t]\!], \\ \#s_1 : [\![t_1]\!] \to [\![t_2 \to \ldots t_n]\!], \\ \ldots, \\ \#s_{n-1} : ([\![t_1]\!], \ldots, [\![t_{n-1}]\!]) \to [\![t_n \to t]\!] \end{array} \right\}$$

$$nsigs'(f\ p_1\ \ldots\ p_n\ =\ e) = nsigs(f : typeof(f))$$

$$nrules(s : d) = \{\}$$

$$nrules(s : t_1 \to \ldots \to t_n \to d) = \left\{ \begin{array}{l} @_{[t_1 \to \ldots \to t_n \to t]}(\#s_0, v_1 : [\![t_1]\!]) = \#s_1(v_1), \\ @_{[t_2 \to \ldots \to t_n \to t]}(\#s_1(v_1 : [\![t_1]\!]), v_2 : [\![t_2]\!]) = \\ \qquad \#s_2(v_1, v_2), \ldots, \\ @_{[t_n \to t]}(\#s_{n-1}(v_1 : [\![t_1]\!], \ldots, v_{n-1} : [\![t_{n-1}]\!]), \\ \qquad v_n : [\![t_n]\!]) = s(v_1, \ldots, v_n) \end{array} \right\}$$

$$nrules'(f\ p_1\ \ldots\ p_n\ =\ e) = nrules(f : typeof(f))$$

Fig. 4. Definition of closure constructors and dispatch functions.

In a translated program, all functions appearing in expressions are fully applied, so no applicative expression ever mentions a function. Thus, solutions of a goal under the translated program never mention the new *dispatch* functions, though they may mention the new #s constructors. Solutions may be translated back into a higher-order form that doesn't contain these constructors by translating each construction $\#s_0$ into the symbol name s, and each construction $\#s_k(e_1, \ldots, e_k)$ into the application $(s\ e_1 \ldots e_k)$. A complete inverse translation for expressions is given in Figure 5.

4.1   Example

Consider again the small example problem of the previous section. Our translation gives the following target problem

```
z : nat
s : nat -> nat
#twice₀ : d1
#twice₁ : d2 -> d2
#s₀ : d2
twice (F:d2, X:nat) = @d2(F,@d2(F,X))
@d1(#twice₀:d1, F:d2) = #twice₁(F)
@d2(#twice₁(F:d2), X:nat) = twice(F,X)
@d2(#s₀:d2, X:nat) = s(X)
(G:d1) @d2(@d1(G,#s₀),z) == @d2(#s₀,@d2(#s₀,z))
```

where

$$d1 = \$_{[\text{nat} \to \text{nat}] \to [\text{nat} \to \text{nat}]} = [\![(\text{nat} \to \text{nat}) \to (\text{nat} \to \text{nat})]\!]$$
$$d2 = \$_{[\text{nat}] \to [\text{nat}]} = [\![\text{nat} \to \text{nat}]\!]$$

An evaluation of the translated problem produces the following (incomplete) narrowing sequence:

$$@_{d2}(@_{d1}(G,\#s_0),z) \;==\; @_{d2}(\#s_0,@_{d2}(\#s_0,z))$$
$$\rightsquigarrow_{\{G \mapsto \#twice_0\}} @_{d2}(\#twice_1(\#s_0),z) \;==\; @_{d2}(\#s_0,@_{d2}(\#s_0,z))$$
$$\rightsquigarrow_{\{\}} twice(\#s_0,z) \;==\; @_{d2}(\#s_0,@_{d2}(\#s_0,z))$$
$$\rightsquigarrow_{\{\}} @_{d2}(\#s_0,@_{d2}(\#s_0,z)) \;==\; @_{d2}(\#s_0,@_{d2}(\#s_0,z))$$

The solution substitution $\{G \mapsto \#twice_0\}$ to the translated problem is mapped by the inverse translation back to the substitution $\{G \mapsto twice\}$, which is a solution of the original problem.

$$[\![v]\!]^{-1} = v$$
$$[\![\#s_0]\!]^{-1} = s$$
$$[\![\#s_k(e_1,\ldots,e_k)]\!]^{-1} = (s\ e_1 \ldots e_k)$$
$$[\![c]\!]^{-1} = c \qquad \text{(for other constructors } c\text{)}$$
$$[\![(e_1,\ldots,e_n)]\!]^{-1} = ([\![e_1]\!],\ldots,[\![e_n]\!])$$

Fig. 5. Inverse Translation Rules.

4.2 Discussion

We have tried to present the translation in the simplest and most uniform way possible. As a result, the translated code is substantially more inefficient than necessary; this can be corrected by using a more sophisticated translation or by post-translation optimization, using standard simplification techniques. For example, we replace *all* source applications by dispatch function applications, whereas in fact *only* applications whose operators are variables need to be dispatched; when the operator is a known symbol, the dispatch function call could be inlined. As another example, translated functions are called in only one place, from within the (type-appropriate) dispatch function, so they could be inlined there without increasing code size. Note, however, that one cannot in general perform *both* these transformations simultaneously without risking a blow-up in the size of the translated program.

Our translation relies fundamentally on having a monomorphic source program, so that each source function can be assigned unambiguously to a closure-constructor type and associated dispatch function in the target. It is obviously desirable to extend the translation to polymorphic problems. One straightforward approach is to generate (automatically) multiple *specialized* versions of the program's polymorphic functions, one for each type at which the function is used, before applying the translation [12]. This method works for problems that combine polymorphic programs with monomorphic goals. For example, given the program

```
u : foo
v : bar
id (Z:α) = Z
```

where α is a type variable, we can solve the goals

```
(X:foo, Y:bar) (id X, id v) == (u,Y)
(F:foo->foo,G:bar->bar) (F u, G v) == (u,v)
```

by first specializing id into two functions

```
id_foo (Z:foo) = Z
id_bar (Z:bar) = Z
```

and then translating to first-order and solving in the normal way. For the latter goal, we obtain the solution $\{F \mapsto id\_foo, G \mapsto id\_bar\}$; we can transform both the monomorphic function names appearing in the solution back into id for presentation to the user. Note that the type annotations on variables F and G are needed to guide the specialization process.

This approach fails to handle goals with polymorphic function-typed variables. For example, given the above program, consider the goal

```
(F u, F v) == (u,v)
```

Here $\{F \mapsto id\}$ is the (sole) solution to the polymorphic goal; no single monomorphic instance can possibly be a solution. Solving this problem appears to require dynamic (runtime) type manipulation. For example, Hanus [8] has shown that a system using explicit type annotations on all terms together with runtime type unification can express the Warren transformation using a single polymorphic dispatch function; there are static analyses that permit the runtime types to be omitted *provided* there are no function-valued goal variables [7]. If there *are* function-valued variables, some runtime type operations will need to remain, and it is not clear what level of static type checking can be guaranteed to the programmer; we are currently investigating this question.

Our translation is presented as operating on an entire program at one time, but this is not a fundamental requirement. If the source program is given incrementally, the translation can be performed incrementally too, provided that it is possible to add new constructors to an existing algebraic datatype and new rules for an existing dispatch function on an incremental basis.

5   Correctness

In this section we formulate the correctness of our translation and sketch its proof. Intuitively, a translation of a source problem into a target problem is correct if solutions of the source problem can be computed by means of the target problem, i.e., if the following diagram commutes:

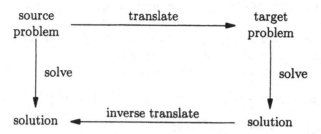

More specifically, it should make no difference whether we compute the solutions of a source program directly or through its translation. To formalize this idea, we need the following notation and definitions. If θ is a substitution, we define $[\![\theta]\!]$ as the substitution that, for any variable v, $[\![\theta]\!](v) = [\![\theta(v)]\!]$. We say that a substitution θ is *applicative* if, for any variable v, $\theta(v)$ is an applicative term. Two substitutions are *equivalent* if each one can be obtained by the other through a renaming of variables. If θ is a substitution and g is a goal, then $\theta_{|Var(g)}$ denotes the *restriction* of θ to the variables of g. If P is a problem, then $solve(P)$ is the set of its solutions. If S is a set, then $[\![S]\!] = \{[\![x]\!] \,|\, x \in S\}$. The comparison of two sets of substitutions is always implicitly intended modulo equivalence of substitutions.

Let P be a source problem. We say that a translation $[\![\,]\!]$ is *complete* iff, for every source problem P, $solve(P) \subseteq [\![solve([\![P]\!])]\!]^{-1}$. We say that a translation $[\![\,]\!]$ is *sound* iff, for every source problem P, $solve(P) \supseteq [\![solve([\![P]\!])]\!]^{-1}$.

Note that the soundness and completeness of a narrowing strategy used to compute a problem solution are not an issue for the soundness and completeness of a translation, though we envision that a sound and complete strategy will be used for the target program.

We express the completeness of our translation as:

> Let θ be a solution (applicative substitution) of a problem (p, g), where p is an ATRS. There exists a substitution θ' such that $[\![g]\!] \overset{*}{\underset{[\![p]\!]}{\leadsto}} \theta'$ true and $[\![\theta']\!]^{-1}_{|Var(g)}$ is equivalent to θ.

The proof of the completeness of our translation is in two parts. First, one proves the completeness claim when all the steps of a computation are rewriting steps by induction on the length of the computation. Then, one proves the completeness claim of a narrowing computation by lifting the completeness result for the corresponding rewrite computation.

The intuition behind the completeness of our translation is that a computation in the source program is "simulated" by a computation in the target program. For example, the evaluation presented in Section 4.1 simulates the corresponding evaluation presented in Section 3.4.

Each application in the source program is replaced by at most two applications in the target program (before optimization). Consequently, the derivation in the target program takes more steps than in the source program, but only by a constant factor. Moreover, all the target program steps are first-order. In addition, the optimized translation of a first-order source application is just itself. Thus, there is no loss of efficiency in the target program for purely first-order narrowing computations in the source program.

We express the soundness of our translation as:

Let (p, g) be a problem, where p is an $\mathcal{ATRS}$. If $[g] \overset{*}{\underset{[p]}{\leadsto}} \theta$ true, then $[\theta]^{-1}_{|Var(g)}$ is a solution of (p, g).

The proof of the soundness of our translation stems directly from González-Moreno's work [5]. His translation of a problem can be obtained from our translation of the same problem by collapsing all our dispatch functions into a single untyped dispatch function. Some consequences of this difference are discussed in Section 6. For example, his translation of Example 4.1 yields the following first-order program (where we have added type annotations):

```
twice (F:nat->nat, X:nat) = @(F,@(F,X))
@(#twice₀:(nat->nat)->(nat->nat), F:nat->nat) = #twice₁(F)
@(#twice₁(F:nat->nat), X:nat) = twice(F,X)
@(#s₀:nat->nat, X:nat) = s(X)
(G:(nat->nat)->(nat->nat)) @(@(G,#s₀),z) == @(#s₀,@(#s₀,z))
```

Therefore, every solution (substitution) of a problem computed via our translation is also computed by González-Moreno's translation of the same problem. Thus, [5, Th. 1] directly implies that our translation is sound.

6   Related Work

The benefits of our approach to higher-order narrowing computations can be better understood by comparing it with related work.

6.1   Smaller Narrowing Space

The approach to higher-order narrowing closest to ours is [5]. The major difference between these approaches is that our target programs are well-typed whereas the target programs in [5] are not. We show the effects of this difference on the narrowing space of the example discussed in Section 5. Figure 6 shows a portion of the goal's narrowing space computed with the translation proposed in [5], where 2 is an abbreviation of $s(s\ z)$. The same portion of narrowing space generated by our target program contains only the left branch. Both middle and right branches of Figure 6 contain ill-typed terms. The right branch is infinite due to

$$@(G,\#s_0) \overset{.}{\leadsto} @(G',@(G',\#s_0)) \overset{.}{\leadsto} @(G''@(G'',@(G'',\#s_0))) \overset{.}{\leadsto} \ldots$$

These conditions, neither of which arises with our translation, have far reaching consequences. An increase in the branching factor of the nodes of a narrowing

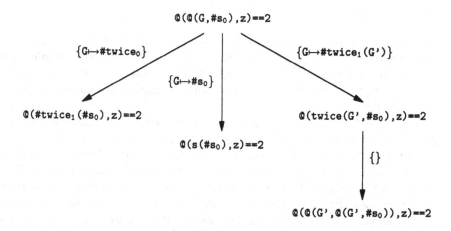

Fig. 6. Portion of the search space of $@(@(G,\#s_0),z)==2$

space implies an exponential growth of the number of nodes that may be generated during a computation. The presence of infinite branches in the search space implies that sequential implementations of complete narrowing strategies may become operationally incomplete. Even if these extreme consequences can be avoided in many cases, we expect in most cases a substantial slowdown of narrowing computations that discard type information. This observation is also made in [10].

Of course, even branches containing only type-correct terms may be infinite, making the use of sequential implementations problematic. We believe, however, that the behavior of such implementations will be much easier for the programmer to understand if they are guaranteed to proceed in a well-typed manner. Gratuitous alteration of the size or finiteness of the narrowing space which cannot aid in finding solutions is surely unacceptable.

6.2   Expanded Programs

Our overall approach has a significant difference with respect to both [6,10]. We reduce higher-order narrowing computations to first-order ones by means of a program translation that is largely independent of both the class of source programs and the narrowing strategy applied to these programs. This decoupling opens new possibilities. For example, there is no published work on higher-order narrowing in both constructor based, weakly orthogonal rewrite systems and inductively sequential, overlapping rewrite systems. It is easy to verify that our translation preserves many common properties of rewrite systems, including weak orthogonality and inductive sequentiality. Since sound, complete, and efficient first-order narrowing strategies are known for both weakly orthogonal rewrite systems [2] and inductively sequential, overlapping rewrite systems [1], our approach immediately provides a means for higher-order narrowing computations in these classes.

6.3   Efficiency

Another difference of our approach with respect to both [6,10] is the granularity of the steps. Both [6,10] perform narrowing computations by means of inferences whereas our approach promotes the use of strategies that perform true narrowing steps. Generally, we expect an overhead when a narrowing step is broken into many inferences.

A noteworthy feature of our approach is that when no variable of function type is instantiated, higher-order narrowing computations do not cost significantly more than first-order narrowing computations. This feature is essential for powerful functional logic languages. For example, the current proposal for Curry defines the dispatch function as *rigid*, thus excluding higher-order narrowing computations from the language, "since higher-order unification is an expensive operation" [4, Sect. 2.6]. Our translation is a step toward lifting exclusions of this kind. Indeed, the above feature extends (at least for monomorphically typed programs) the behavior of modern narrowing strategies in that when no variable is instantiated, narrowing computations should not cost significantly more than functional computations.

6.4   Partial Applications in Patterns

There is a significant difference between [6] and the other higher-order narrowing approaches referenced in this paper. In [6], the patterns of a rule may consist of or contain higher-order patterns [9]. For example, [6, Ex. 1.2] defines a higher-order function *diff*, where *diff*(F, X) computes the differential of F at X in the form of a higher-order pattern. The rules of *diff* include higher-order patterns for symbols such as *sin*, *cos*, and *ln*. Although intuitively these symbols stand for functions sine, cosine, and logarithm, the program defines neither the symbols nor the functions by means of rewrite rules. Our approach supports and extends this feature. The following definitions, where for readability we omit type declarations, allow us to express polynomial functions.

```
const N _ = N
x X = X
plus F G X = F X + G X
times F G X = F X * G X
```

For example, the function $x^2 + 1$ would be expressed using the above rules as

```
plus (times x x) (const 1)
```

The following program defines our *diff* function. Similar to [6], narrowing allows us to use *diff* to compute symbolic integration, although *diff* alone would be inadequate in most cases. By contrast to [6], we use *diff* to compute both the symbolic derivative with respect to x of a polynomial and the differential of a polynomial at $x = X$ — in our framework the former evaluates to a function and the latter evaluates to a number.

```
diff (const _) = const 0
diff x = const 1
```

```
diff (plus F G) = plus (diff F) (diff G)
diff (times F G) = plus (times (diff F) G) (times F (diff G))
```

For example

```
plus (times x x) (const 1) 2 ⇝* 5
diff (plus (times x x) (const 1)) 2 ⇝* 4
diff (plus (times x x) (const 1)) ⇝*
    plus (plus (times (const 1) x) (times x (const 1)))
         (const 0)
```

A "simplification" function with rules such as the following ones would be useful to improve the latter and necessary to compute non-trivial symbolic integration.

```
simpl (plus F (const 0)) = F
simpl (times F (const 1)) = F
...
```

Our approach eases understanding the appropriateness of this unusual programming style. Intuitively, both functions and constructors of the source program become (closure) constructors of the target program, hence function symbols in patterns of the source program need not be harmful. Indeed, higher-order programming is, loosely speaking, allowing a function f to be the argument of a function g. A rule of g has generally a variable, of functional type, to match or unify with f, but there is no reason preventing the use of the symbol f itself in the rule of g. Furthermore, since we do not allow fully applied functions in patterns, the use of functions in patterns does not compromise the confluence of the program, although the lack of confluence would not be an issue for our translation in any case.

7 Conclusion

We have presented a translation from source to target programs that allows us to perform higher-order narrowing computations with first-order narrowing strategies. This has several noteworthy advantages.

Our approach immediately provides sound, complete and efficient higher-order narrowing computations for large classes of systems for which no sound, complete and/or efficient higher-order narrowing strategies were known.

Our approach refines previous translation attempts by preserving in the target program type information of the source program. It is easy to verify that even in trivial examples this has a dramatic effect on the size of the narrowing space.

Our approach allows and justifies the presence of function symbols in the patterns of a rewrite rule. This feature extends the use of higher-order patterns, increases the expressive power of a language and simplifies metaprogramming tasks.

Acknowledgments

The authors are grateful to J. C. González Moreno and M. Hanus for discussions and suggestions on the topics of this paper.

References

1. S. Antoy. Optimal non-deterministic functional logic computations. In *Proc. of the 6th Int. Conference on Algebraic and Logic Programming (ALP'97)*, pages 16–30, Southampton, UK, Sept. 1997. Springer LNCS 1298.

2. S. Antoy, R. Echahed, and M. Hanus. Parallel evaluation strategies for functional logic languages. In *Proc. of the 14th Int. Conference on Logic Programming (ICLP'97)*, pages 138–152, Leuven, Belgium, July 1997. MIT Press.

3. J. M. Bell, F. Bellegarde, and J. Hook. Type-driven defunctionalization. In *Proc. 2nd International Conference on Functional Programming*, pages 25–37, June 1997.

4. Curry: An integrated functional logic language. M. Hanus (ed.), Draft Jan. 13, 1999.

5. J.C. González-Moreno. A correctness proof for Warren's HO into FO translation. In *Proc. GULP' 93*, pages 569–585, Gizzeria Lido, IT, Oct. 1993.

6. M. Hanus and C. Prehofer. Higher-order narrowing with definitional trees. In *Proc. 7th International Conference on Rewriting Techniques and Applications (RTA'96)*, pages 138–152. Springer LNCS 1103, 1996.

7. Michael Hanus. Polymorphic higher-order programming in prolog. In *Proc. 6th International Conference on Logic Programming*, pages 382–397. MIT Press, June 1989.

8. Michael Hanus. A functional and logic language with polymorphic types. In *Proc. International Symposium on Design and Implementation of Symbolic Computation Systems*, pages 215–224. Springer LNCS 429, 1990.

9. D. Miller. A logic programming language with lambda-abstraction, function variables, and simple unification. *Journal of Logic and Computation*, 1(4):497–536, 1991.

10. K. Nakahara, A. Middeldorp, and T. Ida. A complete narrowing calculus for higher-order functional logic programming. In *Proc. 7th International Symposium on Programming Languages, Implementations, Logics and Programs (PLILP'95)*, pages 97–114. Springer LNCS 982, 1995.

11. J. C. Reynolds. Definitional interpreters for higher-order programming languages. In *ACM National Conference*, pages 717–740. ACM, 1972.

12. A. Tolmach and D. Oliva. From ML to Ada: Strongly-typed language interoperability via source translation. *Journal of Functional Programming*, 8(4):367–412, July 1998.

13. D.H.D. Warren. Higher-order extensions to PROLOG: are they needed? In *Machine Intelligence 10*, pages 441–454, 1982.

14. *Proc. Workshop on Types in Compilation (TIC97)*, June 1997. Boston College Computer Science Technical Report BCCS-97-03.

15. *Proc. Second Workshop on Types in Compilation (TIC98)*. Springer LNCS 1473, March 1998.

A Semantics for Program Analysis in Narrowing-Based Functional Logic Languages

Michael Hanus[1]* and Salvador Lucas[2]**

[1] Informatik II, RWTH Aachen, D-52056 Aachen, Germany
hanus@informatik.rwth-aachen.de
[2] DSIC, UPV, Camino de Vera s/n, E-46022 Valencia, Spain.
slucas@dsic.upv.es

Abstract. We introduce a denotational characterization of narrowing, the computational engine of many functional logic languages. We use a functional domain for giving a denotation to the narrowing space associated to a given initial expression under an arbitrary narrowing strategy. Such a semantic description highlights (and favours) the operational notion of evaluation instead of the more usual model-theoretic notion of interpretation as the basis for the semantic description. The motivation is to obtain an abstract semantics which encodes information about the real operational framework used by a given (narrowing-based) functional logic language. Our aim is to provide a general, suitable, and accurate framework for the analysis of functional logic programs.

Keywords: domain theory, functional logic languages, narrowing, program analysis, semantics.

1 Introduction

The ability of reasoning about program properties is essential in software design, implementations, and program manipulation. Program analysis is the task of producing (usually approximated) information about a program without actually executing it. The analysis of functional logic programs is one of the most challenging problems in declarative programming. Many works have already addressed the analysis of certain run-time properties of programs (e.g., [3,11,13,15,23]). Nevertheless, most of these approaches have been done in a rather ad hoc setting, gearing the analysis towards the application on hand. Up to now, there is no general approach for formulating and analyzing arbitrary properties of functional logic programs in an arbitrary operational framework. In this paper we address this problem.

The key of our approach is domain theory [19,20] since it provides a junction between semantics (spaces of points = denotations of *computational processes*)

---

* Partially supported by the German Research Council (DFG) grant Ha 2457/1-1.
** Partially supported by EEC-HCM grant ERBCHRXCT940624, Spanish CICYT grant TIC 98-0445-C03-01, and Acción Integrada hispano–alemana HA1997-0073.

A. Middeldorp, T. Sato (Eds.): FLOPS'99, LNCS 1722, pp. 353–368, 1999.

and logics (lattices of properties of processes) [2,20,22]. The computational process we are interested in is evaluation. In a programming language, the notion of *evaluation* emphasizes the idea that there exists a distinguished set of syntactic elements (the values) which have a predefined mathematical interpretation [10]. The other syntactic elements take meaning from the program definitions *and* the operational framework for the program's execution. In this way, the evaluation process (under a given operational framework) maps general input expressions (having an *a priori* unknown meaning) to values. This point of view favours the operational notion of evaluation instead of the more usual model-theoretic notion of interpretation as the basis for the semantic description.

Since functional logic languages with a complete operational semantics are based on narrowing, we center our attention on it. The idea of using narrowing as an *evaluation mechanism* for integrated languages comes from Reddy's [18]: narrowing is the operational principle which computes the *non-ground value (ngv)* of an input expression. Given a domain D, a *ngv* is a *mapping* from valuations (on D) to values (in D). In moving valuations from being parameters of semantic functions (as usual in many approaches, e.g., [9,16]) to be components of a semantic domain, we understand narrowing as an *evaluation* mechanism which incorporates the instantiation of variables as a part of such evaluation mechanism. Since *ngv*'s are functional values, we use the domain-theoretic notion of *approximable mapping* [19,20] to give them a computable representation. We argue that this is a good starting point for expressing and managing *observable* properties of functional logic programs (along the lines of [2,22]). Moreover, it reveals that, within an integrated framework, there exist semantic connections between purely functional and logic properties of programs. Termination and groundness are examples of such related properties. On the other hand, thanks to including operational information into the semantic description, we are able to derive interesting optimizations for program execution.

Section 2 gives some preliminary definitions. Section 3 introduces a domain theoretic approach to pure rewriting and narrowing computations. Section 4 discusses a semantic-based analysis framework for functional logic languages. Section 5 contains our conclusions.

2 Preliminaries

In this section, we give some preliminary definitions (further details in [6,21]). Given sets A, B, B^A is the set of mappings from A to B and $\mathcal{P}(A)$ denotes the set of all subsets of A. An *order* $\sqsubseteq$ on a set A is a reflexive, transitive and antisymmetric relation. An element $\bot$ of an ordered set $(A, \sqsubseteq)$ is called a *least element* (or a *minimum*) if $\bot \sqsubseteq a$ for all $a \in A$. If such an element exists, then $(A, \sqsubseteq, \bot)$ is called a *pointed ordered set*. Given $S \subseteq A$, an element $a \in A$ is an *upper bound* of S if $x \sqsubseteq a$ for all $x \in S$. In this case we also say that S is a *consistent set*. An upper bound of S is a *least upper bound* (or *lub*, written $\bigsqcup S$) if, for all upper bounds b of S, we have $\bigsqcup S \sqsubseteq b$. A set $S \subseteq A$ is downward (upward) closed if whenever $a \in S$ and $b \sqsubseteq a$ ($a \sqsubseteq b$), we have that $b \in S$. If

$S = \{x, y\}$, we write $x \sqcup y$ instead of $\bigsqcup S$. A non-empty set $S \subseteq A$ is *directed* if, for all $a, b \in S$, there is an upper bound $c \in S$ of $\{a, b\}$. An ideal is a downward closed, directed set and $Id(A)$ is the set of ideals of an ordered set A. A pointed ordered set $(A, \sqsubseteq, \bot)$ is a *complete partial order* (*cpo*) if every directed set $S \subseteq A$ has a *lub* $\bigsqcup S \in A$. An element $a \in A$ of a *cpo* is called *compact* (or *finite*) if, whenever $S \subseteq A$ is a directed set and $a \sqsubseteq \bigsqcup S$, then there is $x \in S$ such that $a \sqsubseteq x$. The set of compact elements of a cpo A is denoted as $K(A)$. A cpo A is *algebraic* if for each $a \in A$, the set $\text{approx}(a) = \{x \in K(A) \mid x \sqsubseteq a\}$ is directed and $a = \bigsqcup \text{approx}(a)$. An algebraic cpo D is a *domain* if, whenever the set $\{x, y\} \subseteq K(D)$ is consistent, then $x \sqcup y$ exists in D. Given ordered sets $(A, \sqsubseteq_A)$, $(B, \sqsubseteq_B)$, a function $f : A \to B$ is monotonic if $\forall a, b \in A, a \sqsubseteq_A b \Rightarrow f(a) \sqsubseteq_B f(b)$; $f : A \to A$ is idempotent if $\forall a \in A, f(f(a)) = f(a)$.

By V we denote a countable set of *variables*; Σ denotes a *signature*, i.e., a set of *function symbols* $\{\mathbf{f}, \mathbf{g}, \ldots\}$, each with a fixed *arity* given by a function $ar : \Sigma \to \mathbb{N}$. We assume $\Sigma \cap V = \emptyset$. We denote by $\mathcal{T}(\Sigma, V)$ the set of (finite) terms built from symbols in the signature Σ and variables in V. A k-tuple $t_1, \ldots, t_k$ of terms is denoted as $\bar{t}$, where k will be clarified from the context. Given a term t, $Var(t)$ is the set of variable symbols in t. Sometimes, we consider a fresh constant $\bot$ and $\Sigma_\bot = \Sigma \cup \{\bot\}$. Terms from $\mathcal{T}(\Sigma_\bot, V)$ are ordered by the usual *approximation ordering* which is the least ordering $\sqsubseteq$ satisfying $\bot \sqsubseteq t$ for all t and $f(\bar{t}) \sqsubseteq f(\bar{s})$ if $\bar{t} \sqsubseteq \bar{s}$, i.e., $t_i \sqsubseteq s_i$ for all $1 \leq i \leq ar(f)$.

Terms are viewed as labeled trees in the usual way. *Positions* $p, q, \ldots$ are represented by chains of positive natural numbers used to address subterms of t. By Λ, we denote the empty chain. The set of positions of a term t is denoted by $\mathcal{P}os(t)$. A *linear term* is a term having no multiple occurrences of the same variable. The subterm of t at position p is denoted by $t|_p$. The set of positions of non-variable symbols in t is $\mathcal{P}os_\Sigma(t)$, and $\mathcal{P}os_V(t)$ is the set of variable positions. We denote by $t[s]_p$ the term t with the subterm at the position p replaced by s.

A *substitution* is a mapping $\sigma : V \to \mathcal{T}(\Sigma, V)$ which homomorphically extends to a mapping $\sigma : \mathcal{T}(\Sigma, V) \to \mathcal{T}(\Sigma, V)$. We denote by ε the "identity" substitution: $\varepsilon(x) = x$ for all $x \in V$. The set $Dom(\sigma) = \{x \in V \mid \sigma(x) \neq x\}$ is called the *domain* of σ and $Rng(\sigma) = \cup_{x \in Dom(\sigma)} Var(\sigma(x))$ its *range*. $\sigma_{|U}$ denotes the *restriction* of a substitution σ to a subset of variables $U \subseteq Dom(\sigma)$. We write $\sigma \leq \sigma'$ if there is θ such that $\sigma' = \theta \circ \sigma$. A *unifier* of two terms t_1, t_2 is a substitution σ with $\sigma(t_1) = \sigma(t_2)$. A *most general unifier* (*mgu*) of t_1, t_2 is a unifier σ with $\sigma \leq \sigma'$ for all other unifiers σ' of t_1, t_2.

A *rewrite rule* (labeled α) is an ordered pair (l, r), written $\alpha : l \to r$ (or just $l \to r$), with $l, r \in \mathcal{T}(\Sigma, V)$, $l \notin V$ and $Var(r) \subseteq Var(l)$. l and r are called *left-hand side* (*lhs*) and *right-hand side* (*rhs*) of the rule, respectively. A *term rewriting system* (*TRS*) is a pair $\mathcal{R} = (\Sigma, R)$ where R is a set of rewrite rules. A TRS (Σ, R) is *left-linear*, if for all $l \to r \in R$, l is a linear term. Given $\mathcal{R} = (\Sigma, R)$, we consider Σ as the disjoint union $\Sigma = \mathcal{C} \uplus \mathcal{F}$ of symbols $c \in \mathcal{C}$, called *constructors*, and symbols $f \in \mathcal{F}$, called *defined functions*, where $\mathcal{F} = \{f \mid f(\bar{l}) \to r \in R\}$ and $\mathcal{C} = \Sigma - \mathcal{F}$. A *constructor-based* TRS (*CB-TRS*) is a TRS with $l_1, \ldots, l_n \in \mathcal{T}(\mathcal{C}, V)$ for all rules $f(l_1, \ldots, l_n) \to r$.

For a given TRS $\mathcal{R} = (\Sigma, R)$, a term t *rewrites* to a term s (at position p), written $\overset{[p,\alpha]}{\rightarrow}_{\mathcal{R}}$ (or just $t \overset{p}{\rightarrow}_{\mathcal{R}} s$, $t \rightarrow_{\mathcal{R}} s$, or $t \rightarrow s$) if $t|_p = \sigma(l)$ and $s = t[\sigma(r)]_p$, for some rule $\alpha : l \rightarrow r \in R$, position $p \in \mathcal{P}os(t)$ and substitution σ. A term t is in *normal form* if there is no term s with $t \rightarrow_{\mathcal{R}} s$. A TRS $\mathcal{R}$ (or the rewrite relation $\rightarrow_{\mathcal{R}}$) is called *confluent* if for all terms t, t_1, t_2 with $t \rightarrow^*_{\mathcal{R}} t_1$ and $t \rightarrow^*_{\mathcal{R}} t_2$, there exists a term t_3 with $t_1 \rightarrow^*_{\mathcal{R}} t_3$ and $t_2 \rightarrow^*_{\mathcal{R}} t_3$. A term t *narrows* to a term s, written $t \leadsto_{[p,\alpha,\sigma]} s$ (or just $t \leadsto_\sigma s$), if there is $p \in \mathcal{P}os_\Sigma(t)$ and a variant (i.e., a renamed version) of a rule $\alpha : l \rightarrow r$ such that $t|_p$ and l unify with (idempotent) mgu σ, and $s = \sigma(t[r]_p)$. A narrowing derivation $t \leadsto^*_\sigma s$ is such that either $t = s$ and $\sigma = \varepsilon$ or $t \leadsto_{\sigma_0} t_1 \leadsto_{\sigma_1} \cdots t_{n-1} \leadsto_{\sigma_{n-1}} s$ and $\sigma = \sigma_{n-1} \circ \cdots \circ \sigma_1 \circ \sigma_0$. In order to show the progress of a narrowing derivation w.r.t. the computed answer and the evaluated goal, we also define the narrowing relation on substitution/term pairs by $\langle \sigma, t \rangle \leadsto \langle \sigma', s \rangle$ if $t \leadsto_\theta s$ and $\sigma' = \theta_{|Var(t)} \circ \sigma$ (i.e., we consider only the substitution of goal variables).

3   The Semantic Approach

A (first-order) program $\mathcal{P} = (\mathcal{R}, t)$ consists of a TRS $\mathcal{R}$ (which establishes the distinction between constructor and defined symbols of the program), and an initial expression t to be *fully* evaluated. We make t explicit since the differences between the purely functional and functional logic styles arise in the different status of the variables occurring in the initial expression: in functional programming, those variables are not allowed (or they are considered as constants and cannot be instantiated). Functional logic languages deal with expressions having *logic* variables and narrowing provides for the necessary instantiations.

We characterize the information which is *currently* couched by a term by means of a mapping $(\!|\ |\!)$ from terms to (partial) values (remind that values are expected to be especial syntactic objects). We call $(\!|\ |\!)$ an *observation* mapping. The adequacy of a given mapping $(\!|\ |\!)$ for observing computations performed by a given operational mechanism should be ensured by showing that $(\!|\ |\!)$ is a homomorphism between the relation among syntactic objects induced by the operational mechanism and the approximation ordering on values. This means that the operational mechanism refines the meaning of an expression as the computation continues.

As a preliminary, simple example, consider pure rewriting computations: The syntactic objects are terms $t \in T(\Sigma_\perp, V)$ and the values are taken from $(\mathcal{T}^\infty(\mathcal{C}_\perp), \sqsubseteq, \perp)$, the domain of infinite, ground constructor (partial) terms[1]. $(\mathcal{T}^\infty(\mathcal{C}_\perp, V), \sqsubseteq, \perp)$ is the domain $(\mathcal{T}^\infty(\mathcal{C}_\perp \cup V), \sqsubseteq, \perp)$, where $\forall x \in V, ar(x) = 0$. For functional computations, we use $(\!|\ |\!)_F : T(\Sigma_\perp, V) \rightarrow T(\mathcal{C}_\perp, V)$ given by

$$(\!|x|\!)_F = x \qquad\qquad (\!|\perp|\!)_F = \perp$$
$$(\!|c(\vec{t})|\!)_F = c((\!|\vec{t}|\!)_F) \quad \text{if } c \in \mathcal{C} \qquad (\!|f(\vec{t})|\!)_F = \perp \quad \text{if } f \in \mathcal{F}$$

---

[1] Formally, $(\mathcal{T}^\infty(\mathcal{C}_\perp), \sqsubseteq, \perp)$ is obtained from $T(\mathcal{C}_\perp)$, which is not even a cpo, as (isomorphic to) its ideal completion $(Id(T(\mathcal{C}_\perp)), \subseteq, \{\perp\})$ (see [21]).

Proposition 1 (Reduction increases information). *Let $\mathcal{R}$ be a TRS and $t, s \in T(\Sigma_\perp, V)$. If $t \rightarrow^* s$, then $(\!(t)\!)_F \sqsubseteq (\!(s)\!)_F$.*

The function $Rew : T(\Sigma_\perp, V) \rightarrow \mathcal{P}(T(\mathcal{C}_\perp, V))$ gives a representation $Rew(t) = \{(\!(s)\!)_F \mid t \rightarrow^* s\}$ of the rewriting space of a given term t.

Proposition 2. *Let $\mathcal{R}$ be a confluent TRS. For all $t \in T(\Sigma_\perp, V)$, $Rew(t)$ is a directed set.*

The semantic function $CRew^\infty : T(\Sigma_\perp, V) \rightarrow T^\infty(\mathcal{C}_\perp, V)$ gives the meaning of a term under evaluation by rewriting: $CRew^\infty(t) = \bigsqcup Rew(t)$. Thus, $CRew^\infty(t)$ is the most defined (possibly infinite) value which can be obtained (or approximated) by issuing rewritings from t. Note that the use of infinite terms in the codomain of $CRew^\infty$ is necessary for dealing with non-terminating programs.

3.1   Narrowing as the Evaluation Mechanism

In the context of a program, a term t with variables denotes a continuous function $t_D \in [D^V \rightarrow D]$ which yields the evaluation of t under each possible valuation[2] $\phi \in D^V$ of its variables on a domain D. This is called a *non-ground value (ngv)* in [18] and a *derived operator* in [8].

Given domains D and E, the set $[D \rightarrow E]$ of (strict) continuous functions from D to E (pointwise) ordered by $f \sqsubseteq g$ iff $\forall x \in V$, $f(x) \sqsubseteq g(x)$, is a domain [10,21]. For proving that $[D^V \rightarrow D]$ is a domain whenever D is, assume that V contains a distinguished (unused) variable $\perp$. Thus, V supplied by the least ordering $\sqsubseteq$ such that $\perp \sqsubseteq x$ and $x \sqsubseteq x$ for all $x \in V$ is a domain. The set $D^{V-\{\perp\}}$ of arbitrary valuations from $V - \{\perp\}$ to D is isomorphic to the domain $[V \rightarrow_\perp D]$ of continuous, strict valuations. We assume this fact from now on by removing $\perp$ from V and considering that D^V is a domain. Therefore, $[D^V \rightarrow D]$ is a domain and, in particular, $[T^\infty(\mathcal{C}_\perp)^V \rightarrow T^\infty(\mathcal{C}_\perp)]$ also is.

Our syntactic objects, now, are substitution/term pairs $\langle \sigma, t \rangle$. We could naïvely extend $(\!(\ )\!)_F$ to deal with those pairs: $(\!(\langle \sigma, s \rangle)\!)_F = \langle (\!(\sigma)\!)_F, (\!(s)\!)_F \rangle$ where $(\!(\sigma)\!)_F$ is a substitution given by $(\!(\sigma)\!)_F(x) = (\!(\sigma(x))\!)_F$ for all $x \in V$. Unfortunately, the semantic progress of a narrowing evaluation might not be captured by the computational ordering $\sqsubseteq$ (extended by $(\phi, \delta) \sqsubseteq (\phi', \delta')$ iff $\forall x \in V.\phi(x) \sqsubseteq \phi'(x)$ and $\delta \sqsubseteq \delta'$) and such an extension of $(\!(\ )\!)_F$.

Example 1. Consider the TRS

```
0+x      → x                0   ≤ x     → true
s(x)+y → s(x+y)            s(x) ≤ s(y) → x ≤ y
```

and the narrowing step $\langle \varepsilon, [\mathtt{x,x+y}] \rangle \rightsquigarrow \langle \{\mathtt{x}\mapsto\mathtt{0}\}, [\mathtt{0,y}] \rangle$ ($[\cdot,\cdot]$ denotes a 2-element list). We have $(\!(\langle \varepsilon, [\mathtt{x,x+y}] \rangle)\!)_F = \langle \varepsilon, [\mathtt{x},\perp] \rangle$ and $(\!(\langle \{\mathtt{x}\mapsto\mathtt{0}\}, [\mathtt{0,y}] \rangle)\!)_F = \langle \{\mathtt{x}\mapsto\mathtt{0}\}, [\mathtt{0,y}] \rangle$. Therefore, we do not get the desired increasing computation, because $\varepsilon \not\sqsubseteq \{\mathtt{x}\mapsto\mathtt{0}\}$ and $[\mathtt{x},\perp] \not\sqsubseteq [\mathtt{0,y}]$.

---

[2] By abuse, we say that the 'domain' of a valuation $\phi \in D^V$ is $Dom(\phi) = \{x \in V \mid \phi(x) \neq \perp\}$.

The problem is that narrowing introduces a new computational mechanism for increasing the information associated to a given term, i.e., instantiation of *logic* variables. Thus, we introduce the observation mapping $(\!| \ |\!)_{FL} : \mathcal{T}(\Sigma_\perp, V) \to \mathcal{T}(\mathcal{C}_\perp)$ which interprets uninstantiated variables as least defined elements:

$$(\!|x|\!)_{FL} = \perp \qquad\qquad (\!|\perp|\!)_{FL} = \perp$$
$$(\!|c(\bar{t})|\!)_{FL} = c((\!|\bar{t}|\!)_{FL}) \quad \text{if } c \in \mathcal{C} \qquad (\!|f(\bar{t})|\!)_{FL} = \perp \quad \text{if } f \in \mathcal{F}$$

Note that $(\!|t|\!)_{FL} = \perp_{Subst}((\!|t|\!)_F)$ and $(\!|\sigma|\!)_{FL} = \perp_{Subst} \circ (\!|\sigma|\!)_F$.

Example 2. Now, $(\!|\langle \varepsilon, [\mathtt{x}, \mathtt{x+y}] \rangle|\!)_{FL} = \langle \perp_{Subst}, [\perp, \perp] \rangle \sqsubseteq \langle \{\mathtt{x} \mapsto 0\}, [0, \perp] \rangle = (\!|\langle \{\mathtt{x} \mapsto 0\}, [0, \mathtt{y}] \rangle|\!)_{FL}$, i.e., $(\!| \ |\!)_{FL}$ satisfies the desired property.

Narrowing computations are compatible with the new observation mapping.

Proposition 3. *Let $\mathcal{R}$ be a TRS. If $\langle \sigma, t \rangle \leadsto^* \langle \sigma', s \rangle$, then $(\!|\langle \sigma, t \rangle|\!)_{FL} \sqsubseteq (\!|\langle \sigma', s \rangle|\!)_{FL}$.*

3.2   The Narrowing Space as an Approximable Mapping

Analogously to $Rew(t)$, we can build a semantic description $Narr(t)$ of the narrowing evaluation of t. Nevertheless, since $Narr(t)$ is intended to be a representation of a *ngv*, i.e., a *functional* value, we need to use the corresponding standard Scott's construction of *approximable mappings* [20,21].

A *precusl* is a structure $P = (P, \sqsubseteq, \sqcup, \perp)$ where $\sqsubseteq$ is a preorder, $\perp$ is a distinguished minimal element, and $\sqcup$ is a partial binary operation on P such that, for all $a, b \in P$, $a \sqcup b$ is defined if and only if $\{a, b\}$ is consistent in P and then $a \sqcup b$ is a (distinguished) supremum of a and b [21]. Approximable mappings allow us to represent arbitrary continuous mappings between domains on the representations of those domains (their compact elements) as relations between approximations of a given argument and approximations of its value at that argument [21].

Definition 1. [21] *Let $P = (P, \sqsubseteq, \sqcup, \perp), P' = (P', \sqsubseteq', \sqcup', \perp')$ be precusl's. A relation $f \subseteq P \times P'$ is an approximable mapping from P to P' if*

1. $\perp f \perp'$.
2. $a \ f \ b$ and $a \ f \ b'$ imply $a \ f \ (b \sqcup b')$.
3. $a \ f \ b$, $a \sqsubseteq a'$, and $b' \sqsubseteq' b$ imply $a' \ f \ b'$.

The ideal completion $(Id(P), \subseteq, \{\perp\})$ of a precusl is a domain (see [21]). An approximable mapping defines a continuous function between $Id(P)$ and $Id(P')$: $\overline{f} : Id(P) \to Id(P')$ is given by $\overline{f}(I) = \{b \in P' \mid \exists a \in I \text{ with } a \ f \ b\}$.

Proposition 4. *Let $P = (P, \sqsubseteq, \sqcup, \perp), P' = (P', \sqsubseteq', \sqcup', \perp')$ be precusl's, and $f, f' \subseteq P \times P'$ be approximable mappings from P to P'. If $f \subseteq f'$, then $\overline{f} \sqsubseteq \overline{f'}$.*

Given a term t, $NDeriv(t)$ is the set of narrowing derivations issued from t. We associate an approximable mapping $Narr^A(t)$ to a given narrowing derivation $A \in NDeriv(t)$.

Definition 2. *Given a term $t \in T(\Sigma_\perp, V)$ and a narrowing derivation*

$$A : \langle \varepsilon, t \rangle = \langle \sigma_0, t_0 \rangle \leadsto \langle \sigma_1, t_1 \rangle \leadsto \cdots \leadsto \langle \sigma_{n-1}, t_{n-1} \rangle \leadsto \langle \sigma_n, t_n \rangle$$

we define $Narr^A(t) = \cup_{0 \le i \le n} Narr_i^A(t)$ where:

$$Narr_i^A(t) = \{\langle \varsigma, \delta \rangle \mid \exists \phi \in T(C_\perp)^V . (\!| \phi \circ \sigma_i |\!)_{FL} \sqsubseteq \varsigma \wedge \delta \sqsubseteq (\!| \phi(t_i) |\!)_{FL}\}$$

Proposition 5. *Let $\mathcal{R}$ be a TRS, t be a term, and A be a narrowing derivation starting from t. Then, $Narr^A(t)$ is an approximable mapping.*

Definition 3. *Given a term $t \in T(\Sigma_\perp, V)$, we define the relation $Narr(t) \subseteq T(C_\perp)^V \times T(C_\perp)$ to be $Narr(t) = \bigcup_{A \in NDeriv(t)} Narr^A(t)$.*

Unfortunately, these semantic definitions are not consistent w.r.t. rewriting.

Example 3. Consider the TRS

```
f(f(x))  → a
c        → b
```

and $A : \langle \varepsilon, t \rangle = \langle \varepsilon, f(x) \rangle \leadsto \langle \{x \mapsto f(x')\}, a \rangle$. If $m = Narr^A(t)$, then $\{x \mapsto a\}\ m\ a$ (we take $\phi = \perp_{Subst}$, $\sigma = \{x \mapsto f(x')\}$ in Definition 2; hence, $(\!| \phi \circ \sigma |\!)_{FL} = \perp_{Subst} \sqsubseteq \{x \mapsto a\} = \varsigma$). Thus, $\overline{Narr^A(t)}(\{x \mapsto a\}) = a$. However, $\{x \mapsto a\}(t) = f(a) \not\rightarrow^* a$.

The problem here is that $(\!|\ |\!)_{FL}$ identifies (as $\perp$) parts of the bindings $\sigma(x)$ of a computed substitution σ which can be semantically refined by instantiation (of the variables in $\sigma(x)$) and other which cannot be further refined by instantiation (the operation-rooted subterms in $\sigma(x)$). If we deal with left-linear CB-TRS's and choose (idempotent) *mgu*'s as unifiers for the narrowing process, the substitutions which we deal with are *linear* constructor substitutions, i.e., for all narrowing derivations $\langle \varepsilon, t \rangle \leadsto^* \langle \sigma, s \rangle$ and all $x \in V$, $\sigma(x)$ is a constructor term and $\{\sigma(x) \mid x \in Dom(\sigma)\}$ is a linear set of terms (i.e., no variable appears twice within them). Hence, the substitutions computed by narrowing have *no* partial information apart from the variable occurrences. In this case, $(\!|\sigma|\!)_F = \sigma$, $(\!|\sigma|\!)_{FL} = \perp_{Subst} \circ (\!|\sigma|\!)_F = \perp_{Subst} \circ \sigma$, and we have the following result.

Proposition 6. *Let σ be a linear constructor substitution and $\phi, \varsigma \in T(C_\perp)^V$. If $\phi \circ \sigma \sqsubseteq \varsigma$, then there exists $\phi' \in T(C_\perp)^V$ such that $\phi \sqsubseteq \phi'$ and $\phi' \circ \sigma = \varsigma$.*

Thus, we obtain a simpler, more readable expression for the approximable mapping which is associated to a given left-linear CB-TRS by noting that

$$Narr_i^A(t) = \{\langle \varsigma, \delta \rangle \mid \exists \phi \in T(C_\perp)^V . (\!| \phi \circ \sigma_i |\!)_{FL} \sqsubseteq \varsigma \wedge \delta \sqsubseteq (\!| \phi(t_i) |\!)_{FL}\}$$
$$= \{\langle \varsigma, \delta \rangle \mid \exists \phi \in T(C_\perp)^V . \phi \circ \sigma_i = \varsigma \wedge \delta \sqsubseteq (\!| \phi(t_i) |\!)_{FL}\}$$

The union of approximable mappings (considered as binary relations) need not to be an approximable mapping. Nevertheless, we have the following result.

Proposition 7. *Let $\mathcal{R}$ be a left-linear, confluent CB-TRS and t be a term. Then $Narr(t)$ is an approximable mapping.*

We define the semantic function $CNarr^\infty : \mathcal{T}(\Sigma_\perp, V) \to [\mathcal{T}^\infty(\mathcal{C}_\perp)^V \to \mathcal{T}^\infty(\mathcal{C}_\perp)]$ as follows: $CNarr^\infty(t) = \overline{Narr(t)}$, i.e., $CNarr^\infty(t)$ is the continuous mapping associated to the approximable mapping $Narr(t)$ which represents the narrowing derivations starting from t. This semantics is consistent w.r.t. rewriting.

Theorem 1. *Let $\mathcal{R}$ be a left-linear, confluent CB-TRS. For all $t \in \mathcal{T}(\Sigma_\perp, V)$, $\phi \in \mathcal{T}(\mathcal{C}_\perp)^V$, $CNarr^\infty(t)\,\phi = CRew^\infty(\phi(t))$.*

Narrowing strategies. A narrowing strategy $\mathcal{N}$ is a restriction on the set of possible narrowing steps. Given a narrowing strategy $\mathcal{N}$ and a term t, we can consider the set $NDeriv_\mathcal{N}(t) \subseteq NDeriv(t)$ of derivations which start from t and conform to $\mathcal{N}$. By Proposition 5, each $A \in NDeriv_\mathcal{N}(t)$ defines an approximable mapping $Narr^A(t)$ which is obviously contained in $Narr(t)$. By Proposition 4, $\overline{Narr^A(t)} \sqsubseteq \overline{Narr(t)} = CNarr^\infty(t)$. Therefore, $\{\overline{Narr^A(t)} \mid A \in NDeriv_\mathcal{N}(t)\}$ is bounded by $CNarr^\infty(t)$. Since $[\mathcal{T}^\infty(\mathcal{C}_\perp)^V \to \mathcal{T}^\infty(\mathcal{C}_\perp)]$ is a domain, it is consistently complete, i.e., the *lub* of every bounded subset actually exists (Theorem 3.1.10 in [21]). Thus, for left-linear CB-TRSs, we fix

$$CNarr_\mathcal{N}^\infty(t) = \bigsqcup \{\overline{Narr^A(t)} \mid A \in NDeriv_\mathcal{N}(t)\}$$

to be the meaning of t when it is evaluated under the narrowing strategy $\mathcal{N}$. Clearly, for all narrowing strategies $\mathcal{N}$, $CNarr_\mathcal{N}^\infty \sqsubseteq CNarr^\infty$. Thus, $CNarr^\infty$ provides a semantic reference for narrowing strategies. Strategies that satisfy $CNarr_\mathcal{N}^\infty = CNarr^\infty$ can be thought of as correct strategies.

Remark 1. Narrowing is able to yield *the graph* of a function f by computing $CNarr^\infty(f(\overline{x}))$, where $x_1, \dots, x_{ar(f)}$ are different variables. This gives an interesting perspective of narrowing as an operational mechanism which computes denotations of *functions* as a whole, rather than only values of particular function calls. A similar observation can be made for narrowing strategies.

3.3   Computational Interpretation of the Semantic Descriptions

Our semantic descriptions are intended to provide a clear computational interpretation of the semantic information. This is essential for defining accurate analyses by using the semantic description.

Proposition 8. *Let $\mathcal{R}$ be a confluent TRS, $t \in \mathcal{T}(\Sigma_\perp, V)$, and $\delta = CRew^\infty(t)$. If $\delta \in \mathcal{T}(\mathcal{C}, V)$, then $t \to^* \delta$.*

Concerning narrowing computations, we have the following result.

Proposition 9. *Let $\mathcal{R}$ be a left-linear, confluent CB-TRS. Let t be a term, $\varsigma \in \mathcal{T}(\mathcal{C}_\perp)^V$, $m = CNarr^\infty(t)$, and $\delta = m(\varsigma)$.*

1. *If $\delta \in T(\mathcal{C}_\perp)$, there exists a narrowing derivation $\langle \varepsilon, t \rangle \rightsquigarrow^* \langle \sigma, s \rangle$ such that $\phi \circ \sigma = \varsigma$ and $\delta = (\!|\phi(s)|\!)_{FL}$.*

2. *For every narrowing derivation $\langle \varepsilon, t \rangle \rightsquigarrow^* \langle \sigma, s \rangle$ such that $\phi \circ \sigma = \varsigma$, it is $(\!|\phi(s)|\!)_{FL} \sqsubseteq \delta$.*

3. *If $\delta \in T(\mathcal{C})$, then there exists a narrowing derivation $\langle \varepsilon, t \rangle \rightsquigarrow^* \langle \sigma, s \rangle$ such that $s \in T(\mathcal{C}, V)$, $\phi \circ \sigma = \varsigma$, and $\delta = \phi(s)$.*

We are able to refine the computational information couched by the narrowing semantics by introducing a small modification on it.

Definition 4. *Given a term $t \in T(\Sigma_\perp, V)$, and a narrowing derivation*

$$A : \langle \varepsilon, t \rangle = \langle \sigma_0, t_0 \rangle \rightsquigarrow \langle \sigma_1, t_1 \rangle \rightsquigarrow \cdots \rightsquigarrow \langle \sigma_{n-1}, t_{n-1} \rangle \rightsquigarrow \langle \sigma_n, t_n \rangle$$

we define $BNarr^A(t) = \cup_{0 \leq i \leq n} BNarr_i^A(t)$ where:

$$BNarr_i^A(t) = \{\langle \varsigma, \delta \rangle \mid (\!|\sigma_i|\!)_{FL} \sqsubseteq \varsigma \wedge \delta \sqsubseteq (\!|t_i|\!)_{FL}\}$$

Proposition 10. *Let $\mathcal{R}$ be a TRS, t be a term and A be a narrowing derivation starting from t. Then $BNarr^A(t)$ is an approximable mapping.*

If we define $BNarr(t) = \bigcup_{A \in NDeriv(t)} BNarr^A(t)$, we have the following result.

Proposition 11. *Let $\mathcal{R}$ be a left-linear, confluent CB-TRS and t be a term. Then $BNarr(t)$ is an approximable mapping.*

The basic description $BNarr^\infty(t) = \overline{BNarr(t)}$ is closer to the computational mechanism of narrowing. The following proposition formalizes this claim.

Proposition 12. *Let $\mathcal{R}$ be a left-linear, confluent CB-TRS, t be a term, $\varsigma \in T(\mathcal{C}_\perp)^V$, $m = BNarr^\infty(t)$, and $\delta = m(\varsigma)$.*

1. *If $\delta \in T(\mathcal{C}_\perp)$, there exists a narrowing derivation $\langle \varepsilon, t \rangle \rightsquigarrow^* \langle \sigma, s \rangle$ such that $\phi \circ \sigma = \varsigma$ and $\delta = (\!|s|\!)_{FL}$.*

2. *For every narrowing derivation $\langle \varepsilon, t \rangle \rightsquigarrow^* \langle \sigma, s \rangle$ such that $(\!|\sigma|\!)_{FL} \sqsubseteq \varsigma$, it is $(\!|s|\!)_{FL} \sqsubseteq \delta$.*

Proposition 13. *Let $\mathcal{R}$ be a left-linear, confluent CB-TRS, t be a term, and $m = BNarr^\infty(t)$. If $\langle \varepsilon, t \rangle \rightsquigarrow^* \langle \sigma, \delta \rangle$ and $\delta \in T(\mathcal{C})$, then $m((\!|\sigma|\!)_{FL}) = \delta$.*

Since each $BNarr_i^A(t)$ is a special case of $Narr_i^A(t)$, by Proposition 11 and Proposition 4, $BNarr^\infty(t) \sqsubseteq CNarr^\infty(t)$.

4   A Semantics-Based Analysis Framework

Domain theory provides a framework for formulating properties of programs and discussing about them [2,20]: A property π of a program $\mathcal{P}$ whose denotation $[\![\mathcal{P}]\!]$ is taken from a domain D (i.e., $[\![\mathcal{P}]\!] \in D$) can be identified with a predicate $\pi : D \to \mathbf{2}$, where $\mathbf{2}$ is the two point domain $\mathbf{2} = \{\bot, \top\}$ ordered by $\bot \sqsubseteq \top$ (where $\bot$ can be thought of as false and $\top$ as true). A program $\mathcal{P}$ satisfies π if $\pi([\![\mathcal{P}]\!]) = \top$ (alternatively, if $[\![\mathcal{P}]\!] \in \pi^{-1}(\top)$). As usual in domain theory, we require continuity of π for achieving computability (or *observability*, see [22]). The set $[D \to \mathbf{2}]$ of observable properties is (isomorphic to) the family of open sets of the *Scott's topology* associated to D [2]. A *topology* is a pair (X, τ) where X is a set and $\tau \subseteq \mathcal{P}(X)$ is a family of subsets of X (called the *open* sets) such that [21]: $X, \emptyset \in \tau$; if $U, V \in \tau$, then $U \cap V \in \tau$; and if $U_i \in \tau$ for $i \in I$, then $\bigcup_{i \in I} U_i \in \tau$. The Scott's topology associated to a domain D is given by the set of upward closed subsets $U \subseteq D$ such that, whenever $A \subseteq D$ is directed and $\bigsqcup A \in U$, then $\exists x \in A.x \in U$ [21].

The family τ of open sets of a given topology (X, τ) ordered by inclusion is a *complete lattice*. The top element of the lattice is X. Note that, when considering the Scott's topology (D, τ_D) of a domain D, the open set D denotes a trivial property which every program satisfies; $\emptyset$, the least element of lattice τ_D, denotes the 'impossible' property, which no program satisfies.

4.1   Analysis of Functional Logic Programs

A program analysis consists in the definition of a continuous function $\alpha : D \to A$ between topologic spaces (D, τ_D) and (A, τ_A) which expresses concrete and abstract properties, respectively. By the topological definition of continuity, each open set $V \in \tau_A$ maps to an open set $U \in \tau_D$ via α^{-1}, i.e., $\alpha^{-1} : \tau_A \to \tau_D$ is a mapping from abstract properties (open sets of τ_A) to concrete properties (open sets of τ_D). It is easy to see that $(D, \{\alpha^{-1}(V) \mid V \in \tau_A\})$ is a subtopology of D (i.e., $\{\alpha^{-1}(V) \mid V \in \tau_A\} \subseteq \tau_D$). Therefore, each analysis distinguishes a subset of properties of D which is itself a topology. For instance, the Scott's topology of $\mathbf{2}$ is given by $\tau_{\mathbf{2}} = \{\emptyset, \{\top\}, \mathbf{2}\}$. Such a topology permits to express only one non-trivial property, namely, the one which corresponds to the open set $\{\top\}$.

In functional logic languages, the semantic domain under observation is $[D^V \to D]$. Observable properties of functional logic programs are open sets of its Scott's topology. Approximations to such properties can be obtained by abstracting $[D^V \to D]$ into a suitable abstract domain (see below).

Every continuous function $f : D \to E$ maps observable properties of the codomain E into observable properties of D (by $f^{-1} : \tau_E \to \tau_D$). In particular, elements of $[D^V \to D]$, i.e., denotations of functional logic programs, map properties of D (we call them 'functional' properties) into properties of D^V ('logic' properties). This provides an additional, interesting analytic perspective: By rephrasing Dybjer [7], we can computationally interpret this correspondence as establishing the extent that a 'logic property' (concerning valuations) needs to be ensured to guarantee a property of its functional part (computed value). There is a simple way to obtain an abstraction of the logic part D^V of $[D^V \to D]$ from an abstraction of its functional part D.

Definition 5. *Let D, V, A be sets. Let $\alpha_F : D \to A$ be a mapping. Then, $\alpha_L : D^V \to A^V$ given by $\alpha_L(\phi) = \alpha_F \circ \phi$, for all $\phi \in D^V$, is called the logic abstraction induced by α_F.*

If $\alpha_F : D \to A$ is strict (surjective, continuous), then α_L is strict (surjective, continuous). Whenever α_F is a *continuous* mapping from a domain D to **2**, α_F expresses, in fact, a single observable property $\alpha^{-1}(\{\top\})$ of D. We can thought of α_F as a *functional* property. Thus, Definition 5 associates an abstraction α_L of D^V to a given property identified by α_F. Thus, each functional property induces a related *set* of logic properties which is a *subtopology* of τ_{D^V}. In Section 4.3 we show that groundness (a logic property), is induced by the functional property of termination.

4.2   Approximation of Functions

Abstractions $\alpha_D : D \to A$ and $\alpha_E : E \to B$ (A and B being algebraic lattices), induce *safety* and *liveness* abstractions $\alpha^S_{D \to E}, \alpha^L_{D \to E} : (D \to E) \to (A \to B)$, of continuous mappings by [1]

$$\alpha^S_{D \to E}(f)(d) = \sqcup\{(\alpha_E \circ f)(d') \mid \alpha_D(d') \sqsubseteq d\}, \text{ and}$$
$$\alpha^L_{D \to E}(f)(d) = \sqcap\{(\alpha_E \circ f)(d') \mid \alpha_D(d') \sqsupseteq d\}$$

where the following correctness result holds:

Theorem 2 (The semi-homomorphism property [1]). *Let $f : D \to E$, $f^S = \alpha^S_{D \to E}(f)$, and $f^L = \alpha^L_{D \to E}(f)$. Then, $f^L \circ \alpha_D \sqsubseteq \alpha_E \circ f \sqsubseteq f^S \circ \alpha_D$.*

Consider an abstraction $\alpha_E : E \to \mathbf{2}$ which can be thought of as a *property* of elements of the codomain E of $f : D \to E$. For analytic purposes, the correctness condition $f^S \circ \alpha_D \sqsupseteq \alpha_E \circ f$ ensures that, for all $x \in D$, whenever the abstract computation $f^S(\alpha_D(x))$ yields $\perp$, the concrete computation $f(x)$ does *not* satisfy the property α_E, i.e., $\alpha_E(f(x)) = \perp$. On the other hand, the correctness condition $f^L \circ \alpha_D \sqsubseteq \alpha_E \circ f$ ensures that, whenever $f^L(\alpha_D(x))$ yields $\top$, the concrete computation $f(x)$ actually satisfies α_E, i.e., $\alpha_E(f(x)) = \top$. We use this computational interpretation later.

4.3   Termination Analysis and Groundness Analysis

The functional structure of the semantic domain of *ngv*'s reveals connections between apparently unrelated analyses. Consider $h_t : \mathcal{T}^\infty(\mathcal{C}_\perp) \to \mathbf{2}$ defined by

$$h_t(\delta) = \begin{cases} \top \text{ if } \delta \in \mathcal{T}(\mathcal{C}) \\ \perp \text{ otherwise} \end{cases}$$

and let $h_g : \mathcal{T}^\infty(\mathcal{C}_\perp)^V \to \mathbf{2}^V$ be the logic abstraction induced by h_t. Note that both h_t and h_g are strict and continuous. Abstractions h_t and h_g express the observable properties of termination and groundness, respectively: Recall that the only nontrivial open set of the Scott's topology of $\mathbf{2}$ is $\{\top\}$. By continuity of h_t, $h_t^{-1}(\{\top\})$ is the (open) set of finite, totally defined values which actually corresponds to terminating successful evaluations[3]. On the other hand, each open set of $\mathbf{2}^V$ is (isomorphic to) an upward closed collection of sets of variables ordered by inclusion. In this case, $h_g^{-1}(F)$ for a given open set F is a set of substitutions whose bindings for variables belonging to $X \in F$ are ground. This formally relates groundness and termination: groundness is the 'logic' property which corresponds to the 'functional' property of termination. In fact, $\mathbf{2}^V$ is the standard abstract domain for *groundness* analysis in logic programming.

4.4 Using Semantic Information for Improving the Evaluation

Groundness information can be used to improve the narrowing evaluation of a term $t = C[t_1, \dots, t_n]$: if we know that every successful evaluation of t_i grounds the variables of t_j, for some $1 \leq i, j \leq n$, $i \neq j$, then it is sensible to evaluate t by first narrowing t_i (up to a value) and next evaluating t'_j (i.e., t_j after instantiating its variables using the bindings created by the evaluation of t_i) by *rewriting* because, after evaluating t_i, we know that t'_j is ground and we do not need to provide code for unification, instantiation of other variables, etc.

Example 4. Consider the following TRS:

```
0+x        → x            if(true,x,y)  → x
s(x)+y     → s(x+y)       if(false,x,y) → y


even(0)     → true        even(s(s(x))) → even(x)
even(s(0))  → false
```

For an initial (conditional) expression "if even(x) then x+x else s(x+x)" (we use the more familiar notation if then else for if expressions), it is clear that x becomes ground after every successful narrowing evaluation of the condition even(x). Thus, we can evaluate x+x by rewriting instead of narrowing.

Additionally, we need to ensure that the evaluation of t_i is safe under the context C (i.e., that failing evaluations of t_i do not prevent the evaluation of t). Eventually, we should also ensure that the complete evaluation of t'_j is safe. Strictness information can be helpful here: if the (normalizing) narrowing strategy is not able to obtain any value, this means that the whole expression does not have a value. However, we should only use non-contextual strictness analyses (like Mycroft's [17] is). In this way, we ensure that the strict character of an argument is not altered after a possible instantiation of its surrounding context.

---

[3] h_t and Mycroft's abstraction: $halt(d) = \begin{cases} \top \text{ if } d \neq \bot \\ \bot \text{ if } d = \bot \end{cases}$ for termination analysis [17] are similar. However, *halt* only expresses termination if C only contains constant symbols. It is easy to see that, in this case, $h_t = halt$.

In order to ensure that *every* successful narrowing derivation grounds a given variable $x \in Var(t)$, we use the safety abstraction $m^S \in 2^V \to 2$ of $m = BNarr^\infty(t)$ (based on h_t and h_g).

Example 5. (Continuing Example 4) For $t = \texttt{even(x)}$, we have:

$$BNarr^\infty(t) = \{\ \{\texttt{x} \mapsto \perp\} \mapsto \perp, \qquad \{\texttt{x} \mapsto \texttt{0}\} \mapsto \texttt{true},$$
$$\{\texttt{x} \mapsto \texttt{s}(\perp)\} \mapsto \perp, \qquad \{\texttt{x} \mapsto \texttt{s(0)}\} \mapsto \texttt{false},$$
$$\{\texttt{x} \mapsto \texttt{s}(\texttt{s}(\perp))\} \mapsto \perp, \quad \{\texttt{x} \mapsto \texttt{s(s(0))}\} \mapsto \texttt{true}, \ldots\}$$

In general, if we can prove that, for all abstract substitutions $\phi^\# \in 2^V$ with $\phi^\#(x) = \perp$, it is $m^S(\phi^\#) = \perp$, then we can ensure that x is grounded in every successful derivation from t. To see this point, consider a successful derivation $\langle \varepsilon, t \rangle \rightsquigarrow^* \langle \sigma, \delta \rangle$ such that $\delta \in \mathcal{T}(\mathcal{C})$ and $\sigma(x) \notin \mathcal{T}(\mathcal{C})$, i.e., x is not grounded. By Proposition 13, $m(\langle\!| \sigma |\!\rangle_{FL}) = \delta$. By definition of m^S, $m^S(h_g(\langle\!| \sigma |\!\rangle_{FL})) = \top$. Since $\langle\!| \sigma |\!\rangle_{FL}(x) \notin \mathcal{T}(\mathcal{C})$, we have $h_g(\langle\!| \sigma |\!\rangle_{FL})(x) = h_t(\langle\!| \sigma |\!\rangle_{FL}(x)) = \perp$, thus contradicting (a case of) our initial assumption, $m^S(h_g(\langle\!| \sigma |\!\rangle_{FL})) = \perp$.

Example 6. (Continuing Example 5) For $t = \texttt{even(x)}$, we have $m^S = \{\{x \mapsto \perp\} \mapsto \perp, \{x \mapsto \top\} \mapsto \top\}$. Thus, x is grounded in every successful derivation of $\texttt{even(x)}$.

The previous considerations make clear that the semantic dependency expressed by the *ngv*'s has the corresponding translation for the analysis questions.

5 Related Work and Concluding Remarks

The idea of giving denotational descriptions of different operational frameworks is not new. For instance, [5] assigns different *fixpoint* semantics for a program under either call-by-name or call-by-value strategies. This shows that, in some sense, the semantic descriptions also (silently) assume some underlying operational approach (usually, call-by-name like).

In [18], the notion of *ngv* as the semantic object that a narrowing computation should compute was already introduced. It was also noted that narrowing only computes a *representation* of the object, not the object itself. However, it was not clearly explained how this connection can be done.

In [16], domains are used to give semantics to the functional logic language BABEL. However, the style of the presentation is model-theoretic: all symbols take meaning from a given interpretation and the connection between the declarative and operational semantics (lazy narrowing) are given by means of the usual completeness/correctness results. The semantic domain is different from ours because valuations are just a parameter of the semantic functions rather than a component of the domain. Thus, the *Herbrand domain* $\mathcal{T}^\infty(\mathcal{C}_\perp)$ is the semantic domain in [16].

The semantic approach in [9] is much more general than [16] (covering non-deterministic computations), but the style of the presentation is model-theoretic too. The basic semantic domain is also different from ours: no functional domain for denotations is used and, in fact, bounded completeness, which is essential in our setting to deal with the functional construction and with narrowing strategies, is not required in [9].

In [23], a denotational description of a particular narrowing strategy (the needed narrowing strategy [4]) is given. The semantics is nicely applied to demandedness analysis but nothing has been said about how to use it for more general analysis problems. This question is important since the notion of demandedness pattern is essential for the definition of the semantics itself.

We have presented a domain-theoretic approach for describing the semantics of integrated functional logic languages based on narrowing. Our semantics is parameterized by the narrowing strategy which is used by the language. The semantics is not 'model-theoretic' in the sense that we let within the operational mechanism (the narrowing strategy) to establish the 'real' meaning of the functions defined by the program rules. In this way, we are able to include more operational information into the semantic description. As far as we know, previous works have not explicitly considered different arbitrary strategies for parameterizing the semantics of functional logic languages, that is, the operational-oriented denotational description formalized in this work is novel in the literature of the area.

Another interesting point of our work is its applicability to the analysis of functional logic programs. Since we use a functional domain (the domain of *non-ground-values*), we are able to associate a denotation to a term with variables. Thus, narrowing is reformulated as an evaluation mechanism which computes the denotation of the input expression. This was already suggested by Reddy [18] but it is only formally established in this paper by using approximable mappings. Thanks to this perspective, we can easily use the standard frameworks for program analysis based on the denotational description of programs. In other words, the approximation of the domain of non-ground values enables the analysis of functional logic programs. Our description also reveals unexplored connections between purely functional and logic properties. These connections suggest that, within the functional logic setting, we have ascertained a kind of 'duality' between purely functional and purely logic properties. As far as we know, this had not been established before.

Future work includes a more detailed study about how to use this semantics to develop practical methods for the analysis of functional logic programs. Another interesting task is to extend this semantics to more general computation models for declarative languages [12].

References

1. S. Abramsky. Abstract Interpretation, Logical Relations, and Kan Extensions. *Journal of Logic and Computation* 1(1):5-40, 1990.
2. S. Abramsky. Domain Theory in Logic Form. *Annals of Pure and Applied Logic* 51:1-77, 1991.

3. M. Alpuente, M. Falaschi, and F. Manzo. Analyses of Unsatisfiability for Equational Logic Programming. *Journal of Logic Programming*, 22(3):221-252, 1995.
4. S. Antoy, R. Echahed and M. Hanus. A needed narrowing strategy. In *Conference Record of the ACM Symposium on Principles of Programming Languages, POPL'94*, pages 268-279. ACM Press, 1994.
5. J.W. de Bakker. Least Fixed Points Revisited. *Theoretical Computer Science*, 2:155-181, 1976.
6. F. Baader and T. Nipkow. Term Rewriting and All That. Cambridge University Press, 1998.
7. P. Dybjer. Inverse Image Analysis Generalises Strictness Analysis. *Information and Computation* 90:194-216, 1991.
8. J.A. Goguen, J.W. Thatcher, E.G. Wagner, and J.B. Wright. Initial Algebra Semantics and Continuous Algebras. *Journal of the ACM* 24(1):68-95, 1977.
9. J.C. González-Moreno, M.T. Hortalá-González, F.J. López-Fraguas, and M. Rodríguez-Artalejo. An approach to declarative programming based on a rewriting logic. *Journal of Logic Programming* 40(1):47-87, 1999.
10. C.A. Gunter. Semantics of Programming Languages. The MIT Press, Cambridge, MA, 1992.
11. M. Hanus. Towards the Global Optimization of Functional Logic Programs. In P.A. Fritzson, editor, *Proc. 5th International Conference on Compiler Construction, CC'94*. LNCS 786:68-82, Springer Verlag, Berlin, 1994.
12. M. Hanus. A Unified Computation Model for Functional and Logic Programming. In *Conference Record of the 24th Symposium on Principles of Programming Languages POPL'97*, pages 80-93, ACM Press, 1997.
13. M. Hanus and F. Zartmann. Mode Analysis of Functional Logic Programs. In B. Le Charlier, editor, *Proc. of 1st International Static Analysis Symposium, SAS'94*. LNCS 864:26-42, Springer Verlag, Berlin, 1994.
14. J.-M. Hullot. Canonical forms and unification. In *Proc. 5th Conference on Automated Deduction, CADE'80*, LNCS:318-334, Springer-Verlag, Berlin, 1980.
15. J.J. Moreno-Navarro, H. Kuchen, J. Mariño, S. Winkler and W. Hans. Efficient Lazy Narrowing using Demandedness Analysis. In M. Bruynooghe and J. Penjam, editors, *Proc. of 5th International Symposium on Programming Language Implementation and Logic Programming, PLILP'93*. LNCS 714:167-183, Springer-Verlag, Berlin, 1993.
16. J.J. Moreno-Navarro and M. Rodríguez-Artalejo. Logic programming with functions and predicates: the language BABEL. *Journal of Logic Programming*, 12:191-223, 1992.
17. A. Mycroft. The theory and practice of transforming call-by-need into call-by-value. In B. Robinet, editor, *Proc. of the 4th International Symposium on Programming*, LNCS 83:269-281, Springer-Verlag, Berlin, 1980.
18. U.S. Reddy. Narrowing as the Operational Semantics of Functional Languages. In *Proc. of IEEE International Symposium on Logic Programming*, pages 138-151, 1985.
19. D. Scott. Domains for Denotational Semantics. In M. Nielsen and E.M. Schmidt, editors, *Proc. of 9th International Colloquium on Automata, Languages and Programming, ICALP'82*, LNCS 140:577-613, Springer-Verlag, Berlin, 1982.
20. D. Scott. Lectures on a mathematical theory of computation. Monograph PRG-19. Computing Laboratory, Oxford University, 1981.
21. V. Stoltenberg-Hansen, I. Lindström, and E.R. Griffor. Mathematical Theory of Domains. Cambridge University Press, 1994.

22. S. Vickers. Topology via Logic. Cambridge University Press, 1989.
23. F. Zartmann. Denotational Abstract Interpretation of Functional Logic Programs. In P. Van Hentenryck, editor, *Proc. of the 4th International Static Analysis Symposium, SAS'97*, LNCS 1302:141-159, Springer-Verlag, Berlin, 1997.

Author Index

Alpuente, María 147
Antoy, Sergio 335

Bakewell, Adam 225
Barthe, Gilles 53
Beierle, Christoph 251
Boizumault, Patrice 267

Caballero, Rafael 85
Camarão, Carlos 37
Chakravarty, Manuel M. T. 68

Danvy, Olivier 241
De Schreye, Danny 163

Falaschi, Moreno 147
Fernández, Antonio J. 194
Figueiredo, Lucília 37

González-Moreno, J. C. 1

Hanus, Michael 353
Hill, Patricia M. 194
Hinze, Ralf 21
Hortalá-González, M. T. 1

Ida, Tetsuo 319

Johnson, Ernie 284

Kühnemann, Armin 114

López-Fraguas, Francisco J. 85
Lucas, Salvador 353
Lux, Wolfgang 100

Malésieux, Frédéric 267
Marin, Mircea 319
Meyer, Gregor 251
Moor, Oege de 209
Moreno, Ginés 147

Ogawa, Mizuhito 131
Ohlebusch, Enno 179
Ohori, Atsushi 300

Ramakrishnan, C. R. 284
Ramakrishnan, I. V. 284
Rao, Prasad 284
Ridoux, Olivier 267
Rodríguez-Artalejo, M. 1
Runciman, Colin 225

Serpette, Bernard P. 53
Sittampalam, Ganesh 209
Suzuki, Taro 319

Tolmach, Andrew 335

Verbaeten, Sofie 163
Vidal, Germán 147

Lecture Notes in Computer Science

For information about Vols. 1–1650
please contact your bookseller or Springer-Verlag

Vol. 1652: M. Klusch, O.M. Shehory, G. Weiss (Eds.), Cooperative Information Agents III. Proceedings, 1999. XI, 404 pages. 1999. (Subseries LNAI).

Vol. 1653: S. Covaci (Ed.), Active Networks. Proceedings, 1999. XIII, 346 pages. 1999.

Vol. 1654: E.R. Hancock, M. Pelillo (Eds.), Energy Minimization Methods in Computer Vision and Pattern Recognition. Proceedings, 1999. IX, 331 pages. 1999.

Vol. 1655: S.-W. Lee, Y. Nakano (Eds.), Document Analysis Systems: Theory and Practice. Proceedings, 1998. XI, 377 pages. 1999.

Vol. 1656: S. Chatterjee, J.F. Prins, L. Carter, J. Ferrante, Z. Li, D. Sehr, P.-C. Yew (Eds.), Languages and Compilers for Parallel Computing. Proceedings, 1998. XI, 384 pages. 1999.

Vol. 1657: T. Altenkirch, W. Naraschewski, B. Reus (Eds.), Types for Proofs and Programs. Proceedings, 1998. VIII, 207 pages. 1999.

Vol. 1659: D.G. Feitelson, L. Rudolph (Eds.), Job Scheduling Strategies for Parallel Processing. Proceedings, 1999. VII, 237 pages. 1999.

Vol. 1660: J.-M. Champarnaud, D. Maurel, D. Ziadi (Eds.), Automata Implementation. Proceedings, 1998. X, 245 pages. 1999.

Vol. 1661: C. Freksa, D.M. Mark (Eds.), Spatial Information Theory. Proceedings, 1999. XIII, 477 pages. 1999.

Vol. 1662: V. Malyshkin (Ed.), Parallel Computing Technologies. Proceedings, 1999. XIX, 510 pages. 1999.

Vol. 1663: F. Dehne, A. Gupta. J.-R. Sack, R. Tamassia (Eds.), Algorithms and Data Structures. Proceedings, 1999. IX, 366 pages. 1999.

Vol. 1664: J.C.M. Baeten, S. Mauw (Eds.), CONCUR'99. Concurrency Theory. Proceedings, 1999. XI, 573 pages. 1999.

Vol. 1666: M. Wiener (Ed.), Advances in Cryptology – CRYPTO '99. Proceedings, 1999. XII, 639 pages. 1999.

Vol. 1667: J. Hlavička, E. Maehle, A. Pataricza (Eds.), Dependable Computing – EDCC-3. Proceedings, 1999. XVIII, 455 pages. 1999.

Vol. 1668: J.S. Vitter, C.D. Zaroliagis (Eds.), Algorithm Engineering. Proceedings, 1999. VIII, 361 pages. 1999.

Vol. 1669: X.-S. Gao, D. Wang, L. Yang (Eds.), Automated Deduction in Geometry. Proceedings, 1998. VII, 287 pages. 1999. (Subseries LNAI).

Vol. 1670: N.A. Streitz, J. Siegel, V. Hartkopf, S. Konomi (Eds.), Cooperal tive Buildings. Proceedings, 1999. X, 229 pages. 1999.

Vol. 1671: D. Hochbaum, K. Jansen, J.D.P. Rolim, A. Sinclair (Eds.), Randomization, Approximation, and Combinatorial Optimization. Proceedings, 1999. IX, 289 pages. 1999.

Vol. 1672: M. Kutylowski, L. Pacholski, T. Wierzbicki (Eds.), Mathematical Foundations of Computer Science 1999. Proceedings, 1999. XII, 455 pages. 1999.

Vol. 1673: P. Lysaght, J. Irvine, R. Hartenstein (Eds.), Field Programmable Logic and Applications. Proceedings, 1999. XI, 541 pages. 1999.

Vol. 1674: D. Floreano, J.-D. Nicoud, F. Mondada (Eds.), Advances in Artificial Life. Proceedings, 1999. XVI, 737 pages. 1999. (Subseries LNAI).

Vol. 1675: J. Estublier (Ed.), System Configuration Management. Proceedings, 1999. VIII, 255 pages. 1999.

Vol. 1676: M. Mohania, A M. Tjoa (Eds.), Data Warehousing and Knowledge Discovery. Proceedings, 1999. XII, 400 pages. 1999.

Vol. 1677: T. Bench-Capon, G. Soda, A M. Tjoa (Eds.), Database and Expert Systems Applications. Proceedings, 1999. XVIII, 1105 pages. 1999.

Vol. 1678: M.H. Böhlen, C.S. Jensen, M.O. Scholl (Eds.), Spatio-Temporal Database Management. Proceedings, 1999. X, 243 pages. 1999.

Vol. 1679: C. Taylor, A. Colchester (Eds.), Medical Image Computing and Computer-Assisted Intervention – MICCAI'99. Proceedings, 1999. XXI, 1240 pages. 1999.

Vol. 1680: D. Dams, R. Gerth, S. Leue, M. Massink (Eds.), Theoretical and Practical Aspects of SPIN Model Checking. Proceedings, 1999. X, 277 pages. 1999.

Vol. 1681: D. A. Forsyth, J. L. Mundy, V. di Gesú, R. Cipolla (Eds.), Shape, Contour and Grouping in Computer Vision. VIII, 347 pages. 1999.

Vol. 1682: M. Nielsen, P. Johansen, O.F. Olsen, J. Weickert (Eds.), Scale-Space Theories in Computer Vision. Proceedings, 1999. XII, 532 pages. 1999.

Vol. 1683: J. Flum, M. Rodríguez-Artalejo (Eds.), Computer Science Logic. Proceedings, 1999. XI, 580 pages. 1999.

Vol. 1684: G. Ciobanu, G. Păun (Eds.), Fundamentals of Computation Theory. Proceedings, 1999. XI, 570 pages. 1999.

Vol. 1685: P. Amestoy, P. Berger, M. Daydé, I. Duff, V. Frayssé, L. Giraud, D. Ruiz (Eds.), Euro-Par'99. Parallel Processing. Proceedings, 1999. XXXII, 1503 pages. 1999.

Vol. 1686: H.E. Bal, B. Belkhouche, L. Cardelli (Eds.), Internet Programming Languages. Proceedings, 1998. IX, 143 pages. 1999.

Vol. 1687: O. Nierstrasz, M. Lemoine (Eds.), Software Engineering – ESEC/FSE '99. Proceedings, 1999. XII, 529 pages. 1999.

Vol. 1688: P. Bouquet, L. Serafini, P. Brézillon, M. Benerecetti, F. Castellani (Eds.), Modeling and Using Context. Proceedings, 1999. XII, 528 pages. 1999. (Subseries LNAI).

Vol. 1689: F. Solina, A. Leonardis (Eds.), Computer Analysis of Images and Patterns. Proceedings, 1999. XIV, 650 pages. 1999.

Vol. 1690: Y. Bertot, G. Dowek, A. Hirschowitz, C. Paulin, L. Théry (Eds.), Theorem Proving in Higher Order Logics. Proceedings, 1999. VIII, 359 pages. 1999.

Vol. 1691: J. Eder, I. Rozman, T. Welzer (Eds.), Advances in Databases and Information Systems. Proceedings, 1999. XIII, 383 pages. 1999.

Vol. 1692: V. Matoušek, P. Mautner, J. Ocelíková, P. Sojka (Eds.), Text, Speech and Dialogue. Proceedings, 1999. XI, 396 pages. 1999. (Subseries LNAI).

Vol. 1693: P. Jayanti (Ed.), Distributed Computing. Proceedings, 1999. X, 357 pages. 1999.

Vol. 1694: A. Cortesi, G. Filé (Eds.), Static Analysis. Proceedings, 1999. VIII, 357 pages. 1999.

Vol. 1695: P. Barahona, J.J. Alferes (Eds.), Progress in Artificial Intelligence. Proceedings, 1999. XI, 385 pages. 1999. (Subseries LNAI).

Vol. 1696: S. Abiteboul, A.-M. Vercoustre (Eds.), Research and Advanced Technology for Digital Libraries. Proceedings, 1999. XII, 497 pages. 1999.

Vol. 1697: J. Dongarra, E. Luque, T. Margalef (Eds.), Recent Advances in Parallel Virtual Machine and Message Passing Interface. Proceedings, 1999. XVII, 551 pages. 1999.

Vol. 1698: M. Felici, K. Kanoun, A. Pasquini (Eds.), Computer Safety, Reliability and Security. Proceedings, 1999. XVIII, 482 pages. 1999.

Vol. 1699: S. Albayrak (Ed.), Intelligent Agents for Telecommunication Applications. Proceedings, 1999. IX, 191 pages. 1999. (Subseries LNAI).

Vol. 1700: R. Stadler, B. Stiller (Eds.), Active Technologies for Network and Service Management. Proceedings, 1999. XII, 299 pages. 1999.

Vol. 1701: W. Burgard, T. Christaller, A.B. Cremers (Eds.), KI-99: Advances in Artificial Intelligence. Proceedings, 1999. XI, 311 pages. 1999. (Subseries LNAI).

Vol. 1702: G. Nadathur (Ed.), Principles and Practice of Declarative Programming. Proceedings, 1999. X, 434 pages. 1999.

Vol. 1703: L. Pierre, T. Kropf (Eds.), Correct Hardware Design and Verification Methods. Proceedings, 1999. XI, 366 pages. 1999.

Vol. 1704: Jan M. Żytkow, J. Rauch (Eds.), Principles of Data Mining and Knowledge Discovery. Proceedings, 1999. XIV, 593 pages. 1999. (Subseries LNAI).

Vol. 1705: H. Ganzinger, D. McAllester, A. Voronkov (Eds.), Logic for Programming and Automated Reasoning. Proceedings, 1999. XII, 397 pages. 1999. (Subseries LNAI).

Vol. 1706: J. Hatcliff, T. Æ. Mogensen, P. Thiemann (Eds.), Lectures on Partial Evaluation. Proceedings, 1998. IX, 433 pages. 1999. (Subseries LNAI).

Vol. 1707: H.-W. Gellersen (Ed.), Handheld and Ubiquitous Computing. Proceedings, 1999. XII, 390 pages. 1999.

Vol. 1708: J.M. Wing, J. Woodcock, J. Davies (Eds.), FM'99 – Formal Methods. Proceedings Vol. I, 1999. XVIII, 937 pages. 1999.

Vol. 1709: J.M. Wing, J. Woodcock, J. Davies (Eds.), FM'99 – Formal Methods. Proceedings Vol. II, 1999. XVIII, 937 pages. 1999.

Vol. 1710: E.-R. Olderog, B. Steffen (Eds.), Correct System Design. XIV, 417 pages. 1999.

Vol. 1711: N. Zhong, A. Skowron, S. Ohsuga (Eds.), New Directions in Rough Sets, Data Mining, and Granular-Soft Computing. Proceedings, 1999. XIV, 558 pages. 1999. (Subseries LNAI).

Vol. 1712: H. Boley, A Tight, Practical Integration of Relations and Functions. XI, 169 pages. 1999. (Subseries LNAI).

Vol. 1713: J. Jaffar (Ed.), Principles and Practice of Constraint Programming – CP'99. Proceedings, 1999. XII, 493 pages. 1999.

Vol. 1714: M.T. Pazienza (Eds.), Information Extraction. IX, 165 pages. 1999. (Subseries LNAI).

Vol. 1715: P. Perner, M. Petrou (Eds.), Machine Learning and Data Mining in Pattern Recognition. Proceedings, 1999. VIII, 217 pages. 1999. (Subseries LNAI).

Vol. 1716: K.Y. Lam, E. Okamoto, C. Xing (Eds.), Advances in Cryptology – ASIACRYPT'99. Proceedings, 1999. XI, 414 pages. 1999.

Vol. 1717: Ç. K. Koç, C. Paar (Eds.), Cryptographic Hardware and Embedded Systems. Proceedings, 1999. XI, 353 pages. 1999.

Vol. 1718: M. Diaz, P. Owezarski, P. Sénac (Eds.), Interactive Distributed Multimedia Systems and Telecommunication Services. Proceedings, 1999. XI, 386 pages. 1999.

Vol. 1719: M. Fossorier, H. Imai, S. Lin, A. Poli (Eds.), Applied Algebra, Algebraic Algorithms and Error-Correcting Codes. Proceedings, 1999. XIII, 510 pages. 1999.

Vol. 1721: S. Arikawa, K. Furukawa (Eds.), Discovery Science. Proceedings, 1999. XI, 374 pages. 1999. (Subseries LNAI).

Vol. 1722: A. Middeldorp, T. Sato (Eds.), Functional and Logic Programming. Proceedings, 1999. X, 369 pages. 1999.

Vol. 1723: R. France, B. Rumpe (Eds.), UML'99 – The Unified Modeling Language99. XVII, 724 pages. 1999.

Vol. 1726: V. Varadharajan, Y. Mu (Eds.), Information and Communication Security. Proceedings, 1999. XI, 325 pages. 1999.

Vol. 1727: P.P. Chen, D.W. Embley, J. Kouloumdjian, S.W. Liddle, J.F. Roddick (Eds.), Advances in Conceptual Modeling. Proceedings, 1999. XI, 389 pages. 1999.

Vol. 1728: J. Akoka, M. Bouzeghoub, I. Comyn-Wattiau, E. Métais (Eds.), Conceptual Modeling – ER '99. Proceedings, 1999. XIV, 540 pages. 1999.

Vol. 1729: M. Mambo, Y. Zheng (Eds.), Information Security. Proceedings, 1999. IX, 277 pages. 1999.

Vol. 1734: H. Hellwagner, A. Reinefeld (Eds.), SCI: Scalable Coherent Interface. XXI, 490 pages. 1999.

Vol. 1564: M. Vazirgiannis, Interactive Multimedia Documents. XIII, 161 pages. 1999.

Vol. 1591: D.J. Duke, I. Herman, S. Marshall, PREMO: A Framework for Multimedia Middleware. XII, 254 pages. 1999.